THE MOST TRUSTED NAME IN TRAVEL

Frommer's®

TEXAS

by Janis Turk

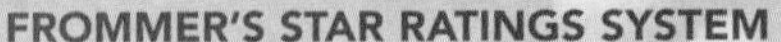

FROMMER'S STAR RATINGS SYSTEM

Every hotel, restaurant, and attraction listed in this guide has been ranked for quality and value. Here's what the stars mean:

★	Recommended
★★	Highly Recommended
★★★	A must! Don't miss!

AN IMPORTANT NOTE

The world is a dynamic place. Hotels change ownership, restaurants hike their prices, museums alter their opening hours, and busses and trains change their routings. And all of this can occur in the several months after our authors have visited, inspected, and written about, these hotels, restaurants, museums and transportation services. Though we have made valiant efforts to keep all our information fresh and up-to-date, some few changes can inevitably occur in the periods before a revised edition of this guidebook is published. So please bear with us if a tiny number of the details in this book have changed. Please also note that we have no responsibility or liability for any inaccuracy or errors or omissions, or for inconvenience, loss, damage, or expenses suffered by anyone as a result of assertions in this guide.

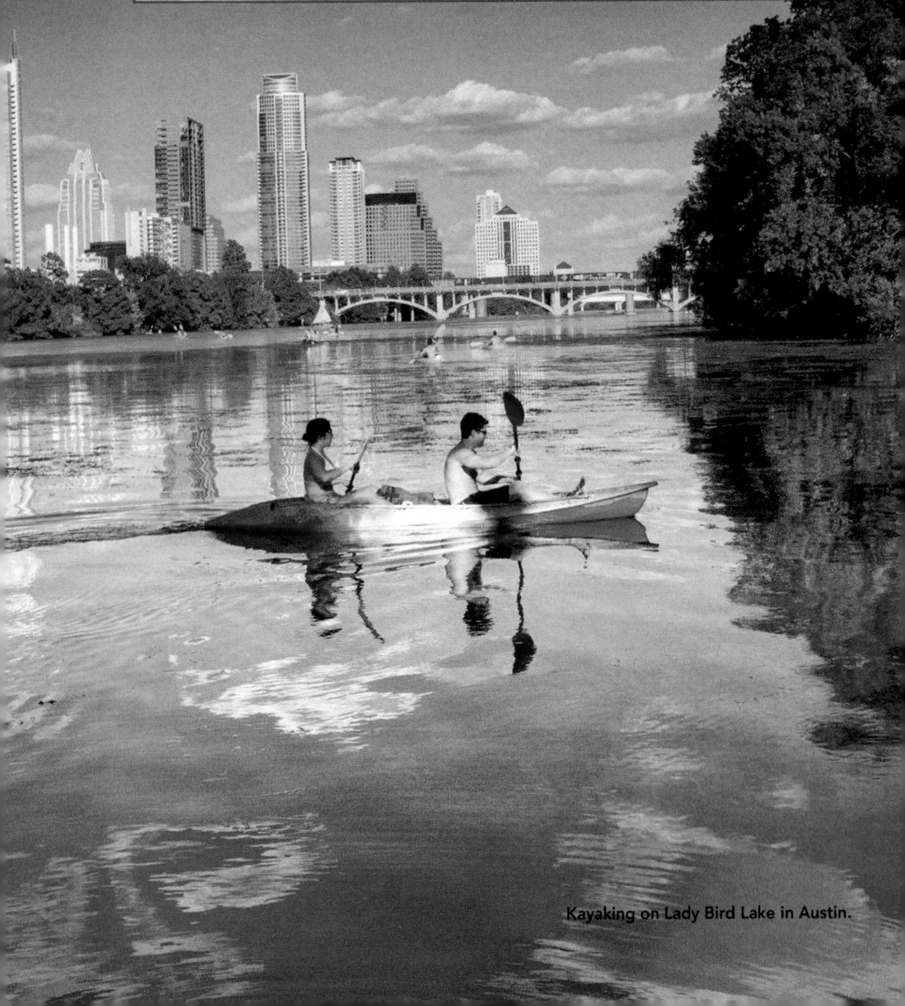

Kayaking on Lady Bird Lake in Austin.

CONTENTS

River Walk in San Antonio.

A LOOK AT TEXAS

For big and colorful, Texas is pretty hard to beat. The state's outsize swagger speaks of the rootin-tootin' Wild West, big oil, and oceans of prairie dotted with desert scrub. Texas sprawl is no cliché—the second-largest state in the union stakes out a big footprint on the U.S. map, zigzagging through climate zones and eco-terrains, from high-country desert to breezy Gulf beaches to gentle hills blanketed in bluebonnets. But Texas is not just starry, big-sky landscapes. It is thoroughly 21st century, with shining cities sheathed in vertical steel and glass; cutting-edge art museums with world-class collections; and locavore farm-to-fork eateries blossoming in every corner of the state. The real Texas is here, but it's also in the small-town fairs, the boot-scooting dance halls, the sizzling Tex-Mex fiestas. High, low; cool, hot: Texas does it all with a big dash of Lone Star panache.

The diverse landscape of Big Bend National Park comprises sun-bleached desert, lush river canyons, and craggy peaks rising out of desert scrub. See chapter 11.

TEXAS CITIES

Spring-fed Barton Springs Pool (p. 295) is Austin's recreational jewel, a 3-acre public swimming hole with crystal-clear water and sloping green banks.

A country band in full toe-tapping swing at the Broken Spoke, one of Austin's classic dancehalls. See p. 336.

A fried chicken-avocado wrap—aka "cone"—at the Mighty Cone, one of the vendors in South Central Austin's celebrated lineup of food trailers (p. 329).

A local sheriff stands at attention before the Alamo mission, site of the famed 1836 battle and an iconic shrine to the state's fight for independence from Mexico. See p. 241.

The leafy pathways of the River Walk trace the curve of the San Antonio River for 15 miles in the heart of San Antonio. See p. 244.

The arched doorway of the 1756 Espada Mission, part of the San Antonio Missions National Historical Park (p. 246).

The Nasher Sculpture Center in Dallas is the only museum in the U.S. completely devoted to sculpture (p. 68). Pictured is *The Bronze Crowd* by Magdalena Abakanowicz.

The tallest Ferris wheel in the U.S., the Texas Star, towers above the horizon at the State Fair of Texas in Dallas. See chapter 4.

A little girl forms the "I" in Dallas's "Big Things Happen Here" logo before a mural in the city's Bishop Arts District (chapter 4).

Get your cowboy duds at M. L. Leddy's boot shop in Fort Worth, which sells classic Western wear like custom boots, handmade belts, and cowboy hats (p. 139).

A mother and baby gorilla in the award-winning Fort Worth Zoo (p. 122), considered one of the country's top zoos.

Kids play in the sprinklers on Sundance Square Plaza with the Chisolm Trail Mural Building in the background, one of Fort Worth's most photographed spots (chapter 5).

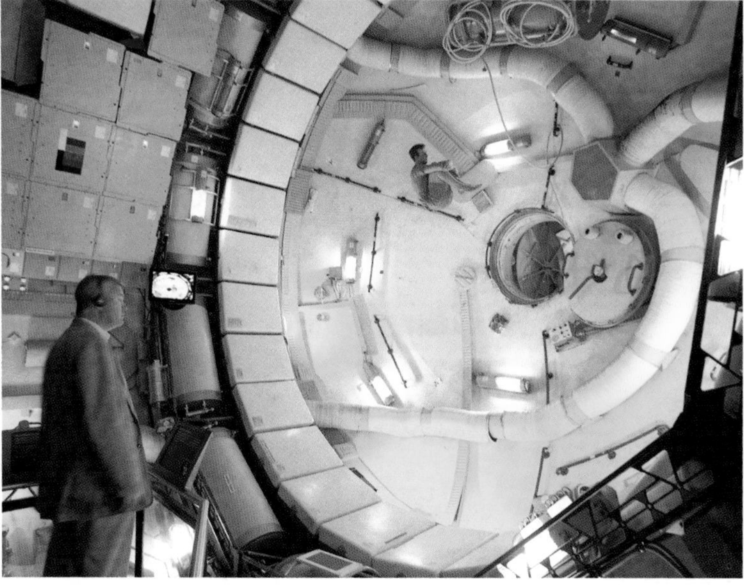

A look at life inside the International Space Station in the interactive "Living in Space" exhibit at NASA's Space Center Houston (p. 157).

The state's largest city, Houston has a gleaming downtown skyline pillowed in green parkland. See chapter 6.

Look closely at the photomosaic of Jackie Kennedy—it's made up of 50,000 photos of President Kennedy. It's in Dallas's Sixth Floor Museum at Dealey Plaza (p. 65), site of President Kennedy's assassination in 1963.

TEXAS OUTDOORS

An old-fashioned ride at the annual State Fair in Dallas's Fair Park (chapter 4).

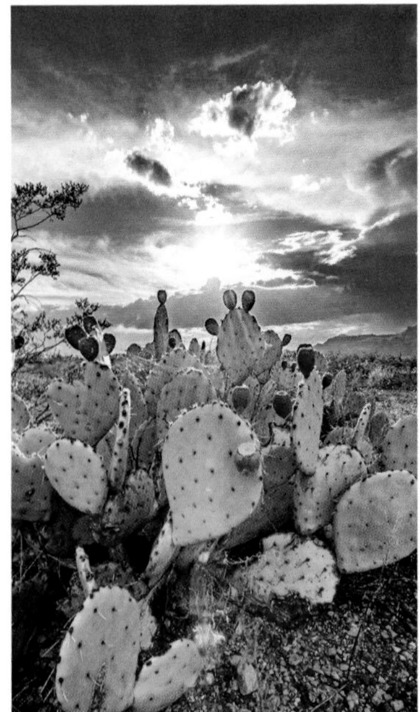

Prickly pear cactus blooming in the desert scrub at Big Bend National Park (chapter 11).

Roseate spoonbills in their natural habitat on South Padre Island (p. 228).

An endangered Kemp's Ridley sea turtle crawls along the sand dunes of Padre Island National Seashore (p. 224) after laying a clutch of eggs on the beach.

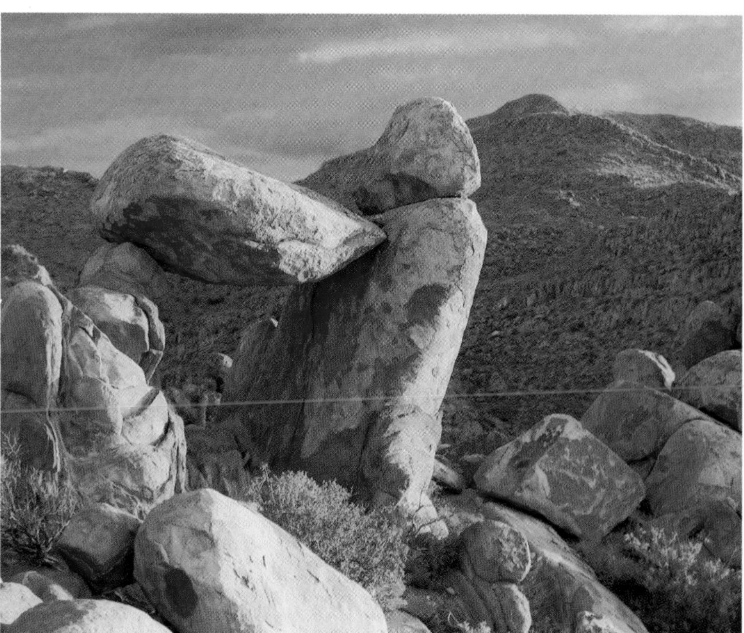

Balanced Rock at Big Bend National Park (chapter 11).

Horseback riders in the lush Hill Country landscape near San Antonio (p. 284).

Port Isabel Lighthouse (p. 229) on South Padre Island.

Whooping crane and a crab at Aransas National Wildlife Refuge (p. 215).

Hitting the beach on horseback at South Padre Island. See chapter 7.

Artist Donald Judd was inspired by the high desert landscape of Marfa (chapter 10), and his concrete art—15 untitled concrete blocks from the early 1980s—makes a bold statement against Marfa's big-sky terrain.

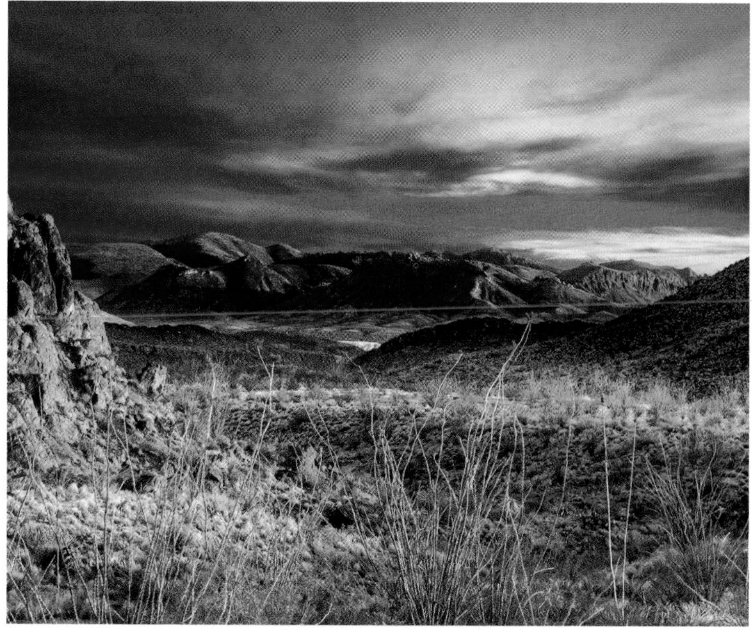

Sunrise over a carpet of ocotillo blooms in Big Bend National Park (chapter 11).

QUINTESSENTIAL TEXAS

Put your own artistic stamp on Cadillac Ranch, a junk-car public sculpture in an old cow pasture in Amarillo, where graffiti is encouraged (p. 425).

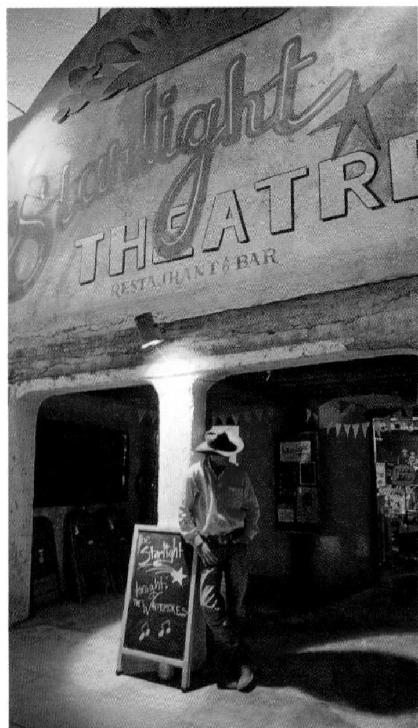

A cowboy pauses at the Starlight Theatre (p. 405), a restaurant and saloon in the ghost town and former Wild West outpost of Terlingua.

With an image of the Alamo licked by flames, a Texas flag, and "Remember the Alamo" stitched on the back, these boots may be the ultimate Texas souvenir.

Texas bluebonnets in a field at sunset in Muleshoe Bend Recreation Area, near Austin.

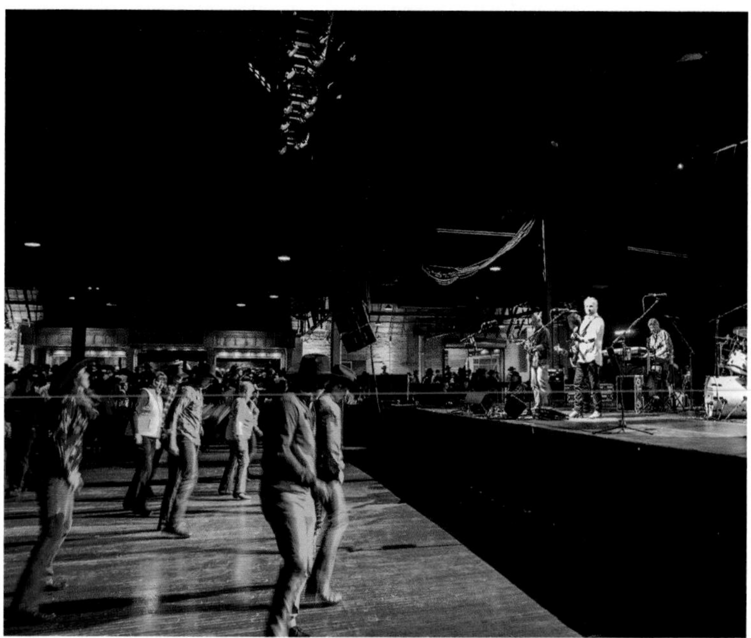

Two-stepping at Gilley's (p. 105), the quintessential country dancehall, made famous in *Urban Cowboy.*

Cowboy roping longhorn cows near San Antonio.

Live rodeo is the weekend action in the Cowtown Coliseum in the Fort Worth Stockyards (chapter 5).

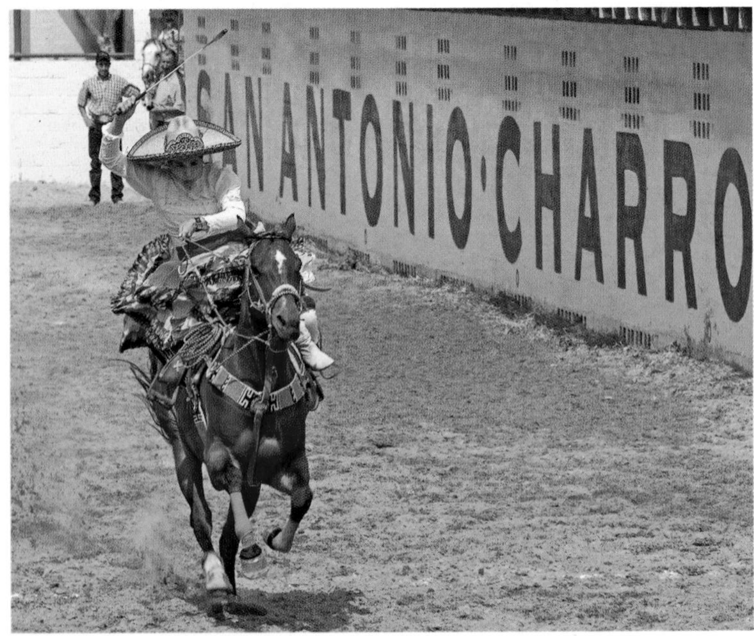

Men and women in colorful Mexican-cowboy dress compete in a *charreada* (Mexican rodeo) in San Antonio.

THE BEST OF TEXAS

1

"You ask me what I like about Texas," sings Austin singer/songwriter Gary P. Nunn, and the lyrics of that old Texas tune list a lot of the things locals love best about the Lone Star State, such as "body surfing the Frio, Saturday night in Del Rio, stories of the Menger Hotel and the Alamo." Many of the things mentioned in that song made the cut as I compiled a list of favorite Texas experiences, destinations, and services. But since it's such a great big state, I added even more, for I wouldn't want you to miss the best parts as I help you plan your own Texas travels. There's more to like about Texas than any one book can show, so explore it on your own to create your own "best-of list," and before long you'll be singing your favorite Texas song.

THE best LONE STAR EXPERIENCES

- **Hopping Aboard the Grapevine Vintage Railroad:** The Old West comes alive aboard the Tarantula Railroad. A vintage train (when running, a restored 1896 steam locomotive called "Puffy" by locals) rumbles along the track from Stockyards Station in Fort Worth, tracing the route of the Chisholm Trail, to the Cotton Belt Depot in historic Grapevine, Texas, a town with 75 restored turn-of-the-20th-century buildings. See p. 120.
- **Lassoing the Fort Worth Stock Show & Rodeo:** Fort Worth ain't called Cowtown for nothing. In late January and early February, the Southwestern Exposition and Livestock Show (as it's officially called) recalls the glory cowboy days with horse shows, auctions, and livestock from beef cattle to llamas to swine. The nightly rodeos are big draws. See p. 122.
- **Attending a Mariachi Mass at Mission San José:** The Alamo may be more famous, but hearing a congregation of San Antonians raise their voices in spirited prayer reminds you that the city's Spanish missions aren't just, well, history. See p. 246.

- **Tubing on the River and Two-Stepping at Gruene Hall:** In central Texas, upstream from the town of Gruene, is a stretch of the Guadalupe River that Texans love to float down "leisurely like" in inner tubes (one tube per person and one for the ice chest). During late spring and early summer, the air is hot, the water is cold, and the "tuber" finds life most agreeable. There is no shortage of outfitters who can set you up with a tube. Then dry off and head up the hill to hear live music at Texas's oldest dancehall, Gruene Hall, just outside New Braunfels. See p. 344.
- **Exploring the Borderlands:** The Texas-Mexico border stretches for nearly 800 miles, and the Rio Grande from the Gulf of Mexico to El Paso is a fascinating region. We are big fans of Ciudad Acuña, across the river from Del Rio, and the amazing canyons in Big Bend National Park, but the entire "borderlands" region is more attractive and diverse than most visitors realize. See chapters 10 and 11.
- **Exploring Big Bend National Park:** Vast and wild, this rugged terrain harbors thousands of species of plants and animals—some seen practically nowhere else on earth. A visit can include a hike into the sunbaked desert, a float down a majestic river through the canyons, or a trek among high mountains where bears and mountain lions rule. See "Big Bend National Park" in chapter 11.
- **Strolling along the San Antonio River Walk, Taking a Rio Taxi to Pearl, and Remembering the Alamo:** The quintessential San Antonio experience is a nighttime walk over arched stone bridges and along slender passageways along the Paseo del Rio, or "River Walk," which wends through downtown San Antonio. Then head over to the Alamo, in the city center, where the story of Texas independence found its battle cry. After that, take a Rio Taxi ride through the lock and dam section of the Museum Reach of the San Antonio River, and pass beneath the art installations hung from bridges and overpasses en route to Pearl, the city's culinary epicenter. See p. 241.

THE best MUSEUMS

- **George W. Bush Presidential Library and Museum** (Dallas): Standing on the Southern Methodist University campus just north of downtown, Texas's second presidential library (LBJ's is on the University of Texas at Austin campus) opened in April of 2013. Sprawling over a 207,000-square-foot area, it is the second-largest presidential library and, naturally, is filled with exhibits geared toward making a somewhat controversial president seem more sympathetic. See p. 71.
- **Nasher Sculpture Center** (Dallas): This world-class collection of modern sculpture is in the downtown Dallas Arts District. Ray Nasher and his wife, Patsy, spent 4 decades assembling what has been called the finest private collection in the world, including superlative works by Miró, David Smith, Brancuşi, Moore, Giacometti, Picasso, Matisse, and Calder. Designed by

Renzo Piano, it has a gorgeous open-air sculpture garden with landscape design by Peter Walker. See p. 68.

- **Meadows Museum of Art** (Dallas): In a building with plenty of room to show off the greatest collection of Spanish masters outside Spain, the Meadows was built by a Dallas oilman fascinated with Spanish art. The museum proudly displays a wealth of works by Velázquez, Goya, Ribera, Murillo, Zurbarán—just about all the biggies from Spain's golden era—as well as the 20th-century masters Picasso, Dalí, and Miró. See p. 73.
- **Perot Museum of Nature and Science** (Dallas): Located in downtown Dallas's Victory Park, this flashy museum, opened in December 2012, is a "world of wonder," as *The Dallas Morning News* calls it, with hands-on interactive exhibits on science, math, technology, and nature, making it a favorite of schoolchildren. See p. 69.
- **Kimbell Art Museum** (Fort Worth): Probably the country's finest small museum, this masterwork by Louis Kahn is a joyous celebration of architecture and a splendid collection of art to boot. Kahn's graceful building, a wonder of technology and natural light, is now a chapter in architectural studies worldwide. The small permanent collection ranges from prehistoric Asian and pre-Columbian pieces to European old masters, Impressionists, and modern geniuses. The Kimbell also gets some of the world's most important traveling shows. See p. 122.
- **Modern Art Museum of Fort Worth** (Fort Worth): In a modernist building designed by Japanese architect Tadao Ando, the Modern—actually the oldest art museum in Texas—is the nation's second largest dedicated to contemporary and modern art. The permanent collection includes works by Picasso, Rothko, Warhol, Rauschenberg, and Pollock. See p. 123.
- **Amon Carter Museum of American Art** (Fort Worth): This museum has one of the finest collections of Western and American art in the country, including the most complete group of works by Frederic Remington and Charles M. Russell, two giants of Western art. It also has a great photography collection and important paintings by Georgia O'Keeffe. See p. 120.
- **Menil Collection** (Houston): One of the great private collections in the world could very well have ended up in Paris or New York, but was graciously bestowed by the collectors on their adopted city. To experience the Menil is pure delight; very little comes between the viewer and the art, which includes works by many 20th-century masters, classical works from the ancients, and tribal art from around the world. See p. 159.
- **The Briscoe Western Art Museum** (San Antonio): Named in honor of the late Texas governor Dolph Briscoe, Jr., and his wife, Janey, this museum, edging the San Antonio River Walk, honors the art, history, and culture of the American West through exhibitions, educational programs, and public events. Housed in a building that once was San Antonio's first public library (and later a circus museum), this attractive museum features a pavilion designed by the nationally recognized architecture firm Lake Flato, as well as an inviting sculpture garden. See p. 242.

- **San Antonio Museum of Art** (San Antonio): Almost as impressive for its architecture as for its holdings, this museum combines several castle-like buildings of the 1904 Lone Star Brewery. The Nelson A. Rockefeller Center for Latin American Art is the most comprehensive collection of its kind in the United States. See p. 244.
- **Marion Koogler McNay Art Museum** (San Antonio): A beautiful collection beautifully located and displayed. This small museum is a delight to visit, especially for fans of modern art, who will devour its collection of works by the modern masters. We love it for its architecture. See p. 245.
- **Elisabet Ney Museum** (Austin): This tiny museum in the Hyde Park neighborhood just north of the UT Campus was once the studio of a fabulous sculptress. Tucked away in the trees by a creek, this is where I love to spend a rainy Austin morning. See p. 301.
- **McDonald Observatory** (northwest of Fort Davis): This observatory is considered one of the world's best astronomical research facilities. Twice a day, visitors can glimpse sunspots, flares, and other solar activity. Nighttime "Star Parties" are held three evenings a week, during which visitors can view constellations and celestial objects through the observatory's high-powered telescopes. See p. 365
- **National Museum of the Pacific War** (Fredericksburg): This world-class museum, set in the small town of Fredericksburg in the Hill Country, grew from its humble beginnings as a small museum in the boyhood home of Fleet Admiral Chester W. Nimitz, who served as Commander in Chief of the United States Pacific Fleet during World War II. Today this 6-acre site is home to the only institution in the U.S. dedicated exclusively to telling the story of the Pacific and Asiatic theaters in World War II. See p. 339.
- **LHUCA: Louise Hopkins Underwood Center for the Arts** (Lubbock): This fantastic little world-class art center and museum put the Lubbock art scene on the map. See p. 434.

THE best OF NATURAL TEXAS

- **The Dallas Arboretum & Botanical Garden:** Who knew Dallas had more than dust, concrete, steel, and glass? This surprising oasis on the edge of White Rock Lake is a great spot to duck the Texas sun. Relax on 70 acres of groomed gardens and natural woodlands, interspersed with a handful of historic homes. The gardens are especially colorful in spring and fall. See p. 69.
- **Fort Worth Botanic Garden:** A rambling, spacious showcase of 2,500 native and exotic species of plants on 100-plus acres, this is the oldest

botanical garden in Texas, created back in the late 1920s. The Texas Rose Garden, with 3,500 roses that bloom in late April and October, and the beautiful Japanese Garden are terrific places to hide out from the world. Bring a picnic, a book, and a Frisbee. See p. 121.

- **Big Thicket National Preserve:** It has been called "the American Ark" for its incredibly rich variety of plants and wildlife, all packed into 100,000 acres of watery bottomland in deepest east Texas. Explore the area on foot or in a canoe, and see how the woods grow so thickly here that they all but blot out the sun and make trailblazing almost impossible. See "Side Trips to East Texas" in chapter 6.
- **Aransas National Wildlife Refuge:** A mecca for birders, with some 300 species sighted here, the refuge is also home to snakes, turtles, lizards, mammals, and a variety of frogs and other amphibians. Aransas has become famous for being the main winter home of the near-extinct whooping crane, the tallest bird in America—5 feet high with an 8-foot wingspan. See "Rockport" in chapter 7.
- **Mustang Island State Park:** This barrier island has more than 5 miles of wide, sandy beach, with fine sand, few rocks, and broken shells, and almost enough waves for surfing. One of the most popular of Texas state parks, it's especially busy on summer weekends. See "Port Aransas" in chapter 7.
- **Lady Bird Johnson Wildflower Center:** Few people remember that Lady Bird Johnson started the program to beautify America's highways—and she began practicing it right here in her home state. This flower-powered research center is a natural outgrowth of the First Lady's lifelong efforts to beautify the state. See p. 296.
- **McKittrick Canyon:** The canyon is forested with conifers and deciduous trees. In autumn, maples, oaks, and other hardwoods burst into color, painting the world in bright hues set off by the rich variety of the evergreens. See "Guadalupe Mountains National Park" in chapter 11.
- **Palo Duro Canyon State Park:** This 60-mile canyon, sculpted by the Prairie Dog Town Fork of the Red River over the past 90 million years, is a grand contrast to the ubiquitous, treeless plains of the Texas Panhandle. Its 800-foot cliffs, striped with orange, red, and white rock and adorned by groves of juniper and cottonwood trees, present an astoundingly stark beauty. See "Canyon & Palo Duro Canyon State Park" in chapter 12.
- **The Canyons on the Rio Grande:** Santa Elena, Boquillas, and Mariscal canyons in Big Bend National Park and Colorado Canyon in Big Bend Ranch State Park have some of the state's best scenery, an unparalleled blend of rock, air, and sky. See "River Running" in chapter 11.

THE best HISTORICAL ATTRACTIONS

- **The Sixth Floor Museum at Dealey Plaza** (Dallas): The events of November 22, 1963, shook the world. John F. Kennedy's assassination in Dallas is remembered by everyone old enough to remember, and argued over still. Visitors can tour the sixth floor of the Texas School Book Depository, from where the Warren Commission concluded that a single sniper, Lee Harvey Oswald, felled the president. The museum also examines the life, times, and legacy of the Kennedy presidency, making it a place to revisit not only the assassination but also an era. See p. 65.
- **The Stockyards National Historic District** (Fort Worth): Still looking the part, this area north of downtown was once the biggest and busiest cattle, horse, mule, hog, and sheep marketing center in the Southwest. Put on your boots and best Western shirt and tour the Livestock Exchange Building; Cowtown Coliseum (the world's first indoor rodeo arena); former hog and sheep pens now filled with Western shops and restaurants; and Billy Bob's Texas, the "world's largest honky-tonk." Then grab a longneck beer at the White Elephant saloon—the oldest bar in Fort Worth and the site of the city's most famous gunfight in 1897—and check in at the historic Stockyards Hotel. Finally, check out the "longhorn cattle drive" that rumbles down Exchange Avenue daily—or take the Vintage Train into Grapevine. See chapter 5.
- **The Alamo** (San Antonio): It's smaller than you might expect, and resides smack in the heart of downtown San Antonio. But the graceful mission church that's come to symbolize the state is a must-see, if only to learn what the fuss is all about. See p. 241.
- **San Jacinto Monument** (Houston): Here on the battlefield of San Jacinto, a small army of Texans led by General Sam Houston charged the much larger, better equipped Mexican army and dealt them a crushing blow. The victory gave Texas its independence. A monument and museum occupy the battlefield to honor and explain the history of the battle and its significance. See p. 155.
- **USS *Lexington* Museum on the Bay** (Corpus Christi): Exploring this huge World War II–era aircraft carrier offers civilians the opportunity to get an idea of what it was like to live in the claustrophobic conditions of such a limited space. In addition to sleeping, dining, and cooking areas, the ship provided a hospital, a rec room, and, numerous working areas. See p. 210.
- **San Antonio Missions National Historical Park** (San Antonio): It's impossible not to remember the Alamo when you're in San Antonio; more difficult is recalling that the Alamo was originally just the first of five missions established by the Franciscans along the San Antonio River. Exploring the other four missions that make up this national park, now Texas's only

UNESCO World Heritage Site, built uncharacteristically close to each other, provides an immersion in the city's early Spanish and Indian history. See p. 246.

- **State Capitol** (Austin): The country's largest state capitol building, second only in size to the U.S. Capitol—but 7 feet taller—underwent a massive renovation and expansion in the 1990s, which left it more impressive than ever. See p. 294.
- **El Paso Mission Trail** (El Paso): Established in the 17th and 18th centuries, these three historic Spanish missions provide a link to El Paso's colonial past. They are among the oldest continually active missions in the country and warrant a visit for their architectural and historic merit. Especially impressive is the large Presidio Chapel San Elceario, near the site of "The First Thanksgiving," said to have taken place in 1598, 23 years before the Plymouth Thanksgiving. See p. 352.

THE best FAMILY ADVENTURES

- **The Stockyards** (Fort Worth): Far from a dry old historic district, the Stockyards are alive with the flavor of the Old West. Kids will adore the twice-daily "cattle drive" of the Fort Worth Herd, which rumbles down the cobbled main drag, led by cowhands in 19th-century duds. They'll also love to find their way around the Cowtown Cattlepen Maze, a human maze made to look like old cattle pens. See "What to See & Do" in chapter 5.
- **Fort Worth's Children's Museums** (Fort Worth): The Fort Worth Museum of Science and History is large and multifaceted, with a domed IMAX theater, a planetarium, and great hands-on science displays. The National Cowgirl Museum and Hall of Fame teaches little cowgirls and cowboys about pioneering women of the American West, but in a way that really brings the culture to life: Jukeboxes pump out country tunes, and kids can ride a simulated bucking bronco, see the film of their adventure on the museum's website, and get their pictures superimposed on Old West film posters. The Fort Worth Zoo is one of the best in the country. See "What to See & Do" in chapter 5.
- **Arlington:** Sandwiched between Dallas and Fort Worth is a kids' suburban dream world: Stumble from the roller coasters at Six Flags Over Texas to the water slides at Hurricane Harbor, visit Ripley's Believe It or Not and the Palace of Wax, and catch a game at the Texas Rangers' ballpark. See "Arlington" in chapter 4.
- **Space Center Houston** (Houston): Always the most popular attraction in the city, NASA's Space Center Houston is a joint effort powered by NASA technology and Disney know-how. It is the epitome of interactive display and simulation, managing to fascinate kids and parents alike. During your visit, check out what's going on at the Johnson Space Center through a tram ride and video feeds. See p. 157.

- **The Gulf Side of South Padre Island:** Fine white sand and warm water lapping at your toes—what more do you want? Although the shore is lined with hotels and condos, the beaches are public and open to everyone. See "Padre Island National Seashore," in chapter 7.
- **Six Flags Fiesta Texas** (San Antonio): Major thrill rides, a huge swimming pool shaped like Texas, and entertainment/food areas with Texas history themes—there's something for every family member at this theme park, and it's even slightly educational. See p. 248.
- **The Austin Bats** (Austin): Most adults and kids tend to finds bats a bit creepy—until they learn more about them, that is. From March to November, you can watch thousands of bats emerge in smoky clouds from under the Ann W. Richards Congress Avenue Bridge—and find out why Austinites adore the little critters. See "Going Batty" on p. 295.
- **Balmorhea State Park** (Balmorhea): This is one of the crown jewels of the Texas state parks system and also, at 45 acres, one of the smallest. The main attraction is a massive 1¾-acre swimming pool—3.5 million gallons of water at a fairly constant 74°F (23°C). Not your typical swimming pool, it's teeming with small fish and laden with rocks. Swimming, snorkeling, and scuba diving are all popular. At a reconstructed *cienega* (desert wetland) you may spot native wildlife such as a Texas spiny soft-shell turtle, a blotched water snake, or a green heron. See p. 367.

THE best LUXURY & HISTORIC HOTELS

- **The Adolphus Hotel** (Dallas): Looking spiffier than ever after a 2016 renovation, this elegant old-school downtown hotel has been a favorite of Dallasites and well-to-do travelers for more than a century. Still, room rates can sometimes be as low as those of far lesser hotels, making an unforgettable Dallas stay at the Adolphus an excellent value for your travel dollar. A landmark Beaux Arts hotel built in 1912 by beer baron Adolphus Busch, the Adolphus is known for its Palm Court–style lobby; warm wood parlors; and fabulous French Room (undergoing renovations at press time), one of Big D's best restaurants. Rooms are spacious and contemporary, and the location is sublime. Be sure to mosey on over to the hotel's casual Rodeo Bar and Grill at street level, with cowboy-kitsch decor and delicious hamburgers. See p. 78.
- **Rosewood Mansion on Turtle Creek** (Dallas): Repeatedly named one of the top five hotels in the United States, this beautiful, high-end hotel in a prime central location draws movie stars, princes, presidents, and luxury mavens. Formerly the grand estate of a cotton magnate in the 1920s and '30s, the Mansion is refined and supremely elegant throughout, with service to match. The revamped restaurant has again vaulted to the top of the heap and is worth a visit even if you haven't snagged a stay. See p. 84.

- **Le Méridien Dallas, The Stoneleigh** (Dallas): A spectacular updating of a landmark 1923 Dallas fixture, this swank Uptown Art Deco hotel, with richly colored rooms, feels more like an intimate boutique hotel than a large, impersonal business hotel. The Stoneleigh Bar and upstairs penthouse, occupying an entire floor, drip with style. See p. 86.
- **Omni Fort Worth Hotel** (Fort Worth): For a taste of progressive Texas luxury, this popular downtown hotel features grand public rooms, a great spa, a rooftop terrace pool and bar, and Bob's Steak & Chop House onsite. The views from the upper floors are some of the best in town. See p. 129.
- **Stockyards Hotel** (Fort Worth): Over-the-top luxury would be gauche in the old Stockyards, so this comfortable and authentic slice of the Old West qualifies as a Fort Worth indulgence: cowboy luxury. Outlaws on the run, cowpokes and their madams, and the country-western elite have all propped up their boots here. Cowtown's cattle-ranching and railroad past are effortlessly evoked in the rooms, each of which is different. See p. 127.
- **Four Seasons Hotel Houston** (Houston): With lots of space to stretch out in and plenty of amenities so you don't have to stretch too far, this hotel offers some of the best services in town. Within a few blocks are the baseball park, the basketball arena, a shopping mall, and the convention center—and just a bit beyond are the city's art district and theater and nightlife hubs. See p. 166.
- **Hotel Derek** (Houston): Here is one of the most comfortable and fun places to stay in Houston's highly popular Uptown/Galleria area. The Derek offers a rare combination of practicality and style, making it a perfect choice for the business traveler or the vacation shopper. Service is smooth, and there's always something happening there. See p. 173.
- **The Lancaster** (Houston): Personal service, charming rooms, and a great location are the keys to this hotel's success. If there's one hotel that makes having a car unnecessary in Houston, this is it. Within easy walking distance are the symphony, the opera, three theaters, the ballet, and several restaurants and clubs. See p. 167.
- **Omni Corpus Christi Hotel** (Corpus Christi): The two towers of the Omni overlook Corpus Christi Bay, and the floor-to-ceiling windows of the 20-story Bayfront Tower afford spectacular views of the Gulf, particularly from its upper floors. Pamper yourself with a massage from the in-house massage therapist or relax in the whirlpool. See p. 212.
- **Isla Grand Beach Resort** (South Padre Island): From the high-ceilinged lobby to the beautiful landscaping around the swimming pools, this resort spells luxury. Many rooms have grand views of the ocean. See p. 232.
- **Omni La Mansión del Río** (San Antonio): Occupying what was once a Catholic seminary, this hotel, standing just behind the Majestic Theatre, was built in the style of a gracious Mexican hacienda, with arresting architectural features and elegant balconies. With a wide frontage along one of the most popular stretches of the River Walk, this is one of the best hotels for those who want an authentic, uniquely San Antonio experience.

Celebrities who play the Majestic often stay here so they can slip in and out of a backstage door facing the hotel. See p. 259.

- **Mokara Hotel & Spa** (San Antonio): If relaxation and pampering are what you seek, the Mokara should be your choice. From the moment you step into the lobby, everything is taken care of effortlessly. Stay in a second-floor room and wear a robe for easy access to the hotel spa—arguably the best in the city. The hotel has a great location overlooking the River Walk, but the rooms are so attractive and comfortable, the service so personal, and the spa so easy to enjoy that you may never want to leave. See p. 259.
- **Hotel Emma** (San Antonio): Arguably the most interesting and exciting new hotel in Texas, Hotel Emma opened in November 2015 inside the 1918 brewhouse of the Pearl Brewery complex. It's the work of the same firm that revamped New York's High Line Hotel. With an aesthetic that is industrial, masculine, and Texan (but still a big hit with the ladies), this hotel is more urban than cowboy and really wows and woos guests, especially in its Sternewirth bar and clubroom set just off the lobby. Emma is home to the restaurant Supper and a gourmet market bistro, Larder, and a "culinary concierge" is on site to help guests navigate the local food scene. Set at the end of the Museum Reach section of the River Walk in the happening Pearl district, this is where to stay if you can afford to splurge. See p. 263.
- **The St. Anthony Hotel** (San Antonio): Old-school elegance (think oversize chandeliers and marble columns) meets a thoroughly modern 2015 renovation at this grand dame in downtown San Antonio, headquarters of many Fiesta festivities and balls each spring. With a rooftop pool, a prime location, and a remarkable restaurant, Rebelle, this swank old hotel bewitches guests with its romantic vibe. See p. 260.
- **The Driskill Hotel** (Austin): If you want to play cattle baron for a day or two, you can't do better than a stay in this opulent 1886 hotel, restored to its glory at the end of the 20th century. The Driskill Grill is one of Austin's most romantic restaurants. See p. 299.
- **South Congress Hotel** (Austin): In the heart of Austin's popular SoCo district, close to clubs like the Continental, shops like Lucy in Disguise, and good eats like Botticelli's, this newish Austin hotel (opened winter 2015) is the hottest spot in town. Sleek, minimalist mid-century–style interiors, hardwood floors, custom furnishings, and pillow-top beds layered with bespoke Mateo linens, the South Congress is trendy and modern but comfortable and oh so SoCo, too. See p. 315.
- **Lake Austin Spa Resort** (Austin): This spa resort has been selected as the best destination spa in the country by the readers of *Condé Nast Traveler,* and nothing spells luxury better than the pampering spa treatments for which this place is known. But you can also find it in the beauty and serenity that surround the place. The guest rooms are not the draw here as much as the resort's riverside location, the pools, the classes and services, and the sublime spa. Set far from downtown, this place is a real retreat. See p. 317.

- **Cíbolo Creek Ranch** (Shafter): Tucked under the Chinati Mountains in some of the most wide-open country in all of Texas, about 40 miles from Marfa, this is a getaway for the most special of occasions, and accordingly priced (it's famously where Justice Antonin Scalia shuffled off this mortal coil). The idyllic setting plays host today to a first-class resort, featuring beautiful guest rooms with red-tile floors, adobe walls, and sumptuous border decor. The recreational opportunities are as impressive as the scenery. See p. 370.
- **Gage Hotel** (Marathon): Located 50 miles north of Big Bend National Park, the historic Gage Hotel opened in 1927 as a social hub for area ranchers and miners, but fell into shambles under the desert sun in the ensuing decades. But that period is long over: The current owners restored the old redbrick's many charms in the early 1980s, melding history and an eye for classic Western style. The historic rooms have cowhide rugs, hardwood floors, Navajo blankets, and charming Old West panache. With a large outdoor courtyard, intimate fire pits, a fine restaurant with a sprawling patio, and family-sized luxury casitas, the Gage is legendary among Texans, many of whom say it's their favorite place to stay in West Texas or when trekking to Big Bend National Park. See p. 404.

THE best BED & BREAKFASTS & BOUTIQUE HOTELS

- **Hôtel St. Germain** (Dallas): Ever wanted to stay with your spouse at a plush bordello? This intimate boutique hotel with its elegant, prix-fixe restaurant is about as close as you'll come to that fantasy. A gorgeous mix of early-20th-century France and New Orleans, the seven suites are so swank, with such pampering features as wood-burning fireplaces, draped Napoléon sleigh beds, bidets, and soaking tubs, you may never want to leave your room. See p. 83.
- **Sinya on Lone Man Creek** (Wimberley): Glamping comes to Texas, and we absolutely love it. An authentic tented African safari suite set high on a bluff overlooking a creek, with a king-size bed, two decks, a living area, a full bathroom, hot tub, outdoor shower and more, Sinya is the most romantic and unusual lodging I've seen since my last luxury safari in Kenya. Reserve this place right now, if you can—it stays solidly booked year-round. See p. 262.
- **The Ashton Hotel** (Fort Worth): Just off Sundance Square, this boutique hotel—one of Fort Worth's only small luxury hotels—offers plush rooms and smooth service, as well as one of the best restaurants in north Texas: Six 10 Grille. See p. 129.
- **Settlers Crossing** (Fredericksburg): Just 5 miles outside of the popular Hill Country hamlet of Fredericksburg, and just up the road from the famous ghost town/tourist draw of Luckenbach, this enchanting 35-acre property features seven individual Pennsylvania Dutch–style cottages, log homes,

and historic farmhouses, most with fireplaces, and all with the comforts of home in German "Sunday Haus" bed-and-breakfast style. See p. 340.

- **Trois Estate at Enchanted Rock** (Fredericksburg): About 16 miles from Main Street, Fredericksburg, this San Miguel Allende–inspired bed-and-breakfast feels like a small, quiet Santa Fe–style village tucked away in the hills, complete with a wedding chapel and underground grotto, a cap-gun museum, saloon, suites, and more. It's unusual, to be sure, and so Texan, of course, but it's also utterly enchanting—as are its views of the pink-marble majesty of Enchanted Rock. See p. 339.
- **Kimber Modern** (Austin): Nothing looks sharper than modern design brilliantly set in natural surroundings. It makes the common terrace of this small hotel an uncommonly beautiful place to linger on a lazy afternoon. Sparse/minimalist, trendy, and clean-lined—this mod little B&B is set on a quiet neighborhood street just behind the Continental Club and the busy boulevard of South Congress Avenue. See p. 314.
- **Hotel Saint Cecilia** (Austin): This oh-so-trendy hotel hidden under massive oak tress just off South Congress Avenue captures the feel for what's fun about the Austin scene. It also takes comfort to an entirely new level: Sleep deeply on a handmade Swedish mattress; greet the morning with your favorite crepes; lounge on your own private deck or patio; or spin some vinyl on your in-room turntable. Stay in the main house, unless you prefer a stark mid-century bungalow instead. Some guests say they've sensed a hipper-than-thou vibe here from management, and the rates are sky-high, but I'd still stay here if I wanted to splurge. See p. 313.
- **Havana Hotel** (San Antonio): Tucked away on a quiet stretch of the River Walk is a fabulous old house turned hipster hotel with a terrace restaurant and bar, Ocho, upstairs and a dark speakeasy-style bar below street level. I adore the vibe at this best-kept-secret hotel of Austin hotelier Liz Lambert, known for her distinctive design aesthetic at Hotel San Jose and the St. Cecelia off Austin's hot SoCo strip. See p. 260.

THE best HOTEL BARGAINS

- **Belmont Hotel** (Dallas): Dallas usually goes gaga over mirrored glass and brand-spanking-new buildings, so it's a refreshing change to find this vintage 1940s motor lodge in Oak Cliff transformed into a funky, retro boutique hotel. With its lounge bar and midcentury-modern decor, it's a dollop of Palm Springs with the attitude of Austin and views of the Dallas skyline—all at affordable rates. See p. 82.
- **Hyatt House Dallas, Lincoln Park** (Dallas): This straightforward, residential-style hotel, formerly known as Hyatt Summerfield Suites, primarily targets businesspeople, but it's also a good value for families. The spacious suites have fully equipped kitchens, and the hotel has a pool, a small spa, and an exercise room. See p. 88.

- **Riverwalk Vista** (San Antonio): I like to think I discovered this place—it's a gem hidden in plain sight right near the River Walk's Commerce Street bridge. Picture Restoration Hardware–style furnishings, tall ceilings, wood floors, exposed brick, fast Wi-Fi, strong coffee, and a great location—all for a surprisingly good rate. See p. 261.
- **Austin Motel** (Austin): Look for the catchy "So Close Yet So Far Out" sign in Austin's hip SoCo area. The rooms of this old motel have been individually furnished, many in fun and funky styles, but the place retains its 1950s character and its lower-than-modern-day prices. See p. 316.
- **Park Plaza Hotel** (Seguin): Just 35 miles from San Antonio, this small-town hotel on an old downtown central park square offers the best rates of any hotel of its kind, yet delivers a contemporary, big-city–style experience. A fresh new hotel in a historic building, this is a good little getaway if you want to venture outside Austin or San Antonio and see a bit more of the area between the two. See p. 283.

THE best RESTAURANTS

- **Fearing's** (Dallas): Cowboy-boot-clad chef Dean Fearing made his name as an innovator of Southwestern cuisine at the Mansion on Turtle Creek, but in 2007, he opened his own place in the swanky Ritz-Carlton in Dallas's Uptown. Since its opening, Fearing's has been named "Restaurant of the Year" and "Table of the Year" by *Esquire* magazine, and #1 in "Hotel Dining in the U.S." by Zagat. See p. 93.
- **Flora Street Cafe** (Dallas): Dallas's other celebrity chef in boots, the man who created the legendary Star Canyon, Stephan Pyles closed his namesake restaurant so he could concentrate on opening this new, exciting eatery in the Arts District, celebrating what he calls "elevated Texas cuisine." See p. 90.
- **Cured** (San Antonio): This charcuterie-board–driven gastropub with house-cured meats and a happening bar scene is our favorite restaurant in San Antonio's popular Pearl culinary district. Chef Steve McHugh is a recent James Beard nominee for Best Chef Southwest, and though the title eluded him this year, all bets are on him next time. See p. 272.
- **Cafe Annie** (Houston): No other restaurant in Houston garners the attention that this place does from foodies and food critics alike. With innovative Southwestern cooking, the best wine list in the city, and a master sommelier (the only "master" in Texas), the restaurant has plenty of credentials. Chef/owner Robert Del Grande offers up wonderful dishes that show just how fertile the crossbreeding of Mexican and American cooking can be. See p. 187.
- **Uchi** (Austin): Don't think of Uchi as just a good place for sushi and Japanese cuisine; it's a great restaurant, period, with creative cooking that transcends its humble roots. Foodies nationwide know it as the best restaurant in Austin (though you could argue there are others as good). Still, this chic, expensive restaurant, set a revamped 1930s house, is always noisy and crowded, a popular spot because it's always so good. See p. 324.

- **Café J** (Lubbock): Who knew Lubbock had such fabulous fine dining? Café J and its Blue Martini Lounge have cuisine to rival the best eateries in Houston and Dallas, with seasonal farm-to-fork fare and clever craft libations. A favorite of Red Raider alums and visiting parents, this quiet, art-filled restaurant sits directly across the street from the sprawling Texas Tech campus. See p. 438.
- **Café Central** (El Paso): Well worth the splurge, Café Central is a sleek urban bistro serving sophisticated international cuisine. The menu changes daily but always offers a wide range of standout fare—most notably creative Southwestern interpretations of traditional Continental dishes. The wine list is one of the city's best, and desserts include the best *tres leches* (Mexican milk cakes) in all of Texas. See p. 360.

THE best TEXAN DINING

- **Sonny Bryan's Smokehouse** (Dallas): Sonny Bryan's has been turning out sweet barbecue since 1910, and the little smoke shack has acquired legendary status. Salesmen perch on their car hoods with their sleeves rolled up and wolf down hickory-smoked brisket, sliced-beef sandwiches, and succulent onion rings. Thinner sorts squeeze into tiny one-armed school desks and get ready to douse their brisket with superb, tangy sauce. A classic. See p. 98.
- **Lonesome Dove Western Bistro** (Fort Worth): This friendly and eclectic restaurant challenges Cowtown to broaden its horizons. The Southwestern menu at this Stockyards eatery successfully stretches the popular theme in new ways, adding unique Texas touches that are both avant-garde and comforting. Pop in for the inexpensive Stockyards lunch special or dive into a blowout dinner. See p. 133.
- **Mi Tierra** (San Antonio): Some people dismiss this cafe as touristy. Not so. It is the practitioner of old San Antonio cooking traditions. Order any of the Tex-Mex specialties and sit back and enjoy the ambience—both the food and the decor are expressions of local tastes when celebrating is called for, and this gem is worth celebrating. Open 24 hours, it's just as good at midnight as it is at noon. Better, maybe. See p. 269.
- **La Gloria** (San Antonio): Owner/chef Johnny Hernandez is kind of a big deal in these parts, with eight restaurants and counting, a catering business, and new eateries in Las Vegas and London—as well as in some Texas airports. Still, San Antonio's favorite native son is the nicest guy, and his "Mexican street food" cuisine makes for an affordable meal with exciting, multilayered flavors. His El Machito restaurant and Fruteria are also good, but La Gloria is heavenly. See p. 273.

- **The Broken Spoke** (Austin): Best known as the quintessential Texas dancehall, the Broken Spoke is also a great place for a down-home dinner of chicken-fried steak, burgers, fries, and more. Don't dare leave Austin without having at least one cold longneck here and checking out the "tourist trap" museum room just off the bar. See p. 336.
- **Franklin Barbecue** (Austin): Possibly the most famous name in Texas barbecue is Franklin. Named the James Beard Best Chef Southwest in 2015, Austin's Aaron Franklin seems as surprised by his success as anyone. He and his brick-and-mortar East Side eatery are unpretentious as they come. The loveable, goofy guy who started with a food truck has become a household name among barbecue aficionados, and Austinites consider him a guru of great barbecue. The long lines that snake around his place each day prove folks will wait hours to eat it. See p. 331.
- **Fiesta Loma Linda** (Houston): When the bubble of a perfectly puffed tortilla smothered in chili con queso bursts, anticipation meets realization in the Tex-Mex experience. The aroma, the texture, the taste . . . words fail us. You can scour the borderlands a long time before coming up with an old-fashioned Tex-Mex joint like this one. The restaurant even has its own special tortilla maker for producing these puffed-up beauties. See p. 182.
- **Gaido's** (Galveston): Proud of its traditional cooking as practiced on the Texas Gulf Coast, Gaidos is the keeper of the flame for seafood devoid of fads and trends. The family has been serving up stuffed snapper, gumbo, and fried oysters for four generations. See p. 207.
- **La Playa** (Port Aransas): This place is in no way connected to La Playa of Corpus Christi (another notable eatery). But the cooking is just as local, with Tex-Mex–style seafood dishes such as *campechana* cocktails and fish tacos. The margaritas transcend cultures. La Playa has that homey, welcoming feel that is as much Texas as anything else. See p. 213.
- **Starlight Theatre** (Terlingua): A 1930s movie palace abandoned when the mines in Terlingua went bust, the Starlight Theatre was reborn as an eatery and watering hole in 1991. The stage is still here, but the silver screen takes a back seat to the food (especially the trademark chili and filet mignon), drink (namely Texas beers and prickly-pear margaritas), and desserts (including a very good *tres leches*). If you're looking for a quirky, cool place to be for New Year's Eve, this is it. See p. 405.
- **Triple J Chophouse** (Lubbock): Triple J is the kind of place that makes you feel like you've really been to Texas. Not just a great brewpub with craft suds, this big, Western-themed restaurant offers chicken-fried steaks, wood-fired pizzas, big fat burgers, and skinny fries. It's located on the old Main Street on Buddy Holly Avenue, drawing Tech Students and locals alike. See p. 439.

THE best SHOPPING

- **Neiman Marcus** (Dallas): Established in 1907, Neiman Marcus is intimately identified with Big D and its shopaholics. The luxury purveyor's annual holiday catalog, with his-and-her fantasies for the rich, has become an institution. The downtown store is classy and retro cool, the best place in north Texas to drape yourself in Prada and Chanel. See p. 99.
- **NorthPark Center** (Dallas): Dallas loves to shop, and while the city has more malls than most people (except Dallasites) know what to do with, NorthPark is the most traditional and elegant (even when a 2007 expansion more than doubled its size). The graceful layout outclasses its more garish competitors. Rotating pieces from Ray Nasher's spectacular collection of modern sculpture are on display throughout. See p. 101.
- **Stockyards National Historic District** (Fort Worth): In Cowtown, looking the part is important. Pick up Western duds—suits and shirts with elegant piping and embroidered yokes that would have made you a star in the Old West, plus cowboy boots and other Western paraphernalia—just steps away from the old Stockyards livestock pens. On the main drag is Maverick, which has upscale Western wear and a bar serving up Lone Star longnecks. M. L. Leddy's is a family-owned shop with a big boot sign out front and top-quality hats, hand-tooled belts, and custom-made boots. And just down the street, plunk down the cash for exquisite custom cowboy boots at Ponder Boot Company. See chapter 5.
- **Uptown** (Houston): In this relatively small district, you can find Houston's Galleria (with over 300 retailers, including Saks, Neiman Marcus, Tiffany's, and Versace) and four other malls fronting Post Oak (with such retailers as Cartier and FAO Schwarz). See "Shopping" in chapter 6.
- **El Mercado** (San Antonio): You'll feel as though you've stepped across the border into an authentic Mexican market, but really you're just steps from downtown River Walk attractions at this indoor Mexican exports center with separate vendor booths at Market Square. See p. 277.
- **Fredericksburg** (Texas Hill Country): It's hard to say how a town founded by German idealists ended up being a magnet for Texas materialists, but Fredericksburg's main street is chockablock with boutiques. This is the place to come for everything from natural chocolate mint–scented room deodorizer to handmade dulcimers. See p. 338.
- **Gallery Hopping in the Big Bend** (Marfa, Alpine, Marathon, Terlingua): Besides being remote, this is one of the most artsy corners of the state, with a wide range of artists and galleries throughout these small towns. See p. 372.

THE best PLACES FOR BOOT-SCOOTIN'

- **Adair's Saloon** (Dallas): Deep Ellum's down-and-dirty honky-tonk is unfazed by the discos, rock clubs, and preppy SMU students in its midst. It sticks with its down-to-earth style, knee-slapping country and redneck rock bands, cheap beer, and tables and walls blanketed in graffiti. See p. 106.
- **Gilley's Dallas** (Dallas): The original Gilley's in Pasadena, Texas, where John Travolta famously rode a bucking bronco in *Urban Cowboy,* no longer stands, but Big D still has a branch of this storied Houston-area honky-tonk. If bigger is better, this one's right up there with the best of them: It's got 90,000 square feet of dance floor, bars, and stages, and even if it primarily draws tourists, it's still a good time. See p. 105.
- **Billy Bob's Texas** (Fort Worth): Kind of like a big-tent country theme park, Billy Bob's has it all: 40 bars, a huge dance floor for two-stepping, pro bull riding, and live performances by big names in country music. Of course, it also has free Thursday-night dance lessons: Learn the Schottische or the Cotton-Eyed Joe, and soon you'll be two-stepping like a Texan. See p. 142.
- **Texas Hill Country** (San Antonio and Austin): South Texas has some of the most wonderful old honky-tonks in the state, and the former ghost town of Gruene, a hopping tourist spot just outside of New Braunfels, has one of the best. The oldest continuously opened country-and-western dance hall in Texas is **Gruene Hall,** still one of the finest places to listen to music. Another great Texas spot, **Arkey Blue's Silver Dollar Bar** is a genuine spit-and-sawdust Hill Country honky-tonk on Bandera's Main Street. When there's no live music, plug a quarter in the old jukebox and play a country ballad by owner Arkey. And look for the table where Hank Williams, Sr., carved his name. See the sections on "Hill Country Side Trips" in chapters 8 and 9.
- **Broken Spoke** (Austin): This is the gen-u-ine item, a Western honky-tonk with a wood-plank floor and a cowboy-hatted, two-steppin' crowd. Still, it's in Austin, so don't be surprised if the band wears Hawaiian shirts, or if tongues are planted firmly in cheeks for some songs. Don't miss the "tourist trap" museum room in the back. See p. 336.

TEXAS IN DEPTH

by Janis Turk & Neil Edward Schlecht

2

Texas looms large in American culture, and Texans are unapologetic in their swaggering embrace of the place they call home. Self-confident and independent almost to a fault, Texas seems to embody all that's good, bad, and especially big about the United States. The former independent Republic of Texas—which shook off the landlord claims of Spain, Mexico, France, and even the U.S.—has diehards who still wish the second-largest state after Alaska would just hurry up and secede.

Texans don't seem to mind too much if outsiders get caught up in the myths and clichés about Texas; they're kind of proud of the rough-and-tumble romance of the state and buy into its mythical "Lonesome Dove" past. Still, locals know there's a lot more to love about the Texas they call home. They know a 10-gallon hat doesn't hold 10 gallons of anything, and Texas isn't all flat, dry, and featureless, filled with cowboys on the range, oilmen watching backyard gushers spit up black gold, and helmet-haired beauty queens. But it's hard to compete with the state's image, the canvas for hundreds of old Western flicks. The big-sky frontier of Texas and the West is the quintessential American landscape, and the mythic cowboy leading his longhorn cattle on drives is a quintessential heroic figure.

Once a separate nation, and today bigger than England and France combined, Texas is a place that dreams big and walks tall. The history of Texas is laced with events and heroes large and legendary, many of which have been catapulted into national lore. In many ways, Texas has come to symbolize the nation's westward expansion, its complicated struggle for independence, and the dearly held mystique of independent living and wide-open spaces. Texas's complex settlement pattern—the territory was claimed by Spain, France, and Mexico before becoming an independent republic and then the 28th state in the Union in 1845—supports its mythic status. "Six flags" really did famously fly over the state from the 16th to the 19th century, during which time there were eight changes of government. Even though the state has increasingly become one of immigrants from other states and other nations south of the border, Texans continue to exhibit a fiercely independent streak. The pages that follow explore the state's history and provide a primer on its unique culture.

TEXAS TODAY

The legendary cowboy still exists, but Texas is now decidedly more urban than it once was. It's home to three of the nation's 10 largest cities: Houston, Dallas, and San Antonio. Texas today is as much a leader of high-tech industries as it is an agricultural and ranching state. Houston, Fort Worth, and Dallas hold world-class art museums and collections where local philanthropists have used their money and influence to import globally celebrated architects to build some of the nation's most talked-about museums. Although Texas is, by and large, a conservative place, Austin has long supported thriving hippie and renegade musician communities, and Dallas is nipping at its heels with a lively music scene. The state is a melting pot with pockets of Czech, German, and Irish communities; bilingual populations in the lower Rio Grande Valley and border towns; and more than 4 million people of Hispanic descent.

This enormous state also has immense geographical diversity: desert plains in the Texas Panhandle, the Piney Woods in east Texas, beaches in the Gulf Coast, north Texas prairies, scenic wildflowers and lakes in central Texas Hill Country, desert canyons in Big Bend National Park, and the rugged Guadalupe Mountains.

Still, some clichés ring true. The second-largest state in the United States in both landmass and population is larger than any country in Europe. You can set out from Amarillo in your car and drive south for 15 hours and still not reach Mexico. Everything is bigger in Texas, of course: The ranches, the steaks, and the cars—Cadillacs with longhorns on the grille and monster pickup trucks with gun racks—really do exist. In Texas, you can carry a concealed handgun—even in church—and the state is known as the capital-punishment capital of the world, though the number of executions has dropped in recent years. "Don't Mess with Texas" is more than an effective anti-litter campaign.

Despite the bluster, Texans are startlingly friendly and hospitable folks. Deals are still completed with handshakes, and adults say "yes, ma'am" and "no, sir" to each other. Also, Texans love their sports, especially football. This is a place where entire towns pack the bleachers for Friday-night high-school games and preachers mention the game in their sermons, praying for victory in a kind of gridiron holy war.

Former Texas governor and owner of the Texas Rangers baseball team—and now former president—George W. Bush maintains a sprawling ranch in Crawford, Texas (outside of Waco), to which he regularly retreated during his presidency. Today, he calls Dallas home. As the Bush presidency perhaps unwittingly illustrated, it's hard for most people—whether in other parts of the U.S. or abroad—to be indifferent about Texas. It's a place to romanticize and ridicule, to dream about and dismiss. Texans can leave the state, but sooner or later they'll admit their weaknesses for Texas dance halls and Old

West saloons, Tex-Mex and barbecue, cowboy boots, and country music. From the big sky and flat plains and the Hill Country highways lined by Texas bluebonnets to the larger-than-life personalities like LBJ, Janis Joplin, Ross Perot, Ann Richards, and Willie Nelson, Texas stays with you.

LOOKING BACK: TEXAS HISTORY

Texas's roots stretch back to some 30,000 different Native American tribes—including the Caddos, Coahuiltecans, Tonkawas, Apaches, and Comanches—who occupied the land long before European settlers arrived in the 16th century. Indeed, the name "Texas" can be traced to Native American tribes: *Tejas* is thought to be the Spanish pronunciation of the Caddo word for "friend." Some of that Native American legacy can still be seen, in the form of pictographs and petroglyphs, at **Lubbock Lake Landmark,** an archaeological and natural history preserve. The **Panhandle Plains Historical Museum** in Canyon, the largest history museum in the state, has an excellent section on paleontology and geology.

Six Flags Over Texas is more than the name of some of the state's most popular amusement parks. The flags of six different nations have flown over Texas: Spain, France, Mexico, the Republic of Texas, the Confederate States of America, and the United States of America. Texas is not only immense; it's a state with a complicated and colorful history.

EUROPEAN CONQUEST Spain was the first European country to claim the territory, and France also ruled over a short-lived colony in Texas. In 1519, the Spanish explorer Alonso Álvarez de Piñeda made a map of the Texas coast, establishing the basis for the first claim to the land. Just like other Spaniards elsewhere in the Americas, Alvar Núñez Cabeza de Vaca was in search of cities of gold when he landed in 1528 in what is now Galveston.

In 1598, the explorer Juan de Oñate formally claimed Texas for Spain, but the first permanent settlement and official mission, Corpus Christi de la Isleta (near El Paso), didn't come for another 84 years. Spain eventually held Texas for 300 years. The 1749 adobe **Spanish Governor's Palace** (the seat of government when San Antonio served as the capital of the Spanish province of Texas), the **El Paso Missions Trail** (including the **Presidio Chapel of San Elceario,** where the "first Thanksgiving" is said to have taken place in 1598), the four Franciscan missions of **San Antonio Missions National Historic Park,** and the **Meadows Museum of Art** in Dallas (with a fine collection of Spanish old masters) are good places to relive the state's Spanish heritage.

In 1690, Spaniards quickly responded to a French territorial claim and settlements in Texas and Louisiana by establishing their own mission, San Francisco de los Tejas, in east Texas. Just 3 decades later, the Mission of San Antonio de Valero—known to all as the **Alamo**—led to the founding of the city of San Antonio (which became the seat of Spanish government in Texas in 1772). The brief French period of rule is evoked at Austin's **French Legation Museum,** built in 1841 for France's representative to the Republic of Texas.

MEXICO'S TURN After winning independence from Spain in 1821, Mexico turned its sights north and granted authorization to Stephen F. Austin to settle in southeast Texas with a colony of 300 families (the "Texas Original 300"). The new colony, made up mostly of people from Tennessee, marked the official beginning of a fast-growing Anglo-American colonization. Austin would become known as the "Father of Texas."

American settlers were forced to accept both Mexican citizenship and Roman Catholicism to remain in Texas. Mexico did little to protect its colony or define the state's rights, however. As more Americans settled there, Texas took on the shape of a U.S. outpost, despite the Mexican flag flying over it. Stephen Austin organized a militia (which would become the famous Texas Rangers) to protect the colony. As tensions grew, Mexico denied the entry of additional American settlers in 1830, and further religious, political, and cultural clashes prompted the self-proclaimed president of Mexico, Gen. António López de Santa Anna, to bolster his troops in Texas. Texans requested the status of an independent Mexican state. When their diplomatic initiative failed, Texans declared independence from Mexico on March 2, 1836.

Texas forces attacked San Antonio. Gen. Santa Anna and his troops vastly outnumbered and then ruthlessly crushed the valiant Texans, led by Davy Crockett and Jim Bowie, at the Alamo in a 2-week battle in March 1836. Mexican troops slaughtered more than 300 Texas prisoners at Goliad only days later, unwittingly giving rise to the battle cry of independence: "Remember the Alamo! Remember Goliad!" (Today, of course, the second defeat has been largely wiped from memory.) The Texans, led by Gen. Sam Houston's army, rebounded with a stunning and decisive victory over Santa Anna at the Battle of San Jacinto, winning their independence from Mexico on April 21, 1836.

Besides seeing the famous **Alamo,** visitors interested in reliving the period of Mexican rule over Texas can check out the other four missions in San Antonio, including the **Mission San José,** where mariachi masses are still held. They can also visit **San Jacinto Monument,** outside Houston, where Sam Houston's small band of Texans defeated the Mexican army, or **San Fernando Cathedral** in San Antonio, the oldest cathedral sanctuary in the U.S., from which Gen. Santa Anna raised the flag of "no quarter."

THE REPUBLIC OF TEXAS, STATEHOOD & CIVIL WAR The Lone Star flag flew over the Republic of Texas from 1836 to 1845. The new nation was officially recognized by the United States and Europe, but not Mexico. Six different sites served as the Texas capital, until the town of Austin became the permanent capital in 1839 (visitors can tour the country's largest **state capitol,** built in 1888). The republic's government was based on the U.S. model, with a president, senate, house of representatives, and an army, navy, and militia. Yet the new republic faced daunting problems, including boundary disputes, debt, and continued concerns about Mexican attack. Texas joined the United States as the 28th state in 1845, ceding some western lands (parts of modern-day Oklahoma, New Mexico, and Colorado) to the Union. The state's annexation precipitated the Mexican-American War in 1846, which concluded with

Mexico's surrender to the United States 2 years later. The Treaty of Guadalupe Hidalgo rejected Mexican claims on Texas and the Southwest.

That wasn't the end of tensions and division, however. As a slave state, Texas joined the southern Confederate States of America and seceded from the United States in January 1861. About 90,000 Texans saw military service, and the war devastated the Texas economy. At the end of the Civil War, Texas rejoined the Union in 1870.

THE WILD WEST & TEXAS OIL Texas formed part of the Wild West, and most settlers lived a frontier life. A war-ravaged economy and abundant longhorn cattle in southern Texas led to the great Texas trail drives to northern markets in the 1860s. The drives north from Texas to Kansas City, such as the famous Chisholm Trail, brought prosperity to ranchers and particularly the city of Fort Worth, which became known as "Cowtown" as the site of cattle auctions and shipping companies. Commerce grew exponentially as railroads reached Texas at the end of the 19th century. In 1873, the Houston and Texas Central Railway reached the Red River, where it connected with the Missouri, Kansas, and Texas Railroad to establish the first rail route from Texas to St. Louis (and the East). The boomtown environment attracted opportunistic entrepreneurs, and the Wild West drew outlaws, among them Wild Bill Hickok, John Wesley Hardin, and Billy the Kid (and later, Texas-born Bonnie Parker and Clyde Barrow, who hid out at the Stockyards Hotel in Fort Worth and were later gunned down by Texas Rangers).

But progress was apparent across the state. By 1883, the University of Texas had begun classes in Austin, and the current state capitol was dedicated in 1888. At the turn of the 20th century, the Texas oil and gas boom exploded with the discovery of the Spindletop oil field near Beaumont, transforming the agricultural economy and bringing riches to many other Texans. The discovery of "black gold" produced new Texas boomtowns, drawing an influx of workers—known as wildcatters and mavericks—looking for rapid wealth. Additional oil fields were discovered in east and west Texas, as well as beneath the Gulf of Mexico.

You can explore more of the Lone Star State's Western heritage in Fort Worth at the **Stockyards National Historic District** (including daily longhorn cattle drives, the Stockyards Museum, and vintage railroad to Grapevine), **Texas Cowboy Hall of Fame, National Cowgirl Museum and Hall of Fame,** and **Log Cabin Village.** In Dallas, visit **Old City Park** for a living museum of a late-19th-century village. Some of the finest Western art in the U.S. is found at the **Amon Carter Museum of Western Art** in Fort Worth.

THE 20TH CENTURY TO TODAY Though Texas suffered through the Great Depression along with the rest of the country, the state quickly became the largest producer of oil in the country. The good times were enhanced at **Gruene Hall** in the Hill Country near Austin, the oldest country-and-western dance hall in Texas; and **Floore's Country Store** in San Antonio, a 1940s roadhouse with a half-acre dance floor. Visitors today can relive the early 20th century and enjoy outstanding live music at both establishments.

The 1960s were an especially eventful and tumultuous time in Texas. In 1962, **NASA** opened the Manned Spacecraft Center in Houston (later renamed Lyndon B. Johnson Space Center). But the next real watershed event in Texas was a tragic one. On November 22, 1963, President John F. Kennedy was assassinated as his motorcade passed through downtown Dallas. The presumed assassin, Lee Harvey Oswald, was gunned down on national television by local businessman Jack Ruby. See the grassy knoll and visit the excellent **Sixth Floor Museum at Dealey Plaza,** housed in the infamous Texas School Book Depository, for exhibits that not only detail the assassination but bring to life the times and legacy of the Kennedy presidency.

Kennedy's vice president, Texas's own Lyndon B. Johnson, was sworn in as the 36th president aboard the presidential plane at Dallas's Love Field airport. LBJ's wife, Lady Bird Johnson, would later create her own lasting legacy with a dedication to beautifying Texas with wildflowers on the sides of highways and throughout the Hill Country; visitors today can ramble the gardens at the **Lady Bird Johnson Wildflower Center** in Austin. In 1966, a gunman, Charles Whitman, terrorized the University of Texas in Austin, shooting with a rifle from the observation deck of the campus tower. Seventeen people died that day. By the end of the decade, President Kennedy's mission to go to the moon was accomplished; the Apollo 11 astronaut Neil Armstrong uttered his memorable first words after landing on the moon: "Houston, the Eagle has landed." Visit the **Space Center Houston** for an interactive display of NASA technology.

In 1988, the transplanted Houstonian (also a U.S. congressman with a background in the Texas oil business) **George H. W. Bush** was elected president of the United States. Bush's son, George W. Bush, was elected the 43rd president of the United States in 2000 after a controversial decision by the U.S. Supreme Court, and he served two terms in office. Today, the **George W. Bush Presidential Library and Museum** stands on the SMU Campus near downtown Dallas.

Throughout the late 20th century, the urban areas of Texas continued their explosive growth. Houston, San Antonio, and Dallas rank among the 10 largest cities in the United States. Texas's Hispanic growth also continues, with more than one-third of Texas residents now of Hispanic origin. The major cities and fast-growing, formerly suburban communities successfully attracted firms that relocated their headquarters from around the country, and Texas is now a leader in the technology industry. The capital, Austin, has been transformed from a government and university town to one of the nation's most important clusters of high-tech corporations and computer-chip makers (including Dell, the computer company founded by a University of Texas student in his dorm room). Other high-tech and cutting-edge Texas companies include Texas Instruments, EDS, and Whole Foods. Austin (home to the South by Southwest Music + Film conference and one of the country's most vibrant music scenes), Dallas, Fort Worth, San Antonio, and Houston are today among the most popular cities in the country for young people looking for a better quality of life.

Sadly, Texas also has become associated with controversy and scandal. In 1993, the Branch Davidians, a sect led by David Koresh, sequestered themselves inside the Mount Carmel Center outside Waco; after a 50-day standoff, the storming of the compound by the U.S. ATF (as well as FBI and Texas National Guard) resulted in the deaths of Koresh and 73 other men, women, and children (both followers and agents). In 1998, an African-American man, James Byrd, was dragged to his death by a truck in Jasper, Texas; three young white men were indicted in the racist murder, which prompted the passing of a hate crimes law in Texas. In 2001, the Houston-based Enron Corporation became a national symbol of corporate greed and corruption when it was discovered to have perpetrated a complex accounting fraud that enriched executives while bankrupting employees and investors. In 2008, an arsonist, possibly a member of a local anarchist group, launched a gasoline bomb and heavily damaged the Governor's Mansion in Austin.

But despite its setbacks, the Lone Star State still triumphs: In 2011, despite record snowfall and ice storms, Dallas hosted Super Bowl XLV at the Cowboys' $1.3-*billion* AT&T Stadium, formerly Cowboys Stadium, in Arlington, Texas. That may seem like an incredible amount for a sports stadium, but in Texas, of course, it's hardly scandalous—and besides, it's really big. In 2014, the San Antonio Spurs won the NBA championship.

TEXAS IN POP CULTURE

MUSIC The role that Texas musicians have played in creating a particularly American idiom of popular music, from country to blues, jazz, and rock, is impossible to overestimate. Neither country-and-western nor the blues originated in Texas, but both genres of roots music have been indelibly shaped by talented Texans. The state ranks alongside Tennessee and Louisiana for contributions to the Americana music scene, and the number of individual music greats spawned in Texas is astonishing. They've come from such big cities as Houston, Austin, and Dallas, of course, but most remarkable is how many have rolled out of Lubbock. The barren lands of West Texas have proved incredibly fertile for the creation of homespun music. Texas has spawned so many musicians that a museum honoring their contributions to pop culture, the **Texas Musicians Museum,** in Irving, just celebrated it first anniversary.

Most listeners think of country music when they think of Texas sounds, and the state was certainly instrumental in the form's early development, a product of cowboy songs and folk contributions from new immigrants. **Bob Wills and the Texas Playboys,** who emerged from Lubbock in the 1920s, introduced Western swing (or Texas swing), a combustible mix of hillbilly tunes, fiddle music, jazz, polka, cowboy ballads, and Mexican ranchero music. Texas artists such as **George Jones** in the 1950s popularized honky-tonk, characterized by steel guitars, fiddles, and plaintive vocals. Jones, one of country's finest voices, became a balladeer and top-10 hit maker. Like **Kenny Rogers** of Conroe, Texas, he was more closely identified with Nashville than with Texas.

With characteristic independence, Texas musicians developed their own kind of country. Progressive and outlaw country fused hard-core honky-tonk, folk, rock, and blues. With country music reaching a national audience in the 1970s with the blandly orchestrated Nashville sound, a gang of Texas outlaws, led by **Willie Nelson, Waylon Jennings, Jerry Jeff Walker** (not a native Texan, but closely identified with the scene), and **Kris Kristofferson** seized the stage with a gritty, maverick rejection of the slicker country being produced in Nashville. Waylon and Willie's "Luckenbach, Texas," a song about a town with two dozen people, became a state anthem. Nelson, the braided, bandanna-wearing iconoclast of Texas country, has evolved into one of Texas's most beloved contemporary figures. He began his career as a songwriter of hits for Patsy Cline ("Crazy") and others before positioning himself as a cult artist and finally a crossover country star, daring to dabble in all genres, from traditional country and ballads ("Blue Eyes Crying in the Rain") to potent country poetry and even reggae. Nelson is currently into alternative fuels (marketing a biodiesel fuel called "BioWillie," which is available in eight states, including 16 locations in Texas) as much as he is into exploring new musical genres.

Other Texas singer-songwriters, such as **Guy Clark** and **Townes Van Zandt,** less prone to the outlaw lifestyle but still resolutely independent, mined a territory of lyrical country-folk music. These unjustly overlooked artists laid the foundation for the current generation of Texas songwriters, including **Lyle Lovett, Jimmie Dale Gilmore, Shake Russell,** and **Steve Earle,** musicians at home in country as well as in rock, gospel, and the blues. Western swing has undergone a couple of rounds of revival, in the 1970s and again in the early 1990s. **Asleep at the Wheel,** a multi-piece band that has gone through innumerable changes in lineup, has been present for both revivals. Current stars among Texas singer-songwriters and "Americana" musicians include **Cody Canada, Brandon Rhyder, Wade Bowen, Randy Rogers, Kelly Willis, Sean McConnell, Jason Boland, Bruce Robison,** and **Charlie Robison.**

Texas blues began with such legendary figures as **Blind Lemmon Jefferson** (whose "Black Snake Moan" struck quite a chord in the 1920s) and **Blind Willie Johnson,** both of whom played the area around Deep Ellum in Dallas. **Robert Johnson** may have been from Mississippi, but he made his only known recordings in Dallas and San Antonio in the 1930s. **Sam "Lightning" Hawkins,** of Houston, created a blistering blues guitar style that influenced generations of rockers. Other notable Houston blues musicians include **B. B. King, Albert Collins,** and **Clarence "Gatemouth" Brown.**

Port Arthur's **Janis Joplin**'s raw vocals and blues-inflected rock (not to mention her heroin overdose and posthumous hit, "Me and Bobby McGee") made her an icon of the 1960s. **Stevie Ray Vaughan,** an incendiary guitar wizard from south Dallas, also became a blues-rock star before his light went out prematurely in a helicopter crash in 1990. Austin club regulars **Angela Strehli, Lou Ann Barton,** and **Toni Price** continue the Texas blues tradition.

Texas has produced its share of rock-'n'-roll pioneers, too. Lubbock's **Buddy Holly,** the bespectacled proto-rocker who with his band, the Crickets, influenced Elvis, the Beatles, and countless new-wavers with tunes like "Peggy Sue" and "That'll Be the Day," went down in a 1959 plane crash after just a couple of years at the top. **Roy Orbison,** from Vernon, Texas, began his career in rockabilly, but his high, haunting voice propelled a number of memorable mainstream hits in the 1960s, like "Only the Lonely" and "In Dreams." **ZZ Top,** from Houston, started out in swaggering blues-rock territory, before their belly-length beards and songs like "Legs" and "Tube Steak Boogie" made them MTV darlings. Current Texas faves on the alternative scene include the intellectual pop of **Spoon** (from Austin); the dusty, Neil Young–like **Centro-Matic** (Denton); the trippy, post-rock instrumentalists **Explosions in the Sky** (Midland), whose music is the soundtrack to the football-oriented TV show *Friday Night Lights* and the epic film *Australia;* and the costumed, unwieldy collective **The Polyphonic Spree** (Dallas).

With its Latino roots and large Hispanic population, Texas has given rise to yet another genre that reflects cross-cultural fertilization: Tex-Mex border sounds. Conjunto, *norteña,* and Tejano are all slightly different takes on this definitive Tex-Mex style, anchored by the accordion and 12-string Mexican guitar. **Flaco Jiménez** (San Antonio) is the leading *conjunto* proponent today. **Selena** (Corpus Christi) brought Tejano to national audiences before her death (she was murdered by the founder of her fan club), and reached a wider audience through films and books about her life. Another cross-cultural musical phenomenon is zydeco, a Cajun stew that is especially popular in the Houston and Galveston areas. **Los Lonely Boys,** three Mexican-American brothers from San Angelo, had a huge hit in 2004 with "Heaven" and their radio-friendly brand of Latino-tinged blues pop, which some have labeled "Texican."

In large part, Texas has proved such fecund musical ground because of its strong tradition of live performance. For a couple of decades now, Austin has immodestly declared itself the "Live Music Capital of the World," and its rollicking clubs have presented nightly diverse lineups of homegrown and imported live music acts. From Armadillo World Headquarters to Club Foot and Liberty Lunch, Austin has embraced a disproportionate share of legendary, beloved, and now-defunct live music venues. **Gilley's** and **Billy Bob's,** two huge, slick honky-tonks still going strong in Houston and Fort Worth, are important national showcases for traditional country and redneck rock bands, while classic small-town Texas dance halls such as **Gruene Hall** (in Gruene, pronounced "green," located north of San Antonio/south of Austin, just outside of New Braunfels) keep the flame burning. Dancing to country music is a true Texas art, and while the popularity of individual dances—the Two-Step, Cotton-Eyed Joe, and line dancing (a kind of kickers' aerobics)—rises and falls with the latest hits, in Texas they have amazing staying power. The dance floors of local honky-tonks pack in young boot-scooters, single rodeo queens in tight jeans, as well as nimble older folks two-stepping like there's no tomorrow.

For rock and alternative music lovers, two of the biggest music festivals in the country are held annually in Austin: **South by Southwest (SXSW)** in March, and the outdoor **Austin City Limits Festival** (cruelly held in late September/early October at the tail end of the brutal central Texas summer).

FILM Texas—with its larger-than-life characters and mythic representation of the Southwest—has been featured prominently in film, both popular blockbusters and serious art movies. Foremost among them, of course, were Westerns starring John Wayne, many of which were placed in Texas, including *The Alamo, Red River,* and *Three Texas Steers.* John Ford's 1956 *The Searchers*—also starring Wayne—is generally considered one of the greatest Westerns ever filmed. *Giant* (also from 1956) is expansive like Texas itself, set on a massive ranch location under a huge sky with Rock Hudson as a ranch baron who wins over Elizabeth Taylor. In 1969's *Easy Rider,* Peter Fonda and Dennis Hopper take a motorcycle road trip through Texas and meet up with Jack Nicholson.

More recent mainstream movies include *Boyhood,* from *Dazed and Confused* and *Before Sunrise* director Richard Linklater and staring Ethan Hawke; and *The Dallas Buyers Club* with Uvalde, Texas native Matthew McConaughey. Other iconic Texas films include *Urban Cowboy,* complete with John Travolta in a 10-gallon hat; and the football-themed *Friday Night Lights,* based on the book by H. G. Bissinger.

The art film category is well represented by *No Country for Old Men,* the Oscar-winning Coen Brothers movie based on the violent Cormac McCarthy novel; *The Last Picture Show,* Peter Bogdanovich's film (based on another McMurtry novel) about high school seniors in Anarene, a nowheresville Texas town; *Tender Mercies,* Bruce Bereford's 1983 movie starring Robert Duvall as a former country singer who finds redemption in the hands of a widow on the Texas plains; *Paris, Texas,* about another Texas drifter (played by Harry Dean Stanton), though this time made by a German, Wim Wenders; and *Days of Heaven,* by the Texan Terrence Malick, about a steel worker who flees to the wheat fields of Texas and finds conflict and tragedy when confronted by a wealthy landowner. If that's all too bleak and grown-up, how about *The Texas Chainsaw Massacre,* or Richard Linklater's homages to Austin, *Slacker* and *Dazed and Confused*?

TELEVISION Surely the most famous television series set in Texas was the long-running nighttime soap *Dallas,* which gave rise to the national mantra "Who shot J. R.?" and made people across the globe believe that all Texans had oil rigs in their backyards. *Lonesome Dove,* based on the novel by Texan Larry McMurtry, with an unforgettable screenplay by Austinite Bill Witliff, was a hugely successful miniseries in 1989, featuring Robert Duvall and Tommy Lee Jones and filmed at several Texas ranches. More recently, the critically acclaimed series adapted from the book and film of the same name, *Friday Night Lights,* beautifully explored a small West Texas town where the weekly ritual, the high school football game, is an obsession (the show was shot in Austin). *King of the Hill,* an animated series from Mike Judge, an

Austinite by way of Garland, was set in the fictional small Texas town of Arlen. PBS's *Austin City Limits* is a legendary long-running live-music program featuring diverse artists from all over the country and globe.

BOOKS Fans of James Michener will appreciate his historical novel *Texas.* Michener was an excellent storyteller as well as historian, and his book (exhaustively) brings the state and its people to life. (It's a big state, but couldn't he have done it in fewer than 1,344 pages?)

Two authors who share a "Mc" in their surnames dominate the subject of contemporary fiction set in Texas: Larry McMurtry and Cormac McCarthy. These two writers are much more than an introduction to both the real and mythical Texas. The contributions of McMurtry to the Texas canon are many. *Lonesome Dove* (1985) won the Pulitzer Prize for its depiction of ex–Texas Rangers on a cattle drive. (See the original script and props from the television mini-series at the Wittliff Collections at the Alkek Library of Texas State University in San Marcos.) Other significant works by McMurtry about or set in Texas, many delving into the lives of cowboys and ranchers, include *Leaving Cheyenne; Lonesome Dove; Terms of Endearment; The Last Picture Show; Horseman, Pass By; In a Narrow Grave: Essays on Texas;* and *All My Friends Are Going to Be Strangers.*

Cormac McCarthy, who is not a Texan, is also a Pulitzer Prize winner. The Western and Southern Gothic themes and depiction of brutal violence hone in on weighty matters of life and death, and McCarthy is frequently compared to William Faulkner. His masterworks are *Blood Meridian* (concerning the 19th-century travels of "the kid," largely in Texas) and *All the Pretty Horses* (about a young cowboy and his friend from West Texas who venture to Mexico). McCarthy's *No Country for Old Men* is also set in southwestern Texas, along the Mexico border.

Annie Proulx's *That Old Ace in the Hole* is set in the Panhandle. Texas author Sandra Cisneros's short stories, such as *Women Hollering Creek,* are powerful and critically acclaimed. *The Gates of the Alamo,* by Stephen Harrigan, is a gripping fictionalized version of Texas's most famous battle. Among fiction and nonfiction with somewhat more mass appeal, *Friday Night Lights* is for many readers one of the finest sports books written, chronicling the football obsession of a small West Texas town; and *Semi-Tough,* a novel by Dan Jenkins about two Fort Worth football studs, is one of the funniest books ever. Jenkins's *Baja Oklahoma* offers a funny, poignant, and somewhat raunchy look at what we might call classic modern Texans, at least the Fort Worth trailer-trash variety.

Even readers who don't cook will enjoy *The Only Texas Cookbook,* by Linda West Eckhardt. Interspersed among its 300 recipes—including classics such as Fuzzy's Fantastic South Texas Road Meat Chili and Bad Hombre Eggs—are humorous anecdotes on food-related subjects. Those who savor biting political wit—and don't mind seeing every Texas Republican mercilessly skewered—will thoroughly enjoy any book of essays by the late newspaper columnist Molly Ivins, who is credited with bestowing the nickname "Dubya" on George W. Bush.

EATING & DRINKING

Texans are famous for their love of artery-clogging steaks the size of Volkswagens. Amarillo's Big Texan Steak Ranch restaurant features a 72-ouncer (eat it in under an hour and get it free). Locals are rabidly fond of **chicken-fried steak.** This oddity is a thick slab of inexpensive beef beaten until tender and dipped in batter, deep-fried like chicken, buried under a puddle of cream gravy, doused with pepper, and served with a glob of mashed potatoes (skins on). Home-style veggies such as okra and black-eyed peas are also worthy accompaniments. A good chicken-fried steak—crisp, light, and tender—is weirdly enjoyable, but an inferior one can be like gnawing on an old tire. Note to Yankees who don't want to get laughed out of town: Don't specify "medium" or "medium rare" when ordering a chicken-fried steak. It comes only one way: cooked.

But steak—whether broiled or chicken fried—is only part of the story. The real holy trinity of Texas eats consists of three down-home staples that no true Texan can do without for long: **chili, barbecue,** and **Tex-Mex.** And some like it hot—so Texas is home to *Chile Pepper* magazine in Houston, which only writes about (and provide recipes for) zesty eats.

CHILI A bowl of Texas red (beef chili without beans), hot or hotter than hell, is often thought of as Mexican or Tex-Mex. But it's as Texan as they come, with its origins in San Antonio in the late 1800s. Chili (not *chile,* which is Spanish for pepper) should be thick, meaty, and spicy, and served unadorned. Real Texas chili is made with beef (or occasionally rabbit or venison), but not beans. This standard has been relaxed, though, and plenty of Texans like pinto beans (never kidney beans) in their chili. There are annual chili cook-offs across the state; the most famous is held in the border town of Terlingua. Degrees of fire are usually designated as one-, two-, or three-alarm or indicated by an X, XX, or XXX. Four Xs means that the bowl of devil's soup is guaranteed to scorch your tongue, lips, and entire digestive tract.

Weird food item: **Frito pie,** which is meaty chili, cheese, and diced onions poured over a plate of (or into a bag of) Frito's corn chips. Frito pie is a staple in Texas school cafeterias (or at least it was when I was growing up).

BARBECUE (BBQ) Vying with chili and chicken-fried steak for the honor of state dish is barbecue (though Texans didn't invent it; the word comes from the Spanish *barbacoa,* and the style originated in Spain and evolved in the Caribbean and Latin America). Still, the art of roasting meats over an open fire distinguishes Texans from, say, lesser humans. Texans slow-cook (smoke) beef brisket and ribs (and, to a lesser extent, pork, chicken, turkey, sausage, and *cabrito,* young goat) in pits over mesquite or hickory wood. The slow roasting and wood give it the unique, revered flavor. Texas barbecue, unlike its worthy regional competitors in such places as Memphis and the Carolinas, is almost wholly focused on beef, and it tends to be tangier and spicier than the sweeter pork popular in those places. A plate of brisket or ribs is served with heaps of tangy barbecue sauce (which is often also employed as a basting

TEXAN style

Some Yankees and coastal snobs might be inclined to consider "Texan style" an oxymoron, and they may be right: Texans are probably better known as world-class shoppers than arbiters of taste. But style? Texans have plenty. Beyond oil, championship sports teams, and roots music, Texas's greatest export is the classic Western cowboy style that it embodies. The basics of cowboy style aren't hard to master. The **cowboy hat** will be a top-of-the-line number from a classic Western outfitter such as M. L. Leddy's in Fort Worth. The most fundamental element of the cowboy look is **cowboy boots**, and almost everyone in Texas owns at least one pair. Boot stores stock a bewildering array of leathers: Besides basic calfskin, you'll find showy and more delicate (and often vastly more expensive) exotic skins, such as lizard, eel, alligator, ostrich, snake, stingray, water buffalo, and kangaroo. **Cowboy hats** are serious business. They're worn at all times and not taken off indoors; if you don't think so, check out a Western dance hall on a Friday night, where you'll find cowboys twirling about the dance floor with their best hats firmly in place. The classic Stetson, like the one LBJ wore on the ranch, dates from the 1850s. The key to your new hat? Getting it formed, or creased, for that perfect range or courthouse look. Finish your outfit with the most essential **Western accessories**: belts (with a sterling-silver belt buckle), hatbands, bolo ties, and bandannas.

sauce), along with side dishes such as potato salad, pinto beans, and coleslaw. A proper Texas barbecue will be either a down-and-dirty, ramshackle joint such as Sonny Bryan's in Dallas or Angelo's in Fort Worth; a small-town spot with smoky walls and butcher paper for plates, like Smitty's in Lockhart; or a rustic place in the country with long picnic tables and a huge barbecue pit in full view, such as the Salt Lick in Driftwood, outside of Austin. The South-Central Texas town of Lockhart is considered the "Barbecue Capital of Texas," by the way, and no barbecue lover should come to the Lone Star State without visiting there, if only to help settle the age-old question (inspired by a famous family feud), "Is Smitty's or Kreuz's barbecue better?"

TEX-MEX Neither identifiably Mexican nor strictly Texan, Tex-Mex is, as the name indicates, a hybrid menu of simple dishes. A Texan gets homesick for authentic Tex-Mex cooking just as fast as she does for barbecue or chili. No Texan has ever had good Tex-Mex except in Texas; both barbecue and chili seem a bit easier to reproduce over state lines. Not spicy or intricate like authentic Mexican food, Tex-Mex is greasy, filling, tasty, and cheap, a step above addictive junk food. There is little distinction between dishes and ingredients. Almost all involve corn or flour tortillas, lots of white and yellow cheese, chili, hot sauce, and rice and refried beans. Tex-Mex dishes can be spiced up with Tabasco sauce or scorcher jalapeño peppers, which young Texans learn to gobble up like pickles.

All Tex-Mex meals begin with tortilla chips and salsa (hot sauce) and hot melty *queso* (cheese dip) for dipping; guacamole is also a popular starter. (Trivia: Folks called it *chile con queso* when I was growing up, but just as young Texans no longer use the term "country-and-western music" and just call it "country," most folks only call it "*queso*" now.) Enchiladas, *chiles rellenos, tacos al carbón, flautas,* and burritos have long been the standard-bearers for Tex-Mex, but in the past couple of decades, **fajitas**—grilled beef or skirt steak rolled in flour tortillas and dolled up with guacamole, *pico de gallo*, and cilantro—have become the most popular dish. Less than authentic, but wildly popular, is the substitution of strips of barbecued chicken breast for beef.

BEVERAGES Texans wash down chili and barbecue with plastic glasses of **ice tea** (it's the rare Texan who says *iced* tea) the size of small oil drums, and **Texas beer,** preferably longnecks of Lone Star, Pearl, and Shiner Bock, drunk straight from the bottle. Beverage choices shift slightly in Tex-Mex restaurants. While pitchers of ice tea are fine, the beer should be ice-cold ***cerveza,*** Mexican beer such as Corona, Tecate, Dos Equis, or Bohemia, usually served with a wedge of lime squeezed into the bottle or can. Of course, Texans are becoming more discriminating about their ales, with microbreweries like Real Ale Brewing Company near Blanco popping up across the state. Still, the number-one libation for washing down a plate of Tex-Mex is the **margarita,** a tart concoction of tequila, lime juice, and triple sec, either served on the rocks or frozen. Most margaritas use cheap well tequila, but connoisseurs opt for "top-shelf" margaritas (served on the rocks), made with 100% blue agave tequilas. And the connoisseurs of connoisseurs drink aged tequilas—called *reposado* or *añejo*—straight, followed by a "tequila chaser," like the one served at Javier's restaurant in Dallas: a shot glass of orange juice, lemon juice, V8, pepper, salt, and Tabasco.

Texas also has a surprisingly robust roster of **wineries,** many in the central Texas Hill Country around Fredericksburg and the High Plains near Lubbock. Becker Vineyards wine, Llano Estacado, and Pheasant Ridge are national award winners.

Popular nonalcoholic drinks include Dr. Pepper, Topo Chico Mexican mineral water, and the ever sweet Big Red soda.

WHEN TO GO

High season is summer, when the kids are out of school, and winter the low season, though beaches along the Gulf Coast are busiest in winter—even if seldom really crowded. The Texas heat (see below) makes summer a less desirable time to travel, if it can be avoided (though, of course, Texans are famous for their omnipresent air-conditioning). Unless you're looking for some rowdy spring-break action, you should avoid all resort areas, including the beaches and national parks, in March and early April, when students from colleges across the country descend upon the Gulf Coast. Outside of that, mid-spring and mid-autumn are generally the best times to visit, with moderate temperatures and fewer crowds (especially at big sights such as the Alamo).

One real draw in spring is the display of Texas wildflowers (including the famous bluebonnets) that bloom along roadsides in Hill Country in late March and early April. The South by Southwest Music + Film Conference (SXSW) takes over Austin for more than a week in March, so if you're an indie rock fan, that's the week to go; if not, that's one to avoid. The Texas State Fair takes place in late September/early October in Dallas.

Weather

The weather in Texas is especially mercurial and subject to extremes, following the oft-heard dictum: "If you don't like the weather, wait 5 minutes and it'll change." Although the unprecedented snowfall and ice storm in Dallas that marred Super Bowl XLV in 2011 was odd even for this state, you should expect unusual weather. For the most part, though, Texas weather is mild most of the year, with 200 days of sunshine and an average temperature of 73°F (23°C). Of course, in a state as big as Texas, with such a variety of physiography, climate varies by location, sometimes dramatically, making it difficult to generalize. It can be snowing in the northern Panhandle, while at the same time folks are swimming at South Padre Island. Best rule of thumb when packing for a summer trip to Texas? Plan on it being hotter than you expected. In many parts of the state, summer can mean 100+°F (37+°C) and high humidity.

With its immense size, Texas ranks first in the U.S. for the number of tornadoes, with an average of about 146.7 a year. Like the rest of the Gulf Coast states, Texas experiences its share of hurricanes (and lesser tropical storms) on the coast in summer and autumn.

Spring is mild for most of the state. Frequent, intense thunderstorms, which experts say can "move in squall lines," hit Texas in late spring. The north, central, and east areas of Texas experience the greatest rainfall in May. **Summer** is very hot across the state, making air-conditioning a necessity everywhere. High temperatures average in the high 90s or 100s (high 30s Celsius) across most of the state in July and August. The heat is most excruciating in the upper Rio Grande (including Big Bend National Park), where temperatures climb well above 100°F (38°C). South Texas also sees triple-digit highs from mid-May to late September. Summer is extremely arid in the west, but very humid in the east and south of Texas. Areas within 100 miles of the Gulf Coast have significant rainfall during the late summer.

Autumn is mostly moderate in temperature, although the remnants of the Texas summer heat can extend well into mid-fall. Though most parts of the state are considerably drier than spring, early autumn is extremely wet along the Gulf Coast, which experiences tropical weather disturbances. **Winter** can be much colder than most visitors expect, especially in north Texas. Few areas in the state escape freezing temperatures. Snowfall occurs at least once every winter in the northern half of Texas (though accumulations of more than a couple of inches are rare, except in the High Plains), and freezing rain and ice are common. The Dallas–Fort Worth area usually gets a dusting of snow once or twice a winter (with average snowfall just over 2 inches annually), but in February 2011, it received an unprecedented amount of snow—as much as 11 to 14 inches combined with ice and bitterly cold temperatures—that threatened Super Bowl traffic and dampened commerce.

Holidays

Banks, government offices, post offices, and many stores, restaurants, and museums are closed on the following legal national holidays: January 1 (New Year's Day), the third Monday in January (Martin Luther King, Jr., Day), the third Monday in February (Presidents' Day), the last Monday in May (Memorial Day), July 4 (Independence Day), the first Monday in September (Labor Day), the second Monday in October (Columbus Day), November 11 (Veterans' Day/Armistice Day), the fourth Thursday in November (Thanksgiving Day), and December 25 (Christmas). The Tuesday after the first Monday in November is Election Day, a federal government holiday in presidential-election years (held every 4 years).

Texas Calendar of Events

For an exhaustive list of events beyond those listed here, check **www.traveltexas.com**, where you'll find an up-to-the-minute roster of what's happening in Texas.

JANUARY

Goodyear Cotton Bowl Classic, AT&T Stadium, Dallas. This annual college football bowl game still holds a prestigious place in pigskin circles. See www.attcottonbowl.com. January 1.

River Walk Mud Festival, San Antonio. Each year, the horseshoe bend of the San Antonio River Walk is drained for maintenance, and San Antonians cheer up by electing a king and queen to reign over such events as Mud Stunts Day and the Mud Pie Ball. Call ✆ **210/227-4262.** Mid-January.

San Antonio Cocktail Conference. Craft-cocktail aficionados gather at various venues throughout the city for seminars, tastings, dinners, and parties. Patterned after the Tales of the Cocktail convention in New Orleans, this event is getting good buzz from mixologists nationwide. Go to www.sanantoniococktailconference.com or call ✆ **210/472-2211.** Mid-January.

Super Bull, Amarillo. Don't come expecting football—this is a bull-riding event at the Amarillo Civic Center. Call ✆ **800/692-1338** or 806/376-7767. Mid-January.

Fort Worth Stock Show & Rodeo, Fort Worth. This famous rodeo and livestock show is the nation's oldest, drawing nearly 1 million people to Will Rogers Memorial Center for 30 rodeo performances. It's kicked off by the All-Western Parade, the biggest horse-drawn parade in the world. Go to www.fwssr.com or call ✆ **817/877-2400.** Mid-January to early February.

FEBRUARY

Stock Show & Rodeo, San Antonio. More than 2 weeks of rodeo events, livestock judging, country-and-western bands, and carnivals at the AT&T Center and Freeman Coliseum Grounds. Go to www.sarodeo.com or call ✆ **210/225-5851.** Early February.

Mardi Gras, Galveston. The city's biggest party of the year, with parades, masked balls, and a live-entertainment district around the Strand. Call ✆ **888/425-4753.** Late February to early March.

MARCH

Houston Livestock Show and Rodeo, NRG Park, Houston. Billed as the largest event of its kind, the rodeo includes all the usual events like bull riding and calf roping, plus performances by famed country-and-western artists. A parade downtown kicks off the show. Go to www.rodeohouston.com or call ✆ **713/791-9000.** First 3 weeks of March.

South by Southwest, Austin. The Austin Music Awards kick off this huge conference, with hundreds of concerts at more than 2 dozen city venues. Keynote speakers have included Johnny Cash. Now with film and media components. Go to www.sxsw.com or call ✆ **512/467-7979.** Mid-March (during spring break at the University of Texas).

Dyeing o' the River Green & Pub Crawl, San Antonio. Are leprechauns responsible for turning the San Antonio River into the green River Shannon? Irish dance and music fill the Arneson River Theatre from afternoon 'til night. Call ✆ **210/227-4262.** March 17.

APRIL

Austin Food + Wine Festival, Austin. Book a month in advance for the cooking demonstrations; beer, wine, and food tastings; and celebrity chef dinners. For the food fair, just turn up hungry. Go to www.austinfoodandwinefestival.com or call ✆ **512/329-0770.** First weekend after Easter.

Houston Art Car Parade & Ball, Houston. The parade of decorated cars down Smith Street is marvelous and hilarious and attracts participants from around the country. The spirited ball is in a downtown parking garage. Go to www.thehoustonartcarparade.com. Early April.

San Jacinto Festival and Texas History Day, West Columbia. Highlights include a parade, talent show, arts and crafts show, and barbecue cook-off. The talent show, where you never know what's going to happen next, is the fun part. Call ✆ **800/938-4853** or 979/265-2508. Mid-April.

Fiesta San Antonio, San Antonio. What started as a modest marking of Texas's independence more than 100 years ago is now a huge event, with an elaborately costumed royal court presiding over 10 days of revelry: parades, balls, food fests, sporting events, concerts, and art shows all over town. Go to www.fiesta-sa.org or call ✆ **877/723-4378.** Mid- to late April.

MAY

Tejano Conjunto Festival, San Antonio. This festival celebrates the lively and unique blend of Mexican and German music born in South Texas. The best conjunto musicians perform at the largest event of its kind in the world. Call ✆ **210/271-3151.** Mid-May.

Return of the Chili Queens, San Antonio. An annual tribute to chili, with music, dancing, crafts demonstrations, and, of course, chili aplenty. Bring the Tums. Call ✆ **210/207-8600.** Memorial Day weekend.

JUNE

American Institute of Architects Sandcastle Competition, Galveston. More than 80 architectural and engineering firms from around the state build sand castles and sand sculptures, taking this pastime to new heights. Call ✆ **713/520-0155.** Early June.

Juneteenth Festival, statewide. News of the Emancipation Proclamation didn't reach Texas until June 19, 1865—nearly 3 years after Lincoln signed it. This day is celebrated with blues, jazz, and gospel music, family reunions, and a variety of events. Houston has a major celebration; call ✆ **713/284-8352** for more information. Weekend nearest June 19.

JULY

Gran Fiesta de Fort Worth, Fort Worth. An outdoor festival celebrating Texas's Hispanic culture with Latin music, art, food, and parades. Call ✆ **214/855-1881.** Third week in July.

Great Texas Mosquito Festival, Clute. A joyous celebration to divert everyone from the annoying pest. Go to www.mosquitofestival.com. Late July.

Miss Texas USA Pageant, Lubbock. This annual beauty contest takes place at Lubbock Municipal Coliseum and area hotels. Call ✆ **800/692-4035** or 806/747-5232. Last week in July.

AUGUST

***Austin Chronicle* Hot Sauce Festival,** Austin. The largest hot sauce contest in the world features more than 300 salsa entries, judged by celebrity chefs and food editors. The music at this superparty is hot, too. Call ✆ **512/454-5766.** Last Sunday in August.

Commemorative Air Force Annual AIRSHO, Midland International Airport. Come see vintage aircraft on display and strutting their stuff in flight. Go to www.airsho.org or call ✆ **800/624-6435** or 915/683-3381. Last weekend in August.

SEPTEMBER

Marfa Lights Festival, Marfa. Celebration of the lights that inexplicably appear on the horizon just east of town. Expect street dances, live music, parades, and lots of food. Go to www.visitmarfa.com or call ✆ **800/650-9696** or 915/729-4942. Labor Day weekend.

GrapeFest, Grapevine. Yes, Texas makes wine—some of it pretty decent. It flows freely at this, one of the country's biggest wine festivals, with live music and other entertainment. Go to www.grapevinetexas usa.com/grapefest or call ✆ **817/410-3185.** Early September.

Fiestas Patrias, Houston. One of the largest community-sponsored parades in the Southwest celebrating Mexico's independence from Spain. Houston's several *ballet folklórico* troupes twirl their way through downtown streets in a pageant of color and traditional Mexican music. Call ✆ **713/926-2636.** Mid-September.

Pioneer Days, Fort Worth Stockyards. A festival commemorating Fort Worth's early pioneer and cattle rancher heritage with country music, rodeos, and Wild West shows. Call ✆ **817/336-8791** or 625-7005. Mid-September.

Bayfest, Corpus Christi. This huge festival fills Shoreline Drive from I-37 down to Bayfront Park with music, games, food, arts and crafts, and fireworks over the bay. Call ✆ **800/678-6232** or 361/881-1888. Late September.

State Fair of Texas, Dallas. The nation's biggest state fair, held at the fairgrounds built in 1936 in grand Art Deco style. Go to www.bigtex.com or call ✆ **214/565-9931.** Late September to third week of October.

OCTOBER

Austin City Limits Festival, Austin. Zilker Park fills up with the city's second most popular annual music festival held on two consecutive 3-day weekends each fall. With music on eight stages, the event was inspired by the PBS concert series of the same name, and gets bigger and better each year. Go to www.aclfestival.com or call ✆ **888/512-SHOW (7469)**. Usually first week of October.

Wings over Houston Airshow, Houston. This thrilling event usually features displays of current military aircraft and performances of aerial acrobatics. Go to www.wingsover houston.com or call ✆ **281/531-9461.** Mid-October.

Texas Jazz Festival, Corpus Christi. This free and popular festival attracts hundreds of big-name musicians from across the U.S. Go to www.texasjazz-fest.org or call ✆ **800/678-6232.** Mid- to late October.

Halloween, Austin. About 100,000 costumed revelers take over 7 blocks of historic 6th Street. Call ✆ **800/926-2282.** October 31.

NOVEMBER

South Padre Island Kite Festival, South Padre Island. What could be more fun than flying a kite above blue waters? Or prettier to watch? For all those still young at heart. Call ✆ **800/678-6232** or 361/881-1888. Early November.

Lighting Ceremony and River Walk Holiday Parade, San Antonio. Trees and bridges along the river are illuminated by some 80,000 lights, and Santa Claus arrives on a boat during this floating river parade. Call ✆ **210/227-4262.** Friday after Thanksgiving.

Wurstfest, New Braunfels. A 10-day family-friendly salute to sausage, complete with German polka bands, men dressed in lederhosen, midway rides, German food, and lots of beer. Go to www.wurstfest.com or call ✆ **830/625-9167.** Early November.

DECEMBER

Christmas in the Stockyards, Fort Worth. Cowtown's classic Old West corner is lit up even more than usual for holiday shopping and caroling with a Texas accent. Call ✆ **817/626-7921.** Throughout December.

Fiestas Navideñas, San Antonio. The Mexican market hosts piñata parties, a blessing of the animals, and surprise visits from Pancho Claus. Call ✆ **210/207-8600.** Weekends in December.

Zilker Park Tree Lighting, Austin. The lighting of a magnificent 165-foot tree is followed by the Trail of Lights, a mile-long display of life-size holiday scenes. Call ✆ **512/499-6700.** Sundays through December 24.

Harbor Lights Celebration, Corpus Christi. The harbor is decked out for the holidays. There's an illuminated boat parade, fireworks, entertainment, and a visit from Santa Claus. Call ✆ **800/678-6232** or 361/881-1888. First weekend in December.

Dickens on the Strand, Galveston. This street party in the city's historic district features revelers dressed up in Victorian costume, parades, street vendors, and lots of entertainment. Call ✆ **409/765-7834.** First weekend in December.

Las Posadas, San Antonio. Children carrying candles lead a procession along the river, reenacting the search for lodging in a moving multi-faith rendition of the Christmas story. Call ✆ **210/224-6163.** Second Sunday in December.

RESPONSIBLE TRAVEL

Traveling "green"—seeking sustainable tourism options—is a concern in almost every part of the world today. Although one could argue that any vacation that includes an airplane flight can't be truly "green," you can still go on holiday and contribute positively to the environment. Go with forward-looking companies that embrace responsible development practices and work with local communities to help preserve destinations for the future. An increasing number of sustainable tourism initiatives can help you plan a trip and leave as small a "footprint" as possible on the places you visit.

Home to big oil, some of the most congested road systems in the country, and arctic air-conditioned shopping malls, Texas may not qualify as the greenest state in the Union. Still, the state certainly has pockets of progressive environmental attitudes, beginning with Austin. Most of Texas's ecotourism activities consist of do-it-yourself trips to state and national parks. The **Big Bend Country** region, including the Guadalupe Mountains and Big Bend national parks (p. 390), is the big draw in Texas for naturalists. **Road Scholar (Elderhostel)** (www.roadscholar.org; ✆ **800/454-5768**) organizes a number of guided tours for outdoors types, including birding trips in south Texas and hiking in west Texas.

WWOOF, the World-Wide Opportunities on Organic Farms exchange program (www.wwoofusa.org; ✆ **949/715-9500**), facilitates opportunities to work on farms and learn about organic farming practices and sustainable living. In Texas, its participating "host" members are 45 farms in or near Dallas, Houston, and Austin in particular. Opportunities range from growing vegetables and working with animals to constructing farm buildings and winemaking. It's a terrific experience for families.

The small town of **Bastrop,** near Austin, has been highlighted as one of the National Trust for Historic Preservation's "Dozen Distinctive Destinations": Downtown farmer's markets and independently owned local restaurants support the area's farmers and producers through the "Go Texan" restaurant program. In addition, Bastrop's green zone along the Colorado River is great for water sports, and two state parks allow for hiking and biking on nature trails. Bastrop County has suffered some of the most devastating wildfire damage in Texas history from fires that raged over thousands of acres, destroying homes and taking lives, in September and October 2011 and again in October of 2015.

The BP Gulf Oil Spill

The 2010 BP Gulf oil spill—the worst on record in U.S. waters—had an impact on the Texas Gulf Coast, though ultimately less severe than the devastation it wrought on Louisiana and other coastal states. Tar balls were discovered on beaches around Galveston, and the spill certainly affected the tourist and seafood trade along the Gulf Coast and in cities such as Houston. Long-term environmental damage hasn't been fully assessed, and the debate goes on regarding the continued presence of oil and its impact on coastal fisheries, wildlife, and other aspects of the environment.

Texas Parks and Wildlife devotes part of its literature and website to **Great Texas Wildlife Trails** (www.tpwd.state.tx.us/huntwild/wild/wildlife_trails), which include birding trails. For information on the 51 **Wildlife Management Areas (WMA) of Texas,** where ecosystems are carefully managed but sustainable outdoor recreational opportunities are encouraged, visit www.tpwd.state.tx.us/huntwild/hunt/wma. For WMA nature tours, Limited Public Use Permits ($12) are required.

You can find eco-friendly travel tips, statistics, and touring companies and associations—listed by destination under "Travel Choice"—at the International Ecotourism Society (TIES) website, **www.ecotourism.org**. Also, check out **Conservation International** (www.conservation.org), which, with *National Geographic Traveler,* annually presents **World Legacy Awards** to those travel tour operators, businesses, organizations, and places that have made a significant contribution to sustainable tourism. **Ecotravel.com** is part online magazine and part eco-directory that lets you search for touring companies in several categories (water-based, land-based, spiritually oriented, and so on).

TOURS

Academic Trips & Language Classes

Road Scholar (Elderhostel) ★★★ (www.roadscholar.org; ✆ **800/454-5768**) offers more than three dozen organized, educational Texas trips, many with a naturalist's bent. They include "San Antonio: Conversational Spanish and Culture in the Alamo City"; astronomy in the Davis Mountains of West Texas; the "Great Texas Coastal Birding Trail"; hiking in Big Bend; "Stories, and Cowboy Poetry of the West"; and history and politics in the capital and Texas Hill Country.

Adventure & Wellness Trips

The massive expanse of Texas is dotted with lakes and threaded with rivers, almost 700 miles of Gulf Coast, plenty of forestland, and several mountain ranges. Its two national parks provide ample opportunities for hiking scenic canyons, spectacular caves, and vast areas of rugged desert. General outdoor recreation information can be found online at **www.texasoutside.com**.

For **bicycling tours** in Texas Hill Country and Big Bend, check out the **Adventure Cycling Association** ★★ (www.adventurecycling.org; ✆ **800/755-2453**).

The **World Birding Center** (www.worldbirdingcenter.org), in the lower Rio Grande Valley, offers a wealth of information on birding events, tours, and sites, such as the 50-acre **South Padre Island Birding and Nature Center** (✆ **956/761-3005**).

Among spa and wellness destinations, one stands out for the total luxury rejuvenation package: **Lake Austin Spa Resort** ★★★ (www.lakeaustin.com; ✆ **800/847-5637**), named the top destination spa in North America by readers of *Condé Nast Traveler* in 2010. This spectacular spot, in the Hill Country just outside the capital, has a 25,000-square-foot LakeHouse spa; indoor and outdoor pools; classes on dreams, painting, dog training, gardening, and healthy cooking; a full slate of yoga, fitness, and meditation activities; and excellent spa dining. Another serious contender for the best Austin-area wellness escape is **Travaasa Austin** ★★ (www.travaasa.com/austin; ✆ **877/261-7792**), which has been voted one of the top 100 hotels in the world, but really is more like a luxury version of an adult summer camp with a fabulous spa than a hotel.

For a fabulous "glamping" (glamor-camping) experience, stay in a tipi or a treehouse at **Geronimo Creek Retreat** ★★ (www.geronimocreekretreat.com; ✆ **888/993-6772**) just east of San Antonio near Seguin; or sleep in a luxury tented safari-style camp outside Wimberley at my personal favorite Hill Country getaway, **Sinya at Lone Man Creek** ★★★ (www.hillcountrysinya.com; ✆ **713/502-3997**), just south of Austin.

You'll find great information on fishing, hunting, and Texas's numerous state parks from the **Texas Parks & Wildlife Department** (www.tpwd.texas.gov; ✆ **800/792-1112** or 512/389-8950). Reservations for camping in state parks can be made through the department's website or by calling ✆ **512/389-8900.** Looking for a hunting or fishing guide? Get info on the state's outdoors outfitters, including numerous hunting and fishing guides, from the **Texas Outfitters and Guides Association,** P.O. Box 33141, Kerrville, TX 78029-3141 (✆ **830/238-4207**).

Food & Wine Trips

The Culinary Institute of America (CIA) campus at Pearl in San Antonio ★★ (www.ciachef.edu/cia-texas; ✆ **800/888-7850**) offers special cooking classes for visitors, including 2- to 5-day boot-camp classes ("Flavors of Texas," "Grilling & BBQ," among others). **Texas Wine Tours** (www.fredericksburgtexaswinetours.net; ✆ **830/997-8687**) offers trips to more than a dozen Hill Country wineries, including stops in Fredericksburg and occasional events in such fun places as Luckenbach. Wine tours in white stretch limos are the focus of **Wine Tours of Texas** (www.winetoursoftexas.com; ✆ **877/693-0800** or 512/458-5466). And if you're thirsty for a craft cocktail, don't forget to visit the Alamo City in January during its 5-day/night lineup of parties, cocktail pairing dinners, and seminars of the **San Antonio Cocktail Conference** (www.sanantoniococktailconference.com).

Guided Tours

Star Shuttle/Gray Line Tours (www.grayline.com; ✆ **800/803-5073**) is one of the largest tour operators in the world. Grey Line Tours organizes a number of escorted bus trips, package tours, and day trips in San Antonio and Austin, with jaunts to Hill Country destinations from both those cities. Unfortunately, for some reason they are no longer serving other major cities like Dallas, Fort Worth, and Houston. For more on guided tours, check the "Organized Tours" section in the individual city and regional chapters.

Volunteer Working Trips

If you want to work in Texas while on vacation, what could be more appropriate than working on a real Texas dude ranch? Okay, it's more like playing cowboy, and these jobs are ultimately more about vacation than work, but you'll still get the chance to observe and participate in roping and roundups, herding cattle, going on trail rides, and getting your fill of Texas longhorns. Some dude ranches that offer working vacations are **Beaumont Ranch ★★** (www.beaumontranch.com; ✆ **888/864-6935**), an 800-acre ranch in Grandview, near Fort Worth; **Dixie Dude Ranch ★** (www.dixieduderanch.com; ✆ **880/375-YALL** [9255] or 830/796-7771), a 725-acre ranch in Bandera, northwest of San Antonio; **Rancho Cortez ★★** (www.ranchocortez.com; ✆ **830/460-6221**), a family-owned ranch where you can ride horses through 6,500 acres of Texas Hill Country, including the adjacent Hill Country State Natural Area, near Bandera; and **Mayan Dude Ranch ★** (www.mayanranch.com; ✆ **830/796-3312**), a family-owned ranch near Bandera, with plenty of leisure activities.

SUGGESTED TEXAS ITINERARIES

3

When Texas became a state in 1845, the relevant legislation included a clause allowing it to split into five distinct states if the state legislature approved it. Likewise, planning a Texas road trip can be something like planning a road trip across five states. El Paso, for example, is closer to Tucson, Arizona (319 miles away), than it is to Dallas (634 miles away). Texas has a lot of ground to cover: big cities; beautiful wide-open spaces; and miles and miles of highway in between. With all of this acreage, it's easy to stretch yourself too thin and spend too much time behind the wheel. As always, tailor your itinerary to your interests. If you like cowboy culture, Fort Worth and Amarillo make ideal focal points; hikers and paddlers will want to make a beeline to Big Bend National Park; city slickers might head to Dallas and Houston; and music lovers should flock to Austin. Beach bums love South Padre, and those who crave scenic road trips and quaint small towns will like the Hill Country. As you're driving, take the opportunity to explore places off the beaten path, and enjoy the freedom of the wide-open spaces. Here are some tips for seeing Texas your way.

THE REGIONS IN BRIEF

You can plan your trip to Texas a couple of ways. If you're interested in a particular activity, such as birding, you might choose two or three locations and divide your time among them. Conversely, you could first select a destination, such as one of the state's major cities or national parks, and then build your trip around the destination and surrounding area.

This book is organized geographically. Because this is such a large state, we suggest visitors limit their Texas vacation to one or two regions.

THE DALLAS–FORT WORTH METROPLEX Made famous by both a TV show about a Texas oil family and a football team, and infamous by the assassination of JFK, **Dallas** is a center of commerce and the headquarters for numerous banks, insurance companies, and other businesses. Big D, as it's known to locals, is one of the most sophisticated cities in Texas, with excellent restaurants, glitzy shopping, swank hotels, and the largest contiguous arts district in the USA. Dallas's unpretentious sister, **Fort Worth,** is equal parts Old West and "Museum Capital of the Southwest." Longhorns still rumble through the Stockyards National Historic District, while the city attracts art lovers to its top-notch museums. Both cities make good bases for outdoor recreation, children's activities, and professional sports outings. The city of **Arlington,** sandwiched between Dallas and Fort Worth, is home to several theme parks, AT&T Stadium ("Cowboy Stadium"), which attracts more than 2 million visitors a year, as well as the Texas Rangers baseball stadium.

HOUSTON & EAST TEXAS The state's largest city (and the fourth-most-populous city in the United States), **Houston** is the heart of the nation's oil and gas industry. Although not considered a primary tourist destination, Houston has an abundance of attractions, including several excellent museums, performing arts such as the city's outstanding symphony orchestra, and a variety of outdoor activities. NASA's Johnson Space Center made Houston famous and is the city's most popular attraction. Not far from Houston, the port city of **Galveston** combines small-town easiness with a good mix of museums and children's activities, plus beaches that draw hordes of spring breakers and families throughout the warm months. It's also known for its historic "Galveston Strand" and for being a major port for popular cruise lines. **East Texas,** along the Louisiana border, is a prime destination for anglers, boaters, and other outdoor recreationists.

THE TEXAS GULF COAST A world removed from the rest of the state, the coastal areas fronting the Gulf of Mexico have beach activities as well as good boating and even some surfing (okay, it's no Hawaii, but you *can* surf here). The Texas Gulf Coast is among the nation's top bird-watching regions, and also has superb fishing. In addition, you'll find a handful of good museums and an active art scene. Scrappy little wind-blown, sun-kissed beach towns like **Port Aransas** and **Rockport** bring a Jimmy Buffet vibe to South Texas. Keep heading south, and you'll get to the **Rio Grande Valley** area near South Padre Island, a region that could stand alone as a place to visit, and a special favorite of birdwatchers. "Snow birds," or "Winter Texans" as they're called, are northerners who come and stay in this area each winter to flee the colder climes. Many stay in RVs in little communities near **McAllen.**

SAN ANTONIO The delightful, Mexican-inflected city of **San Antonio** hosts the most famous historic site in Texas: the Alamo, where in 1836 Davy Crockett and about 187 other Texas freedom fighters died at the hands of a much larger Mexican army. San Antonio also has numerous other historic sites, a charming River Walk, its popular Pearl culinary and entertainment

The Regions in Brief

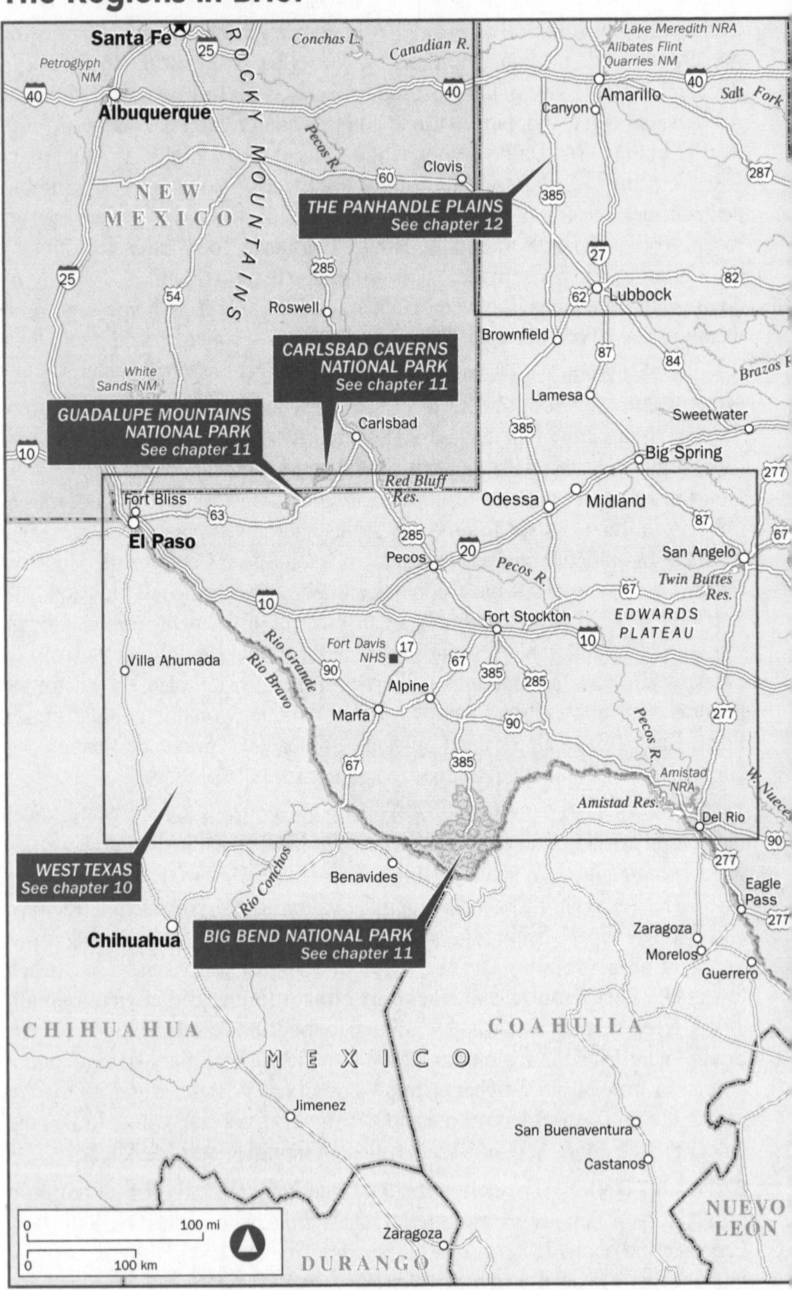

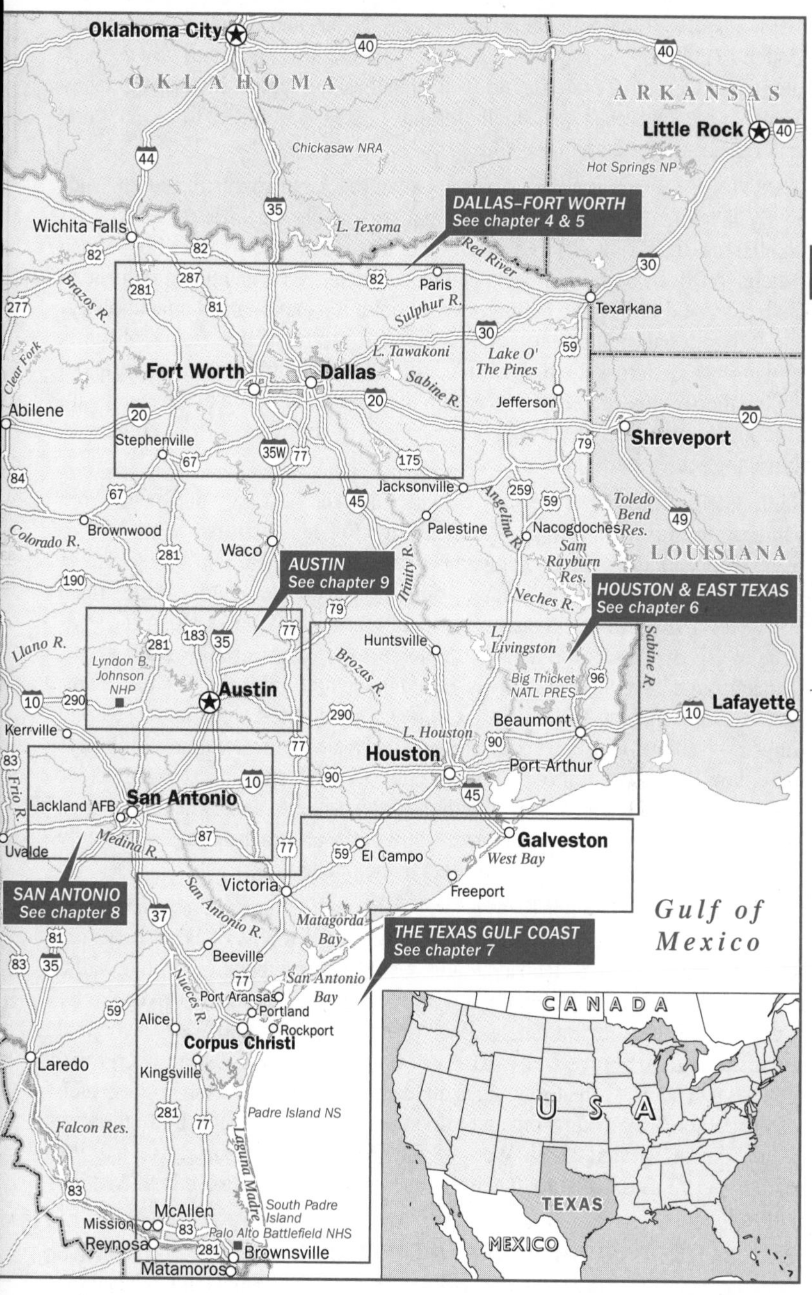

Oklahoma City
OKLAHOMA
ARKANSAS
Little Rock
Chickasaw NRA
Hot Springs NP
DALLAS–FORT WORTH
See chapter 4 & 5
Wichita Falls
L. Texoma
Red River
Paris
Sulphur R.
Texarkana
Brazos R.
Clear Fork
L. Tawakoni
Lake O' The Pines
Fort Worth
Dallas
Sabine R.
Jefferson
Abilene
Shreveport
Stephenville
Jacksonville
Toledo Bend Res.
Angelina R.
Palestine
Nacogdoches
Colorado R.
Brownwood
Waco
Sam Rayburn Res.
LOUISIANA
AUSTIN
See chapter 9
Trinity R.
HOUSTON & EAST TEXAS
See chapter 6
Neches R.
Llano R.
Huntsville
L. Livingston
Sabine R.
Lyndon B. Johnson NHP
Brozas R.
Big Thicket NATL PRES.
Austin
Lafayette
Kerrville
Beaumont
L. Houston
Houston
Port Arthur
Frio R.
Lackland AFB
San Antonio
Uvalde
Medina R.
Galveston
El Campo
West Bay
Freeport
Victoria
SAN ANTONIO
See chapter 8
San Antonio R.
Matagorda Bay
Gulf of Mexico
THE TEXAS GULF COAST
See chapter 7
Beeville
Nueces R.
San Antonio Bay
Port Aransas
Portland
Rockport
Alice
Corpus Christi
Laredo
Kingsville
Padre Island NS
Falcon Res.
Laguna Madre
South Padre Island
McAllen
Mission
Reynosa
Palo Alto Battlefield NHS
Brownsville
Matamoros
CANADA
USA
TEXAS
MEXICO

district, fine cultural attractions, and a madcap schedule of festivals that make it a popular party spot. West and north of the city, the **Texas Hill Country** (see below) is one of the prettiest areas of Texas, cedar- and cypress-covered hills dotted with lakes, rivers, wildflowers, and picturesque small towns with authentic German/Texan flavor. The area has numerous historic "Sunday Haus" inns, antiques stores, small museums, and opportunities for watersports and other outdoor activities.

AUSTIN The state capital, **Austin** is a laid-back but sophisticated and suddenly bustling large city with a distinct personality—a little unusual, a bit intellectual, and a lot different from other Texas cities of its size. It's a place where you'll see bumper stickers that read KEEP AUSTIN WEIRD, an homage to its hipster and old-hippie culture, even though it's experienced a technology-based boom and a huge influx of money and new residents from California and elsewhere across the nation. In addition to museums, historic sites, and a wide range of outdoor activities, Austin has the best nightlife in the state, with live music practically everywhere, any night of the week—from country to blues to rock to swing.

THE HILL COUNTRY Many consider this the best part of Texas. From **Blanco** to **Johnson City, Stonewall** to **Fredericksburg, Comfort** to **Kerrville,** and all the pretty spots in between, this is where you'll see acres of bluebonnets in springtime, where you'll find roadside stands selling fresh Fredericksburg peaches in summer, where you'll enjoy parks along the Pedernales River. This is the area that's home to wineries and lavender farms, **Luckenbach,** and charming towns settled in the mid-1800s by German immigrants. Areas like the **Willow City Loop** and **Enchanted Rock** never cease to impress visitors, and the vistas are so lovely along the two-lane highways here, you'll want to pull over at the scenic overlook spots so you can take it all in—or snap a selfie. It rains big thunderstorms here, gets a dusting of frost in winter, and grows big thick blankets of wildflowers each spring. If you only have time to see one part of Texas, this is the one to pick.

WEST TEXAS Though Texas is largely urban, if you grew up watching TV and movie Westerns, you'd more likely believe the plains of West Texas are the real Texas, a land of dusty roads, weathered cowboys, and huge cattle ranches. Although the shootouts are now staged and the cattle drives are by truck and rail, this region retains much of its small-town Old West flavor, and even the region's biggest city, **El Paso,** is in many ways just an overgrown cowtown. The area's history comes alive at museums and historic sites, such as the combination courtroom and saloon used in the late 1800s by Judge Roy Bean, the self-styled "Law West of the Pecos." West Texas also has the 67,000-acre **Lake Amistad,** a national recreation area along the U.S.-Mexico border.

BIG BEND & GUADALUPE MOUNTAINS NATIONAL PARKS Among America's lesser-visited national parks, Big Bend and Guadalupe Mountains contain rugged mountain scenery, the likes of which is found nowhere else in Texas, or even in surrounding states. Enjoy spectacular views from dizzying peaks, as well as hiking, rafting, and other outdoor activities. **Carlsbad Caverns National Park** is just over the state line in New Mexico, an easy side trip for those visiting Guadalupe Mountains National Park. Here, quirky little towns like **Marathon** and **Terlingua** are not to be missed.

THE PANHANDLE PLAINS A mix of terrain and varied experiences await visitors to this vast, rugged region that occupies the northern reaches of Texas. An entire day's drive from the coast, it's where you'll find small-town charm, good museums, fascinating historic sites, and one of the most outrageous steakhouses in Texas. The main cities—just big towns, actually—are **Amarillo** and **Lubbock,** both with comfortable lodgings and good eats. Lubbock is home to one of the state's largest universities (Texas Tech) as well as a vibrant arts scene. The region has plenty to do and see, including watersports in **Lake Meredith National Recreation Area,** and hiking, horseback riding, and spectacular scenery at **Palo Duro Canyon State Park.** This is also home to a monument to rock-'n'-roll pioneer Buddy Holly and a display of old Cadillacs, noses buried in the ground with their unmistakable fins pointed skyward.

THE BEST OF TEXAS IN 1 WEEK

This route brings you to the four major metro areas in Texas—Dallas/Fort Worth, Austin, San Antonio, and Houston—while including a Gulf Coast getaway on Padre Island National Seashore.

Day 1: Arrive in Dallas–Fort Worth

The Dallas–Fort Worth area is a good starting point for any Texas trip. Rent a car if you don't already have one, and pick lodging accessible to the attractions you want to see in either city and get your bearings. Visit the **John F. Kennedy Memorial** (p. 65) and the **Sixth Floor Museum at Dealey Plaza** ★★ (p. 65), and, if you have time, make an excursion to **Fair Park** ★ (p. 70). After dinner at **Sonny Bryan's Smokehouse** ★ (p. 98) or another Dallas dining staple, check out **Lower Greenville**'s nightlife (p. 104).

Day 2: Explore Dallas–Fort Worth

Split time between the artistic highlights of Dallas and Fort Worth, hitting the Arts District in Dallas (be sure to visit the **Nasher Sculpture Center** ★★★ [p. 68]), but leave plenty of time to meander Fort Worth's incomparable **Cultural District** ★★★ (p. 120), where the **Modern Art Museum of Fort Worth** ★★★ (p. 123) and **Kimbell Art Museum** ★★★ (p. 122) are must-sees. In the evening, have dinner in the **Stockyards National Historic District** ★★ before paying a visit to **Billy Bob's Texas** ★★★ (p. 142), a mega country-music club, or taking in live music at another one of the city's many honky-tonks.

Day 3: Explore Austin

Get going early for the 200-mile drive to Austin. If it's hot, head immediately to **Barton Springs Pool** ★★★ (p. 295) for a dip to cool off. Visit the **Blanton Museum of Art** ★★ (p. 296) in the afternoon, then make it to the **Ann Richards Congress Avenue Bridge** for the sundown bat exodus (p. 295). Have dinner in East Austin and explore the famed **Austin music scene** in the Warehouse District, on Sixth Street, on Red River, on Rainey Street, or along South Congress Avenue. Stay either downtown at **The Driskill Hotel** ★★ (p. 299), on the East Side at the **Heywood Hotel** ★★★ (p. 318), or on South Congress Avenue at the **Austin Motel** ★ (p. 316) or the **South Congress Hotel** ★★★ (p. 315). Want to be near the UT campus and the **Bullock Texas State History Museum**? Stay at the historic yet modern-style **Hotel Ella** ★★ (p. 316).

Day 4: Head to the Hill Country

It's a 78-mile drive west from Austin to the Hill Country town of Fredericksburg. On the way, stop in Johnson City to see the childhood home of **President Lyndon Baines Johnson**, or tour his ranch and home, "The Texas White House," in Stonewall. Wineries like **Becker Vineyards** (www.beckervineyards.com) are popular stops, but you'll want to spend most of your time in downtown Fredericksburg along Main Street, where you can shop, dine at fab bistros like **Vaudeville** ★★★ (p. 341) or visit the **National Museum of the Pacific War** ★★ (p. 339). Then, after dinner, drop by the town made famous by Willie Nelson, Waylon Jennings, and Jerry Jeff Walker, **Luckenbach** ★★★ (p. 340), where someone is always picking and grinning and singing under the oak trees outside the old post office and bar. Spend the night at **Settlers Crossing B&B** (p. 340), or hike **Enchanted Rock** (p. 339) and stay at the nearby **Trois Estate at Enchanted Rock** (p. 339).

Day 5: Explore San Antonio

It's a 70-mile drive from Fredericksburg to San Antonio. Park downtown and stroll along the **River Walk** starting at the Commerce Street Bridge. Walk to the Hyatt River Walk, where you can cut through the lobby past a water-garden area to Alamo Plaza, home of the **Alamo** ★★ (p. 241). From there, cut through the Menger Hotel (see the Teddy Roosevelt Bar), and then walk next door to the Shops at Rivercenter, where you can see the **"Battle for Texas: The Experience"** (p. 277) to learn more about the historic battle and Alamo City. Then cut through the mall to head back to the River Walk and take a **Rio Taxi** to reach the **San Antonio Museum of Art** ★★ (p. 244). Then continue on the Rio Taxi to the Pearl district, passing through a lock-and-dam system and gliding under the city's brilliant $11-million art installations, which hang from bridges and overpasses above the river. Alternatively, you could spend the afternoon visiting the four lesser-known missions that compose the **San Antonio Missions National Historical Park** ★★ (p. 246). Either way, end the

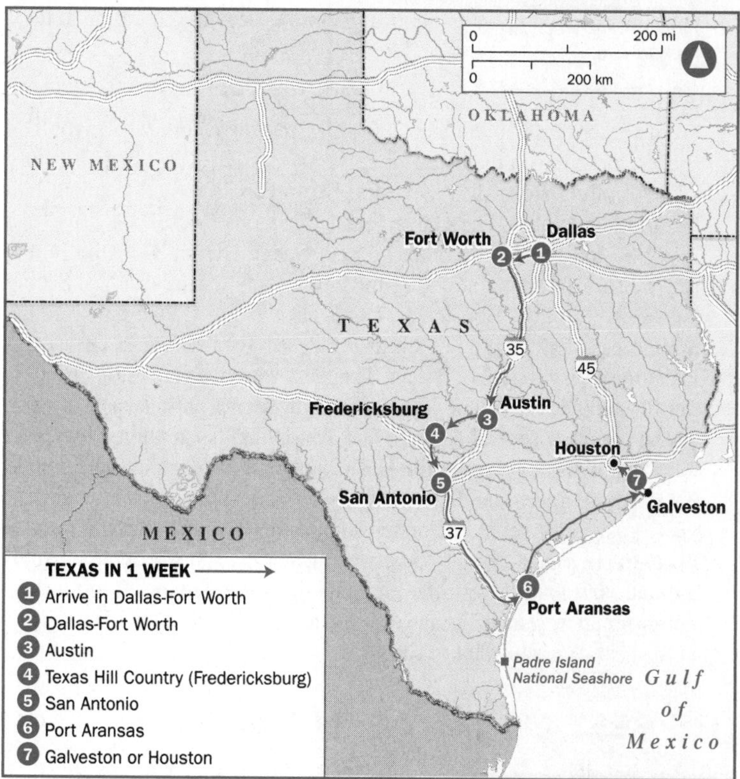

evening with dinner at one of the fabulous restaurants in the Pearl district, such as the fun and affordable **La Gloria** ★★ (p. 273) with its Mexican street foods, or the much-lauded **Cured** ★★★ (p. 272) with its charcuterie selections. Be sure to walk through **Hotel Emma** (p. 263) and peek into its **Sternewirth Clubroom & Bar.** *Note:* The Rio Taxi ride from the Downtown Reach of the River Walk up the Museum Reach to Pearl takes approximately 30 to 45 minutes, even though it's only a 2-mile journey.

Day 6: Explore the Texas Coast

From San Antonio, head down to the coast and take the ferry to Port Aransas. It's a 178-mile drive across coastal plains before you're feeding seagulls, taking dolphin tours, walking along the beach, and enjoying fresh Gulf seafood for dinner. We love **Liberty Hall/Inferno** ★★★, formerly Beulah's, at the Tarpon Inn (p. 223). Head down the beach along **Padre Island National Seashore** ★ (p. 224), and take time to surf, fish, swim, or simply read a book and nap in the sun. Stay at the historic **Tarpon Inn** ★★ (p. 223) or rent a house or condo like our family's favorite three-story **Blue Crab House** (sleeps 10) at **Cinnamon Shore** (p. 222), and remember to return to visit **South Padre Island** (p. 228) on your next trip—it's 212 miles from "Port A," leaving little time to do it this go-round.

Day 7: Explore Galveston or Houston

From Port Aransas it's about 200 miles to **Galveston,** where you can spend more time on the beach or delve into the city's fascinating history while strolling along the **Galveston Strand** (p. 200) and stepping into historic hotels like "The Galvez" and "Tremont House." Or drive east into Houston for the afternoon to visit **Space Center Houston ★★★** (p. 157) before dining at one of the city's many terrific eateries. Seeing both Galveston and Houston in 1 or 2 days is not doable; doing all the driving between them and then trying to see Texas's largest city would make for a very long 2 or 3 days. I suggest you save Galveston or Houston for another trip when you can plan on seeing only these two cities over a period of several days. In fact, for optimal leisurability, I'd spend 2 days in Austin, 2 days in the Hill Country, and 2 days in San Antonio if I only had a week in Texas, and do Dallas and Houston on your next visit. You really shouldn't underestimate the amount of traffic you're likely to encounter along I-35 between Dallas and Austin and San Antonio and how long travel time may take if you're driving. ***Bottom line:*** Allow for about 2 days in each city you pick and about a half day to drive to the next spot you want to see.

THE BEST OF TEXAS IN 2 WEEKS

Start with the first 3 days of the preceding 1-week itinerary, then divert to West Texas and Big Bend Country for a week before working your way back to San Antonio for Day 11, and then continue with the final 3 days of the preceding 1-week itinerary before heading back home.

Day 4: Drive to Del Rio & Explore

From San Antonio, it is only 154 miles to **Del Rio** (p. 382), so you'll have time to get a late start if you want to spend a little more time exploring San Antonio. Or you can get going early, take the scenic drive from Junction to Rocksprings on U.S. 377 to Del Rio, and visit **Amistad National Recreation Area ★** (p. 382), the **Whitehead Memorial Museum ★★** (p. 385), or **Seminole Canyon State Park** (p. 388). Then drive west and stay in **Marathon** (p. 404) or **Alpine** (p. 373) to get a jump on exploring Big Bend.

Days 5–7: Explore Big Bend National Park & Vicinity

From Del Rio, drive west toward **Big Bend National Park ★★** (p. 390). There is plenty to see along the way: You can stop at the Pecos River for a dramatic view or visit Langtry and learn a bit about Judge Roy Bean;

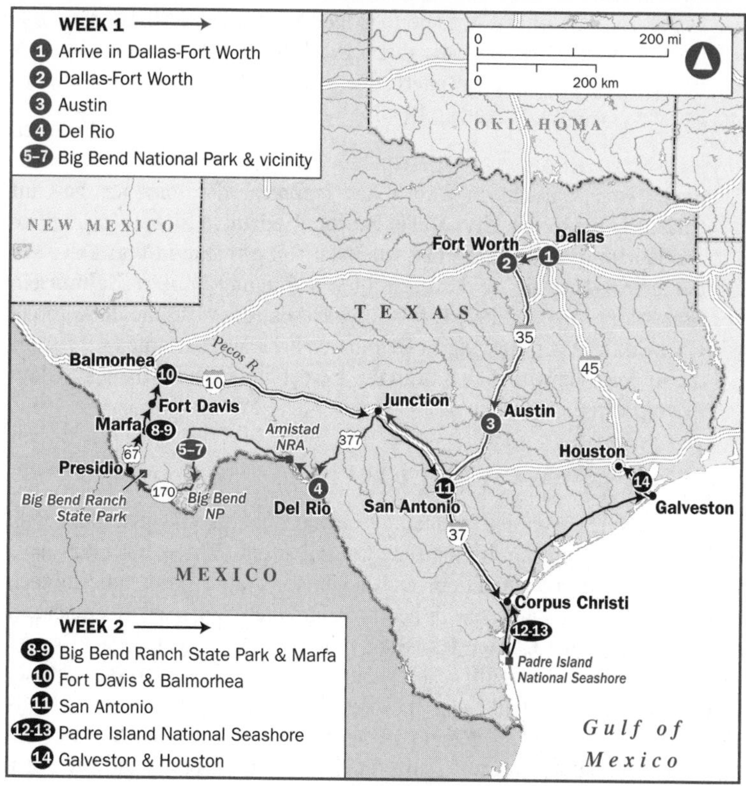

the **Seminole Canyon** (p. 388) is also a worthwhile diversion. Do some hiking and exploring before stopping at the **Gage Hotel** ★★★ in Marathon (p. 404) for the night of **DAY 5.** You can also drive to Terlingua or Study Butte as a base for your Big Bend excursions. Another option is camping in Big Bend National Park or staying in park limits at **Chisos Mountains Lodge** ★★ (p. 402). Make plans to go on day hikes or do a rafting trip on the Rio Grande, a 2-day trip if possible. There are also interesting sights, stores, and restaurants in **Terlingua** (p. 403) and plenty of cultural history along the river in and outside the park.

Days 8 & 9: Explore Big Bend Ranch State Park & Marfa

From Big Bend, drive the Wild and Scenic River portion of FM 170 to Presidio, taking time to get out on a few hikes in **Big Bend Ranch State Park** ★★ (p. 400). From Presidio, take U.S. 67 to **Marfa** (p. 368). Stay and eat in Marfa or **Alpine** (p. 373). On **DAY 9,** check out the **Chinati Foundation**'s ★★ (p. 369) avant-garde installations (full guided tour

10am–4:30pm or 10:30am–4pm) and downtown Marfa while the sun is up. Once it goes down, take U.S. 90 east 9 miles to see **Marfa's Mystery Lights** (p. 371), or else head north to the **McDonald Observatory** ★★★ (p. 365) if there's a Star Party that night. If Marfa's accommodations are booked, Alpine is a great alternative; it has some noteworthy galleries and the **Museum of the Big Bend** ★ (p. 375).

Day 10: Explore Fort Davis & Balmorhea

Spend your final day in West Texas, before heading east for the Gulf Coast, by exploring **Fort Davis National Historic Site** ★ (p. 365) or **Davis Mountains State Park** (p. 364). You can stay in Fort Davis, or continue—stopping at the oasis of a swimming pool at **Balmorhea State Park** ★★ (p. 367) if it's hot—and cut down on the drive to the Gulf Coast. After bunking in Balmorhea or somewhere off I-10 for the night, continue with DAY 5 from the 1-week itinerary for the last 3 days of your trip.

TEXAS FOR FAMILIES

Texas is an excellent choice for a family vacation, but it's a big place, and with kids you'll want to keep driving time to a minimum. The major cities have plenty of kid-friendly attractions and pursuits, so adjust your time in each place accordingly: Families with budding astronauts will want to dedicate a whole day to **Space Center Houston;** other families might want to spend more time in the attraction-packed suburb of Arlington, or in San Antonio where there's a **Sea World** and a **Six Flags Fiesta Texas,** along with a **Schlitterbahn Waterpark and Resort** in nearby New Braunfels. Several San Antonio resort hotels have waterparks on the property, too, like the **JW Marriott San Antonio Hill Country Resort & Spa** and the **Hyatt Regency Hill Country Resort & Spa** with its lazy river out back and kids camps. The Grapevine area near the DFW Airport also has hotels that are like small waterparks and theme parks, like the **Great Wolf Lodge** with its water fun and the **Gaylord Texan,** which has re-created the San Antonio River Walk indoors. Bastrop's **Hyatt Regency Lost Pines Resort and Spa** also has a nice lazy river and fun activities like movie nights on the lawn and marshmallow roasts around a bonfire for the kids.

Day 1: Arrive in Dallas

As mentioned above in the 1-week itinerary, Dallas is a good starting point for any Texas trip. Rent a car if you don't already have one, and pick lodgings accessible to the attractions you want to see. In Dallas, make an excursion to **Fair Park** ★ (p. 70). Eat at **Fireside Pies** ★★ (p. 97) or **Sonny Bryan's Smokehouse** ★ (p. 98), both family-friendly mainstays in Big D.

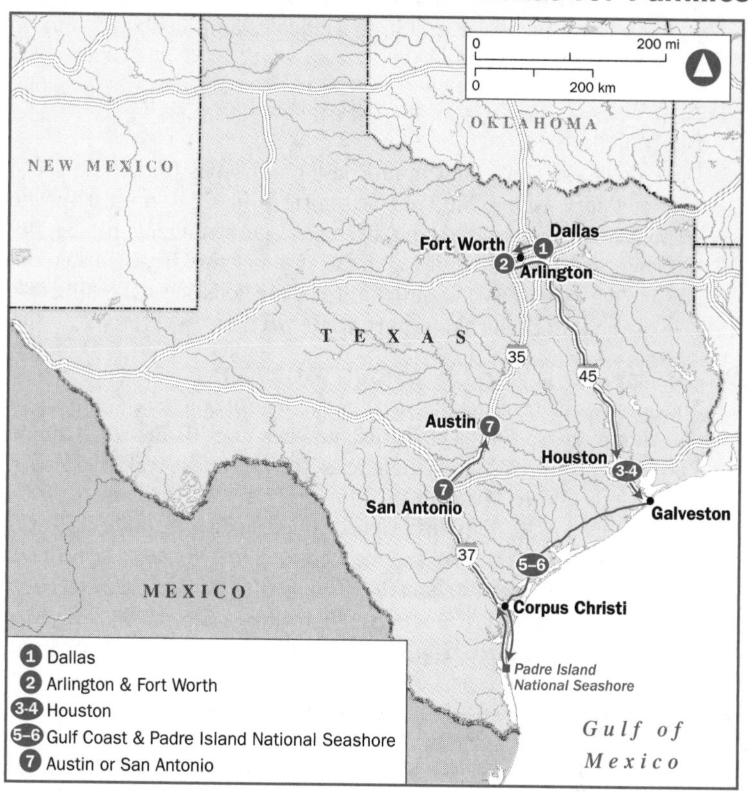

Day 2: Explore Arlington & Fort Worth

Arlington (p. 107) is a top Texas family destination, located roughly midway between Dallas and Fort Worth. The suburb is home to such attractions as **Six Flags Over Texas** (p. 109), the **Legends of the Game Baseball Museum** at the **Texas Rangers Globe Life Park** (p. 108), and the **AT&T "Cowboy" Stadium,** which offers magnificent tours and welcomes about 2 million visitors each year. You can combine the day with some time in Fort Worth or bypass Arlington altogether if you are not sports fans or your kids are old enough to appreciate the fantastic art museums in Fort Worth. The **Cowtown Cattlepen Maze** ★ (p. 118) and the **Fort Worth Zoo** ★★★ (p. 122) are good bets for kids of all ages. That night, stay in Fort Worth after dining at **Joe T. Garcia's** ★ (p. 133).

Days 3 & 4: Explore Houston

Get a good start on your drive to Houston, because you'll have plenty to see and do in the 2 days you'll spend there, among them **Space Center Houston** ★★★ (p. 157), the **Children's Museum of Houston** ★★

(p. 157), the **Orange Show** ★★ (p. 156), the **Downtown Aquarium** (p. 154), the **Kemah Boardwalk** ★ (p. 156), and the **Health Museum** ★★★ (p. 158). **Lupe Tortilla** ★ (p. 186) is a reliable, kid-friendly restaurant in town.

Days 5 & 6: Explore the Gulf Coast & Padre Island National Seashore

Drive down the Gulf Coast from Houston to Corpus Christi and spend time at **Padre Island National Seashore** ★ (p. 224), a great spot to spend a couple of days and burn off some steam swimming, fishing, flying kites, and otherwise playing in the surf and sun. If you venture on down to the beach town of **South Padre Island**, kids and adults alike will love the **Schlitterbahn Waterpark & Resort** there (p. 231).

Day 7: Explore Austin or San Antonio

To cap off your Texas family vacation, in San Antonio take your pick of the **Alamo** ★★ (p. 241) and **HemisFair Park** (p. 250), the **San Antonio Zoo** (p. 247), the **Six Flags Fiesta Texas** (p. 248) theme park, **Sea World** (p. 248), the **Witte Museum** (p. 246), and the cool **DoSeum** (p. 245), which opened in 2015. In Austin, visit **Zilker Park** ★ (p. 303), the **Texas State Capitol** ★★ (p. 294), and the **Thinkery** ★★ (p. 303). In between the two cities in **New Braunfels** is the fun Texas-size **Schlitterbahn Waterpark & Resort** (p. 344). (And if at all possible, do all these cities justice by extending your trip a few days!)

EXPLORING THE HILL COUNTRY

The rolling green hills of central Texas, flanked by Austin to the east and San Antonio to the south, punctuated by crystalline rivers and limestone bluffs, shaded by stands of cedar and cypress trees, make up one of the prettiest spots in the state. With its small German settlement towns, wildflower-filled countryside, wineries. and bed-and-breakfast inns, there is plenty in this region alone to keep a road trip going for a week—or more.

Day 1: Arrive in Austin

The capital of the Lone Star State, **Austin** is also the state's intellectual and cultural center, thanks to the presence of the University of Texas. This is a point of civic pride and the subject of an entire campaign to "Keep Austin Weird." Rife with terrific museums, great parks, and one of the liveliest bar scenes in the country, this is just the place to start your Hill Country excursion. The quirky vintage cowboy style **Ranch 616** ★★ (p. 321) off West Sixth Street is a great choice for dinner.

Days 2 & 3: Explore Austin

Central Austin is very good for a walking tour, but you'll need to drive to many of the city's attractions. In Austin, visit the **state capitol** ★★

Exploring the Hill Country

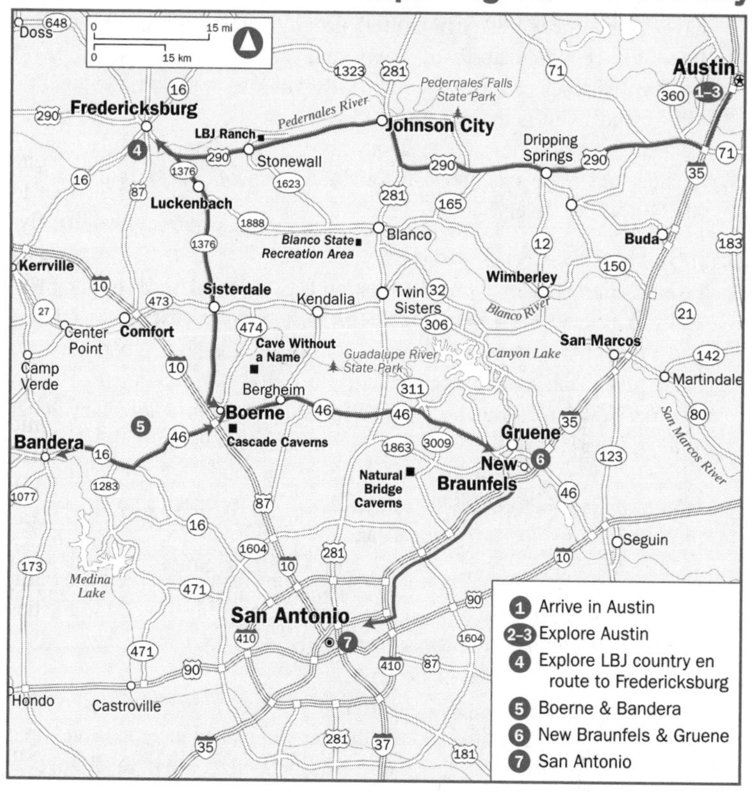

(p. 294) and the **Lady Bird Johnson Wildflower Center** ★★★ (p. 296). The **Barton Springs Pool** ★★ (p. 295) is paradise on a hot day. If you're a night owl, explore the city's terrific venues for live music of every imaginable genre, or just go bar-hopping on Sixth Street or Rainey Street. If it's between March and October, be sure to check out the nightly exodus of over one million **bats** from the **Ann Richards Congress Avenue Bridge** at dusk. Ramble around South Congress and stop by the **Continental Club** ★★ (p. 335), too.

Day 4: Explore LBJ Country en route to Fredericksburg

From Austin, take U.S. 290 west, passing through towns like **Johnson City** and **Stonewall,** stopping to buy peaches at stands along the road in summer, or to see lavender farms and wineries along the way. Don't miss a self-guided driving tour of **Lyndon B. Johnson National Historical Park** and a tour of the "Texas White House," where LBJ and Lady Bird lived at **LBJ Ranch** ★ (p. 342). Then continue on to historic **Fredericksburg** ★ (p. 338), where you can shop along Main Street, visit the

National Museum of the Pacific War ★★ (p. 339), and dine on authentic German fare at restaurants like **Der Lindenbaum** ★★ (p. 341). If you have time, check out **Enchanted Rock State Natural Area** ★★ (p. 339), 18 miles north of town, and stay at the **Trois Estate at Enchanted Rock** ★★ (p. 339): The kids will love to run around the little village and swim in the underground grotto pool or see the world's largest cap-gun collection at the Trois cap-gun museum. Listen to music outside under the oak trees in the little town of **Luckenbach** ★★★ (p. 340) where "everybody is somebody."

Day 5: Boerne & Bandera

From Fredericksburg, backtrack east on U.S. 290 and head south on FM 1376 to Boerne via **Luckenbach** (p. 340). Stop in that famous Texas ghost town for sausage on a stick, a cold drink, and some good music at the Luckenbach post office general store and bar, and then drive to Boerne. Wander downtown **Boerne** (p. 285) to shop along Main Street and stroll its Hill Country Mile, a 1.1-mile-long walking path following River Road Park and historic Main Street. Or tour the **Cave Without a Name** (p. 285) before driving to **Bandera.** There, check into any one of the area's many charming guest ranches, where you can ride tall in the saddle and explore the stunning **Hill Country State Natural Area** (p. 286). If you're up for it, go boot-scootin' that night in Bandera at **Arkey's** (p. 286), a colorful and authentic honky-tonk.

Day 6: New Braunfels & Gruene

After breakfast, take Texas State Highway 46 east about 45 miles to **New Braunfels** (p. 343). If time and weather permit, rent an inner tube and float the Guadalupe River or hit **Schlitterbahn Water Park & Resort** ★ (p. 344). Peruse the art and antiques shops downtown, swim in the spring-fed pool at **Landa Park,** and then check into the **Gruene Mansion Inn** ★ (p. 345) and take in a rollicking show at **Gruene Hall** ★★ (p. 344), the oldest country-and-western dance hall in Texas. For a sublime Texas setting, have dinner next door at the **Gristmill** restaurant (p. 346).

Day 7: San Antonio

From New Braunfels, head south on I-35 about 30 miles to **San Antonio** (p. 234). Spend the day ambling the **River Walk** ★★★ (p. 244), enjoying some Mexican food at **Mi Tierra** ★★★ (p. 269), and shopping the import stalls at **Market Square** ★ (p. 243). Take a tour of one of the famous local attractions, such as the **Alamo** ★★ (p. 241) or the **San Antonio Missions National Historical Park** ★★★ (p. 246). Then don't miss exploring the old brewery complex and dining at one of the restaurants, like **La Gloria** ★★ (p. 273) or **Cured** ★★★ (p. 272), in the Pearl district. It's about 70 miles back up to Austin when heading north on I-35, or if you'd prefer, take Interstate 10 East out of San Antonio and then pop up the Texas 130 Toll Road, on which you can legally drive 85 mph.

DALLAS

Everything is bigger in Texas, and that's certainly true in Dallas, a city of big business and tall buildings, big hats and big hair, flashy corporate suits and hand-tooled cowboy boots. Of its sibling cities—Houston, San Antonio, and Austin—Dallas is the fun and flirty one, unapologetically ostentatious and always flaunting its oil money and cotton-crop wealth. It's also a kingpin of commerce, technology, and higher education.

Still, Dallas is hardly an all-work-and-no-play place. For football fans, it's all about the next big game at the Cowboys' enormous AT&T Stadium (which offers a great building tour). For basketball lovers, it's all about the NBA Mavericks; for baseball buffs, the Texas Rangers rock.

Dallas also boasts the largest arts district in the nation, spanning 68 acres and 19 contiguous blocks, home to outstanding performing-arts centers. And with its world-class museums, and the nation's second-largest presidential library, Big D could be called Texas's capital of culture. It's also a hub of fine restaurants and retail, live music, luxury hotels, happening clubs, theme parks, historic sites, verdant parks, and sparkling lakes.

Yes, Dallas has it all.

Still, some people have grown up with images of Dallas as a city that's sometimes bigger, but not necessarily better. A sniper gunned down President John F. Kennedy as his motorcade snaked through downtown Dallas in 1963; while the nation mourned, a local nightclub owner murdered the presumed assassin, Lee Harvey Oswald, right under the noses of local police. The Dallas Cowboys, a football club that has been called "America's Team," won five Super Bowls and made scantily clad cheerleaders with big hair a required accessory alongside professional sports teams. Bonnie and Clyde began their wanton spree of lawlessness in Dallas. J. R. Ewing presided over an oil empire in the TV soap opera *Dallas,* and propagated an image of tough-talking businessmen who wore cowboy boots with pinstriped suits and had oil rigs pumping in their backyards. The irascible H. Ross Perot made a fortune in technology and thought he deserved to run the country. Although Dallas's Perot Museum of Nature and Science bears his name, Perot's place in pop culture has now been taken over by Mark Cuban, the high-tech billionaire and owner of the Dallas Mavericks.

Dallas–Fort Worth

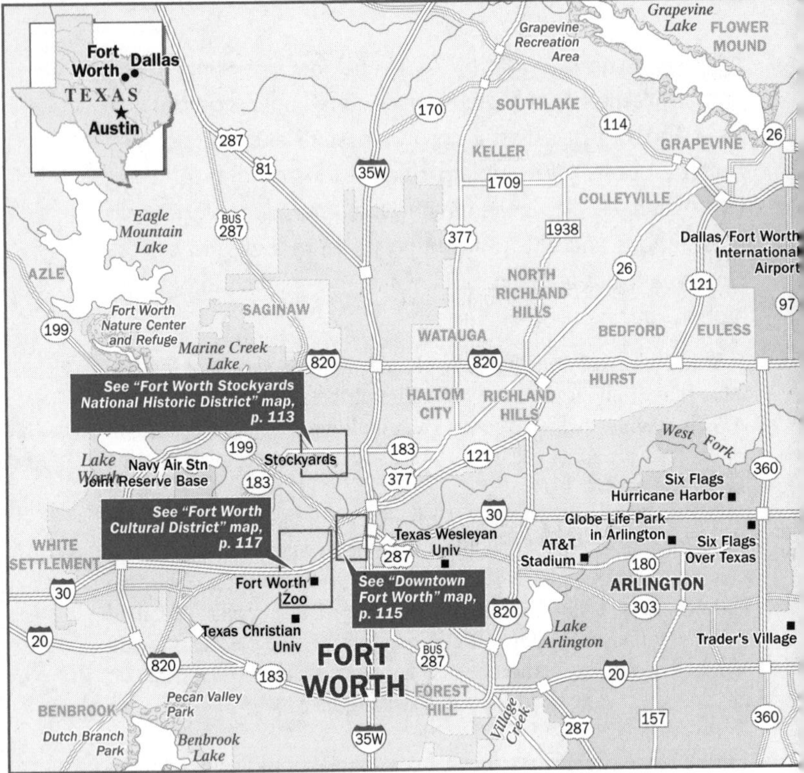

Dallas has come to symbolize the kind of place where such larger-than-life characters live out the American dream. Big D is about dreaming big, so the city—a little more than 400 square miles of flat prairie land broken up by shiny skyscrapers and soaring suburban homes—adopts all things big. Big cars. Big belt buckles. Big attitude.

With 7.1 million inhabitants in the Dallas–Fort Worth Metroplex, and 1,300,092 in Dallas, proper, Big D is the third-largest city in Texas (after Houston and San Antonio), and ranks number nine in the United States. Yet this tenacious, self-made city grew from a little Republic of Texas pioneer outpost in the mid–19th century into a major center for banking, finance, and oil. It is a largely conservative city, and its most famous residents' biggest passions seem to be making money and spending it, often ostentatiously. In the city that spawned Neiman Marcus, shopping is a religion, and megamalls fan out in every direction, part of an endless commercial sprawl.

Dallas, site of Super Bowl XLV in 2011, is fiercely passionate about big-time sports, too, and not only the Cowboys. Just about every professional

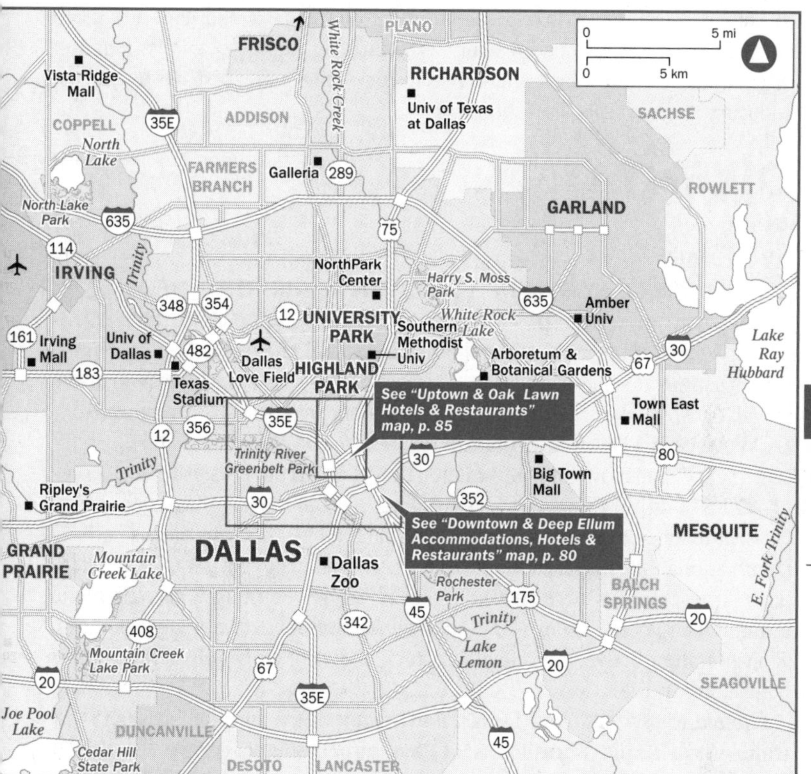

sports league has a franchise in Dallas, and there's also rodeo and the Texas Motor Speedway. This is a place where the top high school football teams routinely sell out playing fields that seat 20,000 and schedule their playoff games in the enormous AT&T "Cowboys" Stadium, to accommodate a fan base that reaches far beyond parents and teachers.

Dallas is also a place where Southern Baptist churches pack in nearly as many people for Sunday services, and, for the most part, conservative politics reign supreme. The George W. Bush Presidential Center, which opened in 2013, includes an institute, presidential library, and museum on the grounds of Dallas's top university, Southern Methodist University (SMU), the alma mater of George's wife, Laura.

Dallas ranks as one of the top business and leisure destinations in Texas (and the sixth-most-popular convention site in the country). The city is more cosmopolitan than ever before, and a great deal of effort and resources have gone into establishing a cultural life on a par with business opportunities. A recent burst of arts philanthropy—and hiring virtually every renowned international architect in the book to build up the Arts District—has catapulted Dallas into the big leagues. Slick and newly sophisticated, Dallas has plenty to entertain visitors, many of whom come on business and stay around to enjoy great hotels, eclectic restaurants, a thriving nightlife, a large museum district, and even a robust alternative music scene—and, lest we forget, the enduring appeal of nonstop shopping.

ORIENTATION

Arriving

BY PLANE

DALLAS/FORT WORTH INTERNATIONAL AIRPORT (DFW) Most visitors will arrive via **DFW Airport** (www.dfwairport.com; ✆ **972/973-3112**), located midway between the two cities and one of the largest airports in the nation. It's the third-busiest airport on the globe and larger than the island of Manhattan, with four terminals connected by a "people mover." **DFW Airport Visitor Information** (✆ **972/574-3694**) provides hotel, sightseeing, and transportation information, and the **Airport Assistance Center** (✆ **972/574-4420**) offers crisis counseling, foreign-language assistance, and car-seat rental. Currency exchange booths and ATMs are in terminals A, B, D (International, the newest terminal), and E. All the major car-rental companies have representatives here (but note that if you're returning a car, the rental terminal is a good 5 miles away, so allow extra time before your departure). Transportation between terminals is quick and easy on **Skylink,** the world's largest airport train.

Ground transportation to Dallas, Fort Worth, or the surrounding area is by **Dallas Area Rapid Transit (DART)** bus, airport shuttle, private car, charter limo, courtesy car, or taxi (www.dfwairport.com/transport; ✆ **972/574-5878**). Many hotels offer courtesy transfers to and from the airport; check to see if yours does. Transport by bus is the cheapest option, but the best value is taking the airport shuttle. Both downtown Dallas and Fort Worth are 18 miles from the airport; expect a drive of 30 minutes to 1 hour, depending on the traffic.

DART (www.dart.org; ✆ **214/979-1111**) offers two principal means of public transportation between DFW Airport and downtown Dallas: the **Trinity Railway Express (TRE)** and **DART.** The **TRE** operates Monday through Saturday (***note:*** not Sun); the 202 express bus runs hourly, 7 days a week, from 6am to 11pm. The single-ride fare east of DFW is $5; west of DFW, it's $3.50. An express 1-day pass costs $7 and is good for unlimited rides on DART and the **TRE** (including your return trip) until 3am the next day. For more information, call ✆ **817/215-8600** or visit www.trinityrailwayexpress.org. Passenger terminals at DFW Airport are served by two **DART** shuttles serving terminals A and C and terminals B and E; both operate from CentrePort/DFW Airport Station: **express route 310** (to/from remote north parking) or **408** (to/from remote south parking). The fare is $1.75 one-way. For more information, call ✆ **214/979-1111** or visit www.dart.org.

Another convenient mode of transportation to and from the airport is **Super Shuttle DFW** (www.supershuttle.com; ✆ **800/BLUE-VAN [258-3826]** or 817/329-2000), which can be reached 24 hours a day. A typical fare to Dallas is $27 to $32, and to Fort Worth, $26 to $33. The **Yellow Checker Shuttle "Airporter"** (✆ **817/267-5150** or 972/222-2000) operates shuttle services between DFW and Fort Worth; the cost to or from the Airporter Park & Ride lot at 1000 E. Weatherford St. in downtown Fort Worth is $15, and to downtown hotels, $19.

Taxis are on hand at airport arrival gates. You can also make airport transportation reservations by calling **Yellow Checker** (✆ **214/426-6262** or 817/426-6262) or **Cowboy Cab** (✆ **214/428-0202**). If you prefer limousine service, try **ExecuCar** (✆ **800/410-4444**), **Agency Limousine** (✆ **800/277-LIMO [5466]** or 817/284-7575), or **DFW Towncars** (✆ **214/956-1880**). The flat-rate taxi fare to downtown Dallas is $45, downtown Fort Worth, $48; limo service is about $59 to $85. **Uber, Fasten,** and **Lyft** are also popular options for shared rides or individual rides; check their apps or websites for pricing

DRIVING FROM DFW AIRPORT International Parkway connects directly to major freeways serving both Dallas and Fort Worth (Hwy. 114 and 635 north, and 183 and 360 south). Signs clearly indicate the route. The distance from the airport to downtown Dallas or Fort Worth is 18 miles, but the drive at peak times can take about an hour.

LOVE FIELD **Love Field** (www.dallas-lovefield.com; ✆ **214/670-6073**) is just 7 miles from downtown Dallas. After DFW Airport was built, Love Field became primarily a private plane and cargo airport for DHL and Federal Express. Southwest Airlines has continued to operate out of it, however, and it has been resurrected as a commercial airport, with Delta and Continental Express building or revamping terminals. While you're hanging around in the Southwest terminal, drop in on the **Frontiers of Flight Museum** (www.flightmuseum.com; ✆ **214/350-3600;** Mon–Sat 10am–5pm and Sun 1–5pm; $10 adults, $8 seniors, $7 children 3–17).

All major car-rental companies have locations here. The same ground transportation services for DFW Airport also travel to Love Field, which is not far from downtown Dallas. A taxi from Love Field to downtown costs about $19; the shared-ride Super Shuttle to downtown, with multiple drop offs, will only save you a few dollars because it costs about $14 from Love Field.

BY CAR

You'll almost surely need a car to get around Dallas and Fort Worth (unless you stick to the downtown areas), so it's not a bad idea to arrive in one. The major roads into Dallas are **I-635** (better known as LBJ Fwy.), which goes from DFW Airport east to Dallas; **I-20,** which joins I-635 and heads west to Fort Worth; **I-35,** north-south from the border towns in south Texas, through San Antonio, Austin, and Dallas, and all the way to Oklahoma; and **U.S. 75** (Central Expwy.), which runs north-south from downtown Dallas to the northern suburbs. From Houston, the drive to Dallas (or Fort Worth) is about 5 hours; from Austin, 4 hours. Dallas is about an hour from Fort Worth.

DFW: The Metroplex

North Texas's two biggest cities, Dallas and Fort Worth, are often referred to as "DFW" or the "Metroplex," as though they were closely intertwined twin cities. Although unrelenting development has filled the flatland gaps between them and created a greater population of some 4 million (and a ranking in the top five in the country for urban sprawl), the two cities remain 30 miles apart and, perhaps more important, worlds apart culturally. Slick and glitzy Dallas, home of the NFL's Cowboys, thrives on an identity of banking and big business; it's "where the East peters out," in the words of Will Rogers. Fort Worth, the "Cowtown" of the legendary cattle drives and now the cultural capital of north Texas, has long identified itself as being where the West *begins.* More laid-back than Dallas, Fort Worth might be considered comparatively pokey were it not for its surprising roster of world-class museums, progressive civic-mindedness, good-natured downtown nightlife, and enduring Western character.

BY TRAIN

Amtrak's Texas Eagle serves Dallas's **Union Station,** 400 S. Houston St. (✆ **214/653-1101**), and Fort Worth's **Intermodal Transportation Center (ITC)** in the southeast corner of the city at 1001 Jones St. and 9th Street (✆ **817/332-2931**). Trains arrive from Chicago, St. Louis, Little Rock, San Antonio, and Los Angeles; Heartland Flyer trains serve Oklahoma City and Fort Worth. For more information and reservations, contact Amtrak at ✆ **800/USA-RAIL (872-7245)** or visit www.amtrak.com or www.texaseagle.com.

The **Trinity Railway Express (TRE)** travels back and forth between Dallas and Fort Worth (day pass, $10; single fare, $5); for more information, call ✆ **214/979-1111** or toll-free 817/215-8600 (www.trinityrailwayexpress.org).

Essentials

VISITOR INFORMATION

The **Dallas Convention & Visitors Bureau** (www.visitdallas.com; ✆ **800/232-5527**) operates a comprehensive website (with online hotel and airfare arrangements) and the **Dallas Tourist Information Center,** located in the historic Old Red Courthouse downtown, 100 S. Houston St. (✆ **214/571-1301,** 24-hr. events hotline; open daily, including most holidays, 9am–5pm). It has Internet terminals and touch-screen computer information kiosks.

To get an immediate handle on what's happening in Dallas, check out the *Dallas Morning News* "Weekend Guide" (www.guidelive.com) or *Dallas Observer* (www.dallasobserver.com), a free weekly paper with arts, entertainment, and dining information.

CITY LAYOUT

Dallas is extremely spread out, covering nearly 400 square miles. Traditionally, most people have worked in the downtown central business district and commuted to their homes in residential districts primarily north and east (but also south and west) of the city. New business attracted to the city has resulted in many more offices in outlying areas, particularly the corridor from Richardson to Plano, north of Dallas along U.S. 75 (Central Expwy.) and west of the city in Carrollton and Irving/Las Colinas.

The West End Historic District, financial center, and Arts District are all downtown, just west of Central Expressway (though Deep Ellum, also part of downtown, is on the east side of U.S. 75). Central, in fact, divides east and west Dallas. LBJ Freeway, or I-635, runs through far north Dallas. It connects to I-20, which runs a loop south of the city. Irving, Grand Prairie, and Arlington are all due west, between Dallas and Fort Worth. I-30 leads directly west to Fort Worth.

Neighborhoods in Brief

In addition to the six major neighborhoods discussed below, the city is surrounded by concentric rings of ever-expanding suburbs. In addition to having bigger homes, these areas, especially north of the city, are marked by megamalls, minimalls, and strip malls of chain stores and restaurants that make the new developments very difficult to distinguish from one another. New stadiums and shopping and entertainment facilities are drawing more and more people to Plano, McKinney, and Frisco.

Downtown Dallas This area encompasses the **Dallas Arts District,** the nexus of downtown Dallas's fine and performing arts, including the Dallas Museum of Art, Nasher Sculpture Center, Meyerson Symphony Center, Crow Collection of Asian Art, Perot Museum of Nature and Science, and others; the **West End Historic District,** a former warehouse district and one of the oldest parts of the city transformed into a popular hotel, restaurant, nightlife, and shopping scene; and the core of downtown offices that extend east from **Reunion Arena** and **Dealey Plaza,** where the flagship Neiman Marcus is the sole remaining department store. Though some urban-minded professionals are finally beginning to renovate residential loft spaces, downtown Dallas remains pretty much a ghost town after 6pm (except for West End and along Main Street behind the Adolphus Hotel). Still, it has a number of major hotels and makes a good place to drop anchor, especially for visiting businesspeople.

Deep Ellum Located east of downtown and bounded by Elm, Main, Commerce, and Canton streets is Deep Ellum. This area once was Big D's best impersonation of Austin, the live-music capital of the Southwest. Unfortunately, Deep Ellum has experienced an eruption of violence, gang-related and otherwise, so the nightlife scene here is not what it once was, though it is definitely on the upswing. Streets were repaved and parking was added in 2014 and 2015, and today you'll find a good number of popular nightclubs and bars here. Simultaneously ragged and chic, the former industrial district is home to alternative, blues, rock, and other music clubs interspersed with discos, honky-tonks, art galleries, furniture and secondhand shops, and upscale restaurants. The area is quiet during the day, but it gets pretty rowdy at night and on weekends. The name is said to be a Southern drawl pronunciation of the main street, Elm.

Uptown & Oak Lawn Located northeast of downtown and promoted as "Uptown," **McKinney Avenue, Knox-Henderson,** and **Victory Park** are destinations with chic restaurants, shopping meccas, and *in* places to live. The pace has slowed a bit, but chic, modern condos continue to go up even in the face of housing slowdowns. McKinney Avenue, once the site of elegant old homes, is now the center of the Dallas art gallery scene, while Knox-Henderson is split right down the middle between trendy restaurants and upscale home-furnishings stores. Some of the hottest shopping and nightlife spots are in **West Village** in Uptown. **Victory Park,** the site of new luxury hotels and the American Airlines Center, hasn't quite taken off as an entertainment enclave, as once envisioned. **Oak Lawn, Cedar Springs,** and **Turtle Creek,** the heart of artsy and gay Dallas, are home to some of its finest hotels, restaurants, shops, and the original Dallas Theater Center, built by Frank Lloyd Wright.

Greenville Avenue & East Dallas The high point of Dallas nightlife, as it has been for decades, is this long strip located northeast of downtown Dallas, from LBJ Freeway south to Ross Avenue. Upper Greenville draws a slightly older and sophisticated crowd, while Lower Greenville (below Mockingbird) swims with nightclubs, bars both shabby and snooty, bohemian restaurants, vintage clothing stores, and resale furniture shops. East Dallas is home to the party district of Deep Ellum, the Lakewood residential neighborhood, and old Dallas sites like the Cotton Bowl and Texas fairgrounds.

Park Cities The traditional haunt of the Dallas elite, Park Cities encompasses one of America's wealthiest residential districts, **Highland Park,** as well as the not-too-shabby **University Park** and the city's major university, preppy SMU, where the George W. Bush Presidential Center, including its museum and presidential library, is located. Park Cities is north of downtown and west of Central Expressway. Plenty of Dallasites tend to refer to the entire zone as Highland Park, if only to use the best-known district as shorthand.

North Dallas The area along the northern edge of the city and southern edge of the suburbs is where the hard-core shopping begins (in places such as the Galleria, Valley View, and Prestonwood malls in Addison). It is also home to an ever-growing contingent of hotels and restaurants away from the downtown business scene.

Oak Cliff For decades, this neighborhood on the other side of I-30 was considered the wrong side of the tracks. But in the last decade (though truly only in the last 2 or 3 years), it has become a hotbed of indie cool. The Bishop Arts District has some of the coolest restaurants, bars, and shops—Dallas's own version of Austin hipness.

GETTING AROUND

By Public Transportation

Until the early 2000s, Dallas was a typical Southern city covering a huge area where there wasn't a lick of public transportation. Things have really improved with the addition of **Dallas Area Rapid Transit (DART) buses and light rail** (www.dart.org; ✆ **214/979-1111**), and its coverage is constantly expanding out from the downtown area. Pick up a map at any visitor information center or at most hotels and major attractions. Two-hour passes (replacing the former bus single-ride and light rail 90-minute fares, allowing transfer between bus and rail) is $2.50 ($1.25 for seniors, students, and children). Day passes are available for $5 ($2.50 for seniors and students with ID, as well as children); for premium routes (serving the suburbs), and a midday pass is $1.75 (for rides between 9:30am–5:30pm). Single tickets and day passes are available at ticket vending machines (TVMs) on all rail station platforms.

Of particular interest to visitors (especially kids) in the downtown area is the free **McKinney Avenue Streetcar Service** (also called the **M-Line Trolley**), which travels from the Dallas Arts District to Cityplace Station and the West Village (it goes along McKinney Ave. from Uptown's Allen St. to downtown's Ross Ave. and St. Paul Ave., next to the Dallas Museum of Art). The vintage trolleys are from 1906, 1913, and 1920, and operate year-round between 7am and 10pm Monday through Friday, 10am and 10pm Saturday and Sunday (every 15 min. during peak and lunch hours and every half-hour during off-peak hours and Sat–Sun). The trolley is perfect for bar, gallery, and

Real Highway Names

To get around Dallas, you'll need to know and adopt the colloquial names of the major local thoroughfares. As a general rule, numbers give way to proper names.

Official Name	Real-Folks Name
U.S. 75	Central Expressway ("Central")
I-635	LBJ Freeway ("LBJ")
Northwest Highway	Loop 12
I-35E	Stemmons Freeway
I-35/U.S. 77/I-635/I-30	R. L. Thornton Freeway

restaurant shopping in Uptown, and great for getting from hotels in the area to the Arts District downtown.

Note: Nearby DART light rail stations are included in the listings in this chapter, but only when one is within a 20-minute walk of the hotel, restaurant, or attraction. For additional route and fare information for DART, call ✆ **214/979-1111,** or log on to www.dart.org.

By Car

You can now actually get around Dallas without a car, if you stick to the major downtown sights, hotels, and restaurants. However, if you want to visit shopping centers in North Dallas or outlying areas, like Arlington and Fort Worth, you'll probably be better off with an automobile. Be advised, though, that if your hotel doesn't have parking, street parking can be an expensive hassle in the downtown area.

The major car-rental agencies, which have outlets at DFW and Love Field airports and at several addresses throughout the Metroplex, include **Advantage** (www.advantage.com; ✆ 800/777-5500), **Alamo** (www.alamo.com; ✆ 800/462-5266), **Avis** (www.avis.com; ✆ 800/230-4898), **Budget** (www.budget.com; ✆ 800/527-0700), **Dollar** (www.dollar.com; ✆ 800/800-3665), **Enterprise** (www.enterprise.com; ✆ 800/736-8222), **E-Z Rent-A-Car** (www.e-zrentacar.com; ✆ 972/574-3360), **Hertz** (www.hertz.com; ✆ 800/654-3131), **National** (www.nationalcar.com; ✆ 800/227-7368), **Sixt Rent-a-Car** (www.sixt.com; ✆ 888/749-8227), and **Thrifty** (www.thrifty.com; ✆ 800/847-4389).

Lyft (www.lyft.com) and **Uber** (www.uber.com/cities/dallas) are popular modes of transport throughout the DFW Metroplex, so be sure to download their apps before you hit Big D.

Note: Yellow lights do little to slow down drivers in Dallas; even the running of red lights seems to have become epidemic in recent years, so be very careful before proceeding when the light turns green.

By Taxi

Don't expect to hail a cab as you would in midtown Manhattan, though you will find taxis parked in front of the bigger, upscale hotels and at the airports. Mostly, though, you'll need to call a cab or go to your Uber app. Among the more than a dozen taxi companies are **Cowboy Cab Company** (✆ **214/428-0202**) and **Yellow Checker** (✆ **214/426-6262**).

Fares are $2.25 (initial drop) and 20¢ each additional ⅑ mile. Extras include a $2 extra passenger charge, a $3.60 airport exit fee, and a $2.60 airport drop-off fee.

[Fast FACTS] DALLAS

Babysitters If your hotel doesn't provide babysitting, contact **Baby Sitters of Dallas** (www.babysittersofdallas.com; ✆ **214/692-1354**) for childcare.

Dentists To find a local dentist, call ✆ **800/DEN-TIST (336-8478).**

Doctors The **Doctor Directory** at University of Texas Southwestern/St. Paul Medical Center, 5509 Harry Hines Blvd. (✆ **214/645-8300**), is a physician's referral service that can direct you to an appropriate health professional or specialist.

Drugstores There are 24-hour **CVS** drugstores located at 10455 N. Central Expwy. at Meadow (✆ **214/369-3872**), and 703 Preston Forest Center (✆ **214/363-1571**). Others include **Kroger,** 17194 Preston Rd. at Campbell Road (✆ **972/931-9371**), and **Albertsons,** 7007 Arapaho Rd. (✆ **972/387-8977**).

Hospitals Major hospitals include the **Baylor University Medical Center,** 3500 Gaston Ave. (www.baylorhealth.com; ✆ **880/4BAYLOR [422-9567],** or for 24-hr. emergency, 214/820-2501); the **Children's Medical Center of Dallas,** 1935 Motor St. (www.childrens.com; ✆ **214/456-7000**); and **Presbyterian Hospital of Dallas,** 8200 Walnut Hill Lane, at Greenville Avenue (www.texashealth.org; ✆ **214/345-6789**).

Internet Access The **Visitor Information Office** (www.visitdallas.com; ✆ **214/571-1301**) at the Old Red Courthouse (Houston, Main, and Commerce sts.) has computers with Internet access for an hourly fee. Decidedly hipper is **Main Street Internet,** 2656 Main St. (✆ **214/237-1121**); it's got a full bar, overstuffed couches, and occasional live music.

Maps The Visitor Information Offices at DFW Airport and the Old Red Courthouse (at Houston, Main, and Commerce sts.) have several maps of varying detail of Dallas and the surrounding area. If that's not enough, contact **MAP Dallas/Fort Worth** (✆ **817/949-2225**), which provides free street maps and visitor guides.

Newspapers & Magazines Both the *Dallas Morning News* "Weekend Guide" (which comes out on Fri; www.guidelive.com) and the *Dallas Observer* (www.dallasobserver.com), a free weekly, have plenty of current information on arts, entertainment, and dining. *D Magazine*, a local monthly, has similar listings, as well as restaurant reviews. *Dallas Voice* is a free weekly serving Dallas's gay and lesbian community, with listings of upcoming events.

Police For a police emergency, dial ✆ **911;** for non-emergencies, call ✆ **214/742-1519** or 972/574-4454. The main precinct headquarters is located at 334 S. Hall, in the central business district (✆ **214/670-5840**).

Post Office The central post office, 400 N. Ervay St. (✆ **800/275-8777** or 214/760-4700), is open Monday through Saturday from 8:30am to 5pm.

Safety In most areas during the day, Dallas is as safe as any big American city. You should exercise particular care, though, around Fair Park and after 7pm in downtown. Gay and lesbian travelers should exercise caution in the Oak Lawn section; though this area has the greatest concentration of gay residents and establishments, harassment has historically been a problem.

Taxes The general sales tax is 8.25%, hotel tax is 15%, and restaurant tax is 7%.

Transit Information For public transportation questions, call ✆ **214/979-1111.**

WHAT TO SEE & DO

Dallas has long been better known for its business and banking instincts than its cultural treasures and must-see attractions—but that's changing with the ever-expanding downtown arts district and the addition of a presidential library. Some claim Fort Worth still gallops ahead of Dallas on the cultural radar, though the playing field has been pretty nearly leveled with the world-class **Nasher Sculpture Center;** the remarkable **Perot Museum of Nature and Science**, which opened December 2012; the **George W. Bush Presidential Center,** which opened in 2013 at SMU; and other prominent local collectors donating valuable works to the city, as well as the stunning $340-million **AT&T Performing Arts Center,** which includes the **Wyly Theater** and **Winspear Opera House** (designed by Rem Koolhaas and Norman Foster, respectively). Of course, plenty of visitors simply come to Dallas and go native: Shop during the day, eat, drink, and attend big-time sporting events on nights and weekends. Big D, a relatively young city, can certainly entertain visitors for a few days or more through its infamous Kennedy legacy (which it has reluctantly embraced), revitalized state fairgrounds, a growing arts scene, and a handful of parks and enjoyable places for the kids—and, of course, loads of shopping. Each fall, the Texas State Fair gets bigger and better than ever, too, drawing visitors from around the globe.

The Top Attractions

HISTORIC DOWNTOWN DALLAS

Dallas County Historical Plaza ★ HISTORIC SITE Just 1 block east of Dealey Plaza, where John F. Kennedy was assassinated in 1963, this open plaza lies in the heart of historic downtown Dallas. It's the site of several attractions, including the **John Neely Bryan Cabin,** a replica of the one-room log structure built by the city's founder in 1841. (The original cabin stood on the banks of the Trinity River.) Across Main Street is the **John F. Kennedy Memorial,** the 1970 work of the architect Philip Johnson, who described this square, spare memorial as a "cenotaph" (empty tomb). Unfortunately, the memorial also feels empty of emotion—not quite the moving testament to a president and event that so affected the American national psyche. Inside the four solemn walls is a granite slab with the words JOHN FITZGERALD KENNEDY painted in shimmering gold. Just west of the Kennedy Memorial, across Record Street, is the **Old Red Courthouse,** built in lavish Romanesque Revival style in 1892 on the site of the city's original log courthouse. The blue granite and red sandstone building today houses the **Dallas Visitor's Center** (www.visitdallas.com; ✆ **214/571-1316**) and a museum with historical artifacts and exhibits.

Junction of Main, Market, Elm, and Record sts. No admission fees for memorial. Memorial open daily 24 hr. year-round. DART: West End.

The Sixth Floor Museum at Dealey Plaza ★★ MUSEUM/HISTORIC SITE The most popular museum in Texas opened to the public in 1989, 25 years after the tragic assassination of President John F. Kennedy. It's

A Dollar Saved . . .

Look for coupons for museums and other attractions in the *Dallas/Fort Worth Area Visitors Guide* and other tourism board publications (available free at the CVB office in the Old Red Courthouse, as well as at some hotels and restaurants in Dallas). Also, out-of-town-visitors should check out the Dallas CityPASS! to save 40% or more off admission to the Perot Museum, the Dallas Reunion Tower GeO Deck, the Dallas Zoo, or the Sixth Floor Museum at Dealey Plaza, and the George W. Bush Presidential Library & Museum or the Dallas Arboretum & Botanical Garden. Find out more at www.citypass.com.

in the very building, the Texas Book Depository, where most historians believe Lee Harvey Oswald squeezed off the fatal shot. The area where Oswald is said to have crouched and pulled the trigger is enclosed in Plexiglass and filled with the same sorts of boxes that would have been there on that fateful day. And if that were all that the museum contained, it would likely still draw thousands of visitors per year. But this savvy museum goes much further in unwinding the facts and theories that surround an event that abruptly altered the course of American history. Your visit starts, as it should, with a focus on JFK, both the man and his times. Well-paced and even erudite at times, the first part of the museum explores the social trends that shaped the 1960s, from the Civil Rights struggles to the Cold War, in photos, videos, and wall texts. Visitors also gain insights into the President himself, some of his foibles (even Marilyn Monroe is mentioned), and his signature achievements while in office. The meat of the museum, of course, deals with the events of November 22, 1963. While none of the original evidence collected by the Warren Commission is on display—that is in the National Archives in Washington, D.C.—some 400 photos tell the tale, as do detailed dioramas of the area, videos, stills from the famous Zapruder film, and absorbing wall text. Conspiracy theories are discussed in a fashion that's both deftly balanced and quite fascinating. Even those who have read books on the assassination—my guess is many visitors have—will walk out having learned something new. And they'll walk right onto Dealey Plaza, which looks shockingly small in real life. An X in the road marks the spot where the President was shot—but please don't try to take a photo there; traffic zooming through makes it quite dangerous. ***Important note:*** Tickets are for timed entry that admits patrons every 30 minutes. It's wise to get tickets in advance.

411 Elm St. at Houston (entrance on Houston St.). www.jfk.org. ✆ **214/747-6660.** Admission (including audio guide) $16 adults; $14 seniors; $13 students and children 7–18; free children 5 and under (unless using an audio guide for $4). Tues–Sun 10am–6pm; Mon noon–6pm. Closed Thanksgiving and Dec 25. DART: West End.

THE ARTS DISTRICT

Art lovers will want to spend the better part of a morning or afternoon in the Arts District, though you could do a drive-by through a couple of the museums in a little over an hour. To get there via public transport, take DART light rail to Pearl or St. Paul station.

The Crow Collection of Asian Art ★ MUSEUM Dedicated to the arts of Asia, the Crow both dazzles the eye and tickles the brain. The constantly changing exhibits are culled from the 7,000-piece collection of real estate moguls Trammel and Margaret Crow, two Texans who became enamored of the Orient midway through their lives and amassed a world-class collection. You might find yourself meandering row upon row of exquisite Chinese marriage boxes, one carved from black rhino horn, another of the purest ivory—and you'll learn that they once held not only the jewels the young woman would take with her to her new home, but also a live cocoon, an important symbol of fertility for the bride. In another room you'll encounter an arch from Myanmar, once part of a temple. Another section might contain a fiberglass Porsche painted with scenes taken from traditional Chinese scrolls. The collection covers all areas of Asia and the Indian subcontinent, and while you never know just what you'll see, chances are it will be spectacular. The Crow hosts a number of weekly events, including a free evening yoga class once a week, music concerts, and more, so check the website before heading over. We'd classify it as a midsize museum, so plan a good 90 minutes to 2 hours for both it and the attached sculpture garden. Crow's non-Asian sculpture collection is on display at the **Trammell Crow Center,** at 2001 Ross Ave. at Harwood. It includes 19th- and 20th-century French bronzes (by Rodin and Maillol) throughout the office building and in the garden.

2010 Flora St. (btw. Harwood and Olive sts.). www.crowcollection.org. ✆ **214/979-6430.** Free admission. Tues–Thurs 10am–9pm; Fri–Sun 10am–6pm. Free guided public tours Thurs 6:30pm and Sat 1pm.

Dallas Museum of Art (DMA) ★ MUSEUM In the century following its formation in 1903, the Dallas Museum of Art slowly amassed a small but choice selection of art—including Impressionist and post-Impressionist works. But the museum's standing in the art world rose exponentially in 2005 when it was bequeathed the world-class modern and contemporary art collections of

Seeing Dallas from the Top of the Tower

Dominating the Big D skyline is sphere-topped **Reunion Tower** (www.reuniontower.com; ✆ **214/651-1234;** DART light rail: Union), the top of which is shaped like a golf ball and, when lit up at night, looks like a giant, brilliant pin cushion. The tower, located in Reunion Park at Reunion Boulevard, rises 50 stories, and the dome rotates very slowly (completing a single rotation in just under an hour, though imperceptibly to the naked eye). Take an exterior elevator to an observation deck for panoramic views of the city and surrounding plains, or have a drink or dinner at the **Dome** cocktail lounge or the Wolfgang Puck restaurant **Five Sixty,** named for the 560-foot height of the landmark tower, where you can blame your spinning head on something other than the libations from the bar.

three prominent local collectors: the Hoffmans, the Rachofskys, and the Roses. The collections, gifted together in an unprecedented deal, totaled more than 800 works as well as future acquisitions. In 2014 the DMA grew again, acquiring the **Rose-Asenbaum Collection of Modern Jewelry,** an exemplary group of some 700 pieces of modern studio jewelry created by more than 150 internationally acclaimed artists from the 1960s through the end of the century.

In a sprawling building designed by Edward Larrabee Barnes in 1984, the museum also contains impressive collections of international art. The Arts of the Americas section is the largest, with valuable contributions from pre-Columbian lost civilizations and Spanish colonial arts. The Art of Europe gallery exhibits only a handful of works by the biggies—Van Gogh, Monet, Cézanne, Gauguin, and Degas—while the small 20th-century collection includes Picasso, Mondrian, Giacometti, Jackson Pollock, Texan Robert Rauschenberg, and Jasper Johns. From 2008 to 2009 the museum hosted **"Tutankhamun and the Golden Age of Pharaohs,"** which proved to be the most popular exhibit in the museum's history.

1717 N. Harwood (at Ross St.). www.dallasmuseumofart.org. ✆ **214/922-1200.** General admission free every day; admission to special exhibitions $16 adults, $14 seniors and military with ID, and $12 students with ID. Tues–Wed and Fri–Sun 11am–5pm; Thurs 11am–9pm; 3rd Fri of month (excluding Dec) 11am–midnight; closed Mon. Guided tours Sat 2pm; gallery talks Wed 12:15pm. Closed Thanksgiving Day, Christmas Day, and New Year's Day.

Nasher Sculpture Center ★★★ MUSEUM/SCULPTURE GARDEN This exquisitely serene indoor/outdoor museum is the only facility in the U.S. exclusively devoted to sculpture. It was founded by the late Raymond and Patsy Nasher, Dallas residents who housed some of their sculptures in the shopping mall that made their fortune. Eventually their collection grew so large that it needed its own space, so the Nashers hired starchitect Renzo Piano to create what was termed a "roofless museum." The building that resulted obviously does have a roof, but an innovative one: Thin sheets of glass were suspended from metal rods that allow filtered natural light to fill the space. It's an extraordinary effect that renders the sculptures shadow-free but still protects them. The architecture is only the beginning of the wonders of the museum, which opened in 2003. Among the Nasher's many highlights are several rare plaster casts (the artists' first medium when creating a metal piece) including a Picasso that's considered the first Cubic sculpture. Though the museum and its sculpture garden are spacious, they aren't big enough to display the 300 works the institution owns, so pieces rotate. You'll likely see works by Jim Dine, Willem De Kooning, Isamu Noguchi, Joan Miro, Auguste Rodin, and George Segal. The Nasher features a lovely on-site **cafe.** It hosts lectures, concerts, and movie screenings, so check the calendar.

2001 Flora St. (btw. Harwood and Olive sts.). www.nashersculpturecenter.org. ✆ **214/242-5100.** Admission (includes audio tour) $10 adults, $7 seniors and military with ID, $5 students, free for children 12 and under, and free for first responders with ID. Free 1st Sat of month from 10am–5pm. Tues–Sun 11am–5pm. Closed Mon (except Mon before New Year's Day), and July 4th, Thanksgiving Day, Dec 25 and Jan 1.

Perot Museum of Nature and Science ★★★ MUSEUM As you'd expect from an exceptionally well-funded science museum that opened its doors in 2012, the Perot uses every contemporary trick in the book to engage its visitors. These range from light shows that visitors can manipulate to learn about the "emissions spectrum" to massive plates one can stand on to experience earthquakes. Visitors are invited to push buttons, touch replicas of dinosaur teeth, and do whatever it takes to make science come to life. Aiding in this process is a veritable army of docents—really, at least four in each exhibit space—who have been coached to be dramatic ("Mars has a volcano the size of Arizona!" one exclaimed in the astronomy pavilion to a group of wide-eyed seniors). This low-tech/high-tech approach works like gangbusters, we must say. Formerly the Dallas Science Museum, the Perot is set on two campuses, the main one being in Victory Park. That building, an enormous cube set atop a plinth (and designed by award-winning architect Thomas Mayne) offers up 180,000 feet of exhibition space on six floors, so choose what interests you most, as you'll likely run out of time. Along with changing exhibits, permanent ones explore such topics as the "Expanding Universe" (astronomy), "Life Then and Now" (evolution), and how energy is created—a nod to the Lone Star State's pet industry. While many of the exhibits are geared toward children, they're so smartly done that adults will enjoy them too. The downside to touring here: School groups crowd the place. To avoid them, come right when the doors open or after 2pm.

2201 N. Field St. www.perotmuseum.org. ✆ **214/428-5555.** General admission $19 adults, $16 military with ID, $13 seniors, $12 youths 2–17. Free admission for K–12 educators with current teaching status in Texas and its bordering states at the museum box office on the day of visit. Mon–Sat 10am–5pm; Sun noon–5pm. Free guided public tours Thurs 6:30pm and Sat 1pm. First Thurs of each month hours extended to 9pm. Special events include late-night film and special interactive programming.

THE OUTSKIRTS OF DOWNTOWN: HISTORIC PARKS, FAIRGROUNDS & MUSEUMS

Dallas Arboretum & Botanical Garden ★ GARDENS Just 15 minutes from the towering skyscrapers of downtown is this welcome oasis. These award-winning gardens and woodlands along the banks of White Rock Lake have become a popular spot, welcoming more than a million visitors in 2016. The 66-acre grounds hold 19 themed gardens, including a Children's Adventure Garden, a Magnolia Glade, and a Pecan Grove. The arboretum is the site of a complete life-science laboratory, and hosts a number of seasonal festivals, including a concert series on Thursday. In spring 2017, the garden held its first annual Food & Wine Festival against a pop-art backdrop of thousands of colorful tulips.

8525 Garland Rd. www.dallasarboretum.org. ✆ **214/515-6615.** Admission $15 adults, $12 seniors, $10 children 3–12, free for children 2 and under. Parking $15, with discounted daytime parking $8 with online reservations. Daily 9am–5pm. Closed Thanksgiving, Dec 25, and Jan 1.

Fair Park ★ PARK/MUSEUMS This 277-acre park complex of classic Art Deco buildings and spacious grounds was created for the 1936 Texas Centennial Exposition. Built to commemorate the Republic of Texas's independence from Mexico, it is the only intact and unaltered pre-1950s World's Fair site in the U.S. recognized as a National Historic Landmark for its architecture (the only such landmark in Dallas). Today in the middle of a revival, Fair Park is the site of the annual State Fair of Texas (last weekend of Sept and first 3 weeks of Oct), a blow-out event like none you've ever seen. It's worth visiting this time of year just to go to the fair, though remember that Dallas is often still hot, weather-wise, in fall.

Fair Park is the site of the old Cotton Bowl Stadium and a 5,000-seat Art Deco bandshell, among a number of impressive structures built in the 1930s. Although several of the museums that once called Fair Park home have closed, city fathers are working to revitalize the park. Here are the highlights:

The **Hall of State,** 3939 Grand Ave. (www.hallofstate.com; ✆ **214/421-4500;** Tues–Sat 9am–5pm, Sun 1–5pm; free admission), is the centerpiece and principal Art Deco legacy at Fair Park. Inside, the **Hall of Heroes** has larger-than-life stalwarts of the Republic of Texas, including Sam Houston and Stephen F. Austin. Venture into the four-story-high Great Hall, yet more proof that bigger is always better in Texas.

The **African American Museum,** 3536 Grand Ave. (www.aamdallas.org; ✆ **214/565-9026;** free admission; Tues–Fri 11am–5pm, Sat 10am–5pm; closed Sun and Mon), is the only museum in the Southwest devoted to the preservation and display of African-American artistic, cultural, and historical materials. It also has one of the largest African-American folk art collections in the U.S. The standout exhibit: a fine collection of African-American folk art, supplemented by African art objects and contemporary African-American art.

First opened in 1936, the beautifully renovated **Children's Aquarium at Fair Park** ★, 1462 First Ave. (www.childrensaquariumfairpark.com; ✆ **479/554-7340;** daily 9am–4:30pm; admission $8 adults, $6 children 3–11), contains a small but diverse collection of marine life. It highlights some of the weirder aquatic specimens in the marine and freshwater world, including walking fish, four-eyed fish, upside-down jellyfish, and desert fish. The newest and largest addition is the Amazon Flooded Forest, a 10,000-gallon tank with 30 species from the Amazon River.

The **Perot Museum of Nature and Science Education and Research,** 3535 Grand Ave. (www.perotmuseum.org; ✆ **214/428-5555;** Sat noon–5pm; admission $1 for all ages), is the sister museum of the flashy Perot Museum of Nature and Science in the Arts District. This smaller museum was originally opened in 1936 as the Dallas Museum of Natural History. It reopened in time for the State Fair in 2016, and will now only be open on Saturdays. Here families can view the kind of wildlife that roamed Texas before steers and longhorns—namely dinosaurs—and explore permanent exhibits like "Paleontology Lab" and "Prehistoric Texas." On the first floor, 52 dioramas showcase

DOWNTOWN DALLAS'S outdoor SCULPTURE

After visiting the Nasher Center and the outdoor sculpture garden at the Dallas Museum of Art, fans of monumental contemporary sculpture should pick up the ***Walking Sculpture*** brochure (available at the Visitor's Center), which details 33 outdoor public sculptures in the downtown area. Along the way, you'll find works by Richard Serra, Ellsworth Kelly, Mark di Suvero, and Henry Moore. On the first and third Saturday of each month, a guided **Arts District Architecture walking tour** is offered at 10:30am, departing from the ceremonial entrance to the Dallas Museum of Art (Flora and Harwood). Presented in partnership with the Dallas Center for Architecture, the tour lasts 90 minutes and is held rain or shine. For required reservations, visit **www.dallasartsdistrict.org/plan-your-visit/architecture-tour**.

native plants and animals from around Texas, many of which date back to the opening of the Museum in 1936. Check out the realistic-looking plant leaves—each one is handmade out of wax! The Lower Level Paleo Lab allows visitors to observe volunteers and scientists working to reveal ancient fossils. The Nature Building, along with many other buildings in Fair Park, is listed on the National Register of Historic Places. Unfortunately, the old planetarium and IMAX are no longer open here, but if you want a great kid-friendly nature and science museum, be sure to visit the big one in Victory Park.

3809 Grand Ave. (bordered by S. Fitzhugh, Washington, and Parry aves. and Cullum Blvd.). www.fairpark.org. ✆ **214/426-3400,** or 421-9600 for museum/event information.

The George W. Bush Presidential Center ★ MUSEUM/LIBRARY
Welcome to the world of presidential libraries, where the agenda is always the same: Prove that the figurehead in question was, without a doubt, one of the best U.S. presidents to ever hold the office. Whether or not you agree with that assertion will definitively shape your experience of the George W. Bush Presidential Library. The tour starts with a bang as you enter the contemporary equivalent of a Greek temple, a $250-million building designed by starchitect Robert A. M. Stern. It's every bit as majestic as the U.S. Capitol or the White House. In fact, it may do one better—a Spielbergian soundtrack of crooning violins and triumphant trumpets greets visitors. Then, before you meet the Bushes—or even purchase your ticket—you'll notice that you're in the middle of the "gift hall" to view the swag foreign dignitaries gifted the First Couple over the years—impressive, if sometimes weird, particularly the downright erotic snake necklace President Berlusconi of Italy presented to Laura Bush.

The central exhibition is highly interactive, with dozens of video clips, photos, documents (such as a page from the President's schedule that shows his day fully packed by 10-minute increments), and artifacts—such as a World Trade Center steel beam twisted by the 9/11 collapse. Interestingly, the full cast of the Bush years has been edited. Condoleezza Rice, both chiefs of staff (Andrew Card and Joshua Bolton), and the Bush family narrate videos and

KID magnets

Older children who have studied the 1960s and President Kennedy should appreciate Dallas's **Sixth Floor Museum ★★** (p. 65). Younger kids are likely to have a better time at the **Dallas Zoo ★** (p. 74), or either the **Children's Aquarium at Fair Park ★** (p. 70) or the **Dallas World Aquarium ★** (p. 74).

Every October, Fair Park is the site of the **State Fair of Texas** (www.bigtex.com), a nearly month-long lollapalooza of music, parades, livestock displays, food (with an emphasis on deep-fried anything), and such state-fair esoterica as butter sculpture, shoe-gluing contests, and pig races. It's all catnip to kids.

The **Gateway Gallery** at the **Dallas Museum of Art ★** (p. 67) has a dedicated kids' space, with interactive art activities, puzzles, books, rubbings and crayons and is continuously staffed with volunteers and art professionals alike. Free weekend programming called "Family Days" includes multiple hands-on art activities, treasure hunts, live music and dance performances, and a host of cultural entertainment.

A former bowling alley turned into two fabulous theaters, the **Dallas Children's Theater** hosts wonderful and engaging family stage productions, performed by a troupe of professional actors, every weekend. Baker Theater (which seats 400) and Studio Theater (a 160-seat venue) are housed in the Rosewood Center for Family (5928 Skillman Dr. at Northwest Highway; www.dct.org; ✆ **214/978-0110**).

Finally, just getting around Dallas can be fun, especially when you ride the **DART Light Rail** around downtown (goes direct to the Dallas Zoo) or hop aboard the **historic trolleys** that patrol McKinney Avenue.

Families pour into the town of **Arlington,** midway between Dallas and Fort Worth, for big-time sports and amusement-park fun. **AT&T Stadium (aka Cowboys Stadium) ★** offers fabulous guided tours of the home turf of the NFL Dallas Cowboys. **Rangers Ballpark ★**, home of the MLB baseball team the **Texas Rangers,** also offers tours. The hugely popular **Six Flags Over Texas ★** is a 212-acre theme park with an adjacent **Hurricane Harbor ★** water park. In the nearby Dallas suburb of Grand Prairie, **Louis Tussaud's Palace of Wax & Ripley's Believe It or Not! ★** is another family fave. For reviews, see "Arlington," p. 107.

A half-hour drive from Dallas, not far from DFW airport, **Grapevine** is home to two mega-resorts that are family destinations in themselves. The **Great Wolf Lodge Resort** (www.greatwolf.com/grapevine; ✆ **800/693-9653**) offers plenty of wet and wild fun for families at its massive (80,000-sq.-ft.) waterpark, with water slides, pools, and a big water-fort treehouse featuring a cool 1,000-gallon tipping bucket. Practically next door to Great Lodge, the grand **Gaylord Texan Resort** (www.marriott.com/hotels/travel/dalgt-gaylord-texan-resort-and-convention-center; ✆ **817/778-1000**) has an indoor/air-conditioned replica of the San Antonio River Walk as well as a New Orleans–style French Quarter neighborhood—all under one enormous rooftop. Set on Lake Grapevine, the resort offers fireworks over the lake on July 4th and an annual **ICE!** exhibit in winter, featuring more than 2 million pounds of colorful, hand-carved ice sculptures. Pile on a heavy parka (the resort provides those, but bring a pair of gloves) and stroll inside a maze of themed ice sculptures kept at a numbing 9 degrees. Kids will love the huge ice slides. ICE! also dazzles with 1.5-million twinkling lights, a 52-foot-tall rotating Christmas tree, and a life-size gingerbread house.

show up in exhibits, but former Vice President Dick Cheney, Donald Rumsfeld, and political operative Karl Rove are conspicuously absent.

The museum's two big crowd pleasers are a perfect replica of the Oval Office (for your own photo op) and the "Decision Points Theater." The latter contains a "situation room" simulation in which participants watch videos of actors explaining the biggest issues that confronted President Bush during his tenure. Visitors then choose between two courses of action. Neither option is the optimal one, in the mind of this reviewer, but they do reveal the mindset of his administration. And then it's off to the gift shop—your own "gift hall"—which carries items commemorating both the Bushes and the office of the president, from Christmas tree ornaments to coffee-table books. Between 1,500 and 3,000 people have visited the Library daily since it opened in May of 2013, and its massive size (14,000 sq. ft.) keeps it from feeling crowded. Still, if you'd like to have it to yourself, get here when it first opens, before the buses arrive.

2943 SMU Blvd. www.bushcenter.org. ✆ **214/200-4300.** Admission $16 adults, $13 seniors, $14 youth 13–17, $10 children 5–12, free for children 4 and under; $15 college students (non-SMU), free to SMU students, faculty, and staff; free for active military with ID, $10 for retired military. Free parking. Mon–Sat 9am–5pm, Sun noon–5pm. Closed Thanksgiving, Dec 25, and Jan 1. DART: Lovers Lane and Mockingbird.

Meadows Museum of Art ★★ MUSEUM When oil baron Algur Meadows (1899–1978) headed to Spain in search of black gold, he came up short. But he didn't come home empty-handed. Having fallen in love with Spanish art, Meadows went on a buying spree and collected what many consider to be the best collection of Spanish art outside of Spain. In his own words, it was to be a "Prado on the Prairie."

The museum had a shaky start—it turned out Meadows had been taken quite a bit by unsavory dealers. But today, the fakes have been culled from the collection, and now it's a parade of great Spanish masters, several of whom have multiple entries (six paintings by Goya alone). Among the "Mona Lisas" here are Ribera's *Retrato de un Caballero de Santiago* and Goya's *El Corral de los Locos*. The collection also features works from Picasso, Dalí, Miró, Velázquez, and Zurbarán. All are hung salon-style (walls are crowded with art from ceiling to near the floor) in a hushed, neoclassical yet modern building on the campus of SMU. Art aficionados will find it all so much catnip, but those who need to be coaxed a bit in museums may be dismayed by the terse wall text and the overwhelming number of paintings on display.

In addition to its permanent collection, the Meadows has forged a partnership with the Prado, which often loans pieces to this smaller collection. So you never know exactly what will be on view when you visit.

Owens Fine Arts Center, SMU Campus, 5900 Bishop Blvd. (1 block north of Mockingbird Lane, west of I-75). www.meadowsmuseumdallas.org. ✆ **214/768-2516.** Admission $12 adults, $8 seniors, $4 students, free for children 11 and under; free for all Thurs after 5pm. Tues–Wed and Fri–Sat 10am–5pm; Thurs 10am–9pm; Sun 1–5pm. Closed Mon. Free Thurs after 5pm. DART: Mockingbird.

Swiss Avenue Historic District ★ HISTORIC DISTRICT At the end of the 19th century, the Dallas elite began to move east, building the McMansions of the day in an array of interesting styles—English Tudor, Georgian, Spanish, you name it—along leafy Swiss Avenue, about 4 blocks of which are listed on the National Register of Historic Places. The Wilson Blocks (2800 and 2900) are especially attractive. The Swiss Avenue Historic District Association hosts a **Mother's Day Home Tour** on Mother's Day weekend ($20 in advance; $25 weekend of event), where guests travel from home to home in air-conditioned mini coaches or vintage horse-drawn carriages.

Northeast of downtown, along Swiss Ave. btw. La Vista Dr. and Fitzhugh Ave. (take Fitzhugh east from I-75). www.sahd.org.

More to See & Do

The Dallas World Aquarium ★ AQUARIUM The Dallas aquarium *not* at Fair Park is a fine place to hide out from the sun downtown. Come to this former warehouse in the West End district to commune with stingrays, sea turtles, and pelagic reef fish. "Orinoco—Secrets of the River," is a seven-story exploration of the South American rainforest, teeming with two-toed sloths, saffron toucanets, monkeys, tree frogs. "Mundo Maya," a tribute to Mayan folklore, is a beauty, with brilliantly hued flamingos, lizards, and snakes.

1801 N. Griffin (West End District). www.dwazoo.com. ✆ **214/720-2224.** Admission (not including tax) is $21 adults, $17 seniors, $15 children 2–12, free for children under 2. Open daily 10am–5pm (times subject to change in spring). Closed Thanksgiving and Dec 25. DART: West End.

Dallas Zoo ★ ZOO The Fort Worth Zoo and the zoo in San Antonio are the tops zoos in Texas, but if Dallas is your only stop and wild animals are what you're craving, this, the oldest zoo in Texas (founded in 1888), will not disappoint. The "Wilds of Africa Adventure Safari" is a newly renovated monorail that takes riders through several African habitats, past giraffes, elephants, chimps, and kudu. Little kids will love the chug-a-lugging T-Rex Express Mini-Train and the Lacerte Family Children's Zoo, the latter with petting goats and pot-bellied pigs; an aviary where you can actually feed the birds; and a crawl-through tunnel to spy on moles and mongoose. Wear sunscreen and bring a hat.

650 S. R. L. Thornton Fwy. (in Oak Cliff, 3 miles south of downtown Dallas). www.dallaszoo.com. ✆ **214/554-7500.** Admission $15 adults, $12 seniors, $12 children 3–11, free for children 2 and under. Reduced admission Dec–Feb. Parking $8. Wilds of Africa Adventure Safari $5 per rider. Daily 9am–4pm.

Organized Tours

Highly rated by visitors, **Dallas City Tour** (www.dallascitytour.com; ✆ **214/310-0700**) offers a range of themed sightseeing tours in the Dallas–Fort Worth area, including bus tours, "cruizers" electric car tours, limo tours, and walking tours.

NorthStar Carriages, starting at its Carriage Stand located at 1800 N. Market St. (www.dfwcarriages.com; ✆ **214/441-9996**), offers horse-drawn carriage tours of historic Dallas 7 days a week, weather permitting (by city ordinance). Standard tours pass by the JFK Museum, Dealey Plaza, the Kennedy Memorial, the John Nealy Bryan Log Cabin, and allow for a magnificent view of the Dallas Skyline, and the ride lasts about 20 minutes ($45). Longer, custom tours and special "romantic tours" can also be arranged.

Architecture enthusiasts will enjoy the 90-minute **Dallas Arts District architecture walking tours** (www.dallasartsdistrict.org/plan-your-visit/architecture-tour; ✆ **214/880-1550**), at 10am on the first and third Saturday of every month, departing from the ceremonial entrance of the Dallas Museum of Art (corner of Flora and Harwood sts.). The tour costs $10 ($5 for seniors and free for kids under 12), but reservations must be made in advance.

Outdoor Activities

BIKING, IN-LINE SKATING & JOGGING White Rock Lake, 5 miles east of downtown Dallas (off Loop 12), is the most popular area for cycling, skating, and running (and, of course, walking). A 12-mile loop traces the banks of the lake. The park is open from 6am to midnight, though we wouldn't advise hanging about too long after darkness falls. Nearby bike and skate shops offer rentals.

GOLF Golf legends such as Byron Nelson, Ben Hogan, and Lee Trevino hailed from north Texas, which has a huge number of golf courses. These range from challenging championship courses to comfortable ones suited to players of all stripes. **TPC Four Seasons Los Colinas** in the Dallas suburb of Irving (www.fourseasons.com/dallas/golf; ✆ **972/717-0700;** greens fees $215), home of the PGA Byron Nelson Classic, is the best and most spectacular course in the area—but you'll have to stay at the Four Seasons (p. 89) to play.

Rated among the top 50 resorts in the United States is **Bear Creek Golf Club,** 3500 Bear Creek Court/DFW Airport (www.bearcreek-golf.com; ✆ **972/456-3200**). With reasonable greens fees and cart costs running between $46 and $56, and with twilight reduced rates available, Bear Creek features two nicely designed championship 18-hole courses on 355 acres of rolling hills.

The City of Dallas operates several courses open to the public, including **Keeton Park Golf Course,** 2323 Jim Miller Rd., southeast of downtown Dallas off I-30 (www.keetonpark.com; ✆ **214/670-8784**), which has pecan tree–lined fairways and numerous ponds. On weekdays, greens fees range from $26 to $33 depending on the time of day (weekends $26–$38). **Park Golf Course,** 3501 Samuell Blvd. (www.tenisonpark.com; ✆ **214/670-1402**), just 5 miles east of downtown, has two 18-hole courses divided by White Rock Creek. Greens fees are $45 to $60, with reduced fees for twilight and sundown times, as well as for students and seniors.

Local duffers (as well as football fans) rave about the **Cowboys Golf Club,** 1600 Fairway Dr., in Grapevine (www.cowboysgolfclub.com; ✆ **817/481-7277;** greens fees all-inclusive VIP package $189, twilight play $130), which is certainly unique: Not only does it boast huge changes in elevation, but it claims to be the "world's first NFL-themed golf course." The clubhouse is

Packin' Heat, Texas Style

Some Texans feel their right to own, use, and brag about firearms is just part of their legally protected birthright. In fact, a controversial 2016 "open-carry" law has actually made it legal for Texans who have passed a required safety course and have a concealed handgun permit to visibly carry their holstered weapons in public. We personally think it's appalling that citizens can even stroll around carrying loaded weapons to church on Sunday—and now museums and cinemas and any business that doesn't want guns on the premises will have to post signs that warn "NO FIREARMS ALLOWED." If, however, you want to play Texan while in Big D, what better way than to fire off a few rounds? If that's your idea of R&R, the **DFW Gun Club & Training Center,** 1607 Mockingbird Lane (www.dfwgun.com; ✆ **214/630-4866**), operates the DFW Gun Range for a little indoor shooting. Featured hilariously in the film *Borat* about the fictional reporter from Kazakhstan, the club offers shooting instruction and even concealed handgun license classes. ***Notable fact:*** About 75 miles southwest of Dallas stands the infamous firing range where real-life *American Sniper* Chris Kyle was killed: the Rough Creek Lodge, an 11,000-acre resort located in Glen Rose, about 25 miles outside of Stephenville.

packed with Dallas Cowboys memorabilia and Super Bowl trophies, and markers along the course pay tribute to key moments in Cowboys lore.

Named among the "Best Places to Play" by *Golf Digest* (and rated one of the top five public courses in Texas) is **Buffalo Creek Golf Club,** 624 Country Club Dr., Rockwall (www.buffalocreekgc.com; ✆ **972/771-4003**), near Lake Ray Hubbard, a healthy drive from Dallas. Greens fees, including cart and range balls, are $37 to $50.

Golf fanatics may want to venture north of Dallas to Flower Mound, Texas, where the **Tour 18 Dallas** course (8718 Amen Corner; www.tour18-dallas.com; ✆ **800/946-5310** or 817/430-2000) reproduces 18 of the best-known holes in golf (from courses such as Winged Foot and Augusta National). The course is west of I-35 E. and Hwy. 121, and greens fees are $29 to $89.

TENNIS Even though tennis in Dallas is mostly confined to swank (and off-limits) private tennis clubs, there are several public courts where visitors can play a few sets. The following are city-owned, but have privately run pro shops: **Fair Oak Tennis Center,** 7501 Merriman Pkwy. (✆ **214/670-1495**), with 14 lighted outdoor hardcourts near White Rock Creek (4 miles north of White Rock Lake); **Fretz Tennis Center,** 14700 Hillcrest Ave. (✆ **214/670-6622**), where I took lessons as a kid, has been renovated and now offers 15 fully lit outdoor, hard-surface tennis courts for public play, a full-service pro shop, and experienced coaching staff.

Spectator Sports

Dallas, home to 2011's Super Bowl LXV, is sports mad, one of only six cities in the U.S. to support teams in all the major professional sports leagues. Tickets to pro sporting events are available from **Central Tickets**

(© **817/335-9000**), **Star Tickets** (© **800/585-3737**), and **Ticketmaster** (© **800/745-3000**).

BASEBALL The **Texas Rangers** (once owned by a group of investors headed by the former president George W. Bush) play from April to October at one of the finest stadiums in the country, the Texas Rangers' **Globe Life Park in Arlington,** I-30 at Hwy. 157 (www.texasrangers.com; © **817/273-5222**), a home field that recalls the glory days of baseball.

The **Frisco Rough Riders** (www.ridersbaseball.com; © **972/731-9300**), the Texas Rangers feeder team, play minor league at the multi-functional Dr. Pepper Ballpark, a 35-minute drive north of downtown at Hwy. 121 S. between Dallas North Tollway and Parkwood Boulevard.

BASKETBALL *Shark Tank* star Mark Cuban has become almost as popular as the team he owns, the **Dallas Mavericks** (www.nba.com/mavericks; © **214/747-MAVS [6287]** or 665-4797). The Mavs, one of the top teams in the NBA, call the American Airlines Center home. This excellent arena, built by the same architect who created the critically acclaimed Rangers Ballpark in Arlington for the Texas Rangers, opened in 2001. Single-game tickets (Ticketmaster: © **214/373-8000**) are $20 to $250 and can be a bit hard to come by, as popular as the Mavs are at home. Tours of the arena are held every Monday, Wednesday, and Friday on non-event days from 11am to 2:45pm.

FOOTBALL The **Dallas Cowboys** (www.dallascowboys.com; © **817/892-4000**), the five-time Super Bowl Champions dubbed "America's Team," played at **Texas Stadium** in Irving, the arena with the famous hole in the roof, for 38 years. The Cowboys' spectacular **AT&T Stadium** opened in 2009; it seats 80,000 and is the largest domed stadium in the country—and it still has a hole in the roof, albeit a retractable one. Individual game tickets, which cost $75 to $200+, aren't easy to come by, so plan ahead if you want to avoid paying high brokers' fees. The tours of this enormous stadium are spectacular, even if you're not a sports fan. There are even Art Tours in the stadium, and you can check out the dressing rooms of not only the players but of the **Dallas Cowboys Cheerleaders,** who led the professional trend of scantily clad women bouncing around on the sidelines to cheer on their teams.

GOLF The **AT&T Byron Nelson Championship,** named for the local legend, is held each May and has a long history in professional golf that traces its roots back to 1944. It's held at the par-70 **TPC Four Seasons Los Colinas** (www.attbyronnelson.org; © **214/943-9700**).

HOCKEY Dallas may not seem like the most logical place for a professional ice hockey team, but Big D has one of the best: the **Dallas Stars** (1999 Stanley Cup winner and 2000 Western Conference Champions)—and Dallasites are wild about them. The Stars play at the American Airlines Center from September through April. The Stars often sell out all their home games, so plan ahead if you want to see a game (www.dallasstars.com; © **214/GO-STARS [467-8277]**). Tickets (available at Ticketmaster; © **214/373-8000**) range from $10 to $300, and family packs (tickets and food) are available.

RODEO One of the top rodeos in Texas, and a huge draw for out-of-towners and travelers from abroad, is the **Mesquite Championship Rodeo,** about 20 miles northeast of downtown at Resistol Arena, 1818 Rodeo Dr. (www.mesquiterodeo.com; ✆ **800/833-9339** or 972/285-8777). From early summer (it varies year to year, but in 2016 the rodeos started up in June) into early October, authentic professional rodeo action—bull riding, saddle and bareback riding, calf roping, and rodeo clown fun—is offered on Saturday nights at 7:30pm (reserved grandstand seating falls into three price zones, $20, $30, and $38 (for VIP seating). (Animal-rights sympathizers might feel a bit uneasy watching some of the roping exercises, which violently snap calves' heads back.) A gift shop is on-site, and before and after the rodeo they offer pony rides for the kids. Boots, hats, bandanas, and big shiny belt-buckles are standard attire for spectators. When I was a kid, I remember getting spiffy new Western wear just for the occasion when we'd mosey on over to the Mesquite Rodeo from our house near White Rock Lake.

SOCCER **FC Dallas** (www.fcdallas.com; ✆ **888/323-4625** or 214/705-6700) draws more than 1.5 million fans to its games at the 20,500-capacity **Toyota Stadium** in Frisco, 30 miles north of Dallas. The season lasts from April to October. Tickets cost $9 to $60.

WHERE TO STAY

If you're in Dallas for a business trip or just a brief vacation, or are hoping to avoid too much time on Dallas freeways, you'll do well to choose your hotel according to neighborhood. Some of the city's best hotels are downtown near the central business area and Dallas Arts District, and in the fashionable area called Uptown, but many more hotels (especially more affordable chains) are nestled in North Dallas and near Irving. For most people, the latter locations will involve considerably more highway time, because Dallas is so spread out.

Most of the hotels in the city are large, well run, and aimed squarely at business travelers, though some very appealing boutique hotels have also taken root. Dallas has a bundle of excellent lodgings at the top end, many chic and modern, but some with a surprisingly old-world feel. The best of the cheaper lodgings are all-suite hotels. ***Note:*** Reservations in Dallas are toughest to come by when conventions take over the city. Check as early as possible with the **Dallas Convention & Visitors Bureau** (www.visitdallas.com; ✆ **800/232-5527**) to find out if your visit coincides with major business events in the city.

Virtually all hotels offer some deals, especially on weekends when the business clientele dries up; check the individual hotels' websites for special online offers. The hotel occupancy tax in Dallas is 15%.

Downtown

EXPENSIVE

The Adolphus Hotel ★★ This is my favorite Dallas hotel, just as it was the favorite of my parents and my in-laws back in their Mad Men/midcentury Dallas days, and just as it has long been for bankers, businessmen, lawyers and lobbyists, politicians and celebs—all the beautiful people for which this brilliant city of excess is known. The equivalent of the Plaza in New York City or the Chateau Frontenac in Quebec City, the Adolphus is the grande dame of Dallas hotels. Built in 1912 by beer magnate Adolphus Busch, it's a landmarked Beaux Arts storehouse of treasures (17th-century Flemish tapestries, magnificent murals in the restaurant, crystal chandeliers). Its lobby is chockablock with majestic paintings, towering vases of plants and flowers, fine antiques, and crannies perfect for high tea (served daily 3–5pm) and stiff martinis come nightfall. The newly renovated rooms are just as spiffy, featuring fine four-poster beds, the finest linens, the finest antiques—the finest of everything, really. While it no longer gets the bold-faced guests that the Rosewood Mansion on Turtle Creek does—the non-exclusive location in the heart of downtown Dallas may account for that—it should still fit the bill for anyone who wants a taste of elegant, old-school Texan hospitality. The longtime favorite **French Room** restaurant, known for its fabulous classic French cuisine and iconic status as a special-occasion room, was undergoing renovations at press time but should be open by the time you read this. Best of all, the Adolphus is actually good value for your travel dollar, with online rates that will surprise you. In my book—this one—it's the quintessential fine downtown Dallas hotel.

1321 Commerce St. (at Akard). www.hoteladolphus.com. ✆ **844/452-4908** or 214/742-8200. 422 units. $167–$299 double; from $299 suite. Special theme packages available. Valet parking $30. DART: Akard. Pets 30 lb. and under accepted with $50 fee. **Amenities:** 2 restaurants, including the French Room (slated to reopen in 2017); bar/grill; free airport transfers; concierge; exercise room; access to nearby health club; room service; Wi-Fi (free).

The Magnolia Hotel Dallas Downtown ★ A red neon Pegasus, the city's most beloved icon, still lights up the night sky above this landmark 1922 skyscraper. Originally built for the Magnolia Petroleum company, which morphed into Mobil, this former office building is within walking distance of most of the city's top sights. Many of the building's original Art Deco flourishes have been lovingly preserved—my favorite aspect of this otherwise merely spiffy business-traveler-type hotel. The Magnolia has an understated stylishness, with oversize rooms done up in contemporary fashion, many with good-looking wooden blinds and leather chairs. The hotel also offers two-bedroom suites with full kitchens, perfect for families or longer stays. Be sure to ask for a room that ends in 07—these feature three sides of windows and a small hallway, yet don't cost a lick more than the standard double rooms. The **Lounge,** which occupies the entire second floor, is a great place to unwind, with a stocked library, TV, bar, and breakfast and evening a la carte dining. The hotel's other perks include a better-than-usual fitness center and a truly devoted staff—they'll bend over backward to help you. Shoppers' alert: The original Neiman Marcus is just down the block.

1401 Commerce St. www.magnoliahoteldallas.com. ✆ **888/915-1110** or 214/915-6500. 330 units. $179–$349 double; $350–$500 suite. Rates include breakfast buffet and complimentary bedtime milk and cookies. Weekend packages available. Valet parking $24. DART: Akard. **Amenities:** Coffee shop adjacent to hotel; bar/lounge; concierge; health club; room service; same-day valet & dry-cleaning; Wi-Fi (free).

Downtown & Deep Ellum Hotels, Restaurants & Attractions

ACCOMODATIONS ■

The Adolphus Hotel **16**
Belmont Hotel **2**
The Corinthian B&B **22**
The Magnolia **17**
SpringHill Suites Dallas Downtown/West End **11**

Dallas-Fort Worth Int'l Airport
Dallas Love Field
DALLAS
Area of detail

TURTLE CREEK PARK
R.E. LEE PARK
UPTOWN
CENTRAL EXPRESSWAY
Blackburn St.
Oak Lawn Ave.
Dallas North Tollway
Harry Hines Blvd.
MARKET CENTER
Maple Ave.
REVERCHON PARK
GREENWOOD CEMETERY
Cedar Springs Rd.
McKinney Ave.
McKinnon St.
Harry Hines Blvd.
Market Center Blvd.
Oak Lawn Ave.
Stemmons Freeway
Woodall Rogers Freeway
Industrial Blvd.
Trinity River
Pearl St.
ARTS DISTRICT
Ross Ave.
WEST END
Pacific Ave.
Elm St.
Main St.
Commerce St.
Ervay St.
Central Expwy.
Pearl Expwy.
Continental St. Viaduct
DEALEY PLAZA
DOWNTOWN
Young St.
Reunion Blvd.
Houston St.
Lamar St.
Griffin St.
Dallas Convention Center
Commerce St. Viaduct
REUNION PARK
TRINITY RIVER GREENBELT PARK
← BISHOP ARTS DISTRICT/ OAK CLIFF
Beckley Ave.
Houston St. Viaduct
Jefferson Blvd. Viaduct
Industrial Blvd.
Lamar St.
Corinth St.

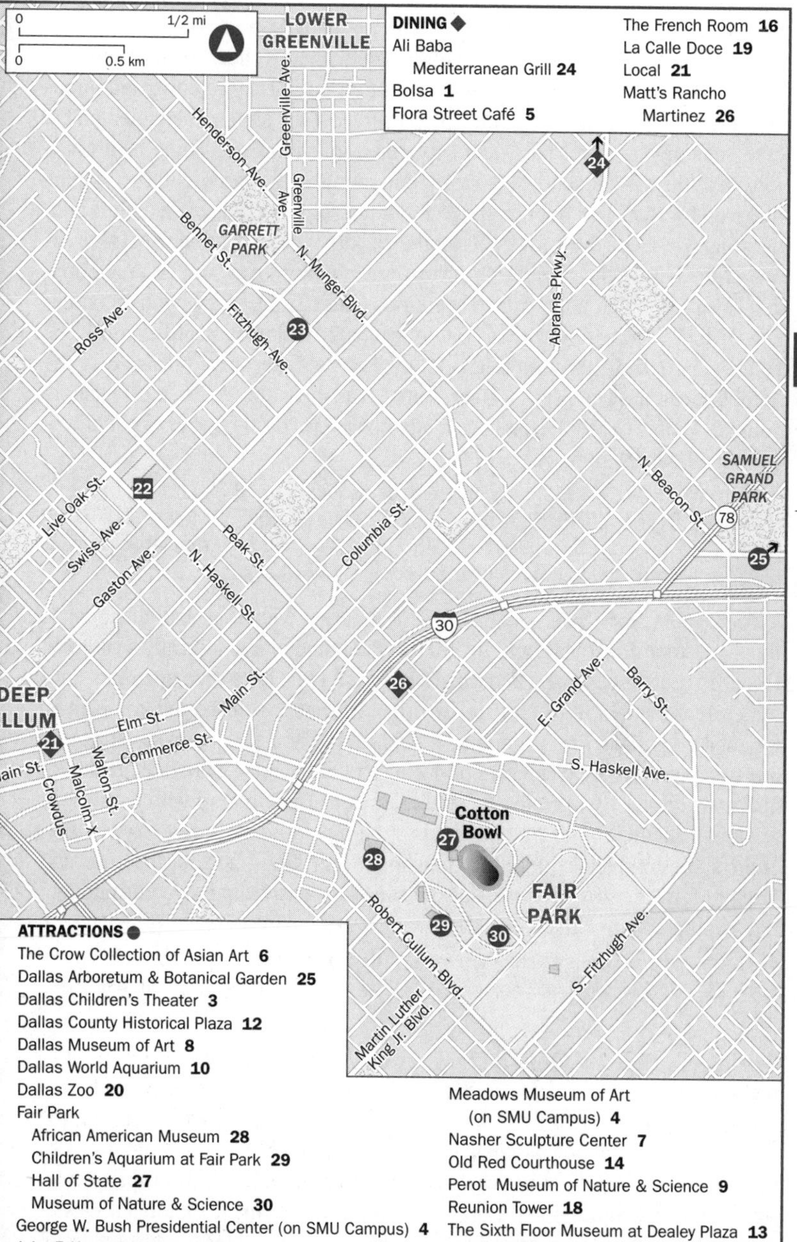
0
1/2 mi
0
0.5 km
LOWER GREENVILLE
DINING ◆
Ali Baba Mediterranean Grill 24
Bolsa 1
Flora Street Café 5
The French Room 16
La Calle Doce 19
Local 21
Matt's Rancho Martinez 26
Henderson Ave.
Greenville Ave.
Greenville Ave.
GARRETT PARK
Bennet St.
N. Munger Blvd.
Abrams Pkwy.
Ross Ave.
Fitzhugh Ave.
Live Oak St.
Swiss Ave.
Gaston Ave.
Peak St.
N. Haskell St.
Columbia St.
N. Beacon St.
SAMUEL GRAND PARK
78
30
DEEP ELLUM
Elm St.
Main St.
Commerce St.
Main St.
Walton St.
Malcolm X
Crowdus
E. Grand Ave.
Barry St.
S. Haskell Ave.
Cotton Bowl
FAIR PARK
Robert Cullum Blvd.
Martin Luther King Jr. Blvd.
S. Fitzhugh Ave.
ATTRACTIONS ●
The Crow Collection of Asian Art 6
Dallas Arboretum & Botanical Garden 25
Dallas Children's Theater 3
Dallas County Historical Plaza 12
Dallas Museum of Art 8
Dallas World Aquarium 10
Dallas Zoo 20
Fair Park
African American Museum 28
Children's Aquarium at Fair Park 29
Hall of State 27
Museum of Nature & Science 30
George W. Bush Presidential Center (on SMU Campus) 4
John F. Kennedy Memorial 15
Meadows Museum of Art (on SMU Campus) 4
Nasher Sculpture Center 7
Old Red Courthouse 14
Perot Museum of Nature & Science 9
Reunion Tower 18
The Sixth Floor Museum at Dealey Plaza 13
Swiss Avenue Historic District 23

MODERATE

Belmont Hotel ★★★ Value and charm are an unusual combination, but that's what this vintage 1940s motel-turned-hotel offers in spades. The owners have embraced the Belmont's midcentury modern roots, meaning the wonderfully colorful and visually jagged tiles in the bathroom are original, and the furnishings suggest a film noir sensibility with a more cheerful color scheme. Ah, but don't worry: The mattresses aren't vintage. They're cushy and modern, as are the amenities—fat duvets, flatscreen TVs, and, in the larger suites, luxe soaking tubs, wet bars, and sometimes full kitchens. Some bathrooms look a little too authentically retro, but rooms with carports-turned-patios make up for that. The Belmont has a fabulous outdoor pool set on a bluff with dazzling views of downtown. Its populist barbecue restaurant, **SMOKE,** is one of the best in the city, serving barbecue of every stripe: coffee-cured brisket, Carolina pulled pork, grilled spare ribs (Chef Tim Byres's book on barbecue, *SMOKE: New Firewood Cooking,* won a 2014 James Beard award). The **Barroom at the Belmont** is the lobby lounge. The only downside is the hotel's location. The view's great, but it isn't near the sights most visitors come to Dallas to see. If you have a car, however, you'll be able to get downtown in about 10 minutes.

901 Fort Worth Ave. (Oak Cliff, 1 block north of the I-30/Sylvan Rd. exit). www.belmontdallas.com. ✆ **866/870-8010** or 214/393-2300. 64 units. $135–$206 double; $180–$240 suite $425 for Terrace Suite. Valet parking $15; self-parking free. **Amenities:** Restaurant; bar; health club; outdoor pool; room service; Wi-Fi (free).

The Corinthian Bed and Breakfast ★★ Victorian with a capital V, this handsome B&B was built in 1905 as the home of a noted Dallas surgeon. Over the years it became a boardinghouse for female telephone operators until the current owners restored it to its original beauty, with period wallpapers, Oriental rugs, and lovely antique furnishings. They've also made sure that creature comforts are taken care of, hiring a chef to create elaborate breakfasts and updating the "water closets" and mattresses (now plump with comfy pillowtops). In addition to four rooms in the original house, guests can rent an entire suite, complete with full kitchen, in the less atmospheric but roomier and brighter former carriage house—also the least expensive option, oddly enough. Savory, ingredients-driven breakfasts served here are a source of pride.

4125 Junius St. www.corinthianbandb.com. ✆ **866/598-9988** or 214/818-0400. 5 units. $149–$209 double. Nonsmoking; adults only; no pets. Free parking. **Amenities:** Wi-Fi (free).

SpringHill Suites Dallas Downtown/West End ★ If you want to be right in the thick of it—within walking distance of the restaurants and rowdy bars of the West End, the Sixth Floor Museum and Dealey Plaza, the Arts District, and downtown's business district—but don't want to burn through your savings or the company per diem, this Marriott property (formerly an AmeriSuites hotel) is a good, safe, and convenient choice. The good-size, comfortable suites have basic kitchenettes and sleeper sofas—nothing fancy, but solid accommodations. Visiting businesspeople should find the business center to their liking, while more leisure-oriented visitors should take to the second-floor outdoor pool, which, though small, has privileged views of the Big D skyline.

1907 N. Lamar St. (at Corbin). www.marriott.com. ✆ **888/287-9400** or 214/999-0500. 148 units. $149–$269 double. Rates include continental breakfast buffet. Valet parking $24. (Self-parking across the street, $8). No pets. DART: West End. **Amenities:** Concierge; exercise room; heated outdoor pool; room service; Wi-Fi (free).

Uptown & Oak Lawn

EXPENSIVE

Hôtel St. Germain ★★★ Attention filmmakers: If you're looking for a place to shoot a movie about the life of Napoleon Bonaparte, this extravagant B&B may be a contender. Seriously, every bedroom at the St. Germain looks like it was lifted—lock, stock, and canopied bed—from the Chateau de Fontainebleau in France. The furniture is of fine antiques, the shimmering palette is taken from a Watteau painting, fireplaces grace many of the suites, and every inch is decorated with Gallic flair. Don't worry though, you won't be using chamber pots: The bathrooms are modern, many marble-clad and with soaking tubs, and each attached to a bedroom. The only downside, and it's a small one, is that the hotel is set in an old mansion, so there is no elevator, meaning guests must climb stairs to their second- and third-floor bedrooms. Grand public spaces on the ground floor turn into a restaurant in the mornings (for the guests) and evenings (for anyone who makes a reservation). We can't think of a more wonderfully over-the-top place in Dallas for a honeymoon. Don't be surprised if reception answers the phone or greets you in French.

2516 Maple Ave. (at Mahon St.). www.hotelstgermain.com. ✆ **214/871-2516.** 7 units. $290–$650 suite. Rates include continental breakfast. No valet parking; no pets. DART: Pearl. **Amenities:** Restaurant; concierge; nearby health club; room service; Wi-Fi (free).

Hotel ZaZa ★★ Some hotels fill common areas with high-priced art in an attempt to impress well-heeled clientele. But few hoteliers have the vision to pick pieces that stop you dead in your tracks. That's one of the things that makes ZaZa so glamorous. The art is museum-quality, often dark in its themes. That artsiness doesn't stop at the doors to the guest rooms. They, too, are blessed with terrifically original works (mostly photos), lush furnishings, and such surreal touches as massive lampshades hanging over the seating and oddball knickknacks placed here and there (different in each room). The smallest rooms are a roomy 400 square feet. All come with quality pillowtop mattresses. Along with the standard rooms are 17 "Concept Suites," each a fantastical pocket of exotica that promises a true getaway, from the "Out of Africa" room with mosquito netting to the "Shag-a-delic," channeling the swinging '60s by way of shag rugs and Lava Lites. Topping that, the "Magnificent Seven" suites are more villa than suite, sumptuously decorated and ranging from 1,300 square feet to 2,200 square feet. In 2013, the hotel added 12 swank bungalows, each with its own kitchen and parking space.

2332 Leonard St. (at McKinney). www.hotelzaza.com. ✆ **800/597-8399** or 214/468-8399. 145 units. $317–$405 double; $450–$1,000 suite or bungalow. Valet parking $30. Pets (nonrefundable $150 fee). DART: Pearl. **Amenities:** Restaurant; bar; babysitting; concierge; fitness center; outdoor pool; room service; spa; Wi-Fi (free).

The Ritz-Carlton, Dallas ★★ Well-heeled guests love this understatedly elegant, supremely comfortable hotel, and because we are bored to tears with the brittle minimalism of today's designer hotels, we love staying here too. Never stuffy or ostentatious, this fabulous high-end high-rise is a wise reminder that less can really be so much more. Gently contemporary (and sure to fare well longer than the edgier hotels in town), Ritz-Carlton Dallas is swathed in sophistication. It's got plenty of diversions, from celebrity chef Dean Fearing's top-rated restaurant **Fearing's ★★★** (p. 93) to a 12,000-square-foot spa, rooftop pool and deck. The huge, impeccably appointed rooms occupy the first eight floors. A staple of Ritz-Carlton properties, higher-priced Club Level Suites give guests unlimited access to the Club Lounge, offering complementary food and drinks daily.

2121 McKinney Ave. www.ritzcarlton.com/en/hotels/dallas. ✆ **214/922-0200.** 218 units. $399–$599 double; suites from $499. Valet parking $32. Pets (nonrefundable $125 fee). DART: Pearl. **Amenities:** Restaurant; bar; club lounge; business center; 24-hour concierge; fitness center; overnight laundry and dry cleaning (for a fee); limousine service, complimentary Rolls Royce car service (within 3 miles of the hotel); outdoor heated pool; 24-hr. room service; complimentary overnight shoe shine; spa; salon; Wi-Fi ($9.95/day).

Rosewood Mansion on Turtle Creek ★★★ Once the swank home of a cotton magnate (in the 1920s and '30s), today this is where the celebrities, politicos, and business tycoons tend to stay. You'll understand why. Guest rooms are huge, with an upgraded country club decor (think pretty pastels, burnished wood furnishings, top-of-the-line soaps, and carpets that feel an inch and a half thick). The **Mansion Restaurant** (p. 94) is one of the finest in town and provides room service. The public areas are even grander, with stained glass, inlaid wood ceilings (sometimes brought over from monasteries in Europe), and acres of marble floors. But the sign of a truly great hotel is its service, and here the Mansion doesn't falter: You'll feel like you have your favorite aunt taking care of your every need. Guests are not only attended to, they also feel coddled—the freshly baked cookies in the lobby go a long way toward accomplishing that. Check online booking sites for mid-week deals: We recently found an unheard-of rate at just over $200 for a king room here!

2821 Turtle Creek Blvd. (off Cedar Springs Rd.). www.mansiononturtlecreek.com. ✆ **888-767-3966** or 214/559-2100. 143 units. $480–$550 double; from $700 suite. Weekend rates and other packages available. Valet parking ($28 per night). Pets (nonrefundable $100 fee). **Amenities:** Restaurant; bar; babysitting; concierge; exercise room; health club; outdoor heated pool; room service; Wi-Fi (free)

Uptown & Oak Lawn Hotels & Restaurants

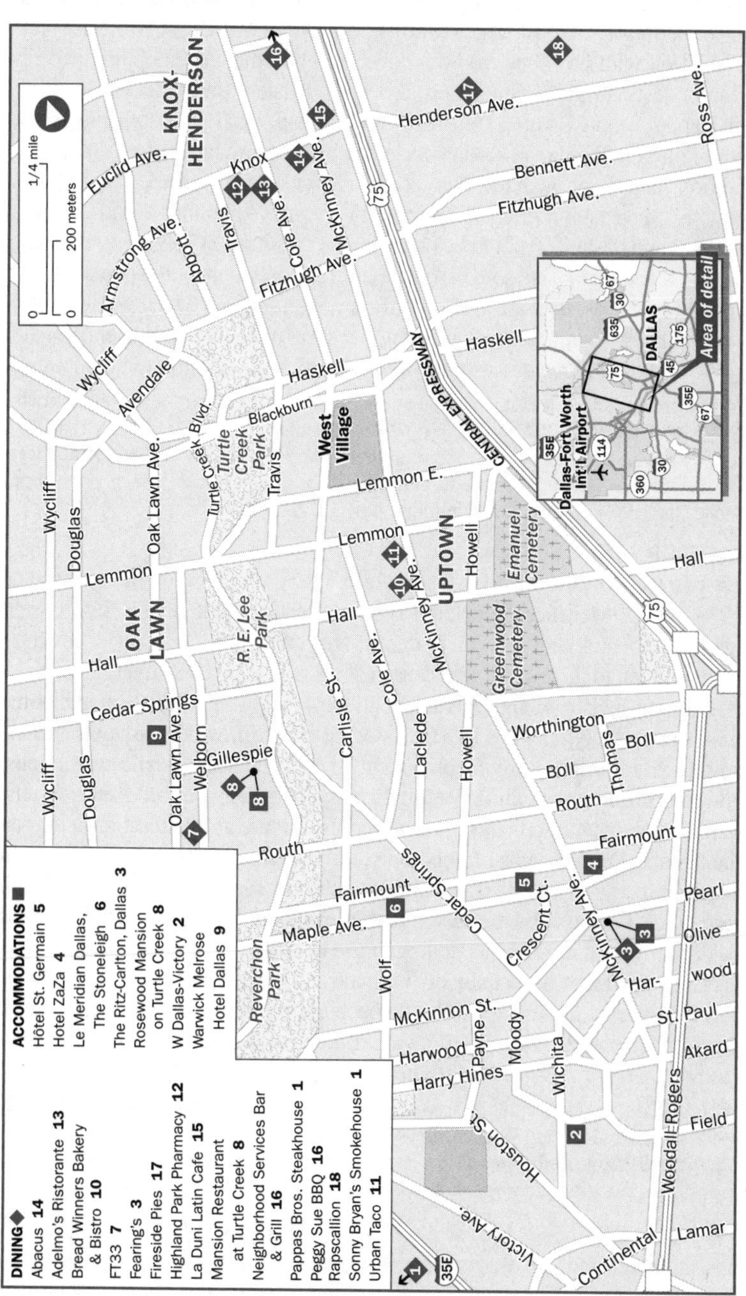

DINING ◆
Abacus 14
Adelmo's Ristorante 13
Bread Winners Bakery & Bistro 10
FT33 7
Fearing's 3
Fireside Pies 17
Highland Park Pharmacy 12
La Duni Latin Cafe 15
Mansion Restaurant at Turtle Creek 8
Neighborhood Services Bar & Grill 16
Pappas Bros. Steakhouse 1
Peggy Sue BBQ 16
Rapscallion 18
Sonny Bryan's Smokehouse 1
Urban Taco 11
ACCOMMODATIONS ■
Hôtel St. Germain 5
Hotel ZaZa 4
Le Meridian Dallas, The Stoneleigh 6
The Ritz-Carlton, Dallas 3
Rosewood Mansion on Turtle Creek 8
W Dallas-Victory 2
Warwick Melrose Hotel Dallas 9
0 1/4 mile
0 200 meters
KNOX-HENDERSON
OAK LAWN
UPTOWN
West Village
Turtle Creek Park
R. E. Lee Park
Reverchon Park
Emanuel Cemetery
Greenwood Cemetery
CENTRAL EXPRESSWAY
Dallas-Fort Worth Int'l Airport
DALLAS
Area of detail

W Dallas-Victory ★ This splashy property, part of the ever-expanding W chain, rises with glass-happy hubris on the Big D skyline, and it's received oodles of attention from locals hip to the newest big thing. Principal among its attractions are the **Living Room Bar** and the casual **Cook Hall** gastropub. The hotel, with proximity to both downtown and the chic shopping and restaurant destinations of Uptown, is a striking, 15-story tower (including pricey residential condos) with a 16th-floor infinity pool. Inside, it's stylishly, if self-consciously, minimalist. Rooms have tile bathrooms, swank furnishings and fabrics, and large windows. Accommodations aren't mere double units; they're "spectacular rooms," "wonderful rooms," "fabulous rooms," "mega rooms," and the suites, not to be outdone, are "wow suites" and "extreme wow suites." That may strike some as just a little too precious, but visitors with toy dogs in tow (yes, pets are welcome for a nonrefundable $100) will undoubtedly be happy here; the Living Room bar is a happening spot evenings after work, and the 5,100-square-foot **Bliss Spa** offers all the required pampering.

2440 Victory Park Lane (next to the American Airlines Center). www.whotels.com/dallas. ✆ **877/946-8357** or 214/397-4100. 252 units. $275–$594 double; from $472 suite. Valet parking $27. Pets (nonrefundable fee $100). DART: Victory. **Amenities:** Restaurant; bar; state-of-the-art exercise room; outdoor heated infinity pool; room service; spa; Wi-Fi ($9.95/day or free for Starwood Preferred Guests).

MODERATE

Le Meridien Dallas, The Stoneleigh ★★★ A fixture in Dallas since 1923, the Le Meridien Stoneleigh is hardly recognizable after a $36-million renovation—and that's a good thing. The once tatty hotel was lovingly brought back to its original grandeur in 2008, and it has style to burn, with the welcoming feel of a large, luxury boutique hotel. Thankfully, the makeover hasn't erased the hotel's Art Deco foundations, most evident in public rooms and the Studio Suites, my favorite rooms here. The decor is all vibrant color and rich surfaces, including deep-red and grass-green walls and shiny black-marble sink countertops in some bathrooms. For a real treat, ask for a tour of the historic Penthouse apartment, one of Dallas's grandest spaces. With bold original art by Texas artists, a 5,000-square-foot spa, a good New American restaurant (**Graze**), and the swank **Bar at Stoneleigh,** the hotel is a haven for business travelers and vacationing hipsters alike. In a quieter section of Uptown, this place has a uniquely intimate and exclusive feel for a large hotel and can even be quite a good deal—check online for significantly discounted prices. We recently even found a special rate for a suite that was lower than the hotel's rate for a standard room.

2927 Maple Ave. (at Randall St.). www.lemeridiendallasstoneleigh.com. ✆ **844/452-4908** or 214/871-7111. 170 units. $214–$268 double; $287–$650 suite. Valet parking $28. Pets ($100 deposit). **Amenities:** Restaurant; bar; babysitting; concierge; state-of-the-art exercise room; room service; spa; Wi-Fi (free).

Warwick Melrose Hotel Dallas ★ This is another one of Dallas's upscale hotels with an old-world, rather than an Old West, atmosphere. In the heart of the Oak Lawn neighborhood, near the nightlife of Cedar Springs and

Turtle Creek, the midsize Melrose feels like a gracious old neighbor. Built in 1924, the eight-floor hotel was once a favorite of artists and entertainers such as Arthur Miller, Elizabeth Taylor, and Luciano Pavarotti. The revamped hotel today is a model of refined taste and caters mostly to executives and couples on weekend getaways. No two rooms are alike, though they are uniformly luxurious and inviting, with 10-foot ceilings, crown molding, antiques, and marble-tiled bathrooms. The renovated **Landmark** restaurant consistently wins accolades, and the stately **Library Bar** is a terrific spot for a nightcap.

3015 Oak Lawn Ave. (at Cedar Springs Rd.). www.warwickmelrosedallas.com. ✆ **214/521-5151.** 184 units. $179–$249 double; $362 suite. Weekend and Internet-only rates available. Pets with $50 deposit. Valet parking $30. **Amenities:** Restaurant; bar; concierge; exercise room; nearby health club; room service; Wi-Fi (free).

North & East Dallas

EXPENSIVE

Cooper Hotel & Conference Center at the Cooper Aerobics Center ★ Worried that every time you go on vacation you seem to put on a few pounds? Then we've got the place for you. This inviting retreat at one of the nation's foremost health facilities, the Cooper Clinic, is set on 30 acres of trees, trails, and duck ponds in North Dallas. The small hotel—called the "second-healthiest hotel in the country" by *USA Today*—remains a well-kept secret, a place to unwind and work off stress and pounds. The spacious, comfortable rooms have French doors that open onto private balconies. But the best part is that guests have complimentary access to the Cooper Fitness Center, which is connected to the famous sports clinic named for Dr. Kenneth Cooper, one of the most influential figures in American fitness training and diagnostics. The facilities include a 40,000-square-foot health club, lighted tennis courts, pools, and a running track, as well as a Mediterranean-style spa for all manner of relaxing body treatments. You can't very well stay at a place like this without eating healthfully, so most guests take full advantage of the complimentary full continental breakfast and heart-healthy fare at the **Colonnade Room** restaurant.

12230 Preston Rd. (at Churchill). www.cooperaerobics.com. ✆ **800/444-5187** or 972/386-0306. 62 units. $206–$269 double; $287–$460 suite. Rates include continental breakfast. Spa packages available. Free parking. **Amenities:** Restaurant; babysitting; health club and spa; heated outdoor pool; room service; tennis courts (lighted); Wi-Fi (free).

The Highland Dallas, Curio Collection by Hilton ★★ Although it's tucked inside an unsightly '60s skyscraper, the Highland retains the soul of a boutique hotel. Formerly the Palomar, it was ceded to Hilton in winter of 2014 to become the first in their new "Curio" line of hotels. The decor is *Mad Men*–esque—think groovy patterned rugs and throw pillows, plus the kind of low-slung, midcentury modern chairs that feel good to sink into after a martini or two. Amenities go beyond the usual: Guests are treated to loaner bikes and free yoga classes (plus mats in each guest room to practice in privacy), and have access to a swank infinity pool on the roof. The parade of amenities continues with a spa, state-of-the-art fitness room, and a respectable restaurant in **Knife,** which has an outdoor patio and service that doesn't miss many beats. Final perk: Dogs are welcome. Those who adore the midcentury modern look will love this place, but recently, when my sister stayed here and I stayed downtown at the Adolphus that same night, I had a bigger room at a lower rate. So really the choice comes down to the style and location you like best.

5300 E. Mockingbird Lane (at North Central Expwy.). www.hotelpalomar-dallas.com. ✆ **888/253-9030** or 214/520-7969. 198 units. $219–$369 double; $369–$489 suite. Valet parking $20. Pets accepted. DART: Mockingbird. **Amenities:** 2 restaurants; bar; concierge; exercise room; outdoor heated infinity pool; room service; spa; Wi-Fi (free).

MODERATE

Embassy Suites Dallas—Park Central Area ★ In far North Dallas, on the edge of the bedroom community of Richardson, this hotel, which not so long ago underwent a multimillion-dollar restoration, is comfortable for families and business travelers alike (especially those with Texas Instruments and the telecom businesses along the corridor just north on Central Expwy.). Rooms, built around a huge, airy atrium, are all suites; they're more comfortable, warmer, and less generic than many at this price, and come with separate living areas and sleeper sofas. The indoor pool and Jacuzzi are an unexpected bonus.

13131 N. Central Expwy. (just north of LBJ Fwy.). www.embassysuites3.hilton.com. ✆ **800/EMBASSY (362-2779)** or 972/234-3300. 279 units. $119–$189 double. Rates include full breakfast and manager's reception. Free parking. No pets. **Amenities:** Restaurant; bar; exercise room; Jacuzzi; indoor pool; room service; Wi-Fi ($10/day).

Hotel Lumen ★ From the trash heap of a 1960s-era motel has risen this smartly chic boutique hotel, with snappy midcentury-modern-inspired rooms, original art, and a good restaurant, the **Front Room Tavern,** serving refined versions of comfort-food classics. It draws a range of guests, from art-loving hipsters to college parents (it's across the street from SMU) to pet lovers (pets stay for free). Accommodations, in black and white monochromes, feature designer writing desks and king-size pillowtop beds; many have comfy sofas or oversize chairs.

6101 Hillcrest Ave. (just north of Mockingbird Lane). www.hotellumen.com. ✆ **214/219-2400.** 52 units. $179–$229 double; $239–$279 suite. Valet parking $13. Pets accepted. **Amenities:** Restaurant; bar; concierge; fitness center; outdoor pool; room service; Wi-Fi (free).

Hyatt House Dallas, Lincoln Park ★ It's appropriate that this property, set in a quiet residential area, has the word house in its name, because it's one of those rare hotels one could comfortably move into for a long stay. Rooms have an apartment-like feel, both in size (roomy) and furnishings, which include a couch, a larger-than-normal desk, and usable kitchens (stovetop burners, microwave or a combo microwave/oven, full-size fridge, and a full complement of pots, pans, and flatware). We also like that the property comes with such unexpected extras as a shuttle that drives guests wherever they want to go in a 3-mile radius; a generous breakfast (including an omelet bar);

twice-weekly cocktail parties; a decent gym; and a very friendly staff. The one downside—and it's a major one—is that you're going to get to know your neighbors. The walls are thin. So in the rare periods when the price pops over $200 (it's usually around $130 to $150), we suggest you look elsewhere.

8221 N. Central Expwy. (U.S. 75 at Northwest Hwy.). https://dallaslincolnpark.house.hyatt.com. ✆ **214/696-1555.** 155 units. $109–$159 1-bedroom suite; $219–$249 2-bedroom suite. Rates include breakfast buffet. Weekend rates available. Parking $12. Pets accepted with $75 nonrefundable fee (plus extra cleaning fee for stays of 7 or more days). **Amenities:** Exercise room; Jacuzzi; outdoor pool; Wi-Fi (free).

Near the Airport

EXPENSIVE

Four Seasons Resort & Club at Las Colinas ★★ It's a Four Seasons property, which bumps it up a big notch in graciousness and comfort all by itself. But this is also the place to stay if you are a sports, specifically golf, fiend. The TPC Four Seasons Las Colinas golf course is the site of the annual PGA Byron Nelson Classic (in May), and it's a beaut, with leafy fairways, undulating greens, and an 18th hole that limns a waterfall-splashed pond. A second 18-hole course, Cottonwood Valley, has a signature 18th hole in the shape of the state of Texas. But golf is not the only game at Las Colinas. Look for 12 Plexihave hardcourt tennis courts, three pools, a Well & Being Spa, and some of most extensive kids' facilities in Dallas (playground, table tennis, volleyball). The spacious rooms, suites, and villas are tastefully luxe, with balconies or patios; some suites and villas have wood-burning fireplaces or outdoor firepits. The hotel is about 15 minutes from DFW Airport.

4150 N. MacArthur Blvd. (at Mills Lane), Irving. www.fourseasons.com/dallas. ✆ **800/819-5053** or 972/717-0700. 431 units. $295–$395 double; from $750 suite. Rates include use of sports club and spa; greens fees $195. Weekend rates, sports and other packages available. Valet parking $20. **Amenities:** 2 restaurants; bar; lounge; babysitting; children's programs; concierge; golf course; exercise room; 1 indoor/2 outdoor pools; room service; spa; 8 lit outdoor/4 indoor tennis courts; Wi-Fi ($10/day).

INEXPENSIVE

Comfort Suites DFW Airport ★ As its name makes clear, this agreeable chain hotel offers convenience to travelers on their way in or out of Dallas, including free airport transportation. What you'll find are good, standard-size rooms (though some are a bit tight) and a range of services and amenities, including a small outdoor pool and fitness center, designed to make your short stay hassle-free. One-bedroom suites feature extra sofa sleepers in the living room and large work desks, while executive rooms sport cathedral ceilings and skylights, and some are equipped with whirlpool tubs. If you're not inclined to stay in your room and work, you can take advantage of the free breakfast.

4700 W. John Carpenter Fwy. (just south of I-114, btw. Esters and International Pkwy.), Irving. www.comfortsuites.com. ✆ **877/424-6423** or 972/929-9097. 101 units. $64–$99 double; $110 suite. Rates include full breakfast. Free parking. **Amenities:** Free airport transfers; exercise room; Jacuzzi; outdoor pool; Wi-Fi (free).

WHERE TO EAT

It wasn't that long ago that the Dallas dining scene was pretty unexciting, mostly run-of-the-mill Mexican and Tex-Mex, with undistinguished steakhouses and half-hearted Southwestern themes. That has changed dramatically, and today the Dallas restaurant scene has exploded and become as sophisticated as anywhere in the country. While you can still get home cooking, Tex-Mex, and barbecue in abundance, Dallas has suddenly become resolutely cosmopolitan, with chic and sophisticated Pan-Asian, Italian, and Southwestern newcomers injecting life into the local dining scene, with a vigor that has even jolted the old stalwarts. Some of the hippest spots are in fashionable hotels, including the excellent **Fearing's** at the Ritz-Carlton, Dallas; **Central 214** at Palomar Dallas; and **Craft** at W Dallas-Victory (see hotel reviews above). The Dallas Visitors Bureau once claimed there were four times more restaurants per capita in Dallas than in New York City; since I am from the former, yet travel and dine out fairly often in the latter, I'm more than a bit dubious about such a claim, but it's certain that you won't suffer from lack of choice.

Downtown & Deep Ellum

EXPENSIVE

Note that the grand and gracious **French Room,** with its elaborate vaulted ceiling and crystal chandeliers in the historic Adolphus Hotel, was undergoing renovations at press time but expected to reopen sometime in 2017. To check, go to www.hoteladolphus.com/dining or call ✆ **214/742-8200.**

Flora Street Café ★★ NEW SOUTHWESTERN & INTERNATIONAL Local celebrity chef Stephan Pyles, a fifth-generation Texan, made his name with Southwestern cooking at Routh Street Café, Star Canyon, and the Stephan Pyles Restaurant downtown in the Arts District. In 2015, Pyles closed his eponymous restaurant and opened Flora Street Café in its stead. At the epicenter of the Arts District, Flora Street feels oh so cosmopolitan, with gleaming wood floors, midcentury furnishings in front, crystal stemware, candlelight, and massive white floral arrangements—all very modern and upscale, the way Dallasites like to see themselves. Tables in the back are laid with creamy linens, and an open kitchen offers seating at a marble counter. A large multicolored silk mural covers one wall, and the menu, which Pyles describes as "elevated Texas" cuisine, is equally colorful. We call it "Texas-eclectic," with odd twists on classic Lone Star dishes, like the current chef de cuisine Peter Barlow's lobster tamale pie with wild paddlefish caviar and ancho glass, or a Serrano-wrapped pork loin and jowl with heirloom tomatoes, eggplant, and basil. The wine list is about as good as it gets in Dallas, with an emphasis on lesser-known finds from around the world, as well as big-spender California cabernets and bordeaux.

2330 Flora St. www.florastreet.com. ✆ **214/580-7000.** Reservations required. Main courses (lunch) $19–$22; (dinner) $42–$52. Mon–Fri 11am–2pm and 5:30–10:30pm (last seating 10pm); Sat 5:30–11pm.

Local ★★ NEW AMERICAN With an arty, intimate, minimalist design that would be perfectly at home in Manhattan or San Francisco, this tiny but chic eatery inhabits Deep Ellum's Boyd Hotel, built in 1908 and the oldest standing hotel in Dallas. Though the neighborhood, once the hip spot downtown, has had a rough time of it, chef-owner Tracy Miller's Local continues to excel. Original walls (one with painted period outdoor advertising that reads TAKE CARDUI THE WOMAN'S TONIC) and hardwood floors have been preserved, adding a warm feel to the Eames chairs and black leatherette booths. With just 50 seats, the restaurant caters to the cognoscenti among Dallas diners, though the food has a decidedly homespun and laid-back angle. The well-executed menu is composed of "tall order" and "short order" dishes, with innovative twists on comfort food, including items such as hazelnut-mustard-crusted halibut, a buffalo burger basket, and mascarpone mac-and-cheese. The wine list has some hard-to-find selections from boutique producers. The chef's tasting menu, seven courses for $70, is a superb deal.

2936 Elm St. (at Malcolm X Blvd.). www.localdallas.com. ✆ **214/752-7500.** Reservations required. Main courses $22–$38. Tues–Sat 6–10pm.

MODERATE

Bolsa ★★ NEW AMERICAN Farm-to-fork is king at this big, colorful revamped garage, with a menu that proudly lists its local producers and an artisanal cocktail menu that includes such ingredients as apple-infused rye and tarragon-infused bourbon. Join friends for drinks and a Texas cheese board or one of the hearty entrees, from the Diamond H quail with local creamer peas and cornbread to the veggie-heavy squash-and-zucchini casserole. Brunch here is affordable and fun, with menu items like maple-bourbon-glazed pork belly with French toast cakes, eggs and smoked fingerling potatoes, crispy scallops, and a bacon-cheddar egg frittata with Creole remoulade. Best of all, the well-selected wine list featuring small producers tops out at $50.

614 W. Davis St. (Oak Cliff). www.bolsadallas.com. ✆ **214/367-9367.** Reservations recommended. Main courses $10–$24. Mon–Fri 11am–10:30pm; Sat 11am–12am; Sun 11am–9pm.

La Calle Doce Restaurante ★ MEXICAN/SEAFOOD This cozy Mexican seafood joint, in a modest old blue house in Oak Cliff, south of Dallas, has been one of the best homestyle Mexican restaurants in the area for more than 25 years. A cult favorite, it deserves to be much better known. The extensive menu focuses on *nuevo* Mexican fish dishes, such as superb ceviche (fish and shrimp marinated with lime), Mexican seafood (such as octopus), mahi-mahi tacos, and other main courses such as *chile relleno de mariscos* (poblano pepper stuffed with shrimp, scallops, octopus, and fish). They even do respectable Spanish paella, or you can opt for the more standard Tex-Mex plates. The soups, such as *sopa de pescado* (fish soup) and *caldo Xochitl* (Oaxacan-style chicken soup), make wonderful appetizers. The margaritas are among the best in town. If your kids like Mexican and Tex-Mex, they will feel like they're eating at Grandma's house—that is, if they call Grandma *abuela.*

415 W. 12th St. (btw. Zang and Tyler sts., west of I-35 E.). www.lacalledoce-dallas.com. ✆ **214/941-4304.** Reservations recommended. Main courses $8–$17. Mon–Fri 11am–10pm; Sat 11am–10:30pm; Sun 11am–9pm.

Greenville Avenue & East Dallas

MODERATE

Ali Baba Mediterranean Grill ★ LEBANESE/MIDDLE EASTERN Family-owned (two brothers and their mom, by way of Syria), Ali Baba—which has moved from its longtime Lower Greenville address to a spot near the Lakewood Theater—still draws crowds for its good, cheap Middle Eastern fare during limited dining hours. Don't be surprised to find a line of customers clamoring to get in. This plain, tiny place packs them in for great rich hummus, marinated beef, grilled chicken, falafel, and Syrian and Lebanese dishes like stuffed kibbe. The tabbouleh and signature rice dish, made with vermicelli and sautéed in seasoned olive oil, are standouts. If you find yourself in North Dallas rather than downtown, check out the newer, larger, and more upscale-looking **Ali Baba** in Richardson at 2103 N. Central Expwy. (✆ **972/437-1222**).

1901 Abrams Pkwy. www.alibabamedgrill.com. ✆ **214/823-8235.** Main courses $10–$18. Tues–Sat 11:30am–2pm and 5:30–9pm.

Matt's Rancho Martinez ★ TEX-MEX In the gently bohemian Lakewood neighborhood east of downtown, Matt's is a Tex-Mex favorite—the real deal. Simple and relaxed, with a nice patio deck, it's Texan to the core, and laid-back as can be (though it can get pretty noisy when the margarita-drinking hordes descend). Start with great chips and salsa, of course (or the renowned Bob Armstrong *queso* dip—stir the ingredients), and move on to the chiles *rellenos* topped with green sauce, raisins, and pecans. If you're not big into Tex-Mex, try the chicken-fried steak: Matt's version of the classic Texas dish even found its way into the pages of *Gourmet* magazine. Matt's has 10 different types of fajitas, grilled specials such as quail, and a dozen daily lunch specials, bargains at $7.25 (Mon–Sat and all day Tues).

6332 La Vista Dr. (at Gaston; Lakewood Theater Plaza). www.mattstexmex.com. ✆ **214/823-5517.** Reservations recommended on weekends. Main courses $8–$20. Mon–Thurs 11am–10pm; Fri–Sat 11am–11pm.

Uptown/Oak Lawn/North Dallas

EXPENSIVE

Abacus ★★ ECLECTIC/NEW AMERICAN The fine-dining, white-tablecloth flagship eatery of Dallas celebrity chef Kent Rathbun's collection of eclectic restaurants, Abacus has been wooing and wowing well-heeled Dallas diners for nearly 2 decades, yet it hasn't lost its edge. Eclectic is such an overused word, but how else would one describe the menu? (One reviewer called it "Shanghai-and-Tokyo-as-seen-from-Abilene.") It offers things like lobster shooters and jumbo lump crab "cannelloni" with a mango wrap, and a hand-chopped

Ranch Akaushi beef tartare. The vibe here is sleek midcentury *Mad Men* with creamy edges—not too formal, but still flashy in the way Dallas does best.

4511 McKinney Ave., Suite 225 (Inwood Village). www.abacus-restaurant.com. ✆ **214/559-3111.** Reservations recommended. Main courses $38–$60. Mon–Thurs 6–10pm; Fri–Sat 6–11pm.

Adelmo's Ristorante ★ TUSCAN After 26 years in its Knox Street location, this always-romantic, old-school Italian restaurant moved to a single-level strip-center suite in Inwood Village in 2016. The charm wasn't entirely lost in translation, thank goodness, as the family-owned Adelmo's still retains its old-fashioned allure. Adelmo's is hardly trendy, but with cuisine this good and service this personable, who cares? Add on good value, and it's no wonder it's a perennial favorite in town. Featuring classic Italian cuisine with what the owner calls "accents" of French and Mediterranean flavors, the menu includes a house lasagna, veal osso bucco, and lighter dishes like a salmon Mediterraneo with tomatoes, capers, and olives—and entrees still come with a green salad.

5450 West Lovers Lane, Suite 225 (Inwood Village). www.adelmos.com. ✆ **214/559-0325.** Reservations recommended. Main courses $22–$39. Mon–Fri 11:30am–2pm; Mon–Sat 6–10pm.

Fearing's ★★★ SOUTHWESTERN/NEW AMERICAN Dean Fearing is one of the pioneers of haute Southwestern cooking. Two bars have become destinations: **Rattlesnake Bar,** the more old-money watering hole, and the outdoor **Live Oak** bar, a magnet for young movers and shakers. Of the four distinct dining areas, each has its own flavor and flair: the bustling Dean's Kitchen; the more refined Gallery; the charming, glass-walled Sendero, beneath a gorgeous Murano chandelier; and the outdoor Ocaso patio (diners' wishes are generally accommodated). It's about one of the most spectacular dining experiences in Big D, even if only part of that is about the food.

2121 McKinney Ave. (in the Ritz-Carlton, Dallas). www.fearingsrestaurant.com. ✆ **214/922-4848.** Reservations required. Main courses $26–$48. Mon–Fri 11:30am–2:30pm; Sat 11am–3pm; Mon–Thurs 6–10:30pm; Fri–Sun 6–11pm; Sun brunch 11:15am–3pm.

FT33 ★★ MODERN AMERICAN Matt McCallister is the chef-owner behind one of Dallas's most exciting upscale eateries in the hip Design District, offering fresh and inventive seasonal farm-to-table fare, just the kind of rare treat Dallas needed. Neither flashy nor ostentatious, FT33 features the kind of low-key elegance you'll find in the best Austin restaurants. FT33 changes its menu often: You might find yourself dining on amberjack crudo with brined green tomatoes, or a Galveston oyster stew with grilled oyster mushrooms, squash, and kale. Like San Antonio's fabulous **Cured** ★★★ (p. 272), FT33 has house-cured charcuterie boards. For a real treat, try the chef's tasting menu, offered on Tuesday, Wednesday, and Thursday nights. It's hard to get a table, so make reservations far in advance.

1617 Hi Line Drive, Suite 250. www.ft33dallas.com. ✆ **214/741-2629.** Reservations well in advance required. Main courses $12–$25. Chef's tasting menu $95. Tues–Thurs 6–10pm (bar 4:30–11pm); Fri–Sat 6–11pm (bar 4:30–midnight).

Mansion Restaurant at Rosewood Mansion on Turtle Creek ★★ NEW AMERICAN Rarefied: That's the best term to describe dining in this extremely upscale hotel restaurant, widely considered one of the best in Dallas. Guests enter through elaborately carved doors that once hung in an ancient Spanish monastery, and they crane their necks to watch Laura and George W. Bush dine in the library (according to staff, they're here about once a month). The setting is downright opulent, with fine art, curving draperies, and lighting that flatters even the most wizened guests. Those with bottomless pockets can partake of the wine list, which once included four bottles of vino smuggled out of Nazi Germany; they sold for $10,000 apiece and all but one have now been consumed. Dinner prix-fixe tasting menus run from $95 to $105 per person. But it's worth it: The food is both exquisite and creative (like truffle raviolo and venison with parsley root and chestnut), sourcing locally wherever possible. If you're in the mood for a celebratory meal, this is a smart place to choose.

2821 Turtle Creek Blvd. (off Cedar Springs Rd.). www.rosewoodhotels.com/en/mansion-on-turtle-creek-dallas. ✆ **214/443-4747.** Reservations required. Main courses $48–$52; seasonal prix-fixe tasting menus $95–$105. Mon–Sat 11:30am–2pm; Sun 11:10am–2:30pm; Sun–Thurs 6–10pm; Fri–Sat 6–11pm.

Neighborhood Services Bar & Grill ★★★ STEAK There is just one thing that's frustrating about this clubby, wildly successful neighborhood eatery (in the parking lot of a shopping center) that executes everything else with aplomb: It doesn't take reservations, and after being named by *D Magazine* as the city's Best New Restaurant in 2010, it takes some patience and even willpower to get a table. But the wait is well worth it. One of three restaurants in Dallas by Nick Badovinus, all similarly named, it's the kind of place where you could easily become a regular—if it weren't for that pesky competition to sit down. This is surefire comfort food: It doesn't try too hard, other than aim for and achieve consistent, good-value pleasure. The big salads are spectacular; main courses such as caramelized Nantucket sea scallops and handmade pastas (among the dishes that change nightly) are delightful. Cocktails are great, and the wine list is interesting and affordable. Although the indoor booths are nice, we usually angle for a table on the covered patio, which is a little less frenetic.

10720 Preston Rd., Ste. 1101. www.nhsbarandgrill.com. ✆ **214/368-1101.** Reservations not accepted. Main courses $17–$29. Mon–Sat 11am–10pm.

Pappas Bros. Steakhouse ★★★ STEAK Consistently ranked one of the top steakhouses in the state, with a twin restaurant in Houston, Pappas Bros. is my husband's favorite place; my Ross Avenue attorney brother likes it, too. It's just so Dallas—the kind of place where J. R. Ewing would have a regular table every Saturday night and his own bottle of bourbon behind the bar. It's got the requisite masculine decor, all dark and clubby. But what truly sets it apart are its steaks. Part of a family-owned chain of Texas restaurants based in Houston, Pappas Bros. is the best of the Pappas family of 80+

restaurants, and its take on the high-end steakhouse is about as good as it gets. The USDA Prime beef, dry aged in house, is the big draw, but the preparations of seafood—especially the bacon-wrapped scallops—are also excellent. It's a classy setting, with red leather booths in a warm, wood-lined dining room with crisp white table linens and gleaming stemware. A cozy bar boasts a deep stock of rare single malts and an expanded cocktail menu that includes classics such as mint juleps and Pimm's Cups. The wine list is a perennial award winner, featuring a mind-boggling selection of fine wines from all over the globe.

10477 Lombardy Ln. www.pappasbros.com. ✆ **214/366-2000.** Reservations recommended. Main courses $26–$50. Mon–Thurs 5–10pm; Fri–Sat 5–11pm. Cocktail lounge opens 4pm.

MODERATE

Bread Winners Bakery & Bistro ★ AMERICAN/BAKERY With patio tables outside under trees and a display case full of scrumptious desserts just inside the door, this charming Uptown neighborhood joint is much more than a place for a quick lunch or dessert and coffee. Step back into the series of dining rooms and you'll find a more serious restaurant, one specializing in well-executed American dishes with incredibly fresh ingredients. In the warren-like house that was once the legendary Andrew's, built around an enclosed courtyard, the restaurant has been transformed into a romantic, easygoing dinner locale—a great date spot. The pulled pork or fish tacos are excellent, and vegetarians will be pleased by a veggie menu (on request) and a long roster of pastas and salads. Of course, if all you want is a burger (okay, smoked-apple-bacon-Gorgonzola burger, please) or any of the many sandwiches for lunch, or one of those diet-busting desserts, Bread Winners is a winner at that, too, and the weekend brunch is a perennial favorite. Check out the New Orleans–style **Quarter Bar** upstairs and its rooftop deck. Additional locations are at Inwood Village, 5560 W. Lover's Lane (✆ **214/351-3339**); NorthPark Center, 8687 N. Central Expressway, on the CenterPark Garden (✆ **469/232-9798**); and 4021 Preston Rd. (✆ **972/312-9300**) in Plano.

3301 McKinney Ave. (at Hall). www.breadwinnerscafe.com. ✆ **214/754-4940.** Reservations recommended on weekends. Main courses $10–$18. Mon 7am–4pm; Tues–Thurs 7am–9pm; Fri–Sat 7am–10pm; Sun 8am–9pm. DART: Cityplace.

La Duni Latin Cafe ★ LATIN AMERICAN/BAKERY How cool is a restaurant that has its own "artisan" car wash next door? One of my favorite spots to take my mom in Dallas, this popular place trots out fresh, carefully prepared, and tasty versions of favorites from across the Americas. Although it may be best known for its sinful desserts and pastries, it's also a terrific spot for lunch and dinner (and brunch on weekends). Good appetizers include the stuffed *arepa* (cornmeal dough patty) and *empanadas criollas* (stuffed turnover pastries). Great for lunch is the array of yummy *tortas* (Latin sandwiches). And classic entrees include *pollo al aljibe,* quite a bit fancier than we've had in Cuba, and grilled *asado* (chimichurri-marinated beef). Desserts are not to be missed; the sweet and moist *cuatro leches* cake is nearly famous, but we're just as fond of the cupcakes and triple-chocolate truffle cake. La Duni's fantastic cocktails, such as the famed "margarinha" (margarita meets mojito with Sauza Silver tequila) and killer *mojito,* also draw aficionados and give it a bit of an evening bar scene. Children will surely enjoy some of the simpler items on the menu, such as chicken-and-cheese enchiladas and quesadillas. But their eyes really light up when they see the dessert counter (or try the old-fashioned hand-spun cotton candy served at La Duni's NorthPark Center location, making for a sweet pit stop during shopping excursions).

4620 McKinney Ave. (just north of Knox). www.laduni.com. ✆ **214/520-7300.** Reservations recommended. Main courses $7.50–$24. Mon–Thurs 7am–8:30pm; Fri 7am–9:30pm; Sat 9am–9:30pm; Sun brunch 9am–8:30pm.

Rapscallion ★ SOUTHERN/NEW AMERICAN Nobody has Southern comfort food down better than this bright, noisy, Lower Greenville gastropub with patio seating outside and a raw bar in (oh, the oysters!). Fresh cornmeal-dusted catfish served with Gulf shrimp, Carolina Gold rice, collard greens, and a smoked ham-hock "gumbo" is what I'm talking about, and big sides like fried pickled green tomatoes; Grammy's Baked Mac with Creole cream cheese; and pork-belly cracklins will have you drooling at the door. With a buzzing bar and he-man menu items like market steak with a side of bone marrow, this is a hip after-work hotspot. For a zesty take on a comfort-food classic, try the "Long Walk to Nashville": an entire chicken, brined, rotisserized, and hot-fried, served with a Szechuan mala sauce. The menu is seasonal, inventive, and ever-changing, but count on it to be good. This place can be pricey, but you don't have to spend a fortune if you choose wisely (*Texas Monthly* listed their burgers among the best in the state) and limit your bar tab. This is the sibling restaurant of the Oak Cliff eatery Boulevardier, another hot concept of owner/brothers Brooks and Bradley Anderson.

2023 Greenville Ave., Suite 110. www.dallasrapscallion.com. ✆ **469/291-5660.** Tues–Wed 4:30–10pm; Thurs 4:30–11pm; Fri 4:30pm–midnight; Sat 11am–3pm and 4:30pm–midnight; Sun 11am–3pm and 4:30–10pm. Bar open/kitchen closed 3-4:30pm on weekends. Closed Mon.

Urban Taco ★ MEXICAN/TACOS This smart, colorful, and cleanly modern little restaurant is deceptive: Yes, it's technically a taco joint, but it also serves subtle and sophisticated authentic Mexican fare, such as ceviche and inspired seafood dishes, like red snapper Acapulco. The guacamole and salsa—surely the barometer of any good *taquería*—are splendid (you can sample all the creative salsas, such as jalapeño avocado or poblano-*pepita* pesto, for just $1 each). The house specialty is, of course, tacos—of the soft, gourmet variety. The spicy ahi tuna tacos, as well as unexpected entries like potato-zucchini tacos, are all excellent. The tostadas of Dos Equis beer–braised beef are a personal favorite, and the margaritas would make a cool cocktail bar proud.

3411 McKinney Ave. www.urban-taco.com. ✆ **214/922-7080.** Reservations not accepted. Main courses $9–$19. Sun–Thurs 11am–10pm; Fri–Sat 11am–11pm.

INEXPENSIVE

Fireside Pies ★★ PIZZA While Fireside serves up the best New York–style pizza in Dallas, locals talk about this funky and energetic place in the revered tones usually used for fine dining—which means it's packed every night. They don't take reservations, so that often means you're in for a wait. But hang in there and have a beer, because the wait is worth it. The hand-stretched pies (baked in a custom pecan-wood-fired oven) are spectacularly fresh and scrumptious, not to mention monstrous in size. Fireside uses a "heavy-handed" cheese blend of mozzarella, fontina, Fontinella, and Parmigiano-Reggiano. Picking favorites from the creative list is difficult, though the Peta Pie (goat cheese, Portobello mushrooms, arugula, roasted red peppers, and roasted piñon nuts) has my name all over it. There are also great fresh salads (also huge) and grinders, and beer by the pitcher, a compact wine list, and a full range of cocktails and soda floats. Whether you're inside the plant-filled main room or out on the patio, you'll be in good company, with a crowd of cheerful regulars. Its success has led to expansion, and there are now four more locations, including one that opened in fall 2016 called Fireside Pies Pronto at Uptown Urban Market at 2600 Cedar Springs Rd. (✆ **214/440-4142**); 7709 Inwood Rd. (✆ **214/357-3800**); 1285 South Main St. in Grapevine (✆ **817/416-1285**); and in Plano at 5717 Legacy Dr. (✆ **972/398-2700**).

2820 N. Henderson Ave. (east of Central Expwy.). www.firesidepies.com. ✆ **214/370-3916.** Reservations not accepted. Main courses $9–$15. Mon–Thurs 5–11pm; Fri 5pm–midnight; Sat 4:30pm–midnight; Sun 4:30–11pm.

Highland Park Pharmacy ★ LIGHT FARE/BREAKFAST/BRUNCH Sad to say, many places like this have disappeared across the country. Amazingly, this one, a Dallas favorite since 1912, is still here, blissfully out of place with all the home-goods stores and high-end restaurants that surround it. An authentic slice of Americana, this old-time soda fountain and lunch counter (and, yes, pharmacy) has stood its ground, even as everything around it has morphed. If you've got a hankering for a grilled pimiento-cheese sandwich, homemade chicken salad, or a limeade, chocolate milkshake, or root beer float, this is the place; just grab a bar stool. It's a good spot for breakfast, too. (Just don't ask the soda jerk for a latte or other fancy fixin's.) I remember going here as a child after a Saturday matinee. Nice to know that some things never change.

3229 Knox St. (at Travis St.). ✆ **214/521-2126.** Reservations not accepted. Dishes $4–$14. Mon–Fri 7am–6pm; Sat 8am–6pm; Sun 10am–5pm.

Peggy Sue BBQ ★ BARBECUE Though this comfy, casual, cheery place looks like it's been around forever, it only opened in 1989 (albeit on the spot where a local barbecue haunt did exist since the 1940s). If it looks and feels like a neighborhood spot—though somewhat incongruously located in fancy Park Cities—stuck in midcentury mode, well, that's exactly the way the owners would have it. With meats smoked on the premises, a salad bar and full roster of fresh vegetables, and fun fare like a "Frito Chili Pie" made with "killer Texas brisket" and melted cheddar, it's a perfect place to bring hungry kids, carnivores, and even vegetarians. Brisket quesadillas and onion rings are great starters for the table; adventurous sorts can try the Texas Torpedoes (cream-cheese-filled, batter-fried jalapeños). Terrific sandwiches include the chopped brisket and Piggy Soo (pulled pork with Carolina slaw), while full-meal standards (served with two veggies) worth a bet are the smoky baby-back ribs and Polish kielbasa sausage. If you can make it to dessert, '50s-style heaven awaits: fried pies, peach cobbler, and root beer floats. You can order ahead of time on the website.

6600 Snider Plaza (at Hillcrest). www.peggysuebbq.com. ✆ **214/987-9188.** Reservations recommended. Main courses $6.50–$14. Sun–Thurs 11am–9pm; Fri–Sat 11am–10pm.

Sonny Bryan's Smokehouse ★ BARBECUE Barbecue is serious business down here. Everybody's got a favorite, whose merits they'll defend as if it were the Alamo, but just about all Dallasites agree that legendary Sonny Bryan's is the original, the one barbecue spot you've got to visit before leaving Dallas. Serving patrons since 1958 in a ramshackle little building in a humble section of Oak Lawn, this place is so popular that even on scorching hot days, you'll see businesspeople with their sleeves rolled up, leaning against their cars, trying in vain not to get barbecue sauce all over themselves. Inside the smoke shack are just two rows of tiny one-armed school desks, under signs that read RESERVED, PHYLLIS, or LITTLE JERRY. Place your order for hickory-smoked brisket, meaty ribs, sliced beef sandwiches, and juicy handmade onion rings at the counter. Then grab a bottle of sauce in a mini Mexican beer bottle and a fistful of napkins, and squeeze into a desk—or grab a spot at one of the picnic tables in the parking lot (or, heck, jump on the hood of your car). Come early, though; Sonny's is open only until the food runs out, which is apt to happen before the stated closing time. If you can't make it to the atmospheric original, several branches of Sonny Bryan's serve up the same great, sloppy barbecue across Dallas and the suburbs—they're good for a fast meal, but don't expect anywhere near the authentic appeal of the original place.

2202 Inwood Rd. (near Harry Hines Blvd.). www.sonnybryans.com. ✆ **214/357-7120.** Reservations not accepted. Dishes $5–$14. Daily 10am–8pm.

SHOPPING

In Big D, shopping is a sport and a pastime, a social activity and entertainment. Dallasites don't pull on sweats or pajama pants and go incognito to the mall; they get dolled up and strut their stuff. Having grown up in Dallas, I know all too well that locals are world-class shoppers. Every time I return home, I initially have a hard time even finding my way around—retail outlets, mostly national chain stores, seem to continually reproduce like a computer virus, blanketing all four corners of every intersection in the bedroom communities that envelop Big D. The Dallas Convention & Visitors Bureau likes to tout that there are more shopping opportunities per capita in Dallas than in any other city in the United States, so if you're a shopper, and come from a place less rich in retail mania, you've got your work cut out.

I suggest focusing your shopping attention toward Western duds (especially Texas-made cowboy boots) and upscale clothing and accessories (this is the home of world-famous Neiman Marcus, after all).

Texans aren't generally fond of taxes (there's still no state income tax), but there is a state sales tax, and it's one of the highest in the country. The Texas state sales and use tax rate is 6.25%, but local taxing jurisdictions (cities, counties, special purpose districts, and transit authorities) may impose sales and use tax up to 2% for a total maximum combined rate of 8.25%.

Great Shopping Areas

Downtown Dallas is largely eviscerated of shopping outlets as inhabitants have flocked to the suburbs. Only Neiman Marcus, the mother of all Dallas purveyors of luxury goods, has stayed put. The **West End MarketPlace** (www.dallaswestend.org) was carved out of an old candy and cracker warehouse to draw hungry tourists and get things going downtown. From Wild Bill's Western Store to Kokopelli Candy, to the bimonthly SideWalk Sale, the West End can be a fun place for unique finds. However, the real high-volume shopping is done north of downtown, in **Uptown** as well as **Highland Park, North Dallas** (north of LBJ Fwy.), and **suburbs** such as Plano and Frisco. The best spot in Plano is the chic **Shops at Legacy** (Legacy Dr. at the Tollway, www.shopsatlegacy.com).

In the area that real estate agents have designated **Uptown,** a vintage trolley line travels along McKinney Avenue, allowing shoppers to jump off to duck into its many antiques shops, art galleries, furniture stores, restaurants, and specialty shops. **West Village** is an outdoor, European-style mall of chic shops, restaurants, bars, and a movie theater at the north end of McKinney Avenue. Knox and Henderson streets, bisected by Central Expressway, are lined with home-furnishing stores and antiques dealers, with an eclectic decoration shop or two mixed in. Routh and Fairmount streets have a large number of art galleries and antiques shops. **Greenville Avenue** is home to a dizzying array of funky shops, including antiques dealers and vintage clothing stores. The avenue gets a little funkier the farther south you travel, with Lower Greenville, in particular, home to plenty of bars and restaurants that make great pit stops. **Deep Ellum,** which rules the alternative scene at night, is loaded by day with offbeat furnishings stores, art galleries, folk art shops, and vintage resale shops. The newest and coolest district, with a smattering of indie-style small boutiques and vintage shops, is the **Bishop Arts District** in Oak Cliff. Of course, most locals tend to head straight for the malls, and if you're in Dallas doing some big-volume shopping, you might do the same; the best are listed below.

Native to Big D

Neiman Marcus ★★★, established in 1907, is a local institution; its annual holiday catalog has become part of pop culture (a once-a-year opportunity to order "His & Her Mummies," say, or perhaps your own personal $20-million submarine). Beyond those attention-grabbing stunts, Neiman Marcus remains one of the classiest high-end retail stores around, and its downtown flagship store (1618 Main St. at Ervay St.; www.neimanmarcus.com; ✆ **214/741-6911**) is a beauty of retro 1960s style that is suddenly very hip again. It's not to be missed, even if you can't fritter away your rent money on a pair of Manolo Blahniks. It's open Saturday through Wednesday 10am to 6pm and Thursdays 10am to 7pm. Stores in NorthPark and Prestonwood malls are open on Sunday and stay open later on weeknights. The downtown store is also known for its little Tiffany-blue-walled **Zodiac** (✆ **214/573-5800**), where the well-heeled ladies of Dallas have been saying, "Let's do lunch," for more than a half-century.

Another department store where customers are often dripping in diamonds and have drivers waiting outside to gather their bags is the sophisticated **Stanley Korshak ★★★**, a purveyor of sleek fashions for men and women in the Crescent Court hotel (Ste. 500) on McKinney Avenue between Maple and Pearl (www.stanleykorshak.com; ✆ **800/972-5959**).

Forty Five Ten ★★★, 4510 McKinney Ave. (www.fortyfiveten.com; ✆ **214/559-4510**), is Dallas's most rarefied and chic emporium, with one-of-a-kind fashion (for both men and women), jewelry, and home decor items. Though it's plenty glitzy, the 8,000-square-foot shop almost qualifies as understated for Dallas; it's a terrific place if you're looking for something unique.

Dallas is an especially good place to pick up Western wear—boots, hats, shirts, and belts—whether you want to look the part of a real cowboy or prefer the more adorned "drugstore cowboy" look. Boots of all leathers and exotic skins, both machine- and handmade, from Texas boot companies (Justin, Lucchese, Nocona, and Tony Lama) are popular in Dallas. You can even order custom-made boots if you've got a grand or so to burn. Compare pricing at any of the following, all of which have excellent selections, and be sure to ask about proper boot fit: **Pink's Western World,** 2475 N Stemmons Fwy. (✆ 214/634-2668); **Wild Bill's,** West End MarketPlace, third floor (✆ 214/954-1050); **Cavender's Boot City,** 5539 LBJ Fwy. (✆ 972/239-1375); and **Cavender's Boot City,** 1610 S. Stemmons Fwy. (✆ 972/353-8407), or 3317 N. Central Expy, Suite100 (✆ 972/881-2668), and 2833 Lyndon B Johnson Fwy. (✆ 972/239-1375), along with more locations in Arlington, Mesquite, and other Texas cities. Fancy Western wear can be found at **Cowboy Cool ★★**, in the West Village at 3699 McKinney Ave., Suite 407 (www.cowboycool.com; ✆ 214/521-4500); it's the place to go if you want to drop $500 on a Western shirt or a grand+ on a unique pair of boots, all with a touch of rock 'n' roll to go with the country.

Vintage Western clothing can be a bit hard to come by. **Dallas Vintage Shop & Costume** in Plano **★★**, 1855 N Central Expressway (www.dallasvintageshop.com; ✆ **214/422-7256**), stocks vintage Western duds, as does jam-packed **Gratitude Vintage Clothing ★★**, 3613 Fairmount St. (www.gratitude-vintage.com; ✆ **214/522-2921**), which has been around for more than 25 years and has something for just about everyone at every price range, from cowboy boots to jewelry, lunch boxes, and funky hats. (If you're looking for Western duds and headed to Fort Worth, several excellent Western wear stores are clustered around the Stockyards; see "Shopping" in chapter 5.) Exclusive gift items for the upscale cowboy—sterling silver money clips, Michel Jordi wristwatches, belt buckles with longhorns and cowboy insignias—can be had for a price at **Bohlin Custom Shop ★**, 4230 Lyndon B. Johnson Fwy. (www.bohlinmade.com; ✆ **800/823-8340** or 972/960-0335).

Dallas's coolest record store is **Good Records ★**, 1808 Lower Greenville Ave. (www.goodrecords.com; ✆ **214/752-4663**), with in-store performances and a great selection of hard-to-find indie rock. **Dallas Farmers' Market ★★**, 1010 S. Pearl Expwy. (www.dallasfarmersmarket.org; ✆ **214/939-2808**), spread over 12 acres just south of downtown Dallas, is one of the nation's largest open-air produce markets. First opened in 1941, this 26,000-square-foot food hall and artisanal vendor market looks across at the glittering Dallas skyline. Farmers from around the area sell directly to the consumer daily from 7am to 6pm. You will find seasonal produce, naturally raised meats, cheese, eggs, and honey, and food artisans who make breads and canned and regional/international foods.

For chocoholics, the must-visit Dallas destination is **Dude, Sweet ★★★**, 408 W. 8th St., in the Bishop Arts District in Oak Cliff (www.dudesweetchocolate.com; ✆ **214/943-5943**); and in Lower Greenville in Dallas (✆ **469/334-0125;** 1925 Greenville Ave); and in Plano (✆ **972/424-6200;** 1016 E. 15th St., as well as at a location in Fort Worth), a funky little purveyor of imaginative, handmade chocolates and an amazing chocolate sauce in a retro medicine bottle. The merchandise makes great gifts.

Department Stores & Malls

It would be impossible to cover the dozens of major shopping malls here—and more difficult still to hit them all on your visit to Dallas. Following are a few of the best, both for the number and quality of stores and for their general ambience.

NorthPark Center ★★★, Northwest Highway/Loop 12 at I-75 (www.northparkcenter.com; ✆ **214/363-7441**), is the most traditional mall and, to my mind, the most elegant. Of course, I'm biased—this is where we went to shop when I was a kid, and the mall-size trees crafted of apples still fill my holiday memories. NorthPark has 160 shops and major anchor stores (including Neiman Marcus, Dillard's, and Nordstrom), as well as natural lighting and, best of all, a rotating display of owner Ray Nasher's fabulous sculpture collection of modern masters throughout the mall (see his full collection at the Nasher Sculpture Center) along with an impressive collection of 20th and 21st-century art, including major works by renowned artists such as Andy Warhol, Frank Stella, Joel Shapiro, Jim Dine, Jonathan Borofsky, James Rosenquist, Antony Gormley, Barry Flanagan and Beverly Pepper, and others. Also, Mark di Suvero's monumentally impressive 48-foot-tall, 12-ton *Ad Astra,* 2005, fills the two-story NorthCourt where it can be viewed from two levels. In 2006, NorthPark underwent a 1.2-million-square-foot, $250-million expansion, making it the largest mall in the Metroplex, while respecting the good taste of the original 1960s structure. Not a mall, but not far from NorthPark, is one of my favorite shopping stops in Dallas: the sprawling flagship store **Half Price Books Records & Magazines ★★** at 5803 E. Northwest Hwy., just east of North Central Expressway (www.hpb.com; ✆ **214/379-8000**). The massive selection of books blows away almost any new bookstore, and everything is half-price or less.

Highland Park Village ★★, Mockingbird Lane at Preston Road (www.hpvillage.com; ✆ **214/443-9898**), is as close as you'll get to Beverly Hills' Rodeo Drive in Dallas. This ultra-chic corner of high-end shopping in Dallas's most exclusive neighborhood was built in the 1930s—reportedly the first shopping mall in the U.S.—and sports an eclectic mix of today's most fashionable boutiques (such as Dior, Céline, Etro, Fendi, and Hermès). Shops aren't enclosed like at a traditional suburban American mall; rather, they face inward for a more enjoyable (or shall we say, European) shopping experience.

The **Galleria,** LBJ Freeway and Dallas Parkway North (www.dallasgalleria.com; ✆ **972/702-7100**), is a huge mall with a light-filled atrium (said to mimic the original Galleria in Milan, Italy). It attracts some of Dallas's most sophisticated shoppers to Coach, Gucci, and Louis Vuitton. You'll also find an ice-skating rink, a Westin Hotel, and a host of restaurants—but many people seem to come just to stroll.

BIG D NIGHTLIFE

Dallas has a very lively nightlife scene, with enough in the way of performing arts and theater (better than ever since the 2009 opening of the AT&T Performing Arts Center) to entertain highbrows, and more than enough bars and clubs to satisfy the young and the restless. If you've come to north Texas to wrangle a mechanical bull, you may have to drop in on Fort Worth, but Big D has a couple of sturdy honky-tonks where you can strap on your boots and your best Stetson and do some two-steppin' and Western swing dancing.

The Performing Arts

In terms of culture, Dallas has had to play catch-up to Fort Worth and Houston, but the downtown Arts District has come a long way in a relatively short time, helped by the contributions of local arts patrons and an influx of buildings by world-renowned architects. The **Morton H. Meyerson Symphony Center ★★**, 2301 Flora St. at North Pearl (www.dallassymphony.com; ✆ **214/TIX-4DSO** [**849-4376**]), is home to the Dallas Symphony Orchestra, a very respectable outfit. The I. M. Pei–designed auditorium is equipped with excellent acoustics and a spectacular pipe organ. Tickets to events are as little as $26 (you may see lower prices online, but they may not include an extra $7 that will be added to the price to cover a building maintenance fee), and free concerts are occasionally held. (Free tours are sometimes available on selected days; call in advance for schedule.)

But the big Arts District buzz belongs to the newest works by international architectural glitterati. The **Dallas Opera,** 2403 Flora St. (www.dallasopera.org; ✆ **214/443-1000**), performs at the stunning **Winspear Opera House ★★★**, a gleaming red horseshoe within a glass box designed by Sir Norman Foster, part of the $340-million, 10-acre **AT&T Center for the Performing Arts** (www.attpac.org; ✆ **214/880-0202**), which opened in 2009. Another star architect, Rem Koolhaas, along with Joshua Prince-Ramus, added an intimate but futuristic 600-seat theater cube to the complex: the **Wyly Theater ★★★**, 2400 Flora St. (www.dallastheatercenter.org; ✆ **214/526-8210**). Other Dallas Theatre Center productions are held at **Kalita Humphreys Theater,** 3636 Turtle Creek Blvd. (✆**214/219-2718**), a gem and the only professional working theater built by the American architect Frank Lloyd Wright.

Traveling Broadway productions, such as *Stomp, Kinky Boots,* and *West Side Story,* play at **Music Hall at Fair Park,** 909 First Ave. (www.liveatthemusichall.com; ✆ **214/421-5678**). I remember seeing *Fiddler on the Roof* here during the Dallas Summer Musicals when I was a child; locals still look forward to Summer Musical season here. Less traditional theater is performed by the acclaimed **Kitchen Dog Theater Company,** at the Trinity River Arts Center, 2600 North Stemmons Freeway (www.kitchendogtheater.org; ✆ **214/953-1055**). Families will be drawn to the fun shows put on by the **Dallas Children's Theater,** 2215 Cedar Springs (www.dct.org; ✆ **214/978-0110**). The colorful **Latino Cultural Center** (2600 Live Oak at Good Latimer; ✆ **214/671-0045**) hosts Latin-themed cultural events, including theater, dance, and music, as well as art exhibitions.

Live Pop, Rock & Jazz

Deep Ellum, the rowdy district east of downtown, continues to struggle after a previous quarter century as the epicenter of live music and late-night dance clubs. Happily, it is undergoing a renaissance after a sustained period when the area became known for crime. While many venerable stalwarts of the Dallas scene (the Bone, Club Clearview, Gypsy Tea Room, and Deep Ellum Blues) have gone under in the past few years, **Trees,** 2709 Elm St. (www.treesdallas.com; ✆ **214/741-1122**), has been resurrected, playing host to punk, rap, alternative, and heavy metal. Still hosting national touring acts of alternative and roots-based rock and country is the spacious **Sons of Hermann Hall ★**, 3414 Elm St. (www.sonsofhermann.com; ✆ **214/747-4422**), a classic Texas dance hall that's equal parts pickup bar, live music venue, and

Ticket Central

You'll want to secure tickets in advance for big sporting events and major musical performances. Go to **Central Tickets** (www.centralticketoffice.com; ✆ **800/462-7979** or 817/335-9000), **Star Tickets** (www.startickets.com; ✆ **888/585-3737**), or **Front Gate Tickets** (www.frontgatetickets.com; ✆ **888/512-7469**).

honky-tonk, hosting indie rock, country, and occasional rockabilly acts. Like many classic Texas dance halls of its era, it's on the endangered list; to make ends meet, it hosts a lot of swing, blues, and "hot rhythm nights" dance lessons. **Double Wide ★★**, 3510 Commerce St. (www.double-wide.com; ✆ **214/887-6510**), is a down-and-dirty music club with a Southern twist; it's the place to go to get your trailer park on, with Lone Star beer, gimme caps, and live, loud rock and country music. Creative drink concoctions like the Yoo-Hoo Yee-Haw and Boone's Farm Sangria will have you yodeling and hollering "yippee ki-yay!" A recent welcome addition to Deep Ellum was the 2011 opening of the **Deep Ellum Brewing Company,** a microbrewery that currently distributes its brews to bars across Texas and hosts public tours at 2823 St. Louis St. (www.deepellumbrewing.com; ✆ **214/888-3322**).

Christian music and culture is picking up some of the Deep Ellum void. For live, all-ages (really all ages—if you're 9 and under, you get in free!) rock and pop gigs, including emo punk rock and Christian acts (sometimes a whole slew of bands in a single night), check out the **Prophet Bar,** 2548 Elm St. (www.thedoordallas.com; ✆ **214/742-3667**), first established in 1985 and then "re-established" in 2007 in the old Gypsy Tea Room theater space. For bigger shows, the club owner's adjacent venue, **The Door,** becomes the Prophet Bar's great room.

Other Deep Ellum delights include delectables from the **Glazed Donut Works,** Chef Tracy Miller's slow-food favorites at long-running **Local** restaurant, the **AllGood Cafe** (✆ **214/742-5362**), and the **Free Man Cajun Cafe and Lounge** (✆ **214/377-9893**).

The **Kessler Theater ★★**, 1230 W. Davis St. (www.thekessler.org; ✆ **214/272-8346**), a resurrected 1942 Oak Cliff–area theater, mostly hosts Texas acts (though many of national renown, such as Joe Ely, Centro-Matic, and the Gourds) playing indie rock, jazz, and alt-country. The **South Side Ballroom** (formerly the Palladium Ballroom), 1135 S. Lamar St. (www.southsideballroomdallas.com; ✆ **214/421-2021**), is somewhere between a club and a large concert hall, with good lighting, sightlines, and sound for mid-size rock, country, and alternative acts (such as the Handsome Ghost) and indie folk bands (like The Head and the Heart).

In Victory Park, just north of downtown, the **House of Blues Dallas ★★**, 2200 N. Lamar St. (www.houseofblues.com; ✆ **214/978-2583**), is no ordinary juke joint; it's a 60,000-square-foot complex with a large concert hall, an outdoor patio, a Southern restaurant, and a members-only VIP club, the Fountain Room. Live acts range from blues to soul and rock. In Uptown, **Renfield's Corner ★**, 2603 Routh St. (www.renfieldscorner.com; ✆ **214/397-0300**), is a nice little bar with a pair of patios, a great beer list, and good local bands playing free shows in the tiny back room. On weekends, it draws a big SMU/college crowd and can feel like a frat party.

Lower Greenville Avenue has been around forever, and is doing its best to fill the bill for bars and clubs in the wake of Deep Ellum's downturn. The **Granada Theater ★★★**, 3524 Greenville Ave. (www.granadatheater.com;

(✆ **214/824-9933**), is a converted old movie theater that now often tops most lists of the best music venues in Dallas. Music legends like Bob Dylan and Leon Russell have played here. **The Crown & Harp English/Irish Pub ★**, 1914 Lower Greenville Ave. (www.thecaverndallas.com; ✆ **214/828-1914**), which for 14 years was called the Cavern before the owners managed a 30-day renovation and changed the course of the club, has an upstairs English pub ("The Crown") and a downstairs Irish counterpart ("The Harp"). With a small bistro menu and an Irish bartender, it's a real neighborhood pub. **Poor David's Pub ★** (www.poordavidspub.com; ✆ **214/565-1295**), a venerable old music club (it opened in 1977) whose stage has been graced by many legendary Texas singer-songwriters (Guy Clark, Jerry Jeff Walker, Lyle Lovett), is smoke-free and occupies decidedly not-poor digs (though it is cash only) at 1313 S. Lamar St. It aims to retain some of the old ambience, and provides a platform for live jazz and blues, albeit with slightly greater capacity.

Once a dark and atmospheric jazz cafe, **Sambuca** has gone upscale now that it's in Uptown, at 2120 McKinney Ave. (www.sambucarestaurant.com; ✆ **214/744-0820**). A spacious, glitzy, thoroughly Dallas supper club, it draws a trendy crowd for cocktails, dinner, and live jazz (much of it jazz fusion to which you can dance) 7 nights a week. Perhaps Dallas's best club for live jazz is **Brooklyn ★★**, 1701 S. Lamar St. (www.brooklynjazzcafe.com; ✆ **214/428-0025**), which has a big space with an outdoor patio. **Balcony Club ★**, 1825 Abrams Rd. at La Vista (www.balconyclub.com; ✆ **214/826-8104**), upstairs from the Landmark (movie) Theater, is a cool, dark Art Deco spot with live jazz nightly and intimate booths, perfect for some relaxing beats and a drink.

Dallas Alley, in the West End, Munger Avenue at Marker Street (✆ **214/880-7420**), is a touristy mix of bars and restaurants primarily aimed at businessmen entertaining clients, and visitors staying in downtown hotels. From karaoke to country to oldies clubs, it's one-stop shopping for most groups looking for a night on the town with skyline views. Don't count on heaps of local flavor and authenticity, but the carousing seems contagious for most. The best spot for big-name touring rock and pop acts is **Verizon Theatre at Grand Prairie ★**, 1001 Performance Place, Grand Prairie (www.verizontheatre.com; ✆ **888/929-7849**), with seating for 6,350 ardent fans.

Honky-Tonk Heaven

Gilley's Dallas ★, 1135 S. Lamar (www.gilleysdallas.com; ✆ **888/445-5397**), a Big D branch of the famous former Houston-area honky-tonk—which shot to fame with John Travolta on a bucking bronco in *Urban Cowboy*—is absolutely Texan in size, with more than 90,000 square feet to accommodate all those boots, hats, and hair. **Cowboys Red River Dancehall ★★**, 10310 Technology Blvd. (www.cowboysdancehall.com/dallas; ✆ **214/352-1796**), has live country music nightly, mechanical bull riding, a huge dance floor, and dance lessons. This is the place lots of young locals go every weekend. Worth the drive if you're a boot-scooter or country music fan is the must-see **Billy Bob's Texas ★★★** in Fort Worth (p. 142).

For a more intimate, down-and-dirty take on the honky-tonk scene, check out **Adair's Saloon ★★**, 2624 Commerce St., in Deep Ellum (www.adairs saloon.com; ✆ **214/939-9900**), which the regulars call "Aay-dares." It gets its share of clean-scrubbed SMU students, but mostly you'll find down-to-earth patrons and infectious country and redneck rock bands that go well with the cheap beer, shuffleboard, and tables and walls blanketed in graffiti. The perfectly greasy burgers with a whole jalapeño on top are surprisingly tasty; some say they're the best in Dallas. The only rule here is in plain English on the sign behind the bar: NO DANCIN' ON TABLES WITH SPURS.

Bars & Lounges

Many of the Dallas spots for scenesters are in Uptown. **Crú,** 3699 McKinney Ave., Ste. 107 (✆ **214/526-9463**), is a wine bar and restaurant that features an excellent wine list; most of its patrons treat it primarily as the former, sampling vintages from the many different wine flights. But the see-and-be-seen spot for wealthy Dallasites and visiting celebs (you'll know immediately if you fit in here) is **Dragonfly,** 2332 Leonard St. (✆ **800/597-8399**), inside the restaurant of trendy Hotel ZaZa. On weekends, it is stuffed to the rafters with guys and gals both busting out of their shirts, but otherwise it's a luxurious spot for a cocktail, such as pre-dinner drinks poolside.

If you're looking for a quieter but still fashionable spot, venture inside **Hotel Lumen,** 6101 Hillcrest Ave. (✆ **214/219-8282**), to the **Front Room Tavern,** a swank lounge and restaurant that's a haunt of trendsetting nightlife types. Among hotel bars, none is more chic than the **Bar at Stoneleigh ★**, 2927 Maple Ave. (✆ **214/871-7111**), at the Le Méridien Stoneleigh Hotel in Uptown, which has a good happy hour on weekdays.

BarBelmont ★★, 901 Fort Worth Ave. (www.belmontdallas.com; ✆ **866/870-8010**), at the ultra-cool, retro Belmont Hotel in Oak Cliff, has a terrace with great views of the Dallas skyline and serves excellent cocktails. It's become a fashionable hangout for hip Bishop Arts types. Standing 560 feet aboveground in the Reunion Tower, **Five Sixty ★★**, 300 Reunion Blvd. (https://wolfgangpuck.com/dining/five-sixty-by-wolfgang-puck-dallas; ✆ **214/571-5784**), is a sleek lounge and restaurant and terrific spot for viewing Dallas from on high and in slow, rotating motion. With a great happy hour and food by Wolfgang Puck, it's a particularly rewarding spot at sunset.

The Old Monk ★, 2847 N. Henderson Ave. (✆ **214/821-1880**), is a dark, down-home bar 1 block east of North Central Expressway with an excellent selection of Belgian beers, single malts, and great pub grub—go with the Belgian mussels with fries and spicy mayo. In Uptown, just off McKinney Avenue, the **Ginger Man,** 2718 Boll St. (✆ **214/754-8771**), has a great beer garden and a beer selection to die for: about 200 beers from around the world.

A step up from karaoke is **Pete's Dueling Piano Bar,** 4980 Belt Line Rd., #200, Addison (www.petesduelingpianobar.com; ✆ **972/726-7383**), a rowdy piano bar where four accomplished players tickle the ivories on two baby grands and everybody sings along (enthusiastically) to crowd favorites by the Stones, Beatles, Johnny Cash, and Eminem.

Dance Clubs

Lizard Lounge ★, 2424 Swiss Ave. at Good Latimer (www.thelizardlounge.com; ✆ **214/826-4768**), is the city's edgiest dance club. Slightly seedy but sexy, it trades in percolating dance beats and a hot crowd, with occasional live bands. The trendiest dance club is **Levu Dallas Nightclub** ★, 2505 Pacific Ave. (www.levudallas.com; ✆ **214/821-2505**), in old East Dallas, with glitter and glam, colorful lighting, reserved VIP banquette seating with throngs of beautiful people, and mirrored pillars. For something out of the ordinary—Latinos dancing to Tejano and ranchero music—check out massive **Escapade 2009,** 10707 Finnell St. (✆ **214/902-6400**).

The Gay & Lesbian Scene

While in Texas, gay country swing and line dancers should check out the **Texas Twisters** (www.texastwisters.org), a group that organizes two-stepping and the like for gays and lesbians around the Dallas area. Though their membership is in decline (and they may not have an event at the time), they will still be happy to point you to the best places to go, like the **Round Up Saloon,** 3912 Cedar Springs Rd., between Reagan and Throckmorton streets (✆ **214/522-9611**), where they sometimes meet to dance. The Round Up has been around for 30 years, a boot-scoot-boogie kind of cowboy club with 12 bars, named by *Instinct* magazine as the "The Best Galdanged Gay Bar in the U.S. of A." It's more cowboys than cowgirls here, and most everyone comes dressed in Stetsons and Wranglers—unless the guys are doing a shirtless line dance.

Another longtime favorite, with a consistently good vibe and a wall of video monitors, is **J. R.'s Bar and Grill** ★, 3923 Cedar Springs Rd. (✆ **214/528-1004**). **Station 4,** 3911 Cedar Springs Rd. (✆ **214/526-7171**), is a popular LGBT-friendly dance club that features "Gender Illusion" (read: drag shows) in its Rose Room and hosts games of Gay Bingo and Trash Disco on other days. For a naughty but nice dance club with hot male dancers and cold libations, the **Tin Room,** 2514 Hudnall St. (✆ **214/526-6365**), is a small, loud, young, DJ-lovin' dance club listed among the "200 Greatest Gay Bars in the World" in 2013 by *Out* magazine (though some warn that it's not for the faint of heart). **Sue Ellen's,** 3014 Throckmorton St. (✆ **214/559-0707**), has a different sort of vibe. It's a friendly LGBT bar with live rock, a lighted dance floor, high-def video screens, private lounge areas, and an outdoor patio.

ARLINGTON

Sandwiched between Dallas and Fort Worth, the medium-size city of Arlington has become known as a pro-sports center and the family playground of the Metroplex. If you're a sports fan, or have kids in tow (or are a kid at heart), it makes a good day trip. To get to Arlington, take I-30 from either Dallas or Fort Worth. If traffic is heavy, plan about an hour's drive from either city. Having your own car is pretty much required to get around to any of the places below.

Arlington's **Visitor Information Center** is located at 1905 E. Randol Mill Rd. (www.arlington.org; ✆ **800/342-4305** or 817/461-3888).

The Top Attractions

Dallas Cowboys AT&T Stadium ★ "America's Team," as Cowboys fans like to call them, reside in one of the finest venues in the country: the stunning, Texas-size AT&T Stadium, which opened in 2009. At full capacity, the stadium can handle over 100,000 ardent fans (there's seating for 80,000, but that doesn't include special suites and more), making this the largest domed stadium in the U.S. I'm not a fervent football fan, but even I was blown away by the VIP guided tour of the stadium (anyone can be a VIP—tickets just cost a bit more than those for self-guided and educational tours). Surprisingly, the stadium even offers a fab art tour of the stadium's impressive contemporary art collection. Even if you're not a sports fan, you'll enjoy this tour, and if you are a football fan, you'll absolutely love it. Plan on spending 2 hours.

1 AT&T Way, Arlington. www.attstadium.com. ✆ **817/892-4000,** or 817/892-5000 for ticket office. VIP guided tours $28 adults, $23 children and seniors. Self-guided tours $18 adults, $15 children and seniors, 5 and under free. Art tours $18 (all ages). $5 discount for military with ID. Mon–Sat tours 10am–6 pm (last tour departs 4:30pm). Sun tours 11am–5pm. (last tour departs 3:30pm). Art tours Tues & Thurs 10am, noon, and 2pm.

Globe Life Park in Arlington ★ Home of the American League's Texas Rangers professional baseball team and the Texas Rangers Baseball Hall of Fame, this is one of the finest ballparks in the country. The retro-style, 50,000-seat stadium, which opened in 1994, was designed by architect David M. Schwarz (a favorite in Fort Worth) to echo classic American baseball parks in the old "jewel box ballpark" style. Billboards in the outfield with retro graphics and the absence of glaring neon give the park an old-school feel. It's a wonderful place to see a game, even for folks who aren't huge baseball fans. And guess what? At press time, a new $1-billion stadium, with a retractable roof and a location adjacent to Globe Life Park, was given the green light and scheduled to be completed by 2021.

1000 Ballpark Way, Arlington. www.texas.rangers.mlb.com. ✆ **817/273-5222,** or 273-5100 ticket office, or 273-5099 tours. Ballpark tours $15 adults, $12 seniors and students with ID, $8 children 4–14. Game days: Tours leave every hour, Mon–Sat 9am–2pm and Sun 11am–2pm. Non-game days: Tours leave every hour, Mon–Sat 9am–4pm and Sun 11am–4 pm. Take I-30 from either Dallas or Fort Worth and exit at Nolan Ryan Expwy./Ballpark Way.

Ripley's Believe it or Not! Grand Prairie ★ Merged under one roof are five weird and wonderful ways to find family fun. **Louis Tussaud's Palace of Wax** features wax dummies of movie stars and historical figures such as Mother Teresa, Tom Hanks as Forrest Gump, Jesus Christ, and Dorothy and her *Wizard of Oz* pals. **Ripley's Believe It or Not! Odditorium** is a collection of the hard-to-swallow and bizarre, such as the giraffe-necked woman of Burma and the double-eyed man of China. Really small kids may get freaked, but most children 12 and older should find the exhibits pretty cool. Other fun attractions here are **Ripley's Impossible LaseRace, Ripley's Enchanted**

Mirror Maze and the bumpy-ride, thrill-filled **7D Moving Theater.** Check out the online coupons. Kids will need at least 2 hours to enjoy this place.

601 E. Palace Pkwy., Grand Prairie. ✆ **972/263-2391.** www.ripleys.com/grandprairie. Admission to single attractions: $19 adults, $13 children 4–12, free children 3 and under. Combination visits for 5 attractions: $35 adults, $27 children 4–12, and free children 3 and under. Combo tickets for 3 attractions: $29 adults, $21 children 4-12. Combo tickets for 2 attractions: $24 adults and $16 children 4–14, and free children 3 and under. Mon–Fri 10am–5pm; Sat–Sun 10am–6pm.

Six Flags Hurricane Harbor ★ The biggest water park in north Texas features such attractions as **Hook's Lagoon** (pirate ships and 12 levels of interactive features), **Black Hole** (a tentacle-like thrill ride that plunges through dark, wet tubes), and the **Bubba Tub** (an inner-tube ride that starts at the top of a 70-ft. tower). Professional lifeguards are on duty.

1800 E. Lamar Blvd., Arlington. www.sixflags.com/hurricaneharbortexas. ✆ **817/640-8900.** $35 adults ($30 online), $30 children 4 ft. tall or under, seniors, and visitors with disabilities; free for children 2 and under. Ticket discounts and passes available online. Mid-May to late Sept.; check website for days and hours.

Six Flags Over Texas ★ Now nearly 50 years old, this 200-acre amusement park is the top draw in Texas (and can be a little crowded on summer weekends). It has Texas-size roller coasters, including the **New Texas Giant** (hitting speeds of more than 65 mph), **Batman the Ride** (a suspended looping coaster with six inversions and corkscrew spirals), and **Mr. Freeze: Reverse Blast** (zooming from 0 to 70 mph in 3.8 seconds, backward). Plus tons of shows, eateries, and nostalgic rides like a classic log flume.

I-30 at Hwy. 360, Arlington. www.sixflags.com/overtexas. ✆ **817/640-8900.** $73 adults ($58 online), $58 children 4 ft. tall or under and seniors, free for children 2 and under. Mid-May to late Aug daily; Mar to mid-May and Sept–Oct weekends only; check website for hours and online ticket discounts/passes.

Traders Village ★ A rollicking and locally famous weekend flea market (spread out over 160 acres), Traders Village has been trading everything under the sun since the early 1970s. It attracts a couple of thousand dealers and tens of thousands of shoppers, who comb through the junk for the occasional find. A midway of rides and games entertains the kids (all-day pass: $9.99).

2602 Mayfield Rd., off Hwy. 360 in Grand Prairie, south of Arlington. www.tradersvillage.com. ✆ **972/647-2331.** Free admission. Parking $4. All-day pass for rides: $9.99. Sat–Sun 8am–dusk.

FORT WORTH

by Janis Turk & Alexis Flippin

Living in the shadow of its big-city sibling has never been easy for Fort Worth, especially since big brother Dallas is a flashy celebrity, an urban-cowboy oasis known worldwide—thanks to that '70s-era namesake TV show. And if suffering second billing weren't bad enough, Fort Worth and Dallas are often lumped together as the "DFW Metroplex"—even though the two cities are really quite different. It hardly seems fair for Fort Worth to forever play second fiddle to Dallas, particularly because many visitors actually like it better than Big D. Even if you come to the Dallas area with little time to spare, Fort Worth—laid-back, historic, friendly, and surprisingly progressive—is absolutely worth a visit. Explore Fort Worth on its own, and you'll find a place that exudes a quiet confidence and sense of comfort, traits often missing in glitzy Dallas.

5

In fact, even though it's only about an hour from Big D on I-35W, this attractive city has plenty for Dallasites to envy (including a 2011 Rose Bowl title for local football heroes the TCU Horned Frogs). It is probably the most authentically Texan city in the state. Long known as "Cowtown"—a sobriquet that the city has shied away from, given its newfound sophistication—Fort Worth still revels in its role as the gateway to the West; the mythic qualities of the American West, the wide-open spaces and even grander dreams, remain palpable here. Yet it turns out this cowboy town with a rough-and-tumble past has a remarkably sophisticated and arts-minded soul.

Fort Worth began as a frontier army town in the mid–19th century, assigned with protecting settlers from Native American attacks on the heels of the war between Texas and Mexico. The outpost became a major stop along the Chisholm Trail, the thoroughfare of the great Texas cattle drives that took ranchers and livestock 450 miles north to the railheads and lucrative markets of Dodge City and Abilene. The trail's importance transformed Fort Worth into a bustling trading post. By 1890, about 9 million head of cattle had been driven through town on their way to market. Saloons, bordellos, and gambling houses staked out the rough-hewn area of town called "Hell's Half Acre."

With the arrival of the railroad, the stampede of cattle north grew exponentially, and strategically positioned Fort Worth became a place for ranchers to keep their herds before moving them for sale. The Fort Worth Stockyards opened in 1890, followed by the arrival of major meatpacking plants, transforming Fort Worth into a major cattle shipping center and one of the country's top livestock markets. Fort Worth had become a wealthy city, a cow town to be reckoned with. The rise of the oil business in West Texas bolstered Fort Worth's commercial prospects, and oil fortunes replaced the cattle-ranching riches of the early–20th century.

If Fort Worth in frontier days was where the East fizzled out and the West began, today the city is a place where cowboy culture meets high culture. The city not only takes a tenacious pride in its Old West past, with plenty of modern-day cowboys and Western flavor, but it's also pretty pleased about its celebrated highbrow art scene. Cultural cognoscenti even call it the "Museum Capital of the Southwest." Local, oil-rich philanthropists have endowed the city with superlative collections of art and hired some of the world's most prestigious architects—Philip Johnson, Louis Kahn, and Tadao Ando—to design places to put them, including the esteemed Kimbell Art Museum (with a 2013 expansion by Renzo Piano), the enlarged Amon Carter Museum of American Art, and the spectacular Modern Art Museum of Fort Worth. The city is also home to a symphony orchestra, an impressive botanical garden, several theater companies, and the Van Cliburn International Piano Competition.

As if by well-devised plan, Fort Worth's downtown, a charming and dignified center of business and entertainment, is almost perfectly equidistant from the Stockyards National Historic District and the Cultural District. Fort Worth natives may like to keep the essential elements of their city separate, but they seem to recognize that they add up to a cohesive whole. Mosey on over to Fort Worth; for me, it is the highlight of north Texas.

ORIENTATION

Arriving

See "Arriving" under "Orientation" in chapter 4 for detailed information on getting to Dallas and Fort Worth by plane, car, and train, as well as transportation options between the city and **Dallas/Fort Worth International Airport (DFW)** (www.dfwairport.com; ✆ **972/973-3112**). Fort Worth is 18 miles from DFW; expect a drive of 30 minutes to 1 hour, depending on traffic.

Essentials

VISITOR INFORMATION

The **Fort Worth Convention & Visitors Bureau** (www.fortworth.com; ✆ **800/433-5747** or 817/336-8791) maintains tourist information centers downtown on Sundance Square at 508 Main St. (✆ **817/698-3300**); in the Stockyards National Historic District at 130 E. Exchange Ave. (✆ **817/624-4741**); and in the

Cultural District at 3401 W. Lancaster Ave. (✆ **817/882-8588**). Of the three, only the Stockyards center is open Sunday (noon–4pm).

The city's events hotline is ✆ **817/332-2000.**

CITY LAYOUT

Fort Worth lies just west of Dallas along I-35W, (which may seem confusing because I-35 also runs north-south and is the road you take between San Antonio, Austin, and Dallas). However, I-35 turns into I-35W and runs straight through Fort Worth. For most visitors, Fort Worth means three distinct districts, which the city calls the Western Triangle: the Stockyards National Historic District, 2 miles north of downtown; historic downtown, which includes Sundance Square, just north of I-30, running east-west; and the Cultural District, 2 miles west of downtown, just beyond the new West 7th Street development. See the Fort Worth map below to help orient yourself.

Neighborhoods in Brief

Stockyards National Historic District This area was the focus of the old cattle-raising and livestock business of Fort Worth. Today, the district retains its Old West feel with rodeos and Wild West shows, as well as daily cattle drives down Exchange Avenue. A handful of hotels and restaurants aimed at visitors are located here, but it's not overly touristy.

Downtown Downtown is the center of the Fort Worth business community and includes **Sundance Square,** where much of the city's restaurant, bar, and theater nightlife and most business-oriented hotels are located. Staying in this area is best if you want to get around easily between the Cultural District, the Stockyards District, and downtown.

Cultural District Fort Worth's outstanding museums, including the Kimbell, Modern, and Amon Carter, are clustered in the Cultural District. Just south are parks and gardens, including the Fort Worth Zoo and Botanic Gardens. Art lovers will want to base themselves here, but the Stockyards District and downtown are better for families.

University/Medical Area Immediately south of downtown, this is the site of major hospitals and several residential areas, and Fort Worth's major university, Texas Christian University (TCU). Many hotels and restaurants are located south of I-30 as well. There's no major benefit to basing yourself here, but it's where you'll find some of the cheaper hotels.

West 7th This neighborhood, occasionally referred to as W7, has steadily risen over the past 10 years, bridging downtown Fort Worth and the Cultural District. It is home to chic shops, bars and restaurants, and condos.

Getting Around

BY PUBLIC TRANSPORTATION

For detailed information on getting to Fort Worth from **DFW,** see "Arriving/By Plane" in chapter 4.

Within the city, the only public transportation most visitors will need are city buses (**"The T"**) that run every 20 minutes among the three major districts, from the Fort Worth Zoo all the way to the Stockyards, making stops downtown on the way. Buses run daily from 6:15am to 10:15pm. The regular one-way fare is $1.50 for adults; 75¢ for seniors, travelers with disabilities, and students ages 6 to 16; and $3 ($1.50 students and seniors) for a day pass. Within the downtown area, service (on red, white, and blue buses) is free.

Fort Worth Stockyards National Historic District

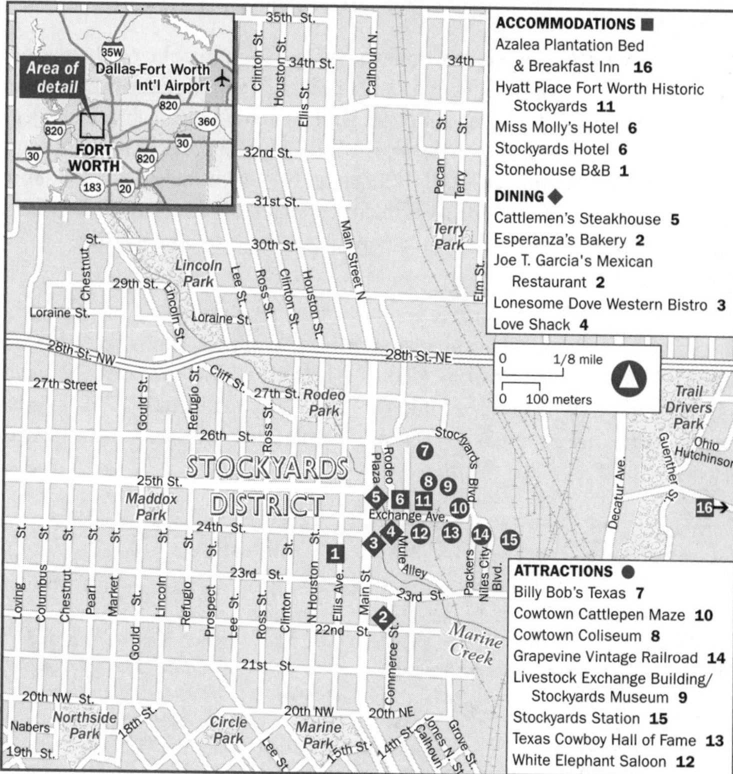

Route 1 (brown) travels from North Main Street to the Stockyards; Route 2 (blue), from Camp Bowie to the Cultural District; and Route 7 (green), from University/Montgomery to the Cultural District. Pick up a schedule at any visitor information center or obtain information on schedules by visiting www.the-t.com or by calling ✆ **817/215-8600.**

Molly the Trolley, a vintage-style trolley, operates three routes around Fort Worth: Downtown Get Around (daily 10am–10pm; free), Stockyards Shuttle (Sat only; $3.50 day pass), and Burnett Plaza Lunch Line (Mon–Fri 11am–2pm; free). Call ✆ **817/215-8600** or see www.mollythetrolley.com for route maps.

The **Trinity Railway Express (TRE)** is the most convenient and hassle-free way to travel to Dallas without having to worry about traffic. It's an express commuter train connecting the two cities, traveling to DFW Airport, Irving, Dallas's American Airlines Center (for Mavericks and Stars games), and Dallas Union Station ($5 one-way; $10 day pass). Pickup and drop-off points are the Texas & Pacific Station and the Intermodal Transportation

Center downtown (at 9th and Jones sts.). Go to www.trinityrailwayexpress.org or call ✆ **817/215-8600** for route and schedule information.

BY CAR

With the city's efficient bus and trolley services, you can quite easily manage to get around Fort Worth without a car. However, if you want to spend time in Dallas or Arlington, you'll be better off with an automobile. Car-rental agencies in Fort Worth include **Avis,** 801 W. Weatherford St. (www.avis.com; ✆ **800/230-4898**); **Budget,** 1001 Henderson St. (www.budget.com; ✆ **800/527-0700**); **Enterprise,** 2832 W. 7th St. (www.enterprise.com; ✆ **800/736-8222**); and **Hertz,** 917 Taylor St. (www.hertz.com; ✆ **800/654-3131**).

BY TAXI

You'll have to call a cab unless you're lucky enough to catch one outside a hotel. The major companies operating in Fort Worth are **Dallas Yellow Cab** (✆ **817/426-6262**) and **Cowboy Cab** (✆ **817/428-0202**). Fares are $2.25 (initial drop) and 20¢ for each additional ⅕ mile. Extras include $2 extra passenger charge, $5 airport exit fee, and $4 airport drop-off fee. **Uber** and **Lyft** are also available in Fort Worth.

[FastFACTS] FORT WORTH

Babysitters If your hotel doesn't offer babysitting services, contact **Baby Sitters of Dallas** (www.babysittersofdallas.info; ✆ **214/692-1354**) for childcare; despite the name, they handle Fort Worth and Tarrant County.

Dentists Call ✆ **800/577-7320** for a dentist referral service.

Doctors Call the **Tarrant County Medical Society** (✆ **817/732-2825**) for a doctor referral.

Drugstores Area locations for **CVS stores** include 4140 E. Lancaster Ave. (✆ **817/534-0261**) and 8560 S. Hulen St. (✆ **817/292-0048**). The CVS store at 3614 Camp Bowie Blvd. (✆ **817/870-1873**) is open 24 hours.

Hospitals The Medical District, south of downtown, has two large, full-service hospitals: **Medical City Fort Worth,** 900 8th Ave. (✆ **817/336-2100**), and **Baylor All Saints Medical Center,** 1400 8th Ave. (✆ **817/926-2544**).

Internet Access One centrally located cybercafe is **BarWired Internet Café in** the **Worthington Renaissance Fort Worth Hotel,** 200 Main St. (✆ **817/870-1000**). Free wireless hot spots include **Corner Bakery Cafe,** 615 Main St. (✆ **817/870-4991**), and **Fox and Hound Pub & Grille,** 604 Main St. (✆ **817/338-9200**).

Maps Any of the Fort Worth tourist information centers can provide you with free maps of all of Fort Worth or individual districts.

Newspapers & Magazines Both the *Fort Worth Star-Telegram* and the *Dallas Morning News* "Weekend Guide" have arts, entertainment, and dining information for Fort Worth and the Metroplex, as does the free *Fort Worth Weekly.*

Police For an emergency, dial ✆ **911.** For non-emergencies, call ✆ **817/392-4000.** The main police station in downtown Fort Worth is located at 350 W. Belknap St. (at Taylor St.).

Post Office The main downtown post office, 251 W. Lancaster Ave. (✆ **817/348-0565**), is open Monday through Friday from 7:30am to 7pm.

Safety For a city of more than 741,000, Fort Worth is a relaxed and for the most

Downtown Fort Worth

2.5 miles to Stockyards
0 1/8 mile
0 100 meters
17.5 miles to DFW Airport
Trinity River
N Main St.
Bluff St.
E Belknap St.
E Weatherford St.
Grove St.
3rd St.
Heritage Park Plaza
Tarrant County Courthouse
Commerce St.
Main St.
Bluff St.
W. Belknap St.
W Weatherford St.
Taylor St.
Cherry St.
Florence St.
1st St.
2nd St.
Henderson St.
3rd St.
Burnett St.
Lamar St.
5th St.
6th St.
7th St.
Throckmorton St.
Houston St.
SUNDANCE SQUARE
6th St.
7th St.
8th St.
Calhoun St.
Jones St.
8th St.
9th St.
Greyhound Trailways Bus Depot
5th St.
7th St.
Macon St.
Cherry St.
Burnett Park
Federal Building
10th St.
10th St.
U.S. Courthouse
City Hall
Fort Worth Convention Center
12th St.
13th St.
Train Station
14th St.
15th St.
Texas St.
Burnett St.
Lamar St.
Taylor St.
Monroe St.
Jennings St.
13th St.
Lancaster Ave. West
35W
Dallas-Fort Worth Int'l Airport
Area of detail
FORT WORTH
820
360
30
183
20
DINING ◆
Bird Café 6
Del Frisco's Double Eagle Steak House 10
Reata 3
ATTRACTIONS ●
Bass Performance Hall 7
Fort Worth Water Gardens 12
Sid Richardson Museum of Art 5
ACCOMODATIONS ■
The Ashton Hotel 8
Etta's Place 4
Hilton Fort Worth 9
Omni Fort Worth Hotel 11
TownePlace Suites Fort Worth Downtown 1
The Worthington Renaissance Fort Worth Hotel 2

part very safe city. Still, as in any large city, visitors should exercise caution and keep an eye on their handbags, especially at night, in major tourist destinations such as the Stockyards and the Cultural District and downtown around Sundance Square. Beyond Sundance Square, which is very lively at night, much of downtown Fort Worth is virtually deserted after midnight. Drive or take taxis late at night.

Taxes The general sales tax and restaurant tax are 8.25% and hotel tax is 15%.

WHAT TO SEE & DO

Despite its laid-back image and manageable size, Fort Worth abounds with sights, sounds, and things to do. Whether you're a cowboy, an aesthete, or a historian—or just plain folk—Fort Worth, an enjoyable, relaxed, and cultured city that's remarkably well organized for visitors, should prove entertaining. There are three distinct parts, each a couple of miles from one another: the **Stockyards National Historic District,** the focus of the city's cattle-raising and livestock auction legacy as the cow town of the cattle drives north in the 19th century; the revitalized, historic **downtown,** a beautifully laid-out, clean, and renovated core built around Sundance Square; and the **Cultural District,** a world-class museum, arts, and architecture center with the superlative Kimbell Art Museum (perhaps Texas's finest art museum), the Amon Carter Museum of American Art, and the fantastic Modern Art Museum. We'll take them in that order, though where you start should match your interest in either art or a living museum of the Old West.

Plenty of the city's attractions are free; go to the website of the **Fort Worth Convention & Visitors Bureau** (www.fortworth.com) under "Things to Do" for a list of free attractions; you'll also find money-saving **discounts and coupons** in the "Deals & Discounts" section under "About."

The Top Attractions

STOCKYARDS NATIONAL HISTORIC DISTRICT ★★

Just 2 miles north of downtown Fort Worth, off North Main Street, is the still-beating heart of Fort Worth's Old West heritage. The Stockyards National Historic District—where female police officers patrol on horseback, and a cattle drive takes place daily on the cobblestones of Exchange Avenue—is part Western theme park and part living-history museum. The roots of the livestock industry lie in this district, which in the 1880s became the biggest and busiest cattle, horse, mule, hog, and sheep marketing center in the Southwest (and quite a pocket of wealth).

The 125-acre district encompasses the **Livestock Exchange Building,** the focus of old livestock business; **Cowtown Coliseum,** the world's first indoor rodeo arena; **Stockyards Station,** the former hog and sheep pens, now overrun with Western shops and restaurants; **Billy Bob's Texas,** known as the world's largest honky-tonk; **Western shops** and authentic **saloons,** such as the **White Elephant;** and the historic **Stockyards Hotel,** where bar stools are topped by saddles and Bonnie and Clyde once camped out while on the lam. Western celebrity heroes like Gene Autry, Dale Evans, Roy Rogers, and Bob Wills are honored in bronze along Exchange Avenue's **Trail of Fame.**

Fort Worth Cultural District

ACCOMMODATIONS ■
Residence Inn Fort Worth Cultural District 4
Texas White House Bed & Breakfast 19
DINING ◆
Angelo's Barbecue 3
Café Moderne 5
Kincaid's Gro. Market Hamburgers 8
Le Cep 2
Michael's Cuisine Restaurant & Ancho Chile Bar 1
Nonna Tata 17
Paris Coffee Shop 16
Railhead Smokehouse 12
Spiral Diner & Bakery 18
ATTRACTIONS ●
Amon Carter Museum of American Art 7
Fort Worth Botanic Garden 11
Fort Worth Museum of Science and History 9
Fort Worth Zoo 15
Kimbell Art Museum 6
Log Cabin Village 14
Modern Art Museum of Fort Worth 5
National Cowgirl Museum and Hall of Fame 10
Thistle Hill House Museum 13
Will Rogers Memorial Center
Farrington Field
Trinity Park
Forest Park
Zoological Park
Newby Park
Colonial Country Club
Thomas Place
Clear Fork Trinity River
Camp Bowie Blvd.
Lancaster Ave.
UNIVERSITY DR.
FOREST PARK BLVD N
WEST FWY
VICKERY BLVD.
6th St. West Bank Landing
7th St.
BNSF RR
UP RR
FW & WR RR
0 1/2 mi
0 0.5 km
Dallas-Fort Worth Int'l Airport
FORT WORTH
Area of detail

SPEND CHRISTMAS IN THE stockyards

Christmas in the Stockyards is perfect for families, featuring games, crafts, roping lessons, a parade, and Cowboy Ride for Toys, all of which is followed by the lighting of a 45-foot tree and Christmas carols. It's held the first Saturday in December (www.fortworthstockyards.org; ✆ **817/624-4741**).

The **Fort Worth Stock Show & Rodeo** (www.fwssr.com; ✆ **817/877-2420**) is held during the last 2 weeks of January and first week of February. Hands down, it's the time in Fort Worth to see a surfeit of rodeo performances, as well as the nation's oldest continuous livestock show.

Cowtown Cattlepen Maze ★ This "Texas-size human maze," constructed to resemble the cattle pens of the Old West, is a fun diversion for kids (and older folks eager to test their skills against the labyrinth). Parents can watch from the observation deck to track how the kids are doing.

E. Exchange Ave. (across from Stockyards Station). www.cowtowncattlepenmaze.com. ✆ **817/624-6666.** Admission $7 adults, $6 children 17 and under. Special group rates and unlimited runs for birthday parties. Daily 9am–dusk (6–7pm in winter, 8–9pm in summer). Closed Thanksgiving, Dec 25, and Jan 1.

Stockyards Museum ★ This small museum is located inside the historic Livestock Exchange building, which dates from 1902 (and holds special livestock sales to this day). Part of the North Fort Worth Historical Society, it displays artifacts from Fort Worth's rootin'-tootin' glory days, from cowboy spurs and saddles to Comanche headdresses. It even displays a Palace Theater lightbulb that's been burning for 107 years and an 1886 Bad Luck Wedding Dress, said to bring "personal misery or disaster to everyone who has worn it." You won't need more than an hour or half-hour to visit the museum.

131 E. Exchange Ave., Suite 113 (just east of N. Main St.). www.stockyardsmuseum.org. ✆ **817/625-5082.** Admission $2 adults; children 12 and under free. Mon–Sat 10am–5pm.

Texas Cowboy Hall of Fame ★ Whereas the Cowgirl Hall of Fame (see p. 123) is decidedly high tech, this little museum, set in a soaring old horse barn (from the days when the Stockyards were first built), is proudly old-fashioned. Each inductee of the Hall of Fame (from Lyle Lovett to famed rodeo clowns to bronco buster Larry Mahan) gets a wooden stall reminiscent of what you'd house a horse in. These are filled with memorabilia, from spurs, saddles, chaps, and hats to posters and award plaques and, often, a video screen which tells, at a sound level that is often barely audible, the story of the cowboy being honored. (A few cowgirls are in the mix, too.) Just as interesting are the beautifully restored Sterquell Wagons dating from the 18th and 19th centuries, each of which had a different function (you'll see a milk wagon, a funeral wagon, a meat wagon, and more). About an hour should be sufficient to take in the cowboys, though some visitors could do a run-through in half that time.

For those who want to broaden their knowledge of the Old West, the **National Multicultural Western Heritage Museum,** east of the Stockyards at 3400 Mount Vernon Ave. (www.cowboysofcolor.org; ✆ **817/534-8801**), pays much-needed tribute to a group of cowboys whose contributions were critical to opening the American West and are sadly often overlooked. The museum is open Saturdays from noon to 4pm or by appointment; admission is $6 adults, $4 seniors, $3 students, free for children 5 and under.

128 E. Exchange Ave., Barn A (just east of N. Main St.) www.texascowboyhalloffame.org. ✆ **817/626-7131.** Admission $6 adults, $5 seniors and students 13–17 with college ID, $3 children 3–12. Mon–Thurs 9am–5pm; Fri–Sat 10am–7pm; Sun 11am–5pm.

HISTORIC DOWNTOWN & SUNDANCE SQUARE ★

Charming, unassuming, and remarkably unhurried, downtown's centerpiece is **Sundance Square** (named for the Sundance Kid, who hid out here with the Hole-in-the-Wall Gang), a prime stop along the Chisholm Trail during the cattle drives of the 1800s. It has 14 blocks of redbrick streets, late-19th-century buildings, and attractions that include the Bass Performance Hall, a couple of museums, and a pair of Art Deco movie theaters. It's a model of urban planning, and a real rarity in Texas: a place with sidewalks that invites non-motored strolling. Downtown Fort Worth is lit up like a Christmas tree at night, and Sundance Square's bars and restaurants are the heart of downtown nightlife.

Bass Performance Hall ★★ This showpiece of a music hall, named one of the world's top opera houses, is 10 stories tall and big enough to seat 2,000 patrons. It was completed in 1998, designed by noted architect David M. Schwarz in a tiered horseshoe shape, topped by a gorgeous dome painted with a cornflower-blue Texas sky. Free guided tours—recommended for architecture buffs—are scheduled most Saturdays at 10:30am and last a little over an hour. Bass Hall hosts the Fort Worth opera, symphony, and dance companies as well as touring Broadway shows and concert performances; see "Fort Worth After Dark," later in this chapter, for more details.

525 Commerce St. (just east of Sundance Sq.). www.basshall.com. ✆ **877/212-4280;** 817/212-4325 information hotline. Free guided public tours Sat 10:30am (performance schedule permitting).

Sid Richardson Museum ★ It may not be as important a collection as that in the Amon Carter Museum of American Art, but those who love Old West art will still want to see this small but smartly curated collection built by a Fort Worth oilman. The collection is centered around a number of important

Cool Break on a Hot Day

Take a breather at the refreshing **Fort Worth Water Gardens,** designed by the famed architect Philip Johnson—4 acres of water (19,000 gal. per min.) cascading over cement and into three pools. It's at Commerce and 15th streets, downtown; call ✆ **817/392-7111** for more information. This is one of the best places in town to visit on a hot summer day.

THE GRAPEVINE vintage RAILROAD

To jump into the turn-of-the-20th-century Old West character of the Stockyards, don your best Western duds and hop aboard the **Grapevine Vintage Railroad** (www.gvrr.com; ✆ **817/410-3185**). You'll ride on trains pulled by one of two locomotives: an 1896 steam engine named "Puffy" (back in service in 2017) or the 1950 diesel train known as "Vinny." The Trinity River Run is a 1-hour trip from Stockyards Station to 8th Avenue in Fort Worth. The Grapevine 5-hour trip to Fort Worth Stockyards is more involved and interesting (as well as more expensive) and begins and ends in historic Grapevine, Texas. Call or visit for exact schedules and the running status of the steam train. The Trinity River Run round-trip fare is $15 first class and $10 regular ride. The Grapevine to Fort Worth Stockyards round-trip fare is $26 first class and $18 regular ride.

paintings by two "titans of Western art," Frederic Remington and Charles M. Russell. Other artists are represented here as well, including Herbert Herget's *Indian Studies* and a wonderful painting of Sid Richardson with a San Jose Island backdrop of horses and cattle by Peter Hurd. The museum was given a new facade and expanded galleries in 2006 in a design by David M. Schwarz. Allow an hour for a visit.

309 Main St. ✆ **817/332-6554.** www.sidrichardsonmuseum.org. Free admission. Mon–Thurs 9am–5pm; Fri–Sat 9am–8pm; Sun noon–5pm. Free tours Tues 2pm; arrange in advance.

THE CULTURAL DISTRICT ★★★

Fort Worth is the cultural capital of the Southwest, with the finest art museums in Texas and the most impressive small art museum in the country. The city essentially ropes off the Cultural District, making it an elite island by placing it safely apart from downtown business interests, a couple of miles west. Arts philanthropy has thrived in Fort Worth to a degree unmatched in Texas and many parts of the United States, where wealthy patrons and an enthusiastic city have welcomed some of the world's most celebrated architects to create splendid buildings to house equally splendid art collections. The presence of the glorious Modern Art Museum, across the street from the Kimbell and down the block from Philip Johnson's expanded Amon Carter, has entrenched Fort Worth as perhaps the top art and architecture city between the two U.S. coasts.

South of downtown is an area of parks, gardens, historic homes, and the Fort Worth Zoo, considered one of the top five zoos in the country.

Amon Carter Museum of American Art ★★ Amon Carter was born in a log cabin and set out to be a wildcatter. He was one of the lucky ones: After digging for years, he finally struck "black gold." He took his oil money and grew it exponentially, founding a newspaper and an airline (a little operation called American Airlines today). With this museum he fundamentally reshaped the skyline and ambitions of his hometown of Fort Worth. The first tenant of the city's Cultural District, this handsome edifice was built by "starchitect" Philip Johnson to house Carter's remarkable collection of Western American art. Carter was amassing the works of such masters as Frederic Remington and Charles M. Russell at a time when no one else was. Carter's daughter Ruth Carter Stevenson expanded both the collection and the museum (with Johnson's help) to showcase the works of other great American masters including photographers Ansel Adams, Man Ray, Walker Evans, and Alfred Stieglitz; and painters Georgia O'Keefe, John Singer Sargent, and Stuart Davis. The original collection of 400 paintings, drawings, and works of sculpture by Remington and Russell has grown to more than 300,000 works and continues to grow, thanks to the foundation Carter established for the museum. Try to get here at 2pm so you can take part in the excellent docent-led tours of the collection.

3501 Camp Bowie Blvd. (at Montgomery St. and W. Lancaster Ave.). www.cartermuseum.org. ✆ **817/738-1933.** Free admission. Tues–Wed and Fri–Sat 10am–5pm; Thurs 10am–8pm; Sun noon–5pm.

Fort Worth Botanic Garden ★★ Get out in the great outdoors and meander among 110 acres of gorgeous manicured gardens at this, the oldest botanical garden in the state. Highlights include the **Japanese Garden,** 7½ acres of shady serenity, with cherry trees that pop in spring and Japanese maples that blaze in fall. Walk the leafy pathways of the Four Seasons Garden, where flower beds bloom with iris, lilies, and scarlet azaleas. Note that the spectacular Rose Garden, laid out in 1933, is replanting in the wake of a deadly rose virus; call to check on its progress. This is an easy place to while away the afternoon.

3220 Botanic Garden Blvd. (south of W. Lancaster Ave. and just west of University Dr.). www.fwbg.org. ✆ **817/392-5510.** Free admission to gardens. Enclosed conservatory $2 adults, $1 seniors and children 4–12, free for children 3 and under. Japanese Garden $7 adults, $5 seniors, $4 children 4–12, free for children 3 and under. Botanic garden daily 8am–5pm. Conservatory Mon–Sat 8am–4pm; Sun 1–4pm. Grounds daily 8am–dusk. Facilities remain open 2 hr. later during daylight saving time.

Longhorn Express: Fort Worth Herd

Amazingly, the Fort Worth Stockyards still retain the look and feel of the Old West. To enhance the atmosphere even more, a twice-daily **"cattle drive"** of the **Fort Worth Herd** takes place on the main drag, Exchange Avenue (at N. Main St.), at 11:30am and 4pm. About 15 head of 1-ton longhorn steers, led by cowhands dressed the part in 19th-century duds, rumble down the red-brick street past the Stockyards, on their way to a graze near the West Fork of the Trinity River and back again to the Stockyards. Claimed to be the world's only daily longhorn cattle drive, it's an ideal photo op. The best places to view the longhorns are on the front lawn of the Livestock Exchange building and from the catwalk above the cattle pens. For more information, go to www.fortworth.com/the-herd or call ✆ **817/336-4373.**

Fort Worth Museum of Science and History ★★ First chartered in 1941, this museum excels in kid-centric learning activities, with a DinoDig (where kids can play amateur paleontologist and hunt for Texas dinosaurs), a planetarium, a domed Omni IMAX theater, and tons of interactive fun. Younger kids are the focus at the **Fort Worth Children's Museum,** a museum within a museum, a play space with a kids' grocery, building blocks, and an outdoor construction area. Allow a couple of hours here.

1729 Gendy St. (south of intersection of Camp Bowie Blvd., W. Lancaster Ave., and Montgomery St.). www.fwmuseum.org. ✆ **817/255-9300.** Exhibit $15 adults, $14 seniors and $12 children 2–12. Omni Theater $9 adults, $7 seniors and children 2–12. Daily 10am–5pm. Closed Thanksgiving and Dec 24–25.

Fort Worth Zoo ★★★ At press time, this award-winning zoo was planning a $100-million expansion, adding acres of space and renovated habitats (including underwater hippo viewing) to further "mimic life in the wild." One of the country's preeminent zoos (founded in 1909), the Fort Worth Zoo hews to a conservation ethos and the use of captive breeding programs to counter the effects of worldwide poaching. Its habitats for critters from around the globe include three generations of elephants, including two calves, Bowie and Belle, born in captivity here in 2013. You can watch these growing youngsters splash around in their big pool—and their habitat will triple in size by 2020. Newly renovated exhibits will aim to more fully imitate the animals' natural ecosystems, among them the **African Savannah,** with giraffes, black rhinos, and hippos; **Predators,** with leopards, lions, and African wild dogs; and **Forests & Jungles,** with okapi, bongo, and the Sumatran orangutan. Allow at least 2 or 3 hours here, though your kids won't want to leave.

1989 Colonial Pkwy. (east of University Dr. and just south of Trinity River). www.fortworthzoo.org. ✆ **817/759-7555.** Admission $12 adults, $10 seniors and children 3–12, free children 2 and under; half-price tickets Wed. Mid-Feb to late Oct daily 10am–5pm; late Oct to mid-Feb daily 10am–4pm (open until 6pm Sat–Sun late Mar to mid-Sept).

Kimbell Art Museum ★★★ One of the world's top small museums, this would be a jewel no matter where it landed. Fortunately for Fort Worth, local philanthropist Kay Kimbell deigned that his superlative art collection would be housed here to help "encourage art in Fort Worth and Texas." The

Ropin' & Rodeo: Fort Worth Stock Show

If you're in Fort Worth at the end of January and first few days of February, you shouldn't miss the **Fort Worth Stock Show** (www.fwssr.com; ✆ **817/877-2400**). Officially known as the Southwestern Exposition and Livestock Show, the rodeo hearkens back to its earliest days at the end of the 19th century. At the Will Rogers Memorial Center near the art museums (on Amon Carter Square), the event features lively rodeos, horse shows and auctions, and livestock, from beef cattle to llamas and swine. There's plenty of entertainment and an all-Western parade on the first Saturday. Tickets are $20 to $28.

American architect Louis Kahn created a classic structure of grace and drama to house the collection, a museum, as he envisioned it, with the "luminosity of silver." Not long ago the museum underwent an expansion including the Renzo Piano Pavilion, two structures connected by two glazed passageways, the work of Pritzker Prize–winning architect Renzo Piano and unveiled in November 2013. And did we mention that general admission is free?

The permanent collection is small, its works ranging from pre-Columbian pieces to 17th-, 18th-, and 19th-century old masters (Velázquez, Rubens, and Rembrandt) and modern masters (Van Gogh, Monet, Cézanne, and Picasso). The sunken **sculpture garden** outside is the work of Isamu Noguchi. In addition, the Kimbell is often the site of heralded national and international shows for which virtually every top-notch museum in the world vies. Plan to spend a good 3 to 4 hours here.

3333 Camp Bowie Blvd. (btw. W. 7th St. and W. Lancaster Ave.). www.kimbellart.org. ✆ **817/332-8451.** Free admission to general collection; special exhibitions (including an audio-guide tour) $12 adults, $10 seniors and students, $8 children 6–11; half-price all day Tues and Fri 5–8pm. Tues–Thurs and Sat 10am–5pm; Fri noon–8pm; Sun noon–5pm. Closed July 4, Thanksgiving, Dec 25, and Jan 1.

Modern Art Museum of Fort Worth ★★★ Japanese architect Tadao Ando created this "Arbor for Art" in 2002, and it's a splendid hymn to glass and concrete, the images of its three pavilions shimmering in a reflecting pond at its base. This sprawling museum, some 50,000 square feet of gallery space, is packed with world-class post–World War II art in galleries suffused with natural light. The Modern may be devoted to modern art, but it is in fact the state's oldest art museum, chartered in 1892. Give yourself half a day (or more) to take in masterworks by Picasso, Rothko, Warhol, Rauschenberg, Pollock, and more. **Café Modern ★★** overlooks the reflecting pool and is one of the better lunch spots in town.

3200 Darnell St. (across from the Kimbell Museum, btw. W. 7th St. and W. Lancaster Ave.). www.themodern.org. ✆ **817/738-9215.** Admission $10 adults, $4 students and seniors, free for children 12 and under; free for all Wed and 1st Sun of each month. Tues–Thurs and Sat–Sun 10am–5pm, Fri 10am–8pm; also Feb–Apr and Sept–Nov Tues until 7pm. Free public tours daily 2pm (no reservations). Artist-led tours 3rd Sun of the month. Closed July 4th, Thanksgiving, Dec 24–25, and Jan 1.

National Cowgirl Museum and Hall of Fame ★ The very first group of women in the history of the world to make a living from a professional sport were the cowgirls who worked the rodeo circuit, and this surprisingly high-tech museum tells their tale and the stories of the women who preceded them (Annie Oakley most prominently). It does so in a majestic Art Deco–esque building in the Cultural District, filling a series of second-floor rooms with videos of these daring dames in action, all sorts of memorabilia (from the sparkly costumes most of the early cowgirls had to sew themselves to rodeo programs and posters) and an entire section on cowgirls in the movies and TV (hello *Toy Story*!). All in all more than 230 women are honored, and there's enough here to keep even those with only a passing interest in this sport engaged, including a very tame mechanical bull that you can videotape yourself riding (you move it with your body motions, rather than the other way around).

1720 Gendy St. (east of intersection of Montgomery and Burnett-Tandy sts., across from Will Rogers Memorial Center). www.cowgirl.net. © **817/336-4475.** $10 adults, $8 seniors, $8 children 6–18, free for children 4 and under. Tues–Sun 10am–5pm. Closed Thanksgiving, Dec 24–25, and Jan 1.

Thistle Hill House Museum ★ Cattle baron W. T. Waggoner wasn't the first big-money Texan daddy to build a mansion for his daughter, and he surely won't be the last. Daughter Electra was pampered, no doubt, known for taking milk baths and spending a whopping $20,000 in one day at Neiman Marcus—and that was way back in 1904! Several owners later, it was salvaged and named a National Historical Landmark (1977), and today this stately brick pile has been handsomely restored with period furnishings. You can climb the gleaming-oak Scarlett O'Hara staircase and imagine your milk bath awaits with the 45-minute tour. The house is a popular place for weddings, although it's said to be spooked by a she-ghost in a long white gown, who likes to make appearances on the landing of the grand staircase as some kind of nuptial omen. Even though it was the first "electric" house in town, it has eight fireplaces. I guess you can't be too warm or too rich. Included in the admission is a tour of the **Ball-Eddleman-McFarland House,** an 1899 Queen Anne at 1110 Penn St. with impressive Victorian flourishes (turrets, gables, parquet floors).

1509 Pennsylvania Ave. (btw. 8th Ave. and Henderson St., south of I-30). www.historicfortworth.org. © **817/332-5875.** Admission $20 and $10 children 10 and under. Tours on the hour Wed–Fri 11am–2pm, Sun 1–3pm.

Organized Tours

Guided daily **Historical Walking Tours** of the Stockyards, with visits to the major sights, leave from the Visitor Information Center at 130 E. Exchange Ave. (www.stockyardsstation.com/attractions/historical-walking-tours; © **817/625-9715**). Tours cost $7 to $9 for adults, $6 to $8 for seniors, and $5 to $7 for children ages 6 to 12, and are given every 2 hours, Monday to Saturday from 10am to 2pm and Sunday noon to 4pm. The **Wrangler Tour** takes in the Livestock Exchange, cattle pens on the Cattleman's Catwalk, Mule Alley, Cowtown Coliseum, Exchange Avenue, and the old Hog and Sheep Barns (Stockyards Station). The **Cowboy Tour** adds a visit to Billy Bob's and a buck to the price.

Other walking tours of Fort Worth, as well as $150 "step-on bus tours" and local author lunches, are offered by **Fort Worth Tours & Trails** (www.fwtoursntrails.com; © **817/731-3875**). Walking tours of historic downtown and the Stockyards are $50 to $60 each; however, they require at least 20 guests for a tour.

Outdoor Activities

BIKING, IN-LINE SKATING & JOGGING Excellent for all outdoor activities are **Trinity Park** (near the Cultural District just north of I-30) and **Forest Park** (south of I-30). Depression-era Trinity Park encompasses the

KID magnets

Fort Worth is loaded with activities for children. The top choice is the **Fort Worth Zoo ★★★** (p. 122), one of the very finest in the country, with a splendid array of exotic animals in natural habitats. Kids can play and learn at the **Fort Worth Museum of Science and History ★★** (p. 122), which has an Omni (IMAX) theater and hands-on science displays, including "DinoDig" for budding paleontologists. If the kids are restless and just need to get outside, take them to the **Fort Worth Botanic Garden ★★** (p. 121), with acres and acres of gardens, exotic plants, and tropical trees.

The **Stockyards National Historic District ★★** (p. 116) has plenty to entertain little cowboys and cowgirls. Twice a day, a herd of longhorn cattle rumbles down brick-paved Exchange Avenue. **Texas Town** in Stockyards Station is a theme park of sorts: an Old West hotel, bar, outhouse, and jail, as well as a vintage ride park, with an antique merry-go-round. Actors in chaps and vests enact *High Noon* gun duels. Nearby, kids can try to find their way through the **Cowtown Cattlepen Maze ★** (p. 118), designed to resemble the cattle pens of the Old West. An enjoyable excursion for families is the **Grapevine Vintage Train ★** (p. 120), a steam locomotive that travels from Stockyards Station to 8th Avenue in Fort Worth and to historic Grapevine. Young cowboys and cowgirls will enjoy **horseback trail rides** at the Stockyard Station Livery (chuck-wagon dinners available for groups of 10 or more; call ✆ **817/624-3446** for more information). The gals may feel empowered by a visit to the **National Cowgirl Museum and Hall of Fame ★** (p. 123), which has cool interactive exhibits (such as filming yourself on a bucking bronco). If the kids are hungry for more Old West adventures, trot them over to the **Cattle Raisers Museum,** now part of the Museum of Science and History (p. 122), which depicts life on the range through talking ranchers and cattle and a theater presentation. The **Log Cabin Village,** 2100 Log Cabin Village Lane (www.logcabinvillage.org; ✆ **817/392-5881**), is a living-history "village" of eight 19th-century cabins transplanted to Forest Park.

For additional family activities, such as Six Flags Amusement Park and professional spectator sports, see "Arlington" in chapter 4.

Botanic Garden and 8 miles of cycling and jogging trails. Forest Park is the site of another well-known Fort Worth landmark, the Fort Worth Zoo. The scenic **Trinity River Trails,** which run 35 miles along the Trinity River, are a good choice for biking, hiking, and in-line skating. Pick up a map at a tourist information center.

For 27 years the **Cowtown Marathon** (www.cowtownmarathon.org; ✆ **817/207-0224**) has drawn runners from around the world to the Stockyards National Historic District in late February. It includes a half-marathon, 10K, 5K, and marathon relay. Get a monthly runners' calendar at ✆ **800/433-5747.**

GOLF Fort Worth has three inexpensive public courses. **Meadowbrooks Golf Course,** 1815 Jenson Rd. (✆ **817/457-4616**), just east of downtown, is one of the top 25 municipal golf courses in Texas. The popular par-71 course is set amid rolling terrain. Also at the top of the list is **Pecan Valley Golf Course,** 6400 Pecan Valley Dr. (✆ **817/249-1845**); it has two 18-hole golf courses: the "River" and the "Hills." The **Sycamore Creek Golf Course,**

Martin Luther King, Jr., Freeway (✆ **817/535-7241**), is a 9-hole layout with narrow tree-lined fairways. For general information about golf courses and events in the Fort Worth area, visit **www.fortworthgolf.org**.

HORSEBACK RIDING **Stockyards Stables,** 128 E. Exchange Ave. Suite 300. (www.fortworthstockyardsstables.com; ✆ **817/575-9506**), offers horseback trail riding for riders of all skill levels (as well as wagon rides and chuckwagon dinners). Trail riding costs $40 for the first hour and $60 for each additional hour.

TENNIS The swanky **Worthington Renaissance** hotel (✆ **817/870-1000**) has two rooftop courts available for guests only. The public can get on an indoor or outdoor court at the **McLeland Tennis Center,** 1600 W. Seminary Dr. (✆ **817/921-2345**), or the **TCU Tennis Center,** 3609 Bellaire Dr. N. on the campus south of downtown (✆ **817/257-7960**), which has 16 lit outdoor courts and five indoor courts. **The Hulen Street Church** kindly opens their clay tennis courts (and swimming pool) to the public at 7100 S. Hulen St. (✆ **817/292-9787**).

Spectator Sports

See "Spectator Sports" in chapter 4 for professional football, baseball, soccer, basketball, and more hockey and golf.

AUTO RACING The **Texas Motor Speedway,** I-35 W. at Hwy. 114, north of Fort Worth (www.texasmotorspeedway.com; ✆ **817/215-8500**), is said to be the third-largest sporting complex in the world. It's the place to see NASCAR, Indy, and truck racing. Plan on joining a crowd; more than 150,000 people attend the races here.

GOLF Fort Worth's stop on the PGA tour is the **Dean & Deluca Invitational,** held every May at Fort Worth's prestigious Colonial Country Club (www.colonialfw.com; ✆ **817/927-4278**). *Note:* The name of the PGA tour is subject to change each year depending on the sponsor of that year's tour.

HOCKEY The professional **Texas Brahmas** of the Central Hockey League (CHL) usually play from January to March at the NYTEX Sports Centre in Rockland Hills; however, they did not play in 2016 and it is not clear if they will continue to play in the future. The amateur **Lone Star Brahmas** are current members of the North American Hockey League, and they continue to play at the same sports center. To learn more about both teams, call ✆ **817/336-3342** or visit www.brahmas.com for news and ticket information.

RODEO/LIVESTOCK SHOWS Fort Worth's famous **Cowtown Coliseum,** 121 E. Exchange Ave. (✆ **817/625-1025**), is the top place to see professional rodeo. Rodeos are usually every Friday and Saturday night (tickets $10–$19). Popping up frequently on the Coliseum schedule is **Pawnee Bill's Wild West Show,** a reenactment of the original, which was once the largest Wild West show anywhere. Events range from trick roping to trick shooting and are accompanied by Western music and an arena full of buffaloes, longhorns, and horses. For information and tickets, call ✆ **817/625-1025,** or visit www.stockyardsrodeo.com.

The big event in Fort Worth is the annual **Fort Worth Stock Show,** which is staged from the end of January to early February (www.fwssr.com; ✆ **817/877-2400**). The nation's oldest livestock show features a Western parade, auctions, and cowboys and cowgirls at the nightly rodeo at **Will Rogers Memorial Center,** located in the Cultural District at 3401 W. Lancaster Ave.

WHERE TO STAY

Fort Worth may not be loaded with ultra-deluxe accommodations, but it does have a nice mix of affordable lodgings, including an attractive roster of Western-flavored small hotels and bed-and-breakfasts. They are spread fairly evenly among the major districts of interest, so you can stay on the main drag of the Stockyards, downtown on Sundance Square, or south of town near the Cultural District. Everything in Fort Worth is pretty close and easily accessible, though, so you needn't choose your hotel strictly according to your primary sightseeing interests.

Breakfast, either continental or buffet, is offered free at several hotels, as noted below. The rates quoted below do not include 15% hotel occupancy tax.

Hotel rates are ever changing; much depends on season, convention traffic, festivals, and other variables. At a minimum, request the lower corporate rate, and ask about special deals. Virtually all hotels offer some deals, especially on weekends when their business clientele dries up. This is not the case in the Stockyards, however, where weekend rates are higher than weekday rates. Check individual hotel websites for special online offers.

Stockyards National Historic District

EXPENSIVE

Stockyards Hotel ★★ Since 1908 the historic Stockyards Hotel has epitomized the spirit of the Old West. From a rough-hewn frame structure on a dusty Western street, the hotel has evolved into the stately three-story brick landmark you see today, albeit with its Old West props intact. We say any place where Bonnie and Clyde once holed up (Room 305) has some serious bona fides. Immerse yourself in the genuine period ambience, from the bordello-red lobby with tufted Victoriana to the atmospheric rooms and suites, some with beamed ceilings and others with stuffed bison heads on the wall. The connected restaurant, the Hunter Brothers' **H3 Ranch,** is a fine place to sample the city's vaunted beef, here grilled over hickory wood. Quench your thirst in one of the Stockyards District saloons nearby, including Booger Red's, with vintage horse-saddle bar stools and icy Buffalo Butt beer.

109 E. Exchange Ave. www.stockyardshotel.com. ✆ **817/625-6427.** 52 units. $199–$319 double; $299–$549 suite. Weekend and other packages available. Valet parking $15. **Amenities:** Restaurant; bar; Wi-Fi (free).

MODERATE

Azalea Plantation Bed & Breakfast Inn ★ Pillowed in a shady oasis of oaks and perfumed magnolias, this white-columned mini-Tara has country relaxation written all over it—even if it's just 10 minutes from Sundance Square. You'll stay in one of four suites in the main inn or the Carriage House out back, some with antique furnishings (four-posters, big wooden headboards, gleaming chiffarobes) and all with comfy king beds and whirlpool tubs for two. The Evening in Paris cottage has country French décor and garden views; the Magnolia Suite even has its own private garden patio. Buffet breakfasts are B&B state-of-the-art (eggs, bacon, the works), and fresh-baked cookies are complimentary.

1400 Robinwood Dr. www.azaleaplantation.com. ✆ **800/687-3529** or 817/838-5882. 4 units. $189 double; $219 cottage suite. Rates include full plantation breakfast. Secure off-street parking. **Amenities:** Wi-Fi (free).

Hyatt Place Fort Worth Historic Stockyards ★ The exterior may say "just another chain hotel," but the Texan touches (Texas stars, limestone accent walls) inside this clean and comfortable Hyatt connects with its Stockyards setting. The location close to all the Stockyards fun is excellent, rooms are contemporary, and the hotel serves a fairly large continental breakfast downstairs each day. The Hyatt may not be as kitschy and fun as the Stockyards Hotel nearby, but it's family-friendly (with an outdoor pool) and offers good value for the travel dollar.

132 E. Exchange Ave. www.stockyards.place.hyatt.com. ✆ **817/626-6000.** 102 units. $149–$375 double; $399–$539 suite. Rates include continental breakfast. **Amenities:** Cafe; outdoor pool; complimentary shuttle service (8am–8pm); Wi-Fi (free).

Miss Molly's Hotel ★ Some say this former bordello is haunted, but even if it's not, all kinds of interesting characters have passed through its doors over the years, including railroad men, oil tycoons, cattle barons, and outlaws. It's been called Cowtown's first B&B, and it does have a romantic sort of Old West style. Set in the heart of the Stockyards on the main drag in a Victorian building dating from 1910, sandwiched amid saloons and Western shops, Miss Molly's has eight cleverly themed rooms, like the **Cattleman's,** with a carved oak bed beneath mounted longhorns, and **Miss Josie's,** the former madam's bedroom (and double the size of other rooms, with a private bath). Though many of the rooms have shared baths, guests seem to like the claw-foot bathtubs. In keeping with true cowboy spirit, there's sometimes a noisy crowd downstairs in the **Star Cafe,** and nearby bars can be clamorous until the wee hours on the weekends. Through the same phone number, guests can book the Stockyard's **Stonehouse Hotel** boardinghouse B&B and the **Cadillac Hotel** above the Cadillac Bar, a hostel-style lodging where young cowhands and college kids like to stay.

109 W. Exchange Ave. www.missmollyshotel.com. ✆ **817/626-1522.** 8 units. $100–$175 double. Special packages available. Self-parking $5. Wi-Fi (free).

INEXPENSIVE

Stonehouse B&B ★ From the moment you enter the front door of the Stonehouse Hotel Bed & Breakfast, you'll know you're in Texas. With log-cabin-like interiors, and cowboy clutter covering every surface, this place is what Texans would call "a hoot." Lassos, cowboy hats, saddles, sombreros, and Longhorn mounts line the walls of this 1936 bunkhouse built with stones from Palo Pinto County. It's no wonder this is called "Fort Worth's authentic cowboy hotel." Rooms are comfortable, though amenities are minimal (no TVs and no central air/heat, just window units); some share a common bath and shower. If you're looking for local color and a "grandma's house" feel (if grandma were a cowgirl), this place is for you. Miss Molly's, the Cadillac Hotel, and the Stonehouse share owners.

2401 Ellis Ave. (at W. Exchange Ave.) ✆ **817/626-2589.** 9 units. $100–$150 double. Limited free parking for Stonehouse Guests only. Wi-Fi (free).

Downtown

EXPENSIVE

The Ashton Hotel ★★★ This small luxury hotel—the only one downtown—comprises the good-boned beauty of two lovingly restored historic brick buildings on Main Street—the 1890 Winfree Building and the 1915 Fort Worth Club Building—with a fine location not far from the Bass Performance Hall and Sundance Square. The boutique property sports a smart and stylish lobby and spacious rooms with mahogany furnishings, king-sized beds, and Italian linens. Some rooms even have large claw-foot tubs with whirlpool jets. The hotel's classy **SIX 10 Grille** features a full a la carte breakfast menu daily, as well as an chic afternoon tea on Saturdays with a seasonally changing menu.

610 Main St. (btw. 5th and 6th sts.). www.theashtonhotel.com. ✆ **817/332-0100.** 39 units. $189–$349 double; $369 suite. Valet parking $25. Pets up to 50 lb. accepted. **Amenities:** Restaurant; fitness center; laundry service; Wi-Fi (free).

Omni Fort Worth Hotel ★★★ Across from the Fort Worth Water Gardens stands this impressive, gleaming, Texas-size high-rise, one of the city's most popular business hotels. The impressive facade is a mix of Texas granite and shining glass, while the interior has the feel of a luxury Montana mountain lodge. The 15-story hotel is popular for its swank **Mokara** spa, classic **Bob's Steak & Chop House** restaurant, big public rooms, and rooftop pool and terrace pool bar. With excellent views of the city and beyond, rooms are elegant without being ostentatious, and all have large bathrooms. The hotel is about 12 blocks from Sundance Square, but it's easy to get around downtown, and the Water Gardens are a cool place to visit on a hot summer day. Look for great packages and special deals online.

1300 Houston St. www.omnihotels.com/findahotel/fortworth.aspx. ✆ **888/444-6664** or 817/535-6664. 614 units. $169–$195 double; from $382–$638 suite. Valet parking $25. **Amenities:** 2 restaurants; 3 bars (including wine bar & pool bar); children's programs; museum shop; rooftop pool; 24-hr. room service; spa; Wi-Fi (free).

The Worthington Renaissance Fort Worth Hotel ★ This massive, 15-story hotel anchors the city with a location near the courthouse downtown, just 3 blocks from Bass Performance Hall, and close to the restaurants, bars and lively fun of Sundance Square. Known as "the Star of Texas," the hotel was fully renovated in 2017, with a big, stylish lobby, and spacious rooms that are modern and understated with cool mineral tones and textures. The **Vidalias Restaurant** serves Southwestern cuisine, and the lobby bar is a nice place to lounge after a day of meetings. Whenever we go to our family reunion outside Fort Worth each year, we always like to add on an extra night at the Worthington.

200 Main St. www.marriott.com/hotels/travel/dfwdt-the-worthington-renaissance-fort-worth-hotel. ✆ **817/870-1000.** 504 units. $199–$239 double; from $329 suite. Romance, weekend, and other packages available. Valet parking $28. Pets accepted with $50 nonrefundable deposit. **Amenities:** Restaurant; coffeehouse; lounge; fitness center; pool; Wi-Fi (free, in lobby; $13/day in room).

MODERATE

Etta's Place ★ If you're looking for a cozy bed-and-breakfast hideaway in Sundance Square, Etta's Place fits the bill. Filling four floors of a landmark building, this boutique B&B is handy to downtown shops and restaurants, and just a trolley ride from the Cultural District and Stockyards. Named for the Sundance Kid's real-life girlfriend (played by Katherine Ross in the movie *Butch Cassidy and the Sundance Kid*), Etta's Place has 10 rooms, each named for a member of Butch Cassidy's Hole in the Wall Gang (and female companions). The simple Old West–style decor includes antique chairs, horseshoe lamps, and Americana quilts. My favorite room is Butch's Hideout, a comfortable 700-square-foot suite with a sitting area and kitchenette. The handsome library and music room, with inviting leather chairs, makes a nice place to chill. Guests enjoy full gourmet breakfasts.

200 W. 3rd St. www.ettas-place.com. ✆ **817/255-5760.** 10 units. $150–$185 double; $190–$310 suite. Rates include full breakfast. Parking $5 weekdays; free weekends. **Amenities:** Library and music room; Wi-Fi (free).

Hilton Fort Worth ★ It was in this historic hotel that John and Jackie Kennedy spent the night before the President's assassination in November 1963. (See the JFK statue just outside the hotel.) Opened in 1921 as the **Hotel Texas,** this Hilton has seen lots of changes since then. An extensive makeover and expansion has ensured its place as one of the city's top business and convention hotels. A large Texas star inlaid in the lobby floor and Western-style art and statues adorn the multi-level lobby; guest rooms feature earthy color schemes and plush bedding. Although many think of this as an unofficial headquarters for conventioneers, it's also a smart family choice—children stay free when occupying their parent's room. The high-end steakhouse **Ruth's Chris** (a New Orleans transplant) is ever-popular with the business folk.

815 Main St. www3.hilton.com/en/hotels/texas/hilton-fort-worth-FTWFWHF/index.html. ✆ **800/445-8667.** 294 units. $179–$200 double. Valet parking $26. No pets. **Amenities:** 2 restaurants; lounge; 24-hr. pantry market; business center; concierge; fitness center; room service (6am–11pm); Wi-Fi (free).

Hotel Chains in a Pinch

If you can't get a room in any hotels reviewed in this section, four additional, good-value chain hotels are especially worthy of consideration: Three **La Quinta Inn & Suites** near downtown (www.lq.com; ✆ **800/531-5900**), all with attractive two-room suites with kitchenettes, a pool, and a gazebo; the **Courtyard Fort Worth University Drive,** 3150 Riverfront Dr. (www.marriott.com/hotels/travel/dfwch-courtyard-fort-worth-university-drive; ✆ **817/335-1300**) and the renovated **Courtyard Fort Worth Downtown/Blackstone,** 601 Main St. (www.marriott.com/hotels/travel/dfwms-courtyard-fort-worth-downtown-blackstone; ✆ **817/885-8700**); and, near the Stockyards, **Country Inn & Suites by Carlson,** 2200 Mercado Dr. (www.countryinns.com/fortworthtx; ✆ **817/831-9200**).

TownePlace Suites Fort Worth Downtown ★ At first glance, this Marriott property at the edge of downtown looks like a standard budget hotel, but it's more than that: In fact, it's surprisingly comfortable, bright, and convenient. Yes, rooms are simple, but they're spacious and well-equipped, with an in-room desk space and all the plug-ins you require. An outdoor pool makes a nice place to cool off after a day of work or travel. This is a good option for business travelers or anyone who needs an affordable place to stay not far from Sundance Square, the Cultural District, and the Stockyards.

805 E. Belknap St. ✆ **817/332-6300.** www.marriott.com/hotels/travel/dfwtd-towne-place-suites-fort-worth-downtown. 140 units. $129–$189 double. Rates include breakfast. Free parking. Pets accepted with $100 fee. **Amenities:** Gym; outdoor pool; Wi-Fi (free).

Cultural District

MODERATE

The Texas White House ★ It may not be as grand as Southfork, but this Fort Worth favorite has the look of a genteel country home, with white columns, a wraparound porch, and a thoroughly Southern gazebo in the backyard. Located near All Saints Episcopal Hospital in the Medical District, this century-old home has a living room warmed by a nice fireplace and hardwood floors throughout. Although the decor includes a sprinkling of antiques (armoires, leather luggage) and the porch is a welcome mat of cushioned wicker, the B&B interior feels more colorfully contemporary than vintage. If you're craving cowboy charm, request the **Lone Star** room, which also has a massive bathroom with a clawfoot tub. For a taste of Tex-Mex, ask for the **Tejas** suite, beautifully done with Mexican folk art and a handmade quilt. In the carriage house out back, the **Treehouse** suite has a private balcony and double Jacuzzi. With a full gourmet breakfast (try the breakfast nachos!) and friendly owners, guests are sure to feel right at home.

1417 8th Ave. www.texaswhitehouse.com. ✆ **817/923-3597.** 5 units. $125–$145 double; $205–$235 suite. Rates include full breakfast. Wi-Fi (free).

INEXPENSIVE

Residence Inn Fort Worth Cultural District ★ This Residence Inn is perfectly located just steps away from 7th Street, Sundance Square, the Will Rogers Center, and a variety of museums, and the hotel also offers a complimentary shuttle service to any Fort Worth attractions within 5 miles. Best of all, the roomy layout is ideal for extended stays. Suites are spread across two floors, and all include kitchens and sitting areas; some have balconies. Because it gets so many families and long-term business-stay travelers, the hotel has a barbecue grill and picnic area so you can eat outside instead of eating out. There's also a spa and a fitness room, outdoor heated pool and whirlpool, and tennis and volleyball basketball court.

2500 Museum Way. www.marriott.com/hotels/hotel-information/restaurant/dfwrw-residence-inn-fort-worth-cultural-district. ✆ **817/885-8250.** 142 units. $140–$165 double; $190–$199 suite. Free parking $5. Pets accepted with $100 nonrefundable fee. **Amenities:** Outdoor pool; fitness room; spa; sport court; Wi-Fi (free; high-speed Internet $4.29 per night).

WHERE TO EAT

Fort Worth's dining scene may not be as lauded or as flashy as the one in Dallas, but it is increasingly sophisticated, with excellent steakhouses as well as innovative Southwestern and haute Mexican cuisine, alongside family-oriented Tex-Mex and barbecue joints. Two areas have emerged as new dining zones: the **West 7th** corridor, roughly 5 blocks of pedestrian-friendly walking streets where there's been immense development in just the last 10 years; and **Magnolia Avenue,** in the Hospital District near TCU, Fort Worth's counterpart to Dallas's cutting-edge Bishop Arts District. In addition to the dining spots below, the Modern Art Museum of Fort Worth has a terrific fine-dining restaurant overlooking a reflective pool: **Café Modern ★★** (✆ **817/840-2157**), headed by a Fort Worth native and CIA graduate, and once named one of the best restaurants in the U.S. by *Gourmet* magazine. It's open for lunch, Sunday brunch, and Friday dinner (and has a kid's menu too). Another great lunch (and even breakfast) spot is the honey-tonk classic **Fred's Texas Café** (✆ **817/332-0083**), known for its great chipotle-topped burgers, quail and eggs, and tacos (Fred's has three locations in Fort Worth).

Stockyards National Historic District

EXPENSIVE

Cattlemen's Steakhouse ★ STEAK The cow on the roof and the weathered wooden saloon-style storefront let visitors know this is not some fancy steakhouse where suits make deals over martinis. It's a laid-back and surprisingly affordable spot with big steaks, baked potatoes, and loads of Stockyards charm. For more than 60 years, this sometimes boisterous and nicely worn place has been a favorite of Fort Worth families in the heart of cattle country, just a short canter from the Stockyards and rodeo ring. Dining rooms have fun names, like the "Sirloin" and the "Branding" and "Longhorn" rooms. The juicy charcoal-broiled cuts of beef come in 13 varieties, from chicken-fried steak to "Rose of Texas Tenderloin" (a center cut) to a 24-ounce Porterhouse steak that's advertised, needlessly, as "guaranteed to satisfy all appetites."

2458 N. Main St. www.cattlemenssteakhouse.com. © **817/624-3945.** Reservations recommended. Main courses $10–$22 lunch, $15–$50 dinner. Mon–Thurs 11am–10:30pm; Fri–Sat 11am–11pm; Sun noon–9pm.

Lonesome Dove Western Bistro ★★★ WESTERN The setting couldn't be more "Cowtown": a historic former warehouse (with a classic pressed-tin ceiling) centered around a long bar. But when you taste the food, look closer at the groovy pieces of Wild West art, and size up the hipster staff, you'll realize this place isn't like anywhere else in Fort Worth, or in Texas for that matter. That's thanks to the talents of chef/owner Tim Love, who takes the same-old, same-old steakhouse concept and turns it on its cowboy-hatted head. Sure there are steaks, and mighty fine ones at that (hand-cut on site), plus standards like Texas red chili. But you'll be missing out if you don't try the menu's more unusual items, like rabbit and rattlesnake sausage or nachos topped with kangaroo carpaccio. The main courses aren't quite as exotic but pack a flavorful punch; recent specialties have ranged from redfish en papillote to Rocky Mountain elk loin with Swiss chard and mushrooms. And if you happen to catch a glimpse of Chef Tim Love and wonder why he looks familiar, here's why: He's been on *Iron Chef* several times, usually as the winning contestant. For lunch, ask about the daily "Stockyard Special"—at $10, a real deal.

2406 N. Main St. (just south of Exchange Ave.) www.lonesomedovebistro.com. © **817/740-8810.** Reservations recommended. Main courses $9–$35 lunch, $25–$55 dinner. Mon 5–10pm; Tues–Sat 11:30am–2:30pm; Tues–Thurs 5–10pm; Fri–Sat 5–11pm.

INEXPENSIVE

Joe T. Garcia's Mexican Restaurant ★ TEX-MEX At this ever popular Cowtown Tex-Mex institution (opened in 1935) just south of the Stockyards, they don't have menus, do only two dinner dishes, and take only cash (or check). But who gives a hoot when the food is this delish? Set in a rambling hacienda-style home with a lush outdoor patio, Joe T. Garcia's is, amazingly enough, large enough to seat 1,200 diners. But that doesn't seem to affect the quality of the food or scene (it never feels crowded). We'd say dining outside is the classic way to "do" Joe's—unless you're wilting from the Texas heat. Ordering couldn't be simpler: Choose between a heaping plate of succulently grilled chicken or beef fajitas, a big family-style dinner with tacos and enchiladas, or *chiles rellenos,* tamales, and chicken *flautas* at lunch. At night, Joe T.'s is a margarita factory, spitting out thousands of them—on the rocks and frozen (pitchers are a good deal if you have a group). Service can be erratic, though it's often lightning fast. A Mexican-style brunch is served on Saturdays and Sundays from 11am to 2pm. A sister restaurant, **Esperanza's Restaurant & Bakery** (2122 North Main St.), is especially good for breakfast.

2201 N. Commerce St. (at NW 22nd St.). www.joets.com. © **817/626-4356.** Reservations not accepted. Main courses $9.25–$15. No credit cards. Mon–Thurs 11am–2:30pm and 5–10pm; Fri–Sat 11am–11pm; Sun 11am–10pm.

Love Shack ★ AMERICAN Right on the main drag, and within spitting distance of his über-successful Lonesome Dove restaurant, this fab burger shack is the creation of star chef Tim Love. With mostly outdoor seating, it's part counter and part kiosk, dispensing delicious burgers on store-bought buns and cardboard trays, with nothing on the menu costing more than 10 bucks. But that burger will hit the spot, especially after a day of exploring Cowtown. A blend of prime tenderloin and brisket, the patties are loosely packed and marvelously juicy and sometimes over-the-top indulgent (the "Dirty Love" burger piles on bacon, fried quail egg, and "love sauce.") Don't feel like a burger? Go for the Flying Texas Dog, a chicken-apple bratwurst with onions and green chiles sided by Crazy Good Onion Rings. Beer and wine, fresh lemonade, root beer on tap, milkshakes (a different one each day), and live country music round out the experience. More live music is next door at the **White Elephant Saloon** (also part of Chef Love's burgeoning honky-tonk empire).

110 E. Exchange Ave. (just east of N. Main Ave.). www.loveburgershackfortworth.com. ✆ **817/740-8812.** Reservations not accepted. Main courses $3–$9.50. No credit cards. Mon–Wed, Sun 11am–8pm; Thurs 11am–9pm; Fri–Sat 11am–12am.

Downtown

EXPENSIVE

Del Frisco's Double Eagle Steak House ★★★ STEAK This is one of Cowtown's top high-end steakhouses, a swank two-level white-tablecloth space with a long Western bar where power brokers, oilmen, business types, and everyday carnivores come for a juicy steak in an uptown setting. In a red-brick corner building (ca. 1890) with an upstairs area edged by a wrought-iron railing, and arched mirrors behind a glittering bar, prime steaks take center stage. Try the butter-broiled filet mignon, the mouth-watering marbled rib-eye, or Santa Fe peppercorn steaks. Desserts are divine, too. All the gleaming Texas-cattleman touches make this as upscale as any Dallas restaurant, so those who prefer a more low-key, family-friendly steakhouse may instead want to mosey on over to **Cattlemen's ★** (see p. 132), though the steaks there may not be on par with Del Frisco's. A **prix-fixe menu** ($58) is available on Sundays.

812 Main St. (at 8th St.) www.delfriscos.com. ✆ **817/877-3999.** Reservations recommended. Main courses $18–$48. Mon–Thurs 4:30–10pm; Fri–Sat 4:30–11pm; Sun 4:30–9pm.

Reata ★ SOUTHWESTERN Named for the Marfa-area ranch in the classic Rock Hudson/Liz Taylor movie *Giant*, Reata opened here in 2002 as an arbiter of "sophisticated cowboy cuisine." It remains one of Fort Worth's highest-rated casual restaurants. It's cowboy to the core, making it a treat for out-of-towners who want a genuine taste of Texas (there's a bison head on one wall, plus chaps and saddles and cowboy art). Waiters wear Western shirts, and dishware and glass doors flaunt Reata's cattle-brand logo. The menu is thoroughly Texan too, with dishes like chicken-fried steak and cowboy rib-eyes, along with Tex-Mex–inspired dishes such as *carne asada* (barbecued meat) with cheese enchiladas. After dinner, check out the view from "Luna

Vista," a weird but wonderful geodesic dome perched atop Reata's rooftop deck, or have a drink at the rooftop bar. Sunday brunch is always a treat at Reata.

310 Houston St. (on Sundance Square). www.reata.net. ✆ **817/336-1009.** Reservations recommended. Main courses $16–$44. Daily 11am–2:30pm; Mon–Thurs and Sun 5–10pm; Fri–Sat 5–10:30pm.

MODERATE

Bird Café ★★★ NEW AMERICAN/GASTROPUB Set in the popular Sundance Square Plaza downtown, the Bird Cafe is open for dinner, but I prefer it as a favorite brunch or lunch spot, though it can get crowded that time of day. It has the kind of yummy-sounding small-plates menu that makes it difficult to decide which delectable dish to order—that is, until a skillet full of something wonderful is set down on the table next to you and it's "I'll have what she's having." We're talking shrimp and grits; comfort-food pot pies filled with rabbit or steak; fresh salads with beets, goat cheese, and salmon; and "stick meats," little kebabs studded with medallions of chicken, tuna, or beef. The dessert and cocktail menus are to die for, too. With a focus on sustainability and supporting local purveyors, the Bird Café is the kind of place you'll want to linger on a lazy Sunday, brunching with friends over small plates and sipping Moscow Mules. The warm, inviting split-level space in an 1889 Victorian building has wood floors and big windows and tables indoors and out.

155 E. 4th St. www.birdinthe.net. ✆ **817/332-2473.** Reservations suggested. Main courses $11–$18. Mon–Thurs 11am–midnight; Fri 11am–1am; Sat 10am–1am; Sun 10am–10pm.

Cultural (& Hospital) District

EXPENSIVE

Le Cep ★★★ FRENCH There are other French restaurants in Fort Worth, but Le Cep is more elegant and authentic than most (and probably pricier). And what could be a better fit for Fort Worth's tony Cultural District than a sweet little Parisian-style restaurant where gentlemen are still expected to wear jackets? The lovechild eatery of Chef Sandra Avila and her husband, David, opened in 2014. This 60-seat contemporary French bistro is set in a strip mall, but don't let the unassuming location fool you. The minimalist space has crisp white tablecloths and waiters in black coats and ties. There's even a trained *fromagier* (cheese expert) who will help with selections for a cheese course from his cheese cart. The outstanding menu offers both an eight-course "Discovery" menu and a four-course tasting menu, and I'd suggest that you and your dinner companion go with the latter, each making different selections so you can share. Additional wine pairings and cheese courses are also offered.

3324 W. 7th St. www.leceprestaurant.com. ✆ **817/900-2468.** Reservations suggested. Main courses $19–$26. Eight-course "Discovery" menu $95 and four-course tasting menu (except Sat; $55) with additional cost for cheese supplement or wine pairings. Jackets requested though not required; no shorts or flip-flops. Tues–Sat 5:30–10pm.

Nonna Tata ★★ ITALIAN The sign at Donatella Trotti's sweet little Hospital District eatery says, "NONNA TATA: A LITTLE TASTE OF ITALY," and this tiny, 21-table spot named after the owner's Italian grandmother gives guests just that—a little slice of pure pasta perfection. Regulars say it's like being in an Italian grandmother's kitchen filled with the wonderful smells of sage and bubbling Bolognese sauce. Take your seat at one of the rustic tables inside the sunshine-yellow dining room, or dine alfresco outside. Regulars know to BYOB and that credit cards or reservations are not taken. The place is small, so it fills up fast, but it's worth the wait to enjoy authentic Italian treats like pappardelle a la Zucca (homemade pasta with roasted pumpkin, butternut squash, hazelnuts, and sage-brown butter) and panna cotta with fresh strawberry marmalade.

1400 W. Magnolia Ave. (btw. Fairmount and 6th aves.) ✆ **817/332-0250.** Reservations not accepted. Main courses $13–$25. No credit cards. Tues–Fri 11am–2pm and 5:30–9:30pm; last Sat of the month 5–9pm.

MODERATE

Michael's Cuisine Restaurant & Ancho Chile Bar ★ STEAKHOUSE/TEXAN This casual "Contemporary Ranch Cuisine" restaurant has in Michael S. Thomson a serious chef, who opened the restaurant in 1992 and is ultra-picky about serving Fort Worth's best steaks. His ideal cut? An aged, 3-inch-thick USDA Prime striploin, seasoned and charbroiled to perfection, cut across the grain, and served with chipotle-mashed potatoes and Thai green beans. The most popular thing on the menu, however, seems to be the pepper-crusted, pan-seared tenderloin with ancho bourbon sauce. Anyway, you get the picture—it's about the beef. Of course, there are other options on the menu that salad and chicken lovers will like, like pecan-crusted goat-cheese chicken and crab cakes. Check out the chef's daily specials.

3413 W. 7th St. www.michaelscuisine.com. ✆ **817/877-3413.** Reservations recommended. Main courses $12–$34. Mon–Fri 11am–2:30pm; Mon–Wed 5:30–10pm; Thurs–Sat 5:30–11pm; Sat brunch 11am–4pm. Ancho Chile Bar Mon–Wed 11am–11pm; Thurs–Sat 11am–midnight. Closed Sun.

Spiral Diner & Bakery ★ VEGAN Vegans and vegetarians may feel unloved in Cowtown, where steakhouses reign on practically every corner. But they will eat well indeed at this little retro-styled vegan cafe in the Magnolia Avenue district, which serves up "vegan comfort food." Relying on organic and (whenever possible) locally sourced seasonal fresh ingredients, Spiral Diner prides itself on cooking up creative fare that even non-vegetarians will crave, including healthful soups, pastas, burritos, and salads. They also have an impressive beer list, with carefully chosen craft and organic brews, as well as fresh juices, smoothies, coffee, and teas. Look for yummy homemade ice cream, cookies, milkshakes, and cupcakes, not to mention deliciously decadent vegan cakes made with organic ingredients.

1314 W. Magnolia Ave. (btw. 6th Ave. and S. Lake St.). www.spiraldiner.com. ✆ **817/332-8834.** Reservations recommended. Main courses $7–$9. Tues–Sat 11am–10pm; Sun 11am–5pm.

INEXPENSIVE

Angelo's Barbecue ★ BARBECUE "I'll take a pound of ribs . . . just for a snack," the strapping 6'4" cowboy-booted fellow in front of me told the counterman, and then he proceeded to order most everything else on the menu, from the famous brisket sandwiches (with the works—raw onion, mustard, mayo, and a side of BBQ sauce) to five of the sides (potato salad, baked beans, you know the drill). Whether the fellow survived this meatapalooza, I don't know. But if he died, he did so a happy man. Because Angelo's has been serving the best barbecue in Fort Worth (and perhaps in the state of Texas) since 1958. Founded by a butcher—of course—the restaurant uses only the best cuts of meat (pork and beef), slathers them with a famed rub, and slow-smokes everything with hickory wood. What emerges is tangy and super-tender, with a slow-building heat that's quenched by beer served Arctic cold. And if this all weren't butch enough, every surface of the barn-like room has some critter's head poking from it (moose, deer, full-sized brown bears—Angelo's doubles as a taxidermy museum). Hey, this is what you came to Texas for, right?

2533 White Settlement Rd. (at N. Vacek St.). https://angelosbbq.com. ✆ **817/332-0357.** Reservations not accepted. Main courses $3.50–$13. Mon–Wed 11am–9pm; Thurs–Sun 11am–10pm.

Kincaid's Gro. Market Hamburgers ★ AMERICAN This nifty hamburger spot isn't fancy, but it sure is fun. There are six Kincaid's locations in the DFW area, but our favorite is the Camp Bowie Blvd. location, a 1940s grocery store turned hopping hamburger joint in the 1960s. The thick, juicy burgers at this venerated Fort Worth institution were once named "best in the U.S." (selling 3,300 hamburgers the next day), and remain in contention to this day, made from veggie-fed, hormone- and preservative-free beef. Look for other all-American basics, like French fries, onion rings, hot dogs, and grilled-cheese sandwiches. Order at the window, then eat at long counters with inflatable toys hanging overhead.

4901 Camp Bowie Blvd. (at Eldridge St.). www.kincaidshamburgers.com. ✆ **817/732-2881.** Reservations accepted. Main courses $1.99–$8.50. Mon–Sat 11am–8pm; Sun 11am–3pm.

Paris Coffee Shop ★ DINER/BREAKFAST/BRUNCH There's more of Paris, Texas, than Paris, France, to this downhome Texas diner, and that's fine with locals who have been eating here for decades. Named after original owner, Vic Paris, who opened a grocery here in the 1920s, the diner moved to its current Hospital District location in the '70s under new owners and has been a favorite of hungry locals for breakfast and lunch ever since. It's a simple place with metal chairs, a few booths, and lots of pictures on the wall. Go here for a Texas-size breakfast, robust helpings of pancakes, omelets, grits, and Southern biscuits and gravy. Sandwiches, plate lunches, and chili are lunch staples, and specials might include enchiladas and ham steak. Paris also serves homemade pies, piled high with peaks of toasted meringue. Texas has hundreds of old-time diners, but Paris Coffee Shop is the only one quite like it in Fort Worth.

704 W. Magnolia Ave. (at Hemphill St.). www.pariscoffeeshop.net. ✆ **817/335-2041.** Reservations not accepted. Main courses $3.95–$7.25. Mon–Fri 6am–2:30pm; Sat 6–11am.

Railhead Smokehouse ★ BARBECUE While Cowtown has many popular Texas barbecue joints, locals claim Railhead is one of the best. This is a traditional old-school-style Texas barbecue joint where you're served generous portions of barbecue on Styrofoam plates along with pickles, slaw, pinto beans, and white bread. The tangy sauce and meat smoked low and slow get raves, and the sliced beef, ribs, and "cheddar peppers" (jalapeños stuffed with cheese) are all winners. Chicken is also on the menu, but folks come mostly for the beef. Railhead's weekday plate specials are often good, and diners can enjoy a cold beer or margarita on the patio or belly up to the bar, which sometimes has live music. In a hurry? You can load up on barbecued meat by the pound to take out.

2900 Montgomery St. (at Vickery Blvd.). ✆ **817/738-9808.** Reservations not accepted. Main courses $6.75–$17. Mon–Thurs 11am–9pm; Fri–Sat 11am–10pm.

FORT WORTH SHOPPING

Fort Worth can't compare to Dallas as a shopping mecca (nor, I suspect, would it want to), but if you're looking for Western clothing and souvenirs of cowtown history, you're in luck. The top tourist area, the **Stockyards National Historic District** (and particularly **Stockyards Station,** a mall of pure Texan shops converted from the old sheep and hog pens), has plenty of authentic Western fashions, antiques, art, and souvenirs, many found in shops inhabiting historic quarters. **Sundance Square** in the downtown historic district is gushing with art galleries, museum gift shops, and fashionable clothing and furnishing stores, most in turn-of-the-20th-century buildings. Along Camp Bowie Boulevard in the **Cultural District** are a number of art galleries and design-oriented shops, and the burgeoning **West 7th** corridor (known to some as W7) has a number of cool boutiques to complement its restaurants, bars, and condos.

The Goods A–Z

ANTIQUES & FURNISHINGS

Bum Steer, 2400 N. Main St. (✆ **817/626-4565**), just a block from the Stockyards' main drag, sells Western home decor including English Tudor chairs in cowhide, metal lamps, bedding, and those lovable antler chandeliers. Just up the street is **Cross-Eyed Moose,** 2340 N. Main St. (✆ **817/624-4311**), run by the same folks and stocking slightly more affordable Western antiques, as well as custom furnishings, game mounts, and Western decorative stuff.

DEPARTMENT STORES & MALLS

Stockyards Station, 140 E. Exchange Ave. (www.stockyardsstation.com; ✆ **817/625-9715**), once the Southwest's largest hog and sheep marketing center, has been converted into a cute center with several dozen restaurants and shops featuring Western apparel, Lone Star wines, country-and-western music, leather goods, Texas products, and arts and crafts.

University Park Village, 2 blocks south of I-30 on South University Drive near Texas Christian University (www.simon.com/mall/university-park-village; ✆ **817/332-5700**), is an upscale shopping center with Anthropologie, Williams-Sonoma, J.Crew, Ann Taylor, and Apple.

MUSIC

Chief Records, 140 E. Exchange Ave., Suite 135 in Stockyards Station (www.chiefrecordsonline.com; ✆ **817/624-8449**), has a great stock of honky-tonk, cowboy, and country-and-western recordings, including old vinyl and hard-to-find stuff.

WESTERN GEAR

Two of the best Western shops—for real ropers, urban cowboys, and rodeo queens—are on the Stockyards' classic Exchange Avenue. Family-owned **M. L. Leddy's** ★, 2455 N. Main at Exchange (www.leddys.com; ✆ **817/624-3149**), with the big neon boot sign out front, is one of the city's oldest Western-wear shops. Originally a boot maker and saddlery, it has fine cowboy duds such as handmade belts, formalwear, custom-made boots, and saddles, and the best-selling top-of-the-line cowboy hat, the pure Beaver. It has another, slightly slicker and "uptown" shop, called **Leddy's Ranch at Sundance,** 410 Houston St., with a full range of boots and Western clothing (✆ **817/336-0800**). Across the street from the Stockyards Hotel, **Maverick** ★★, 100 E. Exchange Ave. (www.maverickwesternwear.com; ✆ **817/626-1129**), has such high-end Western wear as hand-embroidered shirts, saloon-ready 19th-century-style dress jackets, and other swank cowboy duds. It also has a long bar, so you can grab a longneck (plenty of bejeweled shoppers do) and look the part of the cowboy or cowgirl you are (or hope to become).

Also in the Stockyards, **Ponder Boot Company** ★★, 2358 N. Main St. (www.ponderboot.com; ✆ **817/626-3523**), is the place to go for custom boots. Step inside and choose your leather and get your own brand or initial on a boot that will last you a lifetime and cost not much more than a top-of-the-line factory-made boot (most will run $600–$850). Georgia, the owner, will demonstrate the superior quality of one of her handmade, custom boots using a pair of dissected boots (if you ask nicely). I've had trouble reaching the proprietors by phone; however, they are easily accessible in person or online.

Downtown near Sundance Square, **Peters Brothers Hats** ★, 909 Houston St. (www.pbhats.com; ✆ **800/897-4287**), has been around since 1911, stocking Stetsons and hats of all kinds, including Western fedoras and custom-made cowboy hats. Also check out **Retro Cowboy,** 404 Houston St. in Sundance Square (✆ **817/338-1194**), for women's Western apparel and sterling silver jewelry.

FORT WORTH NIGHTLIFE

Despite its decent size, Fort Worth still feels like a small town, and some young people looking for a bigger scene continue to split for Big D on weekends. Still, Fort Worth has a few good nightlife options, especially at the two extremes of the scale: high culture and cowboy culture. Whether you're inclined toward opera, symphony, and theater, or up for some boot-scootin', Fort Worth has some fine venues. **Exchange Avenue** in the Stockyards is where you want to be on weekends for some hot Western swing, Texas shuffle, and honky-tonk tunes. The street becomes a cruising strip of souped-up trucks, guys and dolls in cowboy and cowgirl finery strutting their stuff, and dancers ducking into honky-tonks and cowboy discos. Meanwhile, **Sundance Square** is full of bars, restaurants, cafes, and movie theaters, and is mobbed on weekend nights (luckily, there's plenty of free parking after 5pm and on weekends right in and around the square).

For listings, check out the "Entertainment" section of the *Fort Worth Star-Telegram* or the weekly listings on its website (www.dfw.com). For tickets, try Arts Line at **Ticketmaster** (www.ticketmaster.com; ✆ **817/467-2787**).

The Performing Arts

Elegant **Bass Performance Hall ★★**, located at 4th and Calhoun streets (btw. Commerce and Calhoun sts.; www.basshall.com; ✆ **817/212-4280**) is one of the top places in the country to see a musical or theater performance. Home to the distinguished Fort Worth Symphony Orchestra, its stage has welcomed an eclectic range of productions including *The Nutcracker,* Handel's *Messiah, Madame Butterfly,* Broadway shows (such as *Beautiful: The Carole King Musical, Rent,* and *Annie*), and pop, jazz, and country concerts by the likes of Tony Bennett, k.d. lang, Robert Earl Keen, and Michael Martin Murphy, as well as holiday events like a Mannheim Steamroller Christmas show by Chip Davis. The **Casa Mañana Theater ★**, 3101 W. Lancaster Ave., at University Drive (www.casamanana.org; ✆ **817/332-2272**), is the country's first permanent theater designed for musicals-in-the-round. The aluminum geodesic dome with an oval stage underwent a $3-million renovation in 2008. Casa, as it's known locally, has been around for more than 50 years, and it puts on a wide range of dramas, comedies, and musicals (such as *West Side Story*), and is home to one of the top children's theater operations in the United States, mounting productions such as *The Little Mermaid.*

The **Jubilee Theatre,** 506 Main St. (www.jubileetheatre.org; ✆ **817/338-4411**), stages intimate African-American theater, such dramas as *Brother Mac* (adapted from Shakespeare's *Macbeth*) and *A Raisin in the Sun,* as well as musicals such as *The Beehive.*

The **Rose Marine Theater,** 1440 Main St. (www.artesdelarosa.org; ✆ **817/624-8333**), a movie theater dating from the 1920s just south of the Stockyards, has been restored and converted by the Latin Arts Association; here, you'll find plays in Spanish, Latin films, and other arts targeting the Latino population.

A DAY (OR TWO) IN grapevine

One of the oldest settlements in north Texas, Grapevine—north of DFW Airport, about 25 miles from Fort Worth—is known for its handsomely restored historic Main Street, wineries, and art galleries housed in turn-of-the-20th-century buildings. Among the 75 restored buildings in the historic downtown district, check out the 1845 **Torian Log Cabin,** Liberty Park, 201 S. Main St., and the circa-1888 **Cotton Belt Railroad Depot,** ticketing site for a ride on the **Grapevine Vintage Railroad,** a restored Victorian-era train offering rides along the historic Cotton Belt Route (tickets: ✆ **817/410-3185**). In fact, you can travel roundtrip between the old Stockyards in Fort Worth to Grapevine via these vintage locomotives.

Sample Texan wines on a Grapevine **wine tour.** Wineries offering tours and tastings include **Umbra Winery** (www.umbrawinery.com; ✆ **817/421-2999**), **Sloan & Williams Winery** (www.sloanwilliams.com; ✆ **817/527-7867**), and **Homestead Winery at Grapevine** (www.homesteadwinery.com; ✆ **817/251-9643**).

The area has some fabulous family-friendly hotel resorts, including the **Great Wolf Lodge** hotel and waterpark (www.greatwolf.com/grapevine; ✆ **800/693-9653**) and Marriott's enormous **Gaylord Texan Resort & Convention Center** (www.marriott.com/hotels/travel/dalgt-gaylord-texan-resort-and-convention-center; ✆ **817/778-1000**).

The **Grapevine Visitor Information Center** is located at 701 S. Main St. (www.grapevinetexasusa.com; ✆ **800/457-6338**). If you're driving, take Hwy. 114 NW from Dallas or Hwy. 121 NE from Fort Worth.

For film, probably the best place to catch a current mainstream movie is **Movie Tavern at West 7th Street,** 2872 Crockett St. (✆ **682/503-8101**), where you can also have a movie-themed cocktail (Fantastic Beasts Butter Brew, anyone?) and some cinema grub while you watch.

The Bar Scene

The oldest bar in Fort Worth and the site of the city's most famous gunfight in 1897, **White Elephant Saloon** ★, 106 E. Exchange Ave. (✆ **817/624-1887**), is an authentic Cowtown saloon, a great place to knock back a Lone Star longneck in the afternoon or check out some live Western music nightly on the small stage. The atmospheric bar is decorated with donated hats (from the likes of Ray Wylie Hubbard and Jimmie Dale Gilmore) and cases of porcelain and ceramic white elephants. There's also a nice beer garden, with live bands under the trees. **Booger Red's Saloon,** 109 E. Exchange Ave. (✆ **817/625-6427**), the bar in the Stockyards Hotel, has horse-saddle bar stools and makes a great place to start off the evening with a couple of beers.

On Sundance Square, **Flying Saucer Draught Emporium** ★★, 111 E. 4th St. (www.beerknurd.com/stores/fortworth; ✆ **817/336-7470**), is a beer snob's dream, boasting 80 beers on tap and more than 200 bottles, including a slew of American microbrews and exotics such as Belgian *guerze* and German seasonals. This place has been a local favorite (and favorite of mine) for decades, and it never seems to change except for the better. (My friends held their wedding reception here nearly 2 decades ago.) For the novice or anyone looking for something new, you can sample beer "flights" from around the world. With an outdoor patio and rooftop terrace, the place can get rowdy on weekends with cigar-smoking types and TCU students, but it's still one of the best places in Fort Worth to wet your whistle. Food tends toward such beer-complementary items as bratwurst. It also features an eclectic roster of live music Friday through Sunday.

A swank bar, a good happy hour, and live music in warm months, **8.0,** 111 E. 3rd St. (www.eightobar.com; ✆ **817/336-0880**), on Sundance Square, is frequented by Fort Worth's young and beautiful.

Remaining true to its grungy roots, despite the slick West 7th Street high-rise development going up literally all around it, **Fred's Texas Café ★★**, 915 Currie St. (www.fredstexascafe.com; ✆ **817/332-0083**), remains a classic. Its outdoor covered patio is a great place for a cold beer (and a great Diablo Burger) as well as live bands every night of the week. It's vintage Fort Worth, with—my apologies to locals—a dose of "Keep Austin Weird" thrown in. Part of the burgeoning restaurant-and-bar scene on Magnolia Avenue, in the Fairmont District, the **Usual,** 1408 W. Magnolia Ave. (✆ **817/810-0114**), is a sleekly modern, smoke-free, minimalist space with a midcentury vibe and excellent (if pricey) Prohibition-era cocktails; happy hour is 4 to 7pm daily and all night Sundays and Mondays.

Honky-Tonk Heaven

The one place that's practically a required stop in Fort Worth is **Billy Bob's Texas ★★★**, 2520 Rodeo Plaza (www.billybobstexas.com; ✆ **817/624-7117**). A barn for prize cattle in a former life, this cavernous honky-tonk (according to the proprietors, the world's largest) is a symbol of Texas for many and pretty much a Western theme park. With 26 bar stations, a monster dance floor for hardcore boot-scootin', a rodeo arena, video games, pool tables, and pro bull riding, it's 127,000 square feet (or 7 acres) of honky-tonk heaven. Open more than 35 years now, Billy Bob's continues to draw the biggest names in country music, including LeAnn Rimes, Willie Nelson, and Jerry Jeff Walker. Its fame is such that you'll see real ropers in their best hats and tight jeans, along with drugstore cowboys and a lot of German and Japanese tourists, all soakin' up the flavor. Don't miss the pro live bull riding on Friday and Saturday at 9 and 10pm. Located in the heart of the Stockyards, Billy Bob's does business Monday through Saturday 11am to 2am and Sunday noon to 2am. (***Note:*** It closes from 5 to 6pm on Fri and Sat.) The cover charge varies according to the musical act (general admission $12–$20; reserved seats $20–$80, depending on the performer's popularity). General admission is $2 all day and night on Sunday, Monday, and Tuesday, 'til 7pm on Wednesday and Thursday (after which it's $5, except for special shows/events), and before 5pm on Friday and Saturday; Friday- and Saturday-night pricing varies. Free line-dance lessons are also offered every Thursday night at 7pm.

Another time-tested, Texas-size honky-tonk is the family-owned and -operated **Stagecoach Ballroom ★**, 2516 E. Belknap St. at the corner of Sylvania

Everybody Get in Line

If you want to learn to line dance, do the Cotton-Eyed-Joe, Schottische, and two-step like a Texan, why not do it in one of the most famous honky-tonks in the world, **Billy Bob's Texas**? Wendell Nelson, who's been at Billy Bob's for 2 decades, is the dance man who will lead you through the basics in free line-dance lessons on Thursdays at 7pm. Call ✆ **817/624-7117** for more information. For a more intimate experience, waltz and swing classes are also offered every Wednesday at 6:30pm at **Pearl's Dancehall & Saloon** (✆ **817/624-2800**). At the **Stagecoach Ballroom** (✆ **817/831-2261**), dance lessons are offered from 2:15pm to 4pm.

Ave., off Airport Freeway (www.stagecoachballroom.com; ✆ **817/831-2261**), a real contender for most authentic old-time dance hall in Texas. It offers traditional country music and dance, and is a good spot to pick up some moves if you're not exactly a smooth-footed kicker. It's open Friday from 6pm to midnight, Saturday 7pm to 2am and Sunday 2 to 10pm (dance lessons 2–4pm). General admission is $7 to $8 with additional fees for live music and special shows/events.

I'll always lament the demise of the poetically named **Big Balls of Cowtown,** once a bordello called Pearl's Hotel and later a Western dance hall. However, the space is now inhabited by **Pearl's Dancehall & Saloon ★**, 302 W. Exchange Ave. (www.pearlsdancehall.com; ✆ **817/624-2800**), featuring live traditional, Western swing and honky-tonk music Wednesday to Saturday. Although it's a bit spiffier in its new incarnation, it's still the coolest spot in the Stockyards for non-touristy country music (like Doug Rose and the Last Chance Band) and dancing. Free dance lessons are given on Sunday from 2:15 to 4pm.

Also in the Stockyards District, there's often live country music (and other contemporary music, too) at **Rodeo Exchange,** 221 W. Exchange Ave. (✆ **817/626-0181**), and **Chief Records,** 140 E. Exchange Ave., Suite 135 (✆ **817/624-8449**), the latter only Friday, Saturday, and Sunday.

Other Live Music

Sadly, Fort Worth's legendary jazz venue **Caravan of Dreams** bit the dust more than 15 years ago, and locals still mourn its closing. While nothing has sprung up that could quite fill its big shoes, Fort Worth has a few other jazz clubs, including **Scat Jazz Lounge ★★**, 111 West 4th, Suite 11 (✆ **817-870-9100**), set in the basement of the historic Woolworth building at Sundance Square. Dark and swank, this is a grown-ups only, NY–style jazz club with a great live menu of jazz and blues.

The top rock venue in town is the **Ridglea Theater ★**, 6025 Camp Bowie Blvd. (www.ridgleatheater.net; ✆ **817/738-9500**), a restored 1940s Art Deco theater that plays host to touring alternative rock and (mostly) metal bands. The **Aardvark ★**, 2905 W. Berry St. (www.the-aardvark.com; ✆ **817/926-7814**), is a cool small space that hosts a wide-ranging roster of pop, alternative rock, and neo-folk acts, such as Son Volt and the Gourds, with small cover charges Tuesday through Saturday. For good local and regional acts of mostly indie rock and alt-country, including Texas stalwarts such as Junior Brown and Heartless Bastards, **Lola's Saloon ★★**, 2736 W. 6th St. (www.lolassaloon.com; © **817/877-0666**), is an intimate venue with three bars (including two nice outdoor patios) and daily happy hours.

A sister of the clubs of the same name in Austin and Dallas, **Pete's Dueling Piano Bar,** 621 Houston St. (www.petesduelingpianobar.com; © **817/335-7383**), has shows Wednesday through Saturday at 7pm, when four expert pianists play pop and rock standards and encourage loud audience singalongs. Calling Pete's a "piano bar" probably doesn't do it justice; you won't hear Rachmaninoff, but you will hear Billy Joel's "Piano Man," and maybe even some Johnny Cash.

Rodeo

The **Stockyards Championship Rodeo** is held most weekends on Friday and Saturday nights at Cowtown Coliseum in the Stockyards, 121 E. Exchange Ave. (www.stockyardsrodeo.com; © **817/888-269-8696**). Tickets are $24 in reserved box seats. **Pawnee Bill's Wild West Show** (www.stockyardsrodeo.com/pawnee-bills-wild-west-show) runs during summer months and holiday weekends.

HOUSTON & EAST TEXAS

6

Many visitors, imagining the Texas landscape as it is usually drawn—barren and treeless—are surprised by the verdant environs around Houston. Set on a flat, nearly featureless Gulf Coast plain, the city is green thanks to a location at the tail end of a large belt of natural forest, and a climate much the same as in coastal Louisiana and Mississippi: warm and humid, with ample rainfall. Yes, Houston sprawls out from its center in vast tracts of subdivisions, freeways, office parks, and shopping malls. Yet in undisturbed areas, you'll find marshy grasslands (in the south) and woods (in the north). Meandering across this plain are bayous on whose banks cypress and Southern magnolia trees grow.

It's the fourth-most-populated city in the United States, but if we compare the populations of greater metro areas rather than cities, then Houston ranks only 10th. Yet in geographical expanse, Houston ranks second. The city is more than half as large as the state of Rhode Island and continues to expand outward. In the past several years, however, there has been a shift in residential construction toward downtown and the inner city.

Houston is not your typical tourist destination; most visitors come for business or family reasons and are lured into playing tourist only after arriving. It's a business town, and the oil and gas industry remains the big enchilada, but other sectors have added so much to the local economy that the contribution of oil and gas is now only about 50%. The Texas Medical Center is the largest concentration of medical institutions in the world. It's virtually a city within a city, with 21 hospitals and many clinics, medical schools, and research facilities. Construction and engineering companies also contribute much to the economy, and the newest big player is high-tech.

Houston's society is socially and economically wide open. Houstonians inherently dislike being told what to do, and this dislike cuts across the political spectrum: Opinion surveys show that gun control is highly unpopular, but so is government control over reproductive rights. Among urban planners, Houston is famous (or infamous) as the only major U.S. city that doesn't have zoning, allowing the market to determine land use instead. On the plus side, this love for individual freedoms gives Houston a dynamism that is palpable and has drawn a flood of newcomers from around the world, who have found here a welcoming city. Houston seems to be growing more cosmopolitan every day, as ethnic restaurants and specialty shops spring up throughout the city along with exotic temples and churches—Taoist, Buddhist, Hindu, Islamic, Russian Orthodox—built much as they would be back in the mother country.

On the minus side, this is the land of Enron, the go-go company that preached the gospel of deregulation to state and federal governments and then abused its new freedoms. Also, Houston struggles with an air-pollution problem that has the local government painfully considering unpopular regulations to keep the city in compliance with the Clean Air Act.

In the field of the arts, one can find proof of the city's vigor. Houston has an excellent symphony orchestra, highly respected ballet and opera companies, and an energetic theater scene that few cities can equal in quantity or quality. It has some excellent museums, too, and, if art isn't your bag, there's the world-famous NASA Space Center, which is like nothing else on this planet.

Not only is Houston Texas's largest city; it's still growing. The city's already-sprawling Convention District is undergoing $1.5 billion in renovations and new development, including a new 1,000-room Marriott Marquis and street-level retail space in the GRB that was completed in time for the 2017 Super Bowl, held here at the NRG Stadium. Another seven hotels are under construction or in planning stages across Downtown, so even the hotels we've recommended below are not the newest ones on the block. Still, we selected our favorites in locations around town where the best attractions are.

While you're enjoying those attractions, keep your eyes open and you can appreciate another thing for which Houston is known: its architecture, which stands out for its bold, brash character. This is, after all, home to the nation's first dome stadium—the Astrodome—billed at the time as "the eighth wonder of the world." Several buildings are striking for their dramatic appearance as well as for their irreverence—one skyscraper is crowned with a Mayan pyramid; another wryly samples Gothic flourishes for a bank building, and a pair of towers in the Medical Center unmistakably represent two giant syringes. There is little that is staid about this city, and the more time you spend here, the more you appreciate this fact.

ORIENTATION

Arriving

BY PLANE

Houston has two major airports: the **George Bush Intercontinental Airport (IAH),** 22 miles north of downtown, and the smaller **William P. Hobby Airport (HOU),** 9 miles southeast of downtown. Both shuttle companies listed below offer service between the airports.

George Bush Intercontinental Airport (IAH)

Houston's primary airport (www.fly2houston.com) functions as a hub for Continental Airlines, though it's serviced by all major national and international carriers. The airport has all the facilities of major international airports, including ATMs and currency exchange desks.

GETTING TO & FROM THE AIRPORT Taxi service from IAH to downtown costs $55 to $70 and the ride takes about 30 minutes; getting to the Galleria area costs a few dollars more. **Super Shuttle** (www.supershuttle.com; ✆ **800/258-3826**) ferries passengers to and from this airport to almost all hotels. Prices vary according to the hotel's location. A ride to or from downtown costs $25 per person, but it's only $8 more for each person traveling on the same reservation. A ride to/from the Galleria area costs $30 per person, but only $8 more for each person traveling on the same reservation. Shuttle ticket counters are at all airport terminals. **Houston Metro** (www.ridemetro.org; ✆ **713/739-6968**), Houston's mass transit system, has begun running nonstop buses between downtown and the airport's Terminal C. In the baggage claim area, you'll find a ticket counter labeled "Metro Airport Direct." The fare is $1.25. Buses run every 30 minutes from 5am to 8pm. They drop off (and pick up) passengers downtown at 815 Pierce St., across the street from the Metro Transit Center. Exact change is required, but dollar bills are accepted. Travel time to downtown is 1 hour, or a little longer during rush hour.

The major car-rental companies have counters at each terminal. John F. Kennedy Boulevard is the main artery into and out of the airport. When leaving the airport, you'll see signs pointing toward either the North Freeway (I-45) or the Eastex Freeway (Tex. 59). Both take you downtown, but the Eastex is shorter and usually quicker.

William P. Hobby Airport (HOU)

Hobby Airport (www.fly2houston.com) is served by American Airlines, Delta, JetBlue, and Southwest. All major car-rental agencies have counters here with either staff or a service phone. Taxis from Hobby to the downtown area cost about $30 to $35, and to the Galleria area, $40. Taxis from Hobby to IAH cost about $70 and taxis from Hobby to the Galveston Cruise Terminal cost about $97 and about $160 from IAH to the Galveston Cruise Terminal. For airport shuttle service, see above.

BY CAR

Houston is connected to Dallas and Fort Worth by I-45, and to San Antonio, New Orleans, and Beaumont by I-10. From Austin, you can take either Tex. 71 through Bastrop to Columbus, where it joins I-10, or Tex. 290 east through Brenham.

BY TRAIN

Amtrak (www.amtrak.com; ✆ **800/872-7245**) trains from New Orleans, Chicago, and Los Angeles (and points in between) arrive and depart from the **Southern Pacific Station** at 902 Washington Ave. (✆ **713/224-1577**), close to downtown.

But It's a Wet Heat

Hot and humid, Houston has earned the unofficial title of "Air-Conditioning Capital of the World." If you're unaccustomed to high humidity and its consequences (profuse sweating, bad-hair days), you might want to take it easy at first and work on acquiring some degree of philosophical acceptance. One more thing: Bopping around Houston in summertime means jumping from the frying pan into the freezer. You'll be repeatedly going from steamy outdoors into superchilled shops, restaurants, and so on. The natives are used to it, but many visitors complain—to deaf ears, I might add. Best advice? Bring a light sweater. You'll need one inside most restaurants, theaters, malls, and museums in summer. Some like it hot, but most Houstonites like it really cold indoors.

Visitor Information

The **Greater Houston Convention and Visitors Bureau (GHCVB)** (www.visithoustontexas.com; ✆ **800/466-8786** or 713/437-5556) has an official Houston Visitors Center in a street-level retail space on the east side of the Hilton Americas-Houston facing the Convention Center, 1300 Avenida de las Americas. It offers brochures, a range of city maps, architectural and historical guides, and travel recommendations from the center's staff. Pick up a copy of the *Official Guide to Houston* magazine; it has a helpful calendar of events. The center is open daily from 7am to 10pm. There are a few designated parking spots for visitors; these are free and have a 1-hour limit.

Other websites you might find helpful are operated by the local newspapers. The *Houston Chronicle* (**www.chron.com**) is the daily newspaper, and the *Houston Press* (**www.houstonpress.com**) is the free weekly tabloid that has a large entertainment section.

City Layout

Houston is a difficult city in which to find your way around; it was built with no master plan, and most of its streets are jumbled together with little continuity. The suburban areas look alike and have indistinctive street names, usually ending in "crest," "wood," and "dale." To make matters worse, the terrain is so flat that the only visible points of reference are tall buildings. However, for the visitor, things aren't so bad. Most of the main attractions are not far off the freeways or other main arteries. With a basic knowledge of these, you can keep your bearings and get from one place to another.

To understand the layout of Houston's freeways, it's best to picture a spider web with several lines radiating out from the center, which are connected to each other by two concentric circles. The lines that radiate outward are in the following clockwise order: At 1 o'clock is the Eastex Freeway (Tex. 59 north), which usually has signs saying CLEVELAND, a town in east Texas; at 3 o'clock is the East Freeway (I-10 E. to Beaumont and New Orleans); between 4 and 5 o'clock is the Gulf Freeway (I-45 S. to Galveston); at 6 o'clock is the South Freeway (Tex. 228 to Lake Jackson, Freeport, and Surfside); between 7 and 8 o'clock is the Southwest Freeway (Tex. 59 to Laredo; look for signs that read VICTORIA); at 9 o'clock is the Katy Freeway (I-10 W. to San Antonio); at 10 o'clock is the Northwest Freeway (Tex. 290 to Austin); and at 11 o'clock is the North Freeway (I-45 N. to Dallas). The first circular freeway is Loop 610 (known as "the Loop"), which has a 4- to 5-mile radius from downtown. The second is known alternately as Sam Houston Parkway or Beltway 8. It has a 10- to 15-mile radius and is mostly a toll road except for the section in the area of the Bush Intercontinental Airport.

In addition to the freeways, there are certain arteries that most newcomers would do well to know. Here are brief descriptions of each.

Main Street bisects downtown and then heads south-southwest, changing its name to South Main. It passes through the Museum District, then along Hermann Park and Rice University before reaching the Texas Medical Center. This stretch of South Main has lots of green space and is lined with oak trees. Beyond the Medical Center, the street passes by the NRG Stadium, an exhibition center, and the old Astrodome.

In the middle of the Museum District is a traffic circle called **Mecom Fountain,** where South Main intersects **Montrose Boulevard.** Montrose runs due north from the Mecom Fountain, crossing Westheimer Road and Buffalo Bayou. It gives its name to the Montrose area and is lined by several bistros around the Museum District. After it crosses the bayou, Montrose becomes Studemont and then Studewood when it enters a historic neighborhood known as the Heights.

Westheimer Road is the east-west axis around which most of western Houston turns. It begins in the Montrose area and continues for many miles through various urban and suburban landscapes without ever seeming to come to an end. Past the Montrose area, Westheimer crosses Kirby Drive and then passes by River Oaks, a neighborhood for Houston's rich folk. Farther along is Highland Village Shopping Center, then Loop 610, where it enters the popular commercial district known as the Galleria area or Uptown. Farther west, Westheimer passes an endless series of fast-food restaurants, strip malls, and chain retail stores as it runs through suburbia.

Kirby Drive is an important north-south artery. It intersects Westheimer Road by River Oaks and runs due south, skirting the Greenway Plaza and passing under the Southwest Freeway. Once south of the freeway, Kirby enters University Place, a neighborhood that curls around the western borders of the Rice University campus and is the favorite residential area for Houston's doctors, lawyers, and other professionals. Kirby eventually intersects South Main Street in the vicinity of NRG Stadium.

Neighborhoods in Brief

Downtown Once a ghost town in the evenings and on weekends, downtown Houston is now quite popular. Restaurants and bars are opening (and in some cases closing) in quick succession. Hotels have multiplied, too. In the northwest side of downtown are Old Market Square and the Theatre District, where Houston's symphony orchestra, ballet, opera, and principal theater company all reside. East of Main Street, within walking distance, is the George Brown Convention Center; the area around it which is exploding with new growth and lots of new hotels. Also east of Main Street you'll find the baseball park, Minute Maid Field (formerly Enron Field); and the Toyota Center basketball arena. Also fueling downtown's revitalization is a light rail that runs up and down Main Street and connects to the Museum District and the Medical Center. Beneath downtown is a network of pedestrian tunnels lined by shops and restaurants, forming an underground city. As is typical of Houston, almost all of these tunnels are private, not public, developments. South of downtown is **Midtown,** an area in transition, with town houses and shops gradually replacing vacant lots and small office buildings. Vietnamese shopkeepers and restaurateurs have settled into the western side, especially along Milam Street, where you can find an array of excellent Vietnamese restaurants with reasonable prices.

East End Before Houston was established on the banks of Buffalo Bayou, the town of Harrisburg already existed 2 miles downstream. As Houston grew eastward, it incorporated Harrisburg, leaving behind little of the old town. A small commercial Chinatown lies a couple of blocks east of the convention center; beyond that, the area is residential. The inner East End is an up-and-coming neighborhood of mixed ethnicity. As you move farther east, the residences mix with small-scale manufacturing, auto mechanic and body shops, and service industries for the ship channel. In the far southern part is NASA's Space Center Houston, Kemah (Houston's version of Fisherman's Wharf), and Galveston Island and its cruise terminal area. Most hotels located in this area are along the Gulf Freeway. The main reason for staying here is that hotel rates, for the most part, are economical, and the location between downtown, Hobby Airport, and the above-mentioned attractions makes the East End convenient.

South Main South of downtown and midtown is the **Museum District** and Hermann Park. This lovely part of town has lots of green space. Most of the museums are within a few blocks of one another. Here also are the Houston Zoological Gardens and the Rice University campus. On the south side of the park begins the Texas Medical Center. A bit farther south is a complex of buildings holding NRG Stadium, where the 2017 Superbowl was held, and the old Astrodome. This part of town has many hotels to suit all budgets. The location is convenient, and the city's light rail connects this area with downtown.

Montrose & the Heights Directly west of downtown is the Montrose area, a hip, artsy, and colorful part of town known for its clubs, galleries, and shops. The Museum District extends into this neighborhood to include the famous Menil Collection and its satellite galleries, a must-see for any visitor interested in the arts. Upscale in certain sections, downscale in others, the Montrose contains a broad cross-section of Houston society. It's also the de facto center of Houston's large and active gay community. North of the Montrose area, across Buffalo Bayou, is the Heights. It was conceived and built as an independent, planned residential community in the 1890s and remained so until 1918, when it was annexed by Houston. One curious fact about the Heights is that a 1904 original articles of incorporation requiring it to be "dry" (no sale of alcohol) remained on the books until 2016—when, in a victory for neighborhood groceries and markets, a referendum overturned the restrictions, allowing the off-premise sale of alcohol. The Heights offers great shopping, especially for antiques and folk art. With downtown to the east, the Museum District to the south, and Kirby to the west, the Montrose area and the Heights are well located.

Kirby District & Greenway Plaza The area bordering Kirby Drive from River Oaks to University Place has the most restaurants of any district in Houston. Near Kirby Drive's midway point, where it crosses the Southwest Freeway, is the Greenway Plaza, an integrated development of office buildings, movie theaters, shops, and a sports arena that has been made over into a well-known megachurch called Lakewood. Farther south is Rice Village, a retail development consisting of 16 square blocks of smart shops and restaurants. It is phenomenally popular with Houstonians and visitors and attracts all kinds of shoppers and diners.

Uptown ("Galleria") Farther west, all the way to Loop 610, is where Uptown begins. It is still informally called the **Galleria area,** after the large indoor shopping mall, entertainment, and hotel complex. But the district's business owners had to devise another name for it because the developer of the Galleria protected its name so jealously that it became problematic to use the word in any commercial context. Thus, we have "Uptown." Shops, restaurants, and other businesses front Westheimer Road and Post Oak Boulevard.

North Houston All the neighborhoods described above, except for the Heights, are south of I-10, which bisects Houston into northern and southern halves. North Houston is largely a mix of working- and middle-class neighborhoods and commercial centers and, with the exception of the Heights, has little to offer visitors. Over the years, developers tried to establish upscale communities here, but an inherent quality of suburbanism is that you can always build farther out, and with each successive subdivision, the inner suburbs lose a little more of their luster. Ultimately, the developers took this to its logical extreme, skipping over vast tracts of land to build so far north that the city will never touch them. Thus, Woodlands and Kingwood, two upscale residential developments, are so far out that one can't consider them part of Houston.

Getting Around

BY CAR

Houston is organized around the automobile. Having a car is almost a necessity unless you confine your explorations to the downtown area and the South Main corridor (including the Museum District), which are connected by the light rail. This makes it possible to stay in a downtown or South Main hotel and go up and down this corridor with ease. For trips to other parts of the city, you can use the hotel's shuttle, if available, or the occasional taxi.

Houston's freeways are no place for the meek: Many drivers don't obey speed limits, bob and weave through the lanes, and make their turnoffs at the last possible moment. You should have a clear idea of where you're headed and what exit you need to take before getting on a freeway. All this said, I actually enjoy driving Houston's freeways. It's a good way to grasp what it's like to be a Houstonian. My own practice is not to bother looking down at the speedometer; for all practical purposes, it's irrelevant. It's more important to stay in the flow of traffic at the same speed as most of the cars around you. As freeway systems go, Houston's is logical and has good directional signs. Traffic can be slow during rush hour or anywhere there's construction. You can use the **Texas Department of Transportation Info Hot Line** (✆ **713/802-5074**) to check for lane closures on local freeways. The *Houston Chronicle* provides this information, too, as well as info on street closures. Don't be surprised to encounter construction during your visit.

RENTALS The prices for rental cars in Houston are lower than those for many tourist destinations, but tacked onto the final cost are several taxes that raise the price by as much as 27%. Keep this in mind when the salesperson tries to upgrade you to a higher-priced model. As is the case when renting cars elsewhere, you probably don't need to buy extra insurance if you're already covered by personal auto insurance. The major car-rental companies with locations around the city include **Alamo** (www.alamo.com; ✆ 844/354-6962), **Avis** (www.avis.com; ✆ 800/633-3469), **Budget** (www.budget.com; ✆ 800/218-7992), **Dollar** (www.dollar.com; ✆ 800/800-4000), **Enterprise** (www.enterprise.com; ✆ 855/266-9289), **Hertz** (www.hertz.com; ✆ 800/654-3131), **National** (www.nationalcar.com; ✆ 800/367-6767), and **Thrifty** (www.thrifty.com; ✆ 800/344-1705).

BY PUBLIC TRANSPORTATION

LIGHT RAIL The **Metropolitan Transportation Authority (Metro)** (www.ridemetro.org; ✆ **713/635-4000**) inaugurated its first light rail line in 2004. So far, it's been a big success with locals and is quite helpful for visitors, as it ties together some of the main areas of interest—downtown, the Museum District, the Medical Center, and NRG Stadium. Train tickets cost $1.25 and are valid as bus transfers if the ticket holder is not traveling in the return direction. Train tickets can be purchased at each station from vending machines that accept cash, debit cards, and credit cards. The other option is to buy a "Q fare card" for multiple trips and load it with as much money as you think you'll need. The trains run as frequently as every 6 minutes and in slow times are not more than 20 minutes apart.

Note: In the past few years, there have been collisions involving the light rail train and private vehicles. The train usually wins. Almost all of these accidents occurred because the drivers of the cars were distracted. Pay attention to directional signs and signals when crossing the rail line. There are a few confusing intersections: at the end of the line, where Main Street reaches Buffalo Bayou, in the Medical Center, and where the tracks shift from Main Street to San Jacinto. Otherwise, it's all straightforward.

BUS SERVICE The citywide bus service operated by Metro can get you to most places in the city. To find out what bus to catch and where and when to catch it, your best option is to call the customer service number listed above. The staff can tell you over the phone how to get from point A to point B. If you're planning in advance, you can use the website and click on "Plan Your Trip." Once you know the bus routes you're going to use, you can download schedules from the same website. The standard bus fare is $1.25 for travel inside Loop 610 (seniors pay 60¢ and children 3 and under ride free); exact change is required, and the machines accept dollar bills. If needed, ask for a transfer, which will be good for 3 hours for other buses or the train.

Greenlink buses offer free transportation downtown on three routes (Green, Orange, Silver) with stops at the district's main attractions including the convention center, Discovery Green, and Main Street Square; get the details at www.downtownhouston.org/getting-around.

BY TAXI

Taxis are plentiful in the city, and the number of taxi stands downtown has increased in recent years. In addition, the City of Houston has authorized a **flat $6 fee** for rides anywhere downtown within the Central Business District bounded by I-45, I-10, and U.S. 59.

The principal taxi companies are **Yellow Cab** (✆ 713/236-1111), **Fiesta Cab** (✆ 713/225-2666), **Lonestar Cab** (✆ 713/444-4444), and **United Cab** (✆ 713/699-0000). Rates are set by the city: $2.80 for the first mile and $2.40 for each additional mile, plus a fuel charge, depending on the current price of gas.

Uber and **Lyft** ride-share companies currently serve Houston, as does **ZipCar.**

BY BICYCLE

Houston now has its own public bikeshare program, **Houston BCycle (B-Cycle),** with bikes available throughout the city at B-stations. Get the details, plus B-station locations and bike routes at **https://houston.bcycle.com**. Purchase passes at B-stations for unlimited 60-minute rides ($2 for each additional half-hour). Passes cost $5 (24-hr.), $15 (7 days), and $65 (1 year).

[FastFACTS] HOUSTON

Dentists For a referral, call ✆ **800/922-6588.**

Doctors For minor emergencies or to see a doctor without an appointment, call **Texas Urgent Care** at ✆ **281/477-7490.**

Drugstores **Walgreens,** 3317 Montrose Blvd., at Hawthorne Street (✆ **713/520-7777**), is open 24 hours a day. In the vicinity of the Medical Center, there is a 24-hour **CVS Pharmacy** at 7900 S. Main St. (✆ **713/660-8934**).

Hospitals The **Ben Taub General Hospital,** 1502 Taub Loop, at the Texas Medical Center (✆ **713/873-2000**), has a fully equipped emergency room.

Internet Access If you're not traveling with a computer and your hotel doesn't have a business center, Houston's main library and all its branches have computers for public use; go to **www.houstonlibrary.org** to find locations. Faster connections can be had for a price at **Copy.com**, 1201-F Westheimer Rd., in the Montrose area (www.copydotcom.com; ✆ **713/528-1201**); it has several computers and is open from 7am to midnight on weekdays, 11am to 7pm on Saturdays, and noon to 9pm Sundays. If you have a computer, check out the usual Internet haunts—coffee bars and hotel lobbies.

Maps You can buy standard street maps at many convenience stores, and you'll find some helpful maps of downtown, the Museum District, and other parts of the city at the GHCVB Visitor Center. Today, most travelers rely on smartphones and apps for maps and driving directions.

Newspapers & Magazines The local daily is the *Houston Chronicle*. The *Houston Press*, a free weekly that covers local politics and culture, can be found around town at restaurants, stores, and just about anywhere people congregate.

Police Dial ✆ **911** in an emergency; for non-emergencies, dial ✆ **311.**

Post Office The downtown branch, 700 Smith St. (✆ **713/223-1625**), is open Monday to Friday 10am to 1:30pm and 2:30 to 4pm; closed Saturday and Sunday.

Safety Houston is a safe town for visitors. Exercise caution at night in the downtown areas that lie outside the theater district.

Taxes The local hotel tax is 17%, while the local sales tax is 8.25%.

Transit Information The Texas Dept. of Transportation's hotline is ✆ **713/802-5074.**

WHAT TO SEE & DO

Because Houston isn't a major tourist destination, there isn't much in the way of tourism infrastructure except for the downtown visitor center. Most of the available resources are geared toward conventions and large groups, not independent travelers. From the visitor center, there is often a visitors' tour of downtown that looks at architecture, public sculpture, the tunnel system, and the view from the observation deck of the JPMorgan Chase Tower, the tallest building in Houston.

The Top Attractions

DOWNTOWN

Downtown Aquarium ★ Is it a restaurant, an aquarium, or a kiddie amusement park? Well, it's all that, a 6-acre complex with both indoor and outdoor attractions. The aquarium itself is on the small side, but it's a nice distraction for families and perfect for smaller kids, with a touch tank of velvety stingrays and a range of fun exhibits, like the Louisiana Swampland, a 17th-century Spanish galleon shipwreck, a sunken temple, and rainforest. A ride aboard a miniature train through a glass tunnel in a large shark tank never fails to thrill. Upstairs in the **Aquarium** seafood restaurant, you're surrounded by a 150,000-gallon aquarium teeming with colorful marine life while you dine on their less fortunate brethren. Outside, in a kiddie park, take a spin on one of the old-fashioned rides, like a 100-foot Ferris wheel or the Aquatic Carousel, with dolphins and whales and other sea critters.

410 Bagby St. www.aquariumrestaurants.com/downtownaquariumhouston. ✆ **713/223-3474.** Admission $12 adults; $10 seniors; $9 children 2–12. Shark voyage $6. Mon–Thurs 10am–9pm; Fri–Sat 10am–10:30pm; Sun 10am–9pm.

Downtown Tunnel System ★ It's cool to discover that Houston has an underground, 6 miles of tunnels 20 feet below the streets of downtown connecting 95 city blocks with movie theaters, restaurants, shops, and businesses. You can access the tunnels through two main entry points—at the Wells Fargo Plaza and McKinney Garage on Main—or via stairs, escalators, or elevators in the businesses themselves. Get a map of the tunnels from Houston's visitor centers—a good thing to have, because it's easy to get turned around if you aren't familiar with the downtown area.

Accessible from the visitor center in city hall and all neighboring buildings, as well as most downtown hotels. Free admission. Mon–Fri 6am–6:30pm.

Heritage Society at Sam Houston Park ★ Practically the entire colonized history of Texas is on display here in this serene, leafy park in the shadow of Houston's downtown skyscrapers. Ten of Houston's oldest houses and buildings were moved here from their original locations (except for the Kellum-Noble House, which stands on its original foundations). A cedar log cabin dating from 1823 was moved from Clear Creek to here. The 1847 Kellum-Noble House is the city's oldest surviving building, and a handsome circa-1870 home was built by emancipated slave and minister John Henry Yates. A Lutheran church dates from 1890, and a darling 1893 playhouse has classical columns. All have been restored by the city's Heritage Society and furnished with pieces from the appropriate eras. The only way to see these buildings is by guided tour, which leaves every hour on the hour from the tour office at 1100 Bagby St.; tours take about 45 minutes. The guides are well informed and add a lot to a visit here. You can do a cellphone tour, but you won't get answers to the questions inspired by seeing these houses. The Heritage Museum can be visited without taking the tour; it's free and features permanent exhibits on Texas history. It's just a couple of blocks from Houston's visitor center

1100 Bagby St. ✆ **713/655-1912.** www.heritagesociety.org. Tours $15 adults, $12 seniors, $6 students; free for children 5 and under. Tues–Sat 10am–4pm; Sun 1–4pm. Closed major holidays.

EAST END & BEYOND

Battleship *Texas* and San Jacinto Monument & Museum ★ This site is a historical two-fer: the San Jacinto Battleground and the Battleship Texas. In 1836, Texas won its independence from Mexico on the San Jacinto Battleground in a crushing surprise attack, spurred on by cries of "Remember the Alamo!" One of the most significant battles in American history lasted all of 18 minutes. An obelisk, dedicated in 1936 on the 100th anniversary of the victory, soars 537 feet high, 12 feet taller than the Washington monument—that's Texas pride for you. It's topped, of course, with a Texas Lone Star. You can visit the small museum of Texas history and catch a 35-minute documentary of the battle. Even better: Take the elevator up to the top floor of the tower, and admire the Houston Ship Channel and sweeping views beyond.

Bordering the battlefield and anchored on Buffalo Bayou, the **USS *Texas*** is the last of its kind, the only remaining dreadnought battleship still afloat. The ship fought in both world wars and the Atlantic and the Pacific theaters. Take a guided tour or do your own self-guided tour to climb onto the navigation bridge, inspect the crew's quarters, and check out the engine room. The battleship celebrated its 100th anniversary in 2014.

3523 Battleground Rd. www.sanjacinto-museum.org. ✆ **281/479-2431.** Park admission $6 adults and children 12 and over; free for children 12 and under. Texas Forever! Interactive Experience $6 adults and children 12 and over, $5.50 seniors, free for children 11 and under; free admission to the monument and museum; observation room $6 adults, $5.50 seniors, $4.50 children; A Destined Conflict exhibition $6 adults, $5.50 seniors, $4 children. Daily 9am–6pm. Take the La Porte Fwy. (Tex. 225) east from Loop 610 E. Exit Battleground Rd. (Tex. 134) and turn left.

Houston Ship Channel ★ Take a fascinating 90-minute cruise amid a landscape of refineries and massive container ships in the Houston Ship Channel. These free public boat rides aboard the 1950s-era M/V *Sam Houston* tour the upper 7 miles of the deep-water channel. Reservations are required. The handsome boat, with a cabin trimmed in mahogany, seats 100 passengers, offering air-conditioned seating inside and outdoor deck viewing.

7300 Clinton Dr. at Gate 8. www.porthouston.com. ✆ **713/670-2416.** See website for security regulations, including the prohibition of cameras. Call or visit website to make reservations, which are required. Free admission. Wed and Fri–Sat 10am and 2:30pm; Thurs 10am; Sun 2:30pm. Limited 6pm Fri and Sat tours. Closed Sept and holidays. Take the Gulf Fwy. S.; get on Loop 610 E., which takes you over the ship channel; exit Clinton Dr. Turn right on Clinton (look for small green signs pointing the way); after a mile, you'll come to a traffic light and a sign reading PORT GATE 8. Turn left.

Kemah Boardwalk ★ A waterfront boardwalk, seafood and hot dogs, old-time arcades and amusement-park rides (including a wooden boardwalk): It doesn't get more family-friendly than this. If you're like many visitors to Space Center Houston (see review below) you'll head for dinner afterward to nearby Kemah. This shrimping port on Galveston Bay now has a crowd-pleasing boardwalk complex with restaurants, arcade games and amusement rides, carnival food (funnel cakes, cotton candy), a hotel, and T-shirt and souvenir shops. It's corny, it's touristy, but the sea breezes and the bay views, with shrimp boats skimming the blue horizon, can tame the most ornery curmudgeons.

215 Kipp Ave, Kemah. www.kemahboardwalk.com. ✆ **877/285-3624.**

The Orange Show ★★ In a nondescript, somewhat down-on-its-heels neighborhood, you'll find this extraordinary display of outsider art, the work of a single man, a Houston postal worker named Jeff McKissack. Wishing to extol the health benefits of his favorite fruit—and hard work—McKissack labored for 25 years, constructing an elaborate, rambling, whimsical structure out of materials and objects (wagon wheels, tiles, flagpoles, tractor seats) that he scrapped from junkyards and abandoned buildings. Academics might refer to the creation as a "folk art environment" or a "self-made world," like the Watts Towers in Los Angeles, but for McKissack it was a way of life and a gift that he wanted to share with the entire world. When he died in 1980, the colorful 3,000-square-foot complex languished until a group of local art patrons, including members of ZZ Top, started a foundation to preserve the Orange Show and promote like-minded endeavors. Today the foundation also hosts tours of the **Beer Can House,** spearheads the wildly popular Art Car Parade, and is currently working on Smither Park, a family-friendly, folk-art-inspired park and playground on the half-acre next to the Orange Show.

2401 Munger St. www.orangeshow.org. ✆ **713/926-6368.** Admission $5 adults, free for children 12 and under. Summer Wed–Sun noon–5pm; spring and fall Sat–Sun noon–5pm. From downtown, take Gulf Fwy. Exit Telephone Rd. and make the 3rd right off the feeder road onto Munger (before you get to the Telephone Rd. intersection).

Space Center Houston ★★★ Space Center Houston is the visitor center for NASA's Johnson Space Center, the product of the joint efforts of NASA and Disney Imagineering. Easily the most popular attraction in the Houston area, there's nothing like it anywhere else in the world. You'll find plenty of exhibits and activities to interest both adults and children, and they do a great job of introducing the visitor to different aspects of space exploration. The center banks heavily on interactive displays and simulations on the one hand and actual access to the real thing on the other. For instance, the Feel of Space gallery simulates working in the frictionless environment of space by using an air-bearing floor (something like a giant air-hockey table). Another simulator shows what it's like to land the lunar orbiter. For a direct experience of NASA, a 1½-hour **tram tour** takes you to, among other places, the International Space Station Assembly Building and NASA control center. You get to see things as they happen, especially interesting if a shuttle mission is in progress. You might also see astronauts in training. And, on top of all this, Space Center Houston has the largest IMAX in Texas. Plan on spending 3 to 4 hours here.

1601 NASA Rd. 1, Clear Lake. www.spacecenter.org. ✆ **281/244-2100.** Admission (including tours and IMAX theater) $30 adults, $28 seniors, $25 children 4–11. June–July daily 10am–7pm; Aug–May Mon–Fri 10am–5pm, Sat–Sun 10am–6pm. Closed Christmas. Take the Gulf Fwy. to NASA Rd. 1, turn left, and go 3 miles.

SOUTH MAIN/MUSEUM DISTRICT

Children's Museum of Houston ★★ This hugely popular children's destination hits the sweet spot between fun and learning, with tons of hands-on activities packed into a colorful, 90,000-square-foot facility designed by noted architect Robert Venturi. "Invention Convention" prompts kids to build all sorts of gizmos using magnets, gears, batteries, and Legos; they can even learn the building blocks of robotics. The "Dragons and Fairies" exhibit examines Vietnamese culture through five interactive fairy tales. "PowerPlay" challenges kids physically with a 40-foot climbing tower. For little ones younger than 3, "Tot*Spot" finds creative ways to encourage their emerging motor skills. Thursday nights are a big hit; from 5pm to 8pm, all families get in free. For beleaguered parents, this place is truly a godsend.

1500 Binz St. www.cmhouston.org. ✆ **713/522-1138.** Admission $12 adults and children, $11 seniors, free for children under 1; free family night Thurs 5–8pm. Tues–Sat 10am–6pm; Thurs 10am–8pm; Sun noon–6pm. Closed major holidays. On same street as Museum of Fine Arts, Houston (the street name changes from Bissonnet to Binz), 4 blocks to the east.

Contemporary Arts Museum ★ It's a stunner of a building, a stainless-steel Modernist parallelogram designed by Gunnar Birkerts and opened in 1972. The exterior remains static, while inside, the "non-collecting" museum is ever-changing, where the art on exhibit is constantly replaced and replenished with new exhibits and engaging thematic presentations. It's held many award-winning shows, such as "The Old, Weird America: Folk Themes in Contemporary Art" and "Cinema Remixed and Reloaded: Black Women Artists and the Moving Image since 1970." So although you never know what you might see here, you can count on it to be thoughtfully curated and most likely worth your while. And free.

5216 Montrose Blvd. www.camh.org. ✆ **713/284-8250.** Free admission. Tues–Wed 10am–7pm; Thurs 10am–9pm; Fri 10am–7pm; Sat 10am–6pm; Sun noon–6pm. Closed Thanksgiving, Dec 25, and Jan 1.

The Health Museum ★★ It's only fitting that the city of Houston, home to the Texas Medical Center (the world's largest medical complex), boasts this family-friendly, health-focused museum that illuminates the inner workings of the human body. The museum's standout exhibit, the **Amazing Body Pavilion,** is a grand-scale, hands-on environment where visitors can learn about the body's major organs; walking through the gigantic brain model will get you thinking. **You: The Exhibit** is all about humans, offering a body scanner, a Mirror of Hereditary, and an Age-O-Matic machine that offers users a glimpse of themselves 40 years into the future. (***Warning:*** It can be a bit sobering for some mortality-fearing adults.) The venue also features temporary exhibits, a 4D theater, and a gift shop with the kinds of toys that parents needn't feel guilty about buying for their kids.

1515 Hermann Dr. www.mhms.org. ✆ **713/521-1515.** $10 adults, $8 seniors, $8 children 3–12; free admission Thurs 2–5pm. Mon–Sat 9am–5pm (till 7pm Thurs), Sun noon–5pm.

Hermann Park ★ Houston's popular municipal park was born when real-estate mogul George Hermann deeded some 285 acres of land to the city in 1914. It's now grown to 545 acres, with a Japanese Garden (celebrating its 25th anniversary in 2017), an 18-hole golf course, the Houston Zoo, pedal-boat rentals for skimming 8-acre McGovern Lake, and the Hermann Park Train, a shiny red miniature train that takes visitors on a 2-mile tour of the park grounds ($3.50 per person). The park also has public artworks, a landscaped reflection pool and shimmering fountains, oak-lined walking paths, and playgrounds. Spread a picnic blanket on the sloping green lawn in front of the Miller Outdoor Theater for plays and musical performances. The park is located beyond the Museum District, on the east side of South Main Street.

Fannin St. at Hermann Park Dr. www.hermannpark.org. Open year-round.

Houston Museum of Natural Science ★★★ This diverse, crowd-pleasing museum has only gotten better in recent years. Among its permanent exhibits are the **Morian Hall of Paleontology**, featuring ancient skeletons, including a mummified Triceratops, posed mid-action; a dazzling array of gems and minerals; a state-of-the-art, interactive display on the production of energy (a big deal here in Houston); and an immersive, 10,000-square-foot space detailing ancient Egyptian culture. One of the museum's biggest draws is the **Cockrell Butterfly Center,** where visitors can stroll among the fluttering creatures in a simulated rainforest with a 50-foot waterfall. There's also the 394-seat **Wortham Giant Screen Theatre** with 4K digital projection and 3D capability, plus a planetarium with shows on black holes, asteroids, and

Pink Floyd's "Dark Side of the Moon." Temporary exhibitions may include a peek at an original edition of the Magna Carta, or a collection of objets d'art from the House of Fabergé. Located in the northwest corner of Hermann Park, the museum is about 3 blocks from the Museum of Fine Arts.

5555 Hermann Park Dr. www.hmns.org. ✆ **713/639-4629.** Museum $25 adults, $15 seniors and children 3–11 (free after 2pm Tues); Butterfly Center $9 adults, $8 seniors and children; IMAX tickets $12 adults, $10 seniors and children. Mon–Sun 9am–5pm; hours for Butterfly Center and IMAX may differ.

Houston Zoo ★★ Located in Hermann Park, this revitalized zoological park is on the small size but takes a big approach to conservation and wildlife protection. An infusion of monies in recent years through a public-private partnership has dramatically reversed its fortunes—and it's now the second-most visited zoo in the nation (after the vaunted San Diego Zoo) and the city's most popular attraction, recording some 2.55 million visitors in 2016. Set on 55 acres of landscaped grounds shaded by a canopy of live oaks along flower-filled walkways, the zoo holds a remarkable cross section of animals, from lions and giraffes to a primate exhibit and African wild dogs. The dedicated staff includes a vet clinic that has treated and released some 400 sick and wounded sea turtles back into Galveston Bay.

6200 Herman Park Dr. www.houstonzoo.org. ✆ **713/533-6500.** Admission $17 adults 12–64, $13 children 2–11, $11 seniors. Open daily 9am–5pm.

Museum of Fine Arts, Houston (MFAH) ★★★ This is the big daddy of Houston's art scene. With 65,000 pieces spanning ancient times to the present, these collections cover a lot of ground and include antiquities from Rome, Greece, and Egypt; gold objects from African royal courts; bronze vessels from 11th-century China; American landscapes from the 19th century; and European paintings, including Renaissance, Impressionist and post-Impressionist works. The modern and contemporary holdings are particularly popular, with works by Picasso, Matisse, and Pollock. One of the most striking displays is James Turrell's *The Light Inside,* a mesmerizing tunnel of light that connects the museum's two main buildings. A film department screens a diverse lineup of hard-to-find or overlooked movies. There's also a serene sculpture garden designed by sculptor Isamu Noguchi, which integrates concrete walls with natural elements and contains works by Rodin, Calder, and Ellsworth Kelly. The MFAH has two outposts, **Bayou Bend** and **Rienzi,** River Oaks mansions that showcase American and European decorative arts, respectively (see separate reviews, below).

1001 Bissonnet St. www.mfah.org. ✆ **713/639-7300.** Admission $15 adults, $10 seniors, $7.50 children 13–18, free for children 12 and younger; free for all Thurs. Tues–Wed 10am–5pm; Thurs 10am–9pm; Fri–Sat 10am–7pm; Sun 12:15–7pm.

MONTROSE

Menil Collection ★★★ John and Dominique de Menil's private collection of fine art is a must stop for culture hounds visiting Houston. Only a portion of the 17,000 pieces is on display at any one time, but the collection highlights four major areas: antiquities, Byzantine and Medieval, tribal, and modern art. The main building, designed by acclaimed architect Renzo Piano, is spacious, straightforward, and filled with natural light, fostering an immediate connection between visitors and the works on display. Next door, the **Cy Twombly Gallery,** also designed by Piano, is particularly captivating. Consider a visit to the nearby **Rothko Chapel,** an artsy, non-denominational spiritual sanctuary founded by the Menils.

1533 Sul Ross St. www.menil.org. ✆ **713/525-9400.** Free admission. Wed–Sun 11am–7pm.

KIRBY DISTRICT

Bayou Bend ★★ Oil heiress and philanthropist Ima Hogg, sometimes called the First Lady of Texas, gave the Museum of Fine Arts Houston quite a gift in 1966—her elegant, 28-room River Oaks mansion filled with one of the country's finest collections of American antiques, including furniture, paintings, silver, ceramics, and other decorative objects, some dating back to the Colonial era. The residence sits on 14 lush acres with formal, manicured gardens surrounded by native woodlands and trails; be sure to take time for a leisurely stroll through the peaceful grounds, especially if you're visiting in spring. Two guided tours are offered: an hour-long Highlights Tour and a more intensive 90-minute Study Tour; tours begin every 15 minutes, and reservations are recommended. The self-guided tour does not require reservations.

6003 Memorial Dr. www.mfah.org/bayoubend. ✆ **713/639-7750.** Admission (includes audio tour) $15 adults, $10 seniors, $7.50 youths 13–17, free children 12 and under. Gardens only $7. Guided house tours Tues–Thurs 10–2:30pm; Fri–Sat 10–11:30am. Self-guided house tours: Fri–Sun 1–4pm. Self-guided gardens tours: Tues–Sat 10am–5pm; Sun 1–5pm.

Rienzi ★ Yet another River Oaks mansion donated by a local family, Rienzi is the place to go if you're mad for European decorative arts—and love poking around the insides of a grand pile. The mansion was designed for Houston philanthropist Harris Masterson in a neo-Palladian style by local architect John F. Staub in 1952 and is nestled in 4 acres of sumptuous gardens. This is where the Museum of Fine Arts displays its cache of European decorative arts, including one of the most distinctive collections of Worcester porcelain in the country. The house is outfitted with the Mastersons' own fine English furniture.

1406 Kirby Dr. www.mfah.org/art/departments/rienzi-house. ✆ **713/639-7800.** Admission $8 adults, $5 seniors. Wed–Sat; Sun 1–5pm. Reservations required.

FARTHER AFIELD

George Ranch Historical Park ★ This 400-acre working cattle ranch doubles as an outdoor museum that tells the story of four generations of the George family, who lived and worked here from the 1820s to the 1930s. It's a great chance to experience frontier life from bygone times, and the grounds hold a number of restored landmark buildings to tour, from an 1820s pioneer farm to an 1880s Victorian mansion to a 1930s ranch house. Plan a half-day or more here. The **Dinner Belle Café** was being remodeled at press time, but

KID magnets

Houston is very kid-friendly. Easily half of the above-mentioned attractions are geared toward kids or have a large component especially suitable for them.

A tour of southeast Houston takes you to the **Orange Show** ★ (p. 156), with which young kids display an almost instinctual connection; a boat ride on the **Ship Channel** ★ (p. 156); a visit to the **Battleship *Texas*** ★ (p. 155) or the majestic wonders of **Space Center Houston** ★★★ (p. 157). After that, visit the boardwalk in **Kemah** ★ (p. 156) or **Moody Gardens** ★ in Galveston (see p. 204 in chapter 7).

South of downtown, the Museum District includes the **Children's Museum** ★★ (p. 157), the **Houston Museum of Natural Science** ★★★ (p. 158), and the **Health Museum** ★★ (p. 158). And, of course, the **Houston Zoo** ★★ (p. 159) has just gotten better and better, and is now the second-most-visited zoo in the country. To the north is **Wet 'n' Wild SplashTown** (p. 161), a waterpark; to the southwest is the **George Ranch Historical Park** ★ (p. 160) for cowpokes at heart.

you can still sign up for one of the Historic Lunches on Saturdays, which might include an 1860s Chuckwagon Meal ("son of a gun" beef stew, cowboy beans, and biscuits) or a 1930s Farm Table Lunch (ranch smokehouse pastrami, green beans with fatback and onions, and sweet potato pie). The **Texian Market Days Festival,** held annually in late October, is a big hit, with home tours, cowboy food, folk crafts, and battle reenactments.

10215 FM 762, Richmond. www.georgeranch.org. ✆ **281/343-0218.** Admission $10 adults, $9 seniors 62 and older, $5 children 5–15. Tues–Sat 9am–5pm. Take the Southwest Fwy. (Tex. 59 S.); before getting to the town of Richmond, exit FM Hwy. 762 and go 6 miles south.

Wet 'n' Wild SplashTown ★ If the Texas heat is getting to you, one of the state's most popular water parks is just 45 minutes down the road, located in Spring, Texas. Cool off on a variety of daredevil water slides (including the seven-story Texas Freefall), raft rides, tube rides down lazy rivers, and wave pools. The season generally runs from mid-spring to early fall.

21300 I-45 at Louetts Rd., Spring. www.wetnwildsplashtown.com. ✆ **281/355-3300.** $40 admission, $30 children under 48 in. Daily 11am–9pm during summer months. Hours vary; call or check website. Follow I-45 N. toward Dallas; take exit 69-A.

Organized Tours

If you'd like a bus tour of the city to help you get your bearings, you're out of luck. Companies such as Gray Line offer tours only to conventions and visiting groups, not the general public. The other option is to hire a guide. You can find one through the Web page of Houston's **tour guide association** (www.ptgah.com).

In addition to individual guide services, **Discover Houston Tours** (www.discoverhoustontours.com; ✆ **713/222-9255**) hosts regularly scheduled walking tours of downtown and other places, along with the occasional special-interest tour. For those interested in food tours, you can't go wrong with

Houston Culinary Tours (www.visithoustontexas.com/culinary-tours), run by the Greater Houston CVB, which offers neighborhood food tours, chef-led tours, chocolate tours, and more. See the town by bike on **Bayou City Bike Tours** (www.bayoucitybiketours.com; ✆ **832/387-5631**), which offers trips like the Downtown Historical Tour, Buffalo Bayou Park Tour, and a Cruise the Heights Tour.

SPORTS & OUTDOOR ACTIVITIES

Outdoor Fun

BIKING, JOGGING & WALKING By far the most popular jogging and walking track is in **Memorial Park,** a large and beautiful park clothed in pine trees along Buffalo Bayou west of downtown. It's easy to reach; take Memorial Drive, which follows the north bank of Buffalo Bayou, from downtown to the park. It can be very crowded, however. A lovely hike-and-bike trail runs along the banks of **Buffalo Bayou** from North Shepherd to downtown. It traces both banks of the bayou for 1.5 miles, so you can run a 3-mile loop. It has sweet vistas of the downtown skyline and is dotted with numerous sculptures (and takes you right into the Theater District). During the day it's fine, but I wouldn't advise venturing along the bayou at night. To rent a bike in this area, see **West End Bicycles**, 5427 Blossom St. (www.westendbikes.com; ✆ **713/861-2271**). They can also give you information about good rides.

A 10-mile hike-and-bike trail runs along the banks of **Brays Bayou** from Hermann Park through the Medical Center, where it goes under South Main Street and then heads southwest almost all the way to Beltway 8.

GOLF Houston proper has public golf courses at most of the city's biggest parks, but with the exception of the Memorial Park Golf Course, the best public courses are outside the city. Host to the Shell Houston Open, the **Tournament Course** at **Golf Club of Houston,** 5860 Wilson Rd., Humble (about 12 miles north of Houston and 35 min. from downtown) (www.golfclubofhouston.com; ✆ **281/833-8463**), is one of just 11 public courses with a PGA tour event. One of the loveliest and best-regarded courses in the area is the **Longwood Golf Club,** 13300 Longwood Trace, Cypress (www.longwoodgc.com; ✆ **281/373-4100**), at the northwest edge of Houston; to get there, take Tex. 290 (45 min. from downtown). Fees are $25 to $60 and include cart; tee times should be reserved 7 days in advance. Another course that a lot of people like is **Tour 18 Houston** (www.tour18golf.com; ✆ **281/540-1818**), which copies 18 of the greatest holes in golf. The course is at 3102 FM 1960 East in Humble. Greens fees are $28 to $96; reservations can be made 30 days in advance.

In town are some municipal courses that are cheap, but it can be somewhat tricky to get tee times for them. The **Memorial Park Golf Course** (www.memorialparkgolf.com; ✆ **713/862-4033**) is the most enjoyable. Greens fees are $15 to $40. **Hermann Park's golf course** (✆ **713/526-0077**) is centrally located, with greens fees ranging from $20 to $30.

The **Shell Houston Open** (www.shellhoustonopen.com; ✆ **281/454-7000**) is held in late March or early April.

TENNIS Of course, the best strategy for getting in some tennis is to stay at a hotel with courts. **Memorial Park** has some of the best of the public courses; make reservations well in advance by calling ✆ **832/395-7561.**

Spectator Sports

If you're in Houston and decide on the spur of the moment to get tickets to a game, you can call **Ticket Stop,** 5925 Kirby Dr., Ste. D (www.ticket-stop.com; ✆ **713/526-8889**), a private ticket agency. They charge extra for the tickets, so it's best to buy direct or in advance if possible.

BASEBALL **Houston Astros** fans enjoy the team's indoor/outdoor downtown stadium, **Minute Maid Park** (www.houston.astros.mlb.com; ✆ **877/927-8767**). Its retractable roof is open mostly in the early part of the season before the weather gets too hot. Tickets aren't that hard to come by.

BASKETBALL The **Houston Rockets** (www.nba.com/rockets) play at the **Toyota Center** (www.toyotacenter.com). It's downtown at 1510 Polk St., just south of the convention center and baseball park. The Rockets are a popular team, and tickets must be purchased well in advance. Do so online or by calling ✆ **866/446-8849.**

FOOTBALL The **Houston Texans** (www.houstontexans.com; ✆ **832/667-2390**) play host to opponents at high-tech NRG Stadium (formerly known as Reliant Stadium), which hosted the 2017 Super Bowl. It's located off South Main, not far from the Medical Center, at 1 NRG Parkway.

RODEO Houstonians go all-out "Western" for a couple of weeks in early March, when the **Houston Livestock Show and Rodeo** is held at NRG Park and in NRG Stadium. Billed as the largest of all rodeos, it includes the usual events such as bull riding and calf roping, as well as performances by famous country artists. Call ✆ **832/667-1000,** or go to www.rodeohouston.com for more information. For tickets, call **Ticketmaster** at ✆ **832/667-1134.**

SOCCER The **Houston Dynamo** (www.houstondynamo.com; ✆ **713/276-7500)** compete in America's MLS league and play home games in the **BBVA Compass Stadium.**

WHERE TO STAY

Downtown and the Uptown/Galleria area have most of the city's comfortable hotels. Both are generally good locations for getting to know the city. In choosing a hotel, don't forget to give some thought about where you'll be spending your time in Houston. See "The Neighborhoods in Brief" section, earlier in this chapter. Eastside hotels along the Gulf Freeway work well for those wanting to visit NASA, Kemah, and Galveston. The Montrose Area is great for those wanting to combine shopping with museum visits. And keep in mind that Houston's light rail increases the utility of all the hotels located along its corridor, including the Medical Center and South Main.

Central Houston Hotels

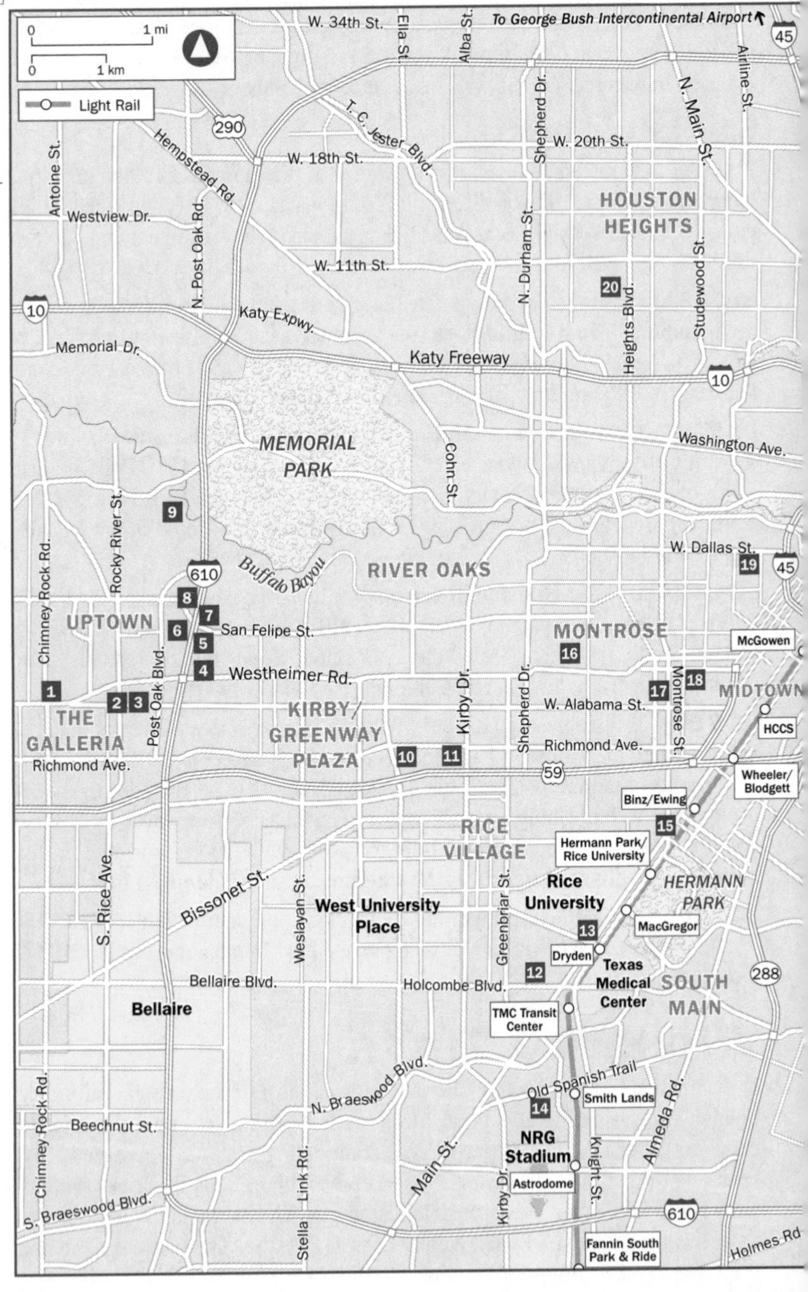

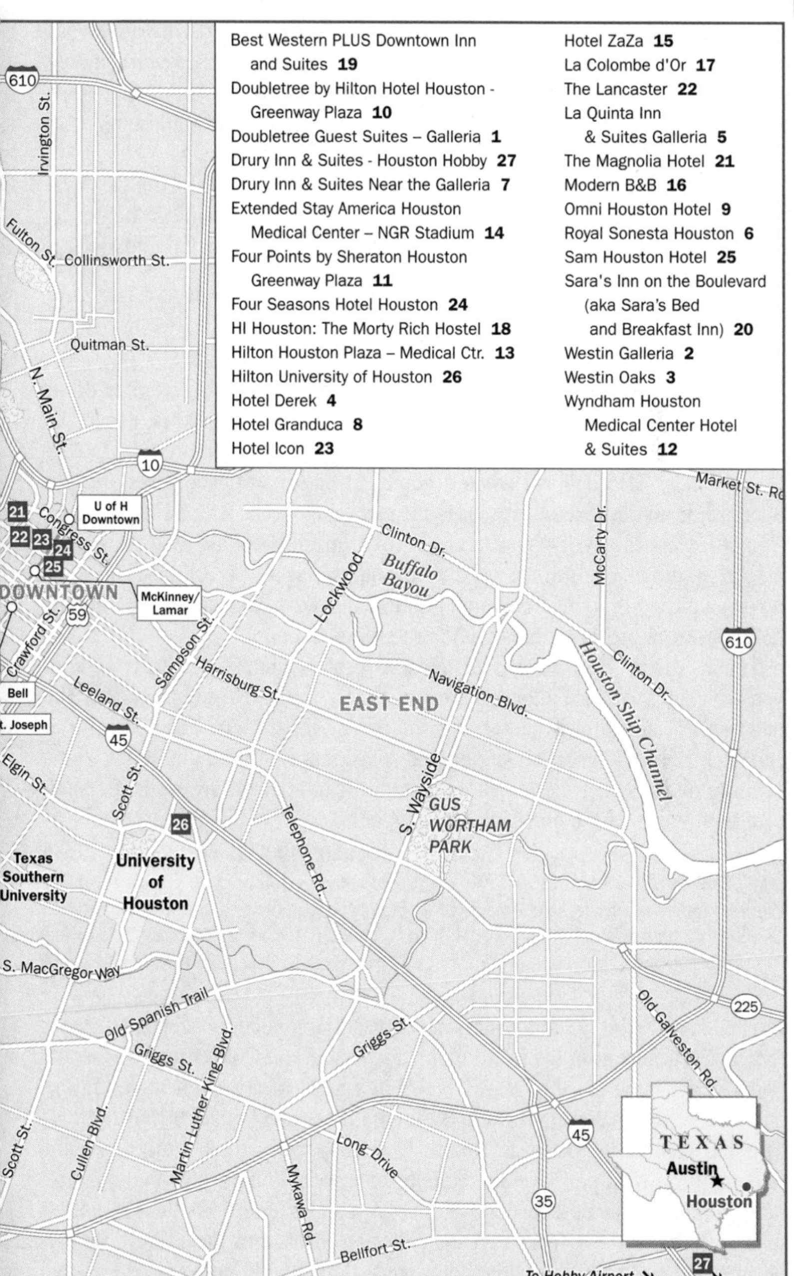
Best Western PLUS Downtown Inn and Suites 19
Doubletree by Hilton Hotel Houston - Greenway Plaza 10
Doubletree Guest Suites – Galleria 1
Drury Inn & Suites - Houston Hobby 27
Drury Inn & Suites Near the Galleria 7
Extended Stay America Houston Medical Center – NGR Stadium 14
Four Points by Sheraton Houston Greenway Plaza 11
Four Seasons Hotel Houston 24
HI Houston: The Morty Rich Hostel 18
Hilton Houston Plaza – Medical Ctr. 13
Hilton University of Houston 26
Hotel Derek 4
Hotel Granduca 8
Hotel Icon 23
Hotel ZaZa 15
La Colombe d'Or 17
The Lancaster 22
La Quinta Inn & Suites Galleria 5
The Magnolia Hotel 21
Modern B&B 16
Omni Houston Hotel 9
Royal Sonesta Houston 6
Sam Houston Hotel 25
Sara's Inn on the Boulevard (aka Sara's Bed and Breakfast Inn) 20
Westin Galleria 2
Westin Oaks 3
Wyndham Houston Medical Center Hotel & Suites 12
610
Irvington St.
Fulton St.
Collinsworth St.
Quitman St.
N. Main St.
10
U of H Downtown
Congress St.
DOWNTOWN
McKinney/ Lamar
59
Crawford St.
Bell
Leeland St.
45
Elgin St.
Scott St.
Sampson St.
Harrisburg St.
Lockwood
Clinton Dr.
Buffalo Bayou
Navigation Blvd.
EAST END
McCarty Dr.
Market St. Rd
Houston Ship Channel
Clinton Dr.
S. Wayside
GUS WORTHAM PARK
Telephone Rd.
Texas Southern University
University of Houston
S. MacGregor Way
Old Spanish Trail
Griggs St.
Martin Luther King Blvd.
Cullen Blvd.
Scott St.
Griggs St.
Long Drive
Mykawa Rd.
Bellfort St.
Old Galveston Rd.
225
35
To Hobby Airport
TEXAS
Austin
Houston

Tip: So many hotels have been built downtown that there is an oversupply of rooms. Rates have fallen, and deals and packages are readily available. Houston is a business-driven city, so discounted weekend rates are quite common. The discounts work to shrink the price difference between a merely acceptable hotel room and a great hotel room, so if you're visiting on a weekend, consider upgrading—for just a few extra bucks, you can get a better room and location.

The hotel listings that follow include the prevailing rates for double occupancy and do not include Houston's 17% hotel tax. Rates will go higher for the rodeo in February and during large conventions, and generally go lower in the summer. Always ask about promotional rates.

Downtown

EXPENSIVE

Four Seasons Hotel Houston ★★★ You'd expect this member of the upscale hotel chain to do things just right—and boy, it delivers, especially when it comes to service. The staff knows what you need before you do. The Four Seasons also delivers when it comes to luxury of space. Everything is oversize, from the spacious rooms to the sweeping lobby, with a Frank-Lloyd-Wright-meets-the-Wild-West feel. A multimillion-dollar renovation has amped up the luxe comfort levels; rooms and suites are stylish nests of down duvets and plump lounge chairs with ottomans. Executive suites separate the bedroom from the living area with frosted French doors.

There's more: The hotel has an enviable location in the CBD, with the convention center, Astros ballpark, and Houston Rockets NBA arena nearby. The newly renovated fitness center and spa is state of the art. The fourth-floor saltwater pool has resort-style lounging sofas, jaunty striped umbrellas, and a decking of Brazilian ipe wood—where you can cool off from the Houston heat with views of the glittering city skyline.

1300 Lamar St. www.fourseasons.com/houston. ✆ **800/819-5053** or 713/650-1300. 468 units. $289–$470 double; $395–$730 executive suite; $1,100 and up specialty suites. Weekend rates available. Valet parking $38. Pets accepted (with restrictions) but no pet deposit/fee. **Amenities:** 2 restaurants; 2 bars; babysitting; complimentary car service throughout downtown; concierge; 24-hour fitness center; large outdoor pool; nail salon; room service; spa; Wi-Fi (free).

Hotel Icon ★★ Good bones, neoclassical architectural elements, and a touch of refinement in the decor make this Autograph Collection by Marriott hotel a handsome place to stay. Housed in a great location downtown in the city's 1912 Union National Bank Building, "The Icon" oozes a sense of history and classical good taste. Rooms feature spacious tiled bathrooms with rain showers, whirlpools, and antique tubs, and many have high ceilings and large windows. The hotel decor used to look a bit boudoir/bordello; I'm happy to report that it now feels statesmanlike, all sleek and gleaming. Perhaps because the walls are thick, the hotel seems remarkably quiet, so guests can count on a good night's sleep. The most fun is to be had in the suites on the top floor, with rooms that are extra-large and plush. I enjoy the way the hotel's original elements, like an original bank vault in the lobby, have been preserved. It's that kind of thing that makes this property unique.

220 Main St. www.hotelicon.com. ✆ **800/323-7500** or 713/224-4266. 153 units. $139–$305 double; from $249 suite. Valet parking $33. Pets under 50 lb. accepted with $100 fee. **Amenities:** Restaurant; bar; concierge; health club and spa; room service; Wi-Fi (free).

The Lancaster ★★ This long-running, family-owned boutique hotel occupies a historic 12-story building in the heart of the Theater District. The Lancaster draws lovers of the arts—Jones Hall, Wortham Center, Alley Theatre, and Bayou Place are all within walking distance—but it makes a strong play for business travelers as well. Guest rooms have received a much-needed makeover; gone are the old-fashioned landscape paintings, dated color schemes, and floral drapes and upholstery. Rooms now have a classic Texas rancher/oilman old-money vibe, with modern, muted tones, plus poster or sleigh beds and spacious bathrooms outfitted in marble and brass. The hotel restaurant and bar, **the Bistro,** is a popular destination for American cuisine.

701 Texas Ave. www.thelancaster.com. ✆ **800/231-0336** or 713/228-9500. 93 units. $169–$250 double; suite starting at $505. Valet parking $30 per night during the week; $20 per night on weekends. No pets. **Amenities:** Restaurant; bar; concierge; exercise room; room service; Wi-Fi (free).

The Magnolia Hotel ★ This stylish, contemporary hotel occupies a stately downtown high-rise built in 1926 as the offices of the old *Houston Post-Dispatch* newspaper (look for the antique letterpress in the lobby). Guest rooms feature luxe bedding, velvet drapes, and spacious bathrooms with granite countertops and oversize tubs; suites with kitchens or kitchenettes are also available. The **Lounge** is a relaxed but sophisticated space where guests can grab a bite to eat, enjoy a cocktail, borrow a book from a small library, or play a game of pool. The Lounge also offers complimentary wine and beer every evening (5:30–6:30pm) and milk and cookies nightly (8–10pm), plus a continental breakfast each morning. The rooftop sports a small pool, a hot tub, a 24-hour fitness center—and stellar views of the downtown area, including Minute Maid Park. If you're looking for charm, this hotel is more standard than boutique in style; on the other hand, it's a good value and has a great location.

1100 Texas Ave. www.magnoliahotels.com. ✆ **888/915-1110** or 713/221-0011. 314 units. $139–$279 double; $159–$389 studio suite; $349 1-bedroom suite. Rates include continental breakfast and evening cocktails. Valet parking $33 weekdays, $29 weekends; pets allowed. **Amenities:** Restaurant/bar; concierge; executive-level rooms; exercise room; Jacuzzi; heated rooftop pool; room service; Wi-Fi (free).

Sam Houston Hotel ★★ This Curio Collection by Hilton hotel, called "The Sam," for short, is a chic, pet-friendly boutique hotel that's a good value for those seeking service and comfort. The Sam dates all the way back to 1924, when it first opened its doors as the Sam Houston Hotel. It shuttered in the 1970s, had another go in the 2000s, switched names a couple of times, and then in 2013, after a redesign, the Sam Houston bounced back as good as ever. Despite its reverence for the past, the Sam sports a cool and contemporary vibe. Rooms feature leather headboards, Herman Miller desk chairs, Keurig coffee makers, and granite bathrooms. The hotel's new restaurant, the **Pearl,** opened in 2017 serving "coastal urban cuisine," as did the **Pearl Bar,** offering a variety of Texas microbrews, cocktails, and crudo; you'll probably spot a few baseball fans during the season (Minute Maid Park is just down the block) having a drink here. Downtown adventurers, as well as business travelers, will find a lot to like here. When the original hotel opened in the '20s, the location wasn't in the best part of downtown; now the location is prime, just 2 blocks from the ballpark and Main Street.

1117 Prairie St. http://curiocollection3.hilton.com/en/hotels/texas/the-sam-houston-curio-collection-by-hilton-HOUTSQQ/index.html. ✆ **832/200-8800.** 100 units. $149–$375 double; from $199 suite. Weekend rates and packages available. Valet parking $32. Pets 50 lb. and under accepted with $100 non-refundable deposit. **Amenities:** Restaurant; bar; fitness center; room service; Wi-Fi (free).

MODERATE

Best Western PLUS Downtown Inn and Suites ★ Pluses: This Best Western has a central downtown location, with clean, comfortable, and roomy doubles and family-friendly suites (fridges, microwaves) and a complimentary full breakfast every morning in the lobby. Minuses: If you're looking for Texas style, or any particular style for that matter, you'll be disappointed. This is a standard-issue American chain hotel. Back to pluses: Location, location, location! Close to the Toyota Center, Minute Maid Park, and the Downtown Aquarium! And prices are pretty reasonable for what you get.

915 W. Dallas St. www.bestwestern.com. ✆ **800/780-7234** or 713/571-7733. 76 units. $132–$217 double; $330 suite. Rates include full breakfast and complimentary beer/wine happy hour. Free parking. **Amenities:** Exercise room; Jacuzzi; outdoor pool; Wi-Fi (free).

East End

EXPENSIVE

Hilton University of Houston ★★ Part of the Conrad Hilton College of Hotel and Restaurant Management, this hotel is staffed by many university students learning the hospitality business—and you can bet they're on their toes. It's got a great location smack-dab on the university campus between downtown and Houston's southeast side attractions. It's got big, comfortable rooms and suites done up in a smart, stylish decor, with ergonomic chairs and sweeping city views. **Eric's,** the hotel restaurant, is better than most, with an American bistro menu. Guests enjoy access to the UH University Center facilities next door, including a health club, large pool, game room, and beauty salon. ***Note:*** It's the perfect place to stay if you're coming for a Cougars football game, so if you're a UH fan, book early for a room on game days.

4450 University Dr. www3.hilton.com/en/hotels/texas/hilton-university-of-houston-HOUUHHF/index.html. ✆ **832/531-6300.** 86 units. $169–$239 double. Self-parking $15. **Amenities:** Restaurant; bar; pool, access to nearby health club and spa; room service; Wi-Fi (free).

MODERATE

Drury Inn & Suites Houston Hobby ★ Look for good weekend rates at this more-than-decent chain hotel near the airport, with roomy suites with a fridge and microwave and a helpful, dedicated staff. It's basic, but bed linens are a notch above, and the perks add a little extra oomph: Guests get free soda and popcorn (3–10pm), a hot breakfast buffet, and an evening reception dinner (tacos, hot dogs, salad), complete with happy-hour drinks. Oh, and it's got a pool and 24-hour fitness center.

7902 Mosley Rd. www.druryhotels.com. ✆ **800-378-7946** or 713/941-4300. 134 units. $79–$139 double; $109–$159 suite. Rates include hot breakfast buffet. Free parking. Pets accepted with $15 pet fee. **Amenities:** 24-hour fitness center; Jacuzzi; heated indoor/outdoor pool; Wi-Fi (free).

South Main

EXPENSIVE

Hilton Houston Plaza/Medical Center ★★ Consider location (near the Medical Center and Rice University), amenities (pool, fitness center, restaurant, bar), and service, and this Hilton is quite the deal—and the hotel has been newly refreshed after a 2017 renovation. It's a popular conference hotel, and even the large, comfy doubles (with king beds) have desks or work stations and ergonomic chairs. The roomy suites start at 720 square feet. The **Garden Court** restaurant is open for breakfast, lunch, and dinner. If you need to travel to the hospital daily, the hotel runs a complimentary shuttle there and back.

6633 Travis St. http://www3.hilton.com/en/hotels/texas/hilton-houston-plaza-medical-center-HOUMCHF/index.html. ✆ **800/HILTONS (445-8667)** or 713/313-4000. 181 units. $99–$259 double; $119–$279 suite; Presidential suite $399–$849. Weekend rates and package deals available. Valet parking $19; self-parking $12. No pets. **Amenities:** Restaurant; bar/coffee shop; health club; outdoor pool; room service; complimentary shuttle to and from Medical Center; Wi-Fi (free).

Hotel ZaZa ★★★ This snazzy, pizazz-y boutique hotel may be the perfect marriage of old property and new owners, with some of the splashiest digs in town, suitable for rock stars, escapist vacationers, and business travelers with time to play. ZaZa rises 12 stories in the heart of the leafy Museum District. At the top of the food chain are the ultra-swanky themed apartments known as the "Magnificent Seven" suites; the "Tycoon," for example, maxes out at about 2,000 square feet with two bedrooms, two-and-a-half bathrooms, white leather furniture, and an iron chandelier, plus an outdoor tub on a spacious balcony. Slightly less decadent (just) are the 10 "concept" suites, such as the Space Age–inspired "Houston, We Have a Problem" and the sultry, Japanese-style "Geisha House." Or you can slum it for what passes as basic here, which might mean a stylish balcony king with a step-out patio, or a cool pool bungalow with easy access to the happening pool scene on the second floor. The venue also boasts a lavish, full-service spa, a fitness center, and a romantic restaurant, **Monarch,** with cocktails and terrace dining overlooking Mecom Fountain. Hotel packages are available with tickets to the Museum of Fine Arts, which is just across the street. There are Hotel ZaZas in Dallas and Austin, and another ZaZa is slated to open in Memorial City Houston in late 2017.

5701 Main St. www.hotelzaza.com/houston. ✆ **888/880-3244** or 713/526-1991. 315 units. $279–$709 double; from $305 suites. Valet parking $30. Pets accepted with $150 fee. **Amenities:** Restaurant; bar; concierge; exercise room; heated outdoor pool; room service; spa; Wi-Fi (free).

MODERATE

Wyndham Houston Medical Center Hotel & Suites ★ This former Holiday Inn is across from the Medical Center and it's a dependable, affordable, clean place to lay one's head—a true comfort for those coming from afar to be with family at MD Anderson. Rooms are comfortable with good bed linens. Deluxe and two-bedroom suites have full kitchens, while others have kitchenettes. In many ways it's feels like your standard business hotel, but it does have the comfy Wyndham beds as well as 10 new "Pure" rooms for asthma- and allergy-friendly lodging. Plus, the hotel sometimes offers better-than-average rates for hospital outpatients (not to mention big discounts on weekend rates), which makes it especially nice.

6800 S. Main St. www.wyndhamhoustonmedcenter.com. ✆ **800/HOLIDAY (465-4329)** or 713/528-7744. 287 units. $149–$209 double; $169–$229 suite; from $219 apt. Special rates available for hospital outpatients. $11/day self-parking; $19/day valet parking. **Amenities:** Restaurant; bar; fitness center; small pool; room service; Wi-Fi (free).

INEXPENSIVE

Extended Stay America Houston Medical Center–NGR Stadium–Fannin ★ The price is right if you're looking for an extended stay in Houston near the Medical Center and the Museum District—or close to the big game. Located a mere 3,200 feet from NRG Stadium, this property is designed for longer stays, with all rooms featuring fully equipped kitchens, coin laundry and ironing facilities, upgraded bedding with extra pillows, and a water filter in every room. I've seen rates as low as $58 a night here, which is amazing for anywhere in Texas—let alone the big city of Houston. It's nice that affordable rooms are available so close to MD Anderson for those who come to Houston for some of the best medical care in the country.

7979 Fannin St. www.extendedstayamerica.com. ✆ **713/797-0000.** 154 units. $58–$80 double. Free parking. Pets allowed ($25/day fee not to exceed $150). **Amenities:** Coin laundry; free shuttle service to airport and nearby shops and locations; fitness room; hot tub; Wi-Fi (free).

Montrose/The Heights

EXPENSIVE

La Colombe d'Or ★★ For luxury lodgings with a sense of grandeur and old-world elegance, splurge on a stay at this five-suite, nine-villa property anchored by a circa-1923 mansion, originally the private residence of oil tycoon W. W. Fondren. Each suite is named after a celebrated French Impressionist and is filled with art and antiques; some boast large formal dining rooms. The hotel also has nine one- and two-bedroom apartments (with full kitchens and living rooms) around a leafy courtyard in the adjacent **Villas at**

the Court of Colombe. A 2,000-square-foot art gallery occupies the third floor of the main building and features original oils by contemporary European artists and rare lithographs from the Picasso estate. In addition to fine art, La Colombe d'Or is known for fine dining. You're probably not going to find a more ambitious hotel eatery in the city than **Restaurant Cinq,** which showcases highly creative New American cuisine. For something a little more intimate, duck into the cozy, classy bar for a choice cocktail or glass of wine. Over the years, the exclusive boutique hotel has attracted its share of the rich and famous, including Bishop Desmond Tutu, Madonna, and President Bill Clinton.

3410 Montrose Blvd. www.lacolombedor.com. ✆ **713/524-7999.** 14 units. $295–$395 suite; $395–$495 villa. Free parking. Small pets accepted with $150 deposit. **Amenities:** Restaurant; bar; library; room service. Wi-Fi (free).

MODERATE

Modern B&B ★ For travelers seeking intimate, non-corporate accommodations—yet who may balk at the old-timey vibe of a stereotypical bed-and-breakfast—the hip, eight-unit Modern B&B should make a nice fit. This slick-looking, four-story townhouse complex in the middle of the bustling Montrose area offers three types of rooms (mod, standard, and top shelf) ranging in size and amenities. Breakfast is a definitely a cut above, with organic ingredients, freshly baked goods, and made-to-order omelets, including vegan options. No pots of burnt coffee here—the dining room includes a fancy espresso machine. A well-outfitted kitchen is available to guests at all hours, and plenty of restaurants, bars, and cafes (West Alabama Ice House, the Chocolate Bar, and Divino Italian) are within walking distance. The owner offers other rentals—the entire townhome next door as well as a couple of apartments around the corner—that are ideal for families or long-term guests.

4003 Hazard St. www.modernbb.com. ✆ **888/512-3113** or 832/279-6367. 18 units. $125–$225 double; guesthouse from $225. Rates include full breakfast. 3-night minimum for holidays. Children accepted with guesthouse rentals. Pets accepted with $30 per day fee. **Amenities:** Exercise room; guest kitchen; Wi-Fi (free).

Sara's Inn on the Boulevard ★ This 11-room bed-and-breakfast occupies a pristine Queen Anne house on a tree-lined stretch of the hip and historic Heights neighborhood. Individually decorated rooms feature antique furniture, king or queen beds with luxe linens, flatscreen TVs, and mini fridges. The atmosphere throughout the property is warm, relaxed, and surprisingly quiet. Parking is free, as is the hearty Texas-size Southern breakfast, which may include made-to-order egg dishes, sweet potato pancakes, and homemade pastries. ***Take note:*** Pets and children younger than 7 are not allowed.

941 Heights Blvd. http://saras.com. ✆ **713/868-1130.** 11 units. $149–$195 double; $205–$215 suite. Rates include full breakfast. Free parking. Children 6 and under not permitted. No pets. **Amenities:** Wi-Fi (free).

INEXPENSIVE

HI Houston: The Morty Rich Hostel ★ Located a block off Westheimer and 3 blocks from Montrose Boulevard, this quirky hostel (formerly the Lovett Hotel) is on a quiet street not far from the busy restaurant and club district of the Montrose area—putting those who want hostel-style rates and accommodations in a good spot not far from the bus station. Occupying a 1917-built Montrose mansion, originally the residence of Houston mayor Joseph Hutchinson, the place offers several multi-bed coed dorm rooms, plus an art-filled lounge area and a billiards room. The best perk, especially at a price point this modest, is the swimming pool in a tree-shaded backyard. Rooms are large and sparse and outfitted with bunk beds (many with their own metal staircases to the top bunk), and most have en-suite bathrooms; a private room gives even more privacy. The hostel offers a free continental breakfast, but it also has a fully operational shared kitchen where you can whip up your own meals with other guests. Some guests rave about this place, while others say it needs a good cleaning.

501 Lovett Blvd. www.hiusa.org/hostels/texas/houston/the-morty-rich-hostel. ✆ **713/636-9776.** 9 units. $33–$66 per guest. Rates include continental breakfast. Free parking. **Amenities:** Outdoor pool; shared kitchen; pool table; Wi-Fi (free).

Kirby District

EXPENSIVE

DoubleTree by Hilton Hotel Houston–Greenway Plaza ★★ This 20-story DoubleTree by Hilton property is the only hotel in the Greenway Plaza (though others are nearby), which means guests have easy access to Greenway's concourse level of shops, including a food court, post office, and movie theater. Guests can also quickly get to downtown or Uptown and the Galleria via the nearby Southwest Freeway. Or hop on the complimentary shuttle, which runs to and from the shops and eateries in the Galleria. Of course, this well-managed property has its own restaurant, bar, and Starbucks coffee shop, not to mention a heated outdoor pool, fitness center, and business center—so all you need may be right here.

6 Greenway Plaza E. http://doubletree3.hilton.com/en/hotels/texas/doubletree-by-hilton-hotel-houston-greenway-plaza-HOUGWDT/index.html. ✆ **713/629-1200.** 388 units. $169–$269 double. Weekend and package rates available. Valet parking $27; self-parking $22. **Amenities:** Restaurant; Starbucks; bar; babysitting; business center; concierge; executive-level rooms; fitness center; outdoor heated pool; room service; sauna; Wi-Fi ($13/day for in-room; free for Hilton honors members; free in lobby).

MODERATE

Four Points by Sheraton Houston Greenway Plaza ★ This smart little Sheraton property is well-located, between downtown, the Rice University/Village area, and the Galleria. Rooms are light, modern, and utilitarian without looking cheap—in fact, the decor is quite stylish for this price point. The hotel's **Upper Kirby Tap Room** is a nice place to nosh and nibble while enjoying craft beer at the end of a long day.

2828 Southwest Fwy. www.starwoodhotels.com. ✆ **713/942-2111.** 216 units. $79–$239 double. Weekend rates available. Self-parking $10. **Amenities:** Restaurant; bar; business center; fitness center; outdoor pool (seasonal); room service; Wi-Fi (free).

Uptown

A number of 3- and 4-star chain hotels are located in and around the Uptown District (Galleria mall area). Many offer a similar level of amenities and service, and all stand a short distance from Houston's best shops, restaurants, and clubs. They include such favorites as the **DoubleTree by Hilton,** 5353 Westheimer Rd. (www.doubletreesuiteshouston.com; ✆ 855/275-4790); **Embassy Suites by Hilton,** 2911 Sage Rd. (www.embassysuites3.hilton.com; ✆ 800/362-2779); **Hotel Indigo,** 5160 Hidalgo St. (www.ihg.com; ✆ 855/743-7676); **La Quinta,** 1625 West Loop S. (www.lq.com; ✆ 800/753-3757); **Omni Houston,** 4 Riverway (www.omnihotels.com; ✆ 800/843-6664); and **Sheraton Suites Houston,** 2400 West Loop S. (www.sheratonsuiteshouston.com; ✆ 888/627-8581).

EXPENSIVE

Hotel Derek ★★ This 312-unit hotel close to the Galleria blends urban sophistication with Texas style—check out the life-size cow sculpture in a lobby decorated with oil derricks. The decor is modern, with bold colors and big windows open to glittering city views. Standard and superior rooms feature platform beds, mod fixtures, contemporary artwork, and wonderful banquettes stretching out beneath large windows. Suites are bigger and even bolder, some with pop art and mod-inflected cowboy motifs. The higher up you go, the bigger the rooms and better the views; the one-bedroom Terrace Suites offer two bathrooms, a glass work desk, and a private terrace. The property also features a sleek restaurant serving updated comfort food such as chicken and waffles and lobster pot pie, and a bar pouring wine and Southern-influenced specialty cocktails. The Splash pool, with a big movie wall, is a great place to cool down in hot Houston. While it's not quite as snazzy as Hotel ZaZa, Derek does have a certain level of style that many adore just as much.

2525 W. Loop South. www.destinationhotels.com/hotel-derek. ✆ **866/292-4100** or 713/961-3000. 312 units. $290–$350 double; $350–$400 studio; from $550 suite. $12 nightly service fee. Weekend and promotional rates available. Valet parking $32, self-parking $23. Pets 65 lb. and under accepted with $100 fee. **Amenities:** Restaurant; 2 bars; Starbucks; chauffeured car service (3-mile radius); concierge; fitness center; outdoor pool; room service; Wi-Fi (free).

Hotel Granduca ★★★ A 16th-century Italian palazzo inspired this independently owned Uptown Park boutique hotel, designed to offer the old-world comfort of a private villa. Pieces from the owners' private homes in Italy were brought in to adorn the space, giving it the well-seasoned feel of treasures collected over time. Rooms and suites have cozy sitting areas, roomy closets, and marble bathroom finishes, and throughout the hotel, walls are awash in the rosy golden sunset colors of the Mediterranean. Equally Old World are the grounds, with a palm-shaded pool area with a Roman-style fountain and statuary, vine-covered walls, terra-cotta pots aside columned pavilions, and breezy cabanas. Even the lobby speaks Italian, with friezes and scrolled iron tables, yet it's more modern and casual than you'd expect. There's even a clubby billiards room and well-equipped health club. Some suites sprawl over 2,000 square feet, so long-term guests are offered monthly rates and VIP status, with attractive perks. The chic **Ristorante Cavour** serves Northern Italian cuisine and has a veranda for alfresco dining, and the **Bar Malatesta** lobby lounge offers live music and happy-hour cocktail snacks. A formal afternoon tea makes this already pleasant place even more pleasing. On Saturdays, "Jazz Con Amore" evenings offer chill live music, classic cocktails from the '50s and '60s, and small-plate specials at affordable prices. One of the hotel's coolest perks? A chauffeur-driven Maserati will take you anywhere you'd like to go within a 3-mile radius, free of charge.

1080 Uptown Park Blvd. www.granducahouston.com. ✆ **888/472-6382** and 713/418-1000. 122 units. $189–$335 double; $340–$400 630-sq-ft suites; $350–$600 825-sq.ft. suites; $750–$900 2-bedroom villa suites; $1,705 3-bedroom villa suites. Valet parking: $28. Pets accepted with $125 fee. **Amenities:** Restaurant; bar; concierge; fitness center; billiards room; Jacuzzi; heated saltwater pool; 24-hr. room service; complimentary Maserati transportation (3-mile radius); Wi-Fi (free).

Westin Galleria (Uptown) ★★ The Westin's massive meeting spaces say big business and conventions, but I like to think of this hotel as shopping central. Adjacent—no, actually attached—to the Galleria, with its high-end stores and indoor ice rink, this Westin property offers a location shoppers love. Completing a large-scale renovation in 2017, the Westin has streamlined the room decor, outfitted in a minimalist style with plush new Westin Heavenly Beds. Standard rooms are good-sized, but ask for a deluxe corner room with views of downtown for a particularly roomy space. The hotel will unveil a new Club Lounge and Fitness Center in late 2017, located on the 24th floor of the hotel, and recently unveiled a new gleaming lobby bar. The rooftop pool has city views. Of the three restaurant/bars in this hotel, my favorite is the casual brasserie-style **Daily Grill,** which opens to the mall. My friends and I found this hotel perfect for a girlfriends' getaway, with nice restaurants, clubs, and shopping options close by. ***Note*:** Guests booking Westin Galleria sometimes accidently book the nearby family-friendly Westin Oaks, which is located on the front side of the Galleria at Post Oak & Westheimer, while the Westin Galleria faces West Alabama Street. Both hotels are equally nice, and both are connected to the mall.

5060 W. Alabama St. www.westingalleriahoustonhotel.com. ✆ **888/627-8514** or 713/960-8100. 487 units. $159 double; $595 suite. Valet parking $33; free self-parking. Pets accepted; no pet deposit. **Amenities:** Restaurant; bar; concierge; 24-hr. exercise room; heated outdoor pool; room service; Wi-Fi ($10/day).

MODERATE

Drury Inn & Suites Near the Galleria ★ Lodging can be pricey in the Galleria/Uptown Park area, but there are bargains to be found if you just need a clean, basic place and a comfy bed. Case in point: this hotel, where prices often hover right around the $100 mark, and rooms are bright, clean, and comfortable, with microwaves and fridges. With good beds, large TVs, and roomy bathrooms, this hotel is a good budget choice in a great location.

There's no restaurant, but the food perks—complimentary breakfast buffet, free evening snacks and drinks—elevate the excellent value. The indoor/outdoor pool is an additional plus for a hotel in this price range.

1615 W. Loop South. www.druryhotels.com. ✆ **713/963-0700.** 134 units. $99–$159 double or king room; $135–$179 suite. Rates include breakfast buffet and free soda and popcorn (3–10pm). Free parking. Pets accepted with restrictions. **Amenities:** Exercise room; Jacuzzi; indoor/outdoor heated pool; Wi-Fi (free).

Royal Sonesta Houston ★ Although this hotel shares the name and ownership of a famous New Orleans French Quarter hotel on Bourbon Street, that's about all they have in common. So if you're expecting lacy balconies and the like, look elsewhere. Formerly the InterContinental Houston, this hotel offers upscale lodgings in a prime location only a block from the Galleria shopping center. Rooms are smartly outfitted with custom furnishings and they are comfortable, with insulated windows that keep them remarkably quiet. The decor includes marble, granite, and leather, with that understated masculine touch Texans embrace. So it's not New Orleans—still, it's not bad at all. Rates are surprisingly affordable, too—making this a good value for Galleria-goers.

2222 W. Loop South. www.sonesta.com/us/texas/houston/royal-sonesta-houston-galleria. ✆ **713/627-7600.** 485 units. $109–$159 double; from $349 suite. Promotional rates and packages available. Valet parking $27; self-parking $16. Pets up to 40 lb. accepted ($50 nonrefundable fee). **Amenities:** Restaurant; bar; coffee & snack shop; concierge; 24-hr health club; Jacuzzi; heated outdoor pool; room service; Wi-Fi ($11/day).

Near Bush Intercontinental Airport

MODERATE

Best Western PLUS Intercontinental Airport Inn ★ Houston's IAH Airport isn't terribly handy to downtown's wealth of destinations, but if you're just here for a layover and want to stick close to the terminals, this is a good choice. A free shuttle service can get you to and from the gate in no time, and rooms are nice-size, comfortable, and equipped with lots of amenities, like cordless phones, outlets for your devices, microwaves, and mini fridges. Standard rooms have two full beds. The hotel may not have a restaurant, but the complimentary hot breakfast buffet or "breakfast-to-go bag" (for those with early fights) is a great way to start the day.

7114 Will Clayton Pkwy, Humble. http://bestwesterntexas.com/hotels/best-western-plus-intercontinental-airport-inn. ✆ **281/548-1402.** 80 units. $78–$91 double. Weekend rates available. Rates include continental breakfast. Free parking. **Amenities:** Free airport transfers; exercise room; outdoor pool; Wi-Fi (free).

Houston Airport Marriott ★ Conveniently situated in the middle of the airport between terminals B and C, this Marriott is easily accessible from the airport TerminalLink train, making it a quick trip from gate to bed. Its advantageous location makes it a popular spot with business travelers. Standard rooms are handsomely furnished with beds in quality linens. The bi-level Loft Suite offers a large space to spread out. Bathrooms could be bigger, but beds are comfortable, and there's surprisingly little air traffic noise. **Flight's**

Lounge & Grill, nicer than restaurants in most Houston airport hotels, is a more-than-decent place for dinner. M Club club-level rooms offer access to the **M Club Lounge,** and its complimentary all-day food and snacks. The hotel's Great Room lobby even has flight status boards, making it easy to keep up-to-date on departure times and gate information.

18700 JFK Blvd. www.marriott.com. ✆ **281/443-2310.** 573 units. $119–$279 double; $349 suite. Weekend and package rates available. Free self-parking. Valet parking $26. **Amenities:** Restaurant; bar; fitness center; Jacuzzi; heated outdoor pool; room service; Wi-Fi ($13/day, free for Marriot Rewards members).

WHERE TO EAT

The Houston restaurant scene, like the city itself, is cosmopolitan. The primary influences come from Louisiana, Mexico, and Southeast Asia, but you can find restaurants serving just about any cuisine here. Houston's native cooking consists of steaks, chili, barbecue, soul food, and Tex-Mex. Expect solid seafood joints, thanks to the close proximity of the Gulf. For locals, the proper accompaniment for any of these is a beer or an extra-large glass of iced tea—the latter a cultural fixture in this town, if not the state. It's the perfect palate cleanser after a bite of something dense and spicy.

Downtown/Midtown

EXPENSIVE

Brennan's of Houston ★★ SOUTHERN/CREOLE Sibling to the famed Commander's Palace in New Orleans, Brennan's is a legend in its own right in Houston, serving up refined Creole cuisine with Southern flair in an elegant atmosphere since 1967. Calamity hit in 2008, when a fire fanned by Hurricane Ike caused major damage to the landmark 1930 building, former home of the Junior League of Houston. Painstakingly rebuilt and reopened in 2010, today it seems like a slightly more casual version of its eponymous culinary counterpart, with exposed brick walls, a solarium, and other large, airy, elegant dining spaces. The menu is an innovative one, yet many loyal diners have a tough time veering from their old favorites—the turtle soup topped with sherry, the shrimp and okra gumbo, the pecan-crusted Gulf fish, and, for dessert, bananas Foster flambéed at the table. The brick-lined interior has sparkling chandeliers and a sunny, New Orleans–inspired courtyard with a fountain and vine-covered walls. "The Kitchen Table" (chef's table), literally in the kitchen, must be reserved in advance and can accommodate between 4 and 12 people (dinner $80 per person, $155 and up per person with wine pairings; lunch $60 per person, $105 and up with wine pairings). Note that Brennan's has a strictly enforced "business casual" dress code: no athletic wear, shorts, flip-flops, torn jeans, or beachwear.

3300 Smith St. (at Stuart St.). www.brennanshouston.com. ✆ **713/522-9711.** Reservations recommended. Main courses $31–$60. Mon–Sat 11am–2pm; Sun 10am–2pm; daily 5:45–10pm. Take Smith St. (one-way headed south from downtown); when it crosses Elgin St./Westheimer Rd., look for the restaurant on your right. Be careful not to pass it, or you'll enter the Southwest Fwy.

Reef ★★★ SEAFOOD James Beard Award nominee Bryan Caswell, who trained under star chef Jean-Georges Vongerichten, is no stranger to fresh seafood, honing his skills in coastal kitchens in Barcelona, the Bahamas, Hong Kong, and New York. So Caswell understands that freshness is fundamental, and seafood dishes needn't be fussy or complicated to be special. Case in point: simple menu options like "redfish on the half shell," served with a comfort-food fave, mac-n-cheese; or almond-crusted snapper swimming in browned butter. Yes, Reef serves satisfying beef and chicken dishes, including the scrumptious pecan-smoked pork chop. Still, my favorite dish resides on the seafood side of the menu: seared scallops with roasted cauliflower splashed with apple vinaigrette. The 8,000-square-foot restaurant, a masterful repurposing of an old auto dealership, has a wall of floor-to-ceiling windows, mother-of-pearl tabletops, and an outdoor patio. Decorated in sea-foam hues, it's an ultra-appealing spot for a casual lunch or dinner.

2600 Travis St. (at McGowan). www.reefhouston.com. © **713/526-8282.** Reservations recommended. Main courses $26–$30. Mon–Thurs 11am–10pm; Fri 11am–11pm; Sat 5–11pm.

Vic & Anthony's ★★ STEAK With sibling steakhouses in Atlantic City, Lake Charles, and Las Vegas, this popular downtown steakhouse is part of a large chain (Landry's Inc.) but is still a cut above most local chophouses. Vic & Anthony's serves prime steaks in a posh, clubby setting of wood, stone, and leather, with sexy lighting and all the sophisticated touches a fine restaurant should have, from impeccable service to a well-crafted wine menu. But it's the steaks that keep 'em coming back, from USDA Prime grain-fed beef from Wisconsin's Strauss Farms to Akaushi-beef skirt steaks and tomahawk cuts from Heart Brand Beef in Yoakum, Texas. The seafood is no slouch, either, whether live Maine lobster or shrimp scampi. Pair your meal with a nice varietal from the restaurant's award-winning wine menu.

1510 Texas Ave. www.vicandanthonys.com. © **713/228-1111.** Reservations recommended. Main courses $28–$51. Mon–Thurs 11am–10pm; Fri 11am–11pm; Sat 5–11pm; Sun 5–10pm. Cocktail lounge opens at 4pm on Sat & Sun.

MODERATE

Hearsay Gastro Lounge ★ GASTROPUB Located on Market Square in the historic W. L. Foley building (one of the oldest structures in Houston), Hearsay is the kind of place you might stumble upon in New York, but it feels equally at home in Houston. A bright, casual space with an enormous crystal chandelier and rugged exposed-brick walls, high-ceilinged Hearsay has banquette seating along one wall and a luminous bar along the other. It seems to be going for a fancy speakeasy vibe—and yes, the craft cocktails fit the bill—but it's really more of a casual after-work spot for drinks and nachos or small plates to share. The menu also offers hearty sandwiches and salads, along with appealing main courses like Atlantic salmon, steak frites, and mahi-mahi tacos. Its sibling restaurant, **Hearsay on the Green,** at 1515 Dallas St. (© **832/377-3362**), has a similar menu with a few small additions, like shrimp

Central Houston Restaurants & Attractions

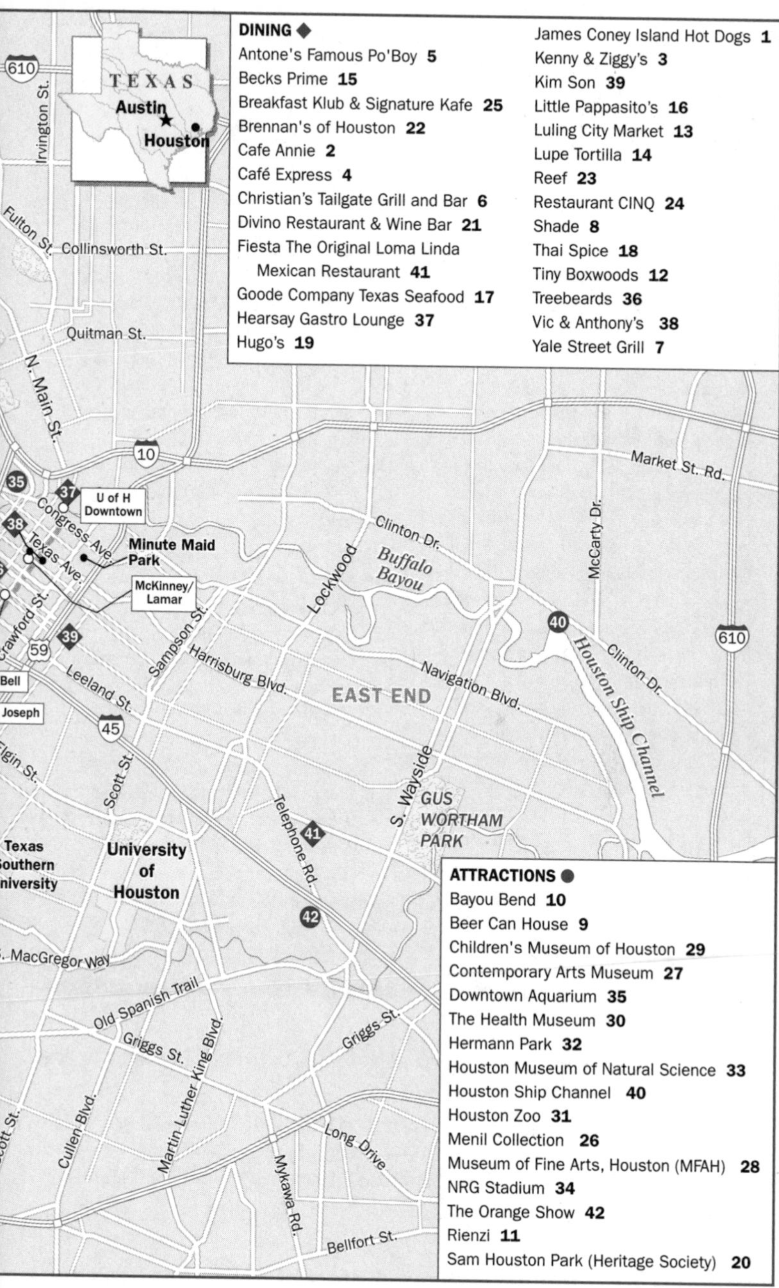
DINING ◆
Antone's Famous Po'Boy 5
Becks Prime 15
Breakfast Klub & Signature Kafe 25
Brennan's of Houston 22
Cafe Annie 2
Café Express 4
Christian's Tailgate Grill and Bar 6
Divino Restaurant & Wine Bar 21
Fiesta The Original Loma Linda Mexican Restaurant 41
Goode Company Texas Seafood 17
Hearsay Gastro Lounge 37
Hugo's 19
James Coney Island Hot Dogs 1
Kenny & Ziggy's 3
Kim Son 39
Little Pappasito's 16
Luling City Market 13
Lupe Tortilla 14
Reef 23
Restaurant CINQ 24
Shade 8
Thai Spice 18
Tiny Boxwoods 12
Treebeards 36
Vic & Anthony's 38
Yale Street Grill 7
ATTRACTIONS ●
Bayou Bend 10
Beer Can House 9
Children's Museum of Houston 29
Contemporary Arts Museum 27
Downtown Aquarium 35
The Health Museum 30
Hermann Park 32
Houston Museum of Natural Science 33
Houston Ship Channel 40
Houston Zoo 31
Menil Collection 26
Museum of Fine Arts, Houston (MFAH) 28
NRG Stadium 34
The Orange Show 42
Rienzi 11
Sam Houston Park (Heritage Society) 20
TEXAS
Austin
Houston
610
Irvington St.
Fulton St.
Collinsworth St.
Quitman St.
N. Main St.
10
Market St. Rd.
U of H Downtown
Minute Maid Park
McKinney/ Lamar
Congress Ave.
Texas Ave.
Crawford St.
59
Bell
Joseph
Clinton Dr.
Buffalo Bayou
Lockwood
McCarty Dr.
Houston Ship Channel
Sampson St.
Harrisburg Blvd.
Navigation Blvd.
EAST END
Leeland St.
45
Elgin St.
Scott St.
S. Wayside
GUS WORTHAM PARK
Telephone Rd.
Texas Southern University
University of Houston
S. MacGregor Way
Old Spanish Trail
Griggs St.
Martin Luther King Blvd.
Cullen Blvd.
Long Drive
Mykawa Rd.
Bellfort St.

fast local FOOD

Sometimes you need to find a meal quickly and cheaply, but you don't want the same-old, same-old from international fast-food chains, where the fare tastes the same whether you're in Houston or Honolulu. A number of small local chains in Houston cook up fast food with character. Here are four worth considering:

Antone's Famous Po'Boy ★ In 1962, the Antone family, originally from Lebanon, opened an exotic import grocery store on Taft Street near Allen Parkway called Antone's. There, they introduced Houston to their now-famous **po'boy (sub) sandwiches,** which caught on in a big way. Today there are three locations across Houston selling New Orleans–style po'boys, deli sandwiches, and gumbo guaranteed to fill you up. Get the original green label or the super red label po'boy, both a combination of ham, salami, cheese, pickles, and special chow chow on fresh baked bread. Or go seafood with a shrimp and oyster po'boy. Antone's Famous Po'Boy (www.antoneshouston.com) locations: West Loop (4520 San Felipe), North Loop (2724 West T.C. Jester), and a new grab-and-go kiosk inside Greenway Plaza (3 Greenway Plaza, Suite C-118); you can also find these po'boys for sale at some of the small grocery stores in town.

Becks Prime This local chain of upscale burger joints is known for big juicy burgers and great shakes. Becks Prime (www.becksprime.com) locations include 2902 Kirby Dr. (near Westheimer Rd.), 1001 E. Memorial Loop (in Memorial Park by the golf course), and 708 Meyerland Plaza.

Café Express Café Express (www.cafe-express.com) operates under the guiding principle that fast food can be nutritious, fresh, and cooked with at least some artistry. It specializes in salads and sandwiches, lively pasta dishes, and juicy roast chicken. Café Express has 11 locations, one in the Fine Arts Museum, and others in the River Oaks Shopping Center (19443 Gulf Fwy., 1422 W. Gray St.); Downtown (650 Main St.), and the Galleria area (1101 Uptown Park, just off Post Oak Blvd.).

James Coney Island Hot Dogs James Coney Island (www.jamesconeyisland.com) started up in Houston in the 1930s, selling Coney Island–style chili dogs for a nickel. (Most Houstonians consider hot dogs without chili as either unfulfilled potential or foreign novelty.) You can also order the chili with or without beans or as a chili pie. For the dawg, I'd go with the Texas chili iteration. Houston has more than 20 locations, including the Kirby District (3607 Shepherd Dr. at corner of Richmond Ave.), the Galleria area (1600 S. Post Oak Blvd.), and along the Gulf Freeway (6955 Gulf Fwy. and 10600 Gulf Fwy.).

and grits. Both are good choices for lunch, dinner, or happy hour in an upbeat, albeit sometimes noisy, setting.

218 Travis St. www.hearsayhouston.com. ✆ **713/225-8079.** Reservations recommended on weekends. Main courses $10–$25 lunch; $12–$34 dinner. Mon–Thurs 11am–midnight, Fri–Sat 11am–2am; Sun 10am–10pm. Brunch Sat–Sun 11am–3pm. Small bites Fri–Sun 3–4pm.

INEXPENSIVE

The Breakfast Klub & Signature Kafé ★★ BREAKFAST/BRUNCH Local radio personality Marcus Davis loved going out for breakfast, but he couldn't find a good diner that served real Southern grits and strong coffee. So when he opened the Breakfast Klub, his self-described "coffee shop that happens to serve great food," he focused on making a great cup of Joe and serving mouthwatering Southern comfort food. "Katfish" and grits, biscuits and gravy, chicken and waffles, pork chops and eggs, and crawfish etouffée all make Davis's menu a stone-cold winner, and he keeps things simple by having guests order at the counter before finding a seat. Of course, a seat is hard to find on Saturday mornings, when a long line snakes through the restaurant and the scent of brewing coffee and good eats fills the air. The hip and attractive dining room is hung with local art and has Southern gospel or soft jazz humming in the background. For lunch, look for salads and sandwiches and hearty Louisiana-inspired specials like crawfish fettuccine. The restaurant is also home to the **Signature Kafé,** a separate dining space behind the Breakfast Klub, serving up mimosas, margaritas, and Bloody Marys with a limited menu of BK signature dishes. And because Davis always loved having breakfast for dinner, he now serves late-night eats from 10pm to 3am on Friday and Saturday. *Good Morning America, USA Today, Esquire,* and *Forbes* have all sung the praises of the Breakfast Klub, and chances are you will too.

3711 Travis St. www.thebreakfastklub.com. ✆ **713/528-8561.** Breakfast $9–$15; sandwiches $9–$13. Mon–Fri 7am–2pm; Sat 8am–2pm.

Treebeards ★★ SOUTHERN CREOLE Louisiana-style Low Country eats—we're talking shrimp gumbo, etouffée, red beans and rice, and jambalaya—are meant to be hearty and filling and served in a snazzy historic space, and that's just what you'll find at Treebeards. With exposed brick walls, high ceilings, and a French Quarter–style alfresco dining gallery, Treebeards is housed in one of Houston's oldest buildings, the Baker-Travis Building (ca. 1861), facing Market Square Park. This is a popular lunch spot for downtown business types, so go early or late to avoid the line. With a full bar, including cocktails, wine, and a big assortment of beers, this is a good place to hit after a day of sightseeing. Look for the funky psychedelic mural outside. Food that is good, inexpensive, and filling is a winning combination, and Treebeards now has four other successful Houston locations: the Cloister (1117 Texas Ave., next to Christ Church Cathedral); in the Tunnel (1100 Louisiana St.); Pennzoil Place (711 Louisiana St.); and the Shops at Houston Center (1200 McKinney #329).

315 Travis St. (btw. Preston and Congress sts.). www.treebeards.com. ✆ **713/228-2622.** Reservations not accepted. Main courses $5–$9. Mon–Fri 11am–2:30pm.

East End

MODERATE

Kim Son ★ VIETNAMESE/CHINESE The menu at this family-owned Bellaire-area restaurant could easily overwhelm a first-time diner with its 100-plus choices; but so many options are actually a plus, for there's no end to the possibilities for a great meal made with fresh ingredients and authentic Asian elements at affordable prices. In fact, you could eat here every day of your

Houston vacation and not sample all its delights. Not sure where to begin? Start simple with the fresh spring rolls and savory noodle dishes, and then maybe try something with more of a local twist, like the pan-seared shrimp with jalapeños and onions. Among the good vegetarian options are the eggplant with garlic sauce and General Tso's Tofu. For more than 3 decades, Kim Son restaurants have pleased Houston diners, and today there are three Houston-area locations, including one in Sugarland.

2001 Jefferson St. (a block east of the Brown Convention Center). www.kimson.com. ✆ **713/222-2461.** Reservations accepted only for parties of 8 or more. Main courses $12–$16. Sun–Thurs 11am–11pm; Sun 11 am–midnight.

INEXPENSIVE

Fiesta The Original Loma Linda Mexican Restaurant ★ TEX-MEX I find that the best Tex-Mex restaurants are homey, unpretentious, and traditional, like this one. Serving tasty Tex-Mex since 1956 in an old motorcycle shop, Loma Linda is the perfect unassuming old-school cantina, a place that seems happily oblivious to all things hip or trendy. With an authentic 1930s tortilla maker, Loma Linda still serves the old-fashioned puffy tortillas that Mexican restaurants always served in Texas when I was a kid—and that should be the first thing you order: a puffy *chili con queso* appetizer and some puffy chicken or beef tacos. Of course, somebody should also order the traditional Tex-Mex enchiladas drowning in cheese and chili gravy. Or just go for a combination plate for a taste of it all. If you've never experienced a real Tex-Mex meal, let this one be your first.

2111 Telephone Rd. (6 blocks off the Gulf Fwy., I-45). www.fiestalomalinda.com. ✆ **713/924-6074.** Reservations not accepted. Main courses $8–$10; lunch specials $7–$10. Mon–Wed 10:30am–9pm; Thurs–Sat 10am–10pm; Sun 10am–4:30pm.

Montrose/The Heights

EXPENSIVE

Divino Restaurant & Wine Bar ★★ ITALIAN/WINE BAR For more than 20 years, this River Oaks restaurant has developed a loyal following with a menu of authentic Northern Italian dishes and a thoughtfully curated array of Italian fine wines. Divino's owner/chef Patrick McCray lived and trained in the Emilia-Romagna region, and his passion for seasonality and freshness comes through in dishes like Emily's Goat Cheese Ravioli, with housemade goat-cheese-and-chive ravioli, or grilled Texas quail with polenta and a sauce of Morello cherries. The restaurant has its own wine newsletter and even sells wine by the case at reasonable prices. Most bottles are under $60, and as many as 30 wines are offered by the glass. On the first Monday of each month, Divino's offers complimentary seminar-style wine tasting events at 6 and 7:30pm; these fill up fast (reservations required). Divino's has good traditional Italian desserts, but the ice cream across the street at the **Chocolate Bar,** 1835 West Alabama (www.theoriginalchocolatebar.com; ✆ **713/520-8599**), is some of the best in town, with several varieties of chocolate and an irresistible white-chocolate lemon. It also has layer cakes, cookies, and pies.

1830 W. Alabama St. www.divinoitalian.com. ✆ **713/807-1123.** Reservations recommended. Main courses $14–$28. Tues–Thurs 5:30–10pm; Fri–Sat 5:30–10:30pm; open every 1st Monday of the month for dinner and free seminar-style wine tasting events.

Hugo's ★★★ MEXICAN Chef Hugo Ortega is a five-time finalist for the James Beard "Best Chef: Southwest" award, and *Eater* named Hugo's one of the "Best Restaurants in America" in 2016. Serving authentic made-from-scratch Mexican dishes given Ortega's brilliant contemporary twist, Hugo's is not your typical Houston Tex-Mex restaurant. Chef Ortega calls upon local purveyors for fresh, seasonal, and sustainable ingredients. For an appetizer, try the tuna ceviche, the spicy shrimp cocktail, or the hot, gooey *queso flameado*. Main courses include smoky grilled chicken with ancho chile sauce and a roasted duck smothered in a traditional Mexican molé sauce. Set in a 1925 Art Deco building, the cavernous dining room has a vintage pressed-tin ceiling and colorful Mexican accents, including tile floors. You can also sit on the sunny patio with adobe walls and a fountain with a shimmering blue-tile backsplash.

1602 Westheimer Rd. (at Mandell St.). www.hugosrestaurant.net. ✆ **713/524-7744.** Reservations recommended. Main courses $19–$34. Mon–Thurs 11am–10pm; Fri–Sat 11am–11pm; Sun 10am–9pm.

Restaurant CINQ ★★★ MODERN EUROPEAN When locals list the chicest restaurants in Houston, CINQ always makes the cut. With an atmosphere of unpretentious elegance (white tablecloths but no fussy attitude) and a menu of modern European cuisine, "5 Restaurant Cinq" is set in La Colombe d'Or Hotel, where many well-heeled Houstonites have attended glittery galas and wedding receptions. At CINQ, guests can choose from five distinctive dining areas, ranging from the terrace to an inviting library to a clubby bar space. All are perfect retreats for cocktails, lunch, afternoon tea, dinner, or just dessert and coffee. At lunch, start with the Jumbo Lump Crab Tower or the crispy foie gras. The chicken hazelnut is also delicious. For dinner, try the smoked octopus to start and the roasted rack of prime Colorado lamb with mint sauce. CINQ is certainly a splurge, but it's worth it.

3410 Montrose Blvd., in the La Colombe d'Or Hotel. http://lacolombedor.com/restaurant-cinq. ✆ **713/524-7999.** Reservations recommended. Main courses: $16–$28 lunch and $26–$49 dinner. Mon–Fri 11am–2pm; Mon–Thurs 6–9pm and Fri–Sat 6–11pm; closed Sun.

Shade ★★ NEW AMERICAN Houston celebrity chef Claire Smith is known for her "global home cooking," as she calls it, a fusion of international flavors underscored by an American sensibility. At Shade, Smith's casual brunch and dinner spot in the Heights, that means the menu may list a Cuban sandwich alongside a duck confit spring roll, and both will reflect Smith's unique sensibilities. The often inventive food includes dishes like Brussels sprouts tartine, a winter vegetable curry, and braised lamb with saffron couscous. The large, minimalist space is high-ceilinged and light-filled. Shade also has a nice bar featuring a popular happy hour every day from 3 to 7pm. Smith also owns the restaurant **Canopy,** as well as its adjacent **Woodbar**—a "spirits and coffee" shop for beer, wine, coffee, lunch and dinner—in Montrose, both neighborhood favorites.

250 W. 19th St. www.shadeheights.com. ✆ **713/863-7500.** Reservations recommended. Main courses $15–$26. Mon 7am–9pm; Tues–Thurs 7am–3pm and 5–10pm; Fri 7am–3pm and 5–10:30pm; Sat 9am–3pm and 5–10:30pm; Sun 9am–3pm.

Tiny Boxwoods ★★★ BISTRO FARE I just adore this lovely little bistro enveloped in the lush green of a nursery. You can shop for flowers and plants next door, and then dine in amid boxwoods under shady awnings at this sunny little brunch, lunch, coffee/tea-time, and dinner spot where much thought has gone into the menu, the service, and the setting. The chef's less-is-more philosophy means that simple, fresh foods are offered in season and in an unfussy style. "When in doubt, use goat cheese," is the mantra here, and that speaks to how they think through each ingredient when creating light, delectable dishes and wood-fired pizzas. In 2011, another location, **Tiny's #5,** was opened near Rice University to serve the West University campus crowd. At this location, a bakery turns out 20 fresh-from-the-oven chocolate chip cookies every 20 minutes, and paired with a cup of coffee, there may be no better finish for a meal.

3614 W. Alabama St. www.tinyboxwoods.com. ✆ **713/622-4224.** Reservations recommended. Main courses $25–$45. Tues–Fri 7–3pm, 3:30–5pm, and 5:30–10pm; Sat brunch 8am–3pm; Sun brunch 9am–2pm. In a nursery setting near River Oaks/Lower Shepherd.

INEXPENSIVE

Christian's Tailgate Grill and Bar ★ BAR/GRILL This is a typical blue-collar happy-hour joint—a sports bar/burger grill with a TV and neon beer signs. It's the sort of place to go after a Rockets or Astros game or to watch the Super Bowl. Christian's hosts beer-pong tournaments on Monday nights, "Geeks who Drink" trivia contests on Tuesdays, "Music Bingo Steak Nights" on Wednesdays, live music on Thursday nights, and karaoke on Friday and Saturday nights. Christian's is a what-you-see-is-what-you-get kind of joint with a pool table, electronic arcade games, and a big menu, with burgers, tacos and jalapeño poppers. For dessert, try the oddly delicious fried Oreos. Happy hour is from 2 to 7pm weekdays. Christian's also offers a "tailgate brunch" on Saturdays and Sundays and has other locations downtown and midtown.

2820 White Oak. www.christianstailgate.com. ✆ **713/863-1207.** Burgers $9–$11. Mon–Fri 10am–9pm; Sat 11am–9pm.

Yale Street Grill ★ AMERICAN Part diner/part antiques store, this vintage lunch counter in the Heights reminds me of a quirky old corner diner we once visited in Queens. Wood paneling, a Formica counter, worn leather booths, and tchotchkes lining walls and ledges give this place a throwback feel—and it's definitely from another era, a business dating to 1923 tucked into a location from 1952. It's attached to Lovejoys Antiques & Collectibles (home, reputedly, to a friendly poltergeist), where guests can browse until the waitress hollers that the food is ready. The walls are framed with photos of musty old celebrities: John Wayne, Johnny Carson, Sonny and Cher, the

Munsters, and even Mr. Ed the talking horse. An entire wall is devoted to Elvis. This is the kind of place that serves chocolate chip pancakes and "patty melts" or diner classics like meatloaf. Shockingly, the kitchen makes a big effort to ensure that ingredients are natural, and you can get gluten-free items too, along with fresh-squeezed juices. It's a popular local breakfast spot (breakfast is served all day on weekends), and milkshakes and malts are made with Blue Bell ice cream in the grill's original mixer. Places like this are disappearing fast in America, and there is no other quite like it in Houston, so soak up the vintage ambience while you still can.

2100 Yale St. ✆ **713/861-3113.** Breakfast $5–$11; sandwiches $5–$9; Specials $7.50. Daily 7am–4:30pm.

Kirby District

MODERATE

Goode Company Texas Seafood ★ SEAFOOD This relaxed barbecue shack is a venerable local institution, smoking its meats—brisket, pork ribs, homemade sausage, chicken, and duck—low and slow over the mesquite logs you see stacked on the side of the building. Made-from-scratch sides, including a jalapeño cheese bread, round out the simple menu. Shuffling along the cafeteria-style line lets you take a gander at richly detailed rustic decor on the walls: historic cowboy photographs, vintage beer bottles, antlers, and a mounted buffalo head looming over the country-music-playing jukebox. You might find a place to sit inside, but your best bet is usually a picnic table on the covered patio. Wash down the savory goodness with an ice-cold Shiner Bock, cap it all off with a sublime slab of pecan pie, and you've got yourself a bona fide Texas experience. This is the original of Goode Company's mini-empire; the family-owned operation currently runs seven other restaurants, including one in Katy, 8911 Katy Fwy. (✆ **713/464-1901**); northwest Houston, 20102 Northwest Fwy. (✆ **832/678-3562**); and Kirby, 5109 Kirby Dr. (✆ **713/522-2530**).

2621 Westpark Dr. www.goodecompany.com. ✆ **713/523-7154.** Reservations not accepted. Main courses $19–$29. Sun–Thurs 11am–10pm; Fri–Sat 11am–11pm.

Little Pappasito's ★ TEX-MEX The Pappas family of restaurants, a Texas-based empire of steakhouses, seafood joints, and more, also serves a quality version of Tex-Mex at the many Pappasito's Cantina restaurants, lending a slightly higher sense of style (and price) to Tex-Mex cuisine, and generally using higher-quality ingredients, too. Folks come here for fire-grilled beef and chicken fajitas, hearty guacamole with fried tortilla chips, and hot, steaming plates of cheese enchiladas. We only have two issues with this Pappasito's: The parking lot is too small for a place this popular, and they don't take reservations. Long waits are not uncommon here, so try to pop in during off-peak hours. But even if you have to wait, you'll be glad you did.

2536 Richmond Ave. www.pappasitos.com. ✆ **713/520-5066.** Reservations not accepted. Main courses $14–$29. Mon–Thurs 11am–10pm; Fri 9:30am–11pm; Sun 9:30am–10pm.

Lupe Tortilla ★ TEX-MEX If we were cynical, we'd say that the playground at this family-owned establishment was a savvy ploy to keep kids occupied while the parents relax nearby at a patio table sipping margaritas. But it's hard to be cynical when you're staring at an enticing menu of Tex-Mex classics. Fajitas are a hit here, as are the grilled and three-pepper-filled cheese steak and the Steak Lupe. Kids will like the nachos and *chalupas* (plus the sombrero lights hanging over the tables), and grownups seem to really go for the crab-stuffed avocados. For dessert, try the fried banana, wrapped in a crisp-fried cinnamon flour tortilla drizzled with chocolate and topped with a scoop of Texas's own Blue Bell ice cream. Lupe's has 10 other Houston-area locations.

2414 Southwest Fwy. www.lupetortilla.com. ✆ **713/522-4420.** Reservations not accepted. Main courses $15–$25. Sun–Thurs 11am–10pm; Fri–Sat 11am–11pm. Happy hour 3–6:30pm.

Thai Spice ★ THAI Popular shopping area Rice Village has several good Thai restaurants, each with its own loyal regulars; we like this place best. The service is consistently good, the dining space is attractive, and the kitchen does Thai with flavorful subtlety—they aren't out to set fire to your tastebuds. If you do like a kick of zesty spice, however, they can bring on the heat, in curries especially, but milder dishes, like drunken chicken and Bangkok Treat (chicken, pork, or shrimp with pineapple, onions, and tomatoes) dominate the menu. Pad Thai Chonburi, with shrimp and chicken, is a house fave. Can't decide? Graze around the menu at the large lunch buffet. This is one of eight Thai Spice locations throughout the greater Houston area.

5117 Kelvin Dr. (at Dunstan St.). www.thaispice.com. ✆ **713/522-5100.** Main courses $10–$16; lunch buffet $9. Mon–Thurs 11am–2:30pm (lunch buffet) and 5–9:30pm; Fri 11am–2:30pm and 5–10pm; Sat 11:30-3pm and 5-10pm; Sun 11:30am–3pm and 5–9pm.

INEXPENSIVE

Luling City Market ★ BARBECUE Call us persnickety, but it bothers us that this Houston barbecue restaurant "borrows" the exact moniker of the famous barbecue joint of the same name in the Texas town of Luling—with which it has no affiliation. Still, this family-owned barbecue hot spot has been a Houston favorite since 1981, and no one else seems to care about the small matter of the name. It's really not much like the original Luling joint anyway, except that the meat here is smoked low and slow over wood fires stoked with Texas Post Oak wood, and the sausage here is made in-house from a 35-year-old family recipe. There's a nice bar on one end, and walls are decorated with a deer mount, a wagon wheel, guitar and hat, and framed flags. Service is cafeteria style, with big pans of ribs and pinto beans, and guests dine at wooden tables. The menu is what you'd expect of a traditional barbecue joint, so brisket and sausage are a good place to start. At night, the bar fills up with regulars who tend to talk football 'til closing time.

4726 Richmond Ave. www.lulingcitymarket.com. ✆ **713/871-1903.** Reservations not accepted. Barbecue sold by weight: brisket, ribs and turkey $9 per half-pound, $17.45 per pound. Mon–Sat 11am–9pm; Sun noon–7pm.

Uptown

EXPENSIVE

Cafe Annie ★★★ SOUTHWESTERN Are we preaching to the choir when we sing this restaurant's praises? We wouldn't be the first. For more than 35 years, no restaurant in Houston has received more coverage and acclaim than Cafe Annie. A little background: In 2009, James Beard Award–winning Chef Robert Del Grande changed Cafe Annie's name to RDG + Bar Annie, debuting a new, two-story eatery on Post Oak Boulevard. In 2016, however, the chef decided it was time the restaurant was reborn again in its original incarnation as Cafe Annie, bringing back many of its most popular signature dishes with it. If you're looking for *the* restaurant in Houston (and especially if you're on a fat expense account), this hits all the high notes. Those of us who aren't so fortunate can save money by going for lunch or ordering from the bar menu. One of Chef Del Grande's signature dishes, crabmeat tostadas, is a wonderful composition of fresh lump crabmeat, avocado, and finely shredded cabbage. Try the bacon-wrapped quail, Gulf crab potpies, or the wood-grilled steaks. The restaurant has an earthy sleekness, with wooden stairs and high ceilings.

1800 Post Oak Blvd. (just south of San Felipe). www.cafeanniehouston.com. ✆ **713/840-1111.** Reservations recommended. Main courses $16–$54. Mon–Thurs 11:30am–10pm; Fri–Sat 11:30am–10:30pm; closed Sun.

MODERATE

Kenny & Ziggy's ★ DELI New York–style delis serving pastrami on rye, corned beef and cabbage, and matzo ball soup are hardly a big thing in Texas. Perhaps that's why this one is so popular. This is a real old-school deli counter. Not far from the shopping fun of the Galleria in the heart of Uptown, this casual space is decorated with movie posters, caricatures, and black-and-white photos on the walls. Deli items (meats, cheeses, and lox) are sold by the pound, and you can also get hearty main-course meals, like roast chicken, baked salmon, and stuffed cabbage. Leave room for authentic New York–style cheese cake. Because there really are not enough delis in town, Kenny & Ziggy's has a second location at 5172 Buffalo Speedway (✆ **832/767-1136**).

2327 Post Oak Blvd. www.kennyandziggys.com. ✆ **713/871-8883.** Sandwiches (served with 2 sides) $12–$20; dinners $20–$33. Mon–Fri 7am–9pm; Sat–Sun 8am–9pm. Look for the strip center at the intersection of Westheimer and Post Oak in the northwest corner.

HOUSTON SHOPPING

If you're anywhere in Houston, you probably aren't that far from a strip center or mall, many more than can be mentioned here. Malls are usually located at or near the intersection of a freeway with the Loop or Beltway 8 or other major artery. One of the biggest and most popular is **The Galleria,** with its ice rink and swank stores. Bargain hunters make a beeline for the city's outlet malls. The top one is **Katy Mills,** a mammoth collection of some 200 factory outlet stores on the far western boundary of Houston in the suburb of Katy.

Take the Katy Freeway (I-10 W.) until you spot the signs; the drive is about 25 miles from the center of town but is handy for those coming into Houston from San Antonio or Austin or those staying in Sugarland or Pearland or Katy. The selection of merchandise is huge, but discounts vary. Katy Mills also has restaurants and a large AMC movie theater with 20 screens.

Top Shopping Areas

Whether you're a purposeful shopper or a last-minute one, you'll need to know something about the shopping terrain of Houston. Of course, the main shopping area in Houston is Galleria/Uptown, but other areas have a diversity of stores that might be just what you're looking for.

DOWNTOWN

Downtown's shopping district is anchored by **GreenStreet** (formerly known as Houston Pavilions), 1201 Fannin St. (http://greenstreetdowntown.com), a mixed-use shopping, entertainment, and dining hub. GreenStreet is home to several big, nationally known shops like Forever 21 and BCBG Max Azria. Two blocks away stand the **Shops at Houston Center** at 1200 McKinney St., across from the Four Seasons (www.shopsathc.com; ✆ **713/759-1442**). with Jos. A Banks, Dress Barn, Radio Shack, and other retail, dining, and fast-food options, including some 40 boutiques and small specialty shops.

EAST END

Just the other side of the freeway from the George Brown Convention Center is a commercial **Chinatown,** where you can find all kinds of goods imported from across Asia. Furniture, foods, curios—you can browse your way through a number of little import stores, all within a 4-block area, between Dowling on the east, Chartreuse on the west, Rusk on the north, and Dallas on the south.

MONTROSE/THE HEIGHTS

Along Westheimer from Woodhead to Mandell, you'll find several junk/antiques shops that are perfect for the bargain shopper on a leisurely hunt for a diamond in the rough. A grouping of similar stores can be found on 19th Street in the Heights. In these stores, merchandise is set down just about anywhere the owners can find a place for it, and dusting is a once-in-a-while practice. Don't ever accept the first price you're offered at these places—they will almost always lower the price. (For more discriminating antiques stores, go to the Kirby District.) Also along Westheimer are vintage clothing stores.

Among the antiques stores on 19th Street, a Latin American folk-art shop called **Casa Ramírez,** 241 W. 19th St. (✆ **713/880-2420**), displays a panoramic collection of Mexican folk art from across the country. And in another part of the Heights, **Hello-Lucky,** 1025 Studewood St. (✆ **713/864-3556**), sells clothing and housewares designed by local artists.

North of Westheimer, on West Gray where it intersects with Shepherd, is Houston's oldest shopping center: the **River Oaks Shopping Center,** 1996 West Gray (www.riveroaksshoppingcenter.com; ✆ **713/880-6129**), set in one of the city's toniest old-money neighborhoods. Home to a chic collection of more than 75 stores and restaurants—including nationally recognized stores, eclectic shops, and good dining options—this fancy little shopping center is 2 blocks long and extends down both sides of West Gray, with its older sections rocking a vintage white-and-black Art Deco style and its newer additions setting a more contemporary tone. It also boasts Houston's oldest movie theatre (1939), an arthouse cinema where you can sip wine while watching the show. This shopping center attracts discriminating shoppers with center-wide valet parking.

KIRBY DISTRICT

Kirby is more uniformly upscale than the Montrose. **Highland Village,** 4000 Westheimer (www.shophighlandvillage.com; ✆ **713/850-3100**), like so much of the retail business in this part of town, is aimed at the upper-middle-class shopper. It has stores like Kate Spade and Restoration Hardware and a few one-of-a-kind boutiques. From this part of Kirby Drive to where it passes Rice Village is a section known informally as **Gallery Row,** a mix of galleries, designer showrooms, and antiques and special-furnishings shops. Finally, **Rice Village** is a 16-block neighborhood of more than 300 shops, including small boutiques mixed with outlets from high-dollar national retailers. This is one of Houston's oldest shopping areas, dating back to the 1930s when it was just a cluster of ad-hoc shops, and a few of the small shops you see today are survivors from those simpler times—now a bit at odds in the environment of day spas, tony shoe stores, and designer boutiques. Rice Village also has a wide variety of restaurants for taking a break from browsing. A popular shopping mall with an indoor ice rink in a nice part of town is **Memorial City Mall,** 303 Memorial City (www.memorialcity.com/shop; ✆ **713/464-8640**).

UPTOWN

The **Galleria,** 5085 Westheimer Rd. (www.simon.com/mall/the-galleria; ✆ **713/966-3500**), is probably Houston's best-known mall—and many people consider the area all around it "The Galleria." The Galleria shopping area occupies a long stretch of land along Westheimer and Post Oak and has 320 stores, including big department stores such as Saks, Neiman Marcus, and Nordstrom, and high-end designer retailers such as Bally, Gucci, Bottega Veneta, and Tiffany & Co. This is where folks from all over Texas come each year to do holiday shopping and go ice skating at the mall's indoor rink. Across Westheimer from the Galleria is another shopping center called **Centre at Post Oak.** If you're looking for the finest in Western wear, go to **Pinto Ranch,** 1717 Post Oak Blvd. (www.pintoranch.com; ✆ **713/333-7900**). This store sells high-end Western clothing, boots, belt buckles, hats, and saddles.

SOUTHWEST

In southwest Houston just beyond the Loop is where the Asian bazaar meets the American suburb. This fascinating area is simultaneously adventure shopping and an exploration into the brave new world of postmodern America. First, drive down **Harwin Drive** between Fondren and Gessner. You will see stores and strip malls selling jewelry, designer clothes, sunglasses, perfumes, furniture, luggage, and handbags. Most of these stores are run by Indian,

Pakistani, Chinese, and Thai shopkeepers, but other cultures are represented, too. Occasionally one will get raided for selling designer knockoffs. Everything is said to be at bargain-basement rates, but buyer beware. What I like the best are the import stores where you never know what you'll find. Farther out, on **Bellaire Boulevard** in the middle of a large commercial Chinatown, is an all-Chinese mall, where you can get just about anything Chinese, including CDs, books, food and cooking items, and wonderful knickknacks.

HOUSTON NIGHTLIFE

The Performing Arts

For fans of the performing arts, Houston is fertile ground. Few cities in the country can equal it for the quality of its resident orchestra, opera, ballet, and theater companies. In addition, a number of organizations bring talented artists and companies here from around the country and the world, everything from Broadway shows to Argentine tango groups to string quartets. Tickets aren't usually discounted for the opera, ballet, or symphony, but ask anyway. For information about performances, visit **ww.visithoustontexas.com** or the websites of the various organizations listed below.

The symphony, the ballet, the opera, and the **Alley Theatre** (the city's largest and oldest theater company) all hold their performances in the theater district downtown. The opera and the ballet share the **Wortham Center,** 501 Texas Ave. (www.houstonfirsttheaters.com/Wortham-Center; ✆ **832/487-700**); the symphony plays a block away at **Jones Hall,** 615 Louisiana St. (✆ **832/487-7050**); and the **Alley Theatre** is one of those rare companies that actually owns its own theater, located at 615 Texas Ave. (www.alleytheatre.org; ✆ **713/220-5700**), adjacent to the symphony. Also in the theater district is **Hobby Center for the Performing Arts,** 800 Bagby St. (www.thehobbycenter.org; ✆ **713/315-2400**), which is shared by the Society for Performing Arts and Theater Under the Stars.

The **Society for the Performing Arts (SPA),** 615 Louisiana St. (www.spahouston.org; box office ✆ **713/227-4772**), is a nonprofit organization that brings to Houston distinguished dance companies, jazz bands, theater productions, and soloists. Within SPA, a program called the Broadway Series brings popular productions from Broadway and London's West End for performances in Jones Hall, the Wortham Center, and the Hobby Center.

Following are brief descriptions of the principal organizations; there are many more, including independent theater companies that present several plays a year.

CLASSICAL MUSIC, OPERA & BALLET

The **Houston Symphony** (www.houstonsymphony.org; ✆ **713/224-7575**) is the city's oldest performing-arts organization. Its season is from September to May, during which it holds about 100 concerts in Jones Hall. The classical series usually contains a number of newer compositions with visits by several guest conductors and soloists from around the world. A pops series and a chamber music series often hold performances at Rice University.

Da Camera of Houston (www.dacamera.com; ✆ **713/524-5050**) brings classical and jazz chamber music orchestras to the city and holds concerts either at the Wortham or in the lobby of the Menil Collection. You can buy tickets from the box office at 1402 Sul Ross St. in the Montrose area.

The nationally acclaimed **Houston Grand Opera** is the fifth-largest opera company in the United States. Known for being innovative and premiering new operas such as *Nixon in China,* its productions of classical works are brilliant visual affairs. The opera season is from October to May. For tickets and information, call or go to the **Wortham Center** box office at 550 Prairie St. (www.houstongrandopera.org; ✆ **713/546-0200**) during regular business hours, or buy tickets online through the website.

The **Houston Ballet** (www.houstonballet.org; ✆ **713/227-2787**) has garnered enormous critical acclaim from across the country. A lot of the credit belongs to director Ben Stevenson, who came to Houston more than 25 years ago under the condition that the company create its own school of dance. Called the **Houston Ballet Academy,** it now supplies the company with 90% of its dancers, and other graduates dance in many top ballet companies. The company tours a great deal, but manages around 80 performances a year at the Wortham Center in Houston.

THEATER

The **Alley Theatre,** 615 Texas Ave. (www.alleytheatre.org; ✆ **713/220-5700**), has won many awards for its productions. It has a large theater and an arena theater, and during the year the company uses both to stage about 10 different productions ranging from Shakespeare to Stoppard and even a musical or two. Ask about half-price tickets sold on the day of the show for weekday and Sunday performances. You can also take advantage of pay-what-you-can days, but you must show up in person to buy the tickets. Box office hours are daily from noon to 6pm and to curtain on performance days.

Theatre Under the Stars, 800 Bagby St. (www.tuts.org; ✆ **713/558-2600**), specializes in musicals that it either brings to town or produces itself, averaging 200 performances annually. The organization got its name from having first worked at Miller Outdoor Theater in Hermann Park. It uses the Hobby Center for the Performing Arts.

The **Ensemble Theatre,** 3535 Main St. (www.ensemblehouston.com; ✆ **713/520-0055**), is the city's largest black theater company. Founded in 1976, the Ensemble has grown from a band of strolling players into a resident professional company of 40 actors and eight directors. Its specialty is African-American and experimental theater.

The Club & Music Scene

To find out what's on, check out the ***Houston Press*** (www.houstonpress.com), a free weekly you can find at many restaurants and shops. It provides a good rundown of the musical and comedy acts in town and includes a lot of

OUT DRINKING? CATCH THE wave

In Houston, as everywhere, it's a terrible idea to drink and drive. If you plan a night on the town, let the Wave transport you. The fixed-route, fixed-rate jitney-shuttle service picks up passengers throughout the city's primary nightlife areas or delivers them from their hotel or home to their destination and back. The Wave jitney runs on Thursdays 6pm to midnight, Fridays and Saturdays midnight to 3am, and Sundays 4pm to midnight. The cost is $8 one-way or $15 all-night roundtrip. Find out more on the Wave website (www.thehoustonwave.com) or call © **713/863-9283.**

advertising from the clubs. A daily paper, the ***Chronicle*** (www.chron.com), has a well-organized entertainment section and a pullout published on Thursdays.

In general, the most popular locations for nightspots are downtown, around the theater district and Old Market Square; and in the Montrose area, along Westheimer, and along Washington streets.

MEGACLUBS

In the theater district in downtown Houston, a developer has converted the old convention center into the **Revention Music Center,** 500 Texas Ave. (www.reventionmusiccenter.com; © **713/230-1600**), a complex of restaurants, clubs, bars, and a concert hall that for a time was called Bayou Place or the Bayou Music Center. Houston is also home to a **Hard Rock Cafe** (www.hardrock.com/cafes/houston; © **713/227-1392**), with some live acts on the weekends; and **Slick Willie's** (http://slickw.com/sites/houston.htm; © **713/522-2525**), a billiards club with four locations in Houston.

Also downtown is the **House of Blues** (www.houseofblues.com/houston; © **888/402-5837**), 1207 Caroline St., part of the national chain. Its size, and the fact that it is also a booking agency, enables it to bring in many name acts, as well as some hot up-and-coming ones. The House of Blues books bands that play every genre of popular music, including the blues. The Houston venue has two restaurants and three stages of varying size.

ROCK

One of the best venues for catching live rock acts is the old Houston institution known as **Fitzgerald's,** 2706 White Oak Dr. (www.fitzlive.com; © **713/862-3838**). It occupies an old Polish dance hall near the Heights neighborhood and gets talented local and touring bands. Look for their ad in the *Houston Press* to see who's playing while you're in town.

One of the most popular clubs for live rock acts in Houston is the **Continental Club,** 3700 Main St. (at Alabama St.) (www.continentalclub.com/houston; © **713/529-9899**). It's an offshoot of the famous Austin club and gets many of the same touring acts. Inside the club, a funky bar area is plastered with old rock concert posters. The crowd can include folks of just about any age, depending on who's playing.

JAZZ

Love jazz? You're in luck in Houston, which has several great jazz clubs. The more formal and expensive club, **Sambuca Jazz Café,** 909 Texas Ave. (✆ **713/224-5299**), is in the old Rice Hotel. It gets a dressed-up crowd and lines up some talented bands. Another favorite is **Cézanne** (www.cezannejazz.com; ✆ **832/592-7464;** $10 cover), a cozy space above the Black Labrador pub at 4100 Montrose Blvd. Often voted one of Houston's best jazz clubs, Cézanne is only open Fridays and Saturdays from 8:30pm until midnight, but expect a packed house. **Café 4212,** 4212 Almeda (www.cafe4212.com; ✆ **713/522-4212**), is a loud and lively place that's always jumping. It's the sometime host of rollicking New Orleans bands guaranteed to take the roof off.

BLUES

The **Big Easy Social and Pleasure Club,** 5731 Kirby Dr. (www.thebigeasyblues.com; ✆ **713/523-9999**), in Rice Village, lines up local blues talent that is uncommonly good, as well as touring zydeco acts. The clientele is a real mix of everything from yuppies to bikers. Admission runs anywhere from $5 to $15, depending on the act.

FOLK & ACOUSTIC

A folk and bluegrass institution in Houston, **McGonigel's Mucky Duck** (www.mcgonigels.com; ✆ **713/528-5999**), 2425 Norfolk St., near Kirby Dr. where it intersects the Southwest Freeway, has live music every night (closed Sun). Monday and Wednesday Irish jam sessions are free. It serves pub grub and burgers, wine, and beer.

Anderson Fair, 2007 Grant St. (www.andersonfair.net; ✆ **832/767-2785**), is a survivor from the 1960s, and looks every bit the product of its age. In its many years, it has nurtured several folk artists who went on to become big names in folk, including Nanci Griffith. It's only open Fridays and Saturdays. People of all ages hang out here, including a lot of former hippies. It's located a block off Montrose, behind the Montrose Art Supply building.

COUNTRY

In the "Urban Cowboy" 1980s, Gilley's in the Houston suburb of Pasadena put Houston's country music and honky-tonk dance scene on the map. A dispute between owners and a bad case of arson closed that place, but country music is alive and kicking (or "kikker dancing" as it's called here) in Houston. They don't call it country-western anymore (do that and they'll know you're a Yankee out-of-towner), but locals still love their country music. A popular place to go is the **Firehouse Saloon,** 5930 Southwest Freeway in the Gulfton area (www.firehousesaloon.com; ✆ **281/513-1995**), which has been in business for longer than 2 decades yet was still nominated best Music Venue of the Year in the Lone Star Music Awards not long ago and always showcases top bands. It's got a large dance hall, but like most Houston honky-tonks, the place is packed on weekend nights. Another hot spot for boot-scoot-boogie nights, Texas-style, is **Neon Boots Dancehall & Saloon,** 11410 Hempstead Rd. in the Lazy Brook/Timbergrove area (www.neonbootsclub.com;

(✆ **713/677-0828**), with a large dance floor and the requisite Gilly's-inspired mechanical bull.

The Bar Scene

La Carafe, 813 Congress St. (✆ **713/229-9399**), has been around for ages, and the small two-story brick building it occupies, even longer. In fact, it is the oldest commercial building in the city and sits slightly askew on a tiny lot facing Old Market Square. Its jukebox is something of a relic, too, with the most eclectic mix possible and some truly obscure choices. The clientele consists of mostly older downtowners who were here before the resurgence, as well as office types, in-line skaters, and reporters from the *Chronicle.* For sheer character, no place can beat it.

Another bar with a unique flavor is **Marfreless River Oaks Bar and Lounge,** an iconic speakeasy-style club hidden behind a nondescript blue door at 2006 Peden St. (www.marfrelesshouston.com; ✆ **281/630-6248**). This is the darkest bar I've ever been in. The background music is always classical, and the ambience is understated. Little alcoves here and there are considered romantic. The only trouble is finding the bar itself. It's in the River Oaks Shopping Center on West Gray. If you stand facing the River Oaks Theater, walk left and then make a right into the parking lot. Look for an unmarked door under a metal stairway. Although the place was renovated and reopened in 2014, it has retained its mysterious vibe.

Gay & Lesbian Nightlife

Most of Houston's gay nightlife centers around the Montrose area, where you'll find more than a dozen gay bars and clubs, mostly along lower Westheimer Road and Pacific Street. For current news, pick up a copy of *Houston Voice.*

For a large and popular dance club, go to **Rich's,** 2401 San Jacinto St. (www.richsnightclub.com; ✆ **281/846-6685**), in the downtown area. Rich's gets a mixed crowd that's mostly gay men and women. It's noted for its lights and decorations and a large dance floor with a mezzanine level, and it is very popular on Saturdays.

SIDE TRIPS TO EAST TEXAS

Piney Woods & Big Thicket National Preserve

From **Beaumont** (from Houston, take I-10 E. toward New Orleans, and you'll arrive in Beaumont in 1½ hr.), if you drive north on Tex. 69, you'll immediately enter the forestland known in Texas as the **Piney Woods.** This is a lovely part of the state that stretches all the way north to Arkansas. Tex. 69 runs through the heart of it and is one of the most enjoyable drives in the state, especially in the fall or the early spring, my favorite times for visiting east Texas. Several of the attractions described below can be reached by this road. The first of these is the **Big Thicket National Preserve.** The information station for the preserve (www.nps.gov/bith; ✆ **409/951-6800**) is 30 miles from

Beaumont, 8 miles past the town of Kountze. It will be on the right, just off the highway at the intersection of Hwy. 69 and Farm Road 420. The station is open daily from 8am to 4:30pm, except for Christmas and New Year's Day.

The Big Thicket is a lowland forest that occupies a region of swamps, bayous, and creeks. It's dotted with the occasional meadow, but for the most part grows so dense as to become impassable. In earlier times, it extended over 3 million acres and was an impenetrable and hostile place for early settlers. Stories abound of people getting lost in these woods and of outlaws using the place for their hideouts. With lumbering, oil exploration, roads, and settlement, the Big Thicket has been reduced to a tenth of its original size. Of what's left, almost 100,000 acres have been preserved by acts of Congress. The preserved area is not one large expanse of land, but 12 separate units, most of which follow the courses of rivers, creeks, and bayous.

The most remarkable thing about the Big Thicket is its diversity of life: The land is checkered with different ecological niches that bring together species coexisting nowhere else. It has been called the American Ark. Hickory trees and bluebirds from the Eastern forests dwell close by cactuses and roadrunners from the American Southwest, and southern cypress trees and alligators from the Southern coastal marshes. The variety is astonishing. Of the five species of North American insect-eating plants, four live inside the Big Thicket.

For the visitor, the area provides opportunities for hiking, canoeing, and primitive camping. Some of the units are closed during hunting season (mid-Sept to mid-Jan) and some might be closed by flooding. You can get maps and detailed information about the hiking trails, free permits for primitive camping, and books about this fascinating area at the information station. The trails here range from .5 to 20 miles. Although leaving the designated hiking trails is permitted, you must be careful not to get lost; trailblazing in this dense brush can be slow going and painful. Canoeing in some ways has an advantage over hiking, though it limits your travel to waterways with easy access for dropping off and picking up the canoes. At the station, you can get information about canoe outfitters that operate from the towns of Kountze and Silsbee, mostly from late spring to early fall. For lodging and food, you'll have to rely on the establishments in one of the nearby towns; the preserve has no such facilities. If you're in Kountze during lunchtime on any weekday, the most interesting place to eat is at the county courthouse, where most of the locals show up.

National Forests

North and west of the Big Thicket, the ecological complexity gives way to pine forest habitat. Inside this large belt of pine forest are four national forests that provide opportunities for hiking, camping, boating, and fishing. These areas are a nice getaway, especially in the non-summer months when the weather is more agreeable. They are much less visited than national parks and forests elsewhere. You can easily get to them from either Beaumont or Houston. Hwy. 69 leads directly into **Angelina National Forest,** about 50 miles north of Kountze. And the **Sam Houston National Forest** is only 55 miles north of Houston (take I-45). The other two are **Davy Crockett National Forest,** north of Sam Houston National Forest, and the **Sabine National Forest,** east of Angelina National Forest, on the Louisiana border. Each of these forests is roughly 150,000 acres, and each has more or less the same activities: hiking, camping, boating, and fishing, with such facilities as boat ramps, camping grounds, and hiking trails. For canoeing, there are a few interesting places in these forests, but they're mostly large expanses of open water and not as fun as what you'll find in the Big Thicket or Caddo Lake (described below).

When the weather is agreeable, the forests are lovely places for hiking, especially in Sam Houston National Forest or Davy Crockett, which have the majority of trails. One hiking trail in Sam Houston is 126 miles long and crosses private property in three or four places; this is a real standout for Texas, which despite its image isn't such a wide-open state. Landowners here are firm believers in barbed-wire fences and the rights of private property, but this trail makes use of the goodwill of local landowners. Fishing draws many visitors, and lots of places rent boats and equipment and can sell a temporary fishing license ($30) in the towns that lie in or next to these national forests. Your best bets for fishing are the Angelina or Sabine forests.

For general information about a specific national forest, visit **www.fs.usda.gov/detail/texas** or call one of the following numbers. The **Sam Houston National Forest** ranger offices are in the town of New Waverly (✆ **936/344-6205**); **Davy Crockett National Forest** ranger offices are in Kennard (✆ **936/655-2299**); **Angelina National Forest** ranger offices are in Zavalla (✆ **936/897-1068**); and the **Sabine National Forest** ranger offices are in Hemphill (✆ **409/625-1940**).

Caddo Lake & Jefferson

Caddo Lake and the town of **Jefferson** (pop. 2,600) share a curious history. The former owes its origin, and the latter its glory days, to an immense, naturally occurring logjam on the Red River, which was known as the "Great Raft." This logjam existed for centuries and stretched from 80 to 150 miles along the river, raising the water level upstream enough to form Caddo Lake and to make Big Cypress Bayou navigable by steamboat as far as Jefferson. The town became the biggest river port in Texas and the sixth-largest city. In fact, commerce was so good in Jefferson during the mid-19th century that, of all the Texas ports, only Galveston shipped more tonnage. But this prosperity came to an abrupt end when the Army Corps of Engineers dynamited the raft in 1873, shrinking the lake and isolating the town. Today the lake is back, thanks to an earthen dam built by the Corps in 1914.

The town is back, too, but now its livelihood depends in large part on B&Bs and antiques stores. The return of good times to Jefferson dates from about 1961, with the restoration of the old Excelsior Hotel (now called **Excelsior House**) by the town's garden club. This sparked a restoration frenzy that has made Jefferson the best-restored town in east Texas. The entire central part of

All Aboard the Texas State Railroad

Many railroad enthusiasts consider a ride on the Texas State Railroad to be one of the best steam-train rides in the country. After passing through the Angelina National Forest, Hwy. 69 continues through Lufkin before reaching the town of Rusk, a drive of about 60 miles. Here, you can ride an old steam locomotive train 25 miles through pine forest to the town of Palestine and back again. Passengers travel in vintage railway cars, in either first class (which has air-conditioning in summer only) or coach. The train runs on a limited schedule (usually weekends) from March to May and August, and Thursday to Sunday from June to July. The round-trip journey through pine forest takes 4 hours. A ride on the steam train costs $36 adults and $24 children ages 2 to 12 for general seating; $69 adults and $44 children for an air-conditioned car seat; rates for the diesel train run $4 lower. For general information and reservations, including holiday POLAR EXPRESS™–inspired special train trips in December, check out the website www.texasstaterr.com, or call ✆ **903/683-3098** or 888/726-7245.

town is listed in the National Register of Historic Places, with a number of antebellum houses (several turned into B&Bs), churches, and commercial buildings listed. It is a very pleasant place to visit and stroll about. Weekends are when the town is most lively, with several tours offered; weekdays are when you get the best lodging rates. One of the top attractions is a tour of robber baron Jay Gould's personal railroad car, the **Atalanta** ($5 guided tour), 211 W. Austin St. (✆ **903/665-2513**). It is in great condition, has a fascinating history, and gives the visitor a wonderful idea of luxury travel in the late 19th century.

Jefferson provides better lodging than what you'll find at Caddo Lake, and when in Jefferson, the place to stay is the **Excelsior House** (www.theexcelsiorhouse.com; ✆ **903/665-2513**) at 211 W. Austin St.—in continuous operation, more or less, since 1850. The 15 rooms are all furnished with antiques, many here before the hotel was purchased by the garden club. Guests are invited to take a fun little tour of the hotel (non-guests $8). Room rates run from $135 to $189. You can also stay at one of the many B&Bs in town. For a list of these as well as information on tours, contact the **Marion County Chamber of Commerce** (www.jefferson-texas.com; ✆ **903/665-2672**). Recommended dining options include **Kitts Cornbread Sandwich & Pie Bar,** 125 N. Polk St. (www.kittskornbread.com; ✆ **903/665-0505**), offering up locally spawned delicacies like Texas cornbread sandwiches (such as the "Irish" with corned beef and Swiss cheese) and chicken and dumpling soup, as well as homemade pies (coconut buttermilk, chocolate pecan); the **Hamburger Store,** 101 Market St. (✆ **903/665-8302**), serving up burgers, chicken fried steak, and po'boys for more than 50 years; and the **Bayou Bakery Restaurant,** 201 W. Austin St. (✆ **903/665-2253**), serving home-cooked breakfast all day long.

Jefferson is situated between two lakes. To the west is **Lake o' the Pines,** which is good for swimming and general recreation, but the real point of interest is **Caddo Lake,** some 10 miles to the east. This is a large, 26,800-acre lake, half of which is in Louisiana. The more interesting half is in Texas, where the lake breaks up into smaller channels removed from most of the boat traffic. The small town of **Uncertain** (pop. 99) is on the western shore of the lake. Here you can take a tour and find lodging. Near Uncertain is **Caddo Lake State Park** (http://tpwd.texas.gov/state-parks/caddo-lake; ✆ **903/679-3351**), in Karnack (home of Lady Bird Johnson). Like several state parks, it has cabins for rent, which must be reserved well in advance by calling the central reservations number at ✆ **512/389-8900.** It also has campsites, which you can reserve by calling the park.

Caddo Lake is for boating or canoeing, but not swimming. Instead of being an open expanse of water, it's more like a watery forest broken up into several smaller areas. Cypress trees draped in Spanish moss crowd the lake's broken shore, their roots rising from the murky water in deformed shapes. The lake also harbors abundant wildlife, including alligators, otters, water snakes, and many types of waterfowl.

Tour-boat companies in this area have changed hands a few times since we last updated this book, so to get the latest update on pontoon-boat tours and other boating excursion experiences and tours in the area, check out the **Caddo Lake Tours** website (www.caddolaketours.com), which lists several reputable companies that offer such outings.

For a very special **private guided tour,** contact **Mystique Tours** (www.facebook.com/MystiqueToursCaddo; ✆ **903/930-2489**), run by Aaron Applebaum, whose late father, David, started the business in 1989. The tour takes 2 to 3 hours on a 14-foot pontoon boat.

Your final option is to rent a canoe and paddle into the quiet parts of the lake. These areas have few motorboats because they're too shallow and have too many roots below the surface. A couple of places to explore are Carter's Lake and Clinton Lake. The state park rangers can point out canoe routes on a map, and also put you in touch with a concessionaire.

THE TEXAS GULF COAST

7

Even though it's technically not on the water, Austin is sometimes referred to as "The Third Coast"—a nickname that has more to do with its outsize social influence than geographical logic. But the Texas coast lies tantalizingly close to the Capital City—and Houston and San Antonio as well. It takes only 2 hours to drive from San Antonio to the beach and even less than that from Houston. When it's sizzling hot, Texans love the coast for sunbathing, sandcastle making, swimming, fishing, and birdwatching. When it's cold, we love making campfires on the beach. And it's nice to know that after a long week of work, by sundown we city folk can be on a ferry feeding the gulls. Drive to Port Aransas and you'll find a line of Texans with smiles on their faces waiting to board the ferry for a sunny beach getaway.

The Texas coast stretches for more than 350 miles between Louisiana and Mexico. It's predominantly flat and sandy, with large bays and slender barrier islands tripling the amount of shoreline. The sand along the coast varies in color from white to light brown, and the water is warm and calm and usually a dull green. Though the natural features along this coast are fairly uniform, there is one notable difference: rainfall. The eastern and central parts of Texas are much wetter than south Texas. Rivers, bayous, and creeks pour into estuaries and marshy wetlands, creating a fertile habitat that supports a broad range of wildlife. Along this coast are several national wildlife refuges, the most famous being the one at Aransas, the winter home of the endangered whooping crane. South of Corpus Christi, the land is arid, which makes the water clearer, especially on the protected side of the barrier islands. South Padre Island has more sand dunes than the barrier islands to the north, and water on its sheltered side is extra salty because evaporation removes water faster than it is added.

The Texas Gulf Coast offers plenty of activities for visitors, including all manner of watersports. Birding and ecotourism are also major draws. Thanks to the short and mild winters, the Gulf Coast attracts a lot of "winter Texans," retired residents of the northern United States and Canada who spend at least part of the winter in the south Texas warmth. Locals call them "snow birds."

The largest cities on this coast are **Corpus Christi** and **Galveston.** Both offer the visitor a good range of recreation, lodging, and dining options. Farther south, at the very tip of the state, is the town of **South Padre Island,** with some of the state's best beaches. This chapter covers everything from Galveston to South Padre Island, but not the bit of coast between Galveston and Port Arthur, at the Louisiana border (and believe me, nobody considers the Port Arthur coast for its recreational activities). Best of all, you'll learn all about my favorite wind-blown beach town, Port Aransas. You're going to like it there.

GALVESTON

50 miles SE of Houston

Galveston is a port city on a barrier island opposite the mainland coast from Houston. Possibly best-known worldwide for the old Glenn Campbell song that bears its name, this enchanting island town is a romantic place. Its main attraction is the Strand, a downtown historic district with Victorian-era commercial buildings and houses. Parts of the town are beautifully restored and ideal for strolling. Only an hour's drive from Houston, Galveston is a good destination for families. It's a quiet town with many points of interest, including Moody Gardens and the tall ship *Elissa,* and it's not far from NASA and the Galveston Island Historic Pleasure Pier. The beaches are another big attraction, drawing crowds of Houstonians and other Texans year-round (not to mention the cruise ships that dock here). Unlike Houston, Galveston is not a boomtown. Its population of 50,000 remains fairly stable.

Essentials

GETTING THERE The nearest commercial airports are in Houston (see chapter 6). Take the Gulf Freeway (I-45 S.) from Houston. After crossing over to Galveston Island, the highway becomes a wide boulevard called Broadway.

ORIENTATION Broadway, Galveston's main street, doesn't cut directly across the island to the seashore; instead, it slants eastward and arrives at the seashore on the east end of the island, in front of Stewart Beach. Streets crossing Broadway are numbered; those parallel to Broadway have letters or names.

The **East End Historic District** and the downtown **Strand District** are north of Broadway. The East End Historic District is the old silk-stocking neighborhood that runs from 9th to 19th streets between Broadway and Church Street. It has many lovely old houses. Three large mansions-turned-museums have regular tours, and the **Galveston Historical Foundation** (www.galvestonhistory.org) has tours of several private historic homes in May. The Strand District is the restored commercial district that runs between 19th and 25th streets between Church Street and the harbor piers. When cotton was king, Galveston was a booming port and commercial center, and the Strand was dubbed the "Wall Street of the Southwest." What you see now are three- and

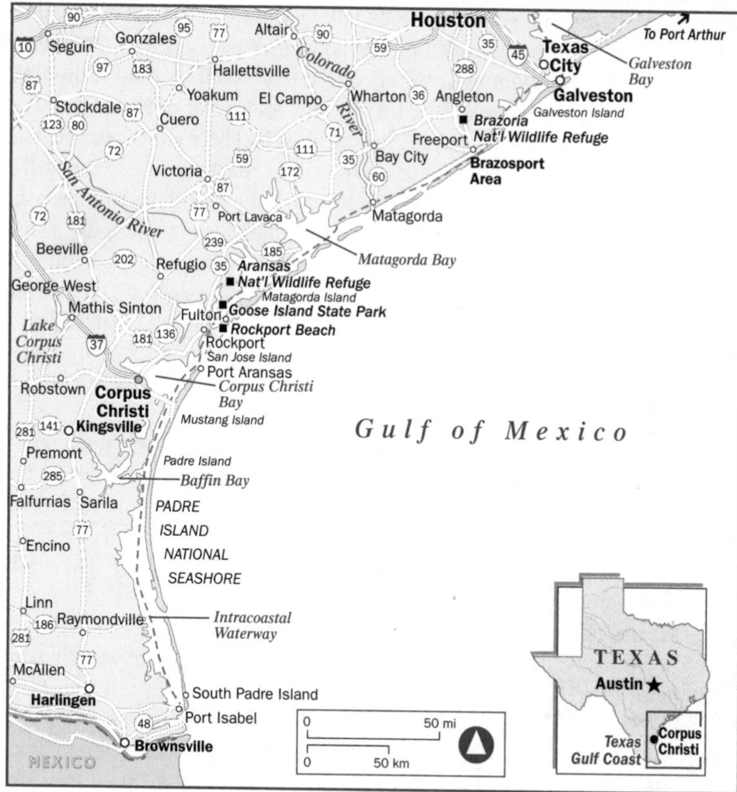

four-story buildings along 6 blocks of the Strand; many are Victorian ironfronts, so called because the facades included structural and decorative ironwork, a common building practice before the turn of the 20th century. Nowadays, the Strand is a shopping and dining area with a variety of stores.

VISITOR INFORMATION The **Galveston Convention & Visitors Bureau** (www.galvestoncvb.com; ✆ **888/425-4753**) has an information center at 2328 Broadway, the carriage house of the Ashton Villa (✆ **409/763-4311**). It's open daily from 9am to 5pm.

GETTING AROUND Most of Galveston's hotels, motels, and restaurants are located along the sea wall from where Broadway meets the shore all the way west past 60th Street.

What to See & Do

Galveston Island's 32 miles of **beaches** are the most popular attraction for Houstonians and other Texans. They may not be quite as nice as those at more popular beach resorts; the sand is closer to brown than white and the water isn't transparent. In the spring and fall, the water is clearer and could almost be considered blue. Beaches here are pure sand, without rocks, and the water has the nice warm temperatures of the Gulf of Mexico. There are five public beach parks in the area, including the popular **East Beach** and **Stewart Beach,** which offer pavilions with dressing rooms, showers, and restrooms, ideal for day-trippers. Stewart Beach is located at the end of Broadway, and East Beach is about a mile east of Stewart Beach. There's a $5-per-vehicle entrance fee. Beaches at other parts of the island are free. Those along the western shore suffered extensive storm erosion, but a multiphase re-nourishment project has added several miles of beach. In the fall of 2016, the island completed an $18-million beach re-nourishment project on the east end that stretched from 12th to 61st streets, offering 4 miles of upgraded recreational space. That same year, Galveston also opened "Babe's Beach," a newly created 15-block beach along Seawall Boulevard west of 61st Street. The American Shore and Beach Preservation Association named the new beach one of the top five "Best Restored Beaches in America."

Another activity popular with visitors and locals alike is to **walk, skate, or ride a bike** atop the **Galveston Seawall,** which extends 10 miles along the shoreline. Couples and families with kids also enjoy the old-fashioned **Galveston Island Historic Pleasure Pier** (www.pleasurepier.com), home to a boardwalk, amusement rides, Midway games, live entertainment, and carnival food as well as a big neon-lit Ferris wheel.

The **Strand Historic District** is perhaps the most famous part of town. This attractive 36-block district is home to ornate Victorian buildings that now house more than 100 shops, restaurants, and art galleries in tall iron-front buildings. The area is home to the **Texas Seaport Museum,** the 1877 tall ship *Elissa,* the Great Storm Theater, the Ocean Star Oil Rig Museum, the interactive museum, and "Pirates! Legends of the Gulf Coast," and is close to harbor-boat dolphin tours (See "Museums" on p. 204 for more information). Many people choose to stay in historic hotels on the Strand, such as **Treemont House,** a sister-property to the glorious **Hotel Galvez & Spa ★★** (see p. 206).

Galveston Harbour Tours, Pier 22 (✆ **409/765-8687**), part of the Texas Seaport Museum, offers 1-hour harbor tours several times daily aboard the 50-foot *Seagull II.* These are entertaining tours, and you'll most likely see dolphins, drilling rigs, and massive cargo ships. The tour costs $10 adults, $8 students 6 to 18, and free children 5 and under. **Duck Tours** (www.galvestonducks.com; ✆ **409/621-4771**) offers its trademark amphibious bus tour. Tours start at the Seawall and 25th Street. The scheduling is irregular, so call for departure times. Tours cost $15 adults and $10 children.

On Broadway, a few massive 19th-century mansions are open for tours: **Ashton Villa,** 2328 Broadway (www.galvestonhistory.org; ✆ **409/762-3933**); the **Bishop's Palace,** 1402 Broadway (www.galvestonhistory.org; ✆ **409/762-2475**); and the **Moody Mansion,** 2618 Broadway (www.moodymansion.org; ✆ **409/762-7668**).

THE great STORM

At the end of the 19th century, Galveston was a thriving port and a fast-growing city with a bright future. In fact, it was the largest city in Texas and had the third-busiest port in the country. Of course, being on the Gulf meant the risk of a hurricane, but the prevailing thought held that the shallow bottom on the western shore of the Gulf of Mexico would prevent the formation of large waves and blunt the force of any approaching storm. This assumption held sway even though a storm in 1886 completely wiped out the Texas port town of Indianola. But more evidence to the contrary came in the form of a massive storm that hit Galveston in September 1900.

It came ashore at night with a 20-foot surge that washed completely over the island. Houses were smashed into matchwood and their dwellers spilled out into the dark waters. By morning, more than 6,000 islanders—one out of every six—were drowned. The city's population dropped even further when many of the survivors moved elsewhere to rebuild their lives on safer shores. Those who remained went to work to prevent a recurrence of the disaster. Galveston erected a stout seawall that now stretches along 10 miles of shoreline with several jetties of large granite blocks projecting out into the sea. It also filled in land under the entire city, raising it 17 feet in some places and jacking up all the surviving houses to the new level. Despite the effort, Galveston would never regain its momentum. The memory of "the storm" proved too compelling for many of Galveston's merchants, who preferred the safety of an inland port and provided impetus for the dredging of the Houston Ship Channel, which was completed in 1914. Houston became a boomtown, taking Galveston's place as the region's commercial center.

Since that storm, more than 15 other hurricanes have hit the area, including Hurricane Ike in 2008, which carried with it 110 mph winds and a huge storm surge that rose high above the seawall and caused horrific destruction. Galveston residents once again came together to rebuild, and today this vibrant city is thriving once more.

Cruise lines bring thousands of visitors to Galveston each year who might otherwise have missed seeing this charming island city. **Port Galveston** is the fourth-busiest cruise port in the United States. Carnival Cruise Lines and Royal Caribbean both offer year-round itineraries, and Disney Cruise Lines has seasonal itineraries, often traveling to destinations in the eastern and western Caribbean. Ships arrive at one of two main cruise terminals: **Terminal Number 1,** 2502 Harborside Dr., and **Terminal 2,** 2702 Harborside Dr.; the **West End Gate** entrance is located at 3870 Port Industrial Rd. (40th St. and Port Industrial Rd.), and the **East End Gate** entrance is located at 1402 Harborside Dr. (14th St. and Harborside Dr.). With most cruises departing between 4pm and 5pm, cruisers can arrive a day or two early and check in at any of the island hotels that offer port shuttle services and free parking during their cruise when booking at least a 1-night stay. For a stay near the port, try Harbor House Hotel & Marina. For a stay on the beachfront, try the San Luis Resort or Hotel Galvez. For a stay on the West End, visit the Moody Gardens Hotel.

MUSEUMS

Except for Moody Gardens and its neighbor, the Lone Star Flight Museum (see below), most of Galveston's museums are in and around the Strand Historic District, the old commercial center. **Pier 21 Theater (✆ 409/763-8808)** shows a short documentary about the 1900 storm that devastated the town, and another about a one-time Galveston resident, the pirate Jean Laffite. Tickets are $4 or $5, depending on the show. On the same pier is the **Texas Seaport Museum** (www.galvestonhistory.org/attractions/maritime-heritage/texas-seaport-museum; ✆ **409/763-1877**) and the *Elissa,* a restored tall ship. Admission for both is $8 for adults, $5 for children 6 to 18, and free for children 5 and under. The museum also offers a boat tour of the harbor (see p. 202).

Next door, at Pier 19, is a one-of-a-kind museum. You may have already noticed the massive offshore rigs parked on the opposite side of the harbor. Tremendous feats of engineering, these rigs are some of the largest free-standing constructions ever built, and are often in the Port of Galveston being reconditioned. Most visitors have never seen one up close; here you have an opportunity to scamper around on one: the ***Ocean Star* Offshore Drilling Rig Museum** (www.oceanstaroec.com; ✆ **409/766-7827**) is an old rig that's been converted into a drilling-rig museum and education center. Through a short film, scale models, actual drilling equipment, and interactive displays, every aspect of the drilling process is explored, including the many rather daunting engineering challenges. Admission is $9 adults, $6 seniors, $5 students 7 to 18, and free for kids 6 and under. Hours for this and the other museums around the Strand are roughly the same, daily from 10am to 5pm (until 6pm in summer).

Moody Gardens ★ Extensive renovations in 2017 have only made this education/entertainment museum, aquarium, 4D Special FX theater, golf course, and hotel bigger and better. The sprawling complex is home to three large glass pyramids: The first built was the rainforest pyramid, which holds trees, plants, birds, fish, and butterflies from several different rainforest habitats. The unusual species of Amazonian fish, birds, and butterflies found here are not often seen in zoos. The aquarium pyramid displays life from four of the world's oceans: penguins from Antarctica, harbor seals from the northern Pacific, and reef dwellers from the Caribbean and South Pacific. It also has a petting aquarium. The discovery pyramid displays space exploration (but doesn't come close to the nearby Space Center Houston). Also of note are two IMAX theaters. On top of all this, there is a pool and a white-sand beach, and an old paddlewheeler that journeys out into the bay. Allow 5 hours to cover the major attractions at Moody Gardens, or 2 hours for only the rainforest habitat. A large hotel, golf course, and spa are also on the grounds.

Just down the road at 2002 Terminal Dr. is the **Lone Star Flight Museum** (www.lonestarflight.org; ✆ **409/740-7722**). Its two hangars are filled with aircraft in varying states of reconstruction. Many are classic planes from World War II, and for a good sum of money, the folks here will take you up in one. Admission to the museum is $10 adults, $8 seniors and kids 5 to 17,

HURRICANE IKE & TREE-TRUNK sculpture

The devastating tidal surge from Hurricane Ike, which hit the island on September 13, 2008, killed a number of the handsome old oak trees that once shaded the island. Many of the trunks of these dead trees were left in place and carved into sculptures. This profusion of new public art—from leaping dolphins to crested herons to a whimsical "Tin Man & Toto"—have become an uplifting symbol of the city's post-storm revival. Download the complimentary self-guided "Tree Sculpture Tour" brochure from the **Galveston Island Convention & Visitors Bureau** (www.galveston.com) or stop by the Visitor Center and pick one up.

and free for kids 4 and under. Allow 1½ hours for a visit. It's open daily 9am to 5pm.

1 Hope Blvd. www.moodygardens.org. ✆ **800/582-4673.** Admission prices for individual exhibits and IMAX vary depending on the season. Full-day pass for all exhibits and theaters $60 (sometimes cheaper off season). Daily 10am–6pm, although hours vary seasonally and by attraction.

Schlitterbahn Galveston Waterpark ★ Home to the world's largest "water coaster," this addition to Galveston's attractions comes from the central Texas town of New Braunfels, where, for the past 40-plus years, the Schlitterbahn water amusement park has pioneered different water rides and even been voted "Best Waterpark" by the Travel Channel. It has since established sister parks here in Galveston and in Corpus Christi and South Padre Island, some of the biggest family destinations on the coast. This one is close to Moody Gardens and has a wealth of tube chutes, wave tanks, and other rides. And, unlike some of the other Schlitterbahn waterparks, it has a large section that can be enclosed and heated for the winter season, keeping the park open throughout December. Although it's not affiliated with Schlitterbahn, the **Inn at the Waterpark,** 2525 Jones Dr., Galveston (www.innatthewaterpark.com; ✆ **409/203-4137**), is located directly next door to it and Moody Gardens, making it a smart choice for families planning on spending a good deal of time there.

2026 Lockheed Dr. www.schlitterbahn.com. ✆ **409/770-9283.** Summer rates $38 adults (12 and older), $32 children 3–11 and seniors. Daily 10am–8pm in summer (closes earlier fall and winter).

FESTIVALS

Mardi Gras (www.mardigrasgalveston.com; ✆ **888/425-4753;** Feb/Mar) is a tremendously popular celebration with parades, masked balls, and a live-entertainment district around the Strand. Mardi Gras here has some advantages over New Orleans—there are fewer tourists, and it's very lively without all the public displays of drunkenness. Be sure to book a hotel room well in advance.

The most unusual local event is the annual **American Institute of Architects (AIA) Sandcastle Competition** (www.aiasandcastle.com; ✆ **713/520-0155;** June). Workers from more than 70 architectural and engineering firms around the state show up on East Beach and get serious about the building of sand castles and sand sculptures, taking this pastime to new heights, literally. It all happens in 1 day, and the results are phenomenal.

For its Christmas celebration, for more than 4 decades Galveston has hosted its **Dickens on the Strand** (© **409/765-7834;** first weekend in Dec), a street party in which revelers dress up in Victorian costumes. The Strand—with its Victorian architecture and association with its namesake—is a natural venue for such a celebration. The party includes performers, street vendors, readings of Dickens, and music. Admission is $8 adults ($4 costumed adults), $5 children ages 7 to 12, and free for children 6 and under.

Where to Stay

Most of the economy chains have properties in Galveston, with higher prices for lodgings along the seawall. Of the big chains, **La Quinta Galveston,** 1402 Seawall Blvd. (www.lq.com/en/findandbook/hotel-details.galveston-east-beach.html; © **800/531-5900**), ranks highly. Galveston also has eight B&Bs, most in Victorian-era houses (www.galvestonbedandbreakfast.com).

Harbor House Hotel & Marina at Pier 21 ★ Built on a pier and overlooking the glittering harbor, this hotel is centrally located near the Strand District and just steps from several popular restaurants, museums, and harbor excursions at the neighboring marina. Harbor House is more contemporary in style than most other lodgings on the island, and recent renovations have made it even more sophisticated. The guest rooms and one-bedroom suites are big and smartly appointed, with custom-built cabinets and original Galveston Island photography (printed on aluminum) beneath a ceiling of exposed wood beams and slender steel rods. "Captain's Quarters" rooms offer a king-size bed, a living area with a sleeper sofa, and a dining area. The spacious king rooms are called "Admiral" quarters, while the "Skipper" rooms feature two queen-size beds. Guests here can enjoy the pool, spa, and restaurants of Harbor House's beachfront sister properties, the Hotel Galvez & Spa and The Tremont House, both Wyndham Grand Hotel properties (see below).

No. 28, Pier 21. www.harborhousepier21.com. © **409/763-3321.** 42 units. $89–$279 double; $149–$299 suite. Rates include continental breakfast. Parking $10. **Amenities:** Room service; Wi-Fi (free).

Hotel Galvez & Spa ★★ This is the grand dame of Galveston Island, a century-old beauty of Spanish colonial splendor. Guests step back in time when they enter the grand lobby, where sunlight streams through huge arched windows, and elegant columns and plush seating speak to the opulence of another era. If you love old-school ambience (with a house ghost) and are looking for a place to relax, the Galvez is an wonderful choice. And, because it's a Wyndham Grand Hotel property, rooms are not too fussy or overdone; in fact, they're quite modern and have all the comforts you'd hope to find. The hotel fronts the seawall in the central part of town, offering nice Gulf views, and the beach across from the hotel is currently being replenished with new sand. But you're only a short drive to Galveston's other beach parks and not far from the Historic Strand District downtown.

2024 Seawall Blvd. www.hotelgalvez.com. ✆ **409/765-7721.** 224 units. $119–$399 double; from $349 1-bedroom suite; from $449 2-bedroom suite. Extra person $20. Valet parking $17; free self-parking. **Amenities:** Restaurant; 2 bars; bikes; fitness center; nearby golf course; Jacuzzi; heated outdoor pool; room service; sauna; spa; Wi-Fi (free).

The Tremont House ★★ Like its sister property the Hotel Galvez (see above), this stylish hotel is also part of the Wyndham Grand Hotel Collection. A former dry goods warehouse built a century ago, the Tremont has been transformed into a boutique hotel with good bones and great character. It's a favorite of many for its prime location in the heart of the Strand Historic District, where restaurants and shops lie just outside its door. This may be a historic hotel, but it feels sophisticated—not old and stuffy. Many rooms have high ceilings, and some have exposed-brick walls and tall windows. Cruise passengers tend to bookend their trips by staying at the Tremont—it's just 2 blocks from the cruise ship terminal, and guests can arrange to leave their cars here. The **Toujouse Bar** has jazz every Friday and Saturday evenings, and the **rooftop bar** is a sublime place to enjoy sunset. Guests here also have the use of the pool, spa, and fitness center in the Hotel Galvez.

2300 Mechanic St. (Strand Historic District). www.thetremonthouse.com. ✆ **409/763-0300.** 119 units. $109–$349. Suites from $386. Valet parking $17. **Amenities:** Restaurant; 2 bars; fitness center; access to spa, pool, & fitness center at Hotel Galvez; nearby golf course; Jacuzzi; heated outdoor pool; room service; sauna; spa; Wi-Fi (free).

Where to Eat

People come to Galveston for seafood, and they won't be disappointed. Local representatives of chain seafood restaurants such as Landry's and Joe's Crab Shack are here, but for the best of Galveston seafood, try one of the places listed below. If you're craving steak, the best in town is at **Steakhouse in the San Luis Resort,** 5222 Seawall Blvd. (www.sanluisresort.com; ✆ **409/744-1500**).

Gaido's ★★ SEAFOOD On the beachfront under a sign with an enormous statue of a blue crab, this large but cozy-feeling family restaurant stands adjacent to the Seaside Inn, a beach bar, and another restaurant. It boasts a kitchen that spans nearly 3 city blocks. Four generations of the Gaido family have toiled in that big kitchen to ensure the restaurant's longtime commitment to quality. Here, the seafood is fresh and service is attentive. Start with the hearty gumbo or the creamy Watkins Bisque, swimming with baby shrimp. Then sample from an array of Gaido's signature dishes, like baked oysters with a lily-gilding topping of fresh jumbo lump crab, panko crumbs, and lemon *beurre blanc* sauce. Then, move on to one of the tasty main dishes: Gulf shrimp stuffed with crabmeat, perhaps, or pork chops dusted in a garlic cracker crust. A sizable bar area is a nice place to wait for a table. Some people dress up to come here, while others wear shorts and sandals, and both feel equally at home.

3800 Seawall Blvd. www.gaidos.com. ✆ **409/762-9625.** Reservations accepted for large parties. Main courses $15–$40. Sun–Thurs 11am–9pm; Fri and Sat 11am–10pm.

Rudy & Paco's ★★ SEAFOOD/STEAK/LATIN AMERICAN Don't be surprised if Chef Paco greets you at the door with a "Baby! Baby!" He calls everyone that, making a point of warmly welcoming guests to his popular, upscale eatery. Filling a small space in a big way in the historic downtown district, the restaurant is located right next to the Grand 1894 Opera House, which means that celebrities are often spotted here on the afternoon of a performance, and Chef Paco's pre-show dinner specials draw theater-goers. Named for Chef Paco and his late business partner, Rudy, the restaurant is famous for its seafood dishes with Latin American flavors, like my favorite, the *filete de pargo simpatico,* pan-sauteed, plantain-encrusted Gulf red snapper, served over a raspberry-chipotle sauce with a topping of jumbo lump crabmeat. This intimate spot with a sparkling bar area may be the only restaurant on the island to have a dress code for dinner: no shorts in the dining room except in the bar (shorts are allowed during lunch).

2028 Post Office St. www.rudyandpaco.com. ✆ **409/762-3696.** Reservations accepted for lunch and dinner and may be made online. Mon–Fri 11am–2pm; Mon–Thurs 5–9pm; Fri–Sat 5–10pm; closed Sun.

Saltwater Grill ★★ SEAFOOD/CREOLE For 2 years running, this popular Strand District spot has snagged Galveston Island's "Restaurant of the Year" title (2016 and 2017). Located directly across the street from the Opera House in a vintage building, Saltwater Grill is a welcoming mix of past and present, formal and informal. Sunlight floods the space, where exposed-brick walls and wooden tables give the place character. Still, the warm ambience isn't the main draw: That would be the daily menus swimming with fresh seafood. A new menu features shrimp tacos, crab lollipops, barbecued redfish, and Pacific fusion recipes like miso-marinated Hong Kong Chilean seabass. Under "From the Kettle" you'll find hearty soups and stews, including two well-seasoned gumbos and a saffron-scented bouillabaisse. Portions are generous, so don't go overboard on the starters, as wonderful as they may be. For instance, I have to remind myself not to fill up on the yummy fried asparagus spears, made with a tempura-style batter so thin as to be translucent—and cooked perfectly.

2017 Post Office St. www.saltwatergrill.com. ✆ **409/762-3474.** Reservations recommended. Main courses $14–$32. Mon–Fri 11am–2pm and 5–9pm; Sat 5–11pm.

Shrimp 'N' Stuff ★ SEAFOOD This small restaurant is about as unassuming as they come, but serves up what many locals say is the island's best seafood for the money. It's more or less a counter, where you stand in line, order, and pick up your food—it has a few seats inside or outside on a leafy deck. The seafood is mostly Southern-fried, but it's ultra-fresh. You can't go wrong with fried oysters, shrimp po'boys, homemade shrimp salad, or shrimp gumbo made from scratch. A second location, **Shrimp 'N' Stuff Downtown** (www.shrimpnstuffdowntown.com), 216 23rd St., offers a few more healthful grilled options and has a slightly more upscale environment than this down-home dive; there you order from a waiter instead of standing in line.

3901 Ave. O. www.shrimpnstuff.com. ✆ **409/763-2805.** Reservations not accepted. Main courses $8–$14. Sun–Thurs 10:30am–8pm; Fri–Sat 10:30am–9:30pm.

CORPUS CHRISTI

207 miles SW of Houston; 377 miles S of Dallas; 143 miles S of San Antonio; 691 miles SE of El Paso

The bay area around Corpus Christi offers visitors the greatest variety of activities of any place along the Texas Gulf Coast. This and the following three sections (Rockport, Port Aransas, and Padre Island National Seashore) cover the major destinations in the bay area. These destinations are only about 45 minutes from one another at most, so you can hop around pretty easily. Whether you stay in Corpus Christi, Port Aransas, or Rockport, you'll find great lodging, good food, and lots to do.

Corpus Christi is a major deepwater seaport with a big, beautiful bay. It has fewer than 300,000 inhabitants, but it feels much less populated. The downtown is easy to enjoy, and probably the best place to stay when visiting. It's relatively calm because most of the locals live on the south side of the bay, along the S.P.I.D. freeway. That's where you'll find most of the traffic, too. There is a Texas A&M University–affiliated campus here, too, and that keeps the island full of college kids during the school year. The three biggest attractions are the State Aquarium, Schlitterbahn water park, and the USS *Lexington* aircraft carrier, which are next to each other on the bay just north of downtown, across Harbor Bridge. High season for Corpus Christi is from May to September. But the weather is so mild that most of the activities can still be enjoyed during the off season, when you can move around without the crowds.

Essentials

GETTING THERE

BY PLANE The **Corpus Christi International Airport (CCIA)** is located within the city limits on the south side of Tex. 44, west of Padre Island Drive/Tex. 358 (www.corpuschristiairport.com; ✆ **361/289-0171**). It's served by **American Eagle** (www.aa.com), **United Express** (www.united.com), and **Southwest** (www.southwest.com). Most major car-rental agencies are here.

BY CAR Tex. 35 follows the Gulf Coast—albeit slightly inland—from the Houston and Galveston area to Corpus Christi. From San Antonio, follow I-37 southeast to Corpus Christi. Before you see the town, you'll pass the city's oil refining complex.

GETTING AROUND

Most visitors to Corpus Christi will use a car to get around. This is an easy city to navigate. Traffic isn't bad except during rush hour. Neither Uber nor Lyft serve Corpus Christi, nor most Texas coastal cities.

In the downtown area, highways I-37 and Tex. 286 (known as the Crosstown Expwy.) intersect. Connected to both is Corpus Christi's busiest freeway, known as South Padre Island Drive, or S.P.I.D., as it appears on signs. It does, in fact, lead to Padre Island. For a nice drive around the bay from the downtown area, take Ocean Drive, which skirts the south shore.

VISITOR INFORMATION

Contact the **Corpus Christi Convention & Visitors Bureau,** 1201 N. Shoreline Blvd. (www.visitcorpuschristitx.org; ✆ **800/678-6232**). A downtown **visitor center,** 1590 N. Shoreline Blvd. (✆ **361/561-2000**), is open daily 9am to 5pm.

FAST FACTS The **Corpus Christi Medical Center** (www.ccmedicalcenter.com) has three locations: Doctors Regional, 3315 S. Alameda St. (✆ **361/761-1400**); Bay Area, 7101 S. Padre Island Dr. (✆ **361/761-1200**); and the Heart Hospital, 7002 Williams Dr. (✆ **361/761-6800**). The main **post office,** 809 Nueces Bay Blvd., is open Monday through Friday from 8am to 5pm.

What to See & Do

THE TOP ATTRACTIONS

Texas State Aquarium ★ A $60-million expansion unveiled in spring 2017 added a new "Caribbean Journey" wing and 71,000 square feet of space, doubling the animal collection at this already wonderful, award-winning aquarium. "Caribbean Journey" includes tropical forest, a Caribbean shark exhibit, a *cenote* (crystal-blue limestone pool), and replicated Mayan ruins. Some half a million visitors already come to the aquarium annually to see "Dolphin Bay," which provides a protected environment for Atlantic bottlenosed dolphins that are unable to survive in the wild. The large "Islands of Steel" exhibit re-creates the marine habitat around deep-sea oil platforms. The aquarium is close to the USS *Lexington* Museum on the Bay.

2710 N. Shoreline Blvd. https://texasstateaquarium.org. ✆ **800/477-4853** or 361/881-1200. Admission $25 adults, $22 seniors 60 and older, $18 children 3–12, free for children 2 and under (online discounts available for Mon–Fri). Mon–Sat 9am–5pm; Sun 10am–5pm. Closed Thanksgiving and Dec 25.

USS *Lexington* Museum on the Bay ★★ The "Lady Lex" is a World War II–era aircraft carrier and floating naval museum and is the pride of Corpus Christi. During the war, the *Lexington* was in almost every major operation in the Pacific theater, and planes from its decks destroyed 372 enemy aircraft in flight and an additional 475 on the ground. It was dubbed "The Blue Ghost" because of the ship's blue-gray color, and because Japanese propaganda radio broadcaster Tokyo Rose repeatedly and mistakenly announced that the *Lexington* had been sunk. The *Lexington* was modernized in the 1950s and served in the U.S. 7th Fleet, including duty during the Vietnam War.

Choose from five self-guided-tour routes. A 3D MEGA Theater shows IMAX movies, and a video details the history of the ship with historic footage. Among several exhibits is a Navy Seal submarine and interpretive displays of ship engines, plus an exciting flight simulator that, for $5 per person, provides a wild 5-minute ride simulating the experience of flying. But a more concrete sense of what life was like on this carrier is gained by boarding the actual ship, climbing up and down ladders between decks, seeing the ship's hospital and mess hall, and exploring its narrow passages. Not many museums can do this sort of thing. On the flight deck are more than a dozen aircraft from the 1930s to the 1960s, including an F-14A Tomcat and a Cobra helicopter. You can also get a close-up look at the ship's 40-millimeter anti-aircraft guns. The *Lexington* has a large gift shop and a snack bar. Allow at least 2 hours for a tour.

Note: Although some parts of the USS *Lexington* are easily accessible to anyone, seeing many of the best parts, such as the flight deck, bridge, and engine room, involves climbing steep metal stairs and ladders, stepping over metal barricades, and maneuvering through tight passageways. Those with mobility problems may have trouble accessing everything.

2914 N. Shoreline Blvd., in Corpus Christi Bay. www.usslexington.com. ✆ **800/523-9539** or 361/888-4873. Admission $15 adults, $13 seniors & military, $10 children 4–12. Free admission to the Hangar Deck for those with disabilities. Daily 9am–5pm; until 6pm Memorial Day to Labor Day.

OTHER ATTRACTIONS

The beach isn't the only wet and wonderful place to cool off in summer. Kids and families adore the **Schlitterbahn Waterpark**, 14353 Commodores Dr. (www.schlitterbahn.com/corpus-christi; ✆ **361/589-4220**), with pools, tube shoots, a pirate ship, rapid river rides, beach and river access areas, and more. Schlitterbahn got its start in New Braunfels but now also has waterparks at South Padre Island and Galveston, and this one is wildly popular with locals and visitors alike.

Just north of downtown is the city's striking convention center, the **American Bank Center** (www.americanbankcenter.com/convention). Nearby are several small to medium-size museums, including the **Art Museum of South Texas** (www.artmuseumofsouthtexas.org), the **Texas State Museum of Asian Cultures Museum** (www.asianculturesmuseum.org), and the **Museum of Science & History** (www.ccmuseum.com). ***Tip:*** Before going to any of them, first step into the **Corpus Christi Visitor Center,** at 1590 N. Shoreline Blvd. ✆ **361/561-2000;** daily 9am–5pm), to see if any coupons are available. I like the Museum of Science & History best of all.

Adding to Corpus Christi's small-town amusements is a minor-league baseball team in the Texas League called the **Corpus Christi Hooks** (www.milb.com; ✆ **361/561-4665**). Home games are played at Whataburger Field, a delightful ballpark at the water's edge, near the foot of the Harbor Bridge, named for a chain of burger joints that started in Corpus Christi in 1950. During your stay here, you'll spot lots of Whataburger restaurants with their trademark orange-and-white roofs.

OUTDOOR ACTIVITIES

Watersports, birding, and fishing are the most popular activities. Certain parts of this area lend themselves to different kinds of watersports. Birding is good throughout; it just depends on the species for which you're looking. Here is a rundown of activities and where best to enjoy them.

FISHING/BOATING For deep-sea fishing, you might be better off going to Port Aransas, which is on Mustang Island facing the open water. You'll save fuel costs that way. For bay fishing, you can find guides and charter boats in Corpus Christi, Rockport, or Port Aransas. Shoreline fishing is popular in these parts, with numerous piers, jetties, and beaches, depending on your tastes. In Corpus Christi, a charter boat usually costs from $300 to $400 for a full-day trip for one or two people. For a good fishing guide, contact the visitor center, or check its website for certified guides. If you prefer a smaller boat, go to **Harrison's Landing** (www.harrisonslanding.net; © **361/881-8503**) at People's Street T-Head pier. This company operates the *Japonica,* an open-air 50-foot boat that cruises the bay on a variety of tours. A basic tour of downtown Corpus Christi highlights is $15 adults, $10 children 10 and under; check website for seasonal hours.

SAILING Corpus Christi has a wonderful bay for sailing and a lively sailing community. Every Wednesday evening, you can watch a friendly sailboat race from the downtown marina. If you want to do some sailing, you can **rent a boat** (if you're a certified captain) or **sail with a captain** (where you would help crew), either by yourself or as part of a group. The outfit with the most flexibility is Harrison's Landing (see above). It has a sailing academy and regularly does introductory sailing cruises. Corpus Christi also has a nonprofit organization that works with people with disabilities who want to sail. **Corpus Christi Sail A.W.A.Y.** (www.ccsailaway.org; © **361/881-3325**) is located on the Coopers Alley L-Head, also at the downtown marina.

SEA KAYAKING Combine a sea kayaking cruise with fishing or nature photography. Most of the interesting sites are near the Rockport/Fulton area—see the "Rockport" section, below—but you can rent kayaks in several places in Corpus Christi, including **Fun Time Rentals,** Lawrence Street T-Head and Shoreline Blvd. (http://funtimerental.tripod.com; © **361/443-0707**), which also rents paddleboats and surries.

WINDSURFING Corpus Christi's reputation for good breezes also draws a lot of windsurfers. Annual windsurfing regattas are held here. An ideal place to windsurf or take lessons is at Bird Island Basin in the Padre Island National Seashore with **Worldwinds Windsurfing** (www.worldwinds.net; © **361/949-7472**).

Where to Stay

Corpus Christi has a number of well-known chain hotels and motels, many of them located along South Padre Island Drive (S.P.I.D.) south of downtown. I prefer staying downtown. Both locations put you close to most of the visitor activities in Corpus Christi, as well as several dining spots. A well-located economical choice, the **Sea Shell Inn,** 202 Kleberg Place (© **361/888-5291**) is on the bay north of downtown, by the USS *Lexington* and the Radisson hotel. Rates are $50 to $100 double.

The highest rates in the Corpus Christi area are in summer.

Omni Corpus Christi Hotel ★★ This full-service hotel hits plenty of high notes for service, amenities, and contemporary style. Many of the rooms in the 20-story Bayfront tower have private balconies, but even rooms without them enjoy spectacular floor-to-ceiling views of the Gulf, particularly from the upper floors. The newly renovated guest rooms are comfortably furnished in a smart, modern style. An outdoor heated pool and the Omni Kids' Crew Program (little kids get a backpack of goodies upon arrival) make this a top family choice. One of the two on-site restaurants is the highly rated **Republic of Texas Bar & Grill** (see "Where to Eat," below). The hotel gets a lot of weekday business travelers, so look for good weekend rates.

900 N. Shoreline Blvd. www.omnihotels.com. © **888/444-0MNI (6664)** or 361/887-1600. 475 units. $129–$159 double; from $300 suite. Valet parking $14; self-parking $9. Pets 25 lb. and under accepted with $50 fee. **Amenities:** 2 restaurants; 2 bars; coffee/snack shop; free airport transfers; bikes; children's programs; concierge; health club and spa; outdoor heated pool; room service; salon; Wi-Fi (free).

CAMPING

RVers have plenty of camping choices in the Corpus Christi area, and although many of the RV parks will accept tents, the rates are often the same as for sites with RV hookups; those in tents will be surrounded by RVs. Visitors in tents should camp at nearby Padre Island National Seashore (see p. 224, later in this chapter) or one of the other public parks in the area.

Among RV parks here, the best is **Colonia del Rey,** 1717 Waldron Rd., near the entrance to Padre Island (www.ccrvresorts.com; © **800/580-2435** for reservations, or 361/937-2435), which has a swimming pool, a Wal-Mart, a library and book exchange, a recreation hall, a playground, and all the other usual amenities, and can accommodate rigs up to 85 feet long. Some sites have telephones, and rates are $34 to $38 for full hookups, including cable TV.

Where to Eat

For a quick bite, try a burger from the chain that began here in Corpus Christi—**Whataburger.** You won't have trouble finding one here; they're everywhere, and they're generally open late. In addition to the places listed below, you might consider dining at **Tavern on the Bay** (www.harrisonslanding.net/restaurant; © **361/881-8503**) if the weather is nice. This outdoor restaurant on the water, located on the Peoples Street T-Head, serves seafood, burgers, and a celebrated lobster bisque.

La Playa ★★ TEX-MEX Cheap and casual Tex-Mex cuisine and beach towns go together like chips and queso, and this popular Tex-Mex spot brings the best of both. La Playa, Spanish for "the beach," offers good tacos, bubbling-hot plates of enchiladas, frosty salt-rimmed margaritas, and a menu large enough to meet everyone's tastes. The fajitas get most of the attention here, and are a safe bet if you're not familiar with Tex-Mex food, but the enchiladas with traditional chili gravy and the green enchiladas with a tangy sauce really sizzle. La Playa calls itself the "home of the stuffed avocado" and these deep-fried treats (stuffed with chicken, beef, or shrimp) may just rock your world. For dessert, try the sopapillas or the traditional Mexican flan.

4201 S.P.I.D. www.laplaya.cc. © **361/853-4282.** Main courses $10–$20. Mon–Sat 11am–10pm; Sun 11am–9pm.

Republic of Texas Bar & Grill ★★★ STEAK/SEAFOOD This glittering hotel steakhouse is the perfect spot to celebrate a special occasion. Located on the 20th floor of the Bayfront Tower at the Omni Corpus Christi Hotel, the restaurant has a terraced dining room that affords breathtaking views of the bay and city through oversize windows. All beef is USDA Prime, hand-cut and grilled over a fire of oak and mesquite. The menu also features seafood (sautéed shrimp, grilled salmon, pan-seared fish of day) and game dishes, such as Texas Bob White quail in a roasted garlic and rosemary sauce. Sides like garlic mashed potatoes and creamed spinach are good, but the house specialty hash browns are exquisite. Service is excellent.

At the Omni Corpus Christi Hotel, 900 N. Shoreline Blvd. www.omnihotels.com. ✆ **361/886-3515.** Reservations recommended. Main courses $19–$50. Mon–Sat 5:30–10:30pm; Sun 5:30–9pm.

Water Street Seafood Company ★★ SEAFOOD Great seafood and good prices and a rockin' raw bar with fresh oysters and more are just a few reasons to like this place and its sister property, Water Street Oyster Bar, in the same building. While the menus are similar in both places, here the cooking combines Southern and Mexican influences, such as the shrimp picayune in a Cajun sauce. Choose from grilled or fried seafood standards, or try one of their house originals, such as pecan-crusted oysters or bacon-wrapped shrimp stuffed with crabmeat. The Water Street Oyster Bar is smaller and less noisy, with somewhat better service. It also has a fabulous sushi bar that made my formerly skeptical husband a believer in the magic of a masterful sushi chef.

314 N. Chaparral St. www.waterstmarketcc.com. ✆ **361/882-8683.** Reservations not accepted. Main courses $14–$34. Sun–Thurs 11am–10pm; Fri–Sat 11am–11pm.

ROCKPORT/FULTON ★★

35 miles NE of Corpus Christi; 182 miles SW of Houston; 161 miles SE of San Antonio

Rockport and its sister town, Fulton (which so seamlessly connect that an outsider might think they're one town), lie on a neighboring bay north of Corpus Christi, sheltered by San Jose Island (or "St. Joe's," as locals sometimes call it.). The two towns fill Aransas County, one of the smallest counties in the state, with a total population of 25,000. Rockport, Texans' favorite fishing village, has more character than its neighbor and has become an art town, with resident artists, galleries, and the Rockport Art Center. The old downtown area is small and colorful, with shops, galleries, and good little restaurants. But Rockport isn't in danger of becoming a fancy place; it's comfortable and feels lived in. Old-style motel courts, still the most common lodging options here, are testaments to a time not so long ago, when Rockport was a summer retreat for Texans looking for a quiet, economical place to enjoy the water. That's changing. A modern subdivision marina community has developed between the two towns, and a Wal-Mart and a slew of chain motels have arrived.

This part of the coast is particularly lovely. Notable are the many windswept oak trees, sculpted by years of harsh weather. They are a favorite subject for artists and emblematic of the area. Of course, water is everywhere. A large, protected wetlands area to the north, the **Aransas National Wildlife Refuge,** is the winter home to the only natural colony of whooping cranes in the world. But this is only one of several natural areas in the region. Birding and fishing are two of the major draws. If a beach is what you're looking for, Rockport has a nice little one, but the best ones by far are at **Port Aransas** and along **Padre Island National Seashore.**

Essentials

GETTING THERE Rockport is 40 minutes from Corpus Christi. Take Tex. 35 over the Harbor Bridge toward Portland. Well after the Aransas Pass turn-off, take the exit labeled MARKET ST. (FM 1069). Both Rockport and Fulton are on Bus. 35, which continues north over the Copano Bay Causeway Bridge, which just opened in 2017 (and is still undergoing some work), leading to the Aransas National Wildlife Refuge.

VISITOR INFORMATION For maps or info, contact the **Rockport–Fulton Area Chamber of Commerce,** 404 Broadway, Rockport, TX 78382 (www.rockport-fulton.org; ✆ **800/242-0071** or 361/729-6445). The office is open Monday to Friday from 9am to 5pm and Saturday from 9am to 2pm.

FAST FACTS The nearest full-service hospital, with a 24-hour emergency room, is **Care Regional Medical Center,** 11 miles south of Rockport at 1711 W. Wheeler Ave., Aransas Pass (✆ **361/758-8585**). The **post office,** located at 1550 FM 2165 in Rockport, is open Monday through Friday from 9am to 4:30pm, Saturday from 9am to noon.

What to See & Do

THE TOP ATTRACTION

This region is among the nation's premier bird-watching destinations, and the best spot for birding here is the **Aransas National Wildlife Refuge ★★** (www.fws.gov/refuge/Aransas; ✆ **361/286-3559**). More than 300 species of birds have been spotted here, but the whooping crane, which winters here from November to April, is the big draw.

In addition to birds, the refuge is home to about 30 species of snakes (only four are poisonous), turtles, lizards, and the refuge's largest reptile, the American alligator. Mammals commonly seen include white-tailed deer, javelinas, wild boar, raccoons, eastern cottontail rabbits, and nine-banded armadillos. Also present, but only occasionally seen, are bobcats and opossums.

A 16-mile paved auto tour loop meanders through a variety of habitats, offering access to a 40-foot observation tower, pier fishing (state permits required), and other viewing areas. The refuge has six walking trails, a picnic area, and an impressive visitor center with information, exhibits, a bookstore, and administration offices. There are also seasons for hunting and saltwater fishing access. Camping is not permitted.

The refuge is located about 36 road miles northeast of Rockport via Tex. 35, FM 774, and FM 2040. It's open daily from just before sunrise to just after sunset; the **Claude F. Lard Visitor Center** is open daily 9am to 4pm October 15 to April 14, and Wednesday to Sunday 9am to 4pm April 15 to October 14. It's closed Thanksgiving and December 25 and most federal holidays. Admission to the refuge is $5 per vehicle ($3 if only one person). Admission is free with the Federal Duck Stamp, Aransas Annual pass, or any of the America the Beautiful Passes, available for purchase at the visitor center. You can borrow binoculars from the visitor center. Insect repellent is recommended year-round.

OUTDOOR ACTIVITIES

BEACHES Rockport is not known for beaches, and most of it rests along a rocky bay; however, **Rockport Beach** (www.rockportbeach-texas.com; ✆ **361/729-6661**) is a nice one. It was the first Texas beach to be designated a Blue Wave Beach by the Texas Beach Watch Program, and it's one of the cleanest strands of sand in the state. Here kids play on waterside playgrounds, and a shady pavilion and restroom are available, as well as 65 covered picnic tables with barbeque grills. No animals/pets are allowed on the beach, and no glass containers are allowed. There is no overnight camping, and no bonfires are permitted (fires in barbecue pits only). All this goes a long way to keep the beach and the water here clean. Most Texans think of this as a good place for a picnic, but to enjoy big, broad beaches, many people turn to Port Aransas.

FISHING There are public fishing piers in Fulton Harbor and at Rockport Beach Park, as well as numerous other areas, including the Aransas National Wildlife Refuge. Fishing guides offer bay and deep-sea fishing trips, and rates vary considerably. Contact **Green Hornet Fishing Guide Service** (www.greenhornetguides.com; ✆ **361/790-9742**), and **Hook Line & Sinker** (www.hook-line.net; ✆ **361/557-1234**).

KAYAKING All the different bays around Rockport are well sheltered by the barrier islands. In some places, the water gets quite shallow and is broken into narrow channels by mangroves. One such place is called Lighthouse Lakes. This is perfect territory for kayaking, which you can combine with birding, fishing, or nature photography. You can rent kayaks, stand-up paddleboards, and golf carts, oddly enough, from **Rockport Birding and Kayak Adventures** (www.whoopingcranetour.com; ✆ **877/892-4737**). This outfit also has pick-up and drop-off services and offers whooping crane and birding boat tours.

PARKS Anglers and birders especially like **Goose Island State Park** (www.tpwd.state.tx.us/park/goose; ✆ **800/792-1112** or 361/729-2858), with camping, fishing, and birding along St. Charles and Aransas bays, and home to the Big Tree, a giant live oak with seemingly countless twisting branches, which is estimated to be more than 1,000 years old. It's more than 35 feet in circumference, 44 feet high, and has a crown spread of 90 feet. The park has a short paved hiking and biking path, picnic tables and grills, a boat ramp, and a lighted 1,620-foot-long fishing pier. Despite being on the coast, it has no beach. You can borrow rods, reels, and tackle boxes at the park through the Tackle Loaner Program and then fish off a pier for speckled trout, redfish, flounder, and sheepshead. Crabbing and oystering are also popular. A fish-cleaning station is by the boat launch area, a spot that is understandably popular with pelicans. There are 44 camping sites by the bay, and 57 sites under oak trees, all with water and electricity, and the park also has restrooms with showers and an RV dump station. Entrance to the park costs $5 per person per day (free for children 12 and under), and camping costs an additional $10 to $22 per night, with reservations available (✆ **512/389-8900**). The park is about 12 miles from Rockport. Follow Tex. 35 north 10 miles to Park Road 13, which you follow 2 miles east to the park entrance. There are several preserves and wildlife sanctuaries in and around the area, which make for good birding.

WHOOPING CRANE TOURS/DOLPHIN TOURS The world-famous **whooping cranes** inhabit the Aransas National Wildlife Preserve from mid-November to mid-April. A number of companies offer 3- to 4-hour whooping crane and birding tours on shallow-draft boats. Most of these boats leave out of Fulton harbor, so you might want to go down and check them out for yourself and find one with a convenient departure time. Several boats do dolphin tours in summer when the whooping cranes have left. Captain Tommy Moore of **Rockport Birding and Kayak Adventures** (www.whoopingcranetours.com; ✆ **877/892-4737**) is a good choice for a whooping-crane tour, a dolphin cruise, a sunset cruise, or even a history tour. Capt. Moore has a good boat with an elevated observation deck, and he works regularly as a guide for serious birders. Check with the Rockport–Fulton Area Chamber of Commerce (see "Visitor Information," p. 215) for information on land-based birding tours.

INDOOR ATTRACTIONS

Fulton Mansion ★ This ornate French Empire–style mansion, listed in the National Register of Historic Places and once called "Oakhurst," is the pride of the Texas coast, and a favorite attraction in Fulton. Constructed between 1874 and 1877 by cattle baron George Fulton, the mansion is a protected architectural landmark and offers hourly tours (except at noon). The house was notable in its day for its indoor plumbing and other modern conveniences. Today the house also has an Education and History Center in back, as well as the **Harriet Fulton Gardens,** which are worth visiting in spring.

316 S. Fulton Beach Rd. www.visitfultonmansion.com. ✆ **361/729-0386.** Admission $6 adults, $4 children ages 6–18, free ages 5 and younger. Tues–Sat 10am–4pm, Sun 1–4pm. Closed major holidays. Educational Center open Tues–Sat 9:30am–4:30pm and Sun 12:30–4:30pm.

Rockport Center for the Arts ★ Rockport has long attracted art lovers, and here artists and art admirers share a creative space for workshops, classes, exhibitions, and events that celebrate the visual arts. In the two galleries, 18 diverse exhibits are presented every year, where the works of local, regional, national, and international artists are displayed. Backed by a strong art-education component, the Art Center hosts a summer art camp and a weekend drop-in program with a take-home art project. Both programs and the materials are offered free of charge. In the Members Gallery and the gift shop, an eclectic array of works by members of the Art Center is available. The Art

Center hosts three events every year: the **Rockport Art Festival** during the July 4th weekend, the **Tour of Homes** in April, and the **Rockport Film Festival** in November. Other attractions include a growing Sculpture Garden collection with the works of renowned sculptors from around the world.

902 Navigation Circle, Rockport. www.rockportartcenter.com. ✆ **361/729-5519.** Free admission. Tues–Sat 10am–4pm; Sun 1–4pm.

Texas Maritime Museum ★ This terrific small museum brings to life the story of the state's maritime heritage, from fishing and shrimping to boatbuilding and offshore drilling. Among the artifacts are vintage fishing gear and old outboard motors. Stand in the life-size ship's bridge and imagine yourself battling the high seas. Check out the scale model of Shell Oil's **Bullwinkle,** the largest offshore drilling platform in the world.

1202 Navigation Circle, Rockport. www.texasmaritimemuseum.org. ✆ **361/729-1271.** Admission $8 adults, $6 seniors 60 and older or active military with ID, $3 children 3–12, free for children 2 and under. Tues–Sat 10am–4pm; Sun 1–4pm; closed Mon and most major holidays.

Where to Stay

Among the national chain motels in the Rockport and Fulton areas are several nice ones, including the **Hampton Inn & Suites** at 3677 Hwy 35 North, Rockport (www.hamptoninn3.hilton.com; ✆ **361/727-2228**); **La Quinta Inn and Suites** at 2921 Hwy 35 North, Rockport (www.lq.com; ✆ **361/727-9824**), a Fairfield Inn at 2950 Hwy 35 North (www.marriott.com/hotels/travel/crprp-fairfield-inn-and-suites-rockport; ✆ **361/727-9007**) and the **Holiday Inn Express & Suites Rockport–Bay View,** 925 Lady Clare St., Rockport (www.ihg.com; ✆ **361/729-4444**).

Crane House ★★★ Set in a privately owned, 824-acre nature preserve bordering the Aransas National Wildlife Refuge, this comfortable coastal bungalow features two bedrooms (one king bed and two twin beds), two bathrooms, a fully equipped kitchen, a living area, and a large screened porch complete with rocking chairs for watching the wildlife—including deer, whooping cranes, snowy egrets, and more. It's a special place, offering privacy, solitude, and an immersion in the region's natural beauty. Best of all, the property enjoys a mile of coastline on St. Charles Bay. You can rent a kayak or fish from your own private beach. The owners partner with the Texas Nature Conservancy to protect more than 200 acres of wetlands. Book well in advance. Crane House is located just across the Capano Causeway in Lamar.

911 S. Water St. www.cranehouseretreat.com. ✆ **361/729-7239.** 1 unit. $225–$300. No credit cards. Pets accepted. **Amenities:** Wi-Fi (free).

The Lighthouse Inn at Aransas Bay ★★ Right away, the classic white nautical-themed exterior sets this handsome boutique inn apart from your typical Texas coast motel. Inside, the Lighthouse Inn doesn't disappoint. I really like staying here, perhaps for its gorgeous setting by the water, or for its good restaurant (the **Palm Room Bar & Grill,** with bay views), or its close proximity to all the town's shops and restaurants. I love that all rooms and suites have balconies or patios with rocking chairs. Standard rooms are comfortably furnished, while suites have a full kitchen and a separate sitting area. There's a private pier for fishing, or you can scan the horizon for dolphins or watch pelicans fish right off the shore. It's a restful place to land after a day of fishing, as much for its elegant lending library as for the outdoor pool and hot tub.

200 S. Fulton Beach Rd. www.lighthousetexas.com. ✆ **866/790-8439** or 361/790-8439. 78 units. $119–$199 double; $149–$209 captain's suite; $299–$399 2-bedroom suite. Rates include full breakfast. **Amenities:** Restaurant; bar; fitness center; Jacuzzi; laundry; outdoor pool; Wi-Fi (free).

Where to Eat

Most of the independent restaurants in the area are clustered on Fulton Beach Road by the Fulton harbor.

495 Chesapeake Eats ★★ SEAFOOD You might not expect to find a chic spot serving up classic Maryland cuisine, craft cocktails, and a whiskey menu in a little fishing town like Rockport, yet here it is. With a menu featuring Baltimore-style shrimp steamed in beer and Old Bay; Maryland crab cakes; local fresh-caught fish; grass-fed steaks; plump and juicy free-range fried chicken; and good veggie sides and healthful salads, the chef aims to please. The restaurant is in the space once occupied by the high-end Hemingway's restaurant. Be sure to say "Go Terps!" for a big smile from the Maryland-mad staff.

1008 E. North St. Rockport. www.495ceats.com. ✆ **361/450-0116.** Main courses $18–$35. Wed–Sat 5–10pm; Sun noon–9pm.

The Boiling Pot ★★★ SEAFOOD My family has vacationed in Rockport every year for more than 20 years, and we always eat here at least once a visit. A meal at the Boiling Pot is like going to a backyard Cajun crawfish boil: tables covered in rolls of butcher paper, bibs and moist towelettes handed out with plastic silverware (you won't need cutlery), and big piles of steamed shrimp, Gulf crab, king crab legs, corn, and potatoes that you greedily eat with your hands until your lips sting from the spices. There's bread and beer and soft drinks, and maybe even dessert—but it's really all about the shrimp. Kids can draw on the butcher paper with crayons while they wait, and mom may sport a bib—it's all part of the fun in Rockport's favorite dive restaurant. Don't miss a meal here when you're in town. The place fills up fast.

201 S. Fulton Beach Rd, Rockport. www.facebook.com/TheBoilingPotRockport. ✆ **361/729-6973.** Most seafood $18/lb.; gumbo and extras $4.50–$5. Mon–Thurs 4–9pm, Fri–Sun 11am–9pm.

Latitude 28°02' ★★ SEAFOOD Its name tells you exactly where you are, and this lovely upscale restaurant serving "coastal cuisine" in the old downtown of Rockport is exactly where you'll want to be for fresh seafood and fine art and a special evening. Here chef/owners Craig and Ramona Day create delightful dishes relying on local producers whenever possible. Nightly specials are always a good pick, and even non-seafood dishes and vegetarian options don't disappoint. Adjacent to the bar is a gallery for the work of local artists, and many of their paintings also grace the walls of the dining room. Like most beach-town restaurants, this place is rather casual, yet somehow it seems more special than most places on the coast, so you may want to wear chinos or a sundress and leave your bathing-suit cover-up at home.

105 N. Austin St., Rockport. www.latituderockport.com. ✆ **361/727-9009.** Reservations recommended. Main courses $15–$37. Mon–Sat 5pm until last table (usually 10pm); closed Sun.

PORT ARANSAS ★★★

30 miles NE of Corpus Christi; 155 miles S of San Antonio

Port Aransas is my favorite funky Texas beach town, and going here is always a treat. Just the thought of driving onto the ferry and feeding the gulls gets my family excited. Located on the north end of Mustang Island, "Port A," as locals lovingly call it, only has about 3,400 permanent residents, but at any given time, at least 2,000 additional vacationing beach lovers descend on the town. Unlike Corpus Christi and Rockport, Port Aransas is set on open water. (Actually, it's open water in one direction, and the bay in the other.) Hence, you get big, broad, sandy beaches, and watersports not available at other destinations.

Port Aransas has many more condos, hotels, and vacation rentals than Rockport/Fulton and even Corpus Christi, and some are quite upscale, making this the most popular place among Texans for a beach holiday. Unlike Rockport, which has other economic activities besides tourism, Port A depends on winter Texans, fishing enthusiasts, surfers, and sun worshipers for its existence. That may be why the town has more of a party spirit, which you can easily discern if you go barhopping here. That party spirit reaches its tipping point during spring break, when college students flood the town and disrupt the calm, small-town feel—perhaps the perfect time *not* to visit. Otherwise, in winter, spring, summer, or fall, Port A is the beach town you'll like best.

Essentials

GETTING THERE & GETTING AROUND Port Aransas is just over 30 minutes from Corpus Christi. One way to get here is to take South Padre Island Drive (S.P.I.D.) out to Mustang Island and then drive north, but that way doesn't take you right into town. The best and most popular way to get here (unless it is a really crowded weekend at the beach) is by taking Tex. 35 north, as you would go to Rockport, but then taking the exit for Aransas Pass East (Hwy. 361) and going until you see signs for the **Port Aransas ferry** (www.txdot.gov/driver/travel/ferry-schedules.html; ✆ **361/749-2850**). Admission is free, the ride is short (10 min.), and each ferry can carry up to 20 passenger vehicles. The ferry drops passengers off in the middle of town; from here you can get the lay of the land (check out the grocery store, restaurants, and shops you'll want to explore later) and then drive on to your hotel or condo. Port Aransas is compact, and most of the watersports activities can be found by just walking around the town harbor. You're allowed to drive your car on most of the beach here as well.

VISITOR INFORMATION The **Port Aransas Chamber of Commerce visitor center** is located on your right just after you get off the ferry, at 421 W. Cotter Ave. (www.portaransas.org; ✆ **800/452-6278** or 361/749-5919).

FAST FACTS The nearest full-service hospital is **Care Regional Medical Center** at 1711 W. Wheeler Ave., Aransas Pass (www.crmctx.com; ✆ **361/758-8585**).

What to See & Do

BEACHCOMBING Okay, so maybe you want a beach that's completely free of cars and all signs of human settlement, where you can walk along in perfect communion with nature. If so, the obvious choice is San José Island (nicknamed "St. Joe's" by locals, or St. Joseph's), right across from Port Aransas. It's privately owned by a Texas oil family and kept pristine. Transporting people to the island is the **Jetty Boat** ($12 adults, $6 children round-trip), which makes 10 trips daily; it's a short 5-minute ride. You'll leave from the dock at **Fisherman's Wharf**, 900 N. Tarpon St. (www.fishermanswharfporta.com; ✆ **800/605-5448** or 361/749-5760), where you also buy tickets. ***Note:*** Bring anything you might need on the island with you. Bring a bag, too: The island is a good place to collect seashells.

BEACH CRUISING Texas beaches tend to be broad and flat and extend for miles. Driving is permitted on most beaches, and cruising is one of the favorite pastimes of the vacationing Texan. The idea is to pack a cooler in the car filled with picnic supplies; take along other essentials such as towels, beach chairs, and perhaps a beach umbrella; and then drive to the beach and slowly cruise along until you find your spot. Always go very slow (it's a matter of safety and courtesy) and stay on the packed sand; don't get into the loose stuff or you may get stuck. The beach on the Gulf side of Mustang Island is miles long, but isn't continuous; there are places where you have to get back on the road. But somewhere along there, you'll find your spot. One possibility is at **Mustang Island State Park** ★★ (www.tpwd.texas.gov/state-parks/mustang-island; ✆ **361/749-5246**), which has more than 5 miles of wide, sandy beach, with fine sand, few rocks, and almost enough waves for surfing.

BIKE RENTAL Port A is a nice town to explore on a bike. You can rent one with **Island Surf Rentals,** located at 130 E. Ave. G. (www.islandsurfrentals.com; ✆ **361/749-0882**). Golf cars, scooters, and buggies are also available for rent all over town.

DOLPHIN TOURS **Neptune's Charters** (www.dolphinwatchnaturetours.net; ✆ **361/749-6969**) offers dolphin and nature tours aboard the *Mustang II.* It's located at Woody's Sports Center, listed below. Kids (and adults) can also fend off a pirate attack and engage in a squirt gun battle on a "Pirates of Lydia Ann" boat tour with Neptune Tours.

FISHING A lot of fishermen complain that the bay around Port A is overfished. Still, my sister and brother-in-law, who have a house in Port A, fish here often, and usually have good luck. The town has more than 200 fishing guides. If you want to try deep-sea fishing from a party boat (rather than chartering your own boat), see the guys at Fisherman's Wharf, under "Beachcombing," above. They have large boats that go out regularly. If you want to charter, ask the good people at **Woody's Sports Center** at 136 W. Cotter (www.woodys-pa.com; ✆ **361/749-5252**).

GOLFING **Newport Dunes** at Palmilla Beach Resort & Golf Community, 132 Palmilla Beach Dr. (www.palmillabeach.com; ✆ **361/693-5729**) was designed by Arnold Palmer, making use of conservation techniques to minimize environmental impact.

SURFING Port A is known in Texas as a favored spot by the local surfers. There are a couple of places on the island to rent boards. I recommend **Boardhouse Surf & Skate** at 509 N. Alister St. (www.boardhousesurfshop.com; ✆ **361/749-3100**), which rents and sells surfboards, body boards, skim boards, stand-up paddleboards, and surfing gear, gives lessons, and is full of pointers on the local surfing and skateboarding scenes.

Where to Stay

There are a number of motels in town, but only one belongs to a national chain: **Best Western Ocean Villa**, 400 E. Ave. G (www.bestwestern.com; ✆ **800/780-7234**). Two local motels I like are **Alister Square Inn,** 122 S. Alister St. (www.portaransas-texas.com/resort/alister-square; ✆ **888/749-3003**), and **Captain's Quarters Inn**, across from the docks at 235 W. Cotter (www.captainsquartersportaransas.com; ✆ **361/749-6005**).

Condos are the most popular form of lodging on the island. The beach condos in the town area are often in smaller, older buildings, but farther south, large condo properties are scattered along several miles of shoreline. Condo owners contract with agencies to rent these out by the week, advertised in town and online. I recommend **Starkey Properties** (www.starkeyproperties.com; ✆ **361/749-3591**). A favorite vacation-rentals property is **Cinnamon Shore** (www.cinnamonshore.com; ✆ **888/893-0658**), which offer high-end multi-story beachfront homes for rent as well as condominiums. It's all set in an attractive, upscale compound with two pools, a firepit, an exercise room, a fine-dining restaurant, and boardwalk access to the beach. For a family weekend with friends in a dreamy three-story beach house just across the boardwalk and dunes from the waves, book a stay at our family favorite, the **Blue Crab House** at Cinnamon Shore, which sleeps 10-plus guests. Our other old standby, which the kids love for its enormous pool and easy access to the beach, is **Port Royal Ocean Resort** (www.port-royal.com; ✆ **800/242-1034**), a gated community with 210 beachfront condominiums that isn't as close to town as Cinnamon Shore (or quite as upscale)—but it's a great place. Book online in advance or (if you're lucky) at the front desk downstairs.

For RVs as well as campsites, try **Mustang Island State Park** (www.tpwd.texas.gov/state-parks/mustang-island; ✆ **512/389-8900** and 361/749-5246). For a nice location closer to town, try **On the Beach RV Park** at 907 Beach Access Rd. 1A (✆ **361/749-4909**).

The Tarpon Inn ★★ This sweet and simple two-story hotel with a long front porch dates to 1886 and is listed on the National Register of Historic Places. Although standard rooms are, for the most part, small, this unique and charming inn has been well maintained. It's a relaxing property. The guest rooms have no phones, and most have no TVs, but the inn has air-conditioning (a must-have in summer) and rocking chairs on the long, breezy porches. Best of all, you can walk to the beach, a good fishing pier, and town with ease, and the hotel restaurant, **Roosevelt's at the Tarpon Inn,** is one of the best in South Texas. Book the premium rooms, which are a bit larger, or, better still, one of the suites. The FDR suite (no, Roosevelt didn't sleep here; he just fished here in 1937) has a king-size bed, a large sitting room, a full kitchen and dining room, a private porch, and a TV. More romantic is the upstairs honeymoon suite (Room 29) with a queen-size bed and a large tub in the bedroom. Also large is the downstairs corner suite (Room 42). The six guest rooms in an adjacent building called Tarpon Flats have televisions. Check out the signed tarpon scales that line the reception walls; one of them is FDR's framed John Hancock.

200 E. Cotter, Port Aransas. www.thetarponinn.com. ✆ **800/365-6784** or 361/749-5555. 24 units. $89–$125 double; $130–$180 premium; $255–$300 suite. 2-night minimum stay on weekends. Pets 35 lb. and under accepted with a one-time $25 fee. **Amenities:** Restaurant; outdoor pool; Wi-Fi (free).

Where to Eat

Port Aransas has a surprising number of good restaurants for a town of its size. Following are the two most interesting ones.

Liberty Hall/Inferno ★★★ NEW AMERICAN/SEAFOOD I've been following this place through its various incarnations over the past 20-some years, first as Beulah's at the Tarpon Inn, then as the wonderful Pelican Club/Beulah's across the street, followed by another two-named spot, Liberty Hall/Inferno. In fact, when I called today and got their recording, it said, "This is Liberty Hall, aka Inferno, aka Beulah's, aka the Pelican Club." Whatever they call it, it's still just as wonderful, and Chef Guy Carnathan is still here. In fact, he's in the kitchen right now preparing fried-oyster BLTs, shrimp nachos, a Tex-Mex shrimp burger, shrimp and grits, and red snapper—all delights. The place is casual and you can wear what you like.

106 E. Cotter St. www.portalibertyhall.com. ✆ **361/749-4888.** Reservations on holiday weekends only. Main courses $12–$27. Wed–Sun 5:30–9pm; closed Mon/Tues.

Venetian Hot Plate ★★ ITALIAN This restaurant's curious name owes its existence to an error in translation, and by the time the Italian owners became aware of their mistake, it was too late to change. There's no problem in translation with the refined Italian food, however. Look for wonderful pasta dishes, a grilled polenta with bits of crumbled Gorgonzola, and savory nightly specials. The set menu changes seasonally. The dining room is comfortable and serene, and dishes are beautifully plated. The owner cares a lot about wine and prices it reasonably. And we dig the name.

232 Beach St. www.venetianhotplate.com. ✆ **361/749-7617.** Reservations recommended. Main courses $13–$20; specials $20–$30. Tues–Sat 5–10pm (Tues–Thurs 5–9pm and Fri–Sat 5–10pm in winter); closed Sun/Mon, except Labor Day and Memorial Day weekends.

PADRE ISLAND NATIONAL SEASHORE ★

31 miles SE of Corpus Christi; 170 miles S of San Antonio; 414 miles S of Dallas

Some 70 miles of delightful white-sand beach, picturesque sand dunes, and warm ocean waters make Padre Island National Seashore a favorite year-round playground along the Texas Gulf Coast. One of the longest stretches of undeveloped coastline in America, this is an ideal spot for swimming, sunbathing, fishing, beachcombing, windsurfing, and camping. It also provides excellent opportunities for bird-watching and a chance to see several species of rare sea turtles. The island was named for Padre José Nicolás Balli, a Mexican priest who, in 1804, founded a mission, settlement, and ranch about 26 miles north of the island's southernmost tip.

Padre Island is a barrier island, essentially a sandbar that helps protect the mainland from the full force of ocean storms. As with other barrier islands, one of the constants of Padre Island is change; wind and waves relentlessly shape and re-create the island, as grasses and other hardy plants strive to get a foothold in the shifting sands. Padre Island's Gulf side, with miles of beach accessible only to those with four-wheel-drive vehicles, has wonderful surf fishing, while the channel between the island and mainland—the Laguna Madre—has excellent windsurfing and a protected area for small powerboats and sailboats.

Essentials

GETTING THERE From Corpus Christi, take Tex. 358 (South Padre Island Dr.) southeast across the JFK Causeway to Padre Island, and follow Park Road 22 south to the national seashore. The drive takes 45 minutes to an hour.

VISITOR INFORMATION For information, contact **Padre Island National Seashore** (www.nps.gov/pais; ✆ **361/949-8068**). The Park Service also maintains a recorded beach- and road-condition information line (✆ **361/949-8175**). The park is open 24 hours a day.

The **visitor center complex,** along Park Road 22 at Malaquite Beach, has an observation deck, a bookstore, and a variety of exhibits, including one on the endangered Kemp's ridley sea turtle.

FEES & REGULATIONS Entry costs $10 per vehicle (good for 7 days) or $5 per individual on foot or a bike. Regulations here are much like those at other National Park Service properties, which essentially require that visitors not disturb wildlife or damage the site's natural features and facilities. Pets must be leashed and are not permitted on the swimming beach in front of the visitor center. Although driving off road is permitted on some sections of beach, the dunes, grasslands, and tidal flats are closed to all vehicles.

WHEN TO GO Summer is the busiest time here, although it is generally very humid and hot, with highs in the 90s (30s Celsius). Sea breezes in late afternoon and evening help moderate the heat. Winters are mild, with highs from the 50s to the 70s (teens to the 20s Celsius), and lows in the 40s and 50s (single digits to the teens Celsius). Only occasionally does the temperature drop below 40°F (4°C), and a freeze is rare. Hurricane season (June–Oct) is the rainiest time of the year and also has the highest surf. September to November is a good time to visit: It's usually still warm enough for swimming, but not nearly as hot or crowded as in summer.

SAFETY Swimmers and those walking barefoot on the beach should watch out for the Portuguese man-of-war, a blue jellyfish that can cause an extremely painful sting. There are also poisonous rattlesnakes in the dunes, grasslands, and mud flats.

RANGER PROGRAMS Various **interpretive programs** are held year-round, ranging from guided beach or birding car tours, to evening talks outside the visitor center. These programs usually last from 30 to 45 minutes and cover subjects such as migrating or resident birds, seashells, the island's plant life or animals, or things that wash up on the beach. There's also a **Junior Ranger Program** for kids 5 to 13, who answer questions in a free booklet and talk with rangers about the national seashore to earn certificates and badges.

What to See & Do

EXPLORING THE HIGHLIGHTS BY CAR

Padre Island National Seashore has an 8½-mile paved road, with good views of the Gulf and dunes, which leads to the visitor center complex. In addition, most of the beaches are open to licensed street-legal motor vehicles; some sections have hard-packed sand that makes an adequate roadbed for two-wheel-drive vehicles, while most of the beach requires four-wheel-drive. See "Four-Wheeling," below.

OUTDOOR ADVENTURES

BEACHCOMBING The best times for beachcombing are usually early mornings and immediately after a storm, when you're apt to find a variety of seashells, seaweed, driftwood, and the like. These items can be collected, but live animals and historical or archaeological objects should be left. Among shells sometimes found at Padre Island are lightning whelks, moon snails, Scotch bonnets, Atlantic cockles, bay scallops, and sand dollars. The best shell hunting is often in winter, when storms disturb the water; and many of the best shells are often found on Little Shell and Big Shell beaches, accessible only to those with 4WD vehicles. Metal detectors are not permitted on the beach.

BIRDING & WILDLIFE VIEWING More than 350 species of birds frequent Padre Island, and every visitor is bound to see and hear at least some of them. The island is a key stopping point for a variety of migratory species traveling between North and Central America, making spring and fall the best time for bird-watching. Since a number of species winter at Padre Island, there's good birding almost year-round except for the summer.

Birding here is very easy, especially with a four-wheel-drive vehicle, which can move down the coast to the more remote stretches of beach. Experienced bird-watchers say it is best to remain in your vehicle, because humans on foot scare off birds sooner than approaching vehicles. As would be expected by its name, Bird Island Basin is also a good choice for birders as long as the marshes have water. The most commonly observed bird is the laughing gull, which is a year-round resident. Other species to watch for include brown pelicans, plus the more common American white pelicans, long-billed curlews, great blue herons, sandhill cranes, ruddy turnstones, Caspian and Royal terns, willets, Harris's hawks, reddish egrets, northern bobwhites, mourning doves, horned larks, great-tailed grackles, and red-winged blackbirds.

In addition to birds, the island is home to the spotted ground squirrel, which is often seen in the dunes near the visitor center, as well as white-tailed deer, coyotes, black-tailed jack rabbits, lizards, and a number of poisonous and nonpoisonous snakes.

BOATING A boat ramp is located at Bird Island Basin, which provides access to Laguna Madre, a protected bay that is ideal for small powerboats and sailboats. Boat launching is not permitted on the Gulf side of the island, except for sailboats and soft-sided inflatables. Personal watercraft are not permitted in Laguna Madre (except to get from the boat ramp to open water outside the park boundaries), but are allowed on the Gulf side beyond the 5-mile marker.

FISHING Fishing is great year-round. Surf fishing is permitted everywhere along the Gulf side, except at Malaquite Beach, and yields whiting, redfish, black drum, and speckled sea trout; anglers in Laguna Madre catch flounder, sheepshead, and croaker. A Texas fishing license with a saltwater stamp is required. For current license information, contact the **Texas Parks and Wildlife Department** (www.tpwd.state.tx.us; ✆ **800/792-1112**).

FOUR-WHEELING Licensed and street-legal motor vehicles (but not ATVs) are permitted on most of the beach at Padre Island National Seashore (but not Malaquite Beach or the fragile dunes, grasslands, and tidal flats). Most standard passenger vehicles can make it down the first 5 miles of South Beach, but those planning to drive farther south down the island (another 55 miles are open to motor vehicles) will need four-wheel-drive vehicles. Markers are located every 5 miles, and those driving down the beach are advised to watch for soft sand and high water, and to carry a shovel, jack, boards, and other emergency equipment. Unless otherwise posted, the speed limit on the beach is 15 mph. Northbound vehicles have the right of way.

HIKING The national seashore has miles of beach that are ideal for walking and hiking. There's also the paved and fairly easy **Grasslands Nature Trail,** a .8-mile self-guided loop trail that meanders through grass-covered areas of sand dunes. Numbered posts correspond with descriptions of plants and other aspects of the natural landscape in a free brochure available at the trail head or the visitor center. You'll need insect repellent to combat mosquitoes, and because western diamondback rattlesnakes also inhabit the area, stay on the trail and watch where you put your feet and hands.

SWIMMING & SURFING Warm air and water temperatures make swimming practically a year-round activity here—January through March is really the only time it's too chilly—and **swimming** is permitted along the entire beach. The most popular swimming area is 4½-mile-long Malaquite Beach, also called Closed Beach, which is closed to motor vehicles. You have to jostle for a spot only at spring break and summer weekends. ***Note:*** There are no lifeguards on duty here.

Disabled Access to the Beach

Specially designed **fat-tire wheelchairs** for use in the sand, and even in the water, are available at no charge at the visitor center. They do require someone to push.

Surfing is permitted in most areas, but not at Malaquite Beach. Although waves are not of the Hawaii or California size, they're often sufficient to catch a wave or two.

WINDSURFING The Bird Island Basin area on Laguna Madre is considered one of America's best spots for windsurfing because of its warm water, shallow depth, and consistent, steady winds. **Worldwinds Windsurfing** (www.worldwinds.net; © **361/949-7472**) sells and rents windsurfing equipment and wetsuits here, and offers windsurfing lessons during the summer. Call for current fees and a schedule.

Where to Stay & Eat

The closest hotels and restaurants are in Corpus Christi; see that section earlier in this chapter. If you want to stay in the park, you'll have to camp.

Malaquite Campground ★, a developed campsite at Padre Island National Seashore about a half-mile north of the visitor center, is a great spot to bed down, with 50 sites ($8 per night) that are available on a first-come, first-served basis year-round. Sites, within 100 feet of the beach, have good views of the Gulf, and the campground has cold showers, restrooms, and picnic tables. There are no RV hookups, but there is a dump station. For those who don't mind its limitations, it's definitely the best place to camp; it gets crowded only during spring break and on summer weekends.

SOUTH PADRE ISLAND ★★★

291 miles south of San Antonio; 314 miles SW of Houston; 366 miles south of Austin; 565 miles S of Dallas; 850 miles SE of El Paso

South Padre Island is a long, long barrier island that shares its name with the resort town at its southern tip. Any farther south and you would be in Mexico. This would be the favorite beach of all Texans if it weren't so far away; many who love it just go to Port Aransas instead because it's so much closer to major Texas cities. Still, the water is clearer and the beaches are better here than in other parts of the state. Padre Island is a great place to stretch out on the beach, feel the Gulf breeze blowing, and hear nothing but the wash of the surf. Restaurants and clubs are good here, and you can busy yourself with boat rides, watersports, or taking the kids to the popular local waterpark.

This part of the island is narrow—2 or 3 blocks wide—and the town starts at the southern tip and extends north for about 5 miles, with a good bit of vacant land the farther north you go. It's a small town, largely comprised of stores, hotels, a small convention center, restaurants, condos, and vacation houses. Regular housing is in short supply because storm insurance and other costs make it prohibitive. Most of the locals commute to work here from the mainland, from either Port Isabel or Brownsville.

South Padre Island gets a lot of families who make the trip by car or RV. Many come from northern Mexico, driving up from cities such as Monterrey and Saltillo. It also gets a number of "snow birds" (winter Texans). Conventioneers and weekenders often come by plane, via the airports at Harlingen or Brownsville. You'll find reasonably priced flights from major cities in Texas, mostly on Southwest Airlines or United. South Padre Island is known for its fame as a spring-break destination. Hotels will fill up with college kids, often several to a room. It's a good time to be somewhere else.

Other Rio Grande Valley–area cities nearby, including **Brownsville, Harlingen,** and **McAllen,** are worth checking out while you're in this part of the state. McAllen in particular is known as a big international shopping hub for Mexican nationals and American shoppers alike, and it has a thriving art district and some spectacular little restaurants, including the wondrous **Salt** (www.saltnewamericantable.com; ✆ **956/627-6304**), the domain of a migrant worker–turned–chef and a fab place to go locavore.

Essentials

GETTING THERE

BY PLANE The closest airports are the **Brownsville/South Padre Island International Airport (BRO)** (www.flybrownsville.com; ✆ **956/542-4373**) in Brownsville (about 28 miles southwest) and the **Valley International Airport (HRL)** (www.flythevalley.com; ✆ **956/430-8600**) in Harlingen (about 40 miles west). Most major car-rental companies have desks at these airports.

BY CAR From U.S. 77/83, which connects to Harlingen, McAllen, and Corpus Christi, take Tex. 100 east to Port Isabel and then across the Queen Isabella Causeway to the south end of South Padre Island. From Brownsville, take Tex. 48 northeast to Tex. 100.

GETTING AROUND

A car is handy on South Padre Island, and parking and traffic congestion are not usually a problem, except during spring break and on summer weekends. The town's main street is Padre Boulevard. It runs north-south down the middle of the island. Running parallel 1 block on either side are Laguna Boulevard (west) and Gulf Boulevard (east). You don't have to drive much once you're here, because many of the major hotels, restaurants, and beaches are within walking distance of one another. Also, there is a free year-round bus service called **the Wave** (www.spadre.com/thewave.htm; ✆ **956/761-1025**), which operates daily from 7am to 7pm. Of the two different buses, both run the length of the town, and one goes into Port Isabel (each is clearly marked). They pass every 30 minutes along Padre Boulevard.

VISITOR INFORMATION

Contact the **South Padre Island Convention and Visitors Bureau** 600 Padre Blvd. (www.sopadre.com; ✆ **800/767-2373** or 956/761-6433), which operates a visitor center. The center is just a few blocks north of the entry point on the east side of the boulevard, beside a Wells Fargo branch office. Hours are Monday to Friday 8am to 5pm and Saturday and Sunday from 9am to 5pm. On weekdays in the summer, the office stays open an extra hour later. You can pick up maps or talk to the staff for suggestions and advice.

FAST FACTS The **post office,** at 4701 Padre Blvd., is open Monday to Friday 8:30am to 4pm and Saturday 10am to noon.

What to See & Do

DISCOVERING THE AREA'S PAST

Shipwrecks, tempests, and war, as well as some of the happier aspects of life along the southern Texas coast, are the focus of the **Museums of Port Isabel,** 317 E. Railroad Ave. (www.portisabelmuseums.com; ✆ **956/943-7602**). It's comprised of the **Port Isabel Historical Museum** ★ (site of the museum headquarters), the **Treasures of the Gulf Museum,** and the **Port Isabel Lighthouse State Historic Site** ★★. In downtown Port Isabel, these are all within easy walking distance of each other, and make for a good activity on a rainy day. Allow a half-hour to 1 hour to visit each museum.

The Port Isabel Historical Museum, located in a restored 1899 Victorian commercial building, houses exhibits that describe the history of the area from the time it was a supply depot during the Mexican-American War through the Civil War and the area's development as a shrimping and fishing port. It has interactive exhibits, a large display of Mexican-American War artifacts, and a fascinating 1906 Victor Morales *Fish Mural.*

Nearby, the Treasures of the Gulf Museum focuses on three Spanish shipwrecks that occurred in 1554 just off the coast. Exhibits include murals, artifacts, and various hands-on activities, such as a children's discovery lab.

At the west end of the Queen Isabella Causeway stands the 72-foot-high Port Isabel Lighthouse, which helped guide ships through Brazos Santiago Pass to Point Isabel from 1852 until 1905. Today the Port Isabel Lighthouse State Historic Site is an enchanting place where you can climb the lighthouse stairs to behold panoramic views of Port Isabel and South Padre Island and the Gulf of Mexico. Also on the property is a replica of the lighthouse keeper's cottage made from the 1850 blueprints.

The museums are open Tuesday to Saturday 10am to 4pm (last entry 3:30pm); the lighthouse and cottage are open Monday to Friday 9am to 5pm and Saturday 9am to 7pm (lighthouse) and 10am to 4pm (cottage). Last entry is 30 minutes before closing. Admission to each site is $4 adults, $3 seniors 55 and older, $2 students with ID, and free for children 4 and under. Combination tickets for all three sites cost $9 adults, $7 seniors, and $4 students.

OUTDOOR ACTIVITIES

BIRD-WATCHING More than 300 species of birds can be found during different times of the year. The **Laguna Madre Nature Trail,** adjacent to the South Padre Island Convention Centre at the north end of town, is a boardwalk that meanders out over the wetlands of the Laguna Madre and around a freshwater pond. There are a few blinds where you can set up a scope and sit for hours unseen by the birds. The boardwalk is wheelchair accessible and open 24 hours, free of charge. For birding tours in the bay, contact George and Scarlet Colley of **Fins to Feathers Photo Safaris ★** (www.fin2feather.com; ✆ **956/739-2473**), which takes small groups out into the Laguna Madre for 3-hour trips. About an hour from South Padre (70 miles) is the city of McAllen, home to a World Birding Center, the historic **Quinta Mazatlán ★**, 600 Sunset Dr. (www.quintamazatlan.com; ✆ **956/681-3370**), where formal tropical gardens encircle a historic Spanish Revival mansion museum. Here birdwatchers may see birds found nowhere else in the country, including plain chachalacas, common pauraques, clay-colored thrushes, green Jays, buff-bellied hummingbirds, and olive sparrows. In fact, more than 230 species of birds have been spotted at Quinta Mazatlán in the past decade. This is well worth the drive for ardent birdwatchers.

DOLPHIN-WATCHING Dolphin tours are a big activity on the island. "Dolphin Whisperer" Captain Scarlet Colley is a dolphin researcher who offers **small-group tours** (limited to six) with the **Dolphin Research & Sealife Nature Center** (www.spinaturecenter.com; ✆ **956/299-1957**) aboard the *Skimmer 2* take to Laguna Madre Bay to spot wild dolphins. The tours last 1½ hours and cost $25 per person. **Fins to Feathers** (listed above) also offers small-group dolphin tours. Another option is to take a large-boat tour. Offering morning, midday, and sunset dolphin tours, **Original Dolphin Watch** (www.theoriginaldolphinwatch.net; ✆ **956/761-4243**), leaves from Sea Ranch Marina on the island's southern end. Tickets are $10 to $13 adults, $10 children.

FISHING There have been record-setting catches made in the waters around South Padre Island. In 2014, the state-record blue marlin was taken offshore, weighing 900 pounds.

The beach and jetties are easily accessible and popular with "winter Texans." Numerous local charter captains specialize in offshore big-game fishing, where anglers try for blue marlin, white marlin, sailfish, swordfish, wahoo, tuna, and mako shark. Offshore fishing also includes red drum, spotted sea trout, snapper, grouper, tarpon, and king mackerel.

The Laguna Madre, on average only 2 feet deep, is perfect for world-class light-tackle sport fishing. The lush carpet of sea grasses on its bottom provides good habitat and food for red drum, spotted sea trout, flounder, black drum, and snook, and locals brag that there are more of these fish per acre than in any other bay on the Texas Gulf.

The **Texas International Fishing Tournament (TIFT)** (www.tift.org) has been going strong for more than 70 years and attracts some 1,000 participants each August. The 5-day event includes bay, offshore, and tarpon fishing divisions, and is open to anglers of all ages. Contact TIFT or the **South Padre Island CVB** (www.sopadre.com; ✆ **800/767-2373**) for details.

SCHLITTERBAHN BEACH WATERPARK This is operated by the same corporation that owns the highly popular waterpark in the German Hill Country town of New Braunfels—hence the German name. It's not as large as the original, but it has a wave pool and several water rides that require sturdy bathing suits. It also has calmer facilities such as wading and floating pools that work well for those just trying to relax. My favorite feature is the river that connects the rides so that you don't have to spend all your time out of the water waiting in line. All-day general admission is $52 adults and $40 children 3 to 11 and seniors 55 and older. It's at 33261 State Park Rd. 100 (www.schlitterbahn.com; ✆ **956/772-7873**).

SUNBATHING & SWIMMING The beaches of South Padre Island are some of the best on the Gulf: The sand is fine and white, and the water is warm and shallow. In town, there are 23 beach access points with free parking, plus the county has a park at each end of town; both have a $4 all-day parking fee. Incidentally, the shoreline and adjacent beaches are public and open to everyone, if they're lined with hotels and condos.

WINDSURFING With winds about 15 mph year-round, these waters are ideal for windsurfing. Spring and fall are best, usually with beautiful weather. Hurricane season runs from August to early November, but is not often a serious problem.

Where to Stay

There are more condo units on this island than there are regular hotel rooms. Most condos rent by the week. Hotel and condo rates vary widely in South Padre Island over the course of the year, with the lowest rates usually in winter. A thorough list of vacation rentals is on the official South Padre Island tourism website (**www.sopadre.com**). Among the national chain motels in

South Padre Island are **Comfort Suites,** 912 Padre Blvd. (✆ **800/424-6423** or 956/772-9020); and **Super 8,** 4205 Padre Blvd. (✆ **800/800-8000** or 956/761-6300). Room tax adds about 17%. Most hotels are nonsmoking.

Isla Grand Beach Resort ★ Formerly a Radisson, this sprawling 10-acre resort enjoys an unobscured swath of beachfront frontage and is easily the nicest full-service hotel in town. The resort's standard rooms, the popular beach cabanas, come with a patio or balcony. Sixty-five high-rise condos have two bedrooms, two full bathrooms, full kitchens, and a spacious living/dining room with a sofa sleeper. The resort has a gorgeous beachside pool (beautifully lit at night) and four tennis courts, plus lots of options for eating and drinking, including a beach bar, a poolside grill, a nightclub with live entertainment, a Starbucks coffee hut, and a full-service beachside restaurant, **Windjammer's,** serving breakfast, lunch, and dinner.

500 Padre Blvd. www.islagrand.com. ✆ **800/292-7704** or 956/761-6511. 193 units. $279–$319 double; $499 condo. **Amenities:** Restaurant; bar; coffee shop; poolside grill; children's programs; exercise room, 2 Jacuzzis; 2 outdoor pools (1 heated); room service; 4 outdoor lit tennis courts; Wi-Fi (free).

The Palms Resort on the Beach ★ Of the three old-time beach motels that still exist, this is the nicest. It's well-maintained and well-managed, with a heated pool and a prime location right on the beach. The newly renovated rooms are spacious and clean, with tile floors and kitchenettes. The newest, the Sunset Suite, is massive, with a king bed (it could fit three or four) and a covered porch. It's even got a popular alfresco restaurant and lounge, the **Café on the Beach,** serving meals all day.

3616 Gulf Blvd. www.palmsresortcafe.com. ✆ **800/466-1316** or 956/761-1316. 30 units. $175–$230 queen suite; $200–$300 palms or king suite. **Amenities:** Restaurant; heated outdoor pool; Wi-Fi (free).

CAMPING

Isla Blanca Park ★★ (www.cameroncountyparks.com/IslaBlancaPark; ✆ **956/761-3700**), on the southern tip of South Padre Island, is our choice for a developed campground on the island, with easy beach access. Part of the Cameron County Park System, this well-maintained facility has 600 paved sites, many of which are pull-through, and more than half have full RV hookups. The park also has restrooms with showers, a dump station, a sandy beach, a fishing jetty, a boat ramp and marina, a bike trail, and beach pavilions with concessions. There is a primitive tent area right on the Laguna Madre. Rates are $25 to $40.

Those looking for a developed resort should head to South Padre Island KOA (www.koa.com/campgrounds/south-padre; ✆ **800/562-9724** or 956/761-5665), just south of the Queen Isabella Causeway on Padre Boulevard. This year-round campground offers 190 sites with full hookups, restrooms with showers, a guest laundromat, and security. There's a large heated pool, spa, boat dock, rec hall and game room, five tent sites, and numerous planned activities. Rates are $49 to $88. There are pet restrictions.

Where to Eat

If you're staying in a condo with a kitchen, and you have many mouths to feed, you'll be going to the grocery store. The island's only full-service supermarket is the **Blue Marlin IGA Supermarket** (✆ **956/761-4966**), 2912 Padre Blvd., which has everything from a deli to a meat market to fresh fruits and veggies. Otherwise, stock up in Port Isabel at the **H.E.B.,** 1679 Hwy. 100 (www.heb.com/heb-store/US/tx/port-isabel/port-isabel-h-e-b-383), or the **Port Isabel Wal-Mart Supercenter,** 1401 State Hwy. (www.walmart.com/store/413).

Dirty Al's ★ SEAFOOD What started as a bait shop and unofficial taco stand by local shrimper Alfonso Salazar is now this bustling, ultra-casual restaurant, going strong since 2003. Dirty Al's claims to serve the World's Best Fried Shrimp, and for our money, they're just fine, as are the fried oysters, peel-and-eat shrimp, po'boys, and tacos stuffed with blackened fish or shrimp. Everything is served on paper plates, and you can wash it down with a cold beer or a glass of wine. The Salazar family now has six restaurants on the island, but this is the original—and it's still a darned good deal.

33396 State Rd. 100. ✆ **956/761-4901.** Reservations accepted before arrival (30 min.). Main courses $9–$15. Daily 11am–8pm.

Ted's Restaurant ★ BREAKFAST/BRUNCH Breakfast is king at this homey establishment, and folks come from miles around to dine on fluffy pecan pancakes, biscuits and gravy, French toast, and fajitas and eggs. For lunch (or brunch), choose from burgers, sandwiches, and salads.

5717 Padre Blvd. ✆ **956/761-5327.** Main courses $5–$8. Daily 7am–2:30pm.

After Dark (or Perhaps After Noon)

On Fridays during the summer, the city puts on a small fireworks show after dark, which folks can enjoy from bayside bars and restaurants. My favorite place with ample deck space above the water is **Louie's Backyard,** 2305 Laguna Blvd. (✆ **956/716-6406**), a big and buzzing establishment serving good food. During high season, there is live music nightly. It's a subline place to listen to reggae and sip a frozen concoction. When in need of a proper beach bar where you can work your toes into the sand while enjoying a cold beer, head to **Wanna-Wanna Beach Bar & Grill,** at the Island Inn, 5100 Gulf Blvd. (www.wannawanna.com; ✆ **956/761-7677**).

SAN ANTONIO

8

Home to the Alamo and rich in Spanish colonial style, San Antonio is a colorful tapestry of influences, from Mexican to Aztec to German. Add a laid-back South Texas charm, and the Alamo City is quite unlike any other in America. Romantic River Walk runs right through it, the Tex-Mex here is hard to beat, and the hot Pearl culinary district is drawing foodies from all over the world. San Antonio has some of the state's most storied historic sites, but modern industry and innovation are welcomed with open arms. And if you're looking for a fun family destination, look no further: The downtown area is comfortable and safe, and on its outskirts are two kid-pleasing theme parks. Best of all, this sunny and inviting city is just a short drive from Austin, so you can see both with ease. San Antonio simply sizzles—and especially in summer when the heat and humidity hit high digits.

For most of its history, San Antonio was the largest city in Texas, the "cosmopolitan" center, where multiple cultures—Native American, Mexican, Anglo, and German, among others—came together and coexisted. In 1718, the native Coahuiltecan Indians sought protection from Apache raids and invited the Spaniards to establish a mission here. A few years later, by order of the king of Spain, 15 families came from the Canary Islands to settle here. (The oldest families in San Antonio can trace their family trees back to these colonists.) The settlement grew and prospered. The church eventually built five missions along the San Antonio River. But during the fight for Mexican Independence and then Texan Independence (1821 and 1836, respectively), San Antonio was the site of several hard-fought battles, including the famous siege of the Alamo. This greatly reduced the population for more than a decade until the city began to attract thousands of German settlers fleeing the revolutions in Europe. So many came that by 1860, German speakers in the city outnumbered both Spanish and English speakers. Throughout the following decades, these different immigrant groups would accommodate each other and forge a unique local culture.

The city continued to grow. In the early 1900s, it showcased the first skyscraper in Texas. But San Antonio wasn't growing fast enough to keep up with Houston or Dallas. By the 1920s, it had become Texas's third-largest city and had arrived at a crossroads.

Would it follow Houston and Dallas in their bull rush toward growth and modernism? Or would it go its own way, preserving what it thought most valuable?

This dilemma took the form of a political dispute over the meandering San Antonio River. A city commission recommended draining the riverbed and channeling the water through underground culverts to free up space for more downtown buildings. This outraged many locals. A group of women's clubs formed to save the river and create an urban green space along its banks (and this was decades before anyone in Texas had ever heard of urban planning). The women's campaign was multipronged and even included a puppet-show dramatization. They were victorious. The river was saved, as was San Antonio's heritage. Plans were laid for the Paseo del Rio, or River Walk, which would eventually became the city's crowning feature and a point of local pride—and which would be expanded in the new millennium with glorious "Museum Reach" and "Mission Reach" sections.

Of course, there are many other aspects to life here that foster pride and a sense of identity. Fiesta celebrations that take place in San Antonio each spring with grand balls, river parades, night parades, parties, food fairs, and street dances are colorful reminders that there's no other city with traditions and celebrations quite like this.

Today, as the Alamo City prepares to celebrate its 300th birthday in 2018, it is bigger and better than ever before, and so much more than many visitors expect. Plan to spend a few days here, and then take a Hill Country side trip to Boerne or Fredericksburg, or head east for Texas barbecue in Lockhart. San Antonio is sprawling, and you'll want to see it all.

ORIENTATION

Arriving

BY PLANE

The **San Antonio International Airport (SAT)** (www.sanantonio-airport.com; © **210/207-3411**) is 8 miles north of downtown. It is compact, easy to navigate, and has two terminals. ***Note:*** At press time, airport construction was affecting access to certain parking garages, so give yourself extra time to navigate the traffic and construction.

GETTING TO & FROM THE AIRPORT Loop 410 and U.S. 281 S. intersect just outside the airport. If you're renting a car here, it should take about 15 to 20 minutes to drive downtown via U.S. 281 S.

Most of the hotels within a radius of a mile or two provide **free shuttle service** to and from the airport (check when you make your reservation). If you're staying downtown, you'll most likely have to pay your own way.

VIA Metropolitan Transit's bus no. 5 is the cheapest ($1.10) way to get downtown, but also the slowest; it'll take from 40 to 45 minutes.

SATRANS (www.supershuttlesa.com; © **800/868-7707** or 210/281-9900), with a booth outside each of the terminals, offers shared van service from the airport to downtown hotels for $19 per person one-way, $34 round-trip. Vans run from about 7am until 1am; phone 24 hours in advance for van pickup from your hotel.

There's a **taxi** queue in front of each terminal. You'll pay approximately $25 to $30 to get downtown by taxi.

BY TRAIN

San Antonio's train station is located at 350 Hoefgen St., in St. Paul's Square, on the east side of downtown near the Alamodome and adjacent to the Sunset Station entertainment complex. Cabs are readily available from here. Lockers are not available, but Amtrak will hold passengers' bags in a secure location for $2 per bag. Information about the city is available at the main counter. For train schedules and fees, go to **Amtrak** (www.amtrak.com).

BY BUS

San Antonio's bustling **Greyhound** station, 500 N. St. Mary's St. (www.greyhound.com; ✆ **210/270-5834**), is located downtown about 2 blocks from the River Walk. The station, open 24 hours, is within walking distance of a number of hotels, and many public streetcar and bus lines run nearby.

Visitor Information

The main office of the **City of San Antonio Visitor Information Center** is across the street from the Alamo, 317 Alamo Plaza (www.visitsanantonio.com; ✆ **800/252-6609** or 210/207-6748). Hours are daily 9am to 5pm, except Thanksgiving, Christmas, and New Year's, when the center is closed.

The center gives visitors a free copy of the magazine "San Antonio Travel and Leisure Guide," published semiannually by the **San Antonio Convention and Visitors Bureau (SACVB).** It has maps and listings and is something you can pore over during an idle moment. Also at the center are racks and racks of brochures and some free magazines heavy on advertisements, such as ***Fiesta,*** with interesting articles about the city, and ***Rio,*** a tabloid focusing on the River Walk. You can find these last two publications at many of the downtown hotels and shops. Both list sights, restaurants, shops, cultural events, and nightlife.

Also free—but more objective—is San Antonio's alternative paper, the ***Current.*** Though skimpy, it is a good source for nightlife listings. The ***San Antonio Express-News*** is the local newspaper. It's got a good arts/entertainment section called "The Weekender," which comes out on Friday and is available around town.

City Layout

San Antonio lies at the southern edge of the Texas Hill Country and is mostly flat. Streets are jumbled, especially in the old parts of town, while a number of the thoroughfares leading in and out of town follow old Spanish trails or 19th-century wagon trails.

MAIN ARTERIES & STREETS Most of the major roads in Texas meet in San Antonio, where they form a rough wheel-and-spoke pattern. There are two loops: I-410 circles around the city, coming to within 6 to 7 miles of downtown in the north and east, and as far out as 10 miles in the west and south; and Hwy. 1604 forms an even larger circle with a 13-mile radius. The spokes of the wheel are formed by highways I-35, I-10, I-37, U.S. 281, U.S. 90, and U.S. 87. Occasionally, two or three highways will merge onto the same freeway. For example, U.S. 90, U.S. 87, and I-10 converge for a while in an east-west direction just south of downtown, while U.S. 281, I-35, and I-37 run together on a north-south route to the east; I-10, I-35, and U.S. 87 bond for a bit going north-south to the west of downtown.

Among the most major of the minor spokes are Broadway, McCullough, San Pedro, and Blanco, all of which lead north from the city center into the most popular shopping and restaurant areas of town. Fredericksburg Road goes out to the Medical Center from just northwest of downtown. You may hear locals referring to something as being "in the loop." That doesn't mean it's privy to insider information, but rather, that it lies within the circumference of I-410, and is therefore in central San Antonio.

Downtown is bounded by I-37 to the east, I-35 to the north and west, and U.S. 90 (which merges with I-10) to the south. Within this area, Durango, Commerce, Market, and Houston are the important east-west streets. Alamo on the east side and Santa Rosa (which turns into South Laredo) on the west side are the major north-south streets.

Neighborhoods in Brief

The older areas described here, from downtown through Alamo Heights, are all "in the loop" (410). The Medical Center area in the Northwest lies just outside it, but the rest of the Northwest, as well as North Central and the West, are expanding beyond even Loop 1604.

Downtown Site of San Antonio's original Spanish settlements, this fun and vibrant area includes the Alamo and other historic sites, along with the River Walk, the Alamodome, the convention center, the Shops at Rivercenter Mall, and many high-rise hotels, restaurants, and shops. It's also the center of commerce and government, so many banks and offices, as well as most city buildings, are located here.

King William The city's first suburb, this historic district directly south of downtown was settled in the mid- to late 1800s by wealthy German merchants who built some of the most beautiful mansions in town. It began to be yuppified in the 1970s, and, at this point, you'd never guess it had ever been allowed to deteriorate. Only a few of the area's many impeccably restored homes are open to the public, but a number have become bed-and-breakfasts. The location is ideal for those who want to explore the central city.

Southtown Alamo Street marks the border between King William and Southtown, an adjoining neighborhood. For years it was a depressed area, but it became trendy a long time ago, thanks to a Main Street refurbishing project and the opening of the Blue Star arts complex. You'll find a nice mix of Hispanic neighborhood shops and funky coffeehouses and galleries here, but few hotels worth booking.

South Side The old, largely Hispanic southeast section of town that begins where Southtown ends (there's no agreed-upon boundary, but we'd say it lies a few blocks beyond the Blue Star arts complex) is home to four of the city's five historic missions. Thus far, it's been left alone and remains a group of quiet working-class neighborhoods with pockets of small businesses.

Monte Vista Area Immediately north of downtown, Monte Vista was established soon after King William by a conglomeration of wealthy cattlemen, politicos, and generals who moved "on to the hill" at the turn of the 20th century. A number of the area's large houses have been split into apartments for students of nearby Trinity University and San Antonio Community College, but many lovely old houses have been restored in the past 30 years. This is a highly desirable place to live. The area has several bed-and-breakfasts, most located on quiet streets within easy reach of downtown. In addition, there are several good dining spots nearby.

Fort Sam Houston Built in 1876 to the northeast of downtown, Fort Sam Houston boasts a number of stunning officers' homes. Much of the working-class neighborhood surrounding Fort Sam is rundown, but renewed interest in restoring San Antonio's older areas is beginning to have some impact here, too.

Alamo Heights Area In the 1890s, when construction in the area began, Alamo Heights was at the far northern reaches of San Antonio. This is now home to San Antonio's well-heeled residents and holds most of the fashionable shops and restaurants. **Terrell Hills** to the east, **Olmos Park** to the west, and **Lincoln Heights** to the north are all offshoots of this area. It is home to the Alamo Quarry, once just that but now a ritzy golf course and popular shopping mall. Shops and restaurants are concentrated along two main drags: Broadway and, to a lesser degree, New Braunfels. Most of these neighborhoods share a single zip code ending in the numbers "09"—thus the local term "09ers," referring to the area's affluent residents. The Witte Museum, DoSeum, McNay Art Museum, San Antonio Botanical Gardens, San Antonio Zoo, and Brackenridge Park are all here.

Tobin Hill Directly north of downtown and part of midtown, Tobin Hill has long been a much-loved part of town, but it is even more popular now as the **Pearl** culinary and entertainment campus has brought new life to the neighborhood. Bordered on the north by Monte Vista and Trinity University; on the west by San Pedro Ave. and San Antonio College; on the east by Hwy. 281, Pearl Brewery, and the River Walk's Museum Reach; and on the south by I-35 and the award-winning River North District, Tobin Hill is seeing more visitors today than it has in years. With the Culinary Institute of America (CIA) campus at Pearl, and with a dozen restaurants, the wildly popular Hotel Emma, bars and music clubs, Pearl is the hottest place in the Alamo City these days.

Northwest These mostly characterless neighborhoods surround the south Texas Medical Center (a large grouping of health-care facilities referred to as the **Medical Center**). The area includes lots of condominiums and apartments, and much of the shopping and dining is in strip malls (the trendy, still-expanding Huebner Oaks retail center is an exception). The farther north you go, the nicer the housing complexes get. The high-end La Cantera Resort & Spa, the exclusive La Cantera and Dominion residential enclave, several tony golf courses, and the Shops at La Cantera (San Antonio's fanciest retail center) mark the direction that development is taking in the far northwest part of town, just beyond Six Flags Fiesta Texas and near Friedrich Park. It's becoming one of San Antonio's prime growth areas.

North Central San Antonio is inching toward Bulverde and other Hill Country towns via this major corridor of development clustered from Loop 410 north to Loop 1604, east of I-10 and west of I-35, and bisected by U.S. 281. The airport and many developed industrial strips line U.S. 281 in the southern section, but the farther north you go, the more the growth will astound you in the Stone Oak part of town. Lots of high-end homes have been built here, and with that has come great shopping and restaurants. The downside of all this growth? Terrific traffic at U.S. 281 and Loop 1604, especially in the afternoons.

West This area around I-10—home to SeaWorld, Six Flags Fiesta Texas, the Shops at La Cantera, and several lovely hotels—is booming these days. The Rim shopping center, La Gloria restaurant, the Santikos Palladium cinemas and IMAX theater, and more make this a hot part of town on the way to the Hill Country along 1-10. Road building hasn't kept pace with growth, however, so traffic can be a bear.

Getting Around

If you're staying downtown, a car is more of a hindrance than an asset: Traffic can be a pain, and public transportation is good. If you're staying in King William or Monte Vista, you can get by without a car, but it would come in handy to see the attractions outside the downtown area. If you're bunking anywhere else in San Antonio, however, you'll definitely want wheels—and you might as well rent them at the airport, where all the major car-rental companies are represented at each of the terminals.

BY PUBLIC TRANSPORTATION

BY BUS **VIA Metropolitan Transit Service** (www.viainfo.net; ✆ **210/362-2020**) offers regular bus service for $1.10, with an additional 15¢ charge for transfers. Express buses cost $2. You'll need exact change. The most convenient of VIA service centers for visitors is downtown at 260 E. Houston St., open Monday to Friday 7am to 6pm, Saturday 9am to 2pm. A helpful bus route is the no. 7, which travels from downtown to the San Antonio Museum of Art, Japanese Tea Garden, San Antonio Zoo, Witte Museum, Brackenridge Park, and the Botanical Garden. ***Tip:*** During large festivals such as Fiesta and the Texas Folklife Festival, VIA offers many Park & Ride lots that allow you to leave your car and take a bus downtown.

BY CAR

If you can avoid driving downtown, by all means do so. The pattern of one-way streets is confusing, and parking is limited. It's not that the streets in downtown San Antonio are narrower or more crowded than those in most old city centers, but driving is unnecessary when public transportation is so convenient and the area is so pedestrian-friendly.

Rush hour lasts from about 7:30 to 9am and 4:30 to 6pm Monday through Friday. The crush may not be bad compared with that of Houston or Dallas, but it's getting worse. San Antonio's rapid growth means you can expect to find major highway construction or repairs going on somewhere in the city at any given time. For updates, go to the Texas Department of Transportation's website at **www.dot.state.tx.us**.

PARKING You'll find plenty of parking lots scattered around the north and east sides of downtown, within a few blocks of the main attractions. These run about $5 to $7 per day. Parking meters are not plentiful in the heart of downtown, but you can find some on the streets near the River Walk and on Broadway. The cost is $1.80 per hour (which is also the time limit) near the courthouse, 75¢ in other locations. ***Note:*** Although very few signs inform you of this fact, meter parking is free after 6pm Monday through Saturday and all day Sunday, except during special events.

BY RIVER TAXI

Rio Taxi Service (www.riosanantonio.com/rio-taxi; ✆ **800/417-4139** or 210/244-5700;) operates daily from 9am to 9pm. Its 39 pickup locations are marked by Rio Taxi signs with black-and-yellow checker flags. You buy your tickets once you board. At $10 one-way, $12 for an all-day pass, $16 for a one-day combination pass, or $25 for a 3-day pass, it's more expensive than ground transport, but it's a real treat to ride on the river. Be sure to use the Rio Taxi for a ride up the Museum Reach to the popular Pearl area. It may take up to 45 minutes to go the 2½-mile distance, but the trip up this part of the river is remarkable; you'll pass through a unique lock-and-dam system gate at one point and then glide underneath overpasses and bridges that have been adorned with $11-million art installations. You can also ride the Rio Taxi to the San Antonio Museum of Art.

BY TAXI

Cabs are available outside the airport, near the Greyhound and Amtrak terminals (only when a train is due, however), and at most major downtown hotels, but they're next to impossible to hail on the street; most of the time, you'll need to phone for one in advance. The best of the taxi companies in town (and also the largest, because it represents the consolidation of two of the majors) is **Yellow-Checker Cab** (www.yellowcabsa.com; ✆ **210/222-2222**), which has an excellent record of turning up when promised. The base charge on a taxi is $4.75; add $2.20 per additional before 8pm, or $3.20 for each mile after 8pm. Download the **Hail a Cab** (www.hailacabapp.com) or **Z-Trip** (www.ztrip.com) smartphone apps to book your cab and pay for it securely from your smartphone. Several rideshare app programs are available in San Antonio, including **Uber** and **Lyft.**

BY BICYCLE

San Antonio now has its own public bikeshare program, **San Antonio BCycle (B-cycle),** with bikes available throughout the city at B-stations. Get the details, plus B-station locations and bike routes at **https://sanantonio.bcycle.com**. Purchase passes at B-stations for unlimited 60-minute rides ($2 for each additional half-hour). A 24-hour pass is $12, and monthly membership is $18 ($100 for entire year).

[FastFACTS] SAN ANTONIO

Dentist To find a dentist near you in town, contact the **San Antonio District Dental Society,** 14603 Huebner Rd., Ste. 2403 (✆ **210/732-1264**).

Doctor For a referral, contact **the Bexar County Medical Society** at 4334 N. Loop 1604 W. (www.bcms.org; ✆ **210/301-4391**), Monday through Friday 8am to 5pm.

Drugstores Most branches of CVS and Walgreens, the major chain pharmacies in San Antonio, are open late Monday through Sunday. There's a CVS downtown at 211 Losoya/River Walk (✆ **210/224-9293**). Call ✆ **800/925-4733** to find the Walgreens nearest you.

Hospitals The main downtown hospital is **Baptist Medical Center,** 111 Dallas St. (www.baptisthealthsystem.com; ✆ **210/297-7000**). The **Children's Hospital of San Antonio,** 333 N. Santa Rosa St. (www.chofsa.org; ✆ **210/704-2011**), is also downtown. Contact the **San Antonio Medical Foundation** (www.samedfoundation.org; ✆ **210/614-3724**) for info about other medical facilities.

Hot Lines Contact **National Youth Crisis Hotline** at ✆ 800/442-HOPE (4673); the **Rape Crisis Hot Line** at ✆ 210/349-7273; **Texas Abuse Hot Line** at ✆ 800/252-5400; **Mental Illness Crisis Hot Line** at ✆ 210/734-3349; and **Poison Control Center** at ✆ 800/764-7661.

Newspapers & Magazines The *San Antonio Express-News* is the only mainstream source of news in town.

Police Call ✆ **911** in an emergency. The nonemergency number is ✆ **311.** The Texas Highway Patrol can be reached at ✆ **210/531-2220.**

Safety The crime rate in San Antonio has risen in recent years, so there's a strong police presence downtown (in fact, both the transit authority and the police department have bicycle patrols); even so, muggings, pickpockets, and purse snatchings in the area are rare. Use common sense as you would anywhere else: Walk only on well-lit, well-populated streets. Also, it's generally not a good idea to stroll south of Durango Avenue after dark.

Taxes The sales tax here is 8.25%, and the city surcharge on hotel rooms increases to a whopping 16.75%.

WHAT TO SEE & DO

San Antonio has a wide selection of attractions that can satisfy a variety of interests. You can easily fill your time hitting each one on your list, but I suggest you set aside a little time for meandering the city's downtown.

Stop in at Visit San Antonio's **Official San Antonio Visitor Information Center,** 317 Alamo Plaza (http://visitsanantonio.com; ✆ **800/447-3372** or 210/207-6700), across the street from the Alamo. The tourism agency's helpful coupon book includes discounts for everything from theme parks to city tours to museums. Many hotels also have a stash of discount coupons for their guests.

The Top Attractions

DOWNTOWN AREA

The Alamo ★★ Tucked tightly between the high-rise buildings and hotels of downtown, San Antonio's most famous of its five missions is a modest little limestone chapel surrounded by well-tended gardens, a few outlying buildings, and a brave but tragic past. Built by the Spanish in 1744 as Mission San Antonio de Valero, the compound today serves as a shrine honoring the memory of its brave protectors and their fight for Texan independence from Mexico. It's one of the state's biggest attractions, drawing more than 2.5 million visitors a year through its wooden church doors.

Throughout the centuries, the compound has served many uses, from mission to Spanish Calvary quarters, but its most important moment came in 1836. A large Spanish army led by General Antonio López de Santa Anna battled with a band of "Texians" fighting for Texas's freedom. Among the defenders were Davy Crockett, William Travis, and Jim Bowie, all of whom died along with the other Texians. The battle cry "Remember the Alamo!" led Texians to victory a month later, on April 21, 1836, at the Battle of San Jacinto.

The Alamo was saved by the Daughters of the Republic of Texas from becoming a hotel in 1902 but today is managed by the General Land Office. (The outlying buildings of the original mission no longer stand, except for the Long Barrack, which was once living quarters for Spanish missionaries who called it the "convento," or "convent.")

The three main buildings—the **Shrine** (church), the **Long Barrack Museum,** and the **Alamo Gift Shop and Museum**—all house exhibits on the Texas Revolution and Texas history. Visitors can also stroll the **Alamo Gardens** behind the church beneath shady pecan trees and oaks. The Alamo shrine, with its famous curved facade, holds a diorama of the mission grounds at the time of the battle. Exhibits display artifacts like Travis's ring, Crockett's buckskin vest, and a period Bowie knife. In the Long Barrack museum, a short video shown every 20 minutes provides a thorough overview of the Texas Revolution and the historic Alamo siege.

To make a visit to the Alamo more meaningful (and fun and educational for the kids), first see the movie *Alamo: The Price of Freedom* (p. 247) in the Alamo IMAX/AMC Rivercenter 11 cinema at the Shops at Rivercenter. Then visit the interactive **Battle for Texas: The Experience** (p. 277) showcasing authentic Alamo artifacts and offering multimedia re-enactments of the battle, also at the Shops at Rivercenter. And don't miss the history talks that are given, free of charge, every 30 minutes in the Calvary Courtyard on the Alamo grounds. Be sure to see the old **Heritage Pecan** tree, planted here in 1850, called the "pampered princess" tree of the Alamo.

300 Alamo Plaza. www.thealamo.org. ✆ **210/225-1391.** Free admission (donations welcome). Peak season (Mar 4–Sept 3): 9am–8pm, Mon–Sat 9am–5:30pm; Sun 10am–5:30pm. Off-peak season (Sept 4–Mar 3): 9am–5:30pm. Last entry 15 min. before closing. Closed Dec 24–25. Streetcar: Red or Blue lines.

The Briscoe Western Art Museum ★★ This elegant museum on the River Walk bend, near the Arneson River Theatre and not far from the Westin hotel and La Contessa, is a delightful place to spend an hour or two seeing glorious depictions of the romantic Wild West. You'll be mesmerized by the collection, from ornate saddles to a wall of shiny spurs, from a re-created Wells Fargo stagecoach to cowboy- and Native American–themed art. It has a small sculpture garden at river level. The building alone is a stunner (it was the city's first public library and once housed a circus museum); you may spend a good deal of time gazing up at the ornate ceilings and Art Deco light fixtures. It's free on Tuesday evenings from 4 to 9pm.

210 W. Market St. www.briscoemuseum.org. ✆ **210/299-4499.** Admission $10 adults, $8 seniors (65 and over) and students and retired military, free for children 12 and younger and active military & family with ID. Free admission Tues 4–9pm. Tues 10am–9pm; Wed–Sun 10am–5pm; closed Mon, Dec 26, and Jan 2.

King William Historic District ★ The Alamo City's first suburb, a 25-block area adjacent to Southtown, was first established in the late 19th century by affluent German merchants who built lavish mansions and named the neighborhood after Kaiser Wilhelm of Prussia. Today visitors walk its shady streets to see the grand homes and their beautifully landscaped yards. First, stop at the headquarters of the **San Antonio Conservation Society,** 107 King William St. (www.saconservation.org; ✆ **210/224-6163**), and pick up a self-guided walking-tour booklet outside the gate. If you stroll at a leisurely pace, the tour should take about an hour. For tours inside the historic homes, visit the **Steves Homestead Museum,** 509 King William St. (✆ **210/227-9160;** daily 10am–3pm), set in a Victorian house built in 1876 for a lumber magnate; and **Villa Finale,** 401 King William St. (✆ **210/223-9800**), the 1876 home of preservationist Walter Mathis. Both tours are worthwhile, and both require reservations. Have breakfast or lunch at the Pioneer Flour Mill family's historic **Guenther House** (p. 272), a Victorian-era home with a small museum (free).

East bank of the river just south of downtown. Streetcar: Blue line.

La Villita National Historic District ★ European settlers first built homes on the east bank of the San Antonio River in the late 18th and early 19th centuries, making La Villita ("little village") the city's oldest neighborhood. Even earlier, this was the place where soldiers camped in rustic huts outside the Mission San Antonio de Valero. Floodwaters destroyed those first structures in 1819, so adobe and brick buildings were erected there. During the famous siege of the Alamo, Gen. Santa Ana set up his cannon line nearby. By 1939, when construction began on the River Walk, La Villita was reclaimed and revitalized by local artists and the San Antonio Conservation Society. Today, art galleries, small crafts shops, and romantic restaurants fill the tiny pueblo adjacent to the River Walk, a movie-set–like village comprising shaded patios, brick-and-tile streets, and some original adobe buildings, including the house of General Cós, the Mexican military leader who surrendered to the Texians in 1835. You may be able to enter the River Walk from the Arneson River Theatre or from the terraced outdoor dining spaces of La Villita restaurants overlooking the river, with their white lights twinkling in the trees at night.

Bounded by Durango, Navarro, and Alamo sts. and River Walk. ✆ **210/207-8610.** Free admission. Shops daily 10am–6pm. Closed Thanksgiving, Dec 25, and Jan 1. Streetcar: Red, Purple, or Blue lines.

Market Square ★★ If you have no time to add a Mexican border town to your vacation to-do list while you're in Texas, San Antonio has the next best thing. Colorful Market Square has the feel of a small Mexican downtown plaza, where food booths, retail kiosks, artist stalls, street performers, and musicians gather on weekends or pleasant spring and summer days. *Ballet folklórico* dancers or mariachi bands at local festivals are held here throughout the year. Inside the adjacent El Mercado building is a mall of Mexican imports vendors re-creating an authentic border-style marketplace where you can buy everything from huge sombreros to scorpion-inlaid paperweights, striped Indian blankets to big bottles of Mexican vanilla and *piñatas.* Kids love to poke around here, as do most adults seeking some of the Old Mexico style for which San Antonio is so well-known. In addition to food stalls, two popular Mexican restaurants edge Market Square, including my favorite, **Mi Tierra ★★★** (p. 269).

Bounded by Commerce, Santa Rosa, Dolorosa, and I-35. www.sanantonio.com/places/el-mercado. ✆ **210/207-8600.** Free admission. El Mercado and Farmers' Market Plaza summer daily 10am–8pm; winter daily 10am–6pm; restaurants and some shops open later. Closed Thanksgiving, Dec 25, Jan 1, and Easter. Streetcar: Red, Purple, or Yellow lines.

The River Walk (Paseo del Río) ★★★ Hidden below street level in downtown San Antonio, another world awaits, romantic and hidden, and a river runs through it. The old-world-style "Paseo del Rio" or "River Walk," is a series of pathways and bridges wending alongside a 15-mile-long stretch of the San Antonio River, part of which flows through 5 miles of downtown. Hotels, outdoor cafes, shops, and restaurants line the more bustling downtown tourist areas, but you can also find places of quiet along the curving riverbanks, shaded by cedar, cypresses, oak, pecan, and willow trees, with an occasional palm tree or two. Rio Taxis, river-cruise tour boats, and floating dinner barges slowly follow a circular section of the Downtown Reach. They also move upriver past the San Antonio Museum of Art and end at Pearl, after passing through an interesting lock-and-dam system that raises the Rio Taxi boats 9 feet.

The River Walk was part of a 1939 federal WPA project designed by architect Robert Hugman, with cobblestone pathways, arched bridges, and entrances steps from street-level locations. Its development more fully expanded just in time for the 1968 World's Fair (or "HemisFair") exposition in San Antonio. In the decades since, many feared that the River Walk would become so overdeveloped and crowded that it would lose its charm. But subsequent expansions have ensured that the River Walk has plenty of quieter stretches.

There are numerous entrances to the River Walk by stair or ramp, with about 50 ADA accessible spots along the way, as well as elevators that take you to River Level. I suggest starting at the Commerce Street Bridge near Casa Rio; nearby you can buy a ticket for a river cruise with a driver/guide to help you get your bearings and decide what parts you want to walk back to later. You can reach Pearl by taking an enjoyable Rio Taxi ride up the Museum Reach. On the way, look up to see (and sometimes hear) public art installations hanging from the overpasses and bridges above your head.

Paseo del Rio Association, 110 Broadway, #500. www.thesanantonioriverwalk.com. ✆ **210/227-4262.**

PEARL

San Antonio Museum of Art ★★ In summer 2017, the San Antonio Museum of Art (SAMA) completed a $10-million facilities overhaul, making this lovely museum along the River Walk's Museum Reach (accessible by road, Rio Taxi, or by foot along River Walk paths) better than it ever was. It's housed in the ornate, fortress-like brick buildings of the 1904 Lone Star Brewery. Exhibits range from early Egyptian, Greek, and Asian collections to 19th- and 20th-century American artworks, but the jewel of the collection is the

Nelson A. Rockefeller Center for Latin American Art. This 30,000-square-foot wing has the most comprehensive collection of Latin American art in the U.S., with pre-Columbian, folk, Spanish colonial, and contemporary works. The **Lenora and Walter F. Brown Asian Art Wing** represents another major collection, the largest Asian art collection in Texas and one of the largest in the Southwest.

200 W. Jones Ave. www.samuseum.org. ✆ **210/978-8100.** Admission $10 adults, $7 seniors, $5 students with ID, free children 12 and younger. Free general admission Tues 4–9pm and Sun 10am–noon (fee for some special exhibits). Tues 10am–9pm; Wed, Thurs, Sat, and Sun 10am–5pm and Fri 10am–9pm. Closed Thanksgiving, Dec 25, Jan 1, Easter, and Fiesta Friday. Bus: 7, 8, 9, or 14.

ALAMO HEIGHTS AREA

The DoSeum ★★ San Antonio's great new children's museum, dubbed the DoSeum, opened in 2015 on a 5½-acre park at the edge of Alamo Heights' busy stretch of Broadway. Two-story exhibit halls in 65,000 square feet of space have been designed to foster creativity and exploration through interactive exhibits with a STEM and arts focus. Kids are crazy about the DoSeum's interactive robot, Baxter, and its clever **Spy Academy** filled with math challenges. There's also an interactive puppet parade and a musical staircase. Powered with solar energy (and the DoSeum recycles its water, too), it was designed with sustainability in mind. The **Big Outdoors,** a 39,000-square-foot outdoor play space, has a lazy stream, climbing structures, and an ADA-accessible treehouse. Although all ages enjoy it, the museum is specially geared for kids up to about 10 years old.

2800 Broadway Ave. www.thedoseum.org. ✆ **210/212-4453.** Admission 1 and older $12. Members free with ID. Fall/winter hours Mon–Thurs 10am–5pm; Fri 9am–5pm; Sat 9am–6pm; Sun noon–5pm. Sun members-only hour 11am–noon. Free family night on 1st and 3rd Tues of each month 5:30pm–7:30pm.

Marion Koogler McNay Art Museum ★★★ If you only have time to visit one San Antonio museum, make it the McNay. Perched atop a hill overlooking a scenic urban panorama, this Spanish Mediterranean–style mansion (ca. 1929) is so picturesque, it's often used as a backdrop for photo shoots. Once the residence of a wealthy art aficionado, the house equals its art collection in charm. The focus of the collection, comprising 20,000 works, is modern art, but it also includes Medieval and Renaissance art, and paintings, sculpture, and photographs from American and European masters of the 19th through 21st centuries, including Van Gogh, Manet, Gauguin, O'Keeffe, Hopper, Matisse, Modigliani, Cézanne, and Picasso. Southwestern prints and drawings, a private collection of art glass, and the **Tobin Collection of Theatre Arts** are also a draw for art lovers. Take it all in at a leisurely pace, and then stroll the beautifully landscaped, 23-acre grounds dotted with sculptures.

6000 N. New Braunfels Ave. www.mcnayart.org. ✆ **210/824-5368.** Admission $10 adults, $5 seniors, $5 students with ID, free for children 12 and under. Tues–Wed and Fri 10am–4pm; Thurs 10am–9pm; Sat 10am–5pm; Sun noon–5pm. Closed Mon. Closed Jan 1, July 4, Thanksgiving, and Dec 25. Bus: 14.

Witte Museum ★★ For more than 90 years, this has been San Antonio's top family-friendly museum, with a focus on the story of Texas as well as nature and science. But after the DoSeum kids' museum opened down the street (p. 245), some lamented that the Witte might be relegated to the back burner. Not to worry: In spring 2017, the **New Witte** museum was unveiled, reopening after 2 years of extensive renovation and expansion created some 170,000 square feet of new space to explore. The pride of San Antonio, the new museum is worth a long, leisurely visit.

The Smithsonian-affiliated museum draws visitors of all ages to its verdant grounds on the banks of the San Antonio River, near Brackenridge Park. Interestingly, the **Acequia Madre** (manmade irrigation canal) and **Diversion Dam** were exposed for the first time in decades during the museum's construction. Spanish settlers and native peoples hand-dug this landmark waterway around 1719 to divert river water to crops around the mission.

Dinosaur skeletons in fearsome poses are the stars at the massive new **Naylor Family Dinosaur Gallery.** The **Texas Wild** exhibit is back bigger and better, with expanded dioramas underneath a big Texas sky. A narrative called "Texas Deep Time" brings to life three important periods in Texas history: millions of years ago when dinosaurs roamed the land; thousands of years ago when prehistoric Indians studied the night sky; and hundreds of years ago when cattle was king and cowboys worked in the saddle across Texas prairie lands.

3801 Broadway (adjacent to Brackenridge Park). www.wittemuseum.org. ✆ **210/357-1900.** Admission $10 adults, $9 seniors and active military with ID, $7 children 4–11, free for children 3 and under, free for all Tues 3–8pm, free for members. Mon and Wed–Sat 10am–5pm; Tues 10am–8pm; Sun noon–5pm. Closed Easter, 3rd Mon in Oct, Thanksgiving, and Dec 24–25. Bus: 7, 9, or 14.

SOUTH SIDE

San Antonio Missions National Historical Park ★★★ The Alamo may be the most famous historic Spanish mission in Texas, but it's just the first of five missions established by the Franciscans along the San Antonio River. Now under the protection of the National Park Service, these four missions are still active parishes for the community under the Archdiocese of San Antonio. The Missions are perhaps the best and most often overlooked of the city's attractions, but perhaps that's because people either don't know they exist (and stand so close to downtown), or they don't realize that the missions were once far more than churches: They were entire communities. Here Spanish priests and indigenous people lived in walled, fortress-like missions where they grew vegetables and raised animals, had barns and stables, schools and shops, wells, granaries, and more. The Park Service has assigned a theme to each mission to educate visitors about the roles they played in San Antonio's 300-year history. If you can, see them all; they stand surprisingly close together and shouldn't take you more than 2 hours to see by car. If time is limited, definitely visit Mission San José and see its film in the visitor center, and try to make it to Mission San Francisco, even though it's the farthest from downtown.

KID magnets

The prime attractions for kids in San Antonio are **Six Flags Fiesta Texas ★** and **SeaWorld ★**. In Alamo Heights, the **DoSeum ★★** provides a wonderful introduction to the city for pint-size folks, including a miniature River Walk, a multicultural grocery store, and even a miniature dentist's office. The popular and newly expanded **Witte Museum ★★** focuses on nature, science, and history, showcasing all things kids love, including humongous dinosaur fossils and cool animal dioramas. For details on these sights, see "What to See & Do," above.

Get the kids psyched for their Alamo visit with the stirring IMAX movie ***Alamo: The Price of Freedom*** on a six-story-high screen with an integrated sound system at the **San Antonio AMC Rivercenter 11 ★**, 849 E. Commerce St., in the Shops at Rivercenter (www.amctheatres.com/movies/alamo-the-price-of-freedom; ✆ **800/354-4629** for recorded schedule information, or 210/247-4629), across the street from the battle site. Also at the Shops at Rivercenter, the loud and exciting **Battle for Texas: the Experience ★★** (www.battlefortexas.com; ✆ **866/633-0195**) is a museum of Alamo artifacts and multimedia reenactments of the Battle of the Alamo.

Live-theater adaptations of beloved children's books are a specialty at **Magik Theatre ★**, 5359 Casa Bella (www.magiktheatre.org; ✆ **210/227-2751**). The professional troupe performs a full season of plays; past shows have included *Junie B. Jones: The Musical* and *The Three Javelinas*.

The **San Antonio Zoo ★**, 3903 N. St Mary's St. (www.sazoo.org; ✆ **210/734-7291**), attracts more than a million visitors each year, and its CEO expects that number to skyrocket much higher as he puts in place his plans for a transformative expansion of the already quite nice Brackenridge Park zoo, home to a wide variety of animals representing 750 species on 56 acres.

There's plenty for families to enjoy in the multimillion-dollar entertainment complex that includes **Louis Tussaud's Waxworks** and **Ripley's Believe It or Not,** 301 Alamo Plaza (www.ripleys.com; ✆ **210/224-9299**). It's all here: the Waxworks, the **Odditorium,** and **Ripley's 4D Moving Theater.** There's something for everyone, from shrunken heads to hearing about the world according to Davy Crockett—as reported by his friend, the bear. Combo tickets are available.

It gets hot in San Antonio; luckily most hotels have pools. But they don't have **Splashtown,** 3600 N. I-35 (www.splashtownsa.com; ✆ **210/227-1100**), with a huge wave pool, hydro tubes nearly 300 feet long, a Texas-size water bobsled ride, more than a dozen water slides, and a two-story playhouse for smaller children.

Mission **Concepción,** 807 Mission Rd. at Felisa, built in 1731, is the oldest unrestored Texas mission—it looks much as it did 286+ years ago. **San José ★★★**, 6701 San José Dr. at Mission Rd. (established in 1720) is the largest, most remarkable, and most beautiful of the five missions, and examines what life was like for native peoples in a mission community. Popular mariachi Masses are held here every Sunday at 12:30pm (come early if you want a seat). Moved from an earlier site in East Texas to its present location in 1731, mission **San Juan Capistrano ★**, 9101 Graf at Ashley, isn't quite as grand as the other missions, but its simple chapel and more rural setting make it feel peacefully anachronistic. The southernmost mission in the San Antonio chain,

San Francisco de la Espada ★★, 10040 Espada Rd., is also arresting, with an iconic three-bell tower facade on its church.

Headquarters: 2202 Roosevelt Ave. Visitor Center: 6701 San José Dr. at Mission Rd. www.nps.gov/saan. ✆ **210/932-1001.** Free admission (donations accepted). All missions daily 9am–5pm. National Park Ranger tours daily. Closed Thanksgiving, Dec 25, and Jan 1. Bus: 42 stops at Mission San José (and near Concepción).

FAR WEST/NORTHWEST

SeaWorld San Antonio ★, 10500 SeaWorld Dr. (www.seaworld.com; ✆ **800/700-7786**), one of the largest marine life adventure parks in the world, is full of thrill rides, wet-'n'-wild fun (a Lost Lagoon, an enormous wave pool, flume rides), and lively shows and attractions. But the deaths of scores of orca whales and dolphins (not to mention four of its trainers in orca attacks) in recent years has put SeaWorld under increased scrutiny from many who feel that keeping these large, wild animals in confined quarters is inhumane. Animal lovers will be happy to know that in 2016, SeaWorld announced a partnership with the Humane Society that included an end to the company's orca breeding program and is making animal protection a bigger part of its mission, investing millions of dollars in ocean conservation efforts. Learn more by seeing the documentary *Blackfish.* The park is 16 miles northwest of downtown.

Six Flags Fiesta Texas ★ In celebration of its 25th anniversary in 2017, this popular 200-acre theme and water park is introducing America's first rocket-blast water coaster, **Thunder Rapids**. This thrilling water coaster, set in Fiesta Texas's new waterpark, White Water Bay, shoots riders uphill at lightning speeds and then thrills them with sudden high drops. Other exhilarating rides include the **Superman Krypton Coaster,** with nearly a mile of twists and turns and two big inversions; the **Iron Rattler,** a wooden coaster with modern steel rails and track; the 60+-mph **Poltergeist** roller coaster; and **Scream!** a 20-story "space shot and turbo drop," to name just a few. Virtual-reality simulators and laser games keep the theme park just tech-y enough to thrill millennials. And in summer, other wet-'n'-wild attractions include the **Lone Star Lagoon,** the state's largest wave pool; and the **Texas Treehouse,** a five-story "drenchfest" with a 1,000-gallon cowboy hat that tips over to pour water on unsuspecting passersby. There's also the **Bugs' White Water Rapids.** The theme park is also home to food stands, shops, crafts, and live shows. This theme park still has some local character, dating back to the days when it was plain old Fiesta Texas, and its themed areas include **Los Festivales,** a Hispanic village where every day feels like Fiesta; a German village called **Spassburg** with a large Sangerfest Halle theater; an old-fashioned Texas town called **Crackaxle Canyon,** where each day is celebrated like the Fourth of July; the **Fiesta Bay Boardwalk** with its Midway vibe and Ferris wheel; and a 1950s town center called **Rockville** with a retro-style Frostee Freeze ice cream shop.

17000 I-10 W. (corner of I-10 W. and Loop 1604). www.sixflags.com/parks/fiestatexas. ✆ **800/473-4378** or 210/697-5050. Admission $55, $40 children 48 in. and under, free for children 2 and under. Special discounts available. Daily late May to mid-Aug; Sat–

Sun Mar to late May and mid-Aug to Oct; open 10am, closing times vary depending on season, as late as 10pm in summer. Call ahead or visit website for current information. Bus: 94 (summer only). Exit 555 (La Cantera Pkwy.) on I-10 W.

More Attractions

DOWNTOWN AREA

San Fernando Cathedral ★ Although tourists probably think of the Alamo as the centerpiece of downtown San Antonio, locals might say that the heart of the city is this handsome Spanish cathedral, portions of it dating back to 1738–1759 when it was first built by Canary Island settlers. Overlooking the town's historic Main Plaza, San Fernando Cathedral was completed in 1749, and the original parts of the structure make it the oldest cathedral sanctuary in the United States and the oldest parish church in Texas. Between 1840 and 1973, the church fell into disrepair until it was rebuilt and consecrated in October of 1873. Alamo defender James "Jim" Bowie married his wife, Ursula, at the cathedral in 1831, before he was killed 5 years later during the siege of the Alamo. The cathedral has undergone major renovations over the centuries, including the addition of a 24-foot-high gilded altarpiece or *retablo*. Interesting note: The church alleges that the marble casket on the left side of the vestibule, or narthex (at the entrance to the cathedral), holds the remains of prominent Alamo defenders, including Bowie, though most historians remain highly skeptical of this. All the same, it's a good place to pay tribute to the fallen.

115 Main Plaza. www.sfcathedral.org. ✆ **210/227-1297.** Free admission. Mon–Thurs 9am–8pm; Fri 9am–5pm; Sat and Sun 9am–6:30pm. Gift shop open Mon–Fri 9am–5pm, Sat 9am–5pm and Sun 8:30am–3:30pm. Streetcar: Purple or Yellow lines.

Spanish Governor's Palace ★ The name makes it sound like a mansion, so you may be surprised when you see this one-story adobe barracks. It's impressive nonetheless, the oldest, best-preserved structure in San Antonio. It was built as a one-room house in 1722, and in 1749, three other rooms were added (along with the insignia of Spanish King Ferdinand VI; the date is shown on one of the doorways,). The house served as the headquarters and residence for the captain of the Spanish garrison and was the capital of the Spanish province of Texas from 1772 to 1821, when Mexico gained its independence. The last captain of San Antonio de Béxar, Juan Ignacio Pérez, and his descendants remained in the house until the 1860s. The house lived many lives—from a saloon to a pawn shop to a tailor's shop—until the city purchased it in 1928. Today the five rooms are filled with period furnishings. Like most Spanish-style dwellings of its time, the house has a shaded garden and a patio with a stone fountain and mosaic flooring. The staff is gracious and helpful, always ready to share information about the house's interesting history. It's within walking distance of the River Walk and downtown hotels and attractions.

105 Plaza de Armas. www.getcreativesanantonio.com/Explore-San-Antonio/Spanish-Governors-Palace. ✆ **210/224-0601.** Admission $5 adults, $3 seniors, $3 children 7–13, free for children 6 and under. Tues–Sat 9am–5pm; Sun 10am–5pm. Closed Jan 1 and for 2 days in late April during Battle of Flowers/Fiesta Flambeaux night parade (usually held around San Jacinto Day, Apr 21), Thanksgiving, Jan 1, Easter, and Dec 25. Streetcar: Purple line.

Parks & Gardens

HemisFair Park ★ Built for the 1968 HemisFair, a World's Fair exposition celebrating the 250th anniversary of the founding of San Antonio, this urban oasis boasts **water gardens** and a **wood-and-sand playground** constructed by children (near the Alamo St. entrance). Among its indoor diversions are the **Institute of Texan Cultures** and the iconic defining skyline symbol, the **Tower of the Americas.** The **Schultze House Cottage Garden ★**, 514 HemisFair Park (✆ **210/229-9161**), created and maintained by Master Gardeners of Bexar County, is also worth checking out for its heirloom plants, varietals, tropicals, and Xeriscape area. Look for it behind the Federal Building. The area is soon to undergo a large-scale expansion project, so after 2017 look for even more parkland acreage and new attractions. Although it may seem touristy, a visit to the top of the **Tower of the Americas** for the view from the observation deck, or for a special dinner with great views of the city at night at the Chart House, is a treat. Our family comes here every December for a special dinner before strolling along the River Walk to see the glittering holiday lights.

Bounded by Alamo, Bowie, Market, and Durango sts. No phone. www.sanantonio.gov/sapar/hemisfair.asp. Streetcar: Blue, Yellow, or Purple lines.

San Antonio Botanical Gardens ★★ Take a horticultural tour of Texas at this gracious 38-acre garden, comprising everything from south Texas scrub to Hill Country wildflowers. Currently at the end of a 2-year expansion project, this glorious garden spot is better than ever. Fountains, pools, paved paths, and examples of Texas architecture provide visual contrast to the flora. The formal gardens include one for the blind, along with Japanese, herb, biblical, and children's gardens. Perhaps most outstanding is the $6.9-million **Lucile Halsell Conservatory** complex, a series of greenhouses replicating a variety of tropical and desert environments. The 1896 **Sullivan Carriage House,** built by Alfred Giles and moved from its original downtown site, serves as the entryway to the gardens. Check the website before your visit for up-to-date information on what's in bloom.

555 Funston Place (at N. New Braunfels Ave.). www.sabot.org. ✆ **210/207-3250.** Admission $10 adults; $8 seniors, students, and military; $7 children 3–13; free for children 2 and under. Daily 9am–5pm. Closed Dec 25 and Jan 1. Bus: 7, 9, or 14.

Organized Tours

San Antonio's organized tours basically provide you with an efficient way to get around and pick up some local lore. The **Alamo Trolley** (www.thealamotrolley.com; ✆ **210/247-0238**) is a bus painted like a trolley offering narrated tours to the city's most popular attractions, including the Alamo, River Walk, Market Square, the Mission Trail, and King William Historic District. You can also opt for a hop-on, hop-off narrated tour. Cost for a 1-hour narrated tour is $22 adults, $11 children 4 to 11; narrated tour with hop pass $26 adults, $13 children 4 to 11.

To get up close and personal with the River Walk, try a **Rio San Antonio River Cruise** (www.riosanantonio.com; ✆ **210/244-5700**). This amusing, informative tour, lasting from 35 to 40 minutes, will take you more than 2 miles down the most built-up sections of the Paseo del Río, with interesting sights pointed out along the way. Ticket offices are at the Rivercenter Mall and River Walk, under the Market Street Bridge. I highly recommend this as a first stop on a River Walk visit; from there, you'll get your bearings and pick out spots you'll want to visit later on.

SPORTS & OUTDOOR ACTIVITIES

Most San Antonians head for the hills—Hill Country, that is—for outdoor recreation. Some suggestions follow for sports in or around town; also see "Hill Country Side Trips from San Antonio," later in this chapter.

BIKING Wending through old neighborhoods and farmlands alongside the San Antonio River, the **Mission Hike and Bike Trail** (see the **San Antonio Missions National Historical Park ★★★** listing, p. 246), gives local and visiting cyclists a good place inside the city to spin their wheels. From Mission Concepción to Mission Espada, there are 8 miles of dedicated paved pathways reserved for the hiker and biker. An easy walk or ride, it is suitable for even young members of the family. The trail is not a loop, so the round-trip path is actually 16 miles. However, walkers and bikers can start at any of the four missions and travel to the next mission, making the round-trip only 6 miles. Water is available at each mission. Food is available near Missions Concepción and San José, but not near Missions San Juan and Espada, so plan accordingly. Other options within San Antonio itself: **Brackenridge Park; McAllister Park** on the city's north side, 13102 Jones Maltsberger Rd. (✆ **210/207-7275** or 207-3120); and around the area near **SeaWorld of Texas.** If you didn't bring your own bike, San Antonio's **B-cycle bike share bicycles** are available all over town, and it's as easy as using a credit or debit card or B-card at any B-station kiosk. Hourly, daily, weekly, and even monthly rates are available. If you'd rather rent from a local who can give you advice, **Blue Star Bike Shop,** in Southtown at 1414 S. Alamo St. (www.bluestarbrewing.com; ✆ **210/212-5506**) will rent cruisers and other bikes ($20/6 hr.).

GOLF Golf has become a big deal in San Antonio, with more and more visitors coming to town expressly to tee off. Of the city's six municipal golf courses, two of the most notable are **Brackenridge,** 2315 Ave. B (✆ **210/226-5612**), the oldest (1916) public course in Texas, featuring oak- and pecan-shaded fairways; and northwest San Antonio's $4.3-million **Cedar Creek,** 8250 Vista Colina (✆ **210/695-5050**), repeatedly ranked as south Texas's best municipal course in golfing surveys. For details on these and other municipal courses, log on to www.sanantonio.gov/sapar/golf.asp. Other options for unaffiliated golfers include the 200-acre **Pecan Valley,** 4700 Pecan Valley Dr.

(✆ **210/333-9018**), which crosses the Salado Creek seven times and has an 800-year-old oak near its 13th hole; the high-end **Quarry,** 444 E. Basse Rd. (www.quarrygolf.com; ✆ **800/347-7759** or 210/824-4500), on the site of a former quarry and one of San Antonio's most popular public courses; and **Canyon Springs,** 24405 Wilderness Oak Rd. (www.canyonspringsgc.com; ✆ **888/800-1511** or 210/497-1770), at the north edge of town in the Texas Hill Country, lush with live oaks and dotted with historic rock formations.

There are a few really nice resort courses in San Antonio, and golfers will especially like those at the **La Cantera Golf Club,** 16401 La Cantera Pkwy. (www.lacanteragolfclub.com; ✆ **800/446-5387** or 210/558-4653)—one designed by Jay Morish and Tom Weiskopf, the other by Arnold Palmer—with knockout designs and dramatic hill-and-rock outcroppings. Equally nice are the resort courses of the **JW Marriott Hill Country Resort & Spa,** 23808 Resort Parkway (www.marriott.com/hotels/travel/satjw-jw-marriott-san-antonio-hill-country-resort-and-spa; ✆ **210/491-5806**), including the AT&T Canyons Course, designed by Pete Dye and PGA TOUR Player Consultant Bruce Lietzke, and the AT&T Oaks Course, designed by Greg Norman and PGA TOUR Player Consultant Sergio Garcia, both built with the infrastructure to host PGA tour tournaments. The JW Marriott resort offers a nice "Stay and Play" golf vacation package, too

Expect to pay $50 to $60 per person for an 18-hole round at a municipal course, plus a $15 (not including tax) fee for a cart, and from $70 up to $205 (Sat–Sun) per person at a private resort course. Twilight (afternoon) rates are often cheaper. To get a copy of the free *San Antonio Golfing Guide,* call ✆ **800/447-3372.**

HIKING The 240-acre **Friedrich Wilderness Park,** 21480 Milsa St. (www.wildtexas.com/parks/fwp.php; ✆ **210/698-1057**), operated by the city of San Antonio as its only nature preserve, is crisscrossed by 5.5 miles of trails that attract bird-watchers as well as hikers; a 2-mile stretch is accessible to people with disabilities. The **Mission Hike and Bike Trail** along the River Walk Mission Reach offers 8 miles of dedicated paved pathways reserved for the hiker and biker (see "Biking," earlier in this section).

RIVER SPORTS For tubing, rafting, or canoeing along a cypress-lined river, San Antonio river rats head 35 miles northwest of downtown to the 2,000-acre **Guadalupe River State Park,** 3350 Park Rd. 31 (www.tpwd.texas.gov/state-parks/guadalupe-river; ✆ **830/438-2656**), near Boerne. About 5 miles north of Hwy. 46, just outside the park, you can rent tubes, rafts, and canoes at the **Bergheim Campground,** FM 3351 in Bergheim (www.bergheimcampground.com; ✆ **830/336-2235**).

TENNIS With a reservation, you can play at the 22 lighted hard courts at the **McFarlin Tennis Center,** 1503 San Pedro Ave. (www.sanantonio.gov/ParksAndRec/Home/tennis; ✆ **210/207-5357**), for the very reasonable fee of $6.25 per adult per hour before 5pm, $7.25 per adult per hour after 5pm; and $3.25 per hour for students/seniors before 5pm, $4.25 for students and seniors after 5pm. For more about this court and others in the area, as well as details about tournaments, contact the **San Antonio Tennis Association** (www.satennis.com; ✆ **210/735-3069**).

Spectator Sports

BASKETBALL Spurs madness hits San Antonio every year from mid-October through May, when the city's only major-league franchise, the **San Antonio Spurs,** shoots hoops. The Spurs are based at the AT&T Center. Ticket prices range from $21 for nosebleed-level seats to $138 for seats on the corners of the court. Tickets are available at the Spurs Ticket Office in the AT&T Center, at One AT&T Center Pkwy. (www.nba.com/spurs; ✆ **210/444-5819**), or via Ticketmaster San Antonio (www.ticketmaster.com; ✆ **210/224-9600**).

GOLF **TPC San Antonio** (www.tpc.com), the private club open to club members and guests of the JW Marriott San Antonio Hill Country Resort & Spa, plays host to the PGA Tour's **Valero Texas Open,** one of the tour's oldest professional golf tournaments, held each spring (March/April) on the AT&T Oaks Course. Visit www.valerotexasopen.com for details.

RODEO If you're in town in early February, don't miss the chance to see 2 weeks of Wild West events, like calf roping, steer wrestling, and bull riding, at the annual **Stock Show and Rodeo** (www.sarodeo.com; ✆ **210/225-5851**). You can also hear major live country music talent each night during the rodeo, including concerts by big-name Nashville and Texas music stars.

WHERE TO STAY

Most visitors to San Antonio want to stay downtown so they can be close to the River Walk and many of the major attractions. Staying downtown is a lot of fun, but to get a feel for San Antonio that you won't get downtown, consider the happening Pearl area, or Southtown/King William Historic District, or Monte Vista. All are interesting places in their own right, are close to downtown, and have dining and entertainment spots nearby. My pick for the don't-miss stay is the new **Hotel Emma ★★★** at Pearl (see review p. 263), which opened in November 2015, within walking distance of some of the city's best restaurants, coffee shops, and clubs.

If the main objective is a relaxing vacation or a family outing at a theme park, then another option would be to stay at one of the resorts or hotels on the west/northwest side of San Antonio, near the two big theme parks: SeaWorld and Six Flags Fiesta Texas. Then you can combine swimming, golfing, and shopping with spa treatments and amusement parks and make the drive into the center of San Antonio when you're up for a change of pace.

DOWNTOWN It's important to shop around. Rates float up and down depending upon occupancy, and occupancy is driven by conventions and smaller conferences. These have their quirks—convention people will tend to group in certain hotels, and many conferences are based at a particular property. Since hotels do not fill up evenly, you should check rates at different

Greater San Antonio Hotels, Restaurants & Attractions

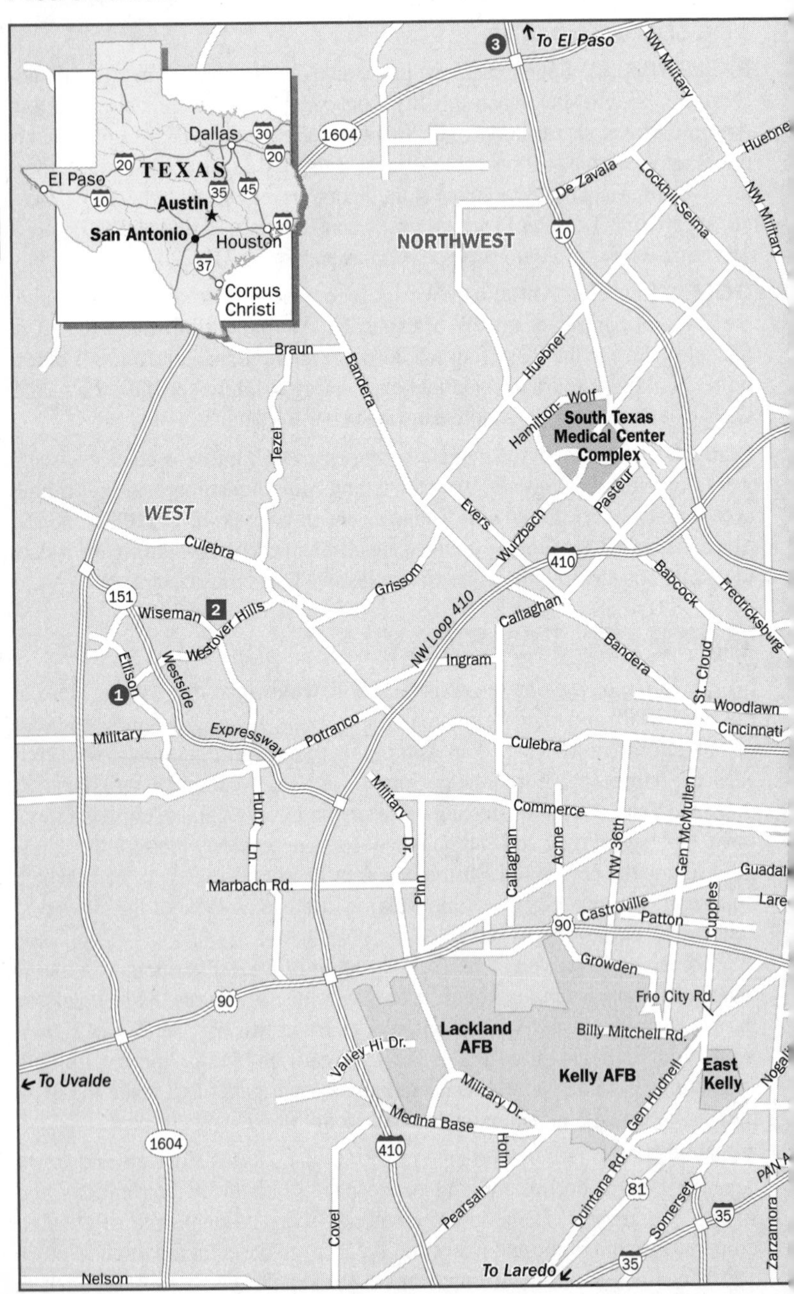

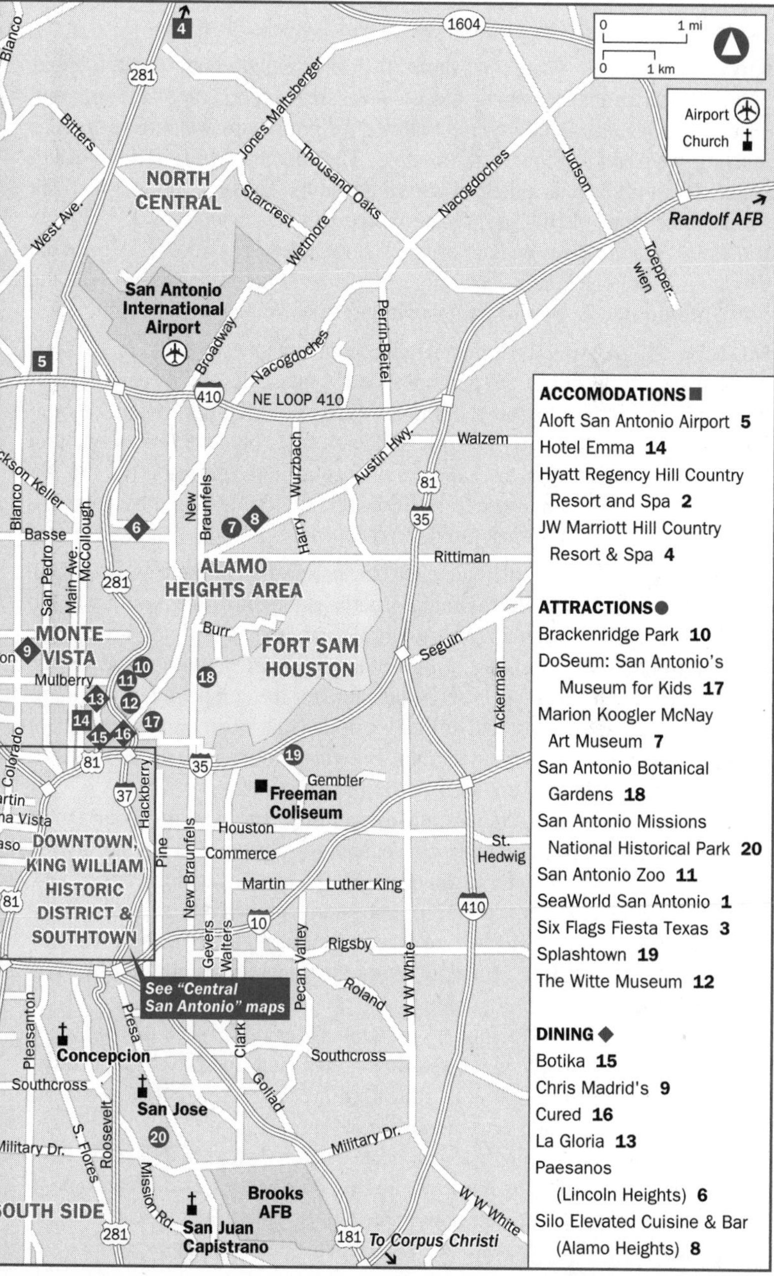
0 1 mi
0 1 km
Airport
Church
ACCOMODATIONS
Aloft San Antonio Airport 5
Hotel Emma 14
Hyatt Regency Hill Country Resort and Spa 2
JW Marriott Hill Country Resort & Spa 4
ATTRACTIONS
Brackenridge Park 10
DoSeum: San Antonio's Museum for Kids 17
Marion Koogler McNay Art Museum 7
San Antonio Botanical Gardens 18
San Antonio Missions National Historical Park 20
San Antonio Zoo 11
SeaWorld San Antonio 1
Six Flags Fiesta Texas 3
Splashtown 19
The Witte Museum 12
DINING
Botika 15
Chris Madrid's 9
Cured 16
La Gloria 13
Paesanos (Lincoln Heights) 6
Silo Elevated Cuisine & Bar (Alamo Heights) 8
NORTH CENTRAL
San Antonio International Airport
ALAMO HEIGHTS AREA
FORT SAM HOUSTON
MONTE VISTA
Freeman Coliseum
DOWNTOWN, KING WILLIAM HISTORIC DISTRICT & SOUTHTOWN
See "Central San Antonio" maps
Concepcion
San Jose
San Juan Capistrano
Brooks AFB
SOUTH SIDE
Randolf AFB
To Corpus Christi
NE LOOP 410
1604
281
410
81
35
37
10
181
Blanco
Bitters
West Ave.
Jones Maltsberger
Thousand Oaks
Starcrest
Wetmore
Nacogdoches
Judson
Toepperwien
Broadway
Perrin-Beitel
Walzem
Austin Hwy.
Wurzbach
Harry
New Braunfels
Basse
San Pedro
Main Ave.
McCollough
Rittiman
Burr
Seguin
Ackerman
Mulberry
Colorado
Hackberry
Gembler
Houston
Commerce
Martin Luther King
St. Hedwig
Pine
Gevers
Walters
Pecan Valley
Rigsby
Roland
W W White
Pleasanton
Presa
Clark
Southcross
Goliad
Roosevelt
S. Flores
Military Dr.
Mission Rd.

properties and, if you have flexibility, inquire about different dates. If you want to see the big picture, check out **http://meetings.visitsanantonio.com/meeting-calendar**, where you can find what conventions are taking place during your travel dates. The high seasons for conventions in San Antonio are fall and spring, and Fiesta is the third week in April (rates will skyrocket then, too).

KING WILLIAM There's no doubt that this neighborhood and the larger Southtown area are happening places these days—more about the arts and leisure than business, and a perfect choice for grown-ups wanting to spend a relaxing weekend, or longer if possible. The monthly street fair on South Alamo (First Fridays) is quite popular with visitors. The best option is to lodge in one of the grand old houses in King William. Downtown is only a 15-minute walk away, via the River Walk or South Alamo Street. Prices don't fluctuate the way they do at large hotels. For a larger selection of properties, check with the **San Antonio Bed & Breakfast Association** (www.sanantoniobb.org).

MONTE VISTA B&Bs in this neighborhood are an especially good value. The houses are beautiful; the neighborhood is quiet, despite its central location; and some interesting neighborhoods are on all sides. It's either a 30-minute walk or a short and easy bus ride to downtown. There are several exciting things happening nearby, including the ongoing redevelopment of the old Pearl Brewery. You can also expect B&Bs to provide fax and other business services, and these days most provide Wi-Fi.

PEARL As of 2017, Pearl had only one hotel (though there were Airbnb spots nearby); however, Hotel Emma is perhaps the only hotel you'll want to stay in anyway, if you can afford a splurge—and especially if you want to get away from the touristy section of the River Walk and enjoy the food-centric part of town that locals love. Pearl is the name for the compound or neighborhood of restaurants, shops, and culinary campus that is set on the grounds of the former Pearl Brewery/San Antonio Brewing Company factory. This area has surged in growth and popularity over the past decade.

With a few exceptions, the vast majority of the other lodgings around town are low-priced chains. The most convenient are clustered in the northwest, near the Medical Center, and in the north-central area, around the airport. For a full alphabetical listing of the accommodations in the city, mapped by area and including rate ranges as well as basic amenities, phone the **San Antonio Convention and Visitors Bureau** (www.visitsanantonio.com; ✆ **800/447-3372**) and request a lodging guide.

Wherever you decide to stay, try to book as far in advance as possible—especially if the property is located downtown. And don't even think about staying downtown during Fiesta (the third week in April) if you haven't reserved a room at least 5 or 6 months in advance.

Note: The rates below are listed rack rates, before taxes (16.75%). They can be both higher or lower, again depending on occupancy, season, and type of room. Almost all the large hotels are nonsmoking properties. Parking fees are always per day and pet fees are per visit, unless specified otherwise.

Central San Antonio Hotels

Emily Morgan Hotel **7**
Holiday Inn Express San Antonio—River Walk **2**
Hotel Contessa **9**
Hotel Havana **1**
Hotel Valencia Riverwalk **3**
Mokara Hotel & Spa **4**
Omni La Mansión del Río **5**
Riverwalk Vista **8**
The St. Anthony Hotel **6**

Downtown

EXPENSIVE

Hotel Contessa ★ Tall twin palm trees wrapped in glittering white lights center a soaring atrium in the grand bi-level lobby of this warm and welcoming all-suites River Walk hotel. Although the palm trees aren't real (you'd never know it) their towering effect is still arresting, as is the indoor/outdoor flow of the lobby to the River Walk and cafe seating outside. The lobby, bar, and restaurant are set along a quiet bend in the river, yet it's all still just steps from jazzy active areas. Because the hotel was originally supposed to be an Embassy Suites before it was sold, mid-build, the rooms are actually large two-room suites with a bedroom (with king-size bed or two double beds), big bathrooms, and living areas with sofabeds and exposed brick walls. Done in saucy red, black, and earth hues, all rooms offer either a river or city view. The best river views are those on lower levels overlooking the cypress-tree–lined pathways, while the top city views are from the higher floors. The hotel is just steps from the **Briscoe Western Art Museum ★★** (p. 242) and within walking distance of area attractions like La Villita, the Arneson River Theatre, and the Alamo. The **Las Ramblas** restaurant was set to undergo a redesign and renaming in 2017. While this may not be the most sophisticated or romantic hotel on the River Walk, it's a smartly stylish place with spacious suites, solid service, and a rooftop pool in which to chill out on a hot San Antonio day. The big suites are great for guests traveling with kids, or business travelers living out of a suitcase. There's also a spa on-site, a rarity among downtown San Antonio hotels. We'd definitely stay here again.

306 W. Market St. (at Navarro). www.thehotelcontessa.com. ✆ **866/435-0900** or 210/229-9222. 265 units. $249–$319 suite; from $329 executive suite. Valet parking $36. Pets 50 lb. and under accepted for $50 per night. **Amenities:** Restaurant/bar; fitness center; pool; spa; Wi-Fi (free).

Hotel Valencia Riverwalk ★ Many consider this hotel to be the hippest on the River Walk, and a brand-new $10-million-dollar renovation in 2017 is expected to make it even more wow-worthy. The hotel has always had a trendy design aesthetic, with sleek and soothing rooms with soft bedding and low lighting, and that hasn't changed. New lights on the entrance columns, flanked by citrus trees in large overscale pots, make the entrance more dramatic than ever, and guests are greeted inside by a flashy new water fountain and mosaic-patterned cow skulls. At reception, help is behind a hand-carved desk. The hotel location on the River Walk (next to the Majestic Theatre) is a big plus. The restaurants have always been outstanding, too, so we have high hopes for the new Buenos Aires–inspired **Dorrego** restaurant and bar (and terrace). It's a safe bet that after renovations, this will be the next big-deal hotel on the River Walk and that the price point will match its magic. Don't miss a margarita and fresh guacamole at Ácenar restaurant, adjacent to Hotel Valencia at river level.

150 E. Houston St. (at St. Mary's). www.hotelvalencia.com. ✆ **866/842-0100** or 210/227-9700. 213 units. $189–$239 double; from $350 suite. Valet parking $34. **Amenities:** Restaurant; bar; concierge; exercise room; room service; spa; Wi-Fi (free).

Mokara Hotel & Spa ★★★ Downtown San Antonio hotels seem to be short on nice spas—but Mokara has one of the best in the area. In fact, everything about this centrally located River Walk hotel feels peaceful and restorative. From the moment you enter the lobby, which seems worlds away from big-city stress, the soft palette of vanilla hues, natural wood, and white limestone creates a sense of calm. Rooms have high ceilings and luxe bedding, and many have balconies overlooking the River Walk. Though the rooms have a comfortable sophistication, touches of a Texan leather-and-wood aesthetic break through. Oversize baths have gleaming marble surfaces with jetted tubs and separate showers. A small rooftop cafe and pool is another pleasant place to relax. And although the Mokara always seems serene, it is located along one of the most popular stretches of the River Walk. It's also close to fine dining along East Houston Street, and the **Majestic Theatre** (p. 279). Second-floor rooms have direct access to the spa (just walk across the hall in your robe). One of the perks of staying here is that guests have charging privileges at sister property **Omni La Mansión del Río** hotel (see below), which happens to be within waving distance of the Mokara, directly across the river. If we were staying at Mokara, we'd have Sunday champagne brunch at Las Canarias at La Mansión.

212 W. Crockett St. (at St. Mary's). www.omnihotels.com/hotels/san-antonio-mokara. ✆ **866/605-1212** or 210/396-5800. 99 units. $279–$509 double; $329–$559 river-view double; from $800 suite. Valet parking $39. **Amenities:** Restaurant; cafe; babysitting; concierge; gym; Jacuzzi; heated outdoor pool; room service; sauna; spa; Wi-Fi (free).

Omni La Mansión del Río ★★ Perhaps nowhere else along the River Walk is the rich, romantic sensibility of Old San Antonio better showcased. Embodying the spirit of the Alamo City, this enchanting hacienda-style hotel is a good choice for first-time visitors. This 1892 Spanish colonial structure encircling a quiet courtyard was originally designed as a seminary that would become St. Mary's College. Today, the hotel's elegant old-world style is expressed in arched passageways, hand-painted tile floors, scrolling wrought iron, and beamed ceilings. Rooms are simple, cool, and spacious, with oversize hand-hewn wood furnishings and subdued Southwestern hues. River-view rooms feature wrought-iron Juliet balconies that stand level with tall cypress and palm trees—book these rooms in December for prime views of the twinkling holiday lights all along the River Walk. (Other rooms have courtyard views.) **Las Canarias** restaurant, which shares a chef with restaurant Ostra, at the Mokara Hotel & Spa (the sister Omni property on the opposite bank of the river, see above), offers one of the best champagne brunches in the city. La Mansión's cantina, **El Colegio Bar,** pays homage to its history as a school, and vaunts a pre-Prohibition theme with splashy craft cocktails. Guests have charging privileges at the Mokara across the river—and the spa there is fabulous.

112 College St. (btw. St. Mary's and Navarro). www.omnilamansion.com. ✆ **800/292-7300** or 210/518-1000. 338 units. $189–$349 double; $329–$599 ambassador room (junior suite); $750–$2,000 suite. Valet parking $39. Pets 25 lb. and under accepted for $50. **Amenities:** Restaurant, 2 bars, coffee shop/snack bar; babysitting; children's programs; concierge, outdoor heated pool; room service; Wi-Fi (free).

St. Anthony Hotel ★★★ For years this downtown hotel was the place to stay in San Antonio (or get married or have Fiesta balls). Today its reputation as the opulent jewel of Alamo City has been restored after an impeccable renovation. With glittering chandeliers, reception walls of white marble, plush peacock green carpet, and Juliet ballrooms, this National Historic Landmark reminds us a little of the lounge and bar of New York's Plaza Hotel. Although the lobby is formally elegant, the rooms and restaurants are actually sleekly contemporary and—dare we say it—even a tad trendy. The restaurant **Rebelle** feels almost *too* trendy (its mod furniture and changing colored lights work great at dinner, but the glam decor can seem a bit much for breakfast). The St. Anthony has a breezy rooftop pool, and after work, locals and visitors alike lurk in the trendy **Haunt** bar (it's said the hotel has ghosts). But the real draw of this Starwood-affiliated hotel is its lavish lobby and prime location on Travis Park—far from the crowds, but close to the River Walk, the Alamo, the Majestic Theatre, and even Mi Tierra—everywhere and anywhere you'll want to go downtown. I always tell guests, for the top two hotels in San Antonio, just remember Emma and Anthony (Hotel Emma at Pearl and this one).

300 E. Travis St. www.thestanthonyhotel.com. ✆ **210/227-4392.** 277 units. $299–$450 double; $500–$5,000 suite. Valet parking $39. **Amenities:** Restaurant, 4 bars, breakfast cafe; 24-hr. business center; concierge; fitness center; Jacuzzi; outdoor heated pool; room service; Wi-Fi (Free).

MODERATE

Emily Morgan Hotel ★★ The Emily Morgan is considerably less expensive than many comparable hotels on the river, and the marriage of style, history, and value makes it a real winner. As the "official hotel of the Alamo," this 1924 landmark tower has a sublime location, towering over Alamo Plaza. Its many rooms overlook the rooftop and sacred grounds of the city's most famous Spanish mission. The location is ideal for other reasons: It's close to downtown attractions, shops, restaurants, the Majestic Theatre and River Walk. Our favorite room is the 12th-floor corner unit with huge arched windows and fantastic views, even from the bathtub. The contemporary rooms are plush and streamlined. Aside from its ornate Gothic Revival facade, studded with gargoyles no less, the hotel is not as fancy or over-the-top as some, and it doesn't sit directly on the River Walk. But it's popular with repeat visitors and a favorite of travel journalists. This historic—and reputedly haunted—hotel is a fun place to stay, and the lobby bar during happy hour is a lively scene filled with friendly locals.

705 E. Houston St. (at Ave. E). www.emilymorganhotel.com. ✆ **800/824-6674** or 210/225-5100. 177 units. $169–$329 double; $229–$379 suite. Valet parking $35. Pets accepted with $50 fee. **Amenities:** Restaurant; bar; concierge; fitness center; Jacuzzi; outdoor heated pool; room service; sauna; Wi-Fi (Free).

Hotel Havana ★★★ In 2010 when Liz Lambert reopened this classic, three-story hotel by the River Walk in the northern part of downtown, it was already one of our favorite boutique properties, a historic hotel built in 1914 in Mediterranean Revival style a la Havana, Cuba. Still, Lambert (developer of Austin's Hotel Saint Cecilia, Austin Motel, and Hotel San Jose) dialed up the hip quotient, giving rooms a spare look (white walls, dark-wood trim, and handsome wood floors) to showcase the building's good bones and furnishing them in a masterful mix of antique and contemporary pieces, like the Penthouse Suite with its midcentury turquoise-blue Smeg refrigerator and mod orange velvet Chesterfield sofa. As with Lambert's other properties, it's all about a retro-modern mashup. Although rooms in the Havana lack closets, they do have dressers and bureaus, and large retro-style refrigerators and minibars are filled with quirky treats like Mexican candies, Topo Chico mineral water, and imported Mexican Coca-Cola. Although the jury's out as to whether Lambert improved on the hotel's already smart decor, she did manage to get the place back on everyone's radar. Now the **Ocho** terrace restaurant, set in a high-ceiling glass conservatory overlooking a quiet River Walk path, is a hot spot with locals and visitors alike—great for a late Sunday breakfast or cocktails after work. Likewise, the **Havana Bar,** hidden below street level, is as cozy and clandestine as they come—the perfect cool hideaway after a sizzling San Antonio day.

1015 Navarro St. (btw. St. Mary's and Martin sts.). www.havanasanantonio.com. ✆ **210/222-2008.** 27 units. $188–$199 double; $209–$599 suite. Self-parking $15. Pets accepted for $25 fee. **Amenities:** Restaurant, bar; concierge; gym; room service; Wi-Fi (free).

INEXPENSIVE

Holiday Inn Express San Antonio—River Walk ★ Don't expect cell-like rooms in this five-story landmark hotel, even though the building was once home to the 1878 Bexar County Jail. A total gut of this historic building created spacious rooms—even the bathrooms are larger than those you might normally see in this price range. The staff here is helpful and friendly, and the free hot breakfast is always a winner. A nicely renovated exercise room and business center round out the good value. The hotel is set in the western part of downtown: a safe area, only a few blocks from the River Walk, El Mercado, Mi Tierra, and the San Fernando Cathedral, and close to the Spanish Governor's Palace. It's only a 10-minute walk to the Alamo, too.

120 Camaron St. (btw. Houston and Commerce). www.holidayexpressriverwalk.com. ✆ **877-545-7015** or 210/281-1400. 82 units. $89–$160 double. Rates include complimentary hot breakfast. Parking $15/day. Service animals only. **Amenities:** Business center; exercise room; Jacuzzi; outdoor heated pool; Wi-Fi (free).

Riverwalk Vista ★★★ This may be the best-kept secret in San Antonio, a centrally located boutique hideaway right in the thick of things, steps from the Alamo and River Walk. Tucked away on the upper floors of a historic 1883 mercantile building, this gem of an inn houses 17 massive rooms in a good location, cater-corner to the Commerce Street Bridge. The location near attractions, restaurants, and the Shops at Rivercenter mall makes this a perfect place for those traveling without a car. (There's no on-site parking, but a multi-level garage is just a block away.) Rooms and suites have high ceilings, long-leaf-pine floors, leather chairs, exposed-brick walls, and handsome

GLAMPING under THE STARS

Deep in the heart of Texas, many travelers are finding that glamping (aka "glamour camping") is more fun than camping. South Texas has a few spots where you can enjoy the beauty of outdoors without having to use an outhouse. My favorite spot of all is **Sinya at Lone Man Creek** (www.hillcountrysinya.com; ✆ **713/502-3997**) in Wimberley (southwest of Austin, northwest of San Antonio), a luxury African safari–style camp built on a high bluff overlooking a creek. Just like the five-star tented bush camps that inspired this place, Sinya features all the comforts of a fine hotel, with a king-size bed, a full bathroom with a claw-foot tub, an outdoor hot tub, decks with brilliant Hill Country vistas, a barbecue grill, and a seating area outside on the hill. There's no roughing it here—and no lions roaring in the middle of the night either. Fully air-conditioned and heated (with a little faux fireplace, too), Sinya is much in demand and requires reservations far in advance.

A bit more family-friendly but as nicely outfitted as a good hotel are the tipi and treehouse-style cabins at the **Geronimo Creek Retreat** (www.besttexastravel.com; ✆ **888-993-6772**) near the tiny hamlet of Geronimo, about 35 miles from San Antonio, just outside the town of Seguin. The property has four cabins (each sleeping up to six guests), and five fully furnished tipis, all with modern perks like A/C and heat, satellite TVs, kitchenettes, queen-size beds, and living room areas. The property also has swimming and fishing spots, a playscape, a recreation room, a hot tub, and more.

The same company that operates Geronimo Creek Retreat also offers tipi and treehouse accommodations in the New Braunfels area about 25 miles from downtown San Antonio along the Guadalupe River at **River Road Treehouses** and **Reservation on the Guadalupe.** You can rent thatched-hut lakeside cabanas for the day at **Son's Island at Lake Placid,** near Seguin, where you can also rent kayaks, paddleboards, hydrobikes, and iFloats for the day on this river-like long lake. For information on these properties, see the Geronimo Creek Retreat contact info above.

wood furnishings along simple lines. The huge in-room windows are lovely, but sometimes let in noise from the street below, with a busy late-night McDonald's next door adding to the din. Still, this is easily one of our favorite places to stay in S.A.—it's homey but stylish, with an Arts and Crafts–meets–Restoration Hardware flair. Quiet communal areas create a friendly, laid-back ambience, the kind of place where we wouldn't mind sipping coffee and poring over *The New York Times* all morning. Don't expect a lobby on the first floor—you'll have to take the elevator or stairs to the second-floor lounge. Access to the River Walk is just across the street and down some stairs to the river level. The Convention Center is nearby, too, though this hotel is not geared toward rowdy conventioneers. Our favorite room? The light-filled Hugman King Suite, with views of the Friendship Torch and the Tower of Americas.

262 Losoya St. (at Commerce St.). www.riverwalkvista.com. ✆ **210/223-3200.** 17 units. $139–$210 double; $187–$233 queen suite $210–$279 king suite. Rates include complimentary breakfast, cookies, afternoon snacks, and wine. Self-parking. **Amenities:** Lounge; business center/conference room; fitness center and pool access; Wi-Fi (free).

Tobin Hill

EXPENSIVE

Hotel Emma ★★★ San Antonio's new urban-cowboy-eclectic hotel is built inside the brick shell of the 19th-century Pearl Brewery. It's the flagship of the popular Pearl district, a wildly popular culinary/retail complex at the end of the River Walk Museum Reach. With the brewery's mammoth cast-iron tanks and steel machinery still standing inside, Emma flaunts grand-scale *nuevo*-Texas style and a bold industrial aesthetic. Fashioned by the designers of New York's stylish High Line Hotel, Emma is the pride of San Antonio—the favorite go-to spot for locals when visitors come to town. Brick, steel, and soft textiles, cool cement and tile, high ceilings and low lighting, big machinery and good bones expose graceful layers of history and style. Where Emma really wows is in its **Sternewirth** bar and clubroom. Here vintage bottling equipment has been repurposed as chandeliers, and elephant-size fermentation tanks hold banquette seating. Nail-head wainscoting and hand-tooled leather wall coverings give a nod to the city's cattle trail tradition. The large standard rooms are high-ceilinged, outfitted with furniture hewn from hardwoods covered in saddle-smooth leather, and king-size poster beds dressed in Frette linens. Much-coveted Mexican Coca-Cola in the "ice box" (minibar) and seersucker robes are nice touches. Exposed layers of original wall paint expose Emma's true colors in the Brewhouse Tower rooms, where cool concrete floors are softened by saddle-blanket-style rugs. French macarons from Pearl's **Bakery Lorraine** are a sweet turndown extra. The spa should be open by the time you read this. Although **Supper** is a great little hotel restaurant, plenty of fabulous others are nearby, too, including Cured, Botika, and La Gloria (my favorites), and a snazzy new music club, **Jazz, TX,** is practically next door. If you can afford to splurge, this is *the* place to stay.

136 E. Grayson St. www.thehotelemma.com. ✆ **844/296-3662** or 210/448-8300. 146 units. $325–$795 double; $795–$3,000 suite. Valet parking $15. Pets 50 lb. and under accepted with $100 nonrefundable deposit per pet. **Amenities:** 3 restaurants, bar/lounge; bikes; concierge; fitness center; library; meeting space; rooftop pool; specialty culinary and cocktail concierge program; Wi-Fi (free).

West/Northwest

EXPENSIVE

Hyatt Regency Hill Country Resort and Spa ★★ If you're looking for a Hill Country cowboy vibe, this resort hotel has it in spades. Kids love this delightful resort's location close to SeaWorld and not far from Six Flags Fiesta Texas. But it's hard to get them to leave when they see the hotel's 950-foot-long man-made Ramblin' River connecting to one of four pools. There they can happily float all day in an inner tube while the gentle current pulls them along a shallow channel. Teens and adults stay busy surfing and body-boarding the cool FlowRider wave. The amusements continue with a 27-hole championship golf course, a tennis court, organized activities for kids and teens, and good restaurants for grown-ups. The lovely setting, on 200 acres of former ranchland, is dotted with bluebonnets in spring, and from the moment you enter the Texas-size lobby—two-story windows, enormous iron chandeliers, grand wood-burning fireplaces—you'll see why this is a special place. It's done up with true Texas touches: native Hill Country white limestone, well-worn leather, and dark wood. Rooms are decorated in earth tones and rustic architectural elements. Some ground-floor rooms have direct access to the pool area, so you don't have to drip through the lobby. The property has six restaurants, but the elegant **Antlers Lodge** is my favorite. The **Windflower,** a Hill Country–style spa housed in a charming barn-like space (made with reclaimed wood from old barns), offers a full range of spa treatments. While you're staying here, be sure to belly up to the longest copper-topped bar in Texas (56 ft.), the aptly named **Charlie's Long Bar,** where you'll really feel like a cowboy.

9800 Hyatt Resort Dr. (off Hwy. 151, btw. Westover Hills Blvd. and Potranco Rd.). https://hillcountry.regency.hyatt.com/en/hotel/home.html. ✆ **800/55-HYATT [554-9288]** or 210/647-1234. 500 units. $260–$440 double; $450–$3,000 suite or villa. Valet parking $15; self-parking free. **Amenities:** 6 restaurants; 4 bars, coffee shop; bikes; children's programs; concierge; concierge-level rooms; golf course; health club; Jacuzzis; jogging trails; 4 outdoor pools; room service; sauna; spa; 3 outdoor tennis courts (1 lit); waterpark; Wi-Fi ($10/day).

JW Marriott Hill Country Resort & Spa ★★ Set on sprawling acreage at the Hill Country's edge, this enormous destination resort is so far from downtown that it becomes a real staycation spot for locals who like to pretend they're getting away from it all. Still, it's not so far from town that you can't run to the River Walk for dinner if you like. But this is where I'd stay if I were traveling with kids during the hot season, when you need a pool to lounge around. In fact, your kids will love this place so much you won't need to spend extra money at a theme park. Why, it's got its own 9-acre waterpark with a lazy river for the little ones. It also boasts a fun River Bluff Water Experience, with seven water sides, including two winding, 250-foot-long semi-enclosed tower slides, and another slide that deposits riders directly into the lazy river. This splashy nine-floor hotel also has an adults-only infinity pool for mom and dad, a 36-hole championship golf course, seven restaurants, and whopping acreage of meeting space. It's got everything that other comparable resorts in the area have, only bigger, with more than 1,000 rooms (including 85 suites). Check out the craft beers and the big, Times Square–like media display in the **High Velocity** bar, or enjoy a healthful lunch in the **Replenish Spa Bistro**. My favorite is **Cibolo Moon,** serving Southwest fare. The multilevel **Lantana Spa** is one of the loveliest and largest in town. The resort fee covers free Wi-Fi if you sign up for the rewards program, so be sure to do so, since that, too, is free.

23808 Resort Pkwy. www.marriott.com. ✆ **210/276-2500.** 1,002 units. $256–$349 double; from $699–$1,569 suite, plus $40 per night resort fee. Valet parking $33; self-parking free**. Amenities:** 6 restaurants, Starbucks; game room; golf course; health club; 4 pools; spa; 7 restaurants; room service; waterpark; Wi-Fi (free in lobby; $16/day in room or free for rewards members).

North Central (Near the Airport)

INEXPENSIVE

Aloft San Antonio Airport ★★ This airport hotel gem is where I'd stay if I were flying in and out of San Antonio on business. A "vision of W Hotels," the Aloft brand of budget inns features trendy touches and cool, business-friendly features, providing a scaled-down version of W Hotel's mod decor and industrial-chic lounge spaces. This Aloft has a pool, a lounge, and a contemporary little bar with lighting that changes to set the mood. A snack area allows guests to pick out treats on the go and charge them to their rooms. Aloft also features a 24/7 gym, fun little Fido-friendly amenities, and room service provided by a local pub. With free parking and Wi-Fi and good rates, it all adds up to great value for travelers. This Aloft is also a budget-friendly place for families, thanks to a location that's fairly convenient to area theme parks and attractions. The hotel offers cool kiddie perks, too, like child-size air mattresses, goody bags, and a splash pool, so your pet isn't the only one getting pampered. Rooms aren't large, but they're streamlined, clean, and well-suited to the young business set who wants to come, plug in, and hit the airport shuttle in the morning. "Plug & Play" connectivity stations allow guests to charge their electronics and link them to 42" LCD TVs. Services here are more help-yourself than pampering, but not in a bad way. There are no real views, but try to avoid a room on the ground level or you may have headlights shining in your windows. One nice perk: The hotel offers a complimentary shuttle to the airport and other area attractions. One important thing to note: Even though it calls itself an airport hotel, the terminal isn't exactly next door, so leave plenty of time to make your flight.

838 NW Loop 410. www.aloftsanantonioairport.com. ✆ **800/716-8143** or 210/541-8881. 141 units. $84–$139 double. Rates include free breakfast buffet. Free parking. Pets accepted for free under 40 lb. **Amenities:** Free airport transfers; exercise room; outdoor splash pool; Wi-Fi (free).

WHERE TO EAT

Nobody does Tex-Mex quite like San Antonio. This cuisine was perfected here over centuries, with a rich array of dishes relying on heaping helpings of tradition. But Tex-Mex restaurants aren't the only places you'll want to sample. The culinary scene in San Antonio is a lot more cosmopolitan than many visitors realize, especially in the hot and happening **Pearl** area, home to the Culinary Institute of America (CIA), a world-class cooking school and pipeline shuttling innovative young chefs into kitchens all across the Alamo City.

The epicenter of the San Antonio food scene, Pearl is a compound of a dozen restaurants set in the former Pearl Brewery factory buildings. Anchored by the fabulous CIA campus, and offering cuisine by some of the city's best-loved chefs, including Andrew Weissman, Steve McHugh, John Brand, and Johnny Hernandez, this is the place foodies will want to go first. In addition to other restaurants, Pearl has the stunning Hotel Emma, a farmer's market on

Saturdays and Sundays year-round, a jazz club (Jazz, TX) and several great bars, a soon-to-open spa, a pop-up food hall, and even two microbreweries, one at Southerleigh and another at the Granary.

Another place that merits special mention is **Southtown,** the eclectic, vivacious area just downstream from the city center. This bohemian district has become a popular place for artists, gallery owners, and innovative restaurateurs. The food scene is predominantly Mexican-American, with neighborhood eateries and *taquerías* (taco shops). But it also has fine-dining spots (**Bliss;** p. 271), hot cocktail and dinner spots (**Feast;** p. 271), and healthful lunch spots (**Liberty Bar;** p. 272).

Downtown

EXPENSIVE

Biga on the Banks ★★ NEW AMERICAN Bruce Auden is a household name in San Antonio, a James Beard "Best Chef" nominee whose restaurant Biga on the Banks (overlooking the River Walk) is a longtime favorite fine-dining choice. Locals claimed chef/owner Auden, a transplanted Brit, as one of their own long ago. Biga on the Banks is located on the ground floor of the International Center building, with dining room and patio views of city lights and the river. Guests enter at St. Mary's Street (not at River Walk level), which means they dine above the din of crowds on the bustling pathways below. The modern dining room has high ceilings and picture windows. Auden's fresh menu changes daily and stays true to the season, but year-round you're likely to find a big, juicy Angus rib-eye served with Shiner Bock–battered onion rings. Snapper is stuffed with Gulf crab, and Hill Country venison and quail comes with 11 spices and juniper sauce. For dessert, Auden's popular sticky toffee pudding rocks the house. For an extra-special dining experience, families or friends can reserve Table 31, an intimate dining space for five to eight people hidden behind a swish of curtains, where guests can enjoy Chef Auden's specially designed five- to eight-course tasting menus.

203 S. St. Mary's St./River Walk. www.biga.com. ✆ **210/225-0722.** Reservations recommended. Main courses $25–$40. 3-course prix-fixe seasonal menu $39 (before 6:30pm and after 9pm). Sun–Thurs 5:30–10pm; Fri–Sat 5:30–11pm.

Bohanan's ★★ STEAK/SEAFOOD What could be more Texan than a big, gleaming high-end steakhouse? The kind where J. R. Ewing strolls in and orders a 14-ounce $95 Akaushi steak for lunch and smokes a fat cigar out on the patio? With a prime location on Houston Street, not far from the Majestic Theatre and just a block or so from the Alamo, Bohanan's is considered by many to be the best steakhouse in San Antonio. It sure *looks* like a fancy Texas steakhouse, all dark wood, creamy white tablecloths, clubby cocktail bar, and humidor stuffed with expensive cigars. This is the kind of place where oilmen and bankers wear Lucchese boots with their suits, ladies have power lunches, couples have romantic dinners, and cowboys remove their hats. Chef/owner Mark Bohanan, an A&M grad who trained at the Culinary Institute of America, opened this restaurant in 2002 in a historic downtown building with

Central San Antonio Restaurants & Attractions

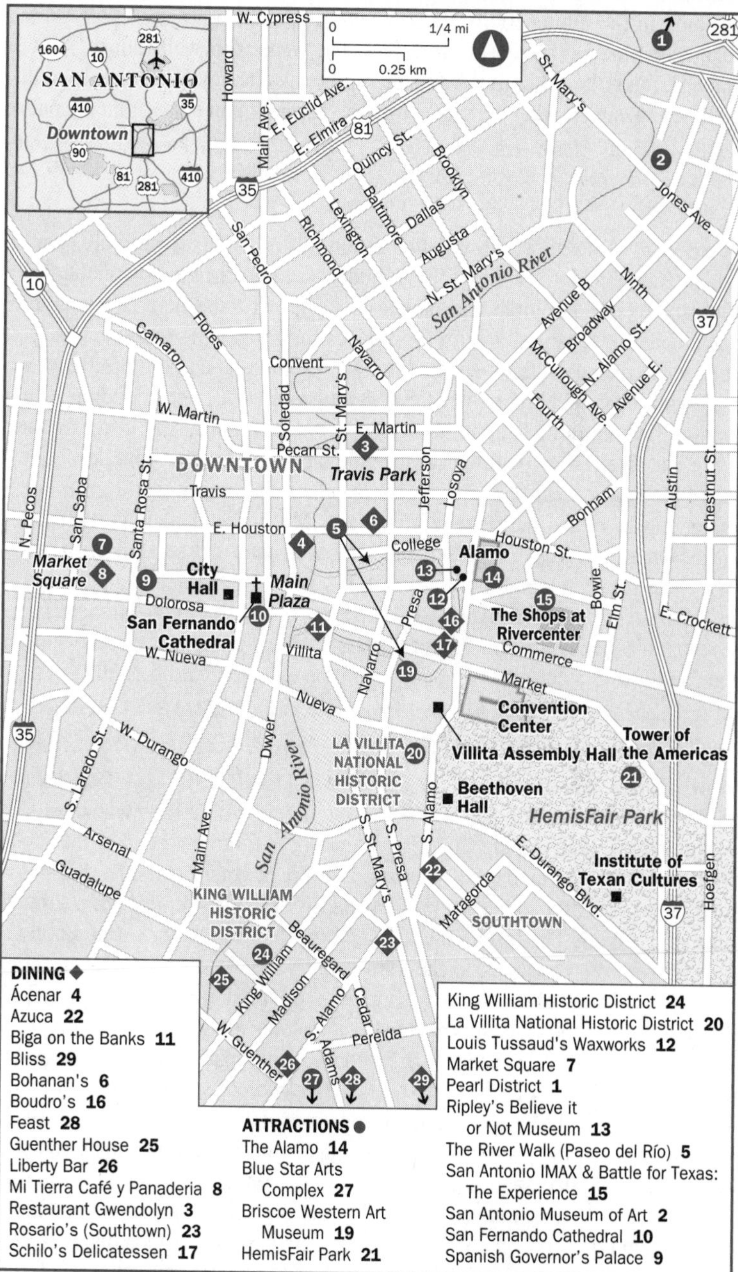
SAN ANTONIO
Downtown
0 1/4 mi
0 0.25 km
DOWNTOWN
Travis Park
Market Square
City Hall
Main Plaza
San Fernando Cathedral
Alamo
The Shops at Rivercenter
Convention Center
Villita Assembly Hall
Tower of the Americas
Beethoven Hall
HemisFair Park
Institute of Texan Cultures
LA VILLITA NATIONAL HISTORIC DISTRICT
KING WILLIAM HISTORIC DISTRICT
SOUTHTOWN
San Antonio River
DINING ◆
Ácenar 4
Azuca 22
Biga on the Banks 11
Bliss 29
Bohanan's 6
Boudro's 16
Feast 28
Guenther House 25
Liberty Bar 26
Mi Tierra Café y Panaderia 8
Restaurant Gwendolyn 3
Rosario's (Southtown) 23
Schilo's Delicatessen 17
ATTRACTIONS ●
The Alamo 14
Blue Star Arts Complex 27
Briscoe Western Art Museum 19
HemisFair Park 21
King William Historic District 24
La Villita National Historic District 20
Louis Tussaud's Waxworks 12
Market Square 7
Pearl District 1
Ripley's Believe it or Not Museum 13
The River Walk (Paseo del Río) 5
San Antonio IMAX & Battle for Texas: The Experience 15
San Antonio Museum of Art 2
San Fernando Cathedral 10
Spanish Governor's Palace 9

long-beam pinewood floors. On the first floor, a pianist tinkles the ivories in **Bohanan's Bar,** with a banquette of tufted leather and a long, slender bar. Upstairs, in the dining room, the kitchen pumps out prime mesquite-grilled steaks, fresh seafood, and a la carte sides. The waitstaff is well-trained, knowledgeable, and ultra-attentive. You can't smoke inside any San Antonio building, but you can buy that big cigar from the humidor and enjoy it on the patio. 219 E. Houston St. www.bohanans.com. ✆ **210/472-2600.** Reservations recommended. Main courses $17–$46; steaks $34–$125. Mon–Fri 11am–2pm; Mon–Thurs 5–10pm; Fri–Sat 5–11pm; Sun 5–9pm.

Boudro's ★ AMERICAN When strolling down the River Walk, you're likely to stumble onto Boudro's, everybody's favorite old standby on the River Walk for fresh guacamole and margaritas. The big thing here is the chunky guacamole, made tableside with fire-roasted tomatoes and serrano chiles (you can get the recipe on the website). Tex-Mex and Gulf seafood top the menu, made with fresh local ingredients. Set in a turn-of-the-century building with a hand-crafted mesquite bar and hardwood floors, the atmosphere inside and out is fun and lively. Start with the guacamole, and then try the "seacakes" (pan-fried blue-crab cakes) or the prime rib, cooked on a pecan-wood grill. For a lighter meal, try the herb-crusted fish filet. My husband likes the whiskey-soaked bread pudding for dessert, and my kids can't get enough of the Key lime chess pie with a butter pastry crust. If you can, eat late to avoid the lunch rush. For the ultimate San Antonio experience, book a Boudro's Dinner Cruise 2 weeks in advance, and for $50 per person (not including tax, tip, and spirits) you can dine on a delicious prix-fixe menu on a barge floating on the river. 421 E. Commerce St./River Walk. www.boudros.com. ✆ **210/224-8484.** Reservations recommended. Main courses $26–$42. Sun–Thurs 11am–11pm; Fri–Sat 11am–midnight.

Restaurant Gwendolyn ★★★ GLOBAL/ARTISINAL Gwendolyn chef/owner Michael Sohocki is a soft-spoken man with a tiny, whisper-quiet restaurant. His unassuming little eatery on a near-forgotten bend in the River Walk, far from the clamor of tourists, is a bit of found treasure. It's got a kitchen the size of a closet, and a Victorian-style dining room with a limited number of tables. The restaurant is named for the chef/owner's grandmother, and the concept is a back-to-the-19th-century rebuke of nearly everything industrial: It's all about locally sourced food prepared without electrical equipment. The cooks use no blenders, mixers, deep fryers, or anything with a motor (other than the fridge, which the health department insisted upon). Serving a fixed menu each night, Chef Sohocki creates mini works of art—food that, like his little restaurant, surprises and delights. Sample fresh-made po'boys at lunch; the changing tasting menu at dinner might include a venison tartare, Caesar salad with charred broccoli, or barbecued quail with stewed collard greens. Sohocki buys whole animals from nearby farms and butchers, dry-ages, and preserves them. He smokes his own bacon, grinds his own sausage, and makes magic in a kitchen smaller than mine. Restaurant Gwendolyn is no stunt; it's a labor of love from a Corpus Christi native with a quiet matter, who just keeps at it, cooking unplugged.

152 E. Pecan St. www.restaurantgwendolyn.com. ✆ **210/222-1849.** Reservations required. Main courses lunch $8–$12; dinner (chef's tasting menu only) $75. Mon–Thurs 11am–1:30pm and 5:30–9pm; Fri 11am–1:30pm and 5:30–10pm; Sat 5:30–10pm. Closed Sun.

MODERATE

Ácenar ★ MEXICAN Finding a shady spot for a bite to eat along the River Walk sounds easy, and sure, you can find lots of Mexican restaurants that will do, but Ácenar does it best. Created by popular restaurateur Lisa Wong of Rosario's in Southtown, this large, elegant restaurant adjacent to the Hotel Valencia features "modern Tex-Mex" fare, including fresh ceviche in lime juice marinade, or guacamole made tableside, as well as original dishes such as crepes with duck in a tamarind–cherry–grilled onion sauce, or the ever-popular *camarones al Diablo* (grilled shrimp in chipotle-butter). Fish tacos are served with sweet and spicy mayo and shredded cabbage. Decorated in bold, modern Mexican hues with midcentury-modern tables and banquettes, the multi-level dining room is bright and inviting. Sip drinks in the **Balcony Lounge** with views of the river, or dine outside on the elevated shaded patio overlooking River Walk. The restaurant is at a slightly secluded spot on the river just before it gets quiet and heads up the Museum Reach, so it's a convenient place to go without being in the thick of the touristy crowds. The restaurant is a fun, bright place for Mexican brunch on Saturdays and Sundays.

146 E. Houston St. (adjacent to Hotel Valencia). www.acenar.com. ✆ **210/222-2362.** Reservations not accepted (priority seating for large parties). Main courses $9–$14 lunch, $13–$28 dinner. Sun–Thurs 11am–10pm; Fri–Sat 11am–11pm.

INEXPENSIVE

Mi Tierra ★★★ TEX-MEX A Tex-Mex tradition since 1941, this family-owned restaurant is not to be missed. Sure, tourists flock here, but locals love it, too. It feels like a giant Mexican fiesta, with strolling mariachis plucking big guitars and pouring out their hearts singing traditional Mexican ballads. Enter from El Mercado, or Market Square, as year-round twinkling Christmas lights and colorful Mexican banners greet you. To the left, a dark lounge has an enormous oak bar, like one you might find in a 19th-century Texas hotel, with Mayan, Aztec, and Mexican symbols carved into the wood. Big glasses of green margaritas are brought on trays. At the front of the restaurant is a traditional *panederia,* or Mexican bakery, with a glass display case full of pink and white *pan dulce* (sweet breads) and colorful Mexican candies. Just beyond the bakery are three dining rooms. Start with a bowl of hot queso and crispy tortilla chips, then move on to traditional Tex-Mex fare, like *enchiladas verdes* and *chile rellenos.* Seasoned diners go for the enchiladas with chocolate-infused *molé* sauce. Even a Yankee is sure to like the chicken *flautas*—corn tortillas stuffed with shredded tender chicken, rolled into flutes, and fried. If you can't decide what to order, go with a *botanas* platter, a generous sampler of various *antojitos* ("little cravings," or appetizers). Be sure to invite the strolling musicians to serenade your table (tip about $5 if you do). Did I mention that it's open 24/7, meaning you can enjoy the same great food and fun at 2am that you get at 7pm? One afternoon I dropped in for a late lunch, and at the table next to me sat President Bill Clinton, Spurs Coach Gregg Popovich, former SA mayor Henry Cisneros, and former SA mayor Julian Castro. Now that's what I call a power lunch! On weekends expect a long wait, but that just gives you time to check out the Mexican imports market nearby; your light-up pager will let you know when your table is ready.

218 Produce Row (Market Sq.). www.mitierracafe.com. ✆ **210/225-1262.** Reservations for 25 people or more only. Breakfast $5–$15; lunch and dinner $11–$35. Open 24 hr.

Schilo's Delicatessen ★★ GERMAN/DELI The locals call it "*Shee*-lo's," and this old-fashioned German delicatessen looks like it's been here since Davy Crockett's days. It actually started as a saloon in Beeville, Texas in the early 1900s, moved to San Antonio in 1914, and settled at its current location in 1942. There's a lot of history here: Schilo's is one of the oldest continuously operated restaurants in the state, serving authentic German cuisine in a downtown mercantile building built in the 1800s. The really great thing about Schilo's is that it never seems to change. I began coming some 30 years ago, and the menu has remained basically the same since: apple and cherry strudels, thick cheesecake, bottled root beer, split-pea soup, hot German potato salad, bratwurst with house-made mustard, and great Reubens. The prices haven't changed all that much either—this is still one of the least expensive restaurants in town. I love Schilo's high-partitioned wooden booths, hexagon-patterned tile floors, big windows, and career waitresses who look like they were born to sling strudels in a *biergarten*. And did I mention the New York–style cheesecake? Best in town. Schilo's is within walking distance of most downtown hotels and attractions, and just steps from the Commerce Street bridge where it crosses one of the most popular stretches of the River Walk.

424 E. Commerce St. www.schilos.com. ✆ **210/223-6692.** Reservations for large groups at breakfast and dinner only. Sandwiches $6–$7; hot or cold plates $5–$10; main dishes $6–$10. Mon–Sat 7:30am–7:30pm.

King William/Southtown

MODERATE

Azuca ★ NUEVO LATINO Southtown isn't like any other San Antonio neighborhood, and Azuca isn't like any other restaurant, either. Azuca, short for *azucar,* or sugar, is no Tex-Mex eatery or hot new "Mexican street food" taco joint. Instead owner/chef Rene Fernandez roams Central and South America, with stops in the Caribbean. So you have a menu that includes refined versions of Brazilian curry, Cuban *ropa vieja* (a stew of shredded beef and veggies), Argentine-style steaks, and plantain fritters from the islands. The boldly decorated restaurant is fun and creative, with folk art, colorful flower-like chandeliers (from its neighbors at Garcia Art Glass), and casual indoor/outdoor spaces. On weekends, live music gets everyone moving, and margaritas, mojitos, and more start flowing. On Sundays, Azuca serves a filling brunch.

713 S. Alamo St. www.azuca.net. ✆ **210/225-5550.** Reservations recommended. Main courses $9.50–$12 lunch, $16–$33 dinner. Mon–Thurs 11am–9:30pm; Fri–Sat 11am–10pm; Sun 11am–2:30pm and 5–9:30pm.

Bliss ★★ NEW AMERICAN This upscale little restaurant is the love-child of Mark Bliss and his wife and business partner, Lisa. Bliss worked under another beloved San Antonio chef Bruce Auden (see **Biga on the Banks,** p. 266) in several of his kitchens before he helped him open **Silo** (p. 274) in 1997, so Bliss has more than 20 years of experience in restaurants across the Alamo City and has harvested quite a following of local fans. Now as the owner/chef of his own fashionable, off-the-beaten-path Southtown restaurant, Bliss brings contemporary American cuisine to new heights. It's set inside what was once a rustic gas station complete with exposed brick, plate-glass windows, and high ceilings. Today the old gas station is a sublimely stylish place with a less-is-more attitude in both decor and menu. Bliss's dishes are elegantly simple, fresh, and masterfully plated, offering main dishes and small plates. You could sate yourself just fine with a big arugula salad and sharable plates: a charcuterie board of house-cured meats, artisanal cheeses and breads, oysters on the half-shell. Or go a little heartier with small dishes like maple-glazed Kurobuta pork belly or roasted bone marrow with beef tenderloin tartare. Main courses include Arctic char with wild mushrooms, and red snapper over a bed of shrimp risotto. The artfully landscaped property makes sitting on the back patio a delight. The restaurant has a chef's table for 10 in the kitchen, which diners can reserve in advance for an unforgettable culinary experience.

926 S. Presa St. www.foodisbliss.com. ✆ **210/225-2547.** Reservations recommended. Shared/small plates $12–$16; main courses $25–$45. Tues–Thurs 5:30–10pm; Fri–Sat 5:30–11pm. Closed Sun/Mon.

Feast ★★ NEW AMERICAN This ultramodern cocktail lounge and restaurant on Southtown/King William's bustling South Alamo Street is the kind of place young business types like to go after work or to meet friends on weekends. The chic decor grabs your attention right away—it's almost Scandinavian in its simplicity, but with lots of trendy touches like industrial lighting; clear Lucite chairs; white, *Mad Men*–style plastic tables; glass bubble chandeliers; and mood lighting in blues, pinks and purples. Because it's so bright and trendy, it's easy to forget why we first fell in love with this place: chef Stefan Bowers's masterful take on New American cuisine. The menu lists dishes under the headings "Oceanic," "Heat," "Chilled," "Grilled," "Crispy," and "Hearty." Start with "Oceanic" and get the cornmeal-fried oysters, then move to "Chilled" for butter-leaf lettuce wraps filled with ground pork. Under "Grilled" we like the lamb belly, or go to "Crispy" for duck breast tostadas. Chef Bowers, a former Navy helicopter rescue swimmer, has worked in fine kitchens from California to Texas, but he's been a longtime San Antonio favorite since teaming with pioneering chef Jason Dady in other restaurants.

Unlike other Southtown eateries that fit well with sneakers-clad tourists, this place feels more fashionable, and Feast's clientele tends to dress that way too.

1024 S. Alamo St. www.feastsa.com. ✆ **210/354-1024.** Reservations recommended. Small/shared plates $7–$12; main courses $12–$22. Tues–Thurs 5–10pm; Fri–Sat 5–11pm; Sun 10:30am–2:30pm. Social-hour drink specials Tues–Fri 5–7pm. Closed Mon.

Liberty Bar ★ NEW AMERICAN/VEGETARIAN-FRIENDLY Back in 2010, the Liberty moved from its 25-year-old perch in an old leaning saloon on Josephine Street to its current location in Southtown. Many locals think that losing the lean took all the magic out of the restaurant, but others were willing to give its current home a shot. (It's quite an arc, moving from a former brothel to a former convent.) Either way, the fare remains pretty much the same, leaning toward fresh, healthful dishes of generous portions and reasonable prices. Vegetarian dishes here are a delight. On my last visit, I sampled the pasta *luego* with housemade fettuccine, pork sausage, mushroom, onion, and cilantro sauce with a mixed green salad with roasted hazelnuts, apples, and bits of Pecorino and prosciutto. Liberty Bar has long been known for its house-made bread, so try one of the innovative sandwiches, such as the Portobello mushroom topped with smoked Gouda and saffron aioli. The Liberty Bar is definitely worth visiting, especially for lunch or brunch.

1111 S. Alamo St. www.liberty-bar.com. ✆ **210/227-1187.** Reservations accepted. Main courses $10–$24; sandwiches $8–$12. Mon–Fri 11am–midnight; Sat–Sun 9am–midnight.

INEXPENSIVE

Guenther House ★ AMERICAN You don't have to stay in a historic King William B&B to step inside a historic Victorian mansion filled with exquisite turn-of-the-century furnishings: Simply have lunch or brunch at Guenther House, set on a serene residential stretch of the River Walk. This is the kind of place you'd take your mom for a special ladies' lunch or stop in for tea and pastries. Set in the original home of the owners of San Antonio's Pioneer Flour Company, the restaurant is a charming place to enjoy a hearty breakfast or a light lunch in the dining room of the former Guenther family residence. When the weather's fine, dine alfresco on the trellised patio. The crenellated castle-like tower in the Guenther family's old flour mill just across the river has become an iconic San Antonio symbol. Biscuits and gravy and other baked goods (using Pioneer flour), are popular here, as are the waffles and pancakes at breakfast, served 'til closing time at 3pm. At lunch I like spinach salad, chicken salad, or the Tex-Mex taco salad. A small museum and a mill store stand adjacent to the restaurant.

205 E. Guenther St. www.guentherhouse.com. ✆ **210/227-1061.** Reservations not accepted. Breakfast $4–$8; lunch $6–$9. Daily 7am–3pm. House and mill store Mon–Sat 8am–4pm; Sun 8am–3pm.

Pearl/Monte Vista Area

MODERATE

Cured ★★★ GASTROPUB/CHARCUTERIE It's considered one of the best restaurants in the whole country—and on that I would agree. Cured reminds me of the carefully crafted menus and cutting-edge kitchens of Manhattan's West Village gastropubs, where chefs design nose-to-tail menus around a hand-crafted, artisanal approach: curing their own meat for a charcuterie board, jarring mustards, canning their own okra, and pickling their own farm-grown cucumbers. That is exactly what James Beard–award finalist Steve McHugh does at Cured. This place works on so many levels—from the wonderful food to the bright, inviting space to the electric atmosphere, which makes Cured a favorite happy-hour and late-night spot. It's set in a gem of a little stand-alone building at Pearl (circa 1904). McHugh, a former Wisconsin farm boy, battled non-Hodgkin's lymphoma only a few years ago but has come back strong. Today the chef is active in the community, giving back to causes that look for a cure. I don't know which impresses me more, Chef McHugh and his wife, Sylvia, who work tirelessly to make this a great restaurant, or the food that comes out of the kitchen. McHugh spent years in the kitchens of several John Besh restaurants, and the menu's subtle nods to New Orleans cuisine show it. (Don't miss the smoked pork gumbo.) Among the powerful craft cocktails, the Bees Knees is made with a local farmer's market honey.

306 Pearl Pkwy. www.curedatpearl.com. ✆ **210/314-3929.** Reservations suggested. Main courses lunch $5–$16 (charcuterie plates $18–$34); dinner $12–$28. Mon–Fri 11am–3pm; Mon–Sat 5–11pm; Sun brunch 10am–3pm.

La Gloria ★★ MEXICAN In the old days, "ice houses" were the quintessential San Antonio gathering places. Many times these family-friendly watering holes were old gas stations or garages converted into taco spots, where beer and Coca-Cola bottles were iced down, and people sat on picnic tables outside while their kids ran around playing tag or marbles. La Gloria has that same vibe, but with a more colorful, contemporary approach. At La Gloria, Chef Johnny Hernandez calls his fare "street foods of Mexico," meaning it's mostly casual, affordable, eat-with-your-hands kind of food. Garage-door walls transform the restaurant into an indoor-outdoor space when the weather allows. You can sit on the patio by the river, and on weekends wander over to the farmer's market, where Hernandez gets much of his produce. The atmosphere is vibrant and bustling and hip: Diners grab a Mexican soda or cold Corona out of a box of ice as they walk in the door. One of the nicest chefs in town, Hernandez has no freezers in his kitchen—why would he need to keep anything overnight? His simple, zesty Mexican fare is made to order fresh. Tacos and *gorditas* in handmade corn tortillas are finished with a crumbling of white farmer's cheese; the dried *cotija* has a drizzle of Mexican cream. Chiles can sometimes burn the lips (making the lime and beer taste better), so alert the waiter if you want to tone down the spice. Hernandez has several other popular eateries in town (El Machito, Fruteria-Botanero, and Casa Hernan) and is meticulously involved in everything, right down to plates designed by Mexican artists. In fact, Chef Johnny (as everybody calls him) is becoming something of a national/international star chef, with a La Gloria and a Fruteria-Botanero now in Caesar's Palace in Las Vegas and in some Texas airports.

Chef Johnny was even invited to cook at the White House for President Obama in 2016.

100 E. Grayson St., Pearl Brewery. www.chefjohnnyhernandez.com. ✆ **210/267-9094.** Reservations not accepted. Main courses $6–$26. Sun–Mon and Wed–Thurs 11am–10pm; Fri–Sat 11am–midnight.

INEXPENSIVE

Botika ★★ PERUVIAN-ASIAN I was a fan of chef Geronimo Lopez (formerly at Nao at Pearl) long before he opened Botika in 2016, a bright, lively Peruvian-Asian restaurant at Pearl, near the Culinary Institute of America where he once was an instructor and executive chef. Botika's innovative menu features "Chifa" (Chinese-Peruvian) and "Nikkei" (Japanese-Peruvian) cuisines, as well as inventive takes on traditional dishes from across Asia and Latin America. Botika's bar offers classic cocktails and a variety of rums, *piscos,* and *cachaças.* The sushi-ceviche bar and late-night dining options are a big hit with locals. Be sure to tell your server your spice/heat tolerance, especially if you can't take the heat. Others who like it hot think it's terrific just as is. You can sit indoors or out—the latter a nice choice in Pearl for great people-watching.

303 Pearl Pkwy. www.botikapearl.com. ✆ **210/670-7684.** Reservations suggested. Main courses $11–$26. Tues–Fri 11:30am–3pm; Sat 11:30am–2pm; Mon–Fri 3–6pm; Sat 2–5pm; Mon–Thurs 5–10pm; Fri–Sat 5pm–midnight.

Chris Madrid's ★★ AMERICAN/TEX-MEX Tex-Mex meets Americana at this fun, down-home hamburger joint known for its extra-large "macho" burger, a supersize version of their standard burgers. The ever-popular "tostada burger" comes with crushed tortilla chips, refried beans, and real cheddar. In its macho variety, the "cheddar cheesy" burger is intimidating, with cheddar oozing out over the large burger, engulfing even the platter. The French fries are made in-house and well worth ordering. The kid-friendly menu also includes chicken sandwiches, nachos, and *chalupas* (tostadas). The main dining area is a large room with a cement floor and high framed ceiling; out back is an outdoor patio. Family-owned since 1977, this place was lovingly run by Chris Madrid, who died in 2012 of an enlarged heart—no surprise to locals who knew he had one of the biggest hearts in town.

1900 Blanco Rd. (just south of Hildebrand). www.chrismadrids.com. ✆ **210/735-3552.** Reservations not accepted. Burgers $6–$10. Mon–Sat 11am–10pm.

Alamo Heights & Olmos Park

EXPENSIVE

Silo Elevated Cuisine & Bar ★★ NEW AMERICAN For the past decade or so, everyone in San Antonio has raved that Silo is one of the best places in town for fine New American cuisine. My chef pals all swore by it. Guess what? Though it's hardly the new kid on the block, Silo is still just as good. Yes, the whole small-plate concept is overdone these days, but foodies never tire of it, and unlike many other trendy farm-to-table restaurants that stylize every dish, Silo fashions simple, pleasing dishes that are understated yet "elevated." The constantly changing menu offers a three-course prix-fixe menu, along with a la carte and main dish offerings like cider-braised Kurobuta pork shank, green chile orzo mac 'n' cheese, and vegetarian risotto with grilled Portobello mushrooms. At lunch, I love to nibble on crispy duck spring rolls or Silo's signature chicken-fried oysters with mustard hollandaise. Downstairs in the front of the Alamo Heights/Austin Highway location also sits aptly named sister restaurant Nosh, where guests snack on small-plate fare and fun items like pizza, chicken wings, and wild-boar sliders. The Silo bar is also downstairs, where guests may order from the full Silo menu. Whether you nosh downstairs or elevate your evening at Silo, you won't be disappointed. There are four Silo locations in San Antonio, but this was the first and is still my favorite.

1133 Austin Hwy. www.siloelevatedcuisine.com. ✆ **210/824-8686.** Reservations recommended. Main courses $17–$40; prix fixe (salad, entree, dessert) $29. Mon–Fri and Sun 11am–2:30pm; Mon–Thurs 5:30–10pm; Fri–Sat 5:30–10:30pm; Sun 5:30–9pm.

MODERATE

Paesanos ★★★ ITALIAN This is my favorite old standby restaurant in San Antonio, and I'm not alone. "A thousand people on a Friday night can't all be wrong," wrote one SA newspaper food critic some 20 years ago. I don't know how many people now pass through Joe Canseco's doors on a weekend night, but it's a big number, though somehow there's rarely a wait. This place isn't fancy or fussy (there are no white tablecloths and it can get noisy), but the food is fabulous. In fact, Paesanos has been consistently wonderful every day and night for more than 4 decades, serving the city's favorite dish: the signature shrimp paesano, lightly breaded and dredged in a buttery lemon sauce whose recipe is often copied but never quite mastered. Little-known fact: The center-cut tenderloin served here is better and less expensive than that at any one of the city's pricey famous steakhouses. Start with the house salad (the dressing is delectable—what is it? They'll never tell) and have an appetizer sampling of the shrimp paesano and the veal cannelloni, then have a steak or the yummy red snapper paesano. All main courses come with a side of pasta (stick with the butter garlic or you'll feel like you've ordered a second meal). There are always house-made breads and good wine and good times here. The Alamo Heights crowd treats this place like it's their personal dining room; you never know who you'll run into, from a Spurs player to a local pol. The kitchen stays open late—a rarity in this town. Paesanos has two other San Antonio locations.

555 East Basse Rd. (Lincoln Heights). www.paesanos.com. ✆ **210/828-5191.** Reservations recommended only for large groups. Main courses $17–$35. Mon–Sat 11am–11pm; Sun 11am–10pm.

SAN ANTONIO SHOPPING

San Antonio provides the shopper with a variety of large malls and little enclaves of specialized shops. You'll find everything here, from the utilitarian to the unusual: a Saks Fifth Avenue fronted by a 40-foot pair of cowboy boots, a mall with a river running through it, and some lively Mexican markets.

Most shops around town are open from 9 or 10am to 5:30 or 6pm Monday through Saturday, with shorter hours on Sunday. Malls are generally open Monday through Saturday 10am to 9pm and on Sunday noon to 6pm. Sales tax in San Antonio is 8.25%.

Shopping Areas

Most out-of-town shoppers will find all they need **downtown,** between the recently renovated **Shops at Rivercenter,** the boutiques and crafts shops of **La Villita,** the colorful Mexican wares of **Market Square,** the **Southwest School of Art and Craft,** and assorted retailers and galleries on and around **Alamo Plaza.** More avant-garde boutiques and galleries, including Blue Star, can be found in the adjacent area known as **Southtown**.

Most San Antonians prefer to shop in the malls along Loop 410, especially **North Star, Huebner Oaks,** and **Alamo Quarry Market.** The city's large-scale, high-end outdoor mall, **Shops at La Cantera,** is out along the outer loop (Loop 1604). More upmarket retail outlets can be found closer to downtown in the fancy strip centers that line Broadway, where it passes through Alamo Heights (the posh Collection and Lincoln Heights are particularly noteworthy). Between Austin and San Antonio along Interstate 35 are two adjacent outlet malls, which have become one of south Texas's largest tourist destinations: the **Tanger Factory Outlet Center** and the **Simon Premium Outlets,** with more than 350 stores and more than 1,000,000 square feet of shopping.

Art

ArtPace, in the northern part of downtown, 445 N. Main St. (www.artpace.org; ✆ **210/212-4900**), and the **Blue Star Arts Complex,** in Southtown, 125 Blue Star 6 (https://bluestarartscomplex.com; ✆ **210/354-3775**), are the best venues for cutting-edge art. Downtown is home to several galleries that show more established artists, and is proud of its enchanting and historic Ursuline-convent-turned-art-school-and-galleries, the **Southwest School of Art and Craft,** 300 Augusta St. (www.swschool.org; ✆ **210/224-1848**), which organizes contemporary art exhibitions and houses a small history museum and a lunch cafe. Adjacent to this, the Santikos Building is the site of the school's contemporary exhibition galleries and its high-tech classrooms and studios for photography, metals, printmaking, digital imaging, paper and book arts, as well as drawing and painting and 3D media. During a typical year, more than 225,000 people attend events, view exhibitions, or enroll in classes at the Southwest School of Art and Craft. In Lincoln Heights, **Nanette Richardson Fine Art,** 555 E. Basse Rd. (www.nanetterichardsonfineart.com; ✆ **210/930-1343**), offers a wide array of oils, watercolors, bronzes, ceramics, and handcrafted wood furnishings.

For more information on other galleries and the art scene in general, visit the **Office of Cultural Affairs website** (www.getcreativesanantonio.com), with listings of several local galleries and schedules for events held during **Contemporary Art Month** in March (www.contemporaryartmonth.com).

Crafts/Folk Art

Mexican folk art and handicrafts make wonderful take-homes from San Antonio, and several of the best places to find them are in Southtown. The top collection is at **San Angel Folk Art,** 1404 S. Alamo St., Ste. 110, in the Blue Star Arts Complex (www.sanangelfolkart.com; ✆ **210/226-6688**), chockablock with colorful, whimsical, and well-made wares. Also in Southtown, **Garcia Art Glass, Inc.,** 715 S. Alamo St. (www.garciaartglass.com; ✆ **210/354-4681**), has beautiful glass bowls, wall sconces, chandeliers, and mobiles. Often, glass blowers are at work behind the store. Downtown, next to the ticket office for the Metropolitan Theatre, is a colorful store filled with Mexican handwork called **Casa Salazar,** 216 E. Houston St. (www.themajestic.com/casa/gallery/index.html; ✆ **210/472-2272**). Just north of downtown, near Monte Vista, the two-level **Alamo Fiesta,** 2025 N. Main St. at Ashby (www.alamo-fiesta.com; ✆ **210/738-1188**), caters to local families with a huge selection of crafts at extremely reasonable prices. Not everything is portable, but the bracelets and other pretty baubles made out of glass beads definitely are. Mexican imports and Mexican folk art, including pottery, may also be found in **Market Square** at **El Mercado,** 110 Produce Row/514 W. Commerce St. (www.getcreativesanantonio.com/Explore-San-Antonio/Market-Square; ✆ **210/207-8600**).

Malls & Shopping Centers

Although it's officially known as the **Alamo Quarry Market,** 255 E. Basse Rd. (www.quarrymarket.com; ✆ **210/824-8885**), no one ever calls this shopping center anything but "The Quarry"—largely because from the early 1900s until 1985 the property was in fact a cement quarry. This unenclosed mall has a series of large shops (like Restoration Hardware and Pottery Barn) and smaller upscale shops, too. Starring Saks Fifth Avenue—the one fronted by the huge pair of cowboy boots—and popular shops such as Abercrombie & Fitch, Victoria's Secret, and Macy's, **North Star Mall,** Loop 410, between McCullough and San Pedro (www.northstarmall.com; ✆ **210/340-6627**), is the crème de la crème of the San Antonio indoor malls. Both the Quarry and North Star Mall are about 15 minutes from downtown.

At the light-filled, bustling, and revamped (2016) **Shops at Rivercenter,** 849 E. Commerce St. (www.shoprivercenter.com; ✆ **210/225-0000**), you can pick up a Rio Taxi or River Walk tour boat from a downstairs dock and listen to bands play on a stage surrounded by water. This popular mall adjacent to the River Walk and accessible to Alamo Plaza features more than 100 retailers, including six restaurants, a Macy's, an IMAX theater and AMC theaters, and a 1,000-room Marriott. It's also home to **Battle for Texas: The Experience,** a multimedia museum that brings the story of the Alamo to life. Upscale shoppers migrate to the far northwest part of the city to the **Shops at La Cantera,** 16401 La Cantera Pkwy. (www.shoplacantera.com; ✆ **210/582-6255**). Nearby, they also visit the **RIM Shopping Center,** 17503 La Cantera Pkwy. (www.therimsa.com; ✆ **210/641-1777**), for shopping, dining, and movies.

Western Wear

Want to buy a pair of authentic Texas cowboy boots while you're in Texas? Look no further than the **Lucchese Gallery,** 255 E. Basse, Ste. 800 (www.lucchese.com; ✆ **210/828-9419**), at the Alamo Quarry Market, where footwear is raised to the level of art (and they can even custom-order/custom-make boots to send to you). It may cost you, but Lucchese's boots are some of the best. Lucchese is far better-known than **Little's Boots,** 110 Division Ave. (www.davelittleboots.com; ✆ **210/923-2221**), but this place—established in 1915—uses as many esoteric leathers and creates even fancier footwear designs. If you're willing to wait awhile, you can have hand-customized leather boots made here, too.

The late Pope John Paul II, Prince Charles, and Dwight Yoakam all had cowboy hats and headgear made for them by **Paris Hatters,** 119 Broadway (www.parishatters.com; ✆ **210/223-3453**), in business since 1917 and still owned by the same family. About half of the sales are special order, but the shelves are stocked with high-quality ready-to-wear hats. For all things Western, visit **Cavender's** at 303 NW Loop 410 (www.cavenders.com; ✆ **210/377-4241**) or one of their other two locations in the Alamo City. For the best and most authentic Western shopping experiences you'll find in Texas, mosey on outside of town about 35 miles east on Interstate 10 to **D&D Farm and Ranch Superstore,** 516 I-10 Frontage Rd. (Exit 609 off I-10), Seguin (www.ddtexasoutfitters.com; ✆ **830/379-7340**), which sells everything from saddles and spurs, horse trailers and firepits to cowboy boots and Western wear, jeans, cowboy hats, home decor, children's Western toys, and more. If it's your first time in Texas, this place will wow you; it's worth the trip.

SAN ANTONIO NIGHTLIFE

San Antonio has its symphony and its Broadway shows, and you can see both at one of the most beautiful old movie palaces in the country. But much of what the city has to offer is not quite so mainstream. Latin influences lend spice to some of the best local nightlife. Don't forget, San Antonio is the birthplace of Tejano music, a unique blend of German polka and northern Mexico *ranchero* sounds (with a dose of pop added for good measure). It also celebrates its Mexican heritage with colorful dance troupes, known as ***ballet folklórico,*** that perform to more traditional Mexican music. And Southtown, with its many Hispanic-oriented shops and galleries, celebrates its art scene with the monthly **First Friday,** a kind of extended block party.

For the most complete listings of what's on while you're visiting, pick up a free copy of the weekly alternative newspaper, the ***Current*** (www.sacurrent.com) or the Friday "Weekender" section of the ***San Antonio Express-News*** (www.mysa.com). Check out the **San Antonio Arts & Cultural Affairs** (www.getcreativesanantonio.com). There's no central office in town for tickets, discounted or otherwise. You'll need to reserve seats directly through the theaters or clubs or, for large events, through **Ticketmaster** (www.

ticketmaster.com; ✆ **210/224-9600**). Generally, box office hours are Monday to Friday 10am to 5pm, and 1 to 2 hours before performance time.

The Performing Arts

The San Antonio Symphony is the city's only resident performing arts company of national stature, but smaller, less professional groups keep the local arts scene lively, and cultural organizations draw world-renowned artists. The city provides them with some unique venues—everything from standout historic structures such as the Majestic, Empire, Arneson, and Sunken Garden theaters to the state-of-the-art AT&T Center.

MAJOR ARTS VENUES

If you're visiting from May to August, catch a performance at the **Arneson River Theatre,** La Villita (www.sanantonio.com/places/arneson-river-theatre; ✆ **210/207-8610**). Built by the Work Projects Administration (WPA) in 1939 as part of architect Robert Hugman's design for the River Walk, this unique theater has a stage on one side of the river, where it narrows considerably, and seating on the opposite side. Most performances are *ballet folklórico.*

The baroque Moorish/Spanish revival–style **Majestic Theatre,** 230 E. Houston St. (www.majesticempire.com; ✆ **210/226-3333**), is the city's best-loved stage theatre and hosts some of the best entertainment in town—the symphony, major Broadway productions, and big-name solo performers.

There's always something happening at the **Guadalupe Cultural Arts Center,** 1300 Guadalupe St. (www.guadalupeculturalarts.org; ✆ **210/271-3151**), the main location for Latino cultural activity in San Antonio. Visiting or local directors put on six or seven plays a year, and the **CineFestival,** running since 1977, is one of the town's major film events.

Smaller than its former rival the Majestic (see above), just down the block, the **Empire Theatre,** 226 N. St. Mary's St. (www.majesticempire.com; ✆ **210/226-5700**), hosts a similarly eclectic array of acts, including musical performances, lectures, and literary events.

CLASSICAL MUSIC

The **San Antonio Symphony,** 711 Navarro St. (www.sasymphony.org; ✆ **210/554-1000** or 223-8624 box office), was founded in 1939, and today the symphony plays at the **Tobin Center for Performing Arts** downtown, offering several Classics Series (including a winter festival concert) and Pops Series concerts, all under music director Sebastian Lang-Lessing. Tickets range from $15 to $81 ($15–$85 for Pops).

THEATER

Most of San Antonio's major road shows turn up at the Majestic or Empire theaters (see "Major Art Venues," above), but several smaller theaters are of interest, too, including the community-based **Josephine Theatre,** 339 W. Josephine St. (www.josephinetheatre.org; ✆ **210/320-0514**), which puts on an average of five productions a year—mostly musicals—at the Art Deco–style theater, only 5 minutes from downtown.

Live children's theater is offered at **Magik Performing Arts Center,** 5359 Casa Bella (www.magiktheatre.org; © **210/227-2751**). This professional troupe offers a full season of plays, many of them adaptations from children's books.

Whether it's an original piece by a member of the company or a work by a guest artist, anything you see at the **Jump-Start Performance Company,** 710 Fredericksburg Rd. (www.jump-start.org; © **210/227-5867**), is likely to push the social and political envelope.

The Club & Music Scene

The closest San Antonio comes to having a main club district is the stretch of North St. Mary's Street between Josephine and Magnolia—just north of downtown and south of Brackenridge Park—known as the **Strip.** This area was hotter about 20 years ago, but it still draws a young crowd to its restaurants and lounges on the weekend. The River Walk clubs tend to be touristy, and many of them close early because of noise restrictions. Pearl has more restaurants than bars and clubs, though it is home to a couple nice ones including **Jazz, TX** and the **Blue Box** bar, and more are slated to open here in the future.

In addition to the **Alamodome,** 100 Montana St. (www.sanantonio.gov/dome; © **210/207-3663**), the major concert venues in town include **Verizon Wireless Amphitheater,** 16765 Lookout Rd., north of San Antonio just beyond Loop 1604 (www.vwatx.com; © **210/657-8300**); and, when the Spurs aren't playing, downtown's **AT&T Center,** One AT&T Center Pkwy. (www.nba.com/spurs; © **210/444-5000**), as well as the **H-E-B Performance Hall at the Tobin Center** (www.tobincenter.org; © **210/223-8624**). The Majestic Theatre (p. 279) also hosts touring singers like Tony Bennett and Don Henley as well as comedians like Jay Leno and Jerry Seinfeld.

COUNTRY MUSIC

John T. Floore, the first manager of the Majestic Theatre, opened up **Floore's Country Store,** 14664 Old Bandera Rd., 2 miles north of Loop 1604 (www.liveatfloores.com; © **210/695-8827**), back in 1942. A couple of years later, he added a cafe and a dance floor—at a half-acre, the largest in south Texas—and since then, the establishment has hosted country greats such as Willie Nelson, Hank Williams, Sr., Lyle Lovett, and Dwight Yoakam. Local boot-scooters, often a college-age crowd, can be found burning up the dance floor at **Cowboy's Dancehall,** 3030 NE Loop 410 (www.cowboysdancehall.com; © **210/646-9378**), a Texas-size place with dance lessons, a mechanical bull, and sometimes even big-name country music bands. Be sure to wear Wranglers and boots when you go there, or folks might mistake you for a Yankee.

JAZZ & BLUES

If you like big bands and Dixieland, there's no better place to listen to music than **Jazz, TX,** 312 Pearl Parkway, Bldg. 6 Suite 6001 (www.jazztx.com; © **210/332-9386**), owned by local bandleader Doc Watkins (who still plays there on weekends). The club is located at Pearl in what was once the cellar of the bottling house of the historic Pearl Brewery. This place combines the class of an upscale jazz club with the grit of a Texas dance hall, featuring jazz, blues, Texas swing, and salsa. It also serves up good eats (and a food hall with pop-up restaurants was slated to open in late 2017 or 2018 upstairs). Jazz great Jim Cullum, known for his American Public Radio program, *Riverwalk, Live from the Landing,* now plays there, among other clubs, now that the Jazz Landing has closed on the River Walk. For a bit grittier place with jazz, blues, and more (including Jim Cullum jazz) and indoor and outdoor stages, go to **Squeezebox,** 2806 N. St. Mary's St. (✆ **210/314-8845**).

The Bar Scene

ALAMO-CITY MICROBREWERIES Preppie and gallery types don't often mingle, but the popularity with college kids of the **Blue Star Brewing Company,** 1414 S. Alamo, no. 105 (www bluestarbrewing.com; ✆ **210/212-5506**), in the Blue Star Arts Complex, demonstrates the transcendent power of good beer (the pale ale is especially fine). Another microbrewery, this one with a great outdoor picnic table and giant beer hall in the shadow of the Hays Street Bridge, **Alamo Beer Company,** 202 Lamar St. (www.alamobeer.com; ✆ **210/872-5589**), is not far from Sunset Station.

A HISTORIC BAR More than 100 years ago, Teddy Roosevelt recruited men for his Rough Riders unit at the dark, woody **Menger Bar,** Menger Hotel, 204 Alamo Plaza (www.mengerhotel.com; ✆ **210/223-4361**); they were outfitted for the Spanish-American War at nearby Fort Sam Houston. Constructed in 1859 on the site of William Menger's earlier successful brewery and saloon, the bar was moved from its original location in the Victorian hotel lobby in 1956, but 90% of its historic furnishings remain intact. You can still see an "X" on the bar put there by prohibitionist Carrie Nation, and Spanish Civil War uniforms hang on the walls. Another of San Antonio's older (and arguably, best) watering holes is the **Esquire Tavern,** 155 E. Commerce St. (www.esquiretavern-sa.com; ✆ **210/222-2521**), which opened in 1933 to celebrate the end of Prohibition and has been a beloved San Antonio institution ever since, with a short hiatus when it was closed from 2006 to 2011. It's still my favorite bar and grill in town and has a nice, cozy, small-plates restaurant downstairs, too. Interestingly, it's on the River Walk but not on tourists' radar; it's said the best chefs in town meet here some nights after they close up shop.

A LOCAL FAVORITE During the week, lawyers and judges unwind at the **Cadillac Bar & Restaurant,** 212 S. Flores St. (www.cadillacbarsa.com; ✆ **210/223-5533**), in a historic stucco building near the Bexar County Courthouse and City Hall; on weekends, singles take the stand.

A COCKTAIL BAR The mixologists at **Cured** at Pearl, 306 Pearl Pkwy., Suite #101 (www.curedatpearl.com; ✆ **210/314-3929**), create some of the city's best craft cocktails and offer great local brews. This is the kind of place where you can sit at the bar and nosh on small-plate gastropub fare and charcuterie boards while sipping great drinks. It's always open later than most places, and day or night it's one of the best cocktail spots in the Alamo City. The **Esquire Tavern** (p. 281) has craft cocktails and local microbrews, too.

A WINE BAR **Zinc Bistro & Bar** (www.zincwine.com; © **210/224-2900**), at 207 N. Presa St. in the downtown area, has a cozy, laid-back feel, with hardwood floors, exposed-brick walls, and shelves of books.

A MARTINI BAR The River Walk's nod to retro chic, **Swig** at 111 W. Crockett St. (www.swigmartini.com; © **210/476-0005**), is so popular it spurred a national chain. Martinis are the top seller, but you can also get single-barrel bourbon, single-malt scotch, and a wide selection of beer and wines.

A SPORTS BAR For a big bar, big televisions, big pool tables, and big fun, go to **On the Rocks Pub**, a popular downtown sports bar at 270 Losoya St. (https://ontherocks.pub; © **210/228-0000**).

The Gay & Lesbian Scene

Tina Turner, Deborah Harry, and La Toya Jackson—the real ones—have all played the **Bonham Exchange,** 411 Bonham St. (www.bonhamexchange.com; © **210/224-9219**), a high-tech dance club near the Alamo that's been a huge SA hotspot for decades. While you may find an occasional drag show here, the mixed crowd of gay and straight, young and old, come mainly to move to the beat under wildly flashing lights. Main Street just north of downtown has several gay clubs in close proximity (it's been nicknamed the "gay bar mall"). **Heat,** 1500 N. Main Ave. (www.heatsa.com; © **210/227-2600**), is a flashy, fun dance club. The **Silver Dollar Saloon,** 1812 N. Main St. (© **210/227-2623**), is loud and fizzy, and **Essence,** 1010 N. Main St. (© **210/223-5418**) is a hot spot with outdoor seating. Other popular LGBT-friendly bars include the **Annex,** 330 San Pedro Ave. (© **210/223-6957**), and **2015 Bar & Pub,** 2015 San Pedro Ave. (© **210/733-3365**), a casual neighborhood bar. The romantic **Candlelight Coffeehouse,** 3011 N. Saint Mary's St. (www.candlelightsa.com; © **210/738-0099**), is not necessarily a gay/lesbian bar or cafe, but it has long been a popular spot in the Tobin Hills neighborhood among LGBT locals and their straight neighbors alike.

SMALL-TOWN TEXAS

If you want to get away from the crowds of San Antonio and see a less touristy part of Texas, then consider this day trip to a few of the old towns to the east of San Antonio. The trip includes a smattering of things: a little history, a historic hotel, a tour of Texas's last independent brewery, and some award-winning barbecue, plus plenty of local color. It's best to go on a weekday, when the brewery is open for tours. Take a relaxing road trip—the roads are good, the traffic is light, and the driving is easy. There won't be any crowds, which is especially important during wildflower season in the spring. Visitors show a strong preference for the Hill Country, but the wildflowers do not.

Seguin

Start by heading out of San Antonio east on I-10 to Hwy. 183 (35 miles) and take exit 609 heading south on Hwy 123 Business into **Seguin.** Seguin rests on the banks of the Guadalupe River and is home to "The World's Largest Pecan" and **Pape Pecan House** nutcracker museum, 5440 S Highway 123 Bypass (www.papepecan.com; ✆ **830/372-2850**). Seguin has a delightful downtown square where the trees are lit with sparkling white lights year-round, and a charming, affordable historic hotel, the **Park Plaza Hotel,** 217 S. River St. (www.parkplazaseguin.com; ✆ **830/584-4400**) overlooks it all. It has a number of antiques shops, a cupcake shop, **Sweet Treats,** at 106 W. Court St. (www.sweettreatsseguin.com; ✆ **830/556-9387**), and the **Court Street Coffee Shop,** 111 W. Court St. (✆ **830/379-7711**), with live music on Friday evenings. To see where real cowboys (and cowgirls) shop, visit the **D&D Farm and Ranch Superstore** (www.ddtexasoutfitters.com; ✆ **830/379-7340**), 516 I-10 Frontage Rd. (Exit 609 off I-10). Seguin is also home to a lovely section of the Guadalupe River by Max Starcke Park.

Shiner

From Seguin take a country road, U.S. Hwy. 90A, through the town of Gonzales to Shiner (pop. 2,198), home to the **Spoetzl brewery,** makers of Shiner beer. It's the last independent brewery in Texas, and in 2009 it celebrated its 100th anniversary. Take Hwy. 90 east for 18 miles. When you drive into Shiner, the brewery will be on your left. It's the tallest structure in town.

Shiner Bock beer, sold in brown longnecks, is now available in various parts of the country, but as late as the 1970s it was available only seasonally and only in central and southeast Texas. But it soon shot up in popularity and is now the default beer in Austin, San Antonio, and most other parts of central Texas. All the Shiner beer sold is made at this small brewery; no production is contracted out to other plants.

Free tours are offered Monday to Friday at 10am, 11am, 1:30pm, and 2:30pm June to August (11am and 1:30pm Sept–May) and take about 30 minutes, with beer tastings before and after in the hospitality room. It's an impressive tour—especially the bottling plant. The bottles moving down the conveyor resemble a long amusement ride. It loops around the entire brewery, guiding bottles in and out of several machines, until capped, labeled, and filled with beer; then they are deposited in boxes ready for shipping.

Luling

If you would rather have beer than barbecue, skip the trip to Shiner and head east leaving Seguin along I-10; exit when you see the signs for **Luling.** You'll *smell* Luling before you get there—it's true. The many oil wells in the area have a rotten-egg sulfur smell that lingers in the air. Luling (pop. 5,400) has some of the best barbecue in the state, even though the town of **Lockhart,** just up Hwy. 183 from Luling, is better known as the "Barbecue Capital of Texas." Still, Luling's pit barbecue is delicious, so you needn't drive farther unless you're a true barbecue aficionado. Luling is divided down the middle by railroad tracks. Where the highway crosses the tracks, look for **City Market** (✆ **830/875-9019**) on the left, a few doors down at 633 E. Davis St. It's open Monday through Saturday until 6pm. Luling is also known for watermelon and celebrates with a late-June festival called the **Watermelon Thump.** If you arrive during the festival, it may be too crowded to score some barbecue. No problem: Head just 15 miles up the road to Lockhart.

Lockhart

Texans flock to this little town (pop. 12,700), which boasts of being the "Barbecue Capital of Texas." It's centered by an ornate sandstone courthouse. My favorite place for wonderful, truly authentic Texas barbecue is **Smitty's Market,** 208 S. Commerce St. (www.smittysmarket.com; ✆ **512/ 398-9344**). Also good is its feuding sibling barbecue joint **Kreuz Market,** 619 N. Colorado St. (www.kreuzmarket.com; ✆ **512/398-2361**), and **Black's Barbecue,** 215 N. Main St. (www.blacksbbq.com; ✆ **512/398-2712**). At Smitty's, even the walls are smoke colored, and you practically have to step over the open fire pits in the floor to get your meat. The town has a pretty little library, several antiques shops, and some nice old houses, and it's a quick jump onto the 130 Toll Road to race back to Seguin and San Antonio when you are ready to get back. The speed limit is 85 mph on this stretch of road, so enjoy the ride but be on the lookout for hogs and deer crossing the road.

HILL COUNTRY SIDE TRIPS FROM SAN ANTONIO

San Antonio lies at the southern edge of the Hill Country, Austin at its eastern edge. The interstate highway (I-35) that runs between these two cities parallels a geological feature called the Balcones Escarpment, a fault zone created when the Edwards Plateau, a thick shelf of limestone, was gently pushed up about 1,000 feet above the coastal plains. This plateau extends for hundreds of miles north and west of San Antonio and Austin; the part closest to these cities is called the Hill Country. The extra elevation makes the climate a little milder, and the water pouring through the limestone creates an abundance of natural springs (and lots of caverns and caves, too).

In the 19th century, these features attracted many German and Czech settlers who were fleeing the social upheavals in Europe. They established small towns that now dot the area and add a little contrast to the prevailing cowboy culture. The mild climate, rolling hills, and abundant springs continue to attract visitors, with summer camps, guest ranches, and resorts celebrating the great outdoors. Wildflowers, especially bluebonnets and Indian paintbrush, line the roadways here in spring. My favorite Hill Country town is **Fredericksburg** (see chapter 9), but the towns below are the most appealing ones closest to San Antonio.

Boerne

The seat of Kendall County, Boerne has more than 10,000 residents. It was founded in 1849 by German settlers who had come to Texas earlier to form a utopian community in an area northwest of Austin. That community disintegrated, thanks, in part, to poor location. This wasn't a problem for Boerne, located on the banks of Cibolo Creek. In fact, it actually developed a reputation for a healthful environment and by the 1880s became a popular health resort.

Despite being so close to San Antonio—so close, in fact, they seem to have grown together on I-10 W—Boerne has retained its charming small-town atmosphere. It's known for the **Boerne Village Band,** an old-time brass band, of which there are several in central Texas but few as good. It occasionally holds concerts in the gazebo on the main plaza and bills itself as the oldest continuously operating German band in the world outside Germany (it first tuned up in 1860). Boerne is also known for its collection of 19th-century limestone buildings in the old downtown area. These buildings include a small historical museum, boutiques, and restaurants. Most are along the *Hauptstrasse,* or main street, which is decorated with old-fashioned lampposts and German street signs. Here, you'll find lots of crafts and antiques shops. The **Dickens on Main** festival is a big draw each December in Boerne. Antiques shopping is a big draw too, as are the many art galleries and restaurants along Main Street.

One of the most popular sights around Boerne is the **Cave Without a Name,** 325 Kreutzberg Rd., 12 miles NE of Boerne (www.cavewithoutaname.com; ✆ **830/537-4212**). Hour-long tours of six large chambers are offered daily. The chambers are well lit, with plenty of stalactites and stalagmites. It's open Memorial Day through Labor Day daily 9am to 6pm (last tour 5pm), and off season daily 10am to 5pm (last tour 4pm). Admission is $20 adults and $10 children. The cave is closed on Thanksgiving and Christmas.

Bandera

Bandera, the self-proclaimed "Cowboy Capital of the World," is a small town of about 850 inhabitants 30 miles west of Boerne. It began as a lumber camp and is now a popular getaway for city folk to come and stay at dude ranches and enjoy rodeos and other cowboy activities. It's a commercial center for all the surrounding guest ranches and working ranches. At first glance, it doesn't look like much, but if you walk around, hang out at the restaurants, and stick your head in some shops, it still feels like you're miles from anywhere. People are open and friendly, and most have an unhurried way about them.

Many people come to Bandera for **horseback riding,** and most of the guest ranches offer horseback rides for day-trippers; the going rate is $35 to $40 an hour. But it's even easier if you elect to stay at a guest ranch like the **Mayan Ranch** (www.mayanranch.com; ✆ **830/796-3312** or 460-3036) or **Rancho Cortez,** 872 Hay Hollar Rd. (www.ranchocortez.com; ✆ **830/460-6221**). It's also one of the best ways to experience the beautiful countryside—many of these ranches are adjacent to the Hill Country State Natural Area, home to 40 miles of multi-use trails in rugged, undeveloped terrain.

You can also go **tubing or kayaking** on pretty little Medina River, which runs right by town. Outfitters include **Bandera Beach Club,** 1106 Cherry St. (https://banderabeachclub.wordpress.com; ✆ **830/796-3227**), and the **Medina River Company,** 1114 Main St. (www.facebook.com/themedinarivercompany; ✆ **830/796-3600**).

Don't miss **Arkey Blue's Silver Dollar Saloon ★★** (✆ **830/796-8826**), a genuine spit-and-sawdust cowboy honky-tonk on Main Street, which is usually called Arkey's. It's been a Bandera bar for almost 50 years. Another popular spot, the **Longhorn Saloon,** 1307 Main St. (www.longhornsaloonbandera.com; ✆ **830/796-3600**), is a Texas honky-tonk and music venue, where in December locals and visitors gather for **Singing in the Saddle,** a Christmas caroling trail ride around town. Rent a horse at the bar, or ride in the wagon. Afterward, enjoy hot cocoa at the chuckwagon.

AUSTIN

The city's unofficial slogan, "Keep Austin Weird," alludes to the capital city's progressive mindset and steadfast bohemian vibe. But this self-proclaimed "Live Music Capital of the World" is not nearly as weird as it is wonderful. Lakes and hills to the west roll into town, creating a verdant urban tableau. Hiking and biking trails, gardens and greenbelts abound. With a smokin' music scene, a world-class university, and a reputation as a creative cultural oasis, Austin is as fun as it is, well, weird.

9

In almost anything you read or hear about Austin, you will be told that it is a laid-back city. In fact, "laid-back" has become Austin's defining trait. First-time visitors get here and expect to find a city whose denizens all move about in the unhurried "Dazed and Confused" manner of Willie Nelson. They must feel a little put upon when they drive into town, only to find debilitating traffic, aggressive drivers, and a brash downtown skyline of skyscrapers and cranes.

Over the years, Austin has gotten bigger, and its once fringe neighborhoods are being gentrified by hipsters, but for the most part it hasn't lost its essential nature. Stay here for a couple of days and the laid-back quality will sink in. Austinites are personable, gracious, and open, and for them, the simple pleasures of life hold a great deal more attraction than the rat race. At times, it seems that everyone you meet is either a musician or a massage therapist, or has some sort of alternative career. The guy behind the convenience store counter could quite possibly have a PhD. People come to the University of Texas and tend to stay after graduation. The city's most recent James Beard award winner for "Best Chef Southwest," Aaron Franklin, only makes barbecue.

Austinites of all walks of life enjoy the outdoors. Barton Springs is the preferred spot for a swim; the popular hike-and-bike trail that encircles Town Lake is a favorite place for either a leisurely walk or a serious run. The city streets and bike lanes are filled with Austin's many cyclists. Just outside of town are several parks, nature preserves, rivers, and lakes. Hand in hand with this love of the outdoors is a strong environmental consciousness, which is reflected in the local government. Austin leads the nation in green energy production, has the most aggressive recycling and energy conservation programs in the state, and, though starting late, has instituted programs to reduce traffic and urban sprawl.

Finally, you can't talk about Austin for very long without mentioning the rather large university at its center. The University of Texas (UT) has brought thousands of bright, young students here who, once they get their degrees, decide they don't want to leave. So they stay and add to a large pool of educated people seeking a livelihood. This has attracted large, high-tech companies that need an educated workforce. Austin has also been fertile ground for many local start-up companies in all kinds of fields.

Austin is now big enough to be many things to many people. To me, it's the creative center and social and environmental conscience of Texas. To borrow a line from "Bennie and the Jets": "Oh, but it's weird and it's wonderful."

ORIENTATION

Arriving

BY PLANE The **Austin-Bergstrom International Airport (AUS)** (www.ci.austin.tx.us/austinairport; ✆ **512/530-ABIA [2242]**) is on the site of the former Bergstrom Air Force Base, just off Hwy. 71 (Ben White Blvd.) and only 8 miles southwest of the capitol. A visitor information booth on the lower level of the terminal is open daily from 7am to 11pm.

Taxis usually form a line outside the terminal, though occasionally you won't find any waiting. To ensure off-hour pickup in advance, phone **American Yellow Checker Cab** (✆ **512/452-9999**) before you leave home. The ride between the airport and downtown costs around $25, including tip.

If you're not in a huge rush to get to your hotel, **SuperShuttle** (www.supershuttle.com; ✆ **800/258-3826** or 512/258-3826) is a less expensive alternative to cabs, offering comfortable minivan service to hotels and residences. Prices range from $15 one-way ($29 round-trip) to a downtown hotel to $33 ($63 round-trip) to a hotel in the northwestern part of town. (***Note:*** Book online, and save $3 on a one-way fare or $6 round-trip.) The drawback is that you often share your ride with several others, who may be dropped off first. You don't have to book in advance for pickups at the airport, but you must phone 24 hours ahead to arrange a pickup when departing.

For $1.75, you can go from the airport to downtown or the university area on a city bus called the **Airport Flyer** (No. 100). It runs until about midnight on weekdays and 2am on weekends. The passenger pickup is outside the arrival gates, close to the end of the concourse. Buses depart about every 30 minutes. You can grab a route schedule from the city's visitor information office, by the baggage carousels. Or you can download it from the **Capital Metro Transit** website (www.capmetro.org).

Most of the **major car-rental companies** have outlets at the airport. The trip from the airport to downtown by car or taxi can take anywhere from 20 to 45 minutes, much more if you're headed to north Austin. During rush hour, there are often backups along highways 290/71.

BY TRAIN The **Amtrak** station (www.amtrak.com; ✆ **512/476-5684**) is at Lamar and West First Street, in the southwest part of downtown. There are generally a few cabs waiting to meet the trains, but if you don't see one, you'll find a list of phone numbers for taxi companies posted near the pay phones. Some of the downtown hotels provide courtesy pickup from the train station. A cab ride shouldn't run more than $6 (there's a $3 minimum charge).

Capital MetroRail has a 32-mile line from Leander, Texas (northwest of Austin) to downtown, and also offers reliable service Monday through Friday between Highland Mall and downtown (with a station outside the Austin Convention Center on 4th St. btw. Neches and Trinity sts.). Visitors may find less expensive lodging near Highland Mall and take the rail into the downtown area. There is also a station at Martin Luther King Blvd. within walking distance of the UT Campus. Bikes are always welcome aboard MetroRail, too. Day passes and 10-pass booklets are available, but a single ride fare is $1.25 for adults and 60¢ for those holding a Reduced Fare ID Card, available through Capital Metro to seniors 65 and older, Medicare card holders, riders with disabilities, and students and members of the military with ID.

BY BUS The Capitol Metro **bus terminal** is near Highland Mall, about 20 minutes north of downtown and close to the I-35 motel zone. There are some hotels within walking distance, and many others a short cab ride away; a few taxis usually wait outside the station. If you want to go downtown, you can catch either bus No. 7 (Duval) or bus No. 10 (Red River) from the bus stop across the street. A cab ride downtown—about 10 to 20 minutes away on the freeway—should cost around $10.

Visitor Information

The **Austin Visitor Center**, downtown at 602 E. Fourth St. (www.austintexas.org; ✆ **866/462-8784**), is open Monday through Saturday 9am to 5pm and Sunday 10am to 5pm (closed Thanksgiving, Christmas, and Easter). You can pick up tourist information pamphlets downtown at the **Old Bakery and Emporium,** 1006 Congress Ave. (✆ **512/974-1300**), open Tuesday to Saturday 9am to 4pm. Don't miss the **Texas Capitol Visitors Center,** 112 E. 11th St. (www.tspb.texas.gov/prop/tcvc/cvc/cvc.html; ✆ **512/305-8400**), a Texas Department of Transportation travel center with info on the entire state—the building alone, in a graciously restored 1856 government building, is worth a visit. It's open Monday through Saturday 9am to 5pm and Sunday noon to 5pm, and it's closed on major holidays.

For entertainment listings, pick up the free alternative newspaper, the ***Austin Chronicle,*** distributed to stores, hotels, and restaurants around town every Thursday. It's got a close rival in ***XLent,*** the free weekend entertainment guide put out by the city's daily newspaper, *Austin-American Statesman,* which also comes out on Thursday.

City Layout

In 1839, Austin was laid out in a grid on the northern shore of the Colorado River, bounded by Shoal Creek to the west and Waller Creek to the east. The section of the river abutting the original settlement is now known as Lady Bird

Lake, and the city has spread far beyond its original borders in all directions. Cities like Round Rock and Georgetown to the north and Cedar Park to the northwest have grown together to create a new north Austin area. To the south, towns like Buda are bumping into the south Austin border. The land to the east is flat Texas prairie; the rolling Hill Country begins on the west side of town.

MAIN ARTERIES & STREETS I-35, forming the border between central and east Austin, is the main north-south thoroughfare; Loop 1, usually called Mo-Pac (it follows the course of the Missouri-Pacific railroad), is the west-side equivalent. Hwy. 290, running east and west, merges with I-35 where it comes in on the north side of town, briefly reestablishing its separate identity on the south side of town before merging with Hwy. 71 (which is called Ben White Blvd. btw. Hwy. 183 and Lamar Blvd.). Hwy. 290 and Hwy. 71 split up again in Oak Hill, on the west side of town. The Pickle Parkway, Austin's infamous 80–85 mph toll road (Texas State Highway 130) edges Austin to the east, making it easy to travel quickly between just above San Antonio at Seguin along Interstate 10 and Georgetown (you can make it from beginning to end in 1 hour, because the speed limit here is the highest in the nation). Not confused enough yet? Hwy. 2222 changes its name from Koenig to Northland and, west of Loop 360, to Bullcreek, while, in the north, Hwy. 183 is called Research Boulevard. (Looking at a map should make all this clear as mud.) Important north-south city streets include Lamar, Guadalupe, and Burnet. If you want to get across town north of the river, use Cesar Chavez Street (once known as First St.), 15th Street (which turns into Enfield west of Lamar), Martin Luther King, Jr., Boulevard (the equivalent of 19th St., and often just called MLK), 38th Street, or 45th Street.

Neighborhoods in Brief

Although Austin, designed to be the capital of the independent Republic of Texas, has a planned, grand city center similar to that of Washington, D.C., the city has spread out far beyond those original boundaries. These days, with a few exceptions detailed below, locals tend to speak in terms of landmarks (the University of Texas) or geographical areas (east Austin) rather than neighborhoods.

Downtown The original city, laid out by Edwin Waller in 1839, runs roughly north from the Colorado River. The river has been dammed in several places, forming a series of lakes. By downtown, it is called Lady Bird Lake (though long-time locals still call it by its former name, Town Lake—it was renamed in honor of former first lady Lady Bird Johnson a few weeks after she died, in July 2007). The first street on the north shore of Lady Bird Lake used to be called First Street; now it's called **Cesar Chavez Street** (though again, long-time locals sometimes still call it First Street). Downtown extends north up to 11th Street, where the capitol building stands. The main north-south street is **Congress Avenue.** It runs from the river to the capitol. Downtown's eastward limit is the I-35 freeway, and its westward limit is Lamar Boulevard. This is a prime sightseeing (it includes the capitol and several historic districts) and hotel area, with music clubs, restaurants, shops, and galleries. There are a lot of clubs on and around **Sixth Street,** just east of Congress, in the **Warehouse District,** centered on Third and Fourth streets just west of Congress, and in the **Red River District,** on (where else?) Red River, between Sixth and 10th streets. A new hot spot? **Rainey Street,** near I-35 and Lady Bird Lake, a recently gentrified area in the southeast corner of downtown that is home to 31 pre-1930s bungalows, most of which have been turned into hipster bars, coffee shops, restaurants, and clubs, with a strip of condos and high-rise residences popping up there too.

South Austin For a long time, not a lot was happening south of Town Lake. This was largely a residential area—a mix of working-class folks and bohemians lived here. **South Congress** (also known as SoCo and the Avenue), the sleepy stretch of Congress Avenue running through the middle of south Austin, was lined with cheap motels. Then, in the 1980s, it started taking off. The area became attractive to store and restaurant owners who liked the proximity to downtown without the high rents. Trendy shops moved into the old storefronts. Yuppies started buying houses in the adjoining neighborhoods. Today, south Austin is one of the preferred places to live. **Fairview Park** and **Travis Heights,** adjoining neighborhoods between Congress and I-35, are perhaps the most popular.

Central Austin This is a larger area that includes downtown and the university campus. It's not a precisely defined area. If you were to travel north from Town Lake through the downtown area and past the capitol, you would come across a complex of state government office buildings (btw. 15th and 19th sts.). Past that would be the University of Texas campus (19th to 26th sts.). Farther north, you get to the **Hyde Park** neighborhood (35th to 51st sts.). Hyde Park got its start in 1891 as one of Austin's first planned suburbs; renovation of its Victorian and early Craftsman houses began in the 1970s, and now there's a real neighborhood feel to this pretty, tree-lined area. Beyond Hyde Park, numbered streets disappear. You pass through a couple of neighborhoods, and eventually you come to Research Boulevard. For a lot of Austinites, this is where central Austin ends and north Austin begins.

West Austin West of Lamar is **Clarksville,** formerly a black community founded in the 1870s by freed slaves. It's now a hilly neighborhood of small, old houses that command high prices. To the west of Clarksville, on the other side of the Mo-Pac Freeway, is a more tony old-school/old-money neighborhood called **Tarrytown,** which extends as far as Lake Austin (upstream from downtown, the Colorado river bends around in a more northerly direction, where another dam creates this long, narrow lake). Just west of the UT Austin campus, between "The Drag" (Guadalupe St.) and Lamar is considered "West Campus."

East Side East of I-35 are several neighborhoods that are predominantly Hispanic and African American. Because it has a central location, this area is gentrifying at a swift pace and is the hot place for new brick-and-mortar restaurants, food trucks, trendy bars, and chic little bungalow hotels. The wildly popular **Franklin Barbecue** restaurant (p. 331) is just off I-35 at East 11th Street.

West Lake The name denotes the townships that are on the opposite side of Lake Austin from west Austin. This is an affluent suburban area that includes the communities of **Rollingwood** and **Westlake Hills.** If you head upstream to the next dam, you come to Lake Travis, a large lake with lots of marinas and lakeside communities, such as **Lakeway.** But you don't have to live here to play here: This is also where those who live in central Austin come to splash around and kick back on nice weekends.

Northwest This is where most of the high-tech industry is located. It is largely suburban. It includes the Arboretum, a large mall and surrounding shopping area, and a tony outdoor shopping village (with condos and hotels) called the Domain. Farther north are the bedroom communities of Round Rock, Georgetown, and Cedar Park.

Getting Around

BY PUBLIC TRANSPORTATION

Austin's public transportation system, **Capital Metropolitan Transportation Authority** (www.capmetro.org), operates more than 50 bus routes. A day pass on Metro costs $2.50; express service from various Park & Ride lots costs $3.50. You'll need exact change or fare tickets (see below) to board the bus. Call ✆ **800/474-1201** or 512/474-1200 (TTY 512/385-5872) for point-to-point routing information. You can also purchase tickets online (https://marketplace.bytemark.co/marketplace/cmta).

Cap Metro now has **light-rail service** between downtown and the bedroom communities in the north (see above). This service only runs during commuting times Monday to Friday. Discussion is underway about expanding service times, so check the Capital Metro website to see if hours have changed.

BY CAR

With its lack of traffic planning, driving in Austin is a bit of a challenge. Don't fall into a driver's daze anywhere in town; you need to be as vigilant on the city streets as you are on highways. The former are rife with signs that suddenly insist LEFT LANE MUST TURN LEFT or RIGHT LANE MUST TURN RIGHT—generally positioned so they're noticeable only when it's too late to switch.

The highways offer their own challenges. I-35—nicknamed "the NAFTA highway" because of the big rigs speeding up from Mexico—is mined with tricky on-and-off ramps and, around downtown, a confusing complex of upper and lower levels; it's easy to miss your exit or find yourself exiting when you don't want to. The rapidly developing area to the northwest, where Hwy. 183 connects I-35 with Mo-Pac and the Capital of Texas Highway, requires particular vigilance, as the connections occur abruptly. If you're driving to San Antonio from Austin, you may want to avoid I-35 altogether by taking the "Pickle Parkway" (locals never call it that, though), Texas State Highway 130, a toll road that will take you from an onramp near the Austin airport all the way to Seguin, 35 miles south of town (about 35 miles east of San Antonio). There's little traffic on the toll road, and it feels like a Texas-version of the Autobahn, with a posted speed of 85 mph on most of that stretch.

PARKING Unless you have congressional plates, you're likely to find the selection of parking spots downtown extremely limited during the week; as a result, lots of downtown restaurants offer valet parking (with hourly rates in the range of $4–$6). There are a number of lots around the area, costing anywhere from $5 to $7 per hour, but the most convenient ones tend to fill up quickly. If you're lucky enough to find a metered spot, it'll run you 75¢ per hour, with a 2-hour limit, so bring change. Although there's virtually no street parking available near the capitol before 5pm during the week, there is a free visitor garage at 15th and San Jacinto streets (2-hr. time limit). It is free for first 2 hours and $1 each 30 mins thereafter.

In the university area, trying to find a spot near the shopping strip (Guadalupe St.) known as the Drag can be just that. However, cruise the side streets and you'll find a pay lot that's not filled. The two most convenient on-campus parking garages are located near San Jacinto and East 26th streets and off 25th Street between San Antonio and Nueces. There's also a (free!) parking lot near the LBJ Library, but it's a good walk from the central campus. Log on to **http://parking.utexas.edu/maps/index.html** to locate additional places to drop off your car.

BY TAXI

The major cab companies in Austin are **Austin Cab** (✆ **512/478-2222**) and **American Yellow Checker Cab** (✆ **512/452-9999**). The flag-drop charge is $2.05, and it's $2.05 for each mile after that. When gas is expensive, taxis will add a fuel surcharge.

Uber and Lyft currently are not available in Austin (though they may be available in its surrounding areas); however, **Fasten, Fare, Get Me, Ride Austin, Wingz,** and **zTrip** are all popular rideshare apps that Austinites depend on when they need a lift.

BY BICYCLE

Austin now has its own public bikeshare program, **Austin BCycle (B-cycle),** with bikes available throughout the city at B-stations. Get the details, plus B-station locations and bike routes at **https://austin.bcycle.com**. Purchase passes at B-stations for unlimited 60-minute rides ($4 for each additional half-hour). A 24-hour pass is $12, a weekender pass is $15, and monthly membership is $11 ($80 for entire year). For more on where to bike in Austin, go to "Staying Active," p. 304.

[Fast FACTS] AUSTIN

Doctor The **Medical Exchange** (✆ **512/458-1121**) and **Seton Medical Center** (✆ **512/324-1000**) both have physician referral services.

Drugstores The city has many Walgreens, CVS, and Randalls drugstores; most HEB grocery stores also have pharmacies. Several Walgreens are open 24 hours. Call ✆ **800/925-4733** to find the Walgreens branch nearest you.

Emergencies Call ✆ **911** for police, the fire department, or an ambulance.

Hospitals **University Medical Center Brackenridge,** 601 E. 15th St. (www.seton.net/locations/brackenridge; ✆ **512/324-7000**); **St. David's,** 3801 N. Lamar Blvd. (www.stdavids.com; ✆ **512/407-7000**); and **Seton Medical Center Austin,** 1201 W. 38th St. (www.seton.net/locations/smc; ✆ **512/324-1000**), have good and convenient emergency-care facilities.

Newspapers & Magazines The daily *Austin American-Statesman* (www.austin360.com) is the only large-circulation mainstream newspaper in town. The *Austin Chronicle* (www.auschron.com), a free alternative weekly, focuses on the arts, entertainment, and politics. Monday through Friday, the University of Texas publishes the surprisingly sophisticated *Daily Texan* (www.dailytexanonline.com) newspaper, covering everything from on-campus news to international events.

Police The nonemergency number for the Austin Police Department is ✆ **311.**

Post Office The city's **main post office** is located at 8225 Cross Park Dr. (✆ **512/342-1259**); more convenient to tourist sights are the **Capitol Station,** 111 E. 17th St., in the LBJ Building, and the **Downtown Station,** 510 Guadalupe St. For information on other locations, call ✆ **800/275-8777.**

Safety Austin has been ranked one of the five safest cities in the United States, but that doesn't mean you can throw common sense to the wind. It's never a good idea to walk down dark streets alone at night, and major tourist areas always attract pickpockets, so keep your purse or wallet in a safe place. Although Sixth Street itself tends to be busy, use caution on the side streets in the area.

Taxes The tax on hotel rooms is 9%. Sales tax, added to restaurant bills as well as to other purchases, is 8.25%.

WHAT TO SEE & DO

Austin is a friendly city, and like most Southerners, Austinites are approachable, hospitable, and happy to offer directions and advice. So don't hesitate to ask for help here. If you'd rather turn to experts for advice, then be sure to visit the city's Visitor Information Center, 209 E. 6th St. There you'll find helpful information, maps, and brochures and can arrange for free walking tours or pick up maps for self-guided tours; this is the point of departure for walking tours and motorized city tours (and the center will know if a tour is cancelled). If you have a car, be sure to drive northwest of town and see the Highland Lake country—or at least drive along scenic FM 2222 toward **The Oasis ★** (p. 329). You'll see how green and lovely Austin is and why so many people love it here.

What sets Austin apart from other Texas cities, and what puts it on all those "most livable" lists, is the amount of green space and outdoor activities available to its citizens, whose attitude toward the outdoors borders on nature worship. From bats and birds to Barton Springs, from the Highland Lakes to the hike-and-bike trails, Austin lays out the green carpet for its visitors. You'd be hard-pressed to find a city that has more to offer fresh-air enthusiasts.

The Top Attractions

DOWNTOWN

Texas State Capitol ★★★ Set on a hill overlooking Austin's downtown, the pink-granite-clad Texas State Capitol opened to the public in 1888 on the 52nd anniversary of the Battle of San Jacinto (after which Texas gained its independence). At the time it was touted as the world's seventh-largest building. Today, skyscrapers and high-rise hotels dwarf the capitol, obstructing its once iconic silhouette. Yet in true "everything's bigger in Texas" fashion, the Texas capitol remains the largest state capitol in the U.S.

Built in Italian Renaissance Revival style using limestone from Austin's Oak Hill area and granite from Granite Mountain, 75 miles away, the capitol took 6 years to build. Nearly a century later, in February 6, 1983, a fire broke out that nearly destroyed the structure. Restoration projects lasted through the 1990s, and by 1993 the $75-million, four-story, underground Capitol Extension was completed, a building that came to be called "the inside out, upside down capitol" because much of the square footage was underground. The light-filled tunnels now connect the capitol and four other state buildings beneath the streets. Later restoration projects refurbished the original capitol and its bucolic 2¼-acre grounds, dotted with monuments, statues, and gardens.

Today visitors come to see the Capitol's regal rotunda and stately dome. Marble statues of Sam Houston and Stephen F. Austin, by Texas sculptress Elisabet Ney, stand near the south entrance. House and Senate chambers are located on the second level at opposite sides of the rotunda, and the third floor has a visitors' balcony overlooking the chambers—a fun place to pop in and see politicians at work when the legislature is in session.

GOING batty

Think Austin isn't all that weird? Then why is one of its top attractions a bridge where folks line up to see bats? It's true: The largest urban bat population in North America is found in Austin, and on many evenings throughout the year, visitors can watch about 1.5-million Mexican free-tailed bats leave their roosts under the Ann W. Richards Congress Avenue Bridge shortly before dusk and fly over Lady Bird Lake (aka Town Lake), moving eerily through the air like a column of smoke above the river.

Each spring (usually around March), free-tailed bats migrate from central Mexico to various roost sites like this in the Southwest. They first came in 1980, following a reconstruction of the South Congress Street bridge, when about 750,000 pregnant bats discovered that it was a perfect place to raise their pups. In time, the bat population grew. By August, each evening around just before sundown, their offspring leave the bridge looking for bugs. Today the bat population taking off from the bridge may consume anywhere from 10,000 to 30,000 pounds of insects in a single night, just another reason why locals go so batty over their bats. By fall (usually Nov), the pups are old enough to fly back south on the winds of a cool blue Norther.

When the bats are in town, a kiosk designed to educate visitors and dispel some scary bat myths is set up on the south bank of the river, east of the bridge. You'll learn, for example, that bats are not rodents, they're not blind, and they're not in the least bit interested in getting in your hair. Austin-based **Bat Conservation International** (www.batcon.org; ✆ **512/327-9721** or 800/538-2287 for catalog) offers interesting bat facts, as well as bat-related retail items. Want to know what time the bats are expected to emerge from the bridge? Simply phone the *Austin American-Statesman* **Bat Hot Line** (✆ **512/327-9721**). Austin is so crazy about its bats that folks here celebrate with an annual **Bat Fest** (www.roadwayevents.com/event/bat-fest; ✆ **512/441-9015**) on the bridge each summer.

Tip: If you think you've arrived at the bridge too late and fear you may have missed the bats, just wait: Sometimes the bats don't leave all at once. If you can still hear chattering sounds from beneath the bridge, sit tight; more bats may yet emerge.

Visitors can take a free 30- to 45-minute guided Capitol tour or simply explore the buildings on their own. Be sure to stop at the **Capitol Complex Visitors Center** (see p. 299).

11th and Congress sts. www.tspb.state.tx.us. ✆ **512/463-0063.** Free admission. Mon–Fri 7am–10pm; Sat–Sun 9am–8pm; hours extended during legislative sessions (held in odd years, starting in Jan, for 140 straight calendar days). Closed major holidays. Free guided tours Mon–Fri 8:30am–4:30pm; Sat 9:30am–3:30pm; Sun noon–3:30. Bus: Multiple bus lines.

SOUTH AUSTIN

Barton Springs Pool ★★★ Some say the pulsing waters of Barton Springs are the beating heart of Austin, and Tonkawa Native Americans who settled along these banks thought the springs sacred for their spiritual purification powers. Many area residents still attest to the springs' refreshing and restorative gifts. Here within Zilker Park's 358 acres, the pool is fed by about

32 million gallons of water, which bubbles to the surface each day from the underground Edwards Aquifer. Although the 300-yard-long pool still has its original limestone bottom (its depths range from 0–18 ft.), the banks of the pool were edged with concrete in the 1920s when the springs were dammed. The bathhouse, now operated by the Parks and Recreation department, was built in the 1940s. Today more than 800,000 people visit this pool each year, and topless sunbathing is even permitted.

Maintaining temperatures of 68°F to 70°F, the cool clear water is invigorating in summer and temperate in winter, when some brave swimmers still take early morning dips. Lifeguards are on duty for most of the day, and the bathhouse offers changing areas and a gift shop.

Zilker Park, 2201 Barton Springs Rd. www.austintexas.gov/department/barton-springs-pool. ✆ **512/476-9044.** Admission $3 adults; $8 non-resident adults; $2 ages 12–17 ($4 non-resident); $1 seniors and children 11 and under ($4 non-resident seniors & children). Admission charged only after 8am mid-Mar to Oct; and free for early birds. Daily 5am–10pm except during pool maintenance (Thurs 9am–7pm). Bus: 30 (Barton Creek Square).

Lady Bird Johnson Wildflower Center ★★★ The late First Lady, Mrs. Lyndon B. Johnson (called "Lady Bird" since childhood) and actress Helen Hayes founded Austin's glorious wildflower center in 1982. This delightful 279-acre botanic garden, moved from its original East Austin site in 1995 and now affiliated with the University of Texas, not only celebrates the state's wildflowers, but has expanded its mission to showcase the state's native plants in a number of gardens and natural areas, including a butterfly garden, 2 miles of trails, and a 16-acre arboretum. With its focus on the study and conservation of native flora, the facility's research library is the largest in the U.S. For visitors, the main attractions include an observation tower, the walking paths, a pleasant cafe, and a large, inviting gift store. Many health-conscious locals and older folks are members at the Wildflower Center and use the paths for their daily walks. Spring is a beautiful time to come, when bluebonnets and Indian paintbrush are in bloom. ***Note:*** Pets are not allowed.

4801 La Crosse Ave. www.wildflower.org. ✆ **512/232-0100.** Admission $10 adults, $8 students and seniors 65 and older, $4 children 5–17, free for children 4 and under. Daily 9am–5pm. Take Loop 1 (Mo-Pac) south to La Crosse Ave. and turn left. Open most major holidays.

CENTRAL AUSTIN

A number of topnotch, well-curated museums, research libraries, and special archives are within walking distance of one another on the University of Texas at Austin campus, collectively known as **Austin's Cultural Campus** (www.austinsculturalcampus.org), including the **Bullock Museum,** the **LBJ Library and Museum,** the **Blanton Museum of Art,** the **Harry Ransom Center**, and the **Texas Memorial Museum.** All are reviewed below.

Blanton Museum of Art ★★ One of many well-curated museums, research libraries, and special archives on the University of Texas at Austin campus, this museum is home to most of UT's remarkable art holdings. It's also one of the largest university art museums in the U.S., its permanent collection comprising almost 18,000 works. Recently reopened after a 2017 renovation—including the introduction of new gallery spaces showcasing nearly twice as many works of art as before—the Blanton's galleries are devoted to European Art, modern and contemporary Latin American art, art from the ancient and Spanish Americas, and Native American art. The museum also offers three rotating galleries: the Paper Vault, Film & Video, and the Contemporary Project. Music events, tours and gallery talks are frequently held throughout the year. The **Blanton Café** is a delightful place to have lunch, and a museum shop sells art-inspired souvenirs.

Martin Luther King Blvd., at Congress Ave. www.blantonmuseum.org. ✆ **512/471-7324** or 512/471-5482 (front desk) and 512/471-7324 (recorded information). $9 adults, $7 seniors (65+), $5 youths 13–21, free for children 12 and under. Free admission on Thursdays. Tues–Fri 10am–5pm; Sat 11am–5pm; Sun 1–5pm. Open 10am–9pm on third Thursday of each month. Closed Mon and major holidays. Bus: UT Shuttle.

Bullock Texas State History Museum ★★★ The bold, 35-foot-tall bronze star out front sets the tone for this dynamic, first-rate museum. In fact, the museum is one of the best in the state, telling the story of Texas in a fresh and entertaining way, through creative thematic exhibits and an eclectic collection of nearly 700 original artifacts—among them ornate Spanish colonial stirrups, a skull cast of a giant prehistoric crocodile, and a tattered 13-star American flag, hand sewn in 1790. The building itself is a beauty, with exterior walls clad in the same pink granite used in the Texas Capitol and topped by a gleaming copper dome. One of the biggest draws is the **La Belle Shipwreck** exhibit, which tells the remarkable story of French explorer Robert La Salle's historic voyage, a trip that spurred Spanish colonization and changed the course of Texas history. The actual ship's preserved and reconstructed hull is here, considered to be one of the most important shipwreck discoveries in North America. The museum offers a number of kid-friendly interactive/hands-on exhibits, and it is also home to the only IMAX with Laser film experience in the state on the biggest screen in Texas. The **Texas Spirit Theater** holds film programs exploring the diversity of Texas cinema and the art of filmmaking. Families can explore the museum and then stop for a snack at the **Story of Texas Cafe.**

1800 N. Congress Ave. www.thestoryoftexas.com. ✆ **512/936-8746.** Exhibit areas: $13 adults, $11 seniors 65 and over, military & college students, $9 youths 4–17, free for children under 4. IMAX Theater (documentaries): $9 adults, $8 seniors, military & college students, $7 youths. IMAX Theater (feature films): $14 adults, $12 seniors, military & college students, $11 youths. Texas Spirit Theater: $7 adults, $6 seniors, military & college students, $6 youths. Combination tickets available. Mon–Sat 9am–5pm; Sun noon–5pm. Phone or check website for additional IMAX evening hours. Closed Jan 1, Easter, Thanksgiving, and Dec 24–25. Bus: UT Shuttle.

LBJ Presidential Library ★★ A presidential library is only as interesting as the president it honors, and since our 36th president Lyndon Baines Johnson was a bigger-than-life, boot-wearing, cigar-smoking character (who may or may not have been involved in ballot-box-stuffing shenanigans), his presidential library and museum on the UT campus is equally fascinating. LBJ's popularity in Texas and his many successes in Washington are sometimes overlooked in light of his handling of the Vietnam War, but that's not the case here. The Library tells the tale of Johnson's long political career—beginning with his early years as a congressman all the way up to the Kennedy assassination, civil-rights battles, and groundbreaking Great Society legislation—through photographs, papers, campaign souvenirs, and personal mementos. LBJ recorded hundreds of hours of telephone conversations, and visitors can pick up one of the many phones in the library and listen to LBJ laconically conducting presidential business. My favorite exhibit is the remarkable (though not quite to scale) replica of LBJ's White House Oval Office. An animatronic LBJ, speaking in his thick Texas drawl, is simultaneously fascinating and creepy. My husband spent half our visit studying LBJ's shiny black, custom-built 1968 Lincoln Continental stretch limo, equipped with then state-of-the-art cassette player, TV, telephone, and reserve gas tank. The library was dedicated in 1971, and until his death in 1973, LBJ kept an office here, no doubt drinking in the impressive views of the UT campus.

University of Texas, 2313 Red River St. www.lbjlibrary.org. ✆ **512/721-0200.** Adults $8, seniors 62 and over and retired military with valid ID $5, children 13–17 and college students with ID $3. Free admission for children 12 and under & active duty military. Daily 9am–5pm. Closed Thanksgiving, Dec 25, and Jan 1. Bus: 15; UT shuttle.

More Attractions

DOWNTOWN

Brush Square Museums ★★ Brush Square, one of the oldest parks in Texas (plotted in 1839), is a mini museum row, with three little museums that are each well worth a visit. A good first stop is the **O. Henry House Museum,** the 1883–1895 home of author William Sidney Porter, who wrote indelible short stories (like "The Gift of the Magi") and novellas under the pen name O. Henry. In Austin, Porter published a popular satirical newspaper called *Rolling Stone* and was a draftsman in the Texas Land Grant office and a teller at the First National Bank of Austin—a business he is said to have embezzled from. The little Victorian cottage where Porter lived with his wife and daughter houses artifacts and memorabilia from his Austin years, including original furniture and personal belongings. If you're visiting in May, check the calendar for the annual O. Henry Pun-Off.

Next door, the 1869 home of Alamo survivor Susanna Dickinson Hannig houses the **Susanna Dickinson Museum.** The story of the life of Susanna Dickinson, one of only 22 survivors of Texas's bloody Battle of the Alamo, is full of heartache, surprises, and changes in fortune. Next door is the little **Austin Fire Museum,** only open on Saturday and Sunday.

The Brush Square museums are all free and centrally located downtown, within walking distance of restaurants, the Sixth Street Entertainment District, and the state capitol.

409 E. 5th St. www.brushsquaremuseums.org. ✆ **512/472-1903.** Free admission. Wed–Sun noon–5pm. Metered street parking only.

Capitol Complex Visitors Center ★ Texas's oldest surviving state office building still in use—older even than the state capitol and listed on the National Register of Historic Places—the historic 1857 General Land Office stands on the capitol grounds in the southeast corner, making it a convenient spot to house the Capitol Complex Visitors Center. With its Norman/Germanic-medieval style, mock-crenellated towers, parapets, and faux stone walls made of scored stucco, the building looks oddly out of place in the heart of downtown—but it also makes it easy for visitors to find. An exhibit on the building's first floor honors short-story writer O. Henry, who worked as a draftsman here from 1887–1891 (and based two stories on his experiences). Also on the first floor is a good gift shop selling books and Texas souvenirs. A tourist information desk on the first floor has a helpful staff and brochures and maps. The second floor is home to engaging exhibits and artifacts that offer an enlightening perspective on Texas history. A stop here before touring the Capitol is highly recommended.

112 E. 11th St. (southeast corner of capitol grounds). www.tspb.state.tx.us/prop/tcvc/cvc/cvc.html. ✆ **512/305-8400.** Free admission. Mon–Sat 9am–5pm; Sun noon–5pm.

The Contemporary Austin ★ Bringing together two very different but equally arresting spaces, the Contemporary Austin is two remarkable museums: the newly renovated **Jones Center** downtown and the 14-acre **Laguna Gloria** in west Austin. The edgy and modern Jones Center is the main exhibition space, with interesting and original exhibits showcasing contemporary art. The Jones's new **Moody Rooftop** is an open-air lounge for galas and gatherings. At Laguna Gloria, a divine turn-of-the-century mansion called the Driscoll Villa houses the lovely exhibition space. The **Betty and Edward Marcus Sculpture Park ★★** is integrated into the lush landscape of the Laguna Gloria grounds—a great place to stroll and enjoy a picnic, even when the villa isn't open.

Jones Center, 700 Congress Ave. (corner of 7th St. and Congress Ave.) and Laguna Gloria, 3809 W. 35th St. (exit W. 35th St. when heading north on MoPac/Loop 1). www.thecontemporaryaustin.org. ✆ **512/495-9224.** Admission $5 adults, $3 seniors 55 and over and students, free for military members and children 18 and under, $1 for all on Tues. Jones Center open Tues–Sat 11am–7pm; Sun Noon–5pm.

The Driskill Hotel ★★ It may seem odd to include a hotel on a list of Austin's best attractions, but we rarely bring visitors downtown without at least once strolling past reception or cutting through the upstairs lobby bar on our way to the Capitol. This place exudes class, Texas style, with inlaid marble floors, massive columns, hand-painted friezes on the walls, and a lounge with leather and cowhide and Remington-style bronze sculptures of cowboys and cattle. Texas legislators and lobbyists gather here on oversize Chesterfield sofas, glasses of bourbon in hand. Built by cattle baron and oilman Col. Jesse Driskill, who opened the hotel in 1886 and promptly named it after himself, the hotel features busts Driskill had made of himself and his two sons over the entrances. In fact, this place was so handsome and grand that the state legislature met here while the 1888 capitol was being built. Feel free to wander the hotel's grand halls. For a full hotel review, see p. 307.

604 Brazos St. www.driskillhotel.com. ✆ **512/439-7039.** Free admission. Open year-round.

Mexic-Arte Museum ★ One of very few Mexican-American art museums in the country, this is home to a small collection of 20th-century Mexican art, photos from the Mexican revolution, and a colorful array of masks from the Mexican state of Guerrero. It's also proud to own several prints by Mexican political printmaker and engraver José Guadalupe Posada. But the museum is perhaps best known for its annual "Young Latino Artists" show held each summer (check website for exact dates), where curators organize a delightful and eclectic exhibition featuring select artists. The museum also hosts the *Viva la Vida* (Live the Life) festival and parade, the city's largest and longest-running annual Day of the Dead celebration (in conjunction with the city of Austin) during the last weekend in October. The festival fills side streets and sidewalks with food booths and vendors' stalls, with music and dancing too. This little art museum stands in the heart of downtown at the corner of Congress Avenue and 5th Street, making it the perfect place to pop in as you're strolling back toward the Driskill Hotel or headed to see the Capitol.

419 Congress Ave. www.mexic-artemuseum.org. ✆ **512/480-9373.** Admission $5 adults, $4 seniors and students, $1 children 12 and under. Free admission on Sun. Mon–Thurs 10am–6pm; Fri–Sat 10am–5pm; Sun noon–5pm.

Texas Governor's Mansion ★ It seems only fitting that a Texas governor should have a classic ivory-hued, Southern-style colonnaded mansion in which to live, and since it's in Austin it should be within walking distance of the Capitol (many folks walk or bike to work in this progressive, "green" city). This Greek Revival–style manor was built in 1856 with a sunny veranda, floor-to-ceiling windows, and broad hallways. It's said to be the oldest continuously inhabited house in Texas and fourth-oldest governor's mansion in the U.S. that has been continuously occupied by a chief executive. The house has 25 rooms and 7 bathrooms. Sam Houston lived here with his large family; President William McKinley visited the mansion in 1901; the nation's second female governor, Miriam "Ma" Ferguson, hosted Will Rogers; and Governor John Connally recuperated here after he was shot in Dallas when President John F. Kennedy was assassinated. Arsonists set fire to the mansion in 2008, causing severe damage; it wasn't until 2013 that the restoration was completed and the house reopened for tours. Among the many historical artifacts is a desk belonging to Stephen F. Austin and portraits of Davy Crockett and Sam Houston.

1010 Colorado St. www.txfgm.org. ✆ **512/305-8524.** Free admission. 30-min. tours Wed–Fri 2–4pm by appointment only (email Mansion.Tours@tspb.texas.gov). All visitors must pass a background security screening and provide their name, date of birth, and government ID information at least a week prior to the tour. Closed some holidays and at the discretion of the governor. Parking in Capitol Visitors Parking Garage, 1201 San Jacinto St., btw. Trinity and San Jacinto sts.

CENTRAL

Elisabet Ney Museum ★★★ Tucked away in the trees along Waller Creek, just north of the UT campus, is artist Elisabet Ney's studio, which she named "Formosa." This unusual castle-like structure seems to spring from the mist like Brigadoon. If it feels as if you've stepped back in time and entered the grand studio of a celebrated sculptress—well, you have. Ney was the first woman trained in the art schools of Munich and Berlin. She became sculptor and confidante to King Ludwig II of Bavaria, for whom she created classically styled Romantic sculptures. Unfortunately, her relations with the democratic left forced her to emigrate to the U.S. in the 1860s. She settled on a farm in southeast Texas. In 1892, she revived her career with the commission for the monumental statues of Stephen F. Austin and Sam Houston now standing at the Texas State Capitol and built Formosa. She lived here until her death in 1907.

Ney became an important figure in the Austin arts community. Today, visitors can stand in her studio and see Ney's exquisite sculptures, including plaster working studies, marble busts, and an enormous plaster cast of Lady Macbeth (the final marble is on display at the Smithsonian). The museum also contains Ney's collection of studio portraits of European dignitaries, which she retrieved from Germany in 1902. The building is small, but you can climb the little tower for a view above the treetops.

304 E. 44th St. www.austintexas.gov/ElisabetNey. ✆ **512/974-1625.** Free admission. Wed–Sun noon–5pm; closed Mon and Tues. Bus: 1, 5, 7 and 338.

Harry Ransom Center ★★★ This place is not only the pride of the University of Texas, it's the pride of the entire state. A museum, research library, and archive, with a focus on cultural and literary artifacts, the Ransom Center is the caretaker and keeper of European and American treasures, including about a million rare books (including a Gutenberg Bible, one of only six complete copies in the U.S.); 42 million literary manuscripts (including works by Ernest Hemingway, James Joyce, John Steinbeck, and Tennessee Williams); 5 million photographs (including the world's first permanent photograph from nature); and more than 100,000 works of art (including works by Picasso and Frida Kahlo). This material is most often accessed by scholars, even though anyone can request to see it, but parts of the collection are regularly exhibited in the gallery on the ground floor. Fascinating exhibits have included handwritten short stories by Hemingway, and poetry scribbled on a lunch bag by e. e. cummings. Woodward and Bernstein's Watergate papers are here, too, along with three copies of the first folio of William Shakespeare's plays, a handwritten journal kept by Jack Kerouac, and Houdini's private papers. There's also an impressive collection of rare and valuable vintage comic books.

University of Texas, Harry Ransom Center, 21st and Guadalupe sts. www.hrc.utexas.edu. ✆ **512/471-8944.** Free admission. Galleries Mon–Wed and Fri 10am–5pm; Thurs 10am–7pm; Sat–Sun noon–5pm; call for reading-room hours. Tours daily at noon, Thurs at 6pm, Sat at 2pm, and Sun at 2pm. Closed university holidays. Bus: UT shuttle. MetroRail: Red Line to MLK, Jr. Station with transfer to 464 MLK, Jr./Capitol Connector or local route 18.

Texas Memorial Museum ★★ Suspended from the ceiling of its Great Hall is this museum's favorite native son, *Quetzalcoatlus northropi,* or Texas pterosaur, a 70- to 66–million-year-old reptile with a 40-foot wingspan. Excavated from a West Texas desert, the skeleton is the largest flying creature ever found. It's as dazzling as the museum's fist-size blue topaz, a 925-karat beauty dug out of the Texas hills. Austin's "first science museum" has many such treasures and outstanding exhibits on prehistoric life, fossils, minerals and meteorites, indigenous wildlife, and biological evolution. The floor below the Great Hall is the main paleontology exhibit, with even more skeletons. The museum has a gift shop, a good place to do early holiday shopping for its cool nature and science toys.

The University of Texas at Austin, 2400 Trinity St. www.tmm.utexas.edu. ✆ **512/471-1604.** Admission $4 ages 13 and up, $3 ages 2–12; college students $2, active or retired U.S. military $1. Tues–Sat 9am–5pm. Closed major holidays. Bus: UT shuttle.

Green Spaces

Umlauf Sculpture Garden & Museum ★★★ More a park than a museum, this is one of the most peaceful places in Austin. "Art framed by nature" is the concept behind this pleasant wooded garden and small studio museum at the edge of the Zilker Park grounds and Barton Springs. In 1985, former UT professor and famed sculptor Charles Umlauf and his wife, Angeline, donated their home, studio, and 168 pieces of sculpture to the city of Austin. Today Umlauf's whimsical and often oversize art, which ranges in style from realistic to abstract expressionism to lyrical abstraction, can be seen in both permanent and changing exhibitions inside the 1991 museum addition. More works are found outside in the garden. Locals recall how late in his life, Umlauf often walked these grounds and warmly greeted visitors. Austin is proud to be home to the largest collection of the sculptor's work, which is also in the collections of the Smithsonian and New York's Metropolitan Museum.

605 Robert E. Lee Rd. www.umlaufsculpture.org. ✆ **512/445-5582.** $5 adults, $3 seniors (60+), $1 students (with ID) and free children 12 & under and active military and their families. Tues–Fri 10am–4 pm; Sat/Sun noon–4pm. Bus: 30.

Zilker Botanical Garden ★★★ Austinites love the natural beauty of their city, and perhaps nowhere is such beauty so gracefully on display as at the Zilker Botanical Garden, set on the south banks of the Colorado River (aka Lady Bird Lake/Town Lake) not far from downtown. These 26 acres of fenced gardens are especially lovely in the spring, or almost anytime from March to October. I like to stroll here on weekend mornings with my daughter, stopping in the **Oriental Garden,** created by Japanese landscape architect Isamu Taniguchi when he was 70 years old. Zilker also has a rose garden, a garden of succulents, and children's gardens. In April and October the **Douglas Blachly Butterfly Trail** is aflutter with migrating butterflies. The dinosaur tracks in the 1½-acre **Hartman Prehistoric Garden** were discovered in the early 1900s and date back 100 million years. And if you come in spring, don't miss the annual creation of the award-winning **Woodland Faerie Trail,** when

KID magnets

Both the **Bullock Museum ★★★** (p. 297) and the **Texas Memorial Museum ★★** (p. 302) are very child-friendly. In addition, kids enjoy the **Thinkery ★★** (at the Meredith Learning Lab, 1830 Simond Ave.; www.thinkeryaustin.org; ✆ **512/469-6200**), a rambling, state-of-the-art facility built on land that was once the Robert Mueller Municipal Airport. Opening there in 2013, the Thinkery has everything from low-tech but creative playscapes for tots to studio soundstages for teens. More than a half-million visitors visit yearly.

Austin's has lots of outdoor attractions for kids. Children will love splashing around at **Barton Springs ★★★** (p. 295), and even kids who find bats creepy are likely to be converted when they see them set flight by the thousands over Lady Bird Lake (see "Going Batty," p. 295). Bats, bees, and crystal caverns are among the subjects of the Discovery Boxes at the 80-acre **Austin Nature & Science Center ★**, Zilker Park, 301 Nature Center Dr. (✆ **512/974-3888**), which also has interactive exhibits on rescued animals; the "Dino Pit" is a lure for budding paleontologists. The scenic 25-minute ride on the narrow-gauge **Zilker Zephyr Miniature Train,** 2100 Barton Springs Rd., just across from the Barton Springs Pool (✆ **512/478-8286**), chugs along at a leisurely pace through **Zilker Park ★★★** along Barton Creek and Town Lake.

Austin-area gardeners, architects, artists, families, and school groups create tiny woodland fairy houses and host tea parties, crafts workshops, and moonlight walks.

2220 Barton Springs Rd. www.zilkergarden.org. ✆ **512/477-8672.** Admission $3 for adults, $2 adult residents, $1 for seniors and children. Cash only. Garden center 7am–7pm daily. Bus: 30.

Zilker Metropolitan Park ★★★ This park serves as Austin's living room, swimming pool, outdoor theater, and park. It's everybody's favorite weekend place, and there's always something fun happening here. Spread out over 347 green acres of rolling hills, Zilker Park is like a big friendly public playground with an awesome swimming hole, the **Barton Springs Pool ★★★** (p. 295). Kids ride the **Zilker Zephyr Miniature Train,** families picnic, and nature lovers rent canoes to take on Lady Bird Lake (aka Town Lake). The summer **Zilker Hillside Theatre** musical productions are free (donations appreciated). Visitors also flock to the nearby **Zilker Botanical Garden ★★★** (p. 302), the **Austin Nature & Science Center ★** (see box above), and the **Umlauf Sculpture Garden & Museum ★★★** (p. 302), a short bike ride from the main part of the park. In addition to athletic fields (nine for soccer, one for rugby, and two multiuse), the park has a 9-hole disk (Frisbee) golf course and a sand volleyball court. There are also greenbelt areas and trails that you can access from the park, and during the holidays Zilker's historic **Moonlight Tower** (made famous in the cult-classic film *Dazed and Confused*) becomes the town's biggest holiday tree. ***Tip:*** Locals simply call this "Zilker Park."

2201 Barton Springs Rd. ✆ **512/476-9044.** Free admission. Daily 5am–10pm. Bus: 30.

Organized Tours

The aquatically inclined might consider taking one of the electric-powered **Capital Cruises** (www.capitalcruises.com; ✆ **512/480-9264**), which ply Lady Bird Lake (aka Town Lake) from March through October. Options include bat-viewing cruises, fajita dinner cruises, and afternoon sightseeing excursions. Similar itineraries are offered by **Lone Star Riverboat** (www.lonestarriverboat.com; ✆ **512/327-1388**), but they go farther upstream and add narration. Both companies depart from the dock near the Hyatt Regency Hotel. Can't decide between sea and land? Board one of the six-wheel-drive amphibious vehicles operated by **Austin Duck Adventures** (www.austinducks.com; ✆ **512/477-5274**). After exploring Austin's downtown and scenic west side, you'll splash into Lake Austin. Tours board in front of the Austin Visitors Center, 602 East 4th St.

Walking Tours

You won't find better guided walks than the informative and entertaining **downtown walking tours ★★** offered by the Austin Convention and Visitors Bureau (www.austintexas.org; ✆ **866/GO-AUSTIN [46-287846]** and 512/462-8784). Tours are about 90 minutes long and cost $10 per person; there's no charge for children under age 12 with paying parents. Three types of tours are offered year-round, weather permitting, including one of Upper Congress Avenue and East Sixth Street; another covering Lower Congress Avenue, Lady Bird Lake, and Second Street; and the third covering Historic Downtown West–Bremond Block and Guadalupe Street. See details online.

STAYING ACTIVE

Outdoor Fun

BIKING Austin has various city bike routes for local bike commuters and visitors who want to pedal around town. If you want to ride on trails, you have a choice of the mellow hike-and-bike trail around Lady Bird Lake (10 miles), or the more challenging Barton Creek Greenbelt (7.8 miles). Contact **Austin Parks and Recreation,** 200 S. Lamar Blvd. (www.austintexas.gov/department/parks-and-recreation; ✆ **512/974-6700**), for more information on these and other bike trails. There is also a paved **Veloway,** a 3.1-mile loop in Slaughter Creek Metropolitan Park, in far south Austin, devoted exclusively to bicyclists and in-line skaters.

Austin now has its own public bikeshare program, **Austin BCycle (B-cycle),** with bikes available throughout the city at B-stations. Get the details, plus B-station locations and bike routes at **https://austin.bcycle.com**. You can also rent bikes and get maps and other information from **University Cyclery,** 2901 N. Lamar Blvd. (www.universitycyclery.com; ✆ **512/474-6696**). A number of downtown hotels rent or provide free bikes to their guests. For information on weekly road rides, contact **Bike Austin,** 1000 Brazos St., Suite 100 (www.bikeaustin.org; ✆ **512/282-7413**). For rougher mountain bike routes, try the **Austin Ridge Riders** (www.austinridgeriders.com). You can also rent mountain and city bikes from notorious Austin Tour de France biker Lance Armstrong at his shop, **Mellow Johnny's Bike Shop,** in the Warehouse District at 400 Nueces between 4th and 5th streets (http://austin.mellowjohnnys.com; ✆ **512/473-0222**). It even has kids' bikes for rent.

CANOEING You can rent canoes at **Zilker Park,** 2000 Barton Springs Rd. (www.zilkerboats.com; ✆ **512/478-3852**), for $15 an hour or $45 per day (open daily year-round, weather permitting). **Capital Cruises,** Hyatt Regency boat dock (www.capitalcruises.com; ✆ **512/480-9264**), also has hourly rentals on Town Lake.

GOLF For information about Austin's six municipal golf courses and to set up tee times, log on to www.austintexas.gov/department/golf. All but the 9-hole Hancock course offers pro shops and equipment rental, and their greens fees are reasonable. The **Hancock** course was built in 1899 and is the oldest course in Texas. The **Lions** course is where Tom Kite and Ben Crenshaw played college golf for the University of Texas.

HIKING Austin's parks and preserves abound in nature trails. Contact the **Sierra Club** (www.texas.sierraclub.org/austin; ✆ **512/472-1767**) if you're interested in organized hikes. **Wild Basin Wilderness Preserve** (www.wildbasin.org; ✆ **512/327-7622**) is another source for guided treks, hosting periodic "Haunted Trails" tours along with its more typical hikes.

SWIMMING The best known of Austin's natural swimming holes is **Barton Springs Pool** ★★★ (see p. 295), but it's by no means the only one. Other scenic outdoor spots to take the plunge include **Deep Eddy Pool,** 401 Deep Eddy Ave. at Lake Austin Boulevard (✆ **512/472-8546**).

For lakeshore swimming, consider **Hippie Hollow** on Lake Travis, 2½ miles off FM 620 (https://parks.traviscountytx.gov/find-a-park/hippie-hollow), where you can let it all hang out in a series of clothing-optional coves, or **Emma Long Metropolitan Park** on Lake Austin (✆ **512/974-1831**).

Spectator Sports

College sports are a big deal, particularly when the **University of Texas (UT) Longhorns** are playing. The most comprehensive source of information on the various teams is www.texassports.com, but you can phone the **UT Athletics Ticket Office** (✆ **512/471-3333**) to find out about schedules and **UTTM Charge-A-Ticket** (✆ **512/477-6060**) to order tickets.

BASEBALL The **University of Texas** baseball team goes to bat February through May at Disch-Falk Field (east of I-35, at the corner of Martin Luther King, Jr., Blvd. and Comal). Many players have gone on to the pros.

Baseball Hall of Famer Nolan Ryan's **Round Rock Express,** a Texas Rangers farm club, compete in the Pacific Coast League. See them play at the Dell Diamond, 3400 E. Palm Valley Rd., in Round Rock (www.roundrockexpress.com; ✆ **512/255-2255**), an 8,688-seat stadium where you can choose from box seats or stadium seating—and an additional 3,000 fans can sit on a grassy berm in the outfield. Tickets range from about $6 to $12.

BASKETBALL The **University of Texas** Longhorn and Lady Longhorn basketball teams, both former Southwest Conference champions, play in the Frank Erwin Center (just west of I-35 on Red River btw. Martin Luther King, Jr., Blvd. and 15th St.) November through March.

FOOTBALL Part of the Big 12 Conference, the **University of Texas** football team often fills the huge Darrell K. Royal/Texas Memorial Stadium (just west of I-35 btw. 23rd and 21st sts., E. Campus Dr., and San Jacinto Blvd.) during home games, played August through November.

FORMULA 1 RACING The highly celebrated opening of the **Circuit of the Americas** (www.circuitoftheamericas.com) Grand Prix racetrack and entertainment venue in 2012 revved the engines of Texans and visitors from all over mad for world-class motorsports. Set on 1,500 acres just southeast of the Austin-Bergstrom Airport, off Pickle Parkway (Texas toll road 130), the Circuit of the Americas hosts the biggest names in racing, action sports, and music and features a 3.41-mile racetrack. It's the first track built in the U.S. specifically for Formula 1.

GOLF World Golf Championship excitement comes to Austin in March 2017, 2018, 2019, and 2020 for the **Dell Technologies Match Play** tournament (www.pgatour.com/tournaments/wgc-dell-technologies-match-play.html) at the **Austin Country Club** (www.austincountryclub.com).

ROLLER DERBY Reincarnated in Austin in 2001, women's roller derby has become a popular pastime in Austin. If you want to celebrate lowbrow culture in a tongue-in-cheek fashion, check out the **Lonestar Rollergirls** (www.txrd.com). Events are usually held every other Sunday at the Palmer Events Center. A flat-track league called the **Texas Rollergirls** (www.txrollergirls.com) has a season that lasts from March to August, with bouts taking place at the Playland Skate Center at 8822 McCann Blvd., close to the intersection of Hwy. 183 and Burnet Road.

WHERE TO STAY

Called the "City of the Velvet Crown," Austin is one of the most popular cities in Texas, drawing Hollywood types and other visitors enamored by the town's thriving music scene, its laid-back culture, and its lovely lake and Hill Country–edge setting. New hotels are popping up all over, and the city is so popular that its tourism offices and hotels don't have to try too hard to court visitors—Austin is enticing enough on its own. This means that hotel rooms don't often discount rates, unless you come during the hottest late-summer days when out-of-towners tend to have enough good sense to stay home in cooler climes.

In looking for discounts, keep in mind the calendars of the state legislature and the University of Texas. Lawmakers and lobbyists converge on the capital from January through May of odd-numbered years, so you can expect tighter bookings. The start of fall term, graduation week, and football weekends—UT's football stadium now seats 100,000—will also fill lots of hotel rooms.

The busiest season, however, is the month of March, when the **South by Southwest (SXSW) music festival** fills entire hotels. It is designed to coincide with UT's spring break, usually the third week of the month. SXSW is the largest gathering of the year for the music industry. It attracts thousands of music fans, music producers, and company execs. Now there's also a **film and media festival** held the week before the music begins. Bottom line: Try to avoid coming in March. Another time when the hotels are busy is in late September/early October for the **Austin City Limits Music Festival.** This immensely popular festival attracts lots of out-of-towners. Hotel rates tend to skyrocket during SXSW and ACL.

If you're coming here to see what Austin's all about, consider staying somewhere in the central part of town. You'll enjoy your stay more because traffic in Austin can be bad, and making your way around an unfamiliar city can be intimidating. You don't have to stay downtown. Consider the hotels in South Austin, in and around South Congress, close to Lady Bird Lake (aka "Town Lake"), or near Rainey Street, like **Hotel Van Zandt** (p. 313). It's a comfortable area to stay, with lively foot traffic, and most of the places of interest are close. Also, consider the areas near the University of Texas, such as Hyde Park, West Campus, or one of the new trendy hotels in East Austin, like the **Heywood** (p. 318). Here, too, it's easy to get around, and you'll get a good feel for Austin.

Tip: If you're on a tight budget and looking for bargains, Austin has two major clusters of economical lodgings. One surrounds the intersection of I-35 and Ben White Blvd. (Hwy. 71), and the other is north of there, where I-35 intersects Hwy. 290 E. The latter cluster is a better location for three reasons: one, it's closer to downtown; two, it has better dining options; and three, you're not limited to using I-35—there are alternative routes for getting around. This cluster includes economy and extended-stay chains, such as **Studio 6,** at 6603 IH-35 (www.staystudio6.com; ✆ **512/458-5453**), and **Orangewood Suites** at 935 La Posada Dr. (www.orangewoodsuites.com; ✆ **512/459-3335**).

Note that rates listed below do not include the city's 9% hotel tax, and represent the rack rates listed during normal times of the year. During festival times and other occasions when hotels fill up, rates will rise.

Downtown

EXPENSIVE

The Driskill ★★★ A wealthy cattle baron built this grand Romanesque hotel in 1886, and it's pretty fancy, with a lobby of hand-inlaid marble floors and tall columns. A dark, Texas-style bar upstairs is topped with a magnificent stained-glass dome. This is Austin's most iconic downtown hotel, Texan to the core, epitomizing old-school luxury but not dated and stuffy. You fully expect *Giant*'s Bick Benedict and Jet Rink to come swaggering into the lobby. The Driskill has welcomed many of the rich and famous. It was here that Lyndon Johnson awaited his election results, and the Texas Rangers gathered to plan

Greater Austin Hotels, Restaurants & Attractions

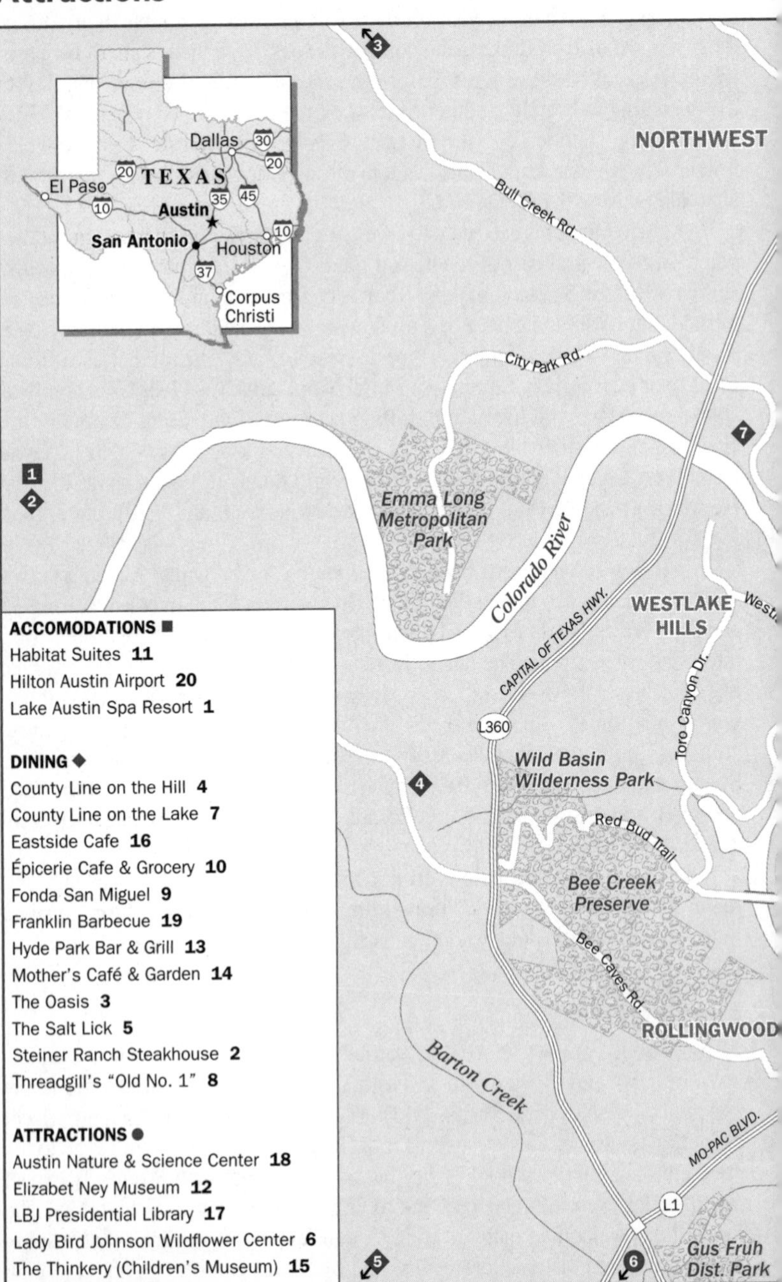
ACCOMODATIONS ■
Habitat Suites 11
Hilton Austin Airport 20
Lake Austin Spa Resort 1
DINING ◆
County Line on the Hill 4
County Line on the Lake 7
Eastside Cafe 16
Épicerie Cafe & Grocery 10
Fonda San Miguel 9
Franklin Barbecue 19
Hyde Park Bar & Grill 13
Mother's Café & Garden 14
The Oasis 3
The Salt Lick 5
Steiner Ranch Steakhouse 2
Threadgill's "Old No. 1" 8
ATTRACTIONS ●
Austin Nature & Science Center 18
Elizabet Ney Museum 12
LBJ Presidential Library 17
Lady Bird Johnson Wildflower Center 6
The Thinkery (Children's Museum) 15
Dallas
TEXAS
El Paso
Austin
San Antonio
Houston
Corpus Christi
NORTHWEST
Bull Creek Rd.
City Park Rd.
Emma Long Metropolitan Park
Colorado River
CAPITAL OF TEXAS HWY.
WESTLAKE HILLS
Toro Canyon Dr.
L360
Wild Basin Wilderness Park
Red Bud Trail
Bee Creek Preserve
Bee Caves Rd.
ROLLINGWOOD
Barton Creek
MO-PAC BLVD.
L1
Gus Fruh Dist. Park

9

AUSTIN Where to Stay

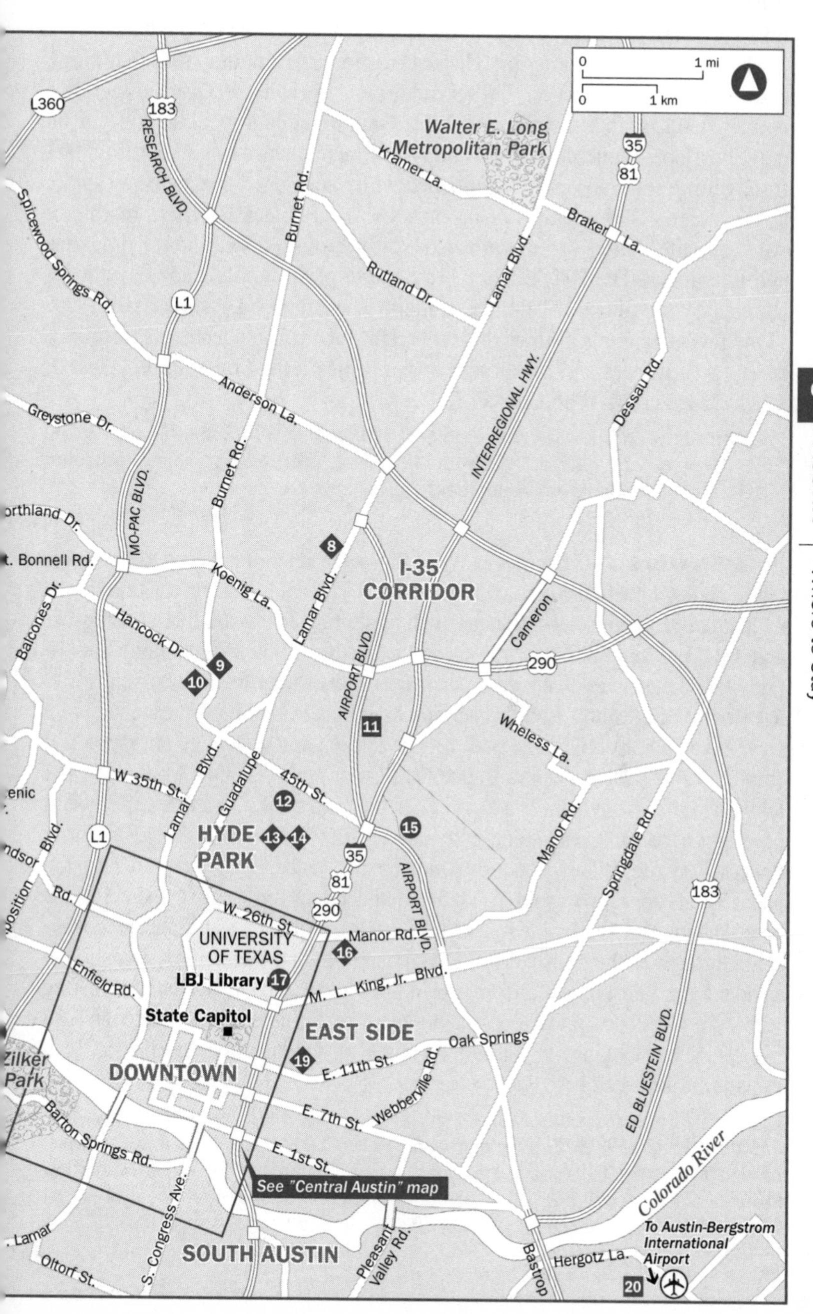

9

AUSTIN | Where to Stay

their ambush of Bonnie and Clyde. The central location is close to the late-night rollicks of Sixth Street and practically at the corner of oh-so-civilized South Congress Avenue. For me, the Driskill is romance—my husband and I had our first date at the Driskill Bar; and I don't think we're alone in saying that.

The hotel has two parts; the Historic section (the original 1886 building), and the Traditional section (a 1929 addition). I prefer the Historic section's corner rooms, with big windows, and I also like the high-ceilinged rooms on the 12th floor. Meticulous renovations and maintenance have kept the hotel from getting stale. Rooms are furnished with understated elegance and subtle Texas touches. The smallish bathrooms are clad in black Brazilian marble or Art Deco tile. Suites are more lavish, softly furnished with heavy draperies and fine linens. The **Driskill Bar** is a favorite of local pols, and is said to be haunted by the ghost of LBJ late at night. The sublime **Driskill Grill** is one of the few restaurants in town that feels right for a truly special occasion, with crystal wineglasses and flickering candles. Enjoy a big Southern breakfast or a light lunch at the **1886 Café & Bakery.**

604 Brazos St. (at E. Sixth St.). www.thedriskill.hyatt.com. ✆ **800/233-1234** or 512/439-1234. 189 units. $259–$328 double; from $429 suites. Valet parking $40. Pets accepted with $100 nonrefundable fee. **Amenities:** 2 restaurants; bar; concierge; exercise room; room service; Wi-Fi (free).

Four Seasons Austin ★★ When big-name celebrities come to town, this high-end hotel is often where you'll find them. The Four Seasons is a fine choice no matter what your celebrity status, with its alluring Texas-size lobby, trendy bar and **TRIO** restaurant, outdoor pool, and exquisite spa, not to mention views of Lady Bird Lake and downtown. Locals meet friends after work in "Austin's Living Room," the **Lobby Lounge,** settling in to blue leather high-back chairs or a cowhide couch. Lobbyists hobnob here over cocktails in the late afternoon and wonder if that's really Sandra Bullock at that far table. TRIO, a level below the lobby with its river views, is a favorite for seafood, steaks, and fine wine. You'll have easy access to the hike-and-bike trails and the boardwalk at Lady Bird Lake. (Guests can rent bikes, stand-up paddleboards, and other watercraft near the lake.) The property was sold in 2015 and underwent some spiffy updates at the time, leaving the hotel modern and traditional in equal measure; Texas touches shine through in the polished stone floors and original Western art. Beds in the standard-size guest rooms are dressed in fine Egyptian cottons. Rooms with city views are nice, but I prefer ones facing the lake. Some even have balconies, so request when booking. If you're traveling with toddlers, the helpful staff can provide strollers and baby seats.

98 San Jacinto Blvd. (at Cesar Chavez St.). www.fourseasons.com/austin. ✆ **512/478-4500.** 291 units. $399–$699 double; from $699 suite. Special packages available. Valet parking $45. Pets 60 lb. or under accepted with $100 nonrefundable fee. **Amenities:** Restaurant; bar; babysitting; bikes; concierge; exercise room; outdoor heated saltwater pool; 24-hr. room service; spa; Wi-Fi (free).

Central Austin Hotels, Restaurants & Attractions

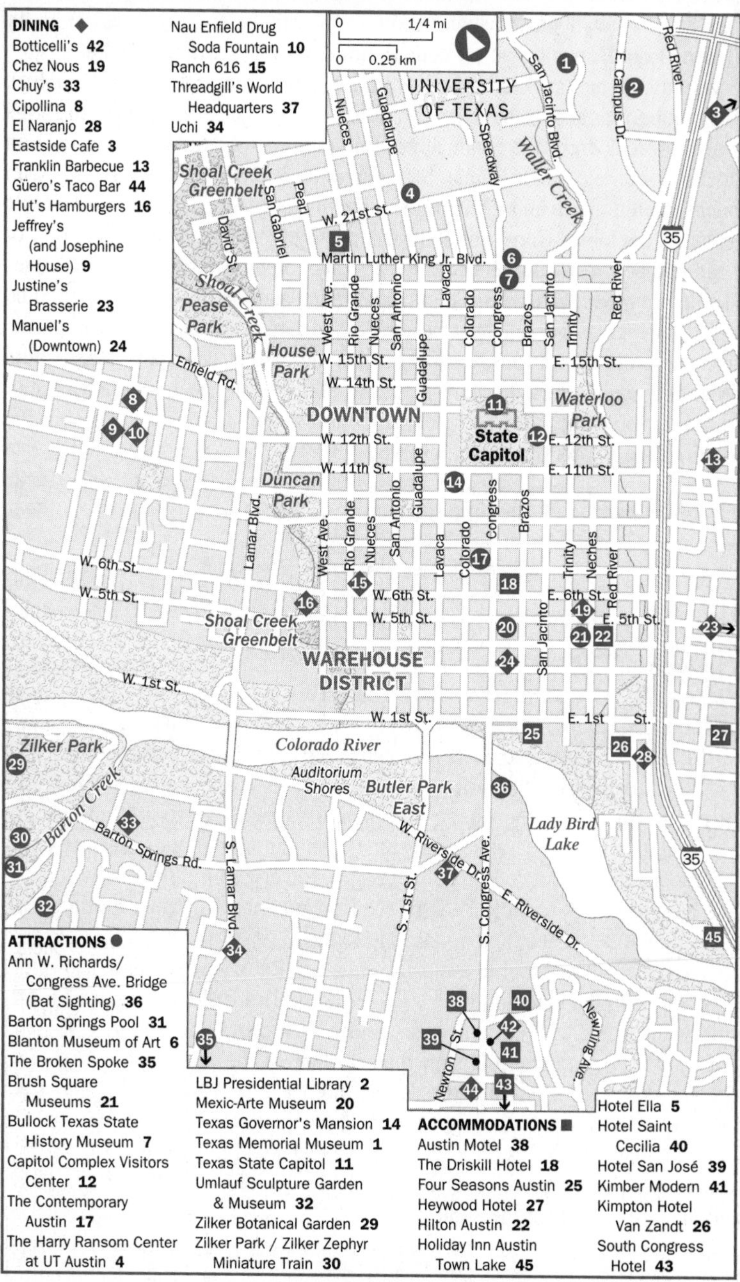

DINING ◆
Botticelli's 42
Chez Nous 19
Chuy's 33
Cipollina 8
El Naranjo 28
Eastside Cafe 3
Franklin Barbecue 13
Güero's Taco Bar 44
Hut's Hamburgers 16
Jeffrey's (and Josephine House) 9
Justine's Brasserie 23
Manuel's (Downtown) 24
Nau Enfield Drug Soda Fountain 10
Ranch 616 15
Threadgill's World Headquarters 37
Uchi 34
0 1/4 mi
0 0.25 km
UNIVERSITY OF TEXAS
Nueces
Guadalupe
Speedway
San Jacinto Blvd.
E. Campus Dr.
Red River
Waller Creek
Shoal Creek Greenbelt
San Gabriel
Pearl
W. 21st St.
David St.
Martin Luther King Jr. Blvd.
Shoal Creek
Pease Park
West Ave.
Rio Grande
San Antonio
Lavaca
Colorado
Congress
Brazos
San Jacinto
Trinity
House Park
W. 15th St.
E. 15th St.
W. 14th St.
Enfield Rd.
DOWNTOWN
Waterloo Park
State Capitol
W. 12th St.
E. 12th St.
W. 11th St.
E. 11th St.
Duncan Park
Lamar Blvd.
Neches
W. 6th St.
W. 5th St.
E. 6th St.
E. 5th St.
Shoal Creek Greenbelt
WAREHOUSE DISTRICT
W. 1st St.
E. 1st St.
Zilker Park
Colorado River
Auditorium Shores
Butler Park East
Barton Creek
Barton Springs Rd.
S. Lamar Blvd.
W. Riverside Dr.
E. Riverside Dr.
S. 1st St.
S. Congress Ave.
Lady Bird Lake
35
Newton St.
Newning Ave.
ATTRACTIONS ●
Ann W. Richards/Congress Ave. Bridge (Bat Sighting) 36
Barton Springs Pool 31
Blanton Museum of Art 6
The Broken Spoke 35
Brush Square Museums 21
Bullock Texas State History Museum 7
Capitol Complex Visitors Center 12
The Contemporary Austin 17
The Harry Ransom Center at UT Austin 4
LBJ Presidential Library 2
Mexic-Arte Museum 20
Texas Governor's Mansion 14
Texas Memorial Museum 1
Texas State Capitol 11
Umlauf Sculpture Garden & Museum 32
Zilker Botanical Garden 29
Zilker Park / Zilker Zephyr Miniature Train 30
ACCOMMODATIONS ■
Austin Motel 38
The Driskill Hotel 18
Four Seasons Austin 25
Heywood Hotel 27
Hilton Austin 22
Holiday Inn Austin Town Lake 45
Hotel Ella 5
Hotel Saint Cecilia 40
Hotel San José 39
Kimber Modern 41
Kimpton Hotel Van Zandt 26
South Congress Hotel 43

MODERATE

Hilton Austin ★ This convention center–area hotel offers good value in a great downtown location with modern minimalist-style rooms, the spiffy **Skyline Pool Bar,** and a sunny central dining spot in **Cannon + Belle,** serving Texas cuisine and cocktail favorites in a bright space with an open kitchen. Even though it's across the street from the Austin Convention Center, the hotel is also a block from the Sixth Street Entertainment District and a few short blocks from the popular Rainey Street area. Rooms have been upgraded with touchscreen lighting and temperature adjustment systems. There's also a Starbucks off the lobby. Conventioneers fill the hotel much of the time, but it's not a bad choice for vacationers who want to stay downtown. On the 8th floor is a health club with an exercise room, spa, sauna and steam room, lap pool, and roof deck lounge with cabanas. The house of famed Battle of the Alamo survivor Susanna Dickinson once sat on this site, but it was moved across the street and made into a museum that now sits next to the O. Henry Museum; both are worth checking out. Look for the coming of a new taco joint, the **Austin Taco Project,** to the hotel in late 2017.

500 E. 4th St. www3.hilton.com/en/hotels/texas/hilton-austin-AUSCVHH/index.html. ✆ **800/445-8667** or 512/482-8000. 800 units. $198–$398 double; from $700 suite. Special packages available. Valet parking $37; self-parking $28. Pets 75 lb. or under accepted with nonrefundable $50 fee. **Amenities:** Restaurant; bar; Starbucks; 24-hr. business center; executive-level rooms; health club and spa; heated outdoor pool; 24-hr. room service; Wi-Fi (standard free; $15/day for high-speed Internet).

INEXPENSIVE

Holiday Inn Austin Town Lake ★ This hotel, with a rowing-themed, open-concept lobby, is a value-friendly find along I-35 on the banks of Lady Bird Lake. With a welcoming staff and rooms that are larger and nicer than you might expect for this price range, this Holiday Inn is spread across two towers with views of the Austin skyline and the lake. All rooms have microwaves and small refrigerators, and some even feature pullout sofa sleepers. A full renovation completed in 2017 has given everything a fresh new look. It also has the family-friendly **Pecan Tree Restaurant,** an outdoor rooftop pool, a private movie theater, and an inviting lounge just off the lobby. It's close to the bars, restaurants, and live-music venues of Rainey Street, and also offers easy access to the hike-and-bike trails on Lady Bird Lake. It's also just a 1.3-mile walk to the convention center, and a boat ramp and a city park stand nearby. Many of the helpful staff have worked at the property for years and are truly knowledgeable about Austin. Another perk: Kids 11 and under eat for free at the hotel restaurant. ***A little history:*** Town Lake, the part of the Colorado River that runs through town, was renamed Lady Bird Lake in 2001 in honor of Texan native Lady Bird Johnson. Locals still call it Town Lake, and this hotel has kept the name.

20 N. I-35 (exit 233, Riverside Dr./Lady Bird Lake). www.ihg.com. ✆ **800/593-5676** or 512/472-8211. 323 units. $119–$249 double. Children 12 and under stay for free in parent's room. **Amenities:** Restaurant, lounge; business center; fitness center; outdoor rooftop pool; private movie theater; Wi-Fi (free).

IT pays TO STAY

Two downtown accommodations at prime locations will save you money. **Extended Stay America Downtown,** 600 Guadalupe St. at Sixth St. (www.extendedstayamerica.com; ✆ **800/398-7829** or 512/457-9994), and **Homestead Studio Suites Austin—Downtown/Town Lake,** 507 S. 1st St. at Barton Springs (www.homesteadhotels.com; ✆ **888/782-9473** or 512/476-1818), will run you from $600 to $900 per week for a room. Full kitchens and coin-op laundries at both bring your costs down even more.

South Austin

EXPENSIVE

Hotel Saint Cecilia ★★ Hip hotelier Liz Lambert, the force behind Austin's Hotel San Jose and San Antonio's Havana Riverwalk Hotel, has really done it this time. This pitch-perfect hideaway is a shrine to the patron saint of music and poetry, with five suites, three studios, and six swanky poolside bungalows on the grounds of a historic house in SoCo. In-room Rega retro-style turntables and Geneva sound systems are a great way to enjoy vintage LPs from the hotel's music library. Suites have lots of little delights: Suite 4 has a yard and outdoor fireplace; Suite 5 an upright piano; Suite 2 a cool outdoor bamboo shower. Beds feature Swedish-made King Hastens beds. Celebrities visiting Austin often stay at the Four Seasons, but some hide out in the bungalows here—how very Chateau Marmont of them. (Frankly, the bungalows are too sparse and garage-like for our taste, but rooms in the main house are sublime.) The hotel stands just a couple short blocks from the heart of the SoCo scene. Even though a much-cooler-than-thou crowd may lounge in the lobby and do laps in the pool, weekday rates at this fab but weird boutique property make an occasional special-event stay here accessible to just about anyone.

112 Academy Dr. (1 block east of S. Congress Ave.). www.hotelsaintcecilia.com. ✆ **512/852-2400.** 14 units. $385–$500 double; $385–$875 suite; $510–$630 bungalow. Rates include full breakfast and free parking. Pets under 25 lb. accepted with $25 fee per day. **Amenities:** Bar; bikes; concierge; outdoor pool; room service; Wi-Fi (free).

Kimpton Hotel Van Zandt ★★ We had a "We're not in Kansas anymore" moment when we walked into this swank property, which opened in late 2015. The place wowed us at the door, and even though it has a wonderful local vibe, it just doesn't feel like the same old, same old Austin. Perhaps that's the charm of it—this old hippie town is finally growing up, holding on to its unique eclecticism while riding a new wave of big-city sophistication. A "rough-around-the-edges kind of sophistication," is the way the hotel staff describes it, and with stabs at midcentury minimalism set against Old West weathered-leather chairs, the Van Zandt feels like a hip club locals would frequent, and they do. This locally owned, Kimpton-managed 16-story hotel stands a stone's throw from Rainey Street—be sure to ask for a room on the highest floor farthest from Rainey, or the din of that lively strip may keep you up all night on weekends. Spacious, modern rooms feature plush bedding, soft carpeting, and draperies tangled up in blue. Some suites even have deep oversize bathtubs with big-window views of the lake. Sip margaritas and local brews at the hotel social hour and pick your underwater playlist for a swim in the rooftop pool. **Geraldine's** restaurant touts "elevated Austin grub," and it jumps with live music every day. Pets are welcome, and the hotel has bikes you can borrow for a free spin around town. We love the lobby light fixtures made from trombones and trumpets—a clever nod to Austin's music capital status. The hotel even has a director of music who curates playlists for each public space; she often spins her favorites on the turntable during social hour.

605 Davis St. (near Rainey St.). www.hotelvanzandt.com. ✆ **800/546-7866** or 512/542-5300. 319 units. $169–$849 double; $750–$4,500 suite. Valet parking $40 per night. Pets stay free with signed waiver, no size or breed restrictions. **Amenities:** Restaurant; bar; snack cafe; fitness center; outdoor rooftop pool; 24-hr. room service; Wi-Fi $13/day (free for Kimpton Karma Members).

Kimber Modern ★★ With its sleek and sophisticated Euro-minimalist style, this little SoCo treasure is perhaps Austin's best-kept secret. Is it a boutique hotel, a B&B, or simply a grownup's treehouse hidden by oak trees? You decide. This architecturally alluring den of designer furnishings oozes austere style, yet at the same time is warm and inviting. It's just a block behind a lively section of South Congress Avenue, meaning you're so close to the Continental Club you could dash over to Kimber Modern to grab a sweater and be back at the club before the next song. This 70-unit midcentury hotel is a quiet compound beneath enormous shade trees. A courtyard deck anchors the hotel's five rooms and two suites and offers conversation-area seating beside a 25-ft. water feature. In the common area indoors, floor-to-ceiling sliding-glass doors bring nature inside. Sink into one of four enveloping Arne Jacobson egg chairs nestled around an Eames surfboard coffee table. The concept here is all-inclusive amenities and seamless convenience, with self-service style: Everything is included in your stay, but the staff doesn't hover. It feels more like you live here, or you're a celebrity who demands privacy. Guests are given a keyless-entry digital code so they can come and go without stopping at a front desk. Complimentary beer and wine are on offer all day and night. The hotel only allows children 15 and older, so it's ideal for singles or couples. The owners say their goal was to create an exceptional architectural work of art tailored toward the independent urban traveler, and their newest project is the 35-room **Kimber SoCo Hotel,** opening in late 2017 behind Güero's Tacos off South Congress Ave.

110 The Circle (1 block east of S. Congress Ave.). www.kimbermodern.com. ✆ **512/912-1046.** 7 units. $250–$295 double; $329–$459 suite. Maximum 3 adults per room, $75 fee for 3rd adult per night. Rates include self-serve gourmet breakfast and 24/7 beverage bar. Children 14 and under not permitted. **Amenities:** Concierge; access to nearby health club; free parking; Wi-Fi (free).

South Congress Hotel ★★★ A few years ago, this big empty lot was the epicenter of the popular Austin food-truck scene. So naturally the neighborhood was up in arms when it was announced that a new hotel would be built here. No one is complaining now. Indeed, SoCo's hot namesake hotel is a huge hit. The three-story midcentury-style hotel has a retro exterior—like a 1960s doctor's office building. But inside it's perfection: rustic chic with warm colors, hardwood floors, and a chill vibe. The *Mad Men* decor (painted white brick, Danish modern furniture, potted cacti) is saved from overkill by the beautiful use of natural elements: lots of wood, stone, and glass. It's a full-service Austin experience, with three restaurants (including **Otoko,** celebrity chef Paul Qui's tiny little sushi bar), boutique shops, a 24-hour fitness center, and even a juice bar/coffee shop. Best of all, shoppers will go crazy with the trendy retail shops nearby, like Allen's Boots, Lucy in Disguise with Diamonds, and Uncommon Objects. You're also close to great little restaurants (Botticelli's, Pearl's, Güero's Taco Bar, Home Slice Pizza). Cool off in the little 4-foot-deep rooftop pool on the second floor. Rooms are spacious and serene, with wood floors, brick walls, fine linens, and a muted color scheme. My favorite room? The apartment-size suite (room 303) with views of the rooftop pool (reserve at a more reasonable rate midweek or off-season). Enjoy oysters, small-plate wonders, craft cocktails, and local brews at the gleaming **Central Standard** restaurant downstairs, where you can sit indoors or out and soak up the SoCo scene. Also onsite is the fun and casual Mexican-style **Café No Sé.** Expect this hotel to be fully booked during SXSW.

1603 South Congress Ave. www.southcongresshotel.com. ✆ **512/920-6405.** 83 units. $249–$449 double; $349–$1,349 suite. Valet parking $32. Pets up to 50 lb. accepted with $125 fee per stay up to 7 days. **Amenities:** 3 restaurants; 2 bars; coffee shop, bike & motorcycle rental; shops; 24-hr. fitness center; nail salon; outdoor pool with bar; car service up to 3 miles from hotel; Wi-Fi (free).

MODERATE

Hotel San José ★★ This boutique "bungalow-style" hotel features the midcentury time-warp vibe many would love to get stuck in: It's minimalist-retro everything, with big TVs, long desk counters, local art, and other über-trendy touches. Originally a 1930s motor court, this hotel hotspot is the brainchild of hotel guru Liz Lambert's Bunkhouse Group and a chic sanctuary in the heart of SoCo, across from the Continental Club. Do the cement floors and stark white walls make it too coolly mod for some tastes? Perhaps. But others embrace the pure minimalist style. Its biggest plus: location, location, location—in the thick of it along the hot SoCo strip. Request a room in the back to avoid traffic noise and partying passersby. The **courtyard lounge** is a pleasant place to unwind in the evenings, amid vine-covered walls and warm breezes.

1316 S. Congress Ave. (south of Nelly). www.sanjosehotel.com. ✆ **800/574-8897** or 512/852-2350. 40 units. $120–$145 double with shared bathroom; $285–$450 double with private bathroom; $328–$570 suite. Free parking. Pets accepted (Up to 2 per room) for $20 per day. **Amenities:** Bar/lounge; rental bikes; outdoor pool; room service; Wi-Fi (free).

INEXPENSIVE

Austin Motel ★ The best lodging bargain on South Congress, the Austin Motel is one of those eccentric local places where the "keep Austin weird" mantra makes sense. An iconic neon sign says "AUSTIN MOTEL: SO CLOSE AND YET SO FAR OUT." An old-school motor court built in 1938, this roadside motel has been in the hands of the same family since the 1950s. A prime (but not quiet) location in the heart of SoCo and competitive rates have long made this midcentury-style motel extremely popular. And lo and behold, in a marriage made in hotel heaven, this quirky property is now operated by celebrated hotelier Liz Lambert's hospitality company, Bunkhouse. Bunkhouse has been a breath of fresh air for the formerly all-too-funky hotel, with new landscaping, a new pool bar and bathhouse, and custom woodwork. Each of the motel's rooms has been given playful, colorful decor, with custom tufted vinyl beds (shaped somewhat like the iconic sign) and '50s-inspired seating. Classic push-button phones, vintage silkscreened music posters, and other eclectic touches make rooms feel retro, local, and fun. The spiffed-up pool (classic kidney-shaped, natch) and lounge area is outfitted with vinyl lounge chairs and vintage tables beneath red-and-white-striped umbrellas. The poolside fun includes punk-rock water ballet, water aerobics, and live music. The reception area is part check-in central/part general store, selling clever retail items. Coolers with beverages and snacks are yours to take back to your room. The hotel location is close to all the best SoCo hotspots, like Güero's Taco Bar and the Continental Club.

1220 S. Congress Ave. www.austinmotel.com. ✆ **512/441-1157.** 41 units. $125 double; $245 king suite. Free parking. Pets accepted for $20 fee. **Amenities:** Outdoor pool and bar; gift shop; Wi-Fi (free).

Central

EXPENSIVE

Hotel Ella ★★ Proud UT parents and Longhorn alums, businessmen, and couples are all regular returning guests to this impeccable West Campus boutique hotel, the former Mansion at Judges Hill. Hotel Ella is known for its casual-chic **Goodall's Kitchen** restaurant, attentive service, and wraparound porches overlooking the city—balconies where my husband and I love to sit and have coffee in the morning. The exterior has a Greek Revival grandeur, but there is nothing grandmotherly or even old-school about the inside, despite its impressive circa-1900 bones. Everything is fresh and modern, from the art photography on the walls (check out the wonderful silver-gelatin Willie Nelson portrait in the lobby) to the midcentury paintings to the comfortable lounge areas in the historic main house. The hotel's adjacent North Wing has an attractive pool area and nice-size guest rooms, but I personally prefer the rooms in the main house, some of which have access to the second-floor wrap-around/columned porch. The bar and restaurant are sublime—elegant but not stuffy. Goodall's Kitchen used to be a white-tablecloth dining spot, but it has become more trendy and less fussy, and now offers fresh seasonal fare in a casual, minimalist atmosphere. It's good enough that I'd go back even if I weren't staying here. ***Tip:*** Be sure to order the seasonal soup. The chef makes a fabulous pumpkin sage in the fall.

1900 Rio Grande St. www.hotelella.com. ✆ **800/311-1619** and 512/495-1800. 47 units. $199–$459 double; $269–$509 suite. Valet parking $25 per night. Pets $150 per night. **Amenities:** Restaurant with bar/lounge; 24-hr. fitness center; outdoor pool, complimentary car service within 3 miles of hotel; Wi-Fi (free).

MODERATE

Habitat Suites ★★ I am much impressed with this friendly little ecotel, located in one of the satellite buildings of Highland Mall. Hidden beneath pleasant shade trees, the hotel looks more like a fancy nursing home or small apartment complex than a hotel, but in many ways it represents the best of what Austin is all about. The all-suites three-story property is probably the greenest little budget hotel in town—and has been since 1991, when its owners made that their goal. Today they recycle, conserve water, grow organic foods, generate electricity, use only natural materials and cleaning products, and even allow guests to cook for themselves—making this a property like none other I know in Austin. This Habitat Suites is a sister-business to the owners' **Casa de Luz** macrobiotic restaurant downtown. Each large suite has a full kitchen and a small outdoor seating area, most overlooking the nicely shaded pool. The furniture is basic and not super stylish (older pieces are sometimes reupholstered to avoid adding to the waste stream). It's set just 2 miles north of the UT Austin campus, but this is not a hotel for college students and partiers. It even has a "quiet time" between 9pm and 9am. Too bad it's not a bit closer to downtown. If you're staying there, though, you can take the daily Capital MetroRail Red Line downtown or ride a Capital Metro Bus downtown.

500 E. Highland Mall Blvd. www.habitatsuites.com. ✆ **800/916-4339** or 512/467-6000. 96 units. $109 1-bedroom suite; $159 2-bedroom suite. Special packages available. Rates include full breakfast and afternoon wine & snacks (except Sun). Free parking. **Amenities:** Jacuzzi; outdoor saltwater pool; Wi-Fi (free).

Westlake/Lake Travis

EXPENSIVE

Lake Austin Spa Resort ★★★ Named the #6 Wellness Retreat in the world in 2017 by *Condé Nast Traveler* readers and ranked the #8 Destination Spa by *Travel + Leisure,* this all-inclusive is the quintessential Austin spa resort. It's a sublime property set along a serene body of water, offering lots of outdoor activities and serving fresh, healthful foods in a picture-perfect setting. Just west of town where the Highland Lakes area and Hill Country begin, the resort is the kind of place where you can sit in a breezy cabana by a pool, take to the water in kayaks, hydro-bikes, and stand-up paddleboards, or venture out on canoe or hiking excursions. Natural herbs and flowers growing in the resort's garden are used for soothing spa treatments, like lavender for the signature "LakeHouse Lavender" sugar scrub, or sourced by the chef for dishes served in the resort restaurants. Three- to seven-night packages are available—but you'll want to stay forever.

Set in adjoining cottages, rooms have private gardens, fireplaces, and hot tubs and are done in a casual French-country style. You'll be torn between the dreamy rooms and the gorgeous lakeside spaces, with yoga zones, reading rooms by the lake, lush gardens and poolside lounges, a large indoor pool, and Swedish-style spa rooms. The resort also has a new luxury watercraft that delivers guests to the Lake Austin shores of its 25,000-square-foot **Lake-House Spa** from downtown Austin or the 360 Bridge. The spa facility is open to the public, and services are available to both day and overnight guests. So even if you aren't able to stay overnight, you can still enjoy a luxury **day-spa package,** including a water-taxi pickup downtown, a gourmet lunch, a floating meditation class, a selection of spa treatments, all gratuities, and a car service back to town (day-spa packages $430–$1,205).

1705 S. Quinlan Park Rd. (at Steiner Ranch, 5 miles south of Hwy. 620). www.lakeaustin.com. ✆ **800/847-5637** or 512/372-7300. 40 units. 3-night package $2,108–$2,445 (per person) double; 7-night package $4,995–$11,990 (per person) double. Rates include all meals, classes, and activities. Alcoholic beverages (beer and wine) extra. Spa treatments/personal trainers extra. Free parking. Dogs accepted in Garden Cottage rooms for $300 fee. Children 13 and under not permitted. **Amenities:** 2 restaurants; standalone lakeside lounges; boutiques; fitness/yoga/meditation classes; 24-hr. fitness center; 1 indoor and 2 outdoor pools; salon; spa; watersports equipment (kayaks, pedalboats, hydrobikes, sculling boats, and stand-up paddleboards); room service; Wi-Fi (free).

East Austin

EXPENSIVE

Heywood Hotel ★★★ Staying here is like crashing at the home of your hippest Austin friends. Austin's best little independently owned boutique hotel is set in in a 1920s-era bungalow in a newly happening section of East Austin. It's very a la mode, with arresting architectural details, reclaimed and repurposed materials (like long-leaf pine flooring), sleek midcentury-style furniture, and high-end textiles. Several rooms have high ceilings and skylights, and all showcase pared-down midcentury-inspired design. You'll easily fall into the chill groove of this casual, comfortable, and contemporary space, with an upstairs courtyard, front porch, and patio. The Heywood is all about the East Austin neighborhood vibe with its food trailers, eclectic restaurants, and residential homes. Special touches, from the art on the walls to throw pillows in the lobby, are created by local artists (and many are for sale). The staff is only on property from 7am to 7pm, so you're on your own at night. Maybe that's why the Heywood makes you feel like you're actually at home. Guests can enjoy a complimentary coffee bar by day and two complimentary beers from a local brewing company at night.

1609 E. Cesar Chavez St. www.heywoodhotel.com. ✆ **512/271-5522.** 7 units. $179–$489 queen double; $289–$559 king double. Free on-site parking. No pets or children under the age of 10. Full property available for rental. **Amenities:** Coffee bar; bikes; Wi-Fi (free).

At the Airport

MODERATE

Hilton Austin Airport ★ So close to the airport you can almost see your gate, this hotel—known as "the Donut" for its round shape—has a central atrium, a restaurant and bar, and a coffee shop. It also has quite a history: It's the former headquarters of Bergstrom Air Force Base and also one of three Cold War bunkers where the president of the United States could be taken for safety in the event of a nuclear attack. So it was built to be solid—which means, for the hotel guest, it's also virtually soundproof. (Ask for the hotel fact sheet on the fascinating history of the Donut, which also served as a strategic air command center during the Vietnam War, the Persian Gulf War, and Desert Storm.) In addition to all that history, the Donut is nicer than most airport hotels. Large, comfortable rooms are equipped with all the amenities, and the hotel has an outdoor saline pool, Jacuzzi, and 24-hour fitness center. If I got stuck in a storm at the airport or had a quick overnight layover, this is where I'd stay. It's also convenient for those heading to the Circuit of the Americas.

9515 New Airport Dr. (½ mile from the airport, 2 miles east of the intersection of hwys. 183 and 71). www3.hilton.com/en/hotels/texas/hilton-austin-airport-AUSAHHF/index.html. ✆ **800/445-8667** or 512/385-6767. 273 units. $139–$199 double; from $189 suite. Special discounts available. Valet parking $20; self-parking $14. Pets accepted with $75 fee. **Amenities:** Restaurant; lounge; free airport transfers; concierge; executive-level rooms; exercise room; outdoor pool; room service; Wi-Fi (free).

WHERE TO EAT

The Austin dining scene has a multitude of barbecue and Tex-Mex joints, but it also has a seriously fine cutting-edge culinary scene. Many restaurants are concentrated in and around downtown and the area immediately south of Lady Bird Lake (aka Town Lake). In other parts of the city, restaurants tend to be set along major commercial corridors like South Lamar. But in some old neighborhoods, you'll find a few tucked away in small clusters on quiet streets. These are some of the city's most interesting local spots, like **Jeffrey's ★★★** on West Lynn (p. 322).

Downtown

EXPENSIVE

Chez Nous ★★ FRENCH This little bistro, French for "our place," has over the years been exactly that: our family's go-to date-night, anniversary, and birthday dinner spot. Set on the busiest part of Sixth Street, this small French hideaway is a mellow respite from the downtown din. It's a pleasant place for a quiet romantic evening with fine wine and appetizing French favorites. It isn't fancy (though the food kind of is); instead, it feels intimate. Small square wooden tables topped with lace doilies and vintage anisette bottles stuffed with fresh flowers sit in a long, narrow dining room of wainscoted walls hung with Paris street signs and French posters. The owners, three friends who came to Austin from Paris in the 1970s, have retained a strong following of loyal locals by consistently providing good service and fine French cuisine at reasonable prices since opening in 1982. A good choice is the prix-fixe dinner (three courses for $33 or two courses for $28) with a choice of soup, salad, or pâté; one of three designated entrees; and crème caramel, chocolate mousse, or brie for dessert. Main courses might include a *saumon au crabe* (Atlantic salmon and crab in vanilla *beurre blanc*–crab remoulade sauce) or a simple grilled Angus sirloin. Everything from the pâtés to the *pommes frites* is made on the premises. Of the main courses, I go for the traditional trout *meunière* with its velvety lemon sauce—reminding me of a great meal I had recently in Paris.

510 Neches St. www.cheznousaustin.com. ✆ **512/473-2413.** Reservations accepted only for parties of 6 or more. Main courses $22–$38; prix fixe $33. Tues–Fri 11:45am–2pm; Tues–Sun 6–10:30pm.

MODERATE

El Naranjo ★★ MEXICAN Ask any Texas chef, and they'll be on a first-name basis with Iliana de la Vega and her husband, Ernesto Torrealba, owners of this popular Rainey Street restaurant. In 1994 they opened a restaurant of the same name in Oaxaca, Mexico, serving traditional Oaxacan cuisine and winning accolades and international acclaim. In 2006, after political unrest came to Oaxaca, the couple moved to Texas, where Iliana was hired as an instructor at the Culinary Institute of America in San Antonio. At the same time, the couple opened a food truck offering traditional Mexican food parked on Rainey Street (at the time not the wildly popular spot it is today). Soon, the two were so busy with their food truck that Iliana quit the CIA. They opened this restaurant in a simple yellow bungalow on Rainey Street, where today you can get some of the city's best *tacos dorados,* here filled with goat cheese, potatoes, or chicken and smothered in green avocado salsa, cream, and crumbled cheese—among other great dishes, including light and delicious fish or shrimp tacos. Iliana bakes fresh bread, Mexican pastries, and tortillas each day and has mastered the art of making spicy fresh salsas and velvet-smooth vegetable-based Oaxacan *molés.* With two dining rooms, a bar, and a lively patio, El Naranjo ("The Orange") is one of Austin's most popular restaurants.

85 Rainey St. www.elnaranjorestaurant.com. ✆ **512/474-2776.** Plates $5–$44. Tues–Sat 5:30–10pm; Brunch Saturday and Sunday 11am–2pm.

Hut's Hamburgers ★★ AMERICAN Sometimes you just want a good burger and fries, some fried onion rings, and a milkshake, and you don't want to spend big bucks. This is the place to go, a classic burger shack that's been an Austin favorite since just about forever. It first opened in 1939 under the name Sammie's Drive-In. Now it's called Hut's, and this Austin favorite offers more than 20 types of burgers, including classic patties made with fresh (never frozen) Texas beef from Johnny G's Meat Market in South Austin. You can also get burgers made with buffalo or chicken, as well as a vegan veggie burger. Regular blue-plate specials include chicken-fried steak, chicken-fried chicken, meatloaf, and fried catfish. I love the Texas-size onion rings.

Decorated with sports pennants, Elvis trinkets, and '50s memorabilia, Hut's is my kids' favorite burger joint, and our family tradition is takeout Hut's for a picnic on the grounds of Zilker Hillside Theatre during the summer musicals. Hut's shares owners with **Frank & Angie's Pizzeria,** located behind Hut's at 508 West St., which serves hand-made pizzas, calzones, New Orleans–style muffaletta sandwiches, salads, and more. Still, I like Hut's burgers best.

807 W. 6th St. www.hutsfrankandangies.com. ✆ **512/472-0693.** Sandwiches and burgers $6–$10; plates $8–$11. Sun–Tues 11am–9:30pm and Wed–Sat 11am–10pm.

Manuel's ★★ MEXICAN With big windows facing Congress Avenue and a bright, glittery vibe inside, this casual but big-city-style restaurant is not your typical Austin Tex-Mex taco joint. For 30 years Manuel's has been pleasing the after-work happy-hour dinner crowd (and made for great date nights) with its dependably fine regional Mexican cuisine. Using high-quality local and seasonal ingredients, Manuel's entrees include *rellenos* and enchiladas of beef, chicken, and pork. Wild-caught fish from certified sustainable waters is never frozen and is hand cut daily. Salad dressings and fried foods are made with canola and virgin olive oils, and Manuel's offers gluten-free, dairy-free, and vegetarian options. My standard order? The *enchiladas suizas* (with a savory Mexican cream sauce) topped with a green chile "verde" sauce. There is often a wait here at night, so reservations are a good idea. Don't miss Manuel's popular Sunday brunch, too.

310 Congress Ave. www.manuels.com. ✆ **512/472-7555.** Reservations recommended. Lunch entrees $12–$16; Dinner main courses $13–$32. Sun–Thurs 11am–10pm; Fri–Sat 11am–11pm; Sunday 10am–3pm. Happy hour daily 4– 6pm. Two locations in Austin (we recommend this downtown one). Reservations recommended.

Ranch 616 ★★ AMERICAN/TEX-MEX/ICEHOUSE They call it a "South Texas–style icehouse," and I love to send visitors here. It's hokey enough to have all that "keep Austin weird" personality, and the food is fabulous. Start with the ever-so-lightly fried oysters and a chilled craft margarita, and you'll see what I mean. It's an immersion in cowboy kitsch, with Christmas lights wrapped around Longhorn mounts, Mexican folk art, and vintage photos of cowboy marching bands and Texas beauty queens on the walls. Sit in the big U-shaped booths or on the patio out front. The menu is hard to pigeonhole—Chef Kevin Williamson and Chef Antonio Vidal offer unique dishes like jalapeño maize chicken or sautéed trout crusted in tortilla chips and topped with mango-chipotle tartar sauce. And it couldn't use the word "ranch" in its name if it didn't serve great steaks, like a Texas Black Angus rib-eye. But here it's paired with enchiladas or house-made tamales instead of boring old steakhouse sides like baked potatoes. Salads are inventive, too, and the cocktail and beer menu can't be beat, so belly up to the bar. This place is fun and cheeky (extra toilet paper rolls in the ladies room are threaded onto the horns of a Longhorn). Just go there. You'll like it.

616 Nueces (just off W. 6th St.). http://theranch616.com. ✆ **512/479-7616.** Reservations recommended. Main courses $9–$20 lunch, $16–$46 dinner. Mon–Thurs 11am–2pm and 5–10pm; Fri 11am–2pm and 5–11pm; Sat 5–11pm; Sun 11am–2:30pm and 5–10pm.

West Austin

EXPENSIVE

Jeffrey's ★★★ NEW AMERICAN If a date brought me to Jeffrey's, I knew he was a keeper. I've been coming here since the 1980s, and it's changed some since, but it's never disappointed in quality and sophistication. This little bistro in the old Clarksville neighborhood west of downtown has been a top destination for Austin food lovers since 1975. In keeping with the tone set by the surrounding neighborhood, the restaurant and bar area are cozy, comfortable, and snazzy. The lighting is low, the art is modern, tables are draped in white linen, and you relax the moment you ease into your chair.

Most of the appetizers rotate with seasons, but our new favorite is the sesame fried oysters. Steaks are always a good choice, like the Niman Ranch Midwest, USDA Prime, Angus center-cut tenderloin. For those wanting to save money and still sample the cuisine, Jeffrey's bar menu features tasty appetizers like king crab avocado toast. You can save even more during happy hour, from 5 to 7pm. ***Tip:*** Want the flavor and fun of Jeffrey's but with a more casual vibe? Pop next door to **Josephine House** (✆ **512/477-5584**), a French-themed sister restaurant to Jeffrey's in a darling Clarksville cottage, offering breakfast, lunch, brunch, happy hour, dinner, and Monday night steak frites.

1204 W. Lynn St. www.jeffreysofaustin.com. ✆ **512/477-5584** or 477-5587. Reservations recommended. Main courses $38–$165. Pre-fixe menus can be arranged in advance. Mon–Thurs 6–10pm; Fri–Sat 5:30–11pm; Sun 6–9:30pm.

MODERATE

Cipollina ★★ ITALIAN/NEW AMERICAN This vine-covered brick West Lynn eatery, with its sweet little bistro tables out front, has long been a neighborhood favorite for delicious wood-fired pizza and sandwiches. But Cipollina is so much more than just a pizzeria. Chef Alex McCurdy likes to say he serves "traditional Italian with an Austin twist," and his fresh seasonal menu offers everything from meatballs to pan-seared snapper, roast chicken to hanger steak, using ingredients sourced locally whenever possible. He still makes his own pasta and gnocchi by hand, and pizza is still on the menu, but McCurdy's pizzas are not your typical pepperoni pies. Look for toppings like bacon with Gorgonzola, apples and arugula, and prosciutto with a rich four-cheese blend drizzled with truffle oil. McCurdy's menu changes with the seasons and often includes a reasonably priced prix-fixe. The roomy dining room has a casual Austin aesthetic with comfy furniture and high ceilings and fans—no fussy tablecloths or mood lighting. It's not that kind of Italian restaurant, after all. From 4 to 6pm, enjoy a happy-hour discount on beer and wine; you can also buy a bottle here to take back to your hotel room—Cipollina has a good wine list with reasonable retail prices.

1213 W. Lynn St. www.cipollina-austin.com. ✆ **512/477-5211.** Main courses $8–$24 lunch, $14–$30 dinner. Daily 11am–10pm. Happy hour 4–6pm.

INEXPENSIVE

Mother's Café & Garden ★ VEGETARIAN/VEGAN This neighborhood vegetarian restaurant has been around since Austin's long-haired-hippie days, yet with warm yellow walls, wooden booths, and an "everyone is welcome" ambience, it's still inviting. The menu is one that should please vegetarians and non-vegetarians alike; favorite dishes include artichoke enchiladas with mushrooms and black olives, and herb- and cheese-filled ravioli. Mother's also serves barbecued tofu, spinach lasagna, stir-fries (garden, Szechuan, Jamaican), and a popular veggie burger. The menu has lots of good entrees built around pasta, which is locally sourced through Pasta & Co. In fact, many of Mother's ingredients and products, from honey to vegan ice cream to coffee beans, are locally sourced. Mother's own cashew-tamari dressing goes well over salads or the steamed vegetables with brown rice. Desserts are made in-house, and smoothies are a treat: Try the Dreamsicle, made with orange juice, banana, and nonfat yogurt. Mother's is home to a popular Sunday brunch from 10am to 3pm.

4215 Duval St. www.motherscafeaustin.com. ✆ **512/451-3994.** Reservations not accepted. Main courses $8–$11. Mon–Fri 11:15am–10pm; Sat–Sun 10am–10pm. Sat–Sun brunch 10am–3pm.

Nau Enfield Drug Soda Fountain ★★★ RETRO SODA FOUNTAIN Some things never change—and that's what locals love about this old West Lynn landmark soda fountain and grill in the Clarksville neighborhood, open since 1951 at the back of an old-fashioned drugstore. It still sells hair nets, gauze bandages, slingshots, and magazines—and a shake or a hamburger or a cup of coffee at the counter with the old-timers. Austin has lots of iconic places that locals wax poetic about: Barton Springs, the (long-gone) Armadillo World Headquarters, the Broken Spoke, Antone's, and Threadgill's. This is one of those places, though sometimes Austinites take it for granted. They'll miss it when it's gone (the family that owns it says it's increasingly hard to keep it going). So go there. Get a strawberry milk shake or chocolate malt. Show your kids an American treasure before it's gone.

1115 W. Lynn St. ✆ **512/476-1221.** Breakfast $2.50–$12; lunch/supper $4.50–$6.50. Mon–Fri 7:30am–8pm; Sat 8am–7pm; Sun 10:30am–4pm.

South Austin

EXPENSIVE

Botticelli's ★★★ ITALIAN When visitors think about dining out in Austin, T-bone steaks, Tex-Mex fare, and chicken-fried steak come to mind. Italian? Not so much. Still, when I crave hand-tossed wood-fired pizza, house-made ravioli, and pasta Bolognese, Botticelli's is my go-to place. This darling little restaurant is tucked beneath a black awning on a popular part of the South Congress strip near the Continental Club. It's got big storefront windows, high ceilings, exposed brick, and a large outdoor patio for alfresco dining. Quiet booths and intimate tables make it the perfect setting for a special meal. The lasagna is superb, as are the house-made raviolis (try the sage butternut squash). The veal/pork/beef meatballs, with a well-seasoned marinara sauce made with freshly diced tomatoes, are outstanding, and fresh fish offerings are often good. The wine list is well-curated, the restaurant serves a good selection of beers, and a flirty little cocktail menu offers drinks like the Hemingway daiquiri and a peach sangria made in-house. I've never made it to dessert here (I fill up on the house-baked focaccia), but friends say the tiramisu is delightful. To eat inside, reserve a table in advance; otherwise, you may have to dine on the patio or out front on the sidewalk. Parking is problematic along South Congress, but a public lot nearby has a credit-card-friendly pay station.

132 South Congress Ave. www.botticellissouthcongress.com. ✆ **512/916-1315.** Reservations accepted. Pizzas $17–$21; pastas and main courses $19–$33. Sun–Wed 5–10:30pm; Thurs–Sat 5–11pm.

Uchi ★★★ ASIAN/JAPANESE Ask any New York foodie what the best restaurant in Austin is—even if they've never been to Texas—and they'll say Uchi. Funny thing is, they'd be right. It's not the atmosphere that makes Uchi so wonderful (although I do like the cozy old bungalow space), it's the food: a playful and inventive take on Asian dishes along with the freshest and finest sushi in town. James Beard award–winning chef and co-owner Tyson Cole is a sushi master who trained at restaurants in Tokyo and New York, and he's deserving of the accolades he receives. His menus change daily but may include such delights as Uchiviche, a whitefish and salmon ceviche with cilantro, chiles, and tomatoes, or the Muru Kai mussels in a dreamy light sauce, or short-ribs cooked low and slow for 72 hours and served with wasabi. But fresh sushi is the main draw. For a near-perfect (though pricey) meal, go with the chef's tasting menu. Pair it with a sake from Uchi's long list of cold sakes. Uchi, Japanese for "house," is set in a converted 1930s bungalow decorated in dark rouge wallpaper with touches of black. Space is limited, and since Uchi has a cult following in Austin, you'll need to make reservations far in advance, or you can wait (hours) for a table at the bar. The only complaint most people have is that it can be far too noisy. I have issues spending $100 on a tasting menu only to have to shout at my dinner companions from across the booth. Still, with food this fresh and fine, it's a hardship I'll put up with. Sister restaurant Uchiko opened in 2010 in a larger, brighter space at 4200 N. Lamar Blvd. (www.uchikoaustin.com; ✆ **512/916-4808**), and there are also Uchi restaurants in Dallas and Houston.

801 S. Lamar Blvd. www.uchiaustin.com. ✆ **512/916-4808.** Reservations recommended. Main courses $18–$30. Chef's tasting menus $100 per person. Mon–Thurs 5–10pm; Fri–Sat 5–11pm.

MODERATE

Güero's Taco Bar ★★★ TEX-MEX This popular hangout has been the go-to Saturday-morning breakfast spot for as long as I can remember. Güero's occupies an old feed store on South Congress, delivering that homey rustic informality that Austinites love. This place is too airy, clean, and bright to feel like a dive, but with well-worn wood floors and stained cement; brick walls exposing peeling paint; and a rattling tin roof, it's too casual and laid-back to be anything else. It's madly popular, and noisy when crowded, so I like to drop in during off hours. Güero's cooks make their own tortillas by hand, and I love the zesty freshness of their fish tacos. Vegetarians will love the spinach enchiladas and big bowls of guacamole. The traditional Tex-Mex combo platters should satisfy big eaters. With margaritas and Mexican beer, Mexican Coca-Cola and Topo Chico mineral water, this is the perfect spot to cool off after shopping the SoCo strip, and it's a hot place to get up and enjoy breakfast tacos on weekends—though half the town wakes up with the same idea.

1412 S. Congress Ave. www.gueros.com. ✆ **512/447-7688.** Reservations not accepted. Main courses $7–$19. Mon–Fri 11am–11pm; Sat–Sun 8am–11pm.

The Salt Lick ★★★ BARBECUE Even my hardcore foodie friends from up north know about the Salt Lick—it's been written up in *The New York Times* more often than many Manhattan eateries. Many think this is the quintessential Austin barbecue spot. Well, it's not actually in Austin: It's 12 miles south of town. You'll start smelling the smoke at least 5 miles before you arrive in the pretty little rural community of Driftwood. As you walk in the door of the original building (on the right as you enter the gate), you'll see a big open-pit barbecue heaving with pounds of juicy turkey and chicken, low-and-slow smoked beef, and pork. Those with extra notches in their belts may enjoy the all-you-can-eat family-style platters of beef, sausage, and pork ribs, served with great sides like slaw, potato salad, pinto beans, and homemade pickles. There are also chopped beef sandwiches, ribs, brisket, and sausage by the pound. But save room for the fresh-baked blackberry or peach cobbler or chocolate pecan pie. Grab a picnic table under heritage oak trees (often with live music) or eat inside in a series of rustic dining rooms. Salt Lick's signature sweet-tangy-sour barbecue sauce is sold here. You may have to wait for a table, so wander next door to the **Salt Lick Cellars** (www.saltlickcellars.com) to sample Texas wines or beers. For years Driftwood was a "dry" community, and the restaurant still doesn't serve alcohol. So you'll need to either buy it next door or BYO. (It's ironic that a community that was dry for so long is now home Stinson Distilling and Winery, the Driftwood Estate Winery, and the nearby Duchman Family Winery—all worth visiting if you're making a day trip to Salt Lick.) If you can't make it out to Driftwood, pick up some brisket at the Salt Lick's Austin airport branch. Salt Lick is a cash-only place, but there's an ATM on-site.

18300 FM 1826, Driftwood. www.saltlickbbq.com. ✆ **512/858-4959** or 888/SALT-LICK (725-8542) mail order. Reservations accepted only for large parties. Main courses $9–$23. Cash only; no credit cards. Daily 11am–10pm. 13 miles south of Austin, from the junction of U.S. 290 W. and FM 1826.

Threadgill's ★★ AMERICAN/SOUTHERN If there is one spot that's considered sacred ground in Austin, this is it. Look for the little plaque on a stick in the parking lot, marking the spot of what was Austin's most famous and most beloved music venue, the Armadillo World Headquarters. From 1970 to 1980 famous folks like Janis Joplin, Lynyrd Skynyrd, Willie Nelson, Arlo Guthrie, Jerry Jeff Walker, and Bruce Springsteen played the 'Dillo before a bank "paved paradise and put up a parking lot" in its place. Nowadays you can pay homage to the Armadillo *and* get a filling Texas-size dinner: chicken-fried steak, burgers, cheese-stuffed jalapeños, fried okra, garlic-cheese grits, black-eyed peas, and more down-home food. Threadgill's owner, Eddie Wilson, was the founder of the Armadillo, and he's filled this location with old photos and music memorabilia from the club, along with a fabulous sound system. Be sure to hit the Sunday brunch buffet with live music from 11am to 1pm, or make it to a "howdy" hour during the week. Both Threadgill's locations, including the original one on North Lamar, double as live-music venues.

301 W. Riverside Dr. www.threadgills.com. ✆ **512/472-9304.** Reservations not accepted. Main courses $8–$13 lunch; $12–$22 dinner. Sunday brunch buffet $13 adults; $5.95 children. Mon–Fri 11am–10pm; Sat 10am–10pm; Sun 10am–9:30pm.

INEXPENSIVE

Chuy's ★★ TEX-MEX Locals have been coming to this wacky den of kitsch since the spring of 1982. They come for the tasty authentic Tex-Mex and zany, good-humored atmosphere. Located on Barton Spring Road just east of Zilker Park, Chuy's feels like a party is perpetually underway, with an entire shrine to Elvis, hubcaps clustered on the ceiling, Christmas lights, wooden fish hanging overhead, and cheesy velvet paintings. The food is consistently good, and servings are more than generous. The jalapeño ranch dip with tortilla chips has just the right amount of zest. My husband's favorite is the *carne guisada* burrito, but I always go for the Chuychanga, a flash-fried flour tortilla filled with hot grilled chicken, grated cheese, and green chiles, topped with a dollop of cold sour cream. Because Chuy's is so popular and doesn't take reservations, expect to wait for a table. Time will pass more quickly if you sit in the bar and order a cold metal bucket of iced-down bottled beer for your party to share. Be careful not to nosh away your appetite at the free nacho bar, or you won't have room for a big hot plate of bubbling enchiladas, Spanish rice, and refried beans. Did I mention that Chuy's margaritas are killer good? Or try the "Mexican martinis" (like margaritas, but bigger and with olives). Other locations have sprouted up all over the USA, but in Austin they can be found on 10520 N. Lamar Blvd. (✆ **512/836-3218**), at 11680 N. Research Blvd. (✆ **512/342-0011**), and at 4301 W. William Cannon Dr. (✆ **512/899-2489**).

1728 Barton Springs Rd. www.chuys.com. ✆ **512/474-4452.** Reservations not accepted. Main courses $8–$14. Sun–Thurs 11am–10pm; Fri–Sat 11am–11pm.

Central

EXPENSIVE

Fonda San Miguel ★★ MEXICAN Fonda San Miguel owners Thomas Gilliland and Miguel Ravago like to reminisce about how George W. Bush proposed to his wife, Laura, at the restaurant. I can see why the former president chose this place for his special night: It's one of Austin's most romantic spots. This landmark restaurant was one of the first to introduce Mexican fine dining to Texas, and even now there are few places quite like it in the state. Fonda San Miguel is the kind of place we like to bring our out-of-town guests for drinks, especially during happy hour. Just inside the enormous hand-carved wooden entry doors lies an interior courtyard. To the right are dining rooms awash in rich colors and soft lighting. The ambience is that of an authentic hacienda, and the cuisine is also true to its regional Mexican roots. This is not a Tex-Mex restaurant, and its prices reflect that difference, as does the menu. From Puebla, Mexico, comes *polle en molé poblano,* baked chicken smothered in a rich chocolaty sauce. The *cochinita pibil* is pork roasted Yucatan-style in a banana leaf. The Sunday brunch buffet is a big (and pricey) event at Fonda San Miguel, with an array of delectable choices (such as fruit gazpacho and *chilaquiles*). Don't want a big dinner? Stick to *antojitos* ("little cravings" or appetizers) and cold margaritas by the bar.

2330 W. North Loop Blvd. www.fondasanmiguel.com. ✆ **512/459-4121.** Reservations recommended. Main courses $18–$42; Sunday brunch $39. Restaurant Mon–Thurs 5:30–9:30pm; Fri–Sat 5:30–10:30pm; Sun 11am–2pm. Bar Mon–Sat 5pm–closing.

MODERATE

Hyde Park Bar and Grill ★★ AMERICAN To quote Yogi Berra, "When you come to a fork in the road, take it." Good advice when looking for this restaurant, known for its landmark giant-size fork out front. Not only is it easy to find, but it's easy to find a parking space and get seated at a table, at least during off-peak hours. If there is a wait, you can always enjoy a drink at the bar. This place is famous (at least locally) for its buttermilk- and pepper-battered fries, arguably the best fries in town. It also serves chicken-fried steak along with more healthful options, like roast chicken. Set in a one-story wooden house with window seating in some of its dining rooms, the atmosphere is cozy and casual, and the service attentive. I had some great dates here back in my '80s college days—that's how long this restaurant has been around. Another location is in South Austin at 4521 Westgate Blvd. (✆ **512/899-2700**).

4206 Duval St. www.hydeparkbarandgrill.com. ✆ **512/458-3168.** Lunch $7–$11; main courses $12–$19. Mon–Thurs 11am–10:30pm; Fri–Sat 11am–11pm; Sun 10:30am–10:30pm.

INEXPENSIVE

Epicerie Cafe & Grocery ★★★ AMERICAN/GROCERY CAFE Stop and smell the beignets at this darling little vine-covered bistro and grocery spot just west of North Lamar. The beignets (powdered-sugar pastries made to order) rival those of New Orleans' Café du Monde, just one of the many delights here. You're wowed from the get-go by a display case of assorted fine cheeses, shelves filled with gourmet foods, and a fine selection of affordable wines. Sit down at one of the cafe tables, and choose from a menu of house-made soups, fresh salads, hot sandwiches, and yes, beignets. I love this little place with its quiet outdoor patio not far from Shoal Creek, but I really need to go easy on the beignets next time. It's not far from Fonda San Miguel, so you could go for a two-fer of beignets and Mexican while you're in the neighborhood.

2307 Hancock Dr. http://epicerieaustin.com. © **512/371-6840.** Main courses $8–$20. Mon–Tues 10:30am–9:30pm; Wed–Thurs 8am–9:30pm; Fri–Sat 8am–10:30pm; Sun 10:30am–3pm.

Westlake/Lake Travis

EXPENSIVE

Steiner Ranch Steakhouse ★★ STEAK/SEAFOOD Take a scenic drive along a curvy canyon-edged road outside Austin for a special evening at this stylish steakhouse. It's a 35-minute drive from Austin to Steiner, but we think it's worth it—the restaurant has sunset views of Lake Travis from every room. Dine outside to live music on the patio, or slide into a big roomy booth in the clubby restaurant, with its casual but upscale vibe. This quintessential Texas steakhouse stands on land that was once part of a 5,200-acre ranch, home base to the founders and livestock of the Steiner rodeo company in the lovely Highland Lake country northwest of town. It's the perfect place to enjoy hand-selected premium cuts of beef. Lighter fare includes blackened Atlantic salmon topped with grilled jumbo shrimp, sautéed spinach, and sun-dried tomato butter. For a romantic winter dinner, sit near the fireplace in the Great Room, or cozy up in a booth and sip a signature cocktail. Steiner has an outstanding selection of fine wines too. The restaurant is not far from the **Lake Austin Spa Resort ★★★**, so if you're staying there, pop on over.

5424 Steiner Ranch Blvd. www.steinersteakhouse.com. © **512/381-0800.** Reservations recommended. Main courses $25–$50. Mon–Thurs 4–10pm; Fri–Sat 4–11pm; Sun 10am–10pm.

MODERATE

County Line on the Hill ★ BARBECUE This County Line on Bee Cave Road, opened in 1975, is the original location of what has become a popular chain. A 1920s speakeasy once stood on this spot, but today it's home to a barbecue joint for those who love big ribs and sunset views of the Hill Country. If you don't mind a heavy midday meal, come for lunch—it's often so crowded at suppertime you may wait as long as an hour to eat. You won't mind too much, though, if you sit on the deck and take in the scenic Hill Country surrounds. County Line is known for its big beef ribs (they also have pork ribs). Unless you request it "moist," the brisket here is generally lean (moist is more flavorful). There are generous servings of chicken and sausage, too. Sides are tasty and include coleslaw, beans, potato salad, and fresh-baked bread. Set in a rustic country house with old signs and photos, the place has a laid-back atmosphere with a 20-mile view (on a clear day). I actually prefer the **County Line on the Lake** location (northwest), 5204 FM 2222 (© **512/346-3664**), because of its attractive setting on Bull Creek just off Lake Austin. It offers the same menu and is also open for lunch and dinner.

6500 W. Bee Cave Rd. www.countyline.com. © **512/327-1742.** Reservations not accepted. Main courses $14–$35 ($6–$8 for children 11 and under). Mon–Thurs and Sun 11:30am–9pm; Fri and Sat 11:30am–9:30pm.

FOOD trailer park IN AUSTIN

Meals-on-wheels takes on a whole new meaning here with a centrally located strip of Airstream and RV eateries in SoCo. In laid-back Austin, no one is in a hurry to eat on the run, so tables have been set up and little lights hung above the gravel parking lot, making this food trailer court a place to grab good food with friends, and stay awhile. For details, visit www.austinfoodcarts.com. Here's a list of a few fun food trailers to try:

- **The Mighty Cone:** Known for hot and crunchy fried wraps—aka "cones"—made with chicken, shrimp, or avocado and served with mango aioli and slaw, SoCo's Mighty Cone was named one of "The Top-10 Trailers in America" by *The Wall Street Journal*. It's no wonder this place gets such raves—it began as the haute cuisine counterpart to the elegant, highly acclaimed Hudson's on the Bend restaurant on Lake Travis, whose then-owner/chef Jeff Blank helped launch this hot food trailer sensation (www.mightycone.com).
- **Paperboy:** This East 11th Street food truck is perfect for breakfast grub, including "hash" (roasted sweet potatoes, poached egg, braised pork belly, grilled onions, coffee mayo) and "sweet" toast (ricotta, tangerine marmalade, granola, strawberry, honey), plus Stumptown coffee (www.paperboyaustin.com).
- **Patrizi's:** Italian food truck fare? Yep. With house-made pastas (truck-made?), meatballs, the simple Roman dish *cacio e pepe*, and a robust signature red sauce, Patrizi's is a favorite go-to food truck. It's located on Manor Rd. just east of I-35 in the Vortex Theater courtyard (www.patrizis.com).
- **Torchy's Tacos:** Go for the green-chile pork tacos topped with *queso fresco*, cilantro, onions, and lime. Torchy's now has brick-and-mortar restaurants all over, like the big one on South Congress Avenue, but a classic Torchy's trailer park still resides on South First (www.torchystacos.com).
- **Hey Cupcake!:** Among the quirky cupcakes is "the Michael Jackson"—chocolate on the inside with cream cheese icing. There are now two Hey Cupcake! trailers and a bakery, but the weird but wonderful concept of a cupcake vending machine (at Lakeline Mall in Cedar Park/NW Austin) is worth seeing, too (www.heycupcake.com).
- **The Holy Cacao:** Ooooh, I love the sweet S'mores on a Stick and chocolate mint grasshopper cakeballs. Located on South First, Holy Cacao also serves frozen hot chocolate and my favorite, a sweet "Cake Shake" (www.theholycacao.com).

The Oasis ★ AMERICAN/TEX-MEX When friends visit from out-of-town, Austinites always take them to the Oasis to see the sunset. An enormous place with multilevel decks burrowed into the hillside hundreds of feet above Lake Travis, the Oasis celebrates the sunset nightly, as guests applaud and whoop it up when the sun finally descends behind the hills. This (and the margaritas) is why they came, and few leave unimpressed. The food can be iffy, however—this is not the place to try your first enchilada or order a big steak. Stick to the basics, like hamburgers, nachos, and chicken-tender-topped salads, and you'll be fine. Then add an icy margarita for the sunset wait, and before the night is over, you'll be planning your next trip back to Austin. The Oasis nearly burned down a few years back, and after the restoration it became a bit more touristy than before (exit by the gift shop), but visitors still like it—it's worth it for the views, not only of the lake, but of the scenery along the way out along Ranch Road 2222 from MoPac.

6550 Comanche Trail, overlooking Lake Travis off RM 620. www.oasis-austin.com. ✆ **512/266-2442.** Reservations not accepted. Main courses $12–$20. Mon–Thurs 11:30am–9pm; Fri 11:30–10:30pm Sat–Sun 11am–10:30pm (closing times may vary with weather).

East Austin

MODERATE

Eastside Cafe ★★ AMERICAN For decades it wasn't even considered a desirable part of town, but these days Austin's East Side is *the* place to open a restaurant. Back in 1988, Carla Blumberg, a forward-thinking, health-conscious Texas millionaire, and Elaine Martin, her business partner, saw something they liked here and opened Eastside Cafe, just east of the UT campus in the Cherrywood neighborhood. Almost 30 years later, Eastside Cafe still remains popular with locals and visitors alike, especially those who want a garden-to-table meal with healthful (and often vegetarian-friendly) menu choices. You can dine on a tree-shaded patio overlooking the gardens or in one of a series of small, homey rooms in the turn-of-the-century wooden house. The menu ranges from panko- and pecan-breaded chicken breasts and artichoke manicotti to sesame-crusted catfish, baked brie, and salads topped with warm goat cheese and pine nuts—all served with the cafe's signature warm jalapeño cornbread. Look for daily chef specials and seasonal soups, too. The cafe offers half-price bottles of wine daily from 4pm 'til closing. Each morning, the gardener and the chef discuss what ingredients are available from the organic garden (and the farm just outside town). An adjacent store carries gardening tools, cookware, and the cafe's salad dressings. Also on the property is **Elaine's Pork & Pie,** serving pulled-pork sandwiches and house-made pies (✆ **512/494-1464**).

2113 Manor Rd. www.eastsidecafeaustin.com. ✆ **512/476-5858.** Reservations recommended; main courses $10–$22. Mon–Thurs 11:15am–9:30pm; Fri 11:15am–10pm; Sat 10am–10pm; Sun 10am–9:30pm (brunch 10am–3pm).

Justine's Brasserie ★★★ FRENCH This old house tucked away on the east side is my favorite restaurant in Austin. It isn't very expensive, so I don't know why I always save Justine's for special-occasion dinners. Justine's is not fancy either—it's got creaky wooden floors, wobbly cafe tables, and vintage Neil Young warbling in the background. Young bohemian types huddle at the bar, and friends sit around the patio firepit. This is the laid-back, unfussy Austin I love, where the atmosphere is beguiling, and the food is solidly pleasing. This Parisian-style bistro offers French fare, like steamed mussels; *pommes frites;* French onion soup; and a Belgian endive, pear, and Roquefort salad with roasted beets and walnuts. Look for chalkboard wine specials daily.

I suggest arriving either very early or very late (the place gets noisy and crowded, and when the dining room gets full you might get seated in what we call Siberia—the tent out front where Justine's tends to lose her charm). I've had dinner here 'round midnight, too—how very European of the place to keep the kitchen open late. If you walked into Justine's in the morning, you might think, *what a dive*—but at night when the music is playing, votive candles are flickering, and the lipstick-red walls cast a warm rosy glow, you may think it's the best place in town.

4710 E. 5th St. www.justines1937.com. ✆ **512/385-2900.** Reservations recommended. Main courses $12–$30. Mon and Wed–Sun 6pm–2am; closed Tues.

INEXPENSIVE

Franklin Barbecue ★★★ BARBECUE No one was more surprised than Aaron Franklin when he won the "Best Chef, Southwest" James Beard award in 2015. He still seems to be scratching his head about that—yet, it couldn't have happened to a nicer guy. The always friendly Franklin and his wife, Stacy, got their start serving barbecue out of a trailer, before popular demand for their tender smoked meats instigated a move to this brick-and-mortar shop. Today Franklin Barbecue is arguably the most popular barbecue joint in the U.S., and Aaron is a media star, appearing on shows like *Jimmy Kimmel Live!* and hosting his own PBS series, *BBQ with Franklin.* Aaron cooks his briskets on a low-heat oak fire for 18 hours, and each morning a line forms that snakes around the block and is filled with folks hoping to get served before he sells out of meat by around 1pm. The only person ever allowed to cut in line? President Obama, who bought lunch for those behind him. Franklin's ribs, brisket, and sausage taste very much like the small-town barbecue found in Lockhart (the "Barbecue Capital of Texas"), and since it may be quicker to get to Lockhart and back than stand in line at Franklin's all morning, you might want to try there first (start at **Smitty's Market,** 208 S. Commerce St., Lockhart, ✆ **512/398-9344**). In addition to more traditional offerings, Franklin serves pulled pork, uncommon in central Texas, and an espresso-flavored barbecue sauce. Plan on taking half a day out of your schedule to stand in line, so bring amusements: lawn chairs, chess sets, card games, magazines. I promise you, the barbecue is worth the wait. ***Tip:*** You can skip the line if you pre-order your meat online for takeout, but there's a 5-pound minimum order if you do.

900 E. 11th St. www.franklinbarbecue.com. ✆ **512/653-1187.** Lunch $8–$20. Tues–Sun 11am–until sold out (usually between 1–3pm).

AUSTIN SHOPPING

The Shopping Scene

Visitors to Austin don't really come for the shopping, but the opportunistic shopper can be rewarded with some wonderful discoveries. Folk art, arts and crafts, music, books—these are the areas where Austin excels (especially along South Congress Avenue). Austin has got the rest of the material world pretty well covered, too.

Shopping Areas

In central Austin, the best concentration of shops and galleries is found along **East Sixth Street** near Congress Avenue, **West Sixth Street and Lamar Boulevard, West Second Street** near Congress Avenue, and **South Congress Avenue** (or **"SoCo"**). SoCo has gotten quite a bit fancier in the past few years. The funkier, less expensive shops moved on to lower-rent **South First Street** and **South Lamar Boulevard.** There is also a cluster of stores in the vicinity of the intersection of **North Lamar and 38th Street.** Many stores on the **Drag**—the stretch of Guadalupe Street between Martin Luther King, Jr., Boulevard, and 26th Street, across from the UT campus—are student-oriented, but a wide range of clothing, gifts, toys, and, of course, books can also be found here.

If you're looking for a shopping center, the growth area seems to be in the northwest, where several upscale shopping centers vie for customers: the **Arboretum,** the **Arboretum Market,** the **Gateway Shopping Centers** (consisting of Gateway Courtyard, the Gateway Market, and Gateway Square), and the **Domain** have earned the area the nickname "South Dallas." If you're a power shopper and want to sleep, shop, eat, repeat, you'll find good little hotels and restaurants in and around the **Domain.**

The Goods A–Z

ART

Austin's commitment to music makes it a perfect location for **Wild About Music,** 615 Congress Ave. (www.wildaboutmusic.com; ✆ **512/708-1700**), a gallery and shop strictly devoted to arts and crafts with a musical theme. **Women & Their Work,** 1710 Lavaca St. (www.womenandtheirwork.org; ✆ **512/477-1064**), highlights more than visual art—it also promotes and showcases women in dance, music, theater, film, and literature. "Outsider" art, created in the rural South, usually by the poor and sometimes by the incarcerated, is the focus of **Yard Dog Folk Art,** 1510 S. Congress Ave. (www.yarddog.com; ✆ **512/912-1613**). Folk art and crafts from Latin America and around the world can be found at **Tesoros Trading Company,** 1500 S. Congress Ave. (www.tesoros.com; ✆ **512/447-7500**); and **Ten Thousand Villages,** 4803 Burnet Rd. (www.tenthousandvillages.com/austin; ✆ **512/440-0440**).

FOOD

To see the ultimate in supermarkets, visit the flagship store of **Whole Foods Markets** at 525 N. Lamar Blvd. (www.wholefoods.com; ✆ **512/542-2200**). It may sound weird, but this store is so big and amazing that it's considered one of top tourist destinations in Austin.

In addition to hosting some of the nation's most lavish grocery stores, Austin has an abundance of farmers' markets. Perhaps the most notable of them is **SFC (Sustainable Food Center) Farmers' Market** (www.sustainablefoodcenter.org/programs/sfc-farmers-market; ✆ **512/236-0074**), held **downtown** at Republic Square Park (422 Guadalupe St.), every Saturday from 9am

FIRST thursday

As if there weren't already enough street theater in Austin, the merchants on South Congress Avenue decided a few years back to host a monthly street festival, keeping their doors open late and providing food, drinks, and, entertainment on the first Thursday of every month. Soon, impromptu open-air markets sprang up, and jugglers, drum circles, and, of course, live bands performed indoors, outdoors, and in between.

First Thursday (www.firstthursday austin.com) has become quite popular for the mix of shopping, entertainment, people-watching, and the surprise factor—you never know what you're going to meet up with. It's also a way for locals to celebrate the approach of the weekend. The street festival occupies about 8 blocks along both sides of South Congress. Traffic along the avenue is not cordoned off, but everyone drives slowly because of the crowds crisscrossing the avenue. It starts around 6pm and runs until about 10pm.

to 1pm March through November. SFC also has a Saturday market in **South Austin** (Toney Burger Center, 3200 Jones Rd.; 9am–1pm) and a Wednesday market in **Triangle Park** (4660 Triangle Ave.; 3–7pm).

MUSIC

Carrying a huge selection of sounds, **Waterloo Records and Video,** 600A N. Lamar Blvd. (www.waterloorecords.com; © **512/474-2500**), is always the first in town to get the new releases. The store has a popular preview listening section, offers compilation tapes of Austin groups, and sells tickets to all major-label shows around town.

TEXAS SOUVENIRS

The gift shop at the **Capitol Visitors Center,** 1100 Congress Ave. (www.tspb.state.tx.us/prop/tcvc/cvc/cvc.html; © **512/475-2167**), sells all kinds of Texas memorabilia, including paperweights made from reproductions of the Texas seal, doorknobs, bookends, and local food products. There is also a variety of educational toys and an excellent selection of historical books.

WESTERN WEAR

Name notwithstanding, **Allen's Boots,** 1522 S. Congress Ave. (www.allens boots.com; © **512/447-1413**), sells a lot more than footwear. Come here too for hats, belts, jewelry, and other boot-scootin' accoutrements (bring the kids, too), but bring your wallet: Manly footwear doesn't come cheap. **Heritage Boot**, 1200 S. Congress Ave. (www.heritageboot.com; © **512/326-8577**), sells only boots, and these are beautifully made, all by hand, using the old ways of craftsmanship—also pricey but worth it. Want a bargain and a great boot? The selection is small, but gently used, quality cowboy boots are available at **Texas Custom Boots,** 1601 South 1st St. (www.texascustomboots.com; © **512/981-5777**), where a boot maker from Mexico can custom-create the perfect pair for you or repair worn-out ones.

AUSTIN NIGHTLIFE

Entertainment in Austin starts with live music. In fact, you might get your first taste of it before you even pick up your bags at the airport, where 11 concerts are held each week to serenade travelers. Live music is what this city is known for. Many famous musicians, such as the Dixie Chicks and Shawn Colvin, call Austin home and frequently perform here. But there are also a large number of lesser-known but great performers, who for one reason or another are content to stay in Austin and enjoy a comfortable and modest level of success, which they supplement occasionally by going on tour, just to pay the bills. The level of virtuosity is impressive.

Austin's music scene is fluid; there's a lot of mixing of styles and genres, some well-known, such as country and rock hybrids, others more incongruous, such as punk and bluegrass. It all makes Austin music really rich and worth exploring. Another aspect of the live music scene here is that it's inexpensive. Some really, really good bands play for tips on weekdays and for starving-artist pay at other times. This has been true for years, and it makes you feel that the city is getting a lot more from this arrangement than it puts out. That's not to say that Austin doesn't try to support its local musicians. Social groups organize benefit concerts, and the city and some companies offer lots of free concerts to promote the local talent.

Check out what's on in the ***Austin Chronicle*** and the ***Austin-American Statesman.*** Both are available in hundreds of outlets across the city.

For information about what's happening in the other performing arts, check out **www.nowplayingaustin.com**. A joint project of the Austin Creative Alliance and the city, the website has a comprehensive, well-organized calendar of events for all the performing arts, and includes museum shows as well. You can also buy tickets through its "Austix" link. If you would rather use the phone, call the **Austix Box Office** (✆ **512/474-8497**). Whether you buy online or by phone, the tickets can be picked up at the event, or at the Austix office in the city's visitor center at 209 E. 6th St. Sometimes Austix offers discount tickets and sometimes half-priced, last-minute tickets. There is a small fee for using the service, which goes to support the performing arts.

The Performing Arts

The **Long Center** (www.thelongcenter.org; ✆ **512/457-5100**) is Austin's venue for symphony orchestra, opera, and ballet, and for visiting performance companies as well. The hall, set on the south shore of Lady Bird Lake, was designed to take advantage of its location. A raised terrace framed by a circular colonnade looks out over the lake to the downtown skyline. The grand concert hall, named for Michael and Susan Dell, seats 2,400 people. A studio theater holds smaller-size performances.

At the University of Texas, the **Texas Performing Arts** (http://texasperformingarts.org; ✆ **512/471-2787**) attracts major Broadway musicals, pop singers, and classical music ensembles. It has six theaters. It also is the venue for performances by university theater and dance groups.

OPERA & CLASSICAL MUSIC

A resident in Austin since 1911, the **Austin Symphony,** 1101 Red River St. (www.austinsymphony.org; ✆ **888/426-3787** or 512/476-6064), performs most of its classical works at Bass Concert Hall. The city's first professional opera company, **Austin Opera,** has its offices at 3009 Industrial Terrace, Suite 100, and performs at the Long Center (www.austinopera.org; ✆ **512/472-5992** for box office), presenting three or four productions annually. The **Austin Chamber Music Center,** 7600 Burnet Rd., Ste. 190 (www.austinchambermusic.org; ✆ **512/454-0026**), features an "Intimate Concert" series, held at private residences, and hosts visiting national and international artists.

THEATER

Austin's oldest professional theater, incorporated in 1933, the **Zach Theatre** (www.zachtheatre.org; ✆ **512/476-0541** [box office] or 476-0594) makes use of two adjacent venues at the edge of Zilker Park: the John E. Whisenhunt Arena at 1510 Toomey Rd., and the theater-in-the-round Kleburg at 1421 W. Riverside Dr., all part of one campus located at 202 S. Lamar.

DANCE

The two dozen professional dancers of **Ballet Austin** (www.balletaustin.org; ✆ **512/476-2163** [box office] or 512/476-9151) leap and bound in such classics as *The Magic Flute* and *The Nutcracker,* as well as in the more avant-garde pieces of the trendsetting "Director's Choice" series. The latter pairs the work of various contemporary choreographers with the music of popular local Latin musicians and singer-songwriters. When in town, the troupe performs at the Long Center (www.thelongcenter.org).

The Club & Music Scene

Music was always important to life in Austin, but it became a big deal in the early '70s with the advent of progressive country (aka redneck rock). Local boy Willie Nelson became its principal proponent, along with several other Austin musicians. The Armadillo World Headquarters, a music hall known for hosting all the '60s rock bands, became the center of events and symbolized the marriage of country with counterculture. The city has since become an incubator for a wonderfully vital, crossbred alternative sound that mixes rock, country, folk, blues, punk, and Tejano. Although the Armadillo is now gone, live music in Austin continues to thrive in bars all across central Austin.

While **Sixth Street** (btw. Congress Ave. and Red River St.) is well known to many outsiders and home to some good bars, just as popular but less famous (at least to non-locals) is the **Warehouse District** (just west of Congress Ave. btw. Second and Fifth sts.), with more glitz than grunge. For those wanting exposure to more of the local sound, there are cheap dives just off Sixth, on **Red River Street** (btw. Sixth and 10th sts.). There also are many venues that don't fall inside these districts, like the **Continental Club** (www.continentalclub.com) on South Congress Ave. and the **Saxon Pub** (www.thesaxonpub.com) on South Lamar. There's a lot to explore.

FOLK & COUNTRY

One of the great country-music dancehalls, **Broken Spoke ★★**, 3201 S. Lamar Blvd. (www.brokenspokeaustintx.net; ✆ **512/442-6189**), dates back to 1964 when this level of South Lamar was the edge of town, surrounded by oak trees, and people would come out here to two-step across the large wood-plank floor. It hasn't changed much (inside at least), except for the occasional busload of tourists stopping by. Today, the Broken Spoke is surrounded by condos; only the big oak tree out front remains.

But do not leave Austin without seeing the Broken Spoke. You don't have to be all duded up for dancing here. Granted, boot-scootin' is nice to do with real boots, but lots of people show up in sneakers and Hawaiian shirts. You can eat in a large, open room out front (the chicken-fried steak can't be beat), or take your longnecks back to a table overlooking the dance floor. Don't miss what the owners call the "tourist trap" room out back, an unofficial sort of Texas country music museum and shrine to the greats, like Bob Wills, Jerry Jeff Walker, Willie Nelson, and the rest. Cover charges (in the dancehall only; sitting in the front room is free) range from $5 to $15.

JAZZ & BLUES

Antone's ★★, 305 W. 5th St. (www.antonesnightclub.com; ✆ **512/814-0361**), has been synonymous with the blues. Stevie Ray Vaughan used to be a regular, and when major blues artists venture this way, you can bet they'll be either playing Antone's or stopping by for a surprise set. The **Elephant Room ★★**, 315 Congress Ave. (www.elephantroom.com; ✆ **512/473-2279**), is an intimate space that's as dark and smoky as any good jazz den should be—Wynton Marsalis listed it among his top 10 favorite jazz clubs in the U.S. It's my favorite music venue in a town with thousands of them.

ROCK

Austin's last word in alternative music, **Emo's,** 2015 E. Riverside Dr. (www.emosaustin.com; ✆ **888/512-7469**), draws acts of all sizes and flavors, from Gang Green to Green Day. It primarily attracts college kids, but those of any age won't really feel out of place.

SINGER/SONGWRITER

A small, dark cavern with great acoustics and a fully stocked bar, the **Cactus Café ★**, Texas Union, University of Texas campus, 24th and Guadalupe (www.cactuscafe.org; ✆ **512/475-6515**), is singer/songwriter heaven. The attentive listening vibes attract the likes of Alison Krauss and Suzanne Vega, along with well-known acoustic combos.

ECLECTIC

Within the rough limestone walls of **Stubb's,** 801 Red River St. (www.stubbsaustin.com; ✆ **512/480-8341**), you'll find great barbecue, three friendly bars, and terrific music ranging from singer/songwriter solos to hip-hop open mics to all-out country jams. Out back, the Waller Amphitheatre hosts some of the bigger acts. The Sunday gospel brunches are an Austin institution. The **Saxon Pub,** at 1320 S. Lamar Blvd. (www.thesaxonpub.com; ✆ **512/448-2552**), is a longtime local favorite. The crowd is older and more laid-back, and the volume is lower than at most of the Sixth Street bars. Check the calendar, and you'll find performers who rarely play in such a small venue.

The Bar Scene

A HISTORIC BAR

Since 1866, when Councilman August Scholz first opened his tavern near the state capitol, every Texas governor has visited **Scholz Garten** ★ (1607 San Jacinto Blvd.; www.scholzgarten.com; ✆ **512/474-1958**) at least once (and many quite a few more times). An extensive menu combines barbecue favorites with traditional bratwurst and sauerkraut; a state-of-the-art sound system cranks out polka tunes; and patio tables and a few strategically placed TV sets help Longhorn fans cheer on their team. This is the perfect place to watch a big sports game and a great place to drink in some Austin history—it's full of great memories for those who went to college in this town.

GAY & LESBIAN SCENE

Its name notwithstanding, **Oilcan Harry's,** 211 W. 4th St. (www.oilcanharrys.com; ✆ **512/320-8823**), attracts a clean-cut, upscale Warehouse District crowd, while the **Highland Lounge,** 404 Colorado St. (www.highlandlounge.com; ✆ **512/649-1212**), is the largest and arguably hottest LGBT club in the Warehouse District—it won the *Austin Chronicle* Readers' Choice award for Best New Club 2015.

LOCAL FAVORITES

The **Cedar Door,** 201 Brazos St. (www.cedardooraustin.com; ✆ **512/473-3712**), remains Austin's favorite neighborhood bar, drawing a group of potluck regulars ranging from hippies to journalists and politicos. This place has moved at least three times in the past 20 years, but it never loses its loyal following. **Mean Eyed-Cat,** 1621 W. 5th St. (www.themeaneyedcat.com; ✆ **512/920-6645**) is a Johnny Cash–themed bar that takes its name from one of the Man in Black's lesser-known songs. A fabulous little dive bar with music out back, this is a favorite best-kept-secret kind of bar. The men's and women's restrooms are marked "Johnny" and "June." The **Moontower Saloon,** 10212 Manchaca Rd. (www.moontowersaloon.com), in South Austin, just a few blocks south of Slaughter Lane, is our favorite of the newer spots. Under a canopy of oak trees strung with white lights are outdoor decks, patio bars, volleyball courts, a firepit, bike racks, and dogs. Did we mention live music? The owners say going here is basically "like you're crashing a really rad backyard/house party already in progress." Yep, this is the Austin we know and love.

HILL COUNTRY SIDE TRIPS FROM AUSTIN

The following destinations in one of the state's prettiest regions can be visited on day trips from Austin, but you really should stay overnight in the area. Trips to the locations detailed here can easily be combined with those described in the "Hill Country Side Trips from San Antonio" section of chapter 8.

Fredericksburg ★★★

Fredericksburg is a town of 10,000 inhabitants located just about 75 miles from either San Antonio or Austin. Fredericksburg is noted for its picturesque main street—old-time storefronts with sidewalk canopies, in the tradition of small-town Texas. It's also known for its German heritage—this was once the center of a large German farming community. These days, the farmers are known for the peaches they grow (available at orchards and roadside stands May–July), and, more recently, vineyards and lavender farms. Fredericksburg is the hub of the Hill Country wineries.

The town is a lovely weekend escape for city dwellers in San Antonio and Austin, with lots of bed-and-breakfasts and guesthouses. Many visitors come to relax, shop, and perhaps taste some wine. Others come to explore the surrounding countryside, including nearby **Enchanted Rock,** the Hill Country's most famous geological feature.

SEEING THE SIGHTS IN TOWN

The **Fredericksburg Visitor Information Center,** 302 E. Austin St. (www.visitfredericksburgtx.com; ✆ **888/997-3600** or 830/997-6523), can direct you to the many points of interest in the town's historic district. These include a number of little **Sunday Houses,** built by German settlers in distant rural areas because they needed a place to stay overnight when they came to town to trade or attend church.

On the town's main square, called Market Square, is an unusual octagonal **Vereins Kirche (Society Church).** It's actually a replica (built in 1935) of the original 1847 building. The original was the first public building in Fredericksburg. It was built to be a church where both Lutheran and Catholic Germans could hold services and, as such, was a symbol of unity for the early pioneers. Inside is a history exhibit of the town, which can be viewed in a half-hour. It's open 10am to 4:30pm Monday to Saturday in the summer and Tuesday to Saturday 10am to 4:30 pm all other seasons. The Vereins Kirche is operated by the Historical Society, which also maintains the **Pioneer Museum Complex** (www.pioneermuseum.net; ✆ **830/990-8441**), 325 W. Main St. Admission to either museum is valid for the other. The cost is $5 adults, $3 students ages 6 to 17, and free for children 5 and under. The Pioneer Museum consists of the 1849 Kammlah House (which was a family residence and general store until the 1920s), as well as the barn and the smokehouse. Later, other historical structures were moved onto the site. These include a one-room schoolhouse and a blacksmith's forge. The complex is open Monday to Saturday 10am to 5pm, and Sunday 1 to 5pm.

The 1852 Steamboat Hotel, originally owned by the grandfather of World War II naval hero Chester A. Nimitz, is now part of the **National Museum of the Pacific War ★★**, 340 E. Main St. (www.pacificwarmuseum.org; ✆ **830/997-8600**), a 9-acre Texas State Historical Park and the world's only museum focusing solely on the Pacific theater. It just keeps expanding and getting better. In addition to the exhibits in the steamboat-shaped hotel devoted to Nimitz and his comrades, there is also the Japanese Garden of Peace, a gift from the people of Japan; the Memorial Wall—the equivalent of the Vietnam War Memorial in Washington, D.C., for Pacific War veterans; the life-size Pacific Combat Zone (2½ blocks east of the museum), which replicates a World War II battle scene; and the George Bush Gallery, where you can see a captured Japanese midget submarine and a multimedia simulation of a bombing raid on Guadalcanal. Indoor exhibits are open daily from 9am to 5pm. Admission is $14 adults; $12 seniors, $10 military and veterans; $4 students and children 6 and older; and free for children 5 and under.

SEEING THE SIGHTS NEARBY

North of town is **Enchanted Rock State Natural Area ★★** (http://tpwd.texas.gov/state-parks/enchanted-rock; ✆ **830/685-3636**), a 640-acre site with a dome of solid-pink granite that was pushed up to the surface by volcanic uplifting. Take FM 965 north for 18 miles. You'll know when you get there: It's a stark sight that shares nothing in common with the surrounding hills, with a dome that's almost 600 feet high. Hiking up and down on the trail takes about an hour. Though the park is fairly large, the parking lot is not, and as soon as it fills, no more visitors are admitted. On weekends, if you get there by 10am, you shouldn't have a problem. The park is open daily 8am to 10pm; day-use entrance fees are $7 adults and free for children 12 and under.

Not far from here, an enchanting San Miguel Allende–inspired village sits within view of Enchanted Rock, where you can stay overnight in one of the lovely B&B–style lodgings of the **Trois Estate at Enchanted Rock ★★** (www.troisestate.net; ✆ **830/685-3415**), a favorite wedding venue. Check out the Trois Estate's underground grotto and chapel while you're there, along with the world's largest collection of cap guns at the Cap Gun Museum.

WHERE TO STAY

Fredericksburg is known for its hundreds of B&Bs and *gästehauses* (guest cottages), or "Sunday Haus" lodgings, as locals call them. Guesthouses or Sunday Haus cottages are more private than the typical B&B. Either breakfast is provided the night before—the perishables are left in a refrigerator—or guests are given coupons to enjoy breakfast at a local restaurant. For many, you simply pick up a key and a map in town and help yourself into the house. *Gästehauses* run anywhere from $120 to $400.

Our favorite go-to places for a romantic weekend getaway or a fun family retreat are the cottages tucked a block off Main Street at the **Austin Street**

Luckenbach: Where Everybody's Somebody

Originally founded as a trading post by German immigrant Jacob Luckenbach in 1849, **Luckenbach ★★★** (www.luckenbachtexas.com; ✆ **888/311-8990** or 830/997-3224), about 10 miles southeast of Fredericksburg, almost faded away until the late John Russell "Hondo" Crouch entered the picture. A political commentator, swimmer, writer, goat farmer, and humorist, Crouch bought the entire town in 1971, primarily so he would have a place to drink beer. Declaring himself mayor, Crouch set to work establishing as many wacky traditions as possible, including women-only chili cook-offs and no-talent contests. The outdoor stage emerged as a favorite venue of Willie Nelson, Jerry Jeff Walker, Waylon Jennings, and other legends, and the catchphrase, "Everybody's somebody in Luckenbach," caught on and became the subject of bumper stickers and T-shirts. Jerry Jeff's famed *Viva Terlingua* album was recorded here live, but it was Willie & Waylon's hit song "Luckenbach, Texas," that put this enchanting ghost town on the map. Centered around the old general store to this day, Luckenbach remains one of the best places to catch live music in all of Texas (shows 7 days a week; tickets are often free, but can run up to about $30). Souvenirs, food, and ice-cold beer are available. Each day, people sit around the stovepipe heater inside the bar and play guitar and sing. Outside, they're singing too. Hondo passed away soon after pushing for the "Non-Buy Centennial" as his personal protest against the commercialization of the bicentennial of the Declaration of the Independence in 1976. His memorial is on-site. ***Tip:*** Luckenbach sometimes tends to shut down early at night on weeknights and even some weekends. Best to get there in the afternoon.

Retreat B&B ★★★, 408 W. Austin St. (www.austinstreetretreat.com; ✆ **866/427-8374**), where nightly rates are $185 to $215. Dogs are allowed in two of the suites for $25 per night. Our other perfect pick is a stand-alone cabin or cottage at **Settlers Crossing B&B ★★★** (www.settlerscrossing.com; ✆ **800/874-1020** or 830/997-2722), where nightly rates are $145 to $209. It's not far from Luckenbach, and both the cottages and setting are delightful.

For something less traditional, consider the **Roadrunner Inn ★** (www.theroadrunnerinn.com), a trendy little B&B above a boutique at 306 E. Main St. The large, uncluttered rooms are furnished in a mix of modern, vintage, and industrial styles. Rates are $159 to $219 double. Although it books through Airbnb, you can e-mail the host at stayattheroadrunner@gmail.com.

Most visitors reserve through one of the main booking services: **First Class Bed & Breakfast Reservation Service,** 909 E. Main St. (www.fredericksburg-lodging.com; ✆ **888/991-6749** or 830/997-0443); **Gästehaus Schmidt,** 231 W. Main St. ★★★ (www.fbglodging.com; ✆ **866/427-8374** or 830/997-5612); or **Main Street B&B Reservation Service,** 337 E. Main St. (www.travelmainstreet.com; ✆ **888/559-8555** or 830/997-0153).

You could also stay in a happening little hotel. The **Hangar Hotel,** 155 Airport Rd. ★★ (www.hangarhotel.com; ✆ **830/997-9990**), has large, comfortable rooms and banks on nostalgia for the World War II flyboy era. Located, as the name suggests, at the town's tiny private airport, this hotel hearkens back to the 1940s with its clean-lined, Art Moderne style, as well as an officers' club (here democratically open to all) and retro diner. The re-creation isn't taken too far: Rooms have all the modern conveniences. Rates range from $149 to $189 double.

For bargain rates, the old **Frederick Motel** ★ (www.frederick-motel.com; ✆ **800/996-6050**), at 1308 E. Main St., has rates from $67 to $90 double, which includes a full breakfast on weekends.

WHERE TO EAT

Fredericksburg's diverse dining scene caters to the traditional and the trendy alike. A jewel of a place is **Vaudeville** ★★★, 230 East Main St. (www.vaudeville-living.com; ✆ **830/992-3234**), a renovated three-story landmark building that houses our favorite Hill Country bistro, a gourmet market, a wine store, a home and giftware showroom, a supper club, and an art gallery. For breakfast takeout, try **Hilda's Tortilla Factory** ★ (✆ **830/997-6105**), at 149 FM 2093/149 Tivydale Rd., which serves good tacos on freshly made flour tortillas. (Be sure to ask for a couple of packs of green sauce.) A line often stretches out the door, but it moves quickly. If you've come to Fredericksburg for German food, try **Altdorf Biergarten** ★, 301 W. Main St. (✆ **830/997-7865**), open Wednesday to Monday for lunch and dinner and Sunday for brunch; or our favorite, **Der Lindenbaum** ★★, 312 E. Main St. (www.derlindenbaum.com; ✆ 830/997-9126), serving fat bratwurst sausages, cool cucumber salads, hot wiener schnitzel, and a display case full of desserts.

Foodies will also love **Otto's** ★★, 316 Elastin St. (www.ottosfbg.com; ✆ **830/307-3336**), and **August E's** ★★, 203 E. San Antonio St. (www.august-es.com; ✆ **830/997-1585**), each featuring fine dining in a casual setting (try August E's spicy spring rolls—our son's favorite).

Lyndon B. Johnson Country

Just 50 miles west of Austin, Johnson City is where the forebears of the 36th president settled almost 150 years ago. A visit to LBJ's boyhood home (in Johnson City) and the sprawling ranch that became known as the Texas White House (14 miles farther west, near Stonewall), and other attractions can fill up a whole day. Even if you're not a history buff, you're likely to be intrigued by the depictions of LBJ and his origins at these sites.

From Austin, take U.S. 290 to **Johnson City,** a pleasant agricultural town named for founder James Polk Johnson, LBJ's first cousin once removed. The modest white clapboard **LBJ Boyhood Home** ★, where Lyndon was raised after age 5, is the centerpiece of this unit of the national historical park. Before exploring, stop at the **visitor center** (www.lbjcountry.com; ✆ **830/868-7128**)—take F Street to Lady Bird Lane and you'll see the signs—to see an educational film and to get details on the Boyhood Home. The Boyhood Home and visitor center are open from 8am to 5pm daily; admission is free.

wild ABOUT TEXAS WILDFLOWERS

Each spring, Texans make a trek out to the Hill Country to see the glorious wildflowers that line the backroads and flood fields there. In mid-to-late March and sometimes early April, the land is ablaze with red-topped Indian paintbrush and blue-and-white-tipped bluebonnets, the state flower of Texas. One of the best drives to see meadows filled with these beautiful blossoms is the **Willow City Loop** (http://txhillcountrytrail.com/plan-your-adventure/historic-sites-and-cities/sites/willow-city-loop), a 13-mile journey down a country road wending through the hills. To get there from Fredericksburg, head north on State Route 16 for approximately 13 miles to Willow City, go east on Ranch Road 1323 for nearly 3 miles, then turn left onto Willow City Loop. (All land along the Willow City Loop is privately owned, so be sure to be respectful of landowners and their property.) The two-lane road passes canyons created by Coal Creek, and as you make a bend in the road you spy what appears to be a pond or lake—but it's really just a sea of bluebonnets. In wildflower season, low-lying meadows are filled with flowers. If you drive 4 or 5 miles and haven't seen many yet, just wait—you'll soon come across the most spectacular flower-filled vistas of all. The Loop is also a popular place for cyclists, so drive slowly and watch for them. Then head to **Wildseed Farms,** 100 Legacy Dr., just outside Fredericksburg on Hwy. 290 ★★ (www.wildseedfarms.com; ✆ **800/848-0078**), which has more than 200 acres of wildflower fields. You can buy seeds, have a bite in the cafe, sit outside in the biergarten, and just drink in those blooms.

From Johnson City, take U.S. 290 W. for 13 miles to the entrance of the **Lyndon B. Johnson State & National Historical Parks at LBJ Ranch ★★**, near Stonewall, jointly operated by the Texas Parks & Wildlife Department (www.tpwd.texas.gov/state-parks/lyndon-b-johnson; ✆ **830/644-2252**) and the National Park Service (www.nps.gov/lyjo; ✆ **830/868-7128**). To visit the ranch, you need to stop at the park and get a permit. The ranch, just the other side of the Pedernales River, was used by LBJ as a second White House, and Lady Bird lived here until she died in 2008. After her death, the park service began giving tours of the 7,500-square-foot ranch house. The tour of the house is the only thing that has a fee (adults $3, 17 and younger free). The house feels eerily like a time warp back to the '60s—LBJ's clothes, hats, and shoes still hang in the closet; it's as though he just walked out the door. The tour really brings home the colorful character that LBJ was.

WHERE TO EAT & STAY

Johnson City has few restaurants. The surest bet is the **Silver K Cafe ★** (✆ **830/868-2911**), at the corner of Main and F streets. For lunch, they serve soups, salads, and sandwiches and a full menu at dinner. For takeout, **Whittington's,** 602 Hwy. 281 S. (www.whittingtonsjerky.com; ✆ **830/868-5500**), is known for its beef and turkey jerky.

The area's top place to dine—and to bed down—is about 16 miles to the west. It's a drive down a rural back road to **Rose Hill Manor ★★**, 2614 Upper Albert Rd., Stonewall (www.rose-hill.com; ✆ **877/ROSEHIL**

[767-3445] or 830/644-2247), a reconstructed Southern manse. The light and airy accommodations—four in the main house, six in separate cottages, and two in a carriage house—are beautifully and comfortably furnished with antiques. All have porches or patios and great Hill Country views. Rates run from $199 to $299 double, including a full three-course breakfast, a wine tasting for two at the winery next door, and a light supper of appetizers and dessert. The inn's New American cuisine, served Wednesday through Sunday evenings in an ultra-romantic dining room, is outstanding. Reservations are essential.

New Braunfels & Gruene

New Braunfels isn't anywhere near Fredericksburg, so don't let the proximity of these two listings throw you off. Closer to San Antonio, New Braunfels sits at the junction of the Comal and Guadalupe rivers along Interstate 35 between Austin and San Antonio. German settlers were brought here in 1845 by Prince Carl of Solms-Braunfels, the commissioner general of the Society for the Protection of German Immigrants in Texas, the same group that later founded Fredericksburg. Although Prince Carl returned to Germany within a year to marry his fiancée, who refused to join him in the wilderness, his colony prospered. By the 1850s, New Braunfels was the fourth-largest city in Texas after Houston, San Antonio, and Galveston. Although you have to look a little to find its quainter side today, this is a good place to enjoy a bit of Germanic history—and lots of watersports. Don't forget to stop in the little town of **Gruene,** a ghost-town-turned-popular-tourist-spot with Texas's oldest continuously open dancehall.

EXPLORING NEW BRAUNFELS

At the **New Braunfels Chamber of Commerce,** 390 S. Seguin St., New Braunfels (www.innewbraunfels.com; © **800/572-2626** or 830/625-2385), you can pick up a pamphlet detailing a **historic walking tour** of downtown. Highlights include the Romanesque-Gothic **Comal County Courthouse** (1898) on Main Plaza; the nearby **Jacob Schmidt Building,** 193 W. San Antonio St., built on the site where William Gebhardt, of canned chili fame, perfected his formula for chili powder in 1896; and the 1928 **Faust Hotel,** 240 S. Seguin St., believed by some to be haunted by its owner. Many antiques shops, restaurants, cafes, and bakeries line San Antonio Street, the town's main thoroughfare.

Several small museums are interesting. In the 11-acre **Heritage Village** complex, 1370 Church Hill Dr. (www.nbheritagevillage.com; © **830/629-6504**), the **Museum of Texas Handmade Furniture ★**, sheds light on local domestic life of the 19th century with its beautiful examples of Texas Biedermeier by master craftsmen. The pieces are displayed at the gracious 1858 Breustedt-Dillen Haus. The complex also includes an 1848 log cabin and a barn with a replica of a cabinetmaker's workshop. Admission is $5 adults, $4 seniors (62 and above), $1 children 6 to 12 ($3 adults with AAA).

HISTORIC GRUENE

Get a more concentrated glimpse of the past at Gruene (pronounced "Green"), which sits high on a bluff overlooking the Guadalupe River, just 2 miles from I- 35 and 4 miles northwest of downtown New Braunfels. First settled by German farmers in the 1840s, Gruene was virtually abandoned during the Great Depression. It remained a ghost town until the mid-1970s, when two investors realized the value of its intact historic buildings and sold them to businesses rather than raze them. These days, tiny Gruene is bursting at the seams, a place crowded with day-trippers browsing specialty shops in the wonderfully restored structures, which include a smoked-meat shop, clothing stores, a wine shop, and antiques and gift shops. Gruene is also home to potters and other artists with galleries here, as well as B&Bs, hotels, restaurants, and other tourist-friendly stops up and down the roads leading into the former ghost town.

But Gruene is perhaps best known for **Gruene Hall** ★★ (www.gruenehall.com; ✆ **830/606-1281**), Gruene Rd., the state's most famous and oldest continually operating dancehall. It's seen everyone from Garth Brooks to Willie Nelson grace its stage. For an unforgettable night in Texas, check out who's playing at Gruene Hall on the weekend, or listen to live music there on a Sunday afternoon. It's still one of the state's most outstanding spots for live music. Do not miss this place.

The **New Braunfels Museum of Art & Music** ★, 1259 Gruene Rd., on the river behind Gruene Mansion (✆ **800/456-4866** or 830/625-5636), focuses on popular arts in the West and South. Subjects of recent exhibits, which change quarterly and combine music and art components, have included Texas accordion music, central Texas dancehalls, and cowboy poetry. Live music includes an open mic on Sunday afternoons, and the recording of *New Braunfels Live* radio show of roots music on Thursday evenings.

WATERSPORTS

Gruene also figures among the New Braunfels area's impressive array of places to get wet, most of them open only in summer. Outfitters who can help you ride the Guadalupe River rapids on a raft, tube, canoe, or inflatable kayak include **Rockin' R River Rides** (www.rockinr.com; ✆ **800/553-5628** or 830/629-9999) and **Gruene River Company** (www.toobing.com; ✆ **888/705-2800** or 830/625-2800), both on Gruene Road just south of the Gruene Bridge.

You can go tubing too, at **Schlitterbahn** ★, Texas's largest waterpark and one of the best in the country, at 305 W. Austin St. in New Braunfels (www.schlitterbahn.com; ✆ **855/246-0273**). Those who like their water play a bit more low-key might try downtown New Braunfels's **Landa Park** (✆ **830/608-2160**), where you can swim in the largest spring-fed pool in Texas or calmly float in an inner tube down the Comal River. Waterski lovers should also check out the **Texas Ski Ranch** (✆ **830/627-2843**), a 70-acre watersports park with a cable water-ski and wakeboard course.

WHERE TO STAY IN NEW BRAUNFELS & GRUENE

The **Prince Solms Inn,** 295 E. San Antonio St., New Braunfels (www.princesolmsinn.com; ✆ **800/625-9169** or 830/625-9169), was built to be a small hotel in 1898 and has been in continuous operation since then. A prime downtown location, tree-shaded courtyard, and High Victorian–style sleeping quarters have made this charming bed-and-breakfast in great demand. Three Western-themed rooms in a converted 1860 feed store next door work for families, and an ultra-romantic separate cabin is in the back of the main house. Downstairs in the "Keller" (cellar/basement), there's a dark piano bar. Rates range from $125 to $195 double. Book the Sophie Suite at the front of the hotel—it's the best room in the house.

A classic old hotel with an ornate lobby and welcoming brewpub, the **Faust Hotel,** 240 S. Seguin St., New Braunfels (www.fausthotel.com; ✆ **830/625-7791**), has standard rooms from $89 to $159 double. Rates go up during town festivals. Rooms are a little too small and old-fashioned for us, but we like the restaurant/bar downstairs. On the other hand, our friend loves this hotel and stays here so often they know him by name.

For a B&B experience, the **Gruene Mansion Inn ★**, 1275 Gruene Rd., New Braunfels (www.gruenemansioninn.com; ✆ **830/629-2641**), has converted the barns that once belonged to the opulent 1875 plantation house into elegant-rustic cottages with decks; some also have cozy lofts (if you don't like stairs, request a single-level room). Accommodations are from $195 to $250 double per night, including breakfast served in the plantation house. Two separate lodges, suitable for families, are available, too ($275–$340).

If you're planning to come to town during the **Wurstfest** sausage festival (late Oct to early Nov), be sure to book well in advance, no matter where you stay—that's high season here.

WHERE TO EAT IN NEW BRAUNFELS & GRUENE

For our money, the **Huisache Grill ★**, 303 W. San Antonio St., New Braunfels (www.huisache.com; ✆ **830/620-9001**), has the best food in town. The American menu has both classic and original dishes. The pecan-crusted pork chop, the mixed grill, and the bleu-cheese steak are among our favorites. Lunch and dinner are served daily. The restaurant is divided into several different dining areas, each with its own character. To find it, drive West San Antonio Street from the courthouse and take the first driveway to the left after you cross the tracks.

The **New Braunfels Smokehouse,** 1090 N. Business at I-35 (www.nbsmokehouse.com; ✆ **830/625-2416**), opened in 1951 as a tasting room for the meats it started hickory-smoking in 1943. Progress arrived in 2008, and the old Smokehouse was torn down (and New Braunfels lost some of the German charm for which it was known). The Smokehouse moved to a smaller building around the corner from the original Highway 46 location, and now it's more of a deli with picnic tables and paper plates, along with a cold box where you can buy packaged meats. Savor the meats on platters or sandwiches; better yet, have it shipped home as a savory souvenir.

In Gruene, the **Gristmill River Restaurant & Bar,** 1287 Gruene Rd. (www.gristmillrestaurant.com; ✆ **830/625-0684**), a converted 100-year-old cotton gin, includes burgers and chicken-fried steak as well as healthful salads on its Texas-casual menu. Kick back on one of its multiple decks and gaze out at the Guadalupe River.

For fine dining (that will strain your purse strings), locals love **Myron's Steakhouse,** 136 N. Castell Ave. (www.myronsprime.com; ✆ **830/624-1024**), with fabulous steaks and seafood and a dark, inviting dining room with booth seating in a historic downtown movie theater space. They have a nice reliable cocktail bar, too. Next door **McAdoo's Seafood Company,** 196 N. Castell Ave. (www.mcadoos.com; ✆ **830/629-FISH [3474]**), is set in a beautifully restored historic former post office building; we love the bar here as well as the decor in the dining room, but we can't say their take on Cajun and Creole cuisine quite hits the mark.

WEST TEXAS

This is the real "old-school" Texas: vast open spaces, longhorn cattle, pickup trucks lined in front of roadside honky-tonks, and cowboys with sweat-stained Stetsons, boot-cut Wrangler jeans, and muddy footwear. While much of Texas has become quite metropolitan, the plains of West Texas retain much of the Old West flavor. Communities here are generally small and far apart, residents seldom lock their doors, and even the region's biggest city, El Paso, feels like an overgrown small town. For those willing to take the time and effort, it's an area filled with gems, with a wide range of people, attractions, and activities amid a landscape that's alternately bleak and beautiful, and sometimes both. No, this isn't the area we'd recommend if you only have one trip to Texas (we prefer the Hill Country and Austin areas); however, if you're passing through on a big I-10 road trip, you'll want to stop and see the "miles and miles of Texas" where true grit and wild West Texas lives on.

10

The region's history and culture come alive in West Texas at Spanish missions from the 17th and 18th centuries and restored frontier forts. It was here that Judge Roy Bean, who called himself "The Law West of the Pecos" presided over a combination courtroom and saloon in the late 1800s. West Texas also offers some surprises, including one of America's most beautiful caves; the state's oldest winery; an oddly out-of-place replica of William Shakespeare's famed Globe Theatre; an avant-garde installation art complex in the much-hyped town of Marfa; and numerous lakes, including 64,900-acre Lake Amistad, a national recreation area and reservoir along the U.S.-Mexico border, which is a joint project of both countries.

EL PASO

46 miles SE of Las Cruces, New Mexico; 551 miles NW of San Antonio; 635 miles W of Dallas

Here, in the sun-swept, mountainous desert of Texas's westernmost corner is the state's sixth-largest city. Built between two mountain ranges on the shores of the Rio Grande, El Paso is an urban history book, with chapters dedicated to Spanish conquistadors, ancient highways, gunfighters, border disputes, and modern sprawl.

El Paso's rich history is a result of its geography. The Franklin Mountains, which now border the downtown area and occupy the city's heart, offered natural defense for the American Indians who inhabited the area for about 12 millennia; the Rio Grande offered water. The mountains slope into a vast canyon, so the Spanish explorers who first crossed the Rio Grande in the 16th century saw it as an ideal north-south route, one that soon became known as "El Camino Real" (or "The King's Highway") and served as a principal trade route for more than 300 years.

With the 17th century came an influx of Catholic missionaries, a group that established numerous missions that survive today. But Spain saw its grip weaken, and a Mexican flag flew over El Paso when independence was established in 1821. This era was short-lived, as Mexico ceded the land north of the Rio Grande to the United States following the Mexican-American War (1846–48). After the railroad arrived in 1881, El Paso became a commercial center and also earned the nickname "Sin City," thanks to the saloons, brothels, and casinos that lined every major street. Many notorious gunfighters—including Billy the Kid and John Wesley Hardin—called the city home.

El Paso boomed in the early 20th century and again following World War II, entrenching itself as a center for agriculture, manufacturing, and international trade, as well as the military: On the east side of town, Fort Bliss is one of the U.S. Army's largest bases, now poised for more growth. El Paso's relationship with Ciudad Juárez has been symbiotic for centuries, even more so since the resolution of a century-old border dispute in the mid-1960s and the signing of the North American Free Trade Agreement in 1994. Unfortunately, increased border security and a wave of drug-related violence in Juárez in the early part of the 21st century put a damper on the sister cities' relationship. The pendulum may be swinging: Pope Francis paid a visit to Juárez in February 2016, and the town has been increasingly lauded for its decrease in crime.

Nevertheless, in comparison with the relative wealth and glitz of Santa Fe or Tucson, El Paso is in many ways the authentic Southwest—unpolished, undiluted, and honest. Separated by a swath of the Rio Grande, El Paso and Ciudad Juárez each is its country's largest border city, and the local culture, a fusion of Mexican and American traditions, is distinct and unique in comparison with the way of life in eastern Texas. A day or two of exploration is worthwhile; take the time to wander downtown, enjoy a meal at one of the city's terrific Mexican restaurants, and gain a better understanding of what a border town is all about.

Essentials

GETTING THERE

BY PLANE More than 90 commercial flights arrive and depart daily from **El Paso International Airport (ELP),** located a mile north of I-10 via Airway Boulevard on the city's east side (www.elpasointernationalairport.com; ✆ **915/212-0330**). **Allegiant Airlines, American, Delta, Southwest,** and **United** all serve El Paso.

West Texas

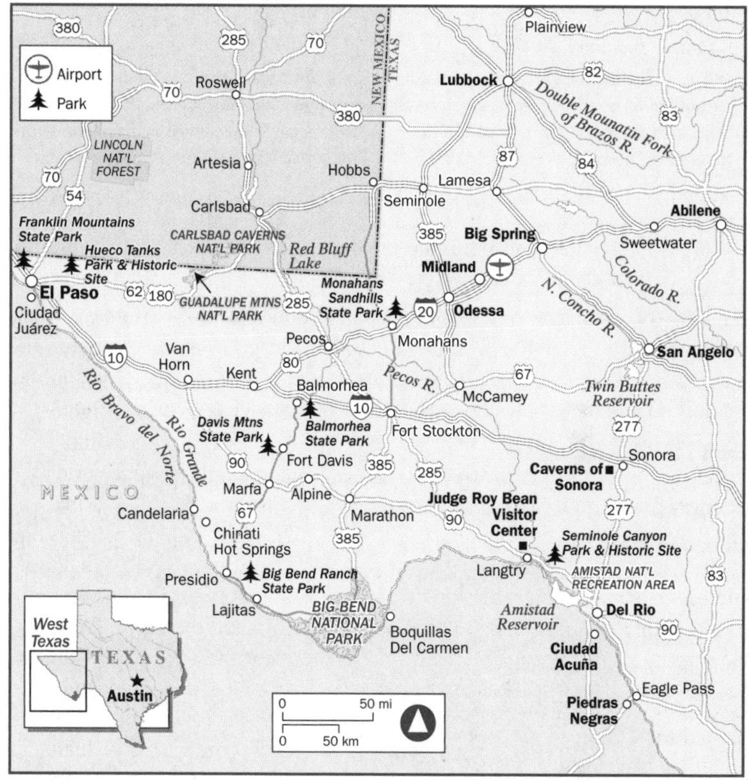

The major car-rental agencies are represented here (www.elpaso internationalairport.com/car-rentals; see "Getting Around," below). **Juárez El Paso Shuttle Service** (www.juarezelpasoshuttle.com; ✆ **915/740-4400**) offers shuttle service to and from the ELP and Ciudad Juárez International airport only; a one-way trip downtown Juárez costs $65.

BY CAR The main artery to the east and west is I-10, bisecting El Paso between downtown and the Franklin Mountains.

From Carlsbad Caverns (149 miles from El Paso) and Guadalupe Mountains National Parks to the east (113 miles), visitors arrive via U.S. 62/180 (Montana Ave.), which eventually skirts the north side of downtown El Paso. For those arriving from Alamogordo, New Mexico (80 miles to the north), U.S. 54 (also known as the Patriot Fwy.) runs through El Paso's east side to the Bridge of the Americas, which crosses the Rio Grande and connects El Paso with Ciudad Juárez, Mexico.

Note: Expect to be asked your citizenship when leaving the city at checkpoints on major highways.

Riding a Vintage Streetcar

Restored vintage streetcars will once more roll along El Paso roadways. The 4.8-mile **El Paso Streetcar project** is expected to open by the time you read this, with six of the city's original PCC streetcars, now refurbished, making loops from downtown El Paso to the University of Texas El Paso. Streetcars are a big part of the city's heritage, running downtown loops from 1948 to 1974. The streetcars will be operated by Sun Metro (www.sunmetro.net).

BY BUS Interstate and intrastate bus service is provided by **Greyhound,** 200 W. San Antonio Ave. (www.greyhound.com; ✆ **915/532-5095**).

BY TRAIN **Amtrak** (www.amtrak.com; ✆ **800/872-7245**) offers westward and eastward rail service. Trains go east to Chicago (via San Antonio) and west to Los Angeles; other major cities on the routes include Houston and Tucson. The depot is downtown at 700 W. San Francisco Ave.

GETTING AROUND

Two natural features—the Rio Grande and the Franklin Mountains—have guided the urban development of El Paso for more than 400 years, so getting around can be tricky for the newcomer. The city is essentially U-shaped, with the Franklin Mountains occupying the center and the downtown area at the bottom.

While El Paso has a public bus system, cars are the norm. Parking is rarely an issue, even downtown.

BY CAR El Paso has numerous car-rental agencies, clustered primarily around the airport in the east and North Mesa Street on the city's west side, including **Advantage** (✆ 915/781-7690), **Alamo** (✆ 915/778-9417), **Avis** (✆ 915/779-2700), **Budget** (✆ 915/779-2532), **Dollar** (✆ 915/778-5445), **Enterprise** (✆ 915/779-2260), **Hertz** (✆ 915/772-4255), **National** (✆ 915/778-9417), **Payless** ✆ 915/779-2052), and **Thrifty** (✆ 915/778-9236).

AAA (American Automobile Association) maintains an office in El Paso at 5867 N. Mesa St. (www.aaa.com; ✆ **915/778-9521**), open Monday through Friday from 9am to 5pm and Saturday from 10am to 2pm.

Street parking is free almost everywhere in El Paso except downtown, where the meters must be fed 50¢ per half-hour. The covered garages downtown typically charge $5 to $10 per day.

BY BUS El Paso's bus system, **Sun Metro** (www.sunmetro.net; ✆ **915/212-3333**), operates one of the world's largest fleets of natural-gas-powered buses. The main transfer station is downtown on Santa Fe and 4th streets. Buses run from about 5am to 10pm on weekdays, with shorter hours on weekends and holidays; the fare is $1.50 for adults; $1 for children, students, and those with disabilities; and 30¢ for seniors. Day passes are $3.50.

BY TAXI **United Independent** (✆ **915/590-8294**), **Border Taxi** (✆ **915/533-4245**), and **Sun City Cab** (✆ **915/544-2211**) offer 24-hour service in El

Paso and the surrounding area. **Uber** rideshare currently serves most locations within the city of El Paso.

BY FOOT Downtown El Paso is well suited for a walking tour, and pedestrians can use the Santa Fe Street Bridge into Ciudad Juárez. ***Note:*** Carry your passport with you when crossing the border. While photo ID once was sufficient for reentry into the United States, it no longer is: All land crossings into Mexico now require a passport upon your return into the U.S.

VISITOR INFORMATION

The **El Paso Convention & Visitors Bureau** (www.visitelpaso.com; ✆ **915/534-0600**) is located at One Civic Center Plaza, next to the El Paso Convention and Performing Arts Center, and also operates an information center at the airport. Request "El Paso: The Official Visitor's Guide" before your trip.

A **Texas Travel Information Center,** located 20 miles northwest of El Paso in Anthony (I-10, exit 0), at the Texas–New Mexico border, has an excellent selection of brochures, maps, and other visitor resources.

[FastFACTS] EL PASO

Dentists Contact **1-800-DENTIST (336-8478).**

Doctors Call the **El Paso County Medical Society** (✆ **915/533-0940**).

Drugstores **Walgreens** has a 24-hour prescription service at 1831 Lee Trevino Dr. (✆ **915/594-1129**).

Emergencies For police, fire, and medical emergencies, call ✆ **911.** To reach the **West Texas Regional Poison Center,** call ✆ **800/222-1222.**

Hospitals Full-service hospitals, with 24-hour emergency rooms, include **Sierra Medical Center (The Hospitals of Providence),** 1625 Medical Center Dr. (www.thehospitalsofprovidence.com/our-locations/sierra-campus; ✆ **915/747-4000**), just northwest of downtown, and **Del Sol Medical Center,** 10301 Gateway W. (www.laspalmasdelsolhealthcare.com; ✆ **915/595-9000**), on the east side of the city.

Newspapers & Magazines The ***El Paso Times*** (www.elpasotimes.com) is the city's only daily English-language newspaper. The Spanish-language newspaper is ***El Diario de El Paso*** (www.diariousa.com). ***El Paso Scene*** (www.epscene.com) is the city's free monthly arts-and-entertainment paper.

Post Office The main post office, located downtown at 219 E. Mills Ave., is open Monday through Friday from 8:30am to 5pm, Saturday from 8:30am to noon.

Safety While El Paso has among the lowest crime rates of any major U.S. city of a comparable size, it is far from crime-free, and drug crimes, burglaries, and auto theft are preeminent problems. It's important to keep aware of your surroundings at all times and ask at your hotel about the safety of a given neighborhood, especially after dark. ***Note:*** When visiting Mexico, it is important to remember that Ciudad Juárez is one of the world's most active drug-smuggling centers, and has been especially bad for drug-related violence in recent years, although that does seem to be changing. Crime against tourists has remained relatively rare; nonetheless, many locals do not recommend driving across the border or crossing alone.

Taxes In the city of El Paso, the total sales tax is 8.25% and 15.5% for lodging.

Time Zone El Paso is in the Mountain Standard Time zone, like nearby New Mexico, but unlike the rest of Texas, which is in the Central Standard Time zone. Set your clock back 1 hour if you enter El Paso from the east.

What to See & Do

THE TOP ATTRACTIONS

Chamizal National Memorial ★ This 55-acre urban park celebrates the peaceful settlement of a century-old border dispute. After the Mexican-American War ended in 1848, the U.S. and Mexico agreed that the center of the deepest channel of the Rio Grande would divide the countries. The river was uncooperative, however, gradually shifting southward. The result? A diplomatic impasse over the border location that lasted until 1964, when the Chamizal Treaty was signed and a permanent concrete channel was built to mark a more predictable boundary.

The Chamizal National Memorial commemorates the dispute's peaceful resolution, with a 55-acre park that's packed with recreational facilities, including 2 miles of foot trails and 1.5 miles of red-gravel bike trails. It has an outdoor amphitheater that hosts free concerts and other events, and a visitor center with a museum, three galleries, and a bookstore. It's a nice open space that's greener than the Franklin Mountains and larger than the other municipal parks. A walkway to the adjacent Bridge of the Americas leads to the memorial's Mexican counterpart, **Museo de Arqueologica de El Chamizal,** with an anthropology and archaeological museum.

800 S. San Marcial Dr., at Paisano Dr. and U.S. 54 (Patriot Fwy.). www.nps.gov/cham. ✆ **915/532-7273.** Free admission, with fees for some events in the amphitheater. Park daily 5am–10pm. Visitor center Tues–Sat 10am–5pm.

El Paso Mission Trail ★ These three historic missions are a direct link to El Paso's Spanish colonial past. Established in the 17th and 18th centuries, the three are among the oldest continually active missions in the country. All are worthy historic destinations, but if you have time to hit only one, drive out to San Elceario; it's a little farther out, but unlike Ysleta and Socorro, it's removed from modern urban development and feels like it's from a different era.

From I-10, exit Zaragoza Road (exit 32) and head south 3 miles to **Mission Ysleta,** 9501 S. Zaragoza Road (www.ysletamission.org; ✆ **915/859-9848**), established in 1682 in what was then Mexico. The silver-domed chapel here was built in 1851 after floods shifted the Rio Grande and washed away all of the previous structure, save the foundation.

Heading southeast on Socorro Road for 3 miles takes you to **Mission Socorro,** 328 S. Nevarez Rd. (✆ **915/859-7718**), established in 1682, 1 day after Mission Ysleta. The original adobe chapel (1692) was washed away by a flood in the 1740s, rebuilt, destroyed again in 1829, and finally replaced in 1843 by the current restored structure.

Presidio Chapel San Elceario (✆ **915/851-2333** for administration or 915/851-1682 for tour information) is the most impressive of the three missions. It was established at its present location in 1789 as a Spanish military outpost 6 miles south of Mission Socorro on Socorro Road. Parishioners built the present-day church in 1877 as the centerpiece of the village plaza, which retains its historical charm to this day. It's the largest of the three missions,

EL PASO'S alligator ART

In El Paso's downtown San Jacinto Plaza, the **Plaza de los Lagartos** (www.visitelpaso.com/places/tabla-s-popup-mercado), a fountain centered by a pile of fiberglass alligators, stands in the sun. The lively 1993 piece by pop artist (and El Paso native) Luis Jimenez harks back to days (for nearly a century) when live alligators actually called the plaza home. In the 1880s, El Paso's mayor first deposited the reptiles in the plaza's fountain as something of a joke; surprisingly, they thrived amid the hustle and bustle of the growing city until they were deemed a potential hazard and removed in the 1960s. There is also another newer popular pop-up market in the same location called **Tabla's PopUp Mercado,** with art, music, fashion, baked goods, pet goodies, handmade objects, food, and other items of interest. It's located in San Jacinto Plaza, bordered on the east and west by Mesa and Oregon streets, and north and south by Main and Mills streets.

and an excellent example of the merging of American Indian and Spanish architectural styles with majestic arches and a pressed-tin ceiling. The surrounding village has been gaining fame in recent years as the site of the "First Thanksgiving," said to have taken place in 1598, 23 years before the Plymouth Thanksgiving.

Visitors are welcome to tour the missions on their own; expect to spend at least 3 hours if you visit all three. Tours are available from the **El Paso Mission Trail Experience** (http://visitelpasomissiontrail.com; ✆ **915/790-0661**) and cost $8 to $40 for 4- or 5-hour trips.

An 8-mile stretch of Zaragoza and Socorro rds., southeast of downtown El Paso via I-10. Call the CVB at ✆ **915/534-0630** for more information. Free admission.

El Paso Museum of Art ★★ This treasure house of a museum showcases an impressive permanent collection of art highlighting the many cultures (American, Mexican, European, Native American) that have commingled in El Paso for the past 400 years. Of particular note is the fine collection of Mexican art from the 17th to 19th centuries, as well as a collection of European art from the 13th to 18th centuries. A collection of American works dates from 1800 to the mid-1900s. Take an unhurried hour or more here; it's very much worth your time.

1 Arts Festival Plaza. www.elpasoartmuseum.org. ✆ **915/532-1707.** Free admission; fees charged for special exhibits (usually $5–$10). Tues–Wed and Fri–Sat 9am–5pm; Thurs 9am–9pm; Sun noon–5pm.

MORE ATTRACTIONS

Oenophiles will want to take a side trip to **Zin Valle Vineyards,** 7315 Canutillo La Union Rd. (www.zinvalle.com; ✆ **915/877-4544**), where the tasting room is open noon to 5pm Friday to Monday (by appt. at other times).

El Paso Holocaust Museum ★ This powerful museum was founded by the late Henry Kellen, a Holocaust survivor from Poland who settled in El Paso in 1946, building a life here for himself and his wife and their 8-year-old

Views of El Paso, Juárez & Beyond: Scenic Drive Overlook

A sightseeing drive up curving Scenic Drive delivers you to the top of the Franklin Mountains cliffs, for amazing views, day or night. You can see downtown El Paso, across the Rio Grande to Juárez, and even parts of New Mexico with the naked eye or using coin-op telescopes provided in the mountaintop municipal park (on Scenic Dr. btw. Rim Rd. and Alabama Ave.). You may also notice the Spanish words "LA BIBLIA ES LA VERDAD. LEELA" ("The Bible is the Truth. Read It") painted on a mountain outside Juárez, Mexico. It's been there for decades. (A newer one, "50TH ANNIVERSARY APOSTLE S. J.F." was painted in 2014 by honor the 50th anniversary of a parishioner from a Guadalajara-based church and may be removed, but in the meantime it is still visible from I-10 and from many spots in El Paso.)

nephew, also survivors of the Holocaust. Henry survived the war thanks to a Lithuanian farmer, but his parents, brother, and sister did not. The museum was Kellen's response to the emergence in the 1980s of Holocaust deniers—and he began collecting artifacts and memorabilia, a collection that grew and was generously supplemented over time. The museum does an excellent job telling a story that's alternately grim and life-affirming. Chronologically arranged exhibits include Nazi anti-Semitic propaganda, a replica of Auschwitz, and stories of the resistance and liberation. The museum is bilingual.

715 N. Oregon St. www.elpasoholocaustmuseum.org. ✆ **915/351-0048.** Free admission; donations accepted. Tues–Fri 9am–5pm; Sat–Sun 1–5pm. Closed major holidays.

El Paso Museum of History ★ This museum opened just over a decade ago, and since then its permanent exhibit, "The Changing Pass," covering the region's evolution from the Ice Age to modern day, gives visitors a rich overview of the multicultural/multinational history of El Paso's unique border region, known as The Pass of the North. Other rotating artifacts and exhibits cover various local Texas-history themed subjects.

510 N. Santa Fe St. www.elpasotexas.gov/history. ✆ **915/351-3588.** Free admission. Tues–Wed and Fri–Sat 9am–5pm; Thurs 9am–9pm; Sun noon–5pm. Closed city holidays.

El Paso Zoo ★ The El Paso Zoo is one of the state's best, a 35-acre home to some 1,700 animals in natural habitat exhibits. It's especially good for young kids, who can hop on the miniature African Star Train ($2 adults, $1.50 children 3–11, free children 2 and under) and spy giraffes and zebras wandering dusty plains, or clamber about the Foster Treehouse Playground, with not one but five treehouses. A wildlife amphitheater offers special performances, such as the "Wings of the World" bird shows. The zoo also has a restaurant and a safari gift shop.

4001 E. Paisano Dr. (across from the El Paso County Coliseum). www.elpasozoo.org. ✆ **915/212-0966.** Admission $12 adults, $9 seniors 60 and over, $7.50 children age 3–12, free for children 2 and under. Mon–Sun 9:30am–5pm year-round.

National Border Patrol Museum ★ The Border Patrol was founded right here in El Paso in 1924, making the city the rightful place for a museum to honor it. Back in the day, recruits patrolled the border between inspection areas on horse and saddle. This modest museum is free (donations accepted) and the only one in the United States dedicated solely to the history of the U.S. Border Patrol, from its genesis in the Old West to its challenges today. Highlights include diaries about the immigrant experience, an array of Border Patrol uniforms (snappy hats), and several Border Patrol vehicles, from ATVs and Jeeps to snowmobiles and a Piper Super Cub plane.

4315 Woodrow Bean (Transmountain Rd.). www.borderpatrolmuseum.com. ✆ **915/759-6060.** Free admission (donations accepted). Tues–Sat 9am–5pm. Closed major holidays.

ESPECIALLY FOR KIDS

With a kid-pleasing miniature-train ride, the **Railroad & Transportation Museum of El Paso,** 400 W. San Antonio Ave. (www.elpasorails.org; ✆ **915/240-8384**), also has plenty of artifacts to keep railroad buffs happy. It's open Monday to Friday 9am to 4pm and Saturday 9am to 2pm. Admission is $2 to $5; weekends are free.

Western Playland Amusement Park ★ Yes, this park is actually in Sunland Park, New Mexico, but that's only about 8 miles northwest of El Paso, not a far drive for some old-fashioned amusement-park fun. Many rides are geared toward younger kids, including "U-boats" and "U-Buggies," a kiddie train, and a merry-go-round, but Western Playland has a few hair-raising humdingers, including the Bandido roller coaster and the Drop zone. Concession stands ensure kids maintain the requisite sugar highs.

1249 Futurity Dr., Sunland Park, NM, across from Sunland Park Race Track and Casino. www.westernplayland.com. ✆ **575/589-3410.** Admission $21 pass for unlimited rides. Mid-Feb to Oct; hours vary throughout the season.

ORGANIZED TOURS

Si! El Paso Tours (www.sielpasotours.com; ✆ **915/541-1308**) offers an El Paso Shopping tour, an Old Mesilla shopping and gallery tour, and a Mission Tour. They also offer large groups (30+) a special cattleman's hayride and dinner evening event. **Border Sights Tours of El Paso** (www.bordersights-tours-of-elpaso.com; ✆ **915/533-5454**) offers a variety of interesting local tours, from home-and-garden tours to food tours for $45 adults, $20 children 18 and under. The **El Paso Convention and Performing Arts Center** (www.visitelpaso.com; ✆ **915/534-0600**) can provide travelers with informative brochures that detail self-guided historic walking tours.

OUTDOOR ACTIVITIES

At nearly 24,300 acres, **Franklin Mountains State Park ★** (www.tpwd.texas.gov; ✆ **915/566-6441**) is the largest urban wilderness park in the United States and a favorite destination of El Pasoans looking to hike, bike, or climb. Rugged and speckled by cacti and ocotillos, the mountains are populated by small mammals, birds, reptiles, deer, and the occasional mountain lion. At

7,192 feet, the summit of North Franklin Mountain is about 3,000 feet higher than the city below.

The mountains, the final southern ridge of the geological phenomenon that created the Rocky Mountains, are home to about 50 miles of developed hiking and mountain biking trails; floods in 2006 washed out many trails, so call for current information. The hikes are primarily moderate to difficult; try the 1.2-mile round-trip to the Aztec Caves or the more difficult 9.2-mile round-trip to the peak of North Franklin Mountain.

If you don't want to break a sweat, take the **Wyler Aerial Tramway** (www.tpwd.texas.gov/state-parks/wyler-aerial-tramway; ✆ **915/566-6622**) to the summit of Ranger Peak ($8 adults, $4 children 12 and under). Beyond the trails and the tram, the park is also a renowned rock-climbing spot with a city-owned outdoor amphitheater (see "The Performing Arts," p. 363).

It takes about 20 minutes to reach the park by car from downtown El Paso. There are numerous primitive campsites, but no water or electricity in the park. Fees are $5 for day use (free for children 12 and under) and $8 for camping, and the park is open from 8am to 5pm year-round (campers receive a combination to the locked gate so they can come and go after day-use hours).

Hueco Tanks State Park & Historic Site (www.tpwd.state.tx.us; ✆ **915/857-1135**), 32 miles northeast of El Paso via U.S. 62/180 and RM 2775, is another popular rock-climbing destination. It is a world-class bouldering site. Centered on three small, rocky outcroppings that loom above the surrounding desert, the park gets its name from the *huecos* (depressions) that catch rainwater and attract life. Many of the rocks are marked by lively pictographs, the work of native tribes over the past 10,000 years. Tours of these fragile sites are offered Wednesday through Saturday at 9 and 11am in the summer and 10:30am and 2pm in the winter; reservations are recommended. Birding and bouldering are also available.

Other than climbing, hiking and camping are popular activities at the park. There are 6.5 miles of trails and a campground with 20 back-in sites (4 with water only, 16 with water and electricity) and showers. Campsite availability is dependent on volunteers; call ahead to see if the campground is open. The park charges $7 for day use and $12 to $16 for campsites. Bikes are not permitted.

GOLF The Tom Fazio–designed **Butterfield Trail Golf Course,** 1858 Cottonwoods Dr. (www.butterfieldtrailgolf.com; ✆ **915/772-1038**), has been ranked as one of the top public courses in the state. Greens fees are $65 to $80, cart included. At the 27-hole **Painted Dunes Desert Golf Course,** located 9 miles northeast of I-10 via U.S. 54 at 12000 McCombs St. (www.painted-dunes.com; ✆ **915/821-2122**), greens fees range from $40 to $50 with cart. Twilight rates are also available. Texan Lee Trevino began his illustrious professional golf career at the course now called the **Horizon Golf Club & Conference Center,** 16000 Ashford St. (www.horizongolfclub.com; ✆ **915/852-3529**). This family-friendly course boasts the lowest greens fees in the El Paso area ($20–$39, cart included) and is the only local course where kids 18 and under play for free with a greens-fee paying adult. Other options include **Ascarate Golf Course** in Ascarate Lake City Park (www.epcounty.com/ascarate/golf.htm; ✆ **915/771-2380**), with greens fees of $29 to $33, cart included; and **Lone Star Golf Club,** 1510 Hawkins Blvd. (www.lonestargolf-club.net; ✆ **915/591-4927**), with greens fees of $38 to $45 with cart.

HIKING The top hiking areas in and around El Paso are at Franklin Mountains State Park and Hueco Tanks State Park & Historic Site (see above).

MOUNTAIN BIKING **Franklin Mountains State Park** (see above) is by far the most popular mountain biking destination in the El Paso area. There are about 40 miles of bike-accessible trails.

SPECTATOR SPORTS

BASEBALL The **El Paso Diablos** relocated to Missouri a few years back, replaced in 2015 by the **El Paso Chihuahuas** (www.milb.com/index.jsp/sid=t4904; ✆ **915/533-2273**). This independent team in the Central League plays a May-to-August schedule at the 10,000-seat Cohen Stadium (9700 Gateway Blvd. N.). Single-game tickets are $7 to $8.

BASKETBALL The **Miners** of the **University of Texas at El Paso** (**UTEP;** www.utepathletics.com; ✆ **915/747-5234**) is a Conference USA team that plays from December to March at the Don Haskins Center (2801 N. Mesa St.). Tickets range from $14 to $29 for single games.

FOOTBALL The **UTEP Miners** (www.utepathletics.com; ✆ **915/747-5234**) football team plays a Conference USA schedule from September to December on campus at the Sun Bowl. Single-game tickets are about $20 to $40. Also, the stadium hosts the second-oldest New Year's bowl game in the nation.

HORSE RACING There is live horse racing just outside of western El Paso (actually in New Mexico) at **Sunland Park Racetrack and Casino,** 1200 Futurity Dr. (www.sunland-park.com; ✆ **575/874-5200**). The racing season runs from December to April (simulcast racing from around the country is featured year-round). There are also restaurants, lounges, and a casino on-site.

RODEO The **Southwestern International PRCA Rodeo** (www.elprodeo.com; ✆ **915/755-2000**) is held every September at Cohen Stadium, 9700 Gateway N.

SHOPPING

El Paso's main shopping district is downtown, targeting both Mexican nationals and American shoppers with all sorts of bargains, and several enclosed malls are scattered around the city. The area is known for Western wear, Southwestern art, and Mexican imports.

The most famous bootmaker in Texas has made El Paso its home since it moved from San Antonio in the 1980s, so that's why **Lucchese** has an outlet store here on 6601 Montana Ave. (www.lucchese.com; ✆ **915/778-8060**). El Paso's **Cowtown Boots,** 11451 Gateway W. (www.cowtownboots.com;

(© **915/593-2929**), claims to be one of the world's largest Western-wear stores, with 40,000 square feet of boots (from alligator to ostrich), jeans, clothing, and accessories. If you want custom boots that are leather works of art, make an appointment at **Rocketbuster Handmade Custom Boots,** 115 S. Anthony St. (www.rocketbuster.com; © **915/541-1300**), but you'll spend almost $1K for a pair. For just about everything else—saddle blankets to yard art to painted longhorn skulls—check the huge, 2-acre showroom of **El Paso Saddleblanket,** 6926 Gateway E. (www.saddleblanket.com; © **800/998-8608**). Oddly enough, you can't shop here without a business tax ID number; however, see something you like there and you can purchase it from the online store on their website.

Shopping centers include **Sunland Park Mall,** 750 Sunland Park Dr. (© **915/833-5596**), and **Cielo Vista Mall,** 8401 Gateway W. (© **915/779-7071**). Located where Pancho Villa and General Pershing once negotiated, **Placita Santa Fe,** 5034 Doniphan Rd. (www.facebook.com/pages/Placita-Santa-Fe/265054740269767; © **915/581-1217**), features 20 quaint shops, specializing in art, designer clothing, antiques, and jewelry.

Where to Stay

You'll find numerous hotels and motels in El Paso, but little in the way of B&Bs and resorts. Most of the accommodations are chain franchises, with a few exceptions, located either near the airport or adjacent to I-10. The city's room taxes add about 15.5% to lodging bills.

In addition to the properties described below, numerous hotels and motels are located off I-10 near El Paso International Airport, including **Best Western Airport Inn,** 7144 Gateway E. (© **800/528-1234**), at $60 to $80 double, and **Comfort Inn,** 900 Yarbrough Dr. (© **800/228-5150**), at $69 to $89 double. Downtown, the **Holiday Inn Express** at 409 E. Missouri Ave. (© **888/465-4329**), has rates of $89 to $149 double. Adjacent to (and blending into) the UTEP campus, the **Hilton Garden Inn,** 111 W. University Ave. (© **915/351-2121**), is a solid choice, with rates of $89 to $169 double. In the Sunland Park area, the pick of the litter is the **Holiday Inn Sunland Park,** 900 Sunland Park Dr. (© **800/658-2744**), at $99 to $179 double.

EXPENSIVE

At press time, the iconic **Camino Real Hotel** (www.caminoreal.com/elpaso; © **915/534-3000**), a century-old National Historic Landmark property with 356 rooms, a stunning two-story lobby, and a spectacular Tiffany stained-glass domed ceiling, had been sold and was undergoing a $70-million "top to bottom" renovation and a return to its original name, Hotel Paso del Norte, built in 1912.

MODERATE

El Paso Marriott ★ This airport-handy Marriott with its inviting **Great Room** restaurant and bar and **Red Rim Bistro** (which serves breakfast) offers a reliably solid El Paso stay for business travelers. Its budget-friendly rates (especially on weekends when the business crowd checks out) makes it popular with families too—not to mention the indoor/outdoor swim-through pool.

Rooms are warm and inviting, done in splashes of amber and sunset red, and a handy shuttle gets you to the airport with ease.

1600 Airway Blvd. (¼ mile S of El Paso International Airport). www.marriott.com. ✆ **915/779-3300.** 296 units. $210–$259 double ($89–$120 weekends). Free parking. **Amenities:** 2 restaurants; business center; Indoor/outdoor pool; airport shuttle bus; Wi-Fi ($13/day).

INEXPENSIVE

DoubleTree by Hilton Hotel El Paso Downtown ★ This smartly modern business hotel in a refurbished older building puts you just steps from downtown restaurants and shops, four museums, and the historic Plaza Theatre. The 17-story hotel (16 guest-room floors and an extra level of meeting space) offers 360-degree city views from its highest floors, an outdoor pool, and a breezy seventh-floor alfresco terrace with bar and firepit. Rooms and suites, done in a pleasant, contemporary earth-and-adobe color scheme, offer one king-size bed or two queens, along with a comfortable armchair, ottoman, and desk; some rooms have enclosed patios with pool views, and two-room suites have separate living areas with sofabeds.

600 N. El Paso St. http://doubletree1.hilton.com. ✆ **915/532-8733.** 296 units. $159–$219 double ($99–$109 on weekends). Free parking. **Amenities:** Restaurant/bar, terrace bar, coffee bar; business center; fitness center; laundry/valet service; pool; Wi-Fi (free).

CAMPING

Several primitive campsites are available at Franklin Mountains State Park, and there are also some tent and RV sites at Hueco Tanks State Historic Site; see "Outdoor Activities," p. 355.

El Paso–West RV Park ★ Located halfway between Las Cruces and El Paso and just west of the New Mexico state line, this self-proclaimed "Little Oasis Out West" is a clean campground with shade trees—a rarity in the desert. With laundry facilities, free cable TV and Wi-Fi, picnic tables and Mexican chimney for outdoor fires, a dog run, and a small grocery store, it's a good spot to stay, especially if you like golf: The 18-hole **Dos Lagos Golf Course** (www.doslagos.com; ✆ **575/882-2830**) is located right across the street at 1150 Duffer Lane.

1415 Anthony Dr., Anthony, NM. www.elpasowestrvpark.com. ✆ **575/882-7172.** 100 sites with full hookups, including 70 pull-throughs. $40 nightly. I-10, exit 162 in New Mexico.

Where to Eat

El Paso cuisine is hard to pigeonhole and defies traditional Texas labels: It's not quite Tex-Mex, nor is it authentic Mexican, and it often contains the green chiles of the traditional dishes of its next-door-neighbor New Mexico. Look for plenty of hearty Texas chili and lots of great hole-in-the-wall eateries. For flavorful Mexican (in sometimes modest environs), we recommend **Kiki's Restaurant & Bar,** 2719 N. Piedras St. (www.kikisrestaurant.com; ✆ **915/565-6713**); **Jalisco Café,** 1029 E. 7th Ave. (✆ **915/532-7174**); **Mexican Cottage,** 904 Texas Ave. (✆ **915/546-9816**); and **Lucky Cafe,** 3831 Alameda Ave. (✆ **915/532-2834**).

Note: Smoking is not allowed in El Paso's restaurants.

EXPENSIVE

Anson 11 ★★ CONTINENTAL Truffle mac-n-cheese, braised lamb shanks, wood-fired pizza, diver sea scallops in El Paso? Yes, you can find fine (but not fussy) dining in El Paso right here at Anson 11, a two-level eatery with a casual (sometimes noisy) bistro section downstairs and a serene, more formal experience on the second floor. Anson 11 added the upstairs area a few years back, and it has become a downtown favorite: a dress-up special-occasion spot with white tablecloths, seductive lighting, and an upscale menu of seafood and steaks. Downstairs, the pub-like menu includes gourmet pizzas, interesting sandwiches (braised short ribs, pork belly tacos, lamb meatball pita), and entrees like roast chicken, meatloaf with smoked tomato gravy, and grilled seafood and meats. Although some complain that the food can be hit or miss, most folks give it a thumb's up—it's easily one of the nicest restaurants in town.

303 N. Oregon St. www.anson11.com. ✆ **915/504-6400.** Reservations recommended. Main courses bistro menu $8–$32; fine-dining menu $19–$48. Sun–Thurs 11am–10pm; Fri–Sat 11am–11pm.

Cafe Central ★★ INTERNATIONAL/CONTEMPORARY SOUTHWESTERN This romantic spot in downtown El Paso is an upscale experience all the way. With a large, gracious dining room (crisp table linens, soft lighting, fresh flowers), a sleek lounge (often with live music), and a courtyard patio, this is our choice for a real treat whenever we're passing through El Paso. The food tastes good and looks good, too, plated with panache. Start with the cold Crab Tower of avocado and lump crab topped by a dollop of spicy remoulade sauce or a cup of cream of green chile soup, and go for the grilled Angus tenderloin with four-cheese Dauphinoise potatoes; the miso Chilean sea bass with ginger jasmine rice; or the Guaymas shrimp with a zesty tequila-cilantro sauce. The award-winning wine list is one of the city's best, with more than 300 bottles, and the desserts include the best *tres leches* (three-milk cake—a Tex-Mex staple) in all of El Paso.

109 N. Oregon St., in the lobby of the Texas Tower (One Texas Court). www.cafecentral.com. ✆ **915/545-2233.** Reservations recommended. Main courses $10–$14 lunch, $13–$35 dinner. Mon–Thurs 11am–10:30pm; Fri–Sat 11am–11:30pm. Bar open later. Closed major holidays.

MODERATE/INEXPENSIVE

The local microbrewery, **Jaxons Restaurant and Brewing Co.,** has three locations: 1135 Airway Blvd. (✆ **915/778-9696**), 4799 N. Mesa St. (✆ **915/544-1188**), and 7410 Remcon Circle (✆ **915/845-6557**). **The Tap,** 408 E. San Antonio St. (✆ **915/532-1848**), might just be the best deal in town, serving huge Mexican plates for under $10.

H&H Car Wash & Coffee Shop ★ MEXICAN You'll love this old dive lunch counter, a genuine car wash married to an old-time coffee shop that serves breakfast and hearty Tex-Mex classics. You wouldn't necessarily think that this weathered cowboy coffee shop—which looks like it landed here straight out of 1958 (when it first opened)—would serve some of the best

THE copper CANYON

El Paso is often a jumping-off point for trips to the Copper Canyon in northwestern Mexico. If you are interested in seeing a rugged and beautiful land, taking one of the most remarkable train trips in the world, or hiking or riding horseback through remote areas to see an astonishing variety of flora and fauna—or if you're simply curious about a land still populated by indigenous people living pretty much the way they have for centuries—the Copper Canyon is the place to go.

Most often, when people say "Copper Canyon," they are referring to a section of the Sierra Madre known commonly in Mexico as the Sierra Tarahumara (after the indigenous people who live there). The area was formed through violent volcanic uplifting, followed by a slow, quiet process of erosion that carved a vast network of canyons into the soft volcanic stone.

Crossing the Sierra Tarahumara is the famed **Chihuahua al Pacífico (Chihuahua to the Pacific)** railway. Acclaimed as an engineering marvel, the 390-mile railroad has 39 bridges (the highest is more than 1,000 ft. above the Chinipas River) and 87 tunnels. It climbs from Los Mochis, at sea level, up nearly 8,000 feet through some of Mexico's most magnificent scenery—thick pine forests, jagged peaks, and shadowy canyons—before descending again to its destination, the city of Chihuahua.

It's easier than ever to get to the region, and there are now Ramada and Hampton Inn by Hilton hotels in Chihuahua city and a Best Western in Chihuahua. Still, this may not be the place to do casual, follow-your-nose traveling—the laidback culture of this area is such anathema to a strict schedule that you may find your vacation itinerary upended. The easiest thing is to contract with one of the tour operators and packagers that run Copper Canyon trips from El Paso. Or you can take a bus to Chihuahua and contact a travel agency there that will book a canyon trip—the cheapest and most flexible way to do it. ***Note:*** Be sure to check U.S. travel advisory updates about travel in Mexico before you go.

Another option is to go with a custom tour operator, which generally allows you more time in the canyon and a better experience. The best of the bunch is **Canyon Travel** (www.canyontravel.com; ✆ **888/629-0718** or +52/1-6241655432), which is pretty much in a class by itself. It has lined up some beautiful lodges in the canyons and staffed them with talented local guides. Another operator that provides good service is the Mexico City–based **Native Trails** (www.nativetrails.com; ✆ +**52/55-53349582**).

For more information on traveling in the Copper Canyon, pick up a copy of *Frommer's Mexico* or check out www.frommers.com/destinations/thecoppercanyon.

cheap Tex-Mex in town. But it does, and uses only the freshest ingredients in the process. The place is packed with locals who keep coming back for *carne picada* (diced sirloin with jalapeños, tomatoes, and onions), *huevos rancheros,* and *chiles rellenos.* You can gas up, get your car washed, and grab a bite to eat, all in one spot. The car wash is open from 9am to 4pm weekdays and from 9am to 3pm on Saturdays, charging $12 to $25 for complete hand cleaning of both the body and interior of your car.

701 E. Yandell Dr. at Ochoa St. ✆ **915/533-1144.** Reservations not accepted. Main courses $5–$8. Mon–Sat 7am–3pm.

> **The Rebirth of the Plaza Theatre**
>
> When "the Showplace of the Southwest" opened in El Paso in 1930, it was a big deal: a state-of-the-art film house and stage theater, the "largest of its kind between Dallas and Los Angeles." The Plaza Theatre had a Mighty Wurlitzer organ, a lavish interior, and a distinctive Spanish Colonial facade, showcasing such stars as the Marx Brothers and the Barrymores. But the advent of television and drive-in theaters led to its decline, and by 1986, the Plaza had a date with the wrecking ball. But preservationists swooped in and saved it, and the landmark has been smashingly restored as a popular concert and entertainment hall—complete with its original refurbished Wurlitzer. Check what's on at **www.elpasolive.com/venues/plaza_theatre**.

L&J Café ★★ MEXICAN "The Old Place by the Graveyard" is a tried-and-true El Paso landmark near Concordia Cemetery. The Duran clan has been running this joint since its opening in 1927, and it has been a casino and a Prohibition-era speakeasy. Today it's a bustling eatery (some say dive) with a bar and savory Tex-Mex food—quite often voted El Paso's best. The green chile chicken enchiladas are a local favorite, but for breakfast we like the *huevos rancheros* (Mexican eggs), chili con queso, and *caldillo* (beef and potato stew with a green chile–and-garlic flavor). But you needn't clog your arteries in queso here; the L&J also serves healthful versions of some entrees, prepared with less cheese and fresh *comal* (griddle)-made tortillas.

3622 E. Missouri Ave. www.landjcafe.com. ✆ **915/566-8418.** Reservations accepted only for parties of 6 or more. Main courses $6–$15. Mon–Wed 9am–9pm; Thurs–Sat 9am–10pm; Sun 9am–9pm. Bar open later. Just north of I-10, exit 22A at Copia St.

Rib Hut ★ BARBECUE Slow-smoked barbecue, cold Texas beer, and a location that's within crawling distance of UTEP: This A-frame hut buzzes day and night. It's good and cheap, too, especially the $2.25 "Rib Nights" on Wednesdays from 4pm to 10pm, when you can score a big plate of beef or pork ribs. The menu includes sandwiches, combo plates, and other platters, mostly barbecue beef, pork, and chicken, but also fried catfish and steak. Suds are always flowing, of course, from a big beer menu that includes Texas microbrews, international imports, and Shiner Bock, brewed in little Shiner, Texas since 1909.

2612 N. Mesa St. www.ribhutep.com. ✆ **915/532-7427.** Reservations accepted. Main courses $7–$15. Mon–Sat 11am–10pm; Sun noon–9pm.

El Paso Nightlife

El Paso's remarkably diverse entertainment scene is spread throughout the city. Look for concerts, national touring acts, and other performances at venues like the El Paso Performing Arts Center, the beautifully restored Plaza Theatre (see box above), the McKelligon Canyon Amphitheatre, the outdoor and indoor stages at Chamizal National Memorial, and the University of Texas at El Paso (UTEP). Fans of rock, country, Tejano, and jazz will likely find what they're looking for in the city's bars and clubs. The lively UTEP college scene is centered around Mesa and Cincinnati streets.

The free monthly *El Paso Scene* and its online counterpart, **www.epscene.com**, are the best places to start for exploring arts-and-entertainment opportunities. The Friday *El Paso Times* (www.elpasotimes.com) also features performance listings, as does *The Prospector,* UTEP's student newspaper. Tickets for many events are available through **Ticketmaster** (www.ticketmaster.com; ✆ **915/533-9889**).

THE PERFORMING ARTS

El Paso Opera, 125 Pioneer Plaza (www.epopera.org; ✆ **915/581-5534**) produces spring and fall shows annually, with a Thursday and Saturday performance of each show held at the Abraham Chavez Theater downtown. Spanish and English subtitles are projected for every performance. Tickets run $15 to $90 for a single event. **El Paso Pro-Musica,** 6557 N. Mesa St. (www.eppm.org; ✆ **915/833-9400**), presents several concerts a year, including the El Paso Chamber Music Festival every January. Concerts are held at numerous locations with ticket prices of $5 to $25. **El Paso Symphony Orchestra,** 1 Civic Center Plaza (www.epso.org; ✆ **915/532-3776**), puts on about a dozen different concerts annually. Tickets for single performances run between $16 and $42, with discounts for students and seniors. At Franklin Mountains State Park, the outdoor **McKelligon Canyon Amphitheatre,** 2 McKelligon Canyon Rd., annually hosts **Viva! El Paso** (www.viva-ep.org; ✆ **915/231-1165**) from mid-June to early August. Tickets are about $18 to $24; barbecue-style dinners are available.

The **El Paso Playhouse,** 2501 Montana Ave. (www.elpasoplayhouse.com; ✆ **915/532-1317**), stages a new production almost every month. Recent productions include *Much Ado About Nothing* and Noel Coward's *Blithe Spirit.* Tickets are usually less than $10. The **University of Texas at El Paso Dinner Theatre,** Union Ballroom on the UTEP campus (www.utep.edu/udt; ✆ **915/747-6060** or 747-5234), is a tradition, producing student musicals since 1983. Today, the theater presents plays Wednesday through Sunday at 7pm during the school year. Show dinners might include prime rib, baked potato, and a cookie sundae. Recent productions have included *August Osage County, Who's Afraid of Virginia Woolf?, It's a Wonderful Life, The Diary of Ann Frank,* and *Driving Miss Daisy.* Tickets run about $30 to $40, except for Sunday matinees (2:30pm), which are $22 to $24 but don't include dinner.

THE CLUB & LIVE MUSIC SCENE

The Union Plaza District on the west side of downtown has blossomed in recent years to emerge as the top club-hopping area in El Paso. The pick of the litter is the **Garden,** 511 Western St. (www.thegardenep.com; ✆ **915/544-4400**), with something for everybody, from great New American cuisine to an outdoor beer garden to a DJ-driven dance floor on the weekends. The **Republic,** 200 Anthony St. (✆ **915/351-7797**), is another Union Plaza standout, a hip nightclub complete with velvet rope.

THE BAR SCENE

Downtown, the **Tap Bar & Restaurant,** 408 E. San Antonio St. (✆ **915/532-1848**), is a classic watering hole serving plenty of cold beer and spicy Mexican dishes. The bar at **Anson 11** downtown, 303 N. Oregon St. (✆ **915/504-6400**), is a popular place for drinks and dinner at the bar. At press time, the **Camino Real Hotel** (✆ **915/534-3010**), 101 S. El Paso St., was under renovation (and renamed as the Hotel Paso del Norte), so call to see if its **Dome Restaurant** bar, one of the most regal places in the Southwest to sip a cocktail, is open. Likewise, **Craft & Social,** 305 E. Franklin (✆ **915/219-7141**) is a great spot with a great selection of more than 25 kinds of beer on tap (including small-batch craft brews) and a respectable wine list, too, as well as some good eats in a casual setting. **Rosa's Cantina,** 3454 Doniphan Dr. (✆ **915/833-0402**), was made famous by country legend Marty Robbins in his 1959 hit "El Paso"—or perhaps merely inspired by it after the fact.

SMALL TOWNS & SITES OF CENTRAL WEST TEXAS ★

Travelers crossing West Texas pass through a smattering of communities with a variety of roadside motels and restaurants. But those who only grab some Zs or a quick bite to eat will be missing out on some fun things to see and do. While most of the areas discussed in this section would not be our choice as a vacation destination in and of themselves, they are definitely worth a stop, and one could easily spend anywhere from a few hours to a few days in each place. The alluring old cowboy outpost hotels and state parks are the real draw here.

Fort Davis & Davis Mountains State Park

200 miles SE of El Paso; 23 miles NE of Alpine; 96 miles NW of Big Bend National Park

A charming small town surrounded by dramatic scenery and steeped in Old West lore, Fort Davis is one of those rare places that can please both city and country types. The town itself is teeming with boutiques and B&Bs, and to the north, outdoors buffs will appreciate Davis Mountains State Park.

The town's origins are tied to Fort Davis, the identically named U.S. Army post established in 1854. The town was initially a ranching center, but the fort's 1891 abandonment and the railroads' decision to bypass the community led to an economic bust. After the fort was designated a National Historic Site in 1961, traffic increased and helped create the tourism-heavy landscape in place today.

ESSENTIALS

Getting There

Fort Davis is located on Tex. 17 between Balmorhea (which has a fabulous spring-fed swimming pool) and Marfa (known for its "ghost" lights). From the north, the town is accessed via I-10 by taking either exit 192 or exit 206 and driving south on the highway for about 40 miles. Tex. 118 also runs through the town, from Kent (on I-10) to the northwest and to Alpine to the southeast. The nearest major commercial airports are 170 miles north in Midland and 205 miles to the northwest in El Paso.

Getting Around

Fort Davis is centered by the town square and historic courthouse. Most of the businesses, lodging establishments, and restaurants are located on Main Street (Tex. 118), which runs north-south through the town square. You can stroll around town, but the attractions discussed below are not easy to access by foot.

Visitor Information

The **Fort Davis Chamber of Commerce,** 4 Memorial Square (www.fortdavis.com; ✆ **432/426-3015**), provides brochures, maps, and trip-planning advice.

FAST FACTS **Big Bend Regional Medical Center,** 25 miles southeast of Fort Davis at 2600 Tex. 118 N. in Alpine (www.bigbendhealthcare.com; ✆ **432/837-3447**), has 24-hour emergency services. The **post office,** located on the town square on Main Street, is open Monday through Friday from 8am to 4pm.

WHAT TO SEE & DO

The Top Attractions

Fort Davis National Historic Site ★ This frontier fort has a picturesque rocky backdrop. A historic military post, Fort Davis was established in 1854 and was named for Jefferson Davis, then U.S. Secretary of War. Surrounded by a natural defense of large rock formations, the fort afforded safety for the six companies of the Eighth U.S. Infantry that were there to battle Comanches, Kiowas, and Apaches in protecting westward pioneers. The fort was abandoned in 1891, having "outlived its usefulness." Today, more than 20 structures on the site have been restored, many precisely decorated in the style of the late 1800s. Expect to spend an hour to tour the fort. There are 5 miles of hiking trails with great views overlooking Sleeping Lion Mountain and Davis Mountains State Park.

Tex. 17/118, 1 mile north of Fort Davis. www.nps.gov/foda. ✆ **432/426-3224.** Admission $7 adults, free for children 15 and under. Daily 8am–5pm. Closed major holidays.

McDonald Observatory ★★★ Stargazers say this is one of the best attractions in West Texas, and we must agree; for here, free of light pollution, McDonald Observatory is a wonderful place to view the majesties of the heavens. In fact, this is one of the world's foremost astronomical research facilities (operated by the University of Texas). Hour-long guided daytime tours reveal live telescope images of the sun and its dramatic flares and sunspots. Three nights a week, the observatory has a **Star Party** (Tues, Fri, and Sat; $12 adults, $10 seniors, $8 children), where you can spy celestial objects and glittering constellations through high-powered telescopes. The **StarDate Café** in the visitor center offers sandwiches, tacos, and snacks. This fabulous observatory is our favorite West Texas attraction, and a membership (donations of $50 and up) allows you to stay in the observatory's **Astronomers Lodge** on-site ($150 double per night, meals included).

Tex. 118 N., 16 miles northwest of Fort Davis. www.mcdonaldobservatory.org. ✆ **877/984-7827** for recorded information, or 432/426-3640. Daytime pass (includes guided tour) $8 adults, $7 children age 6–12, free for children 5 and under, $30 maximum per family. Daily 10am–5:30pm. Guided tours 11am and 2pm daily.

Outdoor Activities

Fort Davis's outdoor recreation is centered around **Davis Mountains State Park,** 4 miles northwest of town via Tex. 118 (www.tpwd.state.tx.us; ✆ **432/426-3337** or 512/389-8900 for campsite reservations). The second-highest range in all of Texas, the Davis Mountains reach their pinnacle at the peak of the 8,382-foot Mount Livermore. Hiking is our activity of choice here; try the moderate, 8-mile round-trip that leads to the Fort Davis National Historic Site. On or off the trails, the park is a great place for wildlife viewing and bird-watching. It's one of the few places in the United States where you might spot a Montezuma quail, and javelinas (the wild boars that roam the Southwest), tarantulas, horned frogs, and pronghorn antelope also live in the park. The entrance fee is $6 for adults, free for children 12 and under. Campsites run $25 for full hookups, $25 for water and electric hookups only, and $15 for tent and primitive sites.

For travelers who've always wanted to be a cowboy when they grew up, just north of the park off Tex. 118 are various guest ranches with a number of fun activities. For horseback riding, mosey over to the **Prude Ranch** (www.prude-ranch.com; ✆ **432/426-3202**), where 1-hour rides run $30 and accommodations and cabins are $75 to $95 double; or the **Harvard Hotel & Lodge and the H.E. Sproul Ranch** (www.sproulranch.com; ✆ **432/426-3097**), with an emphasis on hunting. It has a terrific outdoor pool deck, a 4×4 tour ($55 per person), and well-kept rooms and a cabin with queen and bunk beds for $145 to $225.

WHERE TO STAY

Hotel Limpia ★ This circa-1912 pink-stone hotel is spread out over eight historic buildings. Refurbished rooms are outfitted in tasteful Victorian-era furnishings, with quilted queen- and king-size beds with handsome wooden headboards, writing desks, and swag curtains; all have private bathrooms (both modern and old-fashioned). Welcoming white rockers line the porches of the main building. If you're looking for privacy, try one of the pet-friendly Orchard Suites, about a mile from the main buildings, with original pressed-tin ceilings and clawfoot tubs. Simple, attractive, value-priced rooms are located in the building across from the main hotel. A fun gift shop sells Texas-flavored curios and more. The **Blue Mountain Bistro** has a delicious and eclectic menu that globe-trots from French country cooking to tapas to big Texas rib-eyes—and whets your whistle with the county's only bar.

101 Memorial Square. www.hotellimpia.com. ✆ **800/662-5517.** 31 units, including 10 suites. $109–$125 double; $139–$199 suite. **Amenities:** Pool; Wi-Fi (free).

The Veranda ★★ Sun-dappled courtyards and flower-filled gardens make this quiet, family-owned bed-and-breakfast in the cool mile-high clime of the Davis Mountains a serene retreat. Once the Hotel Lempert, a boarding-house hotel opened in 1883, the aptly named Veranda is the oldest hotel in West Texas, and offers pleasant places to sit amid spring gardens and summer flowers. Each afternoon the owners set out fresh baked goods and organic fair-trade coffee and tea for guests to enjoy. Behind the building's original 135-year-old, 18-inch-thick adobe walls, rooms are decorated with period antiques and offer scenic views of the mountains. Most have king-size beds, although some have two beds and tub-showers. The walled courtyard is a peaceful space amid an orchard of peach trees. Families enjoy the property's spacious two-bedroom Carriage House, with a fully equipped kitchen.

210 Court Ave. www.theveranda.com. ✆ **432/426-2233.** 9 units (including 4 suites, 1 house). From $110 double; $140 suite, $160 house. Rates include "from scratch" buffet breakfast and afternoon baked goods. **Amenities:** Wi-Fi (free).

WHERE TO EAT

Open for dinner daily and weekend breakfast only, the **Blue Mountain Bistro** (www.blue-mountain-bistro.com; ✆ **432/426-3244**) is a surprisingly sophisticated restaurant located inside the **Hotel Limpia,** 101 Memorial Square. In addition to grilled steaks and fish, it serves dishes with a French country accent and has a delectable tapas menu ($7–$30). The bistro has a breakfast buffet on weekends from 7:30 to 10am.

Balmorhea State Park ★★

185 miles E of El Paso; 32 miles N of Fort Davis

Old-timer Texans talk about Balmorhea with the kind of reverence that makes them take off their cowboy hats. Young children have been known to wax poetic over Balmorhea too. A little-known yet well-loved part of the Texas State Park system (and one of the smallest, at 45 acres), **Balmorhea State Park,** 9207 Tex. 17 S. (www.tpwd.state.tx.us; ✆ **432/375-2370**), is home to a massive, 1¾-acre pool cooled and fed by the San Solomon Springs. It's a beautiful natural pool where generation after generation of youngsters have taken a summertime dip in the fairly constant 74°F (23°C) waters.

Size aside, this is no ordinary swimming hole: The water teems with fish, and the floor is covered in rocks. The Civilian Conservation Corps built the pool in the 1930s, planting its V-shaped banks with shade trees and installing a 200-foot circle of limestone and flagstone. Snorkeling and scuba diving are a hit here, and on occasion you might see a nonpoisonous water snake or turtle swimming here, too. A canal system leads from the pool to other areas, creating a habitat for many native fish, two species of which (the Comanche Springs pupfish and Pecos Gambusia) are endangered. There are showers and changing areas, and two diving boards near the pool, which is open daily from 8am to sunset. Forgot your trunks? No worries. Next door, the **Toyahvale Desert Oasis shop,** 9225 Tex. 17 S. (www.toyahvale.com; ✆ **432/375-2572**),

CRUISING THE border & A HOT SPRINGS SOAK

I highly recommend the 48-mile scenic drive along FM 170, which traces the Texas-Mexico border from Presidio to Candelaria. Halfway there, take a side trip to a hidden treasure: the **Chinati Hot Springs,** 7000 N. Hot Springs Rd. (www.chinatihotsprings.net; ✆ **432/229-4165**), a rustic resort that draws guests to the restorative 109°F (43°C) spring waters for which the resort was named. For $13 you can soak in the hot springs ($6 children 12 and under). You can also stay overnight ($105–$140 double) or camp ($25 per person, includes admission). This little side trip is worth it for the scenery, and it also gives travelers a sense of the border as a real place and not just an imaginary line.

provides swimwear, snorkeling and scuba equipment rentals and air fills from 10am to 6pm daily March through October and 10am to 6pm weekends (or by appointment) the rest of the year.

Another park attraction is the reconstructed *cienega* (desert wetland). Set near the campground, **San Solomon Cienega** is a good spot to look for native wildlife: You might spy a Texas spiny soft-shelled turtle, a blotched water snake, or a green heron from the raised wooden platform, or spot a headwater catfish through the underwater viewing window. A path system allows viewing of the fish, reptiles, and amphibians in the canals.

The park has 34 campsites, most with water and electrical hookups, for $11 to $17 a night, in addition to the $7 entrance fee. Additionally, a small motel on the park's grounds has standard rooms for $75 to $135. For groceries, you'll need to head into the town of Balmorhea—the gift shop at the park visitor center stocks mainly souvenirs. The park is located 4 miles south of Balmorhea on Tex. 17. Don't miss this stop in the summertime.

Marfa

98 miles NW of Big Bend National Park; 193 miles SE of El Paso; 21 miles S of Fort Davis

Named after a character in Dostoevsky's *The Brothers Karamazov,* this town of about 1,700 residents is on the brink of one of the last American frontiers. Surrounded by rugged terrain, Marfa is, to say the least, remote. Once an Old West saloon-and-casino outpost, the predominantly Mexican town has evolved into a haven for contemporary artists, its nucleus being the avant-garde Chinati Foundation. This phenomenon makes for some interesting contrasts: 10-gallon hats and berets, wine bars and feed stores, cowboys and intellectuals, all coexisting in the same small town. Marfa has long been touted as "the new Sedona" or "the next Santa Fe," but it remains more than a little bit sleepy—and that's a big part of its charm.

ESSENTIALS

Getting There

Marfa is located at the junction of U.S. 67, U.S. 90, and Tex. 17, 94 miles north of Big Bend Ranch State Park. If you're arriving from the east, take I-10, exit 248, and proceed 82 miles on U.S. 67 through Alpine. From the west,

Marfa is located 74 miles southeast of Van Horn on U.S. 90; from the north, it's 60 miles south of I-10, exit 206, on Tex. 17. The nearest major commercial airport is in Midland.

Getting Around

Tex. 17 (Lincoln St.) is the main north-south artery, and U.S. 90 (San Antonio St.) is the main east-west route. The town square and Presidio County Courthouse are located at Lincoln and Highland streets. You can stroll around downtown Marfa, but in general, a car is necessary to check out the Marfa lights and other attractions.

Visitor Information

Drop by the **Marfa Visitor Center,** 302 S. Highland Ave. (www.visitmarfa.com; © **432/729-4772**) for information, maps, and more; it's open Monday to Friday 8am to 5pm and Saturday and Sunday 10am to 4pm. Contact the **Marfa Chamber of Commerce,** 207 N. Highland Ave. in the Paisano Hotel (© **432/729-4942**), for visitor information.

FAST FACTS The nearest hospital is 35 miles west in Alpine, the **Big Bend Regional Medical Center,** 2600 Tex. 118 N. (© **432/837-3447**). The **post office,** 100 N. Highland Ave., is open Monday through Friday from 8am to 4:30pm.

THE TOP ATTRACTIONS

Besides the attractions listed below, **Big Bend Ranch State Park ★★**, 60 miles south of Marfa (www.tpwd.state.tx.us; © **432/358-4444** for reservations), is Texas's largest state park at over 300,000 acres. It rivals Big Bend as a scenic desert wonderland featuring both the river and mountains—except it only attracts about 7,500 visitors a year, many of whom raft the park's stretch of Rio Grande and never venture into the remote interior. There are primitive campsites and excellent hiking opportunities in and around El Solitario, a huge volcanic swelling in the eastern end of the park. Entrance fees are $5 for adults, and free for kids 13 and under. Campsites are $8 and backcountry camping is $5. There is also lodging available at Sauceda for $35 to $100 per night.

You can catch a ride in that big, blue West Texas sky with **Marfa Gliders** (www.flygliders.com). Rides cost around $160 and last about 15 minutes.

Chinati Foundation ★★ The late New York artist Donald Judd fell in love with the high-desert terrain of Marfa in the 1970s. He bought up acreage and, with help from the Dia Art Foundation, created this nonprofit museum in 1986 to showcase large-scale artworks that are strongly tied to the landscape. In large part, Judd and the Chinati Foundation are responsible for putting this little town of 2,000 on the art map, so to speak—or at least for encouraging others to come enjoy Marfa's charms. Housed in 34 buildings at a former U.S. Army post, the facility has become the centerpiece of Marfa's fertile contemporary arts scene and burgeoning tourist industry. The permanent collection consists of numerous works of modernist, minimalist, and avant-garde art in mediums ranging from paper to steel, fluorescent light to concrete—including 15 Donald Judd works. Chinati also has a rotating calendar of temporary exhibitions, many from the foundation's Artists in Residence program. Marfa's population doubles every October when the foundation hosts a major open house, selling out every hotel within a 100-mile radius.

The entire permanent collection is accessible by guided tours only. Tours start at 10am, break for lunch at noon, then continue from 2 to 3:30pm. Reservations are recommended 3 days in advance for individuals and are required during holiday periods. Call for additional tours of the collection during spring break season, for private viewing or for group tours (reserve 2 weeks in advance).

U.S. 67 (½ mile south of Marfa). www.chinati.org. ✆ **432/729-4362.** Admission $10 adults, $5 students and seniors, free for children 11 and under. Wed–Sun 10am. Artillery sheds tour: $5. Thurs–Sun 3:45pm.

Presidio County Courthouse ★ This Second Empire beauty was built in 1885 for what was then the princely sum of $60,000. A $2.5-million restoration in 2001 made its magnificent domed roof and Victorian woodwork really shine. It's been the site of 19th-century balls and square dances, as well as a little bit of mayhem: Bullet holes remain in the scales of the statue of Lady Justice atop the dome—reputedly the work of a convicted cowboy who shot the scales in the 1890s, proclaiming, "There is no justice in Presidio County." You can climb to the fifth floor for views of Marfa and the surrounding countryside.

Lincoln St. and Highland Ave. www.co.presidio.tx.us. ✆ **432/729-4942.** Free admission. Building Mon–Fri 9am–5pm; grounds 24 hr.

WHERE TO STAY

Cíbolo Creek Ranch ★★★ In the silent shade of the Chinati Mountains, a world away from the noise of city life, this unique 32,000-acre ranch offers an exceptional kind of Texas escape. Three structures built from abandoned 19th-century forts have been meticulously restored and repurposed, resembling traditional Native American houses of Taos or Santa Fe. Each is named for the former fort that inspired it: **El Fortín del Cíbolo, El Fortín de la Ciénega,** and **El Fortín de la Morita.** All feature a distinctive, award-winning Southwestern style, with adobe walls, massive cottonwood beams, and Mexican furniture and period antiques. The Cíbolo fort, the resort's main lodge, has 25 guestrooms, a swimming pool, restaurant, and bar. Thirty miles away is the 10-room Fort Ciénega, with its own pool, hot tub, and industrial kitchen. Some 45 miles from Cíbolo is the more rustic Morita, with oil lamps instead of electricity. All rooms have full bathrooms, tile floors, and small kitchenettes, and most have adobe-style fireplaces. Guests can prepare their own meals in their rooms, or opt to eat at Cíbolo. Adding to the romantic ambience are firepits and outdoor patios with chairs for lounging and stargazing at night. If you like, you can stay busy mountain biking, hiking, swimming, taking guided ranch tours, hunting, or fishing and paddleboating on

MARFA'S mystery LIGHTS

In 1883, an illumination flickered on the horizon east of Marfa, spooking a young cowhand by the name of Robert Ellison. Fearing the lights were Apache campfires, Ellison left behind the cattle he was herding and searched the terrain on horseback. He found nothing. Although this was the first written account of the "ghost lights" of Marfa, it wasn't the first time the Marfa Lights, as they're now called, were observed—people had been talking about them long before Ellison wrote about the lights. For as long as anyone can remember, the **"Marfa Lights"** have puzzled thousands of eyewitnesses, as they appear, disappear, and reappear in an area where there are said to be no roads, no houses, and no human inhabitants. The lights have been described as "conscious beings" (a reference to a *Star Trek* term); some say the lights seem "to play around and hover around the ground and shoot into the sky" as well. When people try to find them, it is said the lights seem to move farther and farther away. Some observers insist the lights are the work of supernatural beings or visiting aliens, while others point to electrostatic discharge, car headlights, campfires, or swamp gas as the real cause. But no one has definitively solved the mystery.

You'll find a nifty viewing area 9 miles east of Marfa on U.S. 90. The lights are best viewed at night from the observation deck: Look to the southwest, just to the right of the mountains, along the horizon for the sporadic flickers of light. If there's a crowd, it's a scene straight out of *Close Encounters of the Third Kind*. If the lights really pique your interest, don't miss the annual **Marfa Lights Festival,** a Labor Day weekend celebration with a parade, street dances, concerts, and arts-and-crafts sales (see www.visitmarfa.com). This festival seems to have little to do with the Marfa Lights anymore, but it's a good time nonetheless for some friendly community fun.

Cíbolo's private lake. Or you can kick back beneath the stars and enjoy an outdoor massage from a local masseuse. Cíbolo Creek is the ultimate getaway—you won't find many places quite this wonderful, even in West Texas. (And yes, this is where Supreme Court Justice Antonin Scalia famously slipped off this mortal coil.)

97139 U.S. Hwy. 67. www.cibolocreekranch.com. ✆ **432/229-3737.** 24 units. $420–$465 double. **Amenities:** Restaurant/bar; pool; Wi-Fi (free).

El Cosmico ★ El Cosmico is popular Austin hotelier/designer Liz Lambert's über-cool concept lodgings, a 21-acre "nomadic hotel and campground" that's just as offbeat and exciting as Marfa itself. The place offers unique accommodations: a mix of campsites, a Mongolian yurt, safari and scout tents, Sioux-style tepees, and fully restored vintage trailers complete with outdoor showers or tubs. Most of the trailers date from the 1940s to the 1960s and are chock-full of funky, nostalgia-laden charm, with A/C and heat, "dry goods" minibars, and fridges. The resort is anchored by **Lobby House and Provision Co.,** a small mercantile with beer and wine, a record player and a nice cache of vintage vinyl, and comfortable places to lounge. There is also an outdoor kitchen, a hammock grove, an outdoor stage, and a bathroom for

GALLERY hopping IN THE BIG BEND

Marfa might be one of the most buzzed-about art towns in the West, but, outside of the Chinati Foundation, it has only a handful of galleries. Art aficionados can cover Marfa's gallery scene in a few hours, but a day can be spent visiting galleries in not only Marfa, but Alpine and Marathon as well. Here are some favorites.

Marfa **Ballroom Marfa** is an installation-oriented space at 108 E. San Antonio St. (www.ballroommarfa.org; ✆ **432/729-3600**) that also hosts film screenings, lectures, and musical performances. Like the Chinati Foundation, **Exhibitions 2d,** 400 S. Highland Ave. (www.exhibitions2d.com; ✆ **432/729-1910**), has a minimalist orientation. The **Baxter Gallery,** 209 W. U.S. 90 (www.baxtergallery.com; ✆ **432/386-0689**), specializes in Big Bend landscapes and wildlife sculptures by the owner, local artisan Mary Baxter. The fine-art photography at the **James Evans Gallery,** 21 S. 1st St. (www.jevansgallery.com; ✆ **432/386-4366**), is sublime and stunning. And don't miss a tour of Donald Judd's home and studios at the **Judd Foundation,** 104 Highland St. (www.juddfoundation.org; ✆ **432/729-4406**), with Judd works and the works of other artists he collected on display.

Alpine Keri Artzt's **Kiowa Gallery,** 105 E. Holland Ave. (www.artwalkalpine.com/locations/kiowa-gallery; ✆ **432/837-3067**), is one of the best in the region, with an eclectic collection of mostly regional work, ranging from elegant to oddball.

Terlingua In Terlingua Ghost Town, edging Big Bend National Park, Bryn Moore's **Leapin' Lizard Guest House** (www.leapinlizardterlingua.com; ✆ **432/371-2775**) offers local jewelry, original watercolor paintings, and folk art. You'll find art and fun souvenirs at the **Terlingua Trading Company** (www.terlinguatradingco.homestead.com; ✆ **432/371-2234**). A lovely (and entirely unexpected) quilt shop in Study Butte/Terlingua, **Quilts, Etc.,** Hwy 118 (www.bigbendquilts.blogspot.com; ✆ **432/371-2292**), not only sells quilts by local artist Marguerite Chanslor but also offers home accessories, paintings, jewelry, and photographs, all created by Big Bend–area artists.

campers and guests staying in tents and yurts. Guests also love El Cosmico's Dutch tubs—wood-fired hot tubs—which they can rent from 6 to 10pm (unless a local burn-ban is in effect). Bikes are also available for rent. If El Cosmico's offbeat style appeals, you may like owner Liz Lambert's more traditional, yet still eclectic, hotels: **Hotel Saint Cecilia** (see p. 313) and **Hotel San Jose** (see p. 315) in Austin, and the **Hotel Havana** (see p. 260).

802 S. Highland Ave. (U.S. 67). www.elcosmico.com. ✆ **877/822-1950** and 432/729-1950. 11 trailers; 21 yurts, teepees, and tents; 25 campsites. $150–$195 trailer; $175 yurt, $150 teepee, or $80 tent; $15 per person for campsite. Pets accepted ($10/night). **Amenities:** Restaurant; bike rental; hammocks; hot tubs; pool; store; Wi-Fi (free).

The Hotel Paisano ★★ How many hotels can say James Dean, Elizabeth Taylor, Dennis Hopper, and Rock Hudson slept here? The Hotel Paisano can, because the cast and crew of the Texas epic cinema sensation *Giant* stayed here in the 1950s when filming on location outside Marfa. (*Giant* was young Dean's last film, which wrapped just before his death.) Set in the heart of downtown Marfa, this is a quintessential old-school Wild West hotel. Built in 1921 and listed on the National Register of Historic places, the hotel has been refurbished and reconfigured in recent years. With 41 rooms, including several suites and original historic hotel rooms, a patio, and a heated pool, this inn seduces with Spanish colonial touches like high arches, stained-glass windows, and a fusion of Prairie and Mission architecture. The small, simple second-floor room where James Dean slept is the most requested room, but the corner suite where Rock Hudson stayed (directly across from Liz Taylor's room), with its kitchenette, wet bar, elevated living room, fireplace, and large rooftop veranda overlooking the pool and courtyard, is nicer by far and the hotel's largest suite. There is no elevator, so request a ground-floor room if you're averse to climbing stairs. Be sure to dine at **Jett's Grill** restaurant, and enjoy local art at the hotel's **Greasewood Gallery.**

Texas St. and Highland Ave. www.hotelpaisano.com. ✆ **432/729-3669.** 41 units, including 9 suites. $99–$159 double; $159–$250 suite. **Amenities:** Restaurant/bar; gallery/shop; pool; Wi-Fi (free).

WHERE TO EAT

Beyond the greasy spoons, Marfa has a few high-end restaurants, including **Jett's Grill** (✆ **432/729-3838**) at the Hotel Paisano (see above). Named after James Dean's character in *Giant,* the restaurant serves dinner only and features Continental fare spiced with a south-of-the-border kick. Most main courses run $15 to $34.

For a quick, cheap bite, it's hard to beat the **Pizza Foundation,** 305 S. Spring St. (www.pizzafoundation.com; ✆ **432/729-3377**), serving East Coast–style thin-crust slices and pies in a newly converted industrial space. (***Insider tip:*** The owners hate it when you call their pies "NY–style" pizza; they claim that East Coast pizza isn't as greasy as New York pies, and boasts both a great thin crust and more cheese.)

SHOPPING

The best bookstore in the entire region is the sophisticated **Marfa Book Company,** located inside the St. George Hotel, 105 S. Highland Ave. (www.marfabookco.com; ✆ **432/729-3906**), which features a coffee and wine bar and a deep inventory of art and architecture titles.

Alpine

80 miles N of Big Bend National Park; 26 miles E of Marfa; 23 miles SE of Fort Davis

The home of Sul Ross State University, Alpine is nicknamed "the Hub of the Big Bend." Long the commercial center of vast Brewster County, this town of about 6,000 residents has numerous amenities that make it a good jumping-off point to Big Bend National Park, or a nice stopover while en route to other area destinations: a vibrant Main Street with plenty of galleries and funky retailers, excellent hiking in all directions, an active railroad depot on the Southern Pacific line, and festivals and museums that are pure West.

ESSENTIALS

Getting There

Alpine is located at the junction of U.S. 67/90 and Tex. 118, just 80 miles north of Big Bend National Park. If you're arriving from the east, take I-10, exit 248, and proceed 56 miles on U.S. 67. From the west, Alpine is located 55 miles south of Balmorhea (I-10, exit 206). **Amtrak** (www.amtrak.com; ✆ **800/872-2745**) serves the train station at 102 W. Holland St., the closest depot to Big Bend National Park. The nearest major commercial airport is in Midland.

Getting Around

U.S. 67/90 (Holland St.) is the main east-west artery and Tex. 119 (5th St.) is the main north-south route; downtown is centered on the intersection of the two. Rental cars are available through **Alpine Auto Rental** (www.alpineauto rental.com; ✆ **800/894-3463** or 432/837-3463).

Visitor Information

Contact the **Alpine Chamber of Commerce,** 106 N. 3rd St., Alpine, TX 79830 (www.alpinetexas.com; ✆ **800/561-3712** or 432/837-2326).

FAST FACTS The **Big Bend Regional Medical Center,** 2600 Tex. 118 N. (www.bigbendhealthcare.com; ✆ **432/837-3447**), has the only 24-hour emergency room in the region. The **post office,** 901 W. Holland Ave., is open Monday through Friday from 8am to 4pm, and Saturday 10am to 1pm.

THE TOP ATTRACTIONS

Elephant Mountain Wildlife Management Area ★ You can spot desert bighorn, mule deer, and javelinas from the comfort of your car on a 15-mile round-trip driving tour through this wildlife management area. The excellent wildlife-viewing opportunities include great bird-watching as well. Morning, before the heat of the day sets in, is the best time to spot fauna in these desert mountains. Hiking and camping are also available, and primitive campsites have fire rings at no extra cost.

26 miles south of Alpine via Tex. 118. www.tpwd.state.tx.us. ✆ **432/837-3251.** Free admission. Portions of the area are open year-round; driving tour May–Aug.

Kokernot Field ★ Once dubbed the "Yankee Stadium of Texas," Alpine's vintage minor-league stadium was actually inspired by Chicago's Wrigley Field. Local rancher Herbert L. Kokernot, Jr., had it built in 1947, spending about $1.25 million ($14 million today) and sparing no expense. It's still a (very) active stadium, home to the Alpine Cowboys of the Pecos League, as well as the Big Bend Cowboys pro team, the Alpine Bucks high school team, and the Sul Ross State Lobos college team. Spend a few minutes to look around; note the grandstand, made with native Texas stone quarried from Kokernot's ranch.

E. Hendryx Dr. and Fighting Buck Ave. www.kokernotfield.com. ✆ **432/837-2326.** Free admission; donations accepted. Grounds open 24 hr., stadium open on game days and for special events.

Museum of the Big Bend ★ Immerse yourself in the Big Bend region's history, from American Indian cultures dating back more than 3,000 years to the legacy of the European settlers. Among the highlights are the Yana and Marty Davis map collection, an exhibit of altar art, or *retablos,* and a cache of ancient arrowheads, the "Livermore Points," which were found on Mount Livermore in the Davis Mountain range. Expect to spend about an hour.

On the campus of the Sul Ross State University. www.sulross.edu/~museum. ✆ **432/837-8143.** Free admission; donations accepted. Tues–Sat 9am–5pm; Sun 1–5pm.

WHERE TO STAY

Besides the option listed below, I also like **Alpine Guest Lodging** (www.alpineguestlodging.rocks; ✆ **877/298-5638**), featuring four units with a queen and king, plus a hideaway or a futon for $69 to $119. One unit has a full kitchen. The rooms are delightful at the **Holland Hotel** (www.thehollandhoteltexas.com; ✆ **432/837-2800**), from suites with hardwood floors, antique reproductions, and jetted tubs to a fourth-floor penthouse, complete with a private hot-tub deck. Double rooms start from $106, with suites from $155 to $325.

Maverick Inn ★ This retro roadside motel has an upscale Route 66 sort of Western sensibility. Here the free-spirited Maverick has created what they call a "roadhouse for wanderers." It's more than that, of course: Look for impeccably understated cowboy decor, all beamed ceilings, cool adobe walls, and Saltillo tile floors. The inviting Maverick lobby is warmed by a Santa Fe–style fireplace, anchored by a big, colorful American Indian rug, and furnished in leather and cowhide. Desert flora borders the pool and patio area outside. Located just across the street from Sul Ross State University and just a few blocks from the center of town, the Maverick is a small treasure.

1200 E. Holland Ave. www.themaverickinn.com. ✆ **432/837-0628.** 21 units. $118–$140 double. Rates include continental breakfast. Pets accepted. **Amenities:** Pool; Wi-Fi (free).

WHERE TO EAT

Named for the ranch in the Edna Ferber novel and James Dean movie *Giant,* the **Reata Restaurant,** 203 N. 5th St. (www.reata.net; ✆ **432/837-9232**), serves regional Texan food and some of the best steaks in the Big Bend; main courses are $10 to $15 for lunch and $11 to $40 for dinner. **Alicia's,** 708 E. Gallego Ave. (✆ **432/837-2802**), is a standby for big burritos and hearty breakfasts (about $3–$8).

MIDLAND & ODESSA

300 miles E of El Paso; 135 miles S of Lubbock

Welcome to oil country, where the ups and downs of the petroleum industry have long defined these twin cities 23 miles apart on I-20. Midland-Odessa sits in the geographic center of the Permian Basin, the home of the country's richest oil fields—about 25% of the United States' reserves. Today, only Alaska produces more oil than the Permian Basin.

Midland's Famous Son, George

Born in New Haven, Connecticut on July 6, 1946, George Walker Bush—later known as Dubya—was on the plains of West Texas by the time he was 2 years old. His father (and the 41st president), George H. W. Bush, moved the family west to seek his fortune in the oil business. The first stop was Odessa, but in 1950, the family moved to Midland, where they lived until 1959. It was this time—young George's formative years—that made the biggest impression on this president-to-be, and in 1975 he returned as an adult to Midland's oil business. The Bushes lived at 1412 W. Ohio Ave. between 1951 and 1955, and this home has been restored to its 1950s appearance and is open to the public Tuesday through Saturday 10am to 5pm and Sunday 2 to 5pm. For additional information, contact the **George W. Bush Childhood Home,** 1412 W. Ohio Ave. (www.bushchildhoodhome.org; ✆ **432/682-1112;**). Additionally, the **Presidential Museum** in Odessa (p. 378) relocated the Bush home in Odessa to its grounds and also restored it for the public.

The area saw the first of several oil booms in the 1920s. However, less than a decade later, the Great Depression brought on the first of several busts. Production increased during World War II, but foreign competition brought on another bust by the mid-1970s. The pendulum again swayed in the boom direction until 1982, when the bottom suddenly fell out of the oil market: Wells were capped, new houses went unsold, and banks failed. In the time since, the industry has diversified and recovered, but Midland and Odessa remain the heart and soul of the Permian Basin's oil industry. As it goes, so do Midland and Odessa.

The one-time home of two presidents—George H. W. Bush and his son George W.—the cities have a handful of noteworthy attractions and offer an educational glimpse at the rewards and the ravages of a volatile, oil-heavy economy. While Midland and Odessa are by no means tourist destinations, they are two of the few actual cities in West Texas, and a good gateway to the Big Bend area.

Essentials

GETTING THERE

Midland is located on the north side of I-20, accessible via exits 131 and 140. Tex. 349 runs north-south through the city. Odessa is located 21 miles west of Midland on the north side of I-20, accessible via exits 112 through 121. U.S. 385 (Grant Ave.) bisects the city north-south, through downtown and to I-20.

Midland International Airport, located between Midland and Odessa at 9506 La Force Blvd. (www.flymaf.com; ✆ **432/560-2200**), is the primary commercial airport in the area (and the closest major airport to Big Bend National Park), served by **American, Southwest,** and **United.** Car-rental companies are on-site.

GETTING AROUND

Laid out on a fairly standard grid that parallels I-20, Midland is a relatively easy city to navigate by car. Most of the accommodations are located on the north and west sides of town. The main downtown thoroughfare is **Wall Street** (Business 20), which continues east through downtown. **Loop 250** circumnavigates the city.

Odessa's busiest street is **Grant Avenue** (U.S. 385, also known as Andrews Hwy.), which runs north-south through downtown. **42nd Street** becomes **Tex. 191** and continues east to Midland. **Loop 338** circles the city.

VISITOR INFORMATION

VisitMidland, 303 W. Wall St. (www.visitmidlandtexas.com; ✆ **800/624-6435**), has an **Information and Travel Center** at 1406 W. Interstate 20 (✆ **432/687-8285**). The **Odessa Convention & Visitors Bureau,** 700 N. Grant Ave., Ste. 200 (www.odessacvb.com; ✆ **432/333-7871**), is on the second floor of the downtown Bank of America building. Both provide maps, itineraries, and travel-planning advice.

FAST FACTS **Midland Memorial Hospital,** 2200 W. Illinois Ave. (www.midland-memorial.com; ✆ **432/221-1111**), has a 24-hour emergency room; Midland's **downtown post office** is at 100 E. Wall St. **Medical Center Hospital,** 500 W. 4th St. (www.mchodessa.com; ✆ **432/640-4000**), is Odessa's largest full-service hospital; the **main post office** is located at 200 N. Texas St.

What to See & Do

THE TOP ATTRACTIONS

Roadside kitsch alert! Don't miss two Odessa landmarks: The **world's largest jackrabbit,** 8th Street and Sam Houston Avenue; and a **70% scale replica of Stonehenge,** University of Texas of the Permian Basin campus, 4901 E. University Blvd.

Globe of the Great Southwest ★ It's not something you'd expect to see on the Texas plains—I'm sure even the Bard would be baffled by it—but here it is, a replica of William Shakespeare's old London haunt, the Globe Theatre, right down to the octagonal design and jutting stage ringed by seating. Adjacent to the 410-seat theater is a replica of the cottage belonging to Shakespeare's wife, Anne Hathaway. Both delightful structures are set on the Odessa College campus. The Elizabethan stage is home to community theater productions, musical performances, concerts and more, and the theater offers about eight plays annually with an emphasis on . . . wait, let me guess . . . Shakespeare. The theater also hosts monthly country-western shows called the "Brand New Opree."

2308 Shakespeare Rd., Odessa. ✆ **432/580-3177.** Admission $5. Tickets for performances $9–$20. Mon–Fri 10am–6pm. Tours available by appointment only.

Museum of the Southwest ★ The historic Turner Mansion (built in 1934) has been reborn as the elegant home of Midland's Museum of the Southwest, with 16,000 square feet of galleries and a collection comprising more than 40,000 works of art and archaeological artifacts. The permanent collection includes pieces by several Taos Society of Artists members and a wide range of indigenous art. The museum's attractive 5-acre campus also has a **children's museum,** with interactive art and science exhibits and a kid-size cityscape with a bank, a Victorian house, a construction site, a mini grocery, and more. In addition, the museum campus is home to a **planetarium** with state-of-the-art 3D digital capabilities and a serene **sculpture garden.** Plan to spend an hour or two here.

1705 W. Missouri Ave., Midland. www.museumsw.org. ✆ **432/683-2882.** $5 adults and teens; $3 seniors and children 3-11; free 2 and under. Tues–Sat 10am–5pm; Sun 2–5pm.

The Permian Basin Petroleum Museum ★ It makes sense that the center of the Texas petroleum industry (Midland) is home to a museum dedicated entirely to oil. Founded in 1975, the museum uses interactive exhibits and educational programs to tell the ancient story of oil and its impact on the world. Discover why there's so much oil underfoot (from a scientific perspective) with such cool exhibits as the newly restored Permian Reef diorama, showing the region as it was 250 million years ago—basically underwater. Interestingly, a small exhibit on "supplemental energies" explains alternative energy sources like solar and wind. This museum also houses a nice collection of oil paintings illustrating life in the oil fields, and car lovers will flock to the Chaparral Gallery, which houses gleaming vintage race cars from Midland's own Chaparral Cars racing team.

1500 I-20. www.petroleummuseum.org. ✆ **432/683-4403.** Admission $12 adults, $6 youths 12–17 and seniors, $5 children 6–11, free for children 5 and under. Mon–Sat 10am–5pm; Sun 2–5pm.

The Presidential Archives and Leadership Library ★ This archive and library is not dedicated just to President George H. W. Bush or his son W. (both famous former area residents), but rather to the office of the U.S. presidency itself. At home on the campus of the University of Texas of the Permian Basin, this unique museum displays portraits of every president from Washington to Trump, and the collection of memorabilia includes such items as campaign buttons, posters, and stickers as well as other artifacts and memorabilia. Originally, it was intended to be a place that paid tribute to JFK after his assassination, but the direction of the archive soon changed to honor all presidents. The 7,500-volume library on site includes rare and first-edition titles and presidential papers. Adjacent to the museum now stands the former Odessa home of Barbara, George, and George W. Bush, a two-bedroom, 800-square-foot house purchased by the Presidential Museum for about $20,000 and moved to this spot on the campus.

4919 E. University Blvd., Odessa. www.shepperdinstitute.com/presidential-archives. ✆ **432/552-2020.** Free admission. Tues–Sat 10am–5pm. Closed major holidays.

OUTDOOR ACTIVITIES

Midland has two public golf courses: the 36-hole **Hogan Park Golf Course,** 3600 N. Fairground Rd. (www.hoganparkgolf.com; ✆ **432/685-7360**), with greens fees for 18 holes of $18 to $30, and carts for $12; and the 18-hole

Nueva Vista Golf Club, 6101 W. Wadley Ave. (www.nuevavistagolf.com; ✆ **432/520-0500**) with greens fees of $28 to $32 and carts for $12 per rider. In Odessa, **Sunset Country Club,** 9301 Andrews Hwy. (✆ **432/366-1061**), is an 18-hole course open to the public year-round. Greens fees are $22 to $27, and carts are $13 per rider. There's also **Ratliff Ranch Golf Links,** 7500 N. Grandview Ave. (www.ratliffranchgolfodessa.com; ✆ **432/550-8181**), with greens fees for 18 holes of $19 to $29, and carts for $13.

SPECTATOR SPORTS

Baseball fans can get their fix in the form of the **Midland RockHounds** (www.midlandrockhounds.org; ✆ **432/520-2255**), the AA Texas League affiliate of the Oakland Athletics. The RockHounds play 70 home dates from April to August at the Citibank Ballpark, 5514 Champions Dr. Tickets cost $5 to $10. The town's **Odessa Jackalopes** (www.jackalopes.org; ✆ **432/552-7825**) play a September-to-April schedule at the Ector County Coliseum, 42nd Street and Andrews Hwy. Tickets run $8 to $23.

But it's high-school football that is the sport of choice in Midland and Odessa, which provides the backdrop to the best-selling book (and popular TV show and movie) ***Friday Night Lights,*** based on the 1988 Permian High School Panthers football team in Odessa.

Where to Stay

DoubleTree by Hilton Hotel Midland Plaza ★ This 11-story, 249-room property is a standard hotel in many ways, but the pluses include a convenient downtown location, reasonable rates, a courtyard pool, and a warm cookie at reception. The average-size rooms are comfortable, and some even have balconies. This is a full-service hotel, with a restaurant, coffee bar, rooftop bar, fitness center, and 24-hour business center.

117 W. Wall St. www.midland.hilton.com. ✆ **432/683-6131.** 249 units. $109–$229 double; $209–$350 suite. **Amenities:** 2 restaurants, 2 bars; business center; fitness center; pool; Wi-Fi (free).

MCM Grandé Hotel FunDome Odessa ★ Like its sibling MCM properties scattered throughout parts of Texas and the Southwest, including the MCM Elegantė Odessa, this MCM Grande is a lodging option that's big

Wink: Roy Orbison's Hometown

Rock-'n'-roll legend Roy Orbison was born near Wichita Falls in Vernon, but grew up in the tiny town of Wink—at age 13, he named his first band the Wink Westerners. Today, the **Roy Orbison Museum,** 205 E. Hendricks Blvd. in Wink, about 20 miles northwest of Monahans, keeps Orbison's legend alive by showcasing photos, mementos, and other relevant artifacts; you can even try on an authentic pair of his trademark sunglasses for a snapshot. Look for the numerous Orbison murals and markers all over town. The museum is open by appointment only; donations accepted (✆ **432/527-3441**).

on family fun. The hotel's "FunDome" is comprised of a large indoor/outdoor pool, miniature golf course, ping-pong tables, a playground, and fitness center and sauna. Families also like the two-room suites, with a sofabed in the living area. Guests enjoy a free hot breakfast with eggs to order at **Polly's Restaurant,** which has a Mexican lunch buffet on Tuesday and Thursday and also serves dinner nightly. Families with young children love this place, and it offers a great break from long car trips when you and the kids need to stretch your legs and relax. (***Note:*** Another nice MCM hotel, the Eleganté Hotel in Lubbock, is popular with many Texas Tech alums and parents. See p. 437.)

5200 E. University Blvd. www.mcmhotels.com. ✆ **432/368-5885.** 245 units, including 36 suites. $99–$209 double; $279–$449 suite. Rates include hot breakfast and complimentary happy-hour drinks. **Amenities:** Restaurant, bar; business center; children's playground; fitness center; indoor/outdoor pool; Wi-Fi (free).

Where to Eat

For a quick bite in the area, head to **Manuel's Crispy Tacos,** 1404 E. 2nd St., Odessa (✆ **432/333-2751**), a fun family joint known for its namesake dish. Main courses are $5 to $16. In Midland, our Mexican go-to is **Gerardo's Casita,** 2407 N. Big Spring St. (www.gerardoscasita.net; ✆ **432/570-8012**), serving tacos, enchiladas, *chiles rellenos,* steaks, and margaritas since 1977. Also recommended is the **Bar,** 606 W. Missouri Ave., Midland (www.thebarmidland.com; ✆ **432/685-1757**), a taxidermy- and petroliana-laden establishment with burgers and pub fare and a wall lined with beer cans.

Wall Street Bar & Grill ★ NEW AMERICAN It's not quite as fancy as it sounds, and is certainly not filled with pinstriped NY stockbrokers. The menu is more down-home chicken-fried steak than lobster Newburgh. Still, for more than 30 years it has offered "casual fine dining" to Midland's business community and enjoyed a strong following from loyal locals. The 1910 building was originally a saddle shop, and the original pressed-tin ceiling gives the dining room a vintage glow. A long mahogany bar and back bar received a commendation from the Texas Historical Foundation for its restoration. The menu may be casual, but that doesn't mean it's not fresh and contemporary. Look for creative dishes like seafood *rellenos* with chipotle-tomatillo sauce, pecan-crusted trout, and charbroiled pork chops, not to mention superb hand-cut steaks. The crawfish étouffée, rich and thick, gives a nod to Texas's Louisiana neighbors. The restaurant has a good wine selection and, yes, white tablecloths, so Wall Street types will feel welcome, too. Many folks come for the nice Sunday brunch.

115 E. Wall St., Midland. ✆ **432/684-8686.** Main courses $9–$25. Mon–Fri 11am–2:30pm; Mon–Sat 5:30–10pm; Sun brunch 10:30am–2:30pm; Sun 5:30–9pm.

A Side Trip to San Angelo

First known as "the town over the river" from Fort Concho, San Angelo stands 111 miles southeast of Midland and 64 miles north of Sonora. This was a rollicking, gunslinging Wild West outpost during the late 1860s and 1870s. In

Paint Rock Pictographs ★

Called a "museum, library, and art gallery" of ancient American Indians, Paint Rock is home to an estimated 1,500 Native American pictographs—primitive paintings on rock—spread out over a half-mile on a 70-foot-high limestone cliff, about 200 yards north of the Concho River. The site is 2 miles northwest of the city of Paint Rock in Concho County and 40 miles southeast of San Angelo along Highway 83, 16 miles south of Ballinger. The pictographs stand on private land owned by Fred and Kay Campbell, two active, enthusiastic 90-year-olds (born a month apart in 1927), whose family has owned the land since the 1870s and who say it is their honor to "share it with the world." On the winter solstice, rays of light reflect off an ornate, otherwise invisible painting known as "Sun Dagger," a picture of a sun on the back of a turtle. Call the Campbells for details on guided tours (appointment only; $6 adults, $3 children—with a minimum charge of $15; ✆ **325/732-4376**).

those early days, soldiers from Texas forts and cowhands would cross the Concho River to get to the town's brothels, casinos, and saloons.

Today San Angelo is a city of about 100,000 residents, but its rowdy past can be revisited in the form of historic **Concho Avenue,** now lined with boutiques and jewelers instead of casinos and bordellos, and old **Fort Concho,** a National Historic Landmark. The city is also one of the few oases of West Texas, with the Concho snaking through town along an attractive River Walk, with a 4-mile walking/jogging trail, bountiful outdoor gardens and water displays, a great playground, a skate park, and a 9-hole golf course (✆ **325/657-4485**). Stroll the River Walk to the **San Angelo Museum of Fine Arts** (www.samfa.org; ✆ **325/653-3333**), historic Concho Avenue, and Fort Concho.

While in town, stop at **Paint Brush Alley,** between Concho Street and Twohig Avenue downtown, an imaginative reinvention of an alley as a drive-through gallery of murals by different artists. Also of note is **Miss Hattie's Bordello Museum,** 18 E. Concho Ave. (www.misshatties.com), a restored brothel offering tours Friday and Saturday every hour from 1 to 4pm and Tuesday through Thursday at 2 and 4pm; admission is $6 per person. Also make time to stop and see the **Fort Concho National Historic Landmark** (www.fortconcho.com; ✆ **325/481-2646**), 630 S. Oakes St., one of the jewels of the old Texas forts, with 17 original buildings and six rebuilt structures.

The Caverns of Sonora ★

Hidden in the middle of nowhere, some 75 miles from San Angelo, are the delightful **Caverns of Sonora** (www.cavernsofsonora.com; ✆ **325/387-3105**). Designated a Registered Natural Landmark by the National Park Service in 1966, these magnificent caves are privately owned and can be explored only on guided tours. You'll see glistening draperies, miles of puffy popcorn, millions of helictites and soda straws, and reflecting pools, plus all the usual stalagmites and stalactites in a wildly fascinating collage of formations. The tour is 2 miles long and takes about 2 hours; admission is $20 adults, $16 children 4 to 11, and free for kids 3 and under.

The caverns are open daily from 8am to 6pm March through Labor Day, and from 9am to 5pm the rest of the year (closed Christmas). From San Angelo, go south on U.S. 277 for 66 miles to the small town of Sonora, then 7 miles west on I-10 to exit 392, then follow signs south to the caverns. Campsites in an attractive, tree-shaded **campground** are available at the caverns. Other than that, the nearest lodging, dining, and other services are in Sonora. For information, contact the **Sonora Chamber of Commerce,** 205 U.S. 277 (www.sonoratx-chamber.com; ✆ **325/387-2880**).

DEL RIO & AMISTAD NATIONAL RECREATION AREA ★

156 miles S of San Angelo; 154 miles W of San Antonio; 268 miles NW of Corpus Christi; 392 miles SW of Dallas

This pleasant little city of about 35,000 people is one of the nicest little border towns you'll find in Texas. (It's one of the places mentioned in the song "You Ask Me What I Like About Texas" by Gary P. Nunn.) Situated along the U.S.-Mexico border across the Rio Grande from Ciudad Acuña, Del Rio is a great base for watersports enthusiasts visiting Amistad National Recreation Area. In a delightful little historic museum in the community of Langtry, 50 miles west of Del Rio, you can learn about Judge Roy Bean, one of the most colorful judges in the history of the American West and famously known as "the Law West of the Pecos." For more about Roy Bean and the museum, see "The Legend of Judge Roy Bean" box, p. 384.

Spanish missionaries originally called Del Rio "San Felipe del Rio" and unsuccessfully tried to start a mission there in 1635, but were thwarted by attacks from American Indians. The name survived, however, and was in use in the mid-1800s when a farming community grew up around the reliable water source of the San Felipe Springs. The springs were also a watering stop for the short-lived U.S. Army Camel Corps, for which camels imported from North Africa were used on the Western frontier as a substitute for horses. The name of the community was shortened to Del Rio in 1883.

In the late 1960s, a dam was built on the Rio Grande near Del Rio, creating a 67,000-acre lake that provides flood protection and irrigation water. It's also a huge water playground in what is generally an arid, rocky land of cactus and sagebrush.

Essentials

GETTING THERE

Del Rio is located at the junction of U.S. 90 and 277/377, along the U.S.-Mexico border. The **Amtrak** station is at 100 N. Main St. (www.amtrak.com; ✆ **800/872-2745**), along the Sunset Limited route. **Del Rio International Airport,** 1104 W. 10th St. (www.cityofdelrio.com/412/International-Airport; ✆ **830/774-8610**) is served by private planes only.

XERF: LEGENDARY border BLASTER

Groundbreaking disc jockey Wolfman Jack got his start in 1963 at Radio XERF, an AM radio station with a famed "border blaster" signal: a superpowerful 500,000 watts emanating from Ciudad Acuña, the Mexican border town just across the International bridge from Del Rio. At the time, that wattage made XERF the most powerful radio station in the world, and some U.S. artists would actually travel there to ensure that their music was played as far and wide as possible—James Brown even climbed XERF's legendary tower. It was at XERF that Wolfman offered mainstream America its first taste of black music: A B. B. King record was his first spin. Earlier, Radio XERF had been a country-music stalwart, showcasing the legendary Carter family (of June Carter Cash fame) from 1936 to 1939. The Carters became known as country music's "First Family" in the process and always opened their radio show with the hillbilly country classic, "Keep on the Sunny Side." Announcer Paul Kallinger came to XERF in 1948, and during the 1950s and 1960s, Billboard Magazine rated him one of country's top five disk jockeys for 8 consecutive years. He played country music and hosted celebrities like Eddie Arnold, Johnny Cash, Tex Ritter, and Ernest Tubb—but refused to play the music of Elvis Presley.

VISITOR INFORMATION

The **Del Rio Chamber of Commerce,** 1915 Veterans Blvd. (www.drchamber.com; ✆ **830/775-3551**), operates a visitor center with maps, self-guided walking-tour brochures, and travel advice. In Ciudad Acuña, the office of the Conventions & Visitors Bureau of Cd. Acuña, **OCV Acuña** (www.ocvacuna.com; ✆ **877/717-9966**), may be your best source for tourism information and advice, though the office is run by volunteers who may or may not be on hand to answer the phone when you call.

FAST FACTS **Val Verde Regional Medical Center,** 801 N. Bedell Ave. (www.vvrmc.org; ✆ **830/775-8566**), has a 24-hour emergency room. The **post office,** 2001 N. Bedell Ave., is open Monday through Friday from 8:30am to 4:30pm, Saturday from 10am to noon.

THE TOP ATTRACTIONS

In addition to the attractions discussed below, Del Rio has some handsome **historic buildings.** A free brochure, which describes and locates some three dozen buildings constructed between 1869 and 1929, is available at the chamber of commerce's visitor center (see "Visitor Information," above). At **San Felipe Springs,** enjoy a nice walk along crystal-clear water; the best access point is at the **Creekwalk** at Moore Park, Calderon Boulevard and De La Rosa Street, where you'll find a spring-fed swimming pool and a small amphitheater.

Many visitors to Del Rio take an excursion across the border to **Ciudad Acuña,** a small Mexican city with a main street lined with shops selling a variety of leather goods, pottery, woven items, jewelry, and other products, plus a number of good restaurants. As with most border towns, American currency is welcome at practically all businesses in Ciudad Acuña. Driving isn't a problem, but walking is a bit of a struggle, especially on hot days. Use care

THE legend OF JUDGE ROY BEAN

Judge Roy Bean, the self-styled "Law West of the Pecos," was a true Wild West character, and definitely the stuff of which legends are made. Born Phantly Roy Bean in Kentucky, probably around 1825, as a teenager he followed his two older brothers west, to California and then New Mexico. Although his brothers were mostly successful and respectable, Roy always seemed to be in trouble, usually related to gambling and gun running, and occasionally he would leave town just a few steps ahead of the hangman.

During the Civil War, Bean reportedly smuggled supplies from Mexico to Confederate troops in Texas. After the war, he ended up in San Antonio, where he cemented his already dubious reputation. There he married and had four children before leaving the family about 16 years later (he would eventually send for them to join him later in life), when he followed a rail-construction crew west to Vinegarroon. It's believed Bean then opened a saloon in a tent, before somehow getting appointed as the local justice of the peace in 1882.

A year later, Bean moved north to a small settlement along the railroad tracks that came to be called Langtry. Bean claimed he had named the town after the beautiful English actress of the day, Lillie Langtry, with whom he was quite infatuated, although according to local historians the town likely garnered its name earlier from a railroad engineer. Bean wrote to Miss Langtry several times, asking her to visit the town "named in her honor."

Bean was elected and reelected Langtry's justice of the peace on and off for about 20 years—legend has it that he was briefly thrown out of office when it became evident that he had received more votes than there were eligible voters (though local historians at the Judge Roy Bean Visitor Center claim there is no proof that this actually happened). Bean's Langtry courtroom, which he called the "Jersey Lillie" after Miss Langtry, was also

when crossing into any Texas border towns at night; it is often best to make your visit to Ciudad Acuña during morning hours, too, as most local shops will close after lunch for an hour or more for *siesta* time (a traditional rest after a midday meal). ***Note:*** Be sure to carry your passport if you cross the border. Passports are required for reentry into the U.S.; a driver's license or birth certificate is not sufficient.

Val Verde Winery ★ The oldest continuously running bonded winery in Texas was established in 1883 by Italian immigrant Frank Qualia, who discovered Lenoir grapes thriving in the Texas soil. Today the winery is owned and run by Thomas Qualia, the founder's grandson. The winery produces from eight to ten varieties of wine (from grapes from adjacent vineyards and other Texas vineyards), and is known for its award-winning Don Luis Tawny Port, aged for 5 years in French oak. It also makes Viognier, rosé, Tempranillo, and Sangiovese wines. Complimentary guided tours are available, and you can also stay and enjoy a wine tasting ($5–$10). Wines are available by the bottle (typically $10–$40). The winery also now makes and sells its own bottled olive oil, from Arbequina olive trees planted here in 2007 and 2008.

100 Qualia Dr. (near intersection with Hudson St.). www.valverdewinery.com. ✆ **830/775-9714.** Free admission. Tastings and tours Tues–Sat 11am–6pm and Sun 1–5pm.

his saloon and home, and he often chose his juries from the saloon's customers.

Numerous stories about Bean's sometimes bizarre rulings have been told, and it's often difficult to tell fact from fiction. When a railroad worker was charged with killing a Chinese laborer, Bean said that although it was against the law to kill your fellow man, he could find no law against killing a "heathen Chinaman," so the case was dismissed. (The killer was, however, required to pay for the funeral.) Another generally accepted story is the case of a dead man found to have a gun and gold coins worth about $40 in his pockets. Bean promptly fined the corpse $40 for carrying a concealed weapon. But perhaps his greatest notoriety came from staging a heavyweight championship fight in 1896. At the time, prizefighting was illegal in Texas as well as in Mexico, so Bean staged the fight on a sandbar in the Rio Grande, a no-man's land between the two. He made a tidy profit at his saloon selling drinks to the spectators.

Bean's reputation as a "hanging judge" is also in question: Although he sentenced people to hang, none of the sentences were ever carried out. Bean died in his saloon on March 16, 1903, after a binge of heavy drinking in Del Rio. Alas, only a few months later his Jersey Lillie, Lillie Langtry, finally arrived in Langtry, spending 30 minutes there during a train stopover on her way to a performance in the region.

To learn more about Bean, drive out to Langtry (60 miles west of Del Rio via U.S. 90) to Bean's restored saloon at the **Judge Roy Bean Visitor Center** (✆ **432/291-3340**), where dioramas and displays in this official state visitor center tell the story of Bean's life. The visitor center and saloon are open daily from 8am to 6pm, and admission is free. *The Life and Times of Judge Roy Bean,* the entertaining 1972 Paul Newman movie based loosely on Bean's life, only built on the judge's legend.

Whitehead Memorial Museum ★★ This little pioneer village in the center of town is a living-history museum that tells the tale of Del Rio and the pioneering life. The museum began with the restoration of the Perry Store, an 1871 mercantile building, and grew to some 21 more structures and exhibits, including a 1925 log cabin, a 1945 caboose, a 1919 American LaFrance fire engine, and the 112-year-old office of Dr. Simon Rodriguez, the community's first Hispanic physician, who is credited with delivering more than 3,000 babies in the area. A re-creation of Judge Roy Bean's saloon brings the legend to life, but perhaps more importantly, both Judge Bean and his son, Sam, are buried here on the property. The star of the museum, however, is the fantastic Cadena Nativity—a 32×20-foot folk-art nativity scene with thousands of figurines of people, animals, miniature buildings, trees, and bushes.

1308 S. Main St. www.whiteheadmuseum.org. ✆ **830/774-7568.** Admission $5 adults, $4 seniors, $3 youths 13–18, $2 children 6–12, free for children 5 and under. Tues–Sat 10am–6pm; Sun 1–5pm. Closed major holidays.

Where to Stay & Eat in Del Rio

Veterans Boulevard, the main drag through town (U.S. 90/277/377), is lined with chain motels. Choices here include **Best Western Inn of Del Rio,** 810

Veterans Blvd. (© **830/775-7511**), with rates of $69 to $79 double; **Hampton Inn,** 2219 N. Bedell Ave. (© **830/775-9700**), with rates of $129 to $144 double; and **Ramada Inn,** 2101 Veterans Blvd. (© **800/272-6232** or 830/775-1511), with rates in the range of $89 to $119 double.

As with lodging, you'll find scads of fast-food chains located along Del Rio's Veterans Boulevard. You'll be better served (in more ways than one) by seeking out one of Del Rio's locally owned restaurants, such as **La Hacienda,** 330 Pecan St. in Pecan Street Station (© **830/774-7094**); **Chinto's Super Taco,** 400 E. 6th St. (© **830/774-1592**); and **Manuel's Steakhouse,** 1312 Veterans Blvd. (www.manuelssteakhouse.com; © **830/488-6044**).

If you want to get a true (and inexpensive) taste of the region, head south to Ciudad Acuña. My picks: **Manuel's,** Morelos #130 (www.manuels-restaurant.com; © **011-52/87-72-59-15**), an upscale Mexican restaurant with good steaks and *chiles rellenos*; **Hosteria de Santa Martha,** Lerdo de Tejada #200 (© **011-52/87-72-38-00**), featuring traditional *burria* (spicy meat stew), paella, and *cuitlacoche* (corn truffles) dishes; and the local favorite, **Tacos Grill,** Guerrero #1490 S. (www.lostacosgrill.com; © **011-52/87-72-40-41**).

A location in the movie *Desperado,* the legendary watering hole/wine bar the **Corona Club,** 2 blocks south of the downtown crossing bridge at Hidalgo #200 (© **011-52/87-72-51-08**), is a classic border dive opening into a pleasant courtyard.

Amistad National Recreation Area ★

This international reservoir is a beautiful spot for boating, fishing, waterskiing, scuba diving, and swimming. Created by the United States and Mexico with the construction of a 6-mile-long dam across the Rio Grande at the international border, Amistad Reservoir provides electricity generation, water storage, flood control, and—most important to anglers and watersports enthusiasts—a 67,000-acre lake and a U.S. National Recreation Area.

The water here is a beautiful blue, thanks to the lake bed's limestone character and lack of loose soil. The lake is actually at the confluence of three rivers, and runs 74 miles up the Rio Grande, 24 miles up the Devils River, and 14 miles up the Pecos River. The shoreline measures 890 miles: 540 miles in Texas and the rest in Mexico.

Byron Velvick's **Amistad Lake Resort** (formerly Amistad Lodge), 11207 U.S. Hwy 90W (www.amistadlakeresort.com; © **800/775-8591**), has 40 rooms (some with lake views), a swimming pool, and 24-hour security near prime fishing waters on Lake Amistad.

The recreation area has five **campgrounds,** with a total of about 60 primitive sites. Campgrounds are generally open, with brush and some low trees but little shade, and have vault toilets, covered picnic tables, and grills. **Governors Landing Campground,** with 15 sites overlooking the lake, is the only campground with potable drinking water (water is available along the Diablo East entrance road, where there is also an RV dump station). **San Pedro Campground** has 35 sites, and **Spur 406, 277 North,** and **Rough Canyon** campgrounds have 6, 17, and 4 sites, respectively. Camping is first come, first served, and is limited to 14 consecutive days, or 60 nights in a 12-month period. **Backcountry camping** from boats is permitted along the lakeshore, except at marinas and other developed areas. Camping costs $4 to $8 per night.

Admission to the park, which is open 24 hours, is free. Ten miles west of Del Rio off U.S. 90, the **Amistad National Recreation Area visitor center** (www.nps.gov/amis; ✆ **830/775-7491**) has maps and a bookstore. It's open daily 8am to 5pm, except Thanksgiving, Christmas, and New Year's Day.

Pets are permitted, but must be leashed at all times. Rangers warn that limestone, which is abundant along the shore, can cut the pads of dogs' feet, and add that pet owners need to provide flea, tick, and mosquito protection.

Here are some of the myriad lakeside activities:

BOATING A dozen or so boat ramps are spread throughout the recreation area, with three developed boat-launching areas. **Diablo East** is 10 miles northwest of Del Rio via U.S. 90; **Rough Canyon** is 23 miles north of Del Rio via U.S. 90 and U.S. 277/377; and **Pecos** is 44 miles northwest of Del Rio via U.S. 90. Boat and slip rentals and sales of supplies are available at Diablo East and Rough Canyon. Motorized-boat use passes cost $4 per day, $10 for a 3-day pass, or $40 per year.

FISHING Forty-pound catfish have been pulled from the lake, as have record striped bass. Among other species caught are largemouth bass, yellowbelly and bluegill sunfish, white and black crappie, and alligator gar. Fishing is permitted from boats and from shore anywhere except in marinas, at boat ramps, and at designated swimming beaches. There are also fishing docks and fish-cleaning stations at several locations. A Texas fishing license (available at convenience stores and most shops along U.S. 90) is required on the U.S. side of the border. A list of licensed fishing guides is available at the headquarters.

PICTOGRAPHS American Indian peoples are believed to have come to this area about 12,000 years ago; however, it was not until about 4,000 years ago that creation of the spectacular rock art began, and it's visible today in several areas in and near the recreation area. These pictographs—designs painted on rocks using colors created from ground iron ore and other minerals mixed with animal fat—are difficult to get to, but well worth the effort.

One of the best rock art sites is **Panther Cave,** at the confluence of the Rio Grande and Seminole Canyon, which is usually accessible by boat and a steep climb up stairs. It has numerous figures that resemble humans or animals, including what looks like a 9-foot panther. Another good site, accessible by boat at average lake levels and by a strenuous hike through tall brush at low-water levels, is **Parida Cave,** located on the Rio Grande. See also the section on "Seminole Canyon State Park & Historic Site," below.

RANGER PROGRAMS Rangers present a variety of programs, including evening programs at the amphitheater at the visitor center. Kiosks with displays on natural history, recreation, and water safety are scattered throughout the recreation area.

SWIMMING **Governors Island** has a swimming area (no lifeguards), and swimming is permitted in most undeveloped areas. Water temperatures range from a chilly 54°F (12°C) in winter to a pleasant 86°F (30°C) in summer. Waterskiing is permitted in open water (away from mooring areas, channels, and swimming beaches) during daylight hours only.

WILDLIFE-WATCHING Among the wildlife you're likely to see are white-tailed deer, javelinas (also called collared peccaries), black-tailed jack rabbits, rock squirrels, and nine-banded armadillos. Birds to watch for include white-winged doves, sandpipers, great blue herons, great egrets, American coots, killdeer, roadrunners, black vultures, ravens, and an occasional bald or golden eagle. A particularly good spot to bird-watch is the San Pedro Campground, which also has lots of butterflies. Rangers lead morning **birding walks** every other Saturday; the group meets at the park visitor center at 8am.

Note: While Amistad has been free of much of the violence that has wracked much of the U.S.-Mexico border and Falcon Lake (near Laredo) in recent years, always pay attention to your surroundings while boating or fishing and be sure to check Texas/Mexico travel advisories.

SEMINOLE CANYON STATE PARK & HISTORIC SITE

Adjacent to Amistad National Recreation Area, about 45 miles northwest of Del Rio via U.S. 90, **Seminole Canyon State Park** (www.tpwd.texas.gov; ✆ **432/292-4464**) provides opportunities for guided hikes to see what many consider to be the best pictographs in North America, possibly 4,000 years old. In addition, Seminole Canyon offers a short nature trail, camping, hiking through a rugged limestone terrain, wildlife viewing and bird-watching, and a museum.

Although it is believed that human beings lived in this area at the end of the last ice age, some 12,000 years ago, they left few signs of their presence. Then, about 7,000 years ago, other civilizations arrived, and within 3,000 years, they began to paint designs on sheltered rock walls. State park rangers lead hiking tours to several of the rock-art sites.

The **Fate Bell Cave Shelter Tour** at Seminole Canyon, in Comstock, Texas, is offered Wednesday through Sunday from 10 to 11:30am year-round and also from 3 to 4:30pm from September through May. (*Note:* Tours may

Scenic View of the Mouth of the Pecos

On the east rim of the 300-foot cliffs above the Pecos River, there is an overlook before the U.S. 90 bridge over the Pecos that is one of the region's best photo opportunities. Heading west on the highway from Del Rio, take the left immediately before the bridge for the most scenic views of the vast surrounding badlands and the untamed Pecos snaking into the Rio Grande below.

be cancelled during hot weather or when it is raining.) The cost is $5 per person for age 13 and over, and reservations are not required. Meet at the Headquarters Building to purchase tickets. This is a moderately rated 2-mile round-trip hike that leads into Seminole Canyon to a huge rock shelter where participants will see hundreds of pictographs.

The 1.75-mile round-trip **Upper Canyon Tour,** which costs $12 per person and takes 2 hours, leads to a normally closed area of the park in the upper section of the canyon to see pictographs and some railroad sites from 1882; and the 8-mile round-trip **Presa Canyon Tour,** which costs $25 per person, is an all-day hike into the lower canyon to see rock-art sites that are normally off limits to the public. The **Rock Art Foundation** (www.rockart.org) takes visitors on a 90-minute tour to the White Shaman site's hallucinogenic pictographs for $10, as well as other tours. They no longer have a phone, but the website has all the information you'll need, including a contact e-mail.

The park has a 6-mile round-trip **hiking/biking trail** along the top of the canyon that leads to a bluff from which you can see **Panther Cave** and its namesake painted panther, across Amistad Reservoir (see the section on "Amistad National Recreation Area," above). Bring your binoculars for great views. The trail has little elevation change, but is rocky with little shade. No one is allowed to go down into the canyon except on guided tours.

The **Windmill Nature Trail,** just behind the visitor center/museum, is an easy .7-mile loop, but it's not shaded, so hiking can be hot going. It meanders through a harsh environment of ocotillo, cacti, yucca, juniper, Texas mountain laurel, and other desert plants on the way to its namesake windmill—actually the remains of two windmills, one from the 1890s and one from the 1920s.

The species of birds and animals to watch for in the park are much the same as at the adjacent Amistad National Recreation Area, and include birds such as great blue herons, black and turkey vultures, scaled quail, killdeer, white-winged and mourning doves, greater roadrunners, and northern mockingbirds. Also watch for great-tailed grackles, northern cardinals, pyrrhuloxia, ash-throated flycatchers, ladder-backed woodpeckers, and black-chinned hummingbirds. Mammals here include desert cottontails, black-tailed jack rabbits, coyotes, raccoons, white-tailed deer, striped skunks, and javelinas.

The small **campground,** with 23 campsites with water and 30-amp electricity, 8 basic campsites with water nearby, and 8 drive-up primitive campsites, rests on an open knoll covered with mesquite, creosote bush, yucca, cacti, and other desert plants. There are hot showers and a dump station. Sites with water nearby only cost $14 per night, and those with water and electricity cost $20 per night, while primitive drive-up campsites cost $8 per night.

The park is open 24 hours a day year-round, except for 1 week in November and 1 week in December when it is open only for properly licensed hunters. The visitor center, with its excellent museum containing exhibits on the area's ancient inhabitants as well as its more recent history, is open daily from 8am to 4:45pm. Admission to the park is $3 adults, free for children 12 and under.

11

BIG BEND & GUADALUPE MOUNTAINS NATIONAL PARKS

Outdoor enthusiasts will love this part of Texas. Here, in Big Bend and Guadalupe Mountains national parks, you'll find Texas's most spectacular mountain scenery, as well as absolutely wonderful opportunities for hiking and other outdoor recreation. These parks have an abundance of wildlife and both prehistoric and historic sites. Big Bend National Park is bounded by the Rio Grande, as it defines the U.S.-Mexico border, while Guadalupe Mountains National Park boasts the highest peak in Texas and a canyon with perhaps the prettiest scenery in the state, especially in the fall.

In addition to these two national parks in Texas, a third, **Carlsbad Caverns National Park,** is just over the state line in New Mexico. This easy side trip from Guadalupe Mountains National Park will lead you to some of the world's most beautiful cave formations, and, if you're so inclined, the thrill of a true caving experience, as you crawl belly to rock through dark, narrow underground passages. There are also some pretty sweet places to stay in this part of the state, like the Gage Hotel in Marathon, where you can sit by a campfire after a fabulous dinner and see "miles and miles of Texas, and all the stars up in the sky," as an old cowboy song goes.

BIG BEND NATIONAL PARK ★★

Vast and wild, Big Bend National Park is a land of extremes—and a few contradictions. Its rugged terrain harbors thousands of species of plants and animals—some seen practically nowhere else on earth. A visit here can include a hike into the sunbaked desert, a

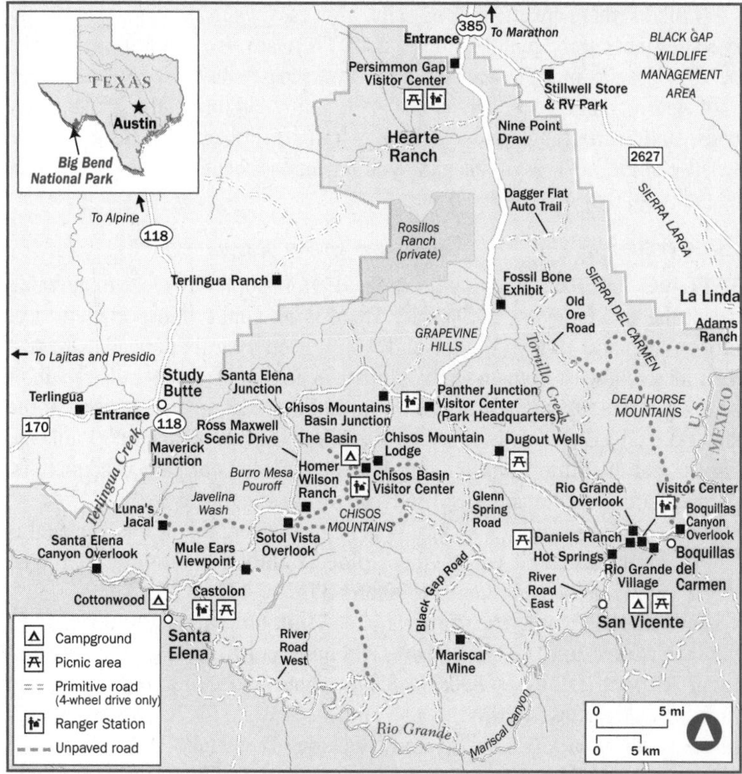

float down a majestic river through the canyons, or a trek among high mountains where bears and mountain lions rule.

Millions of years ago, this area was covered ay an inland sea. As it dried up, sediments of sand and mud turned to rock; mountains were created and volcanoes split the earth. The resultant canyons and rock formations that we marvel at today—colored in red, orange, yellow, and brown hues—make for one of the most spectacular landscapes in the Southwest. This is not a fantasyland of delicate hoodoos, like Bryce Canyon National Park in Utah, but a powerful and dominating terrain. Although the greatest natural sculptures lie in the park's three major river canyons—the Santa Elena, Mariscal, and Boquillas—throughout Big Bend you'll find spectacular examples of what nature can do with rock.

Visitors to Big Bend National Park will also discover a rugged wilderness, populated by myriad desert and mountain plants and animals. Box turtles, black-tailed jack rabbits, piglike javelinas, black bears, and mountain lions are all known to roam here. The park is a birder's paradise, frequented by more bird species than any other national park. It's also a wonderful spot to see wildflowers and delightfully colorful cactus blooms.

For hikers, there are all kinds of trails, from easy walks to rugged backcountry routes that barely qualify as trails at all. There are also opportunities to ride the Rio Grande in rafts, canoes, and kayaks past canyons carved through 1,500 feet of solid rock. Drivers of 4×4s enjoy exploring the backcountry roads, and petroglyphs and old mining ruins bring out the history buffs. Because of the vastness of this park, you'll need to schedule at least 2 full days here, though 3 or 4 would be better.

Essentials

GETTING THERE Big Bend National Park is not really close to anything except the Rio Grande and Mexico. There is no public transportation to or through the park, so to get to the park you'll need a car. Park headquarters is 108 miles southeast of the town of Alpine via Tex. 118, and 69 miles south of the town of Marathon via U.S. 385. From El Paso, 328 miles northwest of the park, take I-10 E. 121 miles to exit 140, follow U.S. 90 southeast 99 miles to Alpine, and then turn south on Tex. 118 for 108 miles to park headquarters. No rideshare app companies currently serve cities in this area.

The closest train and bus service is in Alpine, where the nearest hospital is located. For information, contact the **Alpine Chamber of Commerce,** 106 N. 3rd St. (www.alpinetexas.com; ✆ **800/561-3712** or 432/837-2326).

The nearest commercial airports are **Midland International (MAF)** (www.flymaf.com; ✆ **432/560-2200**), 235 miles north, and **Del Rio International Airport (DRT)** (✆ **830/774-8558**), about 250 miles southeast. From Midland-Odessa, take I-20 W. about 50 miles to exit 80 for Tex. 18, which you follow south about 50 miles to Fort Stockton. There take U.S. 385 S. 125 miles through Marathon to park headquarters. From Del Rio, you take U.S. 90 W. 175 miles to Marathon, and U.S. 385 S. 70 miles to park headquarters.

VISITOR INFORMATION For advance information, go to www.nps.gov/bibe or contact the **Superintendent,** P.O. Box 129, Big Bend National Park, TX 79834 (✆ **432/477-2251;** or 477-1183 weather hotline).

Books, maps, and videos are available from the **Big Bend Natural History Association** (www.bigbendbookstore.org; ✆ **432/477-2236**). The free park newspaper, *The Big Bend Paisano,* published seasonally by the National Park Service, is a great source of current information on special programs, suggested hikes, kids' activities, and local facilities.

The park has five visitor centers: **Panther Junction Visitor Center** (open daily year-round 9am–5pm; reduced hours on Christmas Day) is centrally located at park headquarters; **Persimmon Gap Visitor Center** (open daily Nov–Apr 9:30am–4pm; closed for lunch), at the North Entrance to the park on U.S. 385; **Rio Grande Village Visitor Center** (open daily Nov–Apr 8:30am–4pm; closed for lunch), on the river in the eastern part of the park; **Castolon** (open daily Nov–Apr 10am–4:30pm; closed for lunch), near the river in the southwestern end of the park; and **Chisos Basin Visitor Center** (open daily year-round 8:30am–4:30pm; closed for lunch; reduced hours on Christmas Day), in the Chisos Mountains in the middle of the park, at 5,401 feet in elevation. All visitor centers provide information, backcountry permits, books and maps and have exhibits; Chisos Basin has an impressive display on mountain lions Castolon has informative exhibits on the park's cultural history. Bulletin boards with schedules of ranger programs, notices of animal sightings, and other information are located at each of the visitor centers.

FEES, REGULATIONS & PERMITS Entry into the park for up to a week costs $25 for one private, noncommercial vehicle (15 passengers or fewer), and $12 per person on foot or bicycle for up to 7 days. Entry for one motorcycle is $20 for up to 7 days. The National Park Service operates three developed, front-country campgrounds: **Rio Grande Village Campground, Chisos Basin Campground,** and **Cottonwood Campground.** The cost is $14 per night per site ($7 per night with applicable pass). Limited campsites at Rio Grande Village and Chisos Basin campgrounds are reservable November 15 to April 15 (Nov 15–May 31 at Chisos Basin). Reservations may be made at www.recreation.gov or by calling ✆ **877-444-6777.** (Big Bend National Park cannot make reservations.) Backcountry campsites require a $12 backcountry use permit ($6 with applicable pass), which must be acquired in person at one of the park's visitor centers during normal business hours. Permits are also required for all river-float trips (see "Camping" and "River Running," later in this chapter).

Wood or ground fires are prohibited in the park, and caution is advised when using campstoves, charcoal grills, and cigarettes. Smoking is prohibited on all trails in the Chisos Basin. Check at the visitor centers for current drought conditions and any restrictions that may be in effect when you visit. Horses are not permitted on any paved roads in the park.

WHEN TO GO Weather here is generally mild to hot, although because of the vast range of elevations—from about 1,800 feet at the eastern end of Boquillas Canyon to 7,825 feet on Emory Peak in the Chisos Mountains—conditions can vary greatly throughout the park at any given time. Essentially, the higher you go, the cooler and wetter you can expect it to be, although no section of the park gets a lot of precipitation.

Summers are hot, often well over 100°F (38°C) in the desert in May and June, and afternoon thunderstorms are common July through September. Winters are usually mild, although temperatures occasionally drop below freezing, and light snow is possible, especially in the Chisos Mountains. Fall and spring are usually warm and pleasant.

Average annual visitation is just over 300,000. Although the park is relatively uncrowded much of the year, there are several periods when lodgings and campgrounds are full: college spring break (usually the second and third week in March), Easter weekend, Thanksgiving weekend, and the week between Christmas and New Year's Day. Park visitation is generally highest in March and April, and lowest in August and September.

Although the park's visitor centers, campgrounds, and other developed facilities may be taxed during the busy season, visitors can still be practically alone simply by seeking out less-used hiking trails. Those seeking solitude should discuss their hiking skills and expectations with rangers, who can offer suggestions on the best areas to escape the crowds.

SAFETY Watch for wild animals along the roads, especially at night, when they may be blinded by your vehicle's headlights and stunned into standing still in the middle of the road. Feeding wildlife is strictly prohibited—not only to minimize the risk of injuries to park visitors, but also because it's ultimately bad for the animals.

The **Basin Road Scenic Drive** into the Chisos Mountains has sharp curves and steep grades and is not recommended for trailers longer than 20 feet or motor homes longer than 24 feet. The **Ross Maxwell Scenic Drive** to Castolon is fine for most RVs and trailers but might present a problem for those with insufficient power to handle the steep grade. These roads require extra caution by all users—drivers of motor vehicles, pedestrians, and bicyclists alike.

Desert heat can be dangerous. Hikers should carry at least 1 gallon of water per person per day; wear a hat, long pants, and long sleeves; and use a good sunscreen. Don't depend on springs as water sources, and avoid hiking in the middle of the day in summer. Early mornings and evenings are best. Talk to rangers about your plans before heading out; they can help you plan a hike in accordance with your ability and time frame. They can also advise you on expected weather conditions—sudden summer thunderstorms are common and can cause flash flooding in usually dry washes and canyons.

Swimming is not recommended in the Rio Grande, even though it may look tantalizingly inviting on a hot summer day. Waste materials and waterborne microorganisms have been found in the river and can cause serious illness. Also, strong undercurrents, deep holes, and sharp rocks in shallow water are common.

RANGER PROGRAMS & SPECIAL EVENTS Park ranger naturalists offer a variety of programs year-round. Enjoy guided walks and talks by day and special evening programs as well at the 5,400-foot **Chisos Basin amphitheater** year-round. From November to April, evening programs are held regularly in the amphitheater at **Rio Grande Village** and occasionally at Cottonwood Campground. Subjects include the park's geology, plants, animals, and human history. The ranger-led **nature walks ★★** are especially good, and rangers occasionally lead driving tours. Workshops are also planned, on subjects such as adobe construction or photography. Look for weekly schedules on the bulletin boards scattered about the park. **Personal ranger-guided tours** are also available for $40 an hour with a 4-hour minimum. Call ✆ **432/477-1108** for reservations or to check on availability.

The park has a **Junior Ranger Program** for children of all ages. Kids learn about the park through a range of activities and earn certificates, badges, and patches. Pick up Junior Ranger activity books ($2) at any visitor center.

What to See & Do

EXPLORING THE HIGHLIGHTS BY CAR

The park has several paved roads. In addition, several unimproved roads require high clearance or 4×4 vehicles.

The park has two scenic drives, both with sharp curves and steep inclines and not recommended for certain RVs and trailers (see "Safety," above). The 7-mile **Chisos Basin Drive,** which takes at least a half-hour, climbs up Green Gulch to Panther Pass before dropping down into the basin. Near the pass, there are some sharp curves, and parts of the road are at a 10% grade. The views are wonderful any time of the year, and particularly when the wildflowers dot the meadows, hills, and roadsides. The best months for wildflowers are March and April, and even later on the highest mountain trails.

When you've breathed your fill of clear mountain air, head back down and turn west toward the **Ross Maxwell Scenic Drive** through the Chihuahuan Desert and finally to the Rio Grande. This drive, which will take an hour or so plus stops, winds through the desert on the west side of the Chisos Mountains, providing a different perspective. Afterward, it passes through Castolon, and then continues along and above the river to **Santa Elena Canyon.** Here you should park and hike the trail, which climbs above the river, allowing for great views into the steep, narrow canyon (see "Hiking," p. 398).

Another worthwhile drive, recommended for all vehicles, begins at **Panther Junction Visitor Center** and goes to Rio Grande Village. Allow a half-day. From the visitor center, head southeast through the desert toward the high mountains that form the skyline in the distance. The first half of the drive passes through desert grasses, finally making a comeback after severe overgrazing in the decades before the establishment of the park in 1944. Recovery has been slow in this harsh climate, but the area is beginning to vegetate again.

As the elevation gradually decreases, you progress farther into the desert, and the grasses give way to agave lechuguilla and ocotillo, cacti, and other arid-climate survivors. Off to the south is the long, rather flat **Chilicotal Mountain,** named for the *chilicote,* or mescal-bean bushes, growing near its base. The chilicote's poisonous red bean is used in Mexico to kill rats. Several miles farther, the River Road turns off and heads southwest toward Castolon, more than 50 miles away. This is a primitive road for high-clearance vehicles only.

If you feel adventurous, take the **Hot Springs** turnoff about a mile beyond the Tornillo Creek Bridge. The road follows a rough wash to a point overlooking the convergence of Tornillo Creek and the Rio Grande. A trail along the riverbank leads to several springs. The foundation of a bathhouse is a remnant of the town of Hot Springs, which thrived here about 20 years before the park was established.

Back on the paved road, you'll soon pass through a short tunnel in the limestone cliff, beyond which is a parking area for a short trail to a viewpoint overlooking **Rio Grande Village.** It's just a short drive from here to Rio Grande Village, your destination, where you can take a .75-mile nature trail ending at a high point above the Rio Grande, providing terrific views up and down the river.

HISTORIC SITES

There is evidence that prehistoric American Indians and later Apaches, Kiowas, and Comanches occupied this area. Throughout the park, you can find **petroglyphs, pictographs,** and other signs of early human presence, including ruins of **stone shelters.** There are pictographs along the Hot Spring Trail (see "Hiking," p. 398), and along the river. Watch for **mortar holes** scattered throughout the park, sometimes a foot deep, where Indians would grind seeds or mesquite beans.

Also within the park boundaries are the remains of several early-20th-century communities, a mercury mine, and projects by the Civilian Conservation Corps.

The **Castolon Historic District,** located in the southwest section of the park just off the Ross Maxwell Scenic Drive, includes the remains of homes and other buildings, many stabilized by the National Park Service, that were constructed in the early 1900s by Mexican-American farmers, Anglo settlers, and the U.S. Army. The first is the **Alvino House,** the oldest surviving adobe structure in the park, dating from 1901. Nearby is **La Harmonia Store,** built in 1920 to house cavalry troops during the Mexican Revolution, but never actually used by soldiers because the war ended. Two civilians converted it into a general store and then purchased the building, calling it La Harmonia for the harmony and peaceful relations they hoped to encourage among area residents. The store continues to operate, selling snacks, groceries, and other necessities.

The village of **Glenn Springs,** located in the southeast section of the park and accessible by dirt road off the main park highway, owes its creation to having a reliable water source in an otherwise arid area. It was named for rancher H. E. Glenn, who grazed horses in the area until Indians killed him in the 1880s. By 1916 the area held several ranches, a factory that produced wax from the candelilla plant, a store, a post office, and a residential village divided into two sections—one for Anglos and the other for Mexicans. But then Mexican bandit revolutionaries crossed the border and attacked, killing and wounding a number of people, looting the store, and partially destroying the wax factory. Within 3 years, the community was virtually deserted. Today, the spring still flows, and you can see the remains of several adobe buildings and other structures.

Remains of a small health resort advertised in the 1920s as "the Fountain of Youth that Ponce de León failed to find" can be seen at the **Hot Springs,** accessible by hiking trail or dirt road, along the Rio Grande west of Rio Grande Village in the park's southeast section. Today, you'll see the ruins of a general store/post office, other buildings, and a foundation that fills with natural mineral water, at about 105°F (41°C), creating an almost natural hot tub—except when the river rises above 4½ feet in depth.

To get to the **Mariscal Mine,** you will likely need a four-wheel-drive or high-clearance vehicle. Located in the south-central part of the park, it is most easily accessed by River Road East, which begins 5 miles west of Rio Grande

Village. The mine operated on and off between 1900 and 1943, producing 1,400 76-pound flasks of mercury, which was almost one-quarter of the total amount of mercury produced in the United States during that time. Mining buildings, homes, the company store, a kiln, foundations, and other structures remain in what is now a National Historic District.

Also in the park, you can see excellent examples of the work done by the **Civilian Conservation Corps** in the 1930s and early 1940s, including stone culverts along Basin Road, the Lost Mine Trail, and stone-and-adobe cottages still in use at the Chisos Mountains Lodge.

OUTDOOR ADVENTURES

Local companies that provide equipment rentals and a variety of guided adventures in both the park and the general area include **Desert Sports** (www.desertsportstx.com; ✆ **888/989-6900** or 432/371-2727), located on FM 170, 5 miles west of the junction of FM 170 and Tex. 118; **Big Bend River Tours,** FM 170 just west of Tex. 118 (www.bigbendrivertours.com; ✆ **800/545-4240** or 432/371-3033); and **Far Flung Outdoor Center ★**, FM 170 just west of Tex. 118 (www.ffoc.net; ✆ **800/839-7238** or 432/371-2633).

Bird-Watching & Wildlife Viewing ★★

Big Bend National Park has an absolutely phenomenal variety of wildlife. About 450 species of birds can be found here over the course of the year—that's more than at any other national park and nearly half of all species found in North America. At latest count, there were also about 75 species of mammals, close to 70 species of reptiles and amphibians, and more than three dozen species of fish.

This is the only place in the United States where you'll find the Mexican long-nosed bat, listed by the federal government as an **endangered species.** Other endangered species that make their homes in the park include the black-capped vireo and a tiny "mosquito fish"—the Big Bend gambusia—which I hope prospers and multiplies, because its favorite food is mosquito larvae.

Birders consider Big Bend National Park a key bird-watching destination, especially for those looking for some of America's more unusual **birds.** Among the park's top bird-watching spots are Rio Grande Village and Cottonwood campgrounds, the Chisos Basin, and the Hot Springs. Species to watch for include the colorful golden-fronted woodpecker, often seen year-round among the cottonwood trees along the Rio Grande; and the rare colima warbler, whose range in the United States consists solely of the Chisos Mountains at Big Bend National Park. Among the hundreds of other birds that call the park home (at least part of the year) are scaled quail, spotted sandpipers, white-winged doves, greater roadrunners, lesser nighthawks, white-throated swifts, black-chinned and broad-tailed hummingbirds, acorn woodpeckers, northern flickers, western wood-pewees, ash-throated flycatchers, tufted titmice, bushtits, cactus and canyon wrens, loggerhead shrikes, Wilson's warblers, and Scott's orioles.

Mammals you may see in the park include desert cottontails, black-tailed jack rabbits, rock squirrels, Texas antelope squirrels, Merriam's kangaroo rats, coyotes, gray foxes, raccoons, striped skunks, javelinas (wild desert pigs), mule deer, and white-tailed deer. There are occasional sightings of mountain lions, usually called panthers here, in the Green Gulch and Chisos Basin areas. Four attacks on humans have occurred at the park, with no fatalities. Black bears, which were frequently seen in the area until about 1940, were mostly killed off by area ranchers who saw them as a threat to their livestock. However, with the protection provided by national park status, they began to return in the mid-1980s and have now established a small population.

The park has a number of **reptiles,** including some poisonous snakes, such as diamondback, Mojave, rock, and black-tailed rattlesnakes, plus the Trans-Pecos copperhead. Fortunately, it is unlikely you will see a rattler or copperhead, because they avoid both the heat of the day and busy areas. You are more apt to encounter nonpoisonous western coachwhips, often seen speeding across trails and roadways. Sometimes called "red racers," they're reddish, sometimes bright red, and among America's fastest snakes. Other nonpoisonous snakes that inhabit the park include Texas whipsnakes, spotted night snakes, southwestern black-headed snakes, and black-necked garter snakes.

Among the **lizards** you may see scurrying along desert roads and trails is the southwestern earless lizard—adult males are green with black-and-white chevrons on their lower sides, and often curl their black-striped tails over their backs. You'll also see various whiptail lizards in the desert, but in the canyons and higher in the mountains watch for the crevice spiny lizard, which is covered with scales and has a dark collar. Although rare, there are also **western box turtles** in the park, as well as several types of more common water turtles.

Hiking ★★★

Big Bend National Park is a wonderful park for hikers, with a variety of trails, most of which are easy or moderate. There are a number of short, easy interpretative nature walks, with either booklets available at the trailheads or signs along the trail. One example is the **Panther Path,** outside the Panther Junction Visitor Center, which is a 50-yard round-trip walk through a garden of cacti and other desert plants. I also enjoy the **Window View Trail,** a .3-mile round-trip via the Chisos Basin trailhead. This level, paved, and wheelchair-accessible self-guided nature trail runs along a low hill and has beautiful sunset views through the Window, a V-shaped opening in the mountains to the west. The **Rio Grande Village Nature Trail ★**, .75-mile round-trip, starts at the southeast corner of Rio Grande Village Campground across from site 18 and is a good choice for sunrise and sunset views. It climbs from the surprisingly lush river floodplain about 125 feet into desert terrain to a hilltop with excellent panoramic vistas.

Those interested in historic structures should try the easy 1-mile **Hot Springs Trail,** at the end of an improved dirt road to Hot Springs, off the road to Rio Grande Village. An interpretive booklet available at the trailhead describes the sights, including a vintage health resort and homestead (see "Historic Sites," p. 396), along this loop. Fairly substantial ruins remain of a general store/post office and a foundation that fills with natural mineral water at about 105°F (41°C), creating an inviting hot tub. Also along the trail are pictographs left by ancient Indians, and panoramic views of the Rio Grande and Mexico.

Among other easy hikes is the **Tuff Canyon Trail** (.75-mile round-trip), which is accessed from the Ross Maxwell Scenic Drive, 5 miles south of the Mule Ears Overlook access road. This walk leads into a narrow canyon, carved from soft volcanic rock called tuff, and provides several canyon overlooks. The 1.6-mile **Chisos Basin Loop Trail** (access at the Chisos Basin trailhead) is a fairly easy walk that climbs about 350 feet into a pretty meadow and leads to an overlook with good views of the park's mountains, including Emory Peak, the highest point in the park at 7,825 feet; more adventurous hikers can continue on to the breathtaking South Rim for a 12-mile round-trip. The easy **Grapevine Hills Trail,** which is 2.2 miles round-trip, begins about 6 miles down the unpaved Grapevine Hills Road. It has an elevation change of about 240 feet as it follows a sandy wash through the desert, among massive granite boulders, ending at a picturesque balancing rock.

Among shorter, moderately rated trails, I heartily recommend the .8-mile one-way **Santa Elena Canyon Trail ★★★**, which you'll find at the end of Ross Maxwell Scenic Drive. You may get your feet wet crossing a broad creek on this trail, which also takes you up a series of steep steps; it's one of the most scenic short trails in the park, leading along the canyon wall, with good views of rafters on the Rio Grande, and down among the boulders along the river. Interpretive signs describe the canyon environment. Beware of flash flooding as you cross the Terlingua Creek, and skip this trail if the creek is running swiftly. Another good moderate hike is the **Boquillas Canyon Trail ★**, which is 1.4 miles round-trip and starts at the end of Boquillas Canyon Road. This hike begins by climbing a low hill and then drops down to the Rio Grande, ending near a shallow cave and huge sand dune. There are good views of the scenic canyon and the Mexican village of Boquillas, across the Rio Grande.

Among longer trails, I suggest the moderately rated, 3.8-mile round-trip **Mule Ears Spring Trail ★**, which you'll find at the Mule Ears Overlook parking area along the Ross Maxwell Scenic Drive. This relatively flat desert trail crosses several arroyos and then follows a wash most of the way to Mule Ears Spring. It has great views of unusual rock formations, such as the Mule Ears, and ends at a historic ranch house and rock corral. At 4 miles round-trip, the moderate **Pine Canyon Trail** takes you from desert grasslands dotted with sotols into a pretty canyon with dense stands of pinyon, juniper, oak, and finally bigtooth maple and ponderosa pine. At the higher elevations (it climbs 1,000 ft.), you'll also see Texas madrones—evergreen trees with smooth reddish bark that is shed each summer. At the end of the trail is a 200-foot cliff, which becomes a picturesque waterfall after heavy rains. This trail is located at the end of unpaved Pine Canyon Road (check on road conditions before going).

Visiting Mexico via Big Bend/Boquillas Border Crossing

Big Bend National Park is edged by the Rio Grande, a natural border between the U.S. and Mexico. Travelers who'd like to dip their toes into Mexico can take the Boquillas International Ferry across the Rio Grande or go by foot or rowboat, but they will be required to have a Western Hemisphere Travel Initiative–approved document, such as a valid passport. (Birth certificates alone are not sufficient, even for minors.) Upon returning to Big Bend National Park, crossers are also required to check in at the National Park Service Visitor Center, about a 5-minute walk from the river on the U.S./Texas side. The Boquillas Ferry operates Wednesday to Sunday 9am to 6pm, when the U.S. Port of Entry is open, and costs $5 per person. Once you've crossed the river into Mexico, you can walk, rent a burro or horse, or hail a car for the 1-mile trip into little Boquillas, Mexico, home to a couple cafes and a bar. Locals on the Mexico side offer 90-minute guided canoe trips down the river and tours of a historic silver mine. The federal governments of the United States and Mexico reopened the border crossing at Boquillas in April 2013, 11 years after the U.S. closed the crossing in the aftermath of 9/11. The Trump administration may alter border laws yet again; check www.nps.gov/bibe/planyourvisit/border_travel.htm before your Big Bend border-crossing adventure.

There are additional hiking opportunities in the even less visited **Big Bend Ranch State Park,** located between Terlingua and Presidio via FM 170.

Horseback Riding

Horses are permitted on most dirt roads and many park trails (check with rangers for specifics) and may be kept overnight at many of the park's primitive campsites, although not at the developed campgrounds. The **Government Springs Campsite,** located 3½ miles from Panther Junction, is a primitive campsite with a corral that accommodates up to eight horses. It can be reserved up to 10 weeks in advance (✆ **432/477-2241**). Those riding horses in the park must get free stock-use permits, which should be obtained in person up to 24 hours in advance at any of the park's visitor centers.

Although there are no commercial outfitters for guided rides in the park as of this writing, there are opportunities for rides just outside the park on private land, such as nearby Big Bend Ranch State Park and across the river in Mexico. **Lajitas Stables** (www.lajitasstables.com; ✆ **800/887-4331** or 432/371-3066) offers a variety of guided trail rides, lasting from 2 hours to all day. Some trips follow canyon trails; others visit ancient Indian camps and ghost towns. Typical rates are $60 to $70 for 2 hours, $90 to $100 for 4 hours, and $150 for a full day. A cattle drive in Big Bend Ranch State Park is also offered twice a year. At that same website above, you'll find information on **Big Bend Stables** (✆ **800/887-4331** or 432/371-3064) with horseback rides along North America's Chihuahuan Desert. The company's trail rides are permitted by the U.S. Forest Service.

Mountain Biking

Bikes are not permitted on hiking trails, but are allowed on the park's many established dirt roads. Mountain bikes are available for rent from **Desert Sports** (see p. 397), at a cost of $40 per day, $175 for 5 to 7 days, and $30 for each additional day after 7 days. The company also offers 1-day and multiday guided trips, including a combination hiking/mountain-biking/float trip in the park—3 days for $675. They also offer guided float trips, and there are even canoe and inflatable kayak rentals.

River Running ★

One of the first rivers designated by Congress as part of the Wild and Scenic River System, the Rio Grande follows the southern edge of the park for 118 miles, and extends another 127 miles downstream. The river allows for mostly calm float trips, but it does have a few sections of rough whitewater during high-water times. It can usually be run in a raft, canoe, or kayak. You can either bring your own equipment or rent equipment near the park (none is available in the park), but for novices it's safest to take a trip with one of several river guides approved by the National Park Service.

Those planning trips on their own must obtain the necessary backcountry park permits, which cost $12 for overnight use ($6 with an applicable pass). There is no charge for day-use river or stock permits. You'll need to pick these up in person at the park visitor's center no more than 24 hours before the trip. Permits for the lower canyons of the Rio Grande Wild and Scenic River are available at the **Persimmon Gap Visitor Center;** a self-serve permit station is located here when the visitor center is closed. Permits for the section of river through Santa Elena Canyon can also be obtained at the **Barton Warnock Environmental Education Center,** 1 mile east of the community of Lajitas, Texas, about 20 miles from the park's West Entrance. Park rangers, however, strongly advise that anyone planning a river trip check with them beforehand to get the latest water conditions. A river-running booklet with additional information is available at park visitor centers and from the **Big Bend Natural History Association** (see "Visitor Information," earlier in this chapter).

Rafts, inflatable kayaks, and canoes can be rented from **Desert Sports** (www.desertsportstx.com; ✆ **888/989-6900** or 432/371-2727). Canoe rental costs $50 for the first day and $45 for each additional day or $30 for each additional day after 7 days. Inflatable kayak rentals cost $40 per day for a 1-person kayak and $50 a day for a 2-person kayak. Good to know: Inflatables also include a patch kit and pump. The company also provides shuttle services and offers guided 1-day and multiday canoe and raft trips, where you can either grab a paddle and take an active role, or sit back and let your boatman and the river do the work. Typical prices are $350 per person for 2 days on the river through Santa Elena Canyon; and $600 per person for 3 days on the river through Mariscal Canyon, considered the most remote canyon in the national park. Desert Sports also offers trips that combine a float trip with hiking or mountain biking. Also see "Mountain Biking," above.

Another recommended outfitter on the Rio Grande is **Far Flung Outdoor Center** (www.ffoc.net; ✆ **800/839-7238** or 432/371-2633), offering raft and canoe trips for $79 per person for a half-day float or $145 per person for a full-day canyon float. Multiday trips range from $369 per person for an overnight trip to $899. Rentals run $79 per day for canoes and inflatable kayaks; other gear rentals and shuttles for river trips are also available. In addition, the company provides jeep and ATV tours of the region and several wilderness first-aid courses a year.

Guided trips on the Rio Grande are also available through **Big Bend River Tours** (www.bigbendrivertours.com; ✆ **800/545-4240** or 432/371-3033), which has daily raft trips year-round. Trips range from a delightful half-day float for about $75 per person to 10-day excursions for about $1,900 per person. Among the company's most popular trips is the 21-mile float through beautiful Santa Elena Canyon, which can be explored on a day trip ($135 per person), a 2-day trip ($340 per person), or a 3-day trip ($500 per person), although rates vary based on the number of people making the trip. The longer trips include a stop in a side canyon with waterfalls and peaceful swimming holes. Big Bend River Tours also offers guided canoe and inflatable kayak trips, a shuttle service, and equipment rentals.

Where to Stay

This is an isolated area, so don't expect to find your favorite chain hotel or restaurant right around the corner. There are, however, some pretty special lodging options in Marathon (though some are costly), and some funky ones in Terlingua. Both book up far in advance, so make lodging reservations well in advance, especially in winter—the high season here, when rates are highest. Another busy time is spring when college and high school students come during their spring break vacation, and lodging in the park, campsites, and RV hookup areas are often booked well in advance then, too.

IN THE PARK

Chisos Mountains Lodge ★★ The best place to stay while exploring Big Bend, Chisos Mountains Lodge offers a variety of accommodations, ranging from simple motel rooms to historic stone cottages built by the Civilian Conservation Corps in the 1930s. These six delightful cottages have a rustic feel that fit the setting, with stone floors, wooden furniture, three double beds, and covered porches. Book as far in advance as possible.

The Emory Peak units are also a bit on the rustic side, with one double and one single bed, wood furnishings, and painted brick walls with Western art. The lodge's motel rooms come in two flavors: The Rio Grande rooms are small and simply decorated, with two double beds and terrific views of the Chisos Mountains, and the Casa Grande units have larger and more modern motel rooms with private balconies. All rooms are nonsmoking.

Chisos Basin, Big Bend National Park. www.chisosmountainslodge.com. ✆ **432/477-2291.** 72 units. $120–$160 double. Wi-Fi (free; not available in the cottages and Emory Peak rooms).

THE STUDY BUTTE–TERLINGUA AREA

Just outside the national park's West Entrance, this is the closest community to the park with lodging and other services. **Big Bend Resort & Adventures,** at the junction of Tex. 118 and FM 170 (www.bigbendresortadventures.com; ✆ **877/386-4383** or 432/371-2218; $75–$150 double; $165–$200 two-bedroom apartments with kitchenettes; $300 three-bedroom house) offers simple but comfortable, modern, and well-maintained motel rooms. A restaurant and convenience store are on-site. In Terlingua Ghost Town, the formerly abandoned **Holiday Hotel,** behind the Terlingua Trading Company (www.bigbendholidayhotel.com; ✆ **432/203-6929;** $135–$250 double), has been nicely restored and has four rooms. The proprietors also have numerous historic homes for rent in the area, which are quite nice and have a Southwestern style that is so truly Terlingua. The **Big Bend Campsite, Terlingua Las Ruinas** (formerly Las Ruinas Hostel) ★★ (www.bigbendcampsite.com; ✆ **317-699-7432**), in Terlingua Ghost Town behind the Boathouse restaurant, has six tents and dozens of tent campsites. It features pitch-your-own tent sites, as well as "Terlingua fancy glamping tents," as they call them, complete with beds with memory-foam mattresses, nice bedding, rugs, chairs, and lanterns. Tents are available with either one queen-size bed or two twin beds. The campsite also has smaller two-person tents with a memory-foam mattress on the ground. All tent sites have access to two bathrooms and a shower on-site, and here in the "dark sky" zone, you'll enjoy amazing views of the stars. Guests must bring their own towels and toiletries, and flashlights and closed-toed shoes are recommended. Choose wisely here when selecting your campsite—some are as close as 10 feet from another tent, while others are set farther apart to allow for more privacy.

About 20 miles west of Terlingua, **Lajitas Golf Resort,** HC 70 (www.lajitasgolfresort.com; ✆ **877/525-4827** or 432/424-5000; doubles and suites starting at $199–$320), includes the use of an 18-hole golf course, a spa, and an outdoor pool. It also has condominium suites and cottages ($320–$520). A wing of stylish rooms is located in a former cavalry post once under the command of "Black Jack" Pershing.

Big Bend Casitas at Far Flung Outdoor Center ★★ Longstanding local river outfitter Far Flung built six comfortable and modern *casitas,* or little houses, in 2010, each with 400 square feet of living space. Centered on a nicely landscaped courtyard that's a hummingbird haven, the cabins are comfortable and functional, featuring two queen beds, kitchenettes, and plenty of peace and quiet. The convenience factor is also worth mentioning, especially if you're going on an expedition with Far Flung—you'll meet your guide in the parking lot—and the location is within easy walking distance of a Mexican restaurant and a liquor store.

FM 170 just west of Tex. 118. www.bigbendfarflung.com/lodging. ✆ **800/839-7238** or 432/371-2633. 6 units. $145–$195 double. Children 12 and under stay free; additional guests 13 and older $10 per person per night, except for the Big Bend Bunkhouse, where additional guests are $40 per night. No phone in rooms. Wi-Fi (free).

La Posada Milagro ★ Built on the site of a former ruin that is now incorporated into the structure, La Posada Milagro overlooks Terlingua Ghost Town and is a terrific place to hang your hat in the Big Bend region. It features distinctive West Texas touches (thatched ceilings, corner hearths, great patio seating areas), and three smaller rooms share a full bathroom and a half bathroom. The Chisos Honeymoon Suite is the most elegant of the casitas, with its own private bathroom, and the San Carlos Suite offers great views of the Big Bend to the east, west, and south. Also available is a nearby guesthouse, La Casita.

100 Milagro Rd., Terlingua Ghost Town, Terlingua. www.laposadamilagro.net. ✆ **432/371-3044.** 5 units, 3 with shared bathroom, including 1 guesthouse. $145–$210 double with shared bathroom; $210 double with private bathroom; $350 guesthouse. No phone in room. **Amenities:** Wi-Fi (free).

MARATHON

The Gage Hotel ★★★ For the quintessential Texas hotel experience, go to the Gage. Just an hour's drive from Big Bend National Park in the dusty tumbleweed town of Marathon, it's the stuff of dreamy cowboy lore. Enter the lobby and you'll feel you've stumbled onto the set of *Giant* or *Lonesome Dove.* The 1927 main building has hardwood floors and wood-beam ceilings, hand-carved Mexican furniture, saddles, plush couches, taxidermy mounts, and a 10-gallon hat full of authentic Wild West charm. Rooms in the main building aren't as large and comfortable as other rooms on the property, but rates are lower, especially for those units with a shared bath down the hall. Most guests like **Los Portales,** 20 pueblo-style adobe brick suites surrounding a large courtyard with a firepit, but I prefer the large casitas across the street with fireplaces and patios (some with kitchenettes). Behind the main building stands the Spanish colonial–style **Captain Shepard House,** with guest rooms there and in an adjacent carriage house, also part of the hotel. The Gage also has a pool and spa. Its **12-Gage** restaurant offers fine dining, and the **White Buffalo Bar** is one of the best watering holes in the state. Sip a longneck by a fireplace or around the courtyard firepit. There's nowhere I'd rather be, deep in the heart of Texas, when "the stars at night are big and bright."

U.S. 90 (P.O. Box 46), Marathon. www.gagehotel.com. ✆ **800/884-4243** or 432/386-4205. 45 units (2 with shared bathroom), 5 guesthouses. Double with shared bathroom $99; queen bed with private bathroom $165; king bed with private bathroom $229; Captain Shepard suites $229–$252; casitas $325–$350. **Amenities:** Restaurant; bar; exercise room; outdoor heated pool; gardens; spa; Wi-Fi (free).

Where to Eat

IN THE PARK

The restaurant at **Chisos Mountains Lodge** (see p. 402) is your only dining option within park boundaries. It serves three meals a day, including a breakfast buffet.

THE STUDY BUTTE–TERLINGUA AREA

High Sierra Bar & Grill ★ MEXICAN/PUB FARE When you're in a hot, dusty ghost town in summer, sometimes all you want is cold air-conditioning and a cold drink. Here, you'll find that and more: panoramic balcony views of the Chisos Mountains, a patio for outside dining, good drinks, and good company. It serves standard Texas bar-and-grill menu items like hot wings, burgers, and quesadillas and down-home Tex-Mex fare, like enchiladas and fajitas.

In Terlingua Ghost Town, off FM 170. www.highsierra.homestead.com. ✆ **432/371-3282.** Main courses $5–$15. Sun–Fri noon–midnight; Sat noon–1am.

Starlight Theatre ★★★ MEXICAN/AMERICAN A 1930s movie palace abandoned when the mines in Terlingua went bust, the Starlight Theatre (named for what was formerly visible through a hole in the ceiling) was reborn as an eatery and watering hole in 1991. Now bedecked with murals, artful tables, and longhorn skulls, the theater still has a stage, but the silver screen takes a back seat to the food (especially the trademark chili and filet mignon, as well as a number of vegetarian and seafood options), drink (namely Texas beers and prickly pear margaritas), and desserts (including a very good *tres leches*). The Starlight still occasionally hosts movie nights, as well as plays and live music. This is the place to be on New Year's Eve and a prime destination during any Big Bend/Terlingua trip.

In Terlingua Ghost Town, 631 Ivey Road, off FM 170. www.thestarlighttheatre.com. ✆ **432/371-4300.** Main courses $9–$25. Daily 5pm–10pm; Sun brunch 11am–2pm. Bar open Sun–Fri 5pm–midnight and Sat 5pm–1am.

CAMPING

A $12 camping permit ($6 with an applicable pass), available at any visitor center, is required for use of the primitive backcountry roadside and backpacking campsites. All are open year-round.

In the Park

The National Park Service runs three developed **campgrounds** (no showers, laundry facilities, or RV hookups; $14 per night). An **RV park** is run by a concessionaire. A limited number of campsites in Rio Grande Village and the Chisos Basin campgrounds accept reservations from November 15 to April 15; call ✆ **877/444-6777** or visit **www.recreation.gov**.

Rio Grande Village Campground ★★ is the largest, with 100 sites, flush toilets, running water, and a dump station. It has numerous trees, many with prickly pear cacti growing up around them, and thorny bushes everywhere. Sites are either graveled or paved and are nicely spaced for privacy. Sites are often taken by 1pm in winter (the busy season). One area is designated a "No Generator Zone." Separate but within walking distance is **Rio Grande Village RV Campground** (✆ **432/371-2348**), a concessionaire-operated RV park with 25 sites with full hookups. It looks like a parking lot in the middle of grass and trees, fully paved with curbs and back-in sites (no pull-throughs). Cost is $33 per night for two people with an additional $3 per extra person. Tents are not permitted. A small store has limited camping supplies and groceries, a coin-operated laundry, showers for a fee, propane, and gasoline. Guests must first register at the Rio Grande Village store/service station.

Chisos Basin Campground ★★ (✆ **432/477-1121**), although not heavily wooded, has small pinyon and juniper trees and 60 well-spaced campsites (only 26 of which are reservable, however). The highest-elevation campground in the park at 5,400 feet, it's nestled around a circular road in a bowl below the visitor center. There is a dump station, along with flush toilets and running water. The access road to the campground is steep and curved, so take it slow. The campground is not recommended for trailers over 20 feet or motor homes over 24 feet.

Cottonwood Campground (✆ **432/477-2251**) is named for the huge cottonwood trees that dominate the terrain. The 24 first-come, first-served sites in this rather rustic area at an elevation of 2,169 feet are spacious and within walking distance of the river. Campsites are $14 per night ($7 with applicable passes). Pit toilets, picnic tables, grills, and water are available. There is no dump station, and no generators are allowed. A small picnic area is available across from campsite #23.

Near the Park

About 7 miles east of the park's North Entrance on FM 2627 is **Stillwell Store and RV Park,** HC 65, Alpine, TX (www.stillwellstore.com; ✆ **432/376-2244**), a casual RV park in desert terrain that's open year-round. There are two areas across the road from each other. The west side has full hookups, while the east has water and electric only, but the east side also features horse corrals and plenty of room for horse trailers. There are 65 pull-through hookups ($26 per night) plus almost unlimited space for tenters, who are charged $10 per adult and $5 per child. There's a dump station, showers, a self-serve laundry, and a public phone. The RV park's office is at the Stillwell Store, where you can get groceries, limited camping supplies, and gasoline. There is also a small museum (donations accepted), with exhibits from the Stillwell family's pioneer days.

In Terlingua, the **Big Bend Campsite, Terlingua Las Ruinas** (formerly Las Ruinas Hostel) (✆ **317-699-CAMP [7432]**) is a great option for a comfortable stay in tents with beds or for pitching your own tent. For more information, see p. 403.

GUADALUPE MOUNTAINS NATIONAL PARK ★

Once a long reef below the ocean's surface, then a dense forest, Guadalupe Mountains National Park is today a rugged wilderness of tall Douglas firs and lush vegetation rising out of a vast desert. Here you will find varied hiking trails, panoramic vistas, the highest peak in Texas, plant and animal life unique to the Southwest, and a canyon that may be the prettiest spot in all of Texas.

As you approach from the north, the mountains seem to rise gradually from the landscape, but seen from the south they stand tall and dignified. **El Capitan,** the southern tip of the reef escarpment, watches over the landscape like a sentinel. In the south-central section of the park, **Guadalupe Peak,** at 8,749 feet the highest mountain in Texas, provides hikers with incredible views of the surrounding mountains and desert.

Within its 86,416 acres of land, the park has several hubs of human activity and distinct ecological zones. Park headquarters and the visitor center are at **Pine Springs,** along the park's southeast edge, where you'll also find a campground and several trailheads, including one with access to the **Guadalupe Peak Trail,** the park's premier mountain hike. Nearby, a short dirt road leads to historic **Frijole Ranch,** with a museum and more trailheads. A horse corral is nearby for those traveling with their steeds. The **McKittrick Canyon** section of the park, near the northeast corner, gets my vote as the most beautiful spot in Texas, especially in fall when the oak, maple, ash, and walnut trees produce a spectacular show of color. A day-use area only, McKittrick Canyon has a delightful although intermittent stream, several trailheads, and historic buildings. Along the park's northern boundary, practically in New Mexico, is the secluded and forested **Dog Canyon.**

Particularly impressive about Guadalupe Mountains National Park is its vast variety of flora and fauna. You'll find species here that don't seem to belong in West Texas, such as maple and oak trees. Scientists say these seemingly out-of-place plants and animals are leftovers from a time when the region was cooler and wetter. As the climate changed and the desert spread, some species were able to survive in these mountains, where conditions remained somewhat cooler and moister. At the base of the mountains, at lower elevations, you'll find desert plants such as sotol, agave, and prickly pear cactus; but as you start to climb, especially in stream-nurtured canyons, expect to encounter ponderosa pine, ash, walnut, and oak trees, and ferns. Wildlife abounds, including mule deer, elk, all sorts of birds, and the occasional snake.

It takes several days to fully explore this park, but just a half-day trip to McKittrick Canyon would be well worth your time.

Essentials

GETTING THERE Located on the border of New Mexico and Texas, the park is 55 miles southwest of Carlsbad, New Mexico, along U.S. 62/180. From El Paso, drive east 110 miles on U.S. 62/180 to the Pine Springs Visitor Center.

Air travelers can fly to **Cavern City Air Terminal** (✆ **575/887-3060**), at the south edge of the city of Carlsbad, which has commercial service from Albuquerque with **New Mexico Airlines** (www.flynma.com; ✆ **888/564-6119**) The nearest major airport is **El Paso International Airport** (www.elpaso internationalairport.com; ✆ **915/780-4749**) in central El Paso just north of I-10, with service from most major airlines and car-rental companies; see chapter 10 for more information.

VISITOR INFORMATION Contact **Guadalupe Mountains National Park,** 400 Pine Canyon Rd., Salt Flat, TX 79847 (www.nps.gov/gumo; ✆ **915/828-3251**). Books and maps can be ordered from the **Carlsbad Caverns**

Guadalupe Mountains Association, 3225 National Parks Hwy, Carlsbad, NM 88220 (© **575/785-2232**).

Park headquarters and the main visitor center are located at Pine Springs just off U.S. 62/180. There are three other access points along this side of the park: Frijole Ranch, about a mile east of Pine Springs and a mile north of the highway; McKittrick Canyon (day use only), about 7 miles east and 4 miles north of the highway; and Williams Ranch, about 8 miles south of Pine Springs and 8 miles north of the highway on a four-wheel-drive road. (***Note:*** Keys to locked gates can be checked out at park headquarters.)

The **Pine Springs Visitor Center,** open daily year-round except Christmas, has natural history exhibits, a bookstore, and an introductory slide program. **McKittrick Canyon** has an intermittently staffed visitor contact station with outdoor exhibits and an outdoor slide program on the history, geology, and natural history of the canyon. On the north side of the park is the year-round **Dog Canyon Ranger Station** (© **575/981-2418**), at the end of N.M. 137, about 70 miles from Carlsbad and 110 miles from park headquarters. Information, restrooms, and drinking water are available.

FEES, REGULATIONS & PERMITS Entry into the park runs $5 per person or $20 for an annual pass. Backcountry camping is free, but a $12 permit is required. Corrals are available for those who bring their horses to ride in the park; although use is free, permits are required. All permits are available at the Pine Springs Visitor Center and Dog Canyon Ranger Station and must be requested in person, either the day before or the day of use. Horses are prohibited in the backcountry overnight.

Visitors to McKittrick Canyon, a day-use area, must stay on the trail; entering the stream is not permitted. The McKittrick Canyon **entrance gate** opens at 8am daily and closes at 4:30pm Mountain Standard Time and at 6pm Mountain Daylight Time. Neither wood nor charcoal fires are allowed in the park.

WHEN TO GO In general, summers in the Guadalupe Mountains are hot: highs in the 80s and 90s Fahrenheit/upper 20s and 30s Celsius (and sometimes exceeding 100°F) and lows in the 60s/upper teens Celsius, and winters are mild (highs in the 50s and 60s/teens Celsius and lows in the upper 20s and 30s/around 0° Celsius), but there can be sudden and extreme changes in the weather at any time. In winter and spring, high winds can whip down the mountain slopes, sometimes reaching 100 mph; on hot summer days, thunderstorms can blow up quickly. The sun is warm even in winter, and summer nights are generally cool no matter how hot the afternoon. Clothing that can be layered is best, comfortable and sturdy walking/hiking shoes are a must, a hat and sunscreen are highly recommended, and plenty of drinking water is essential for hikers.

Overall, Guadalupe Mountains National Park is one of America's less-often-visited national parks, with attendance of only about 167,000 each year. This is partly because it is primarily a wilderness park, where you'll have to tackle rugged hiking trails to get to the best vistas, but also because of its isolation. The only time the park might be considered even slightly crowded is during spring-break time, usually in March, when students from area colleges bring their backpacks and hit the trails. Quite a few families visit during the summer, but even then the park is not usually crowded; and visitation drops considerably once schools open in late August.

An exception is McKittrick Canyon, renowned throughout the Southwest for its beautiful fall colors, at their best in late October and early November. The one road into McKittrick Canyon is a bit busy then, but once you get on the trails, you can usually walk away from the people.

SAFETY This is extremely rugged country, with sometimes unpredictable weather, and hikers need to be well prepared, with proper hiking boots and plenty of water. Because the park's backcountry trails often crisscross each other and can be confusing, rangers strongly recommend that hikers carry topographical maps.

RANGER PROGRAMS In March, summer, and fall, rangers lead a variety of programs and activities. Check at the visitor center for the current schedule.

What to See & Do

EXPLORING THE HIGHLIGHTS BY CAR

This is not the place for the vehicle-bound visitor. There are no paved scenic drives traversing the park; roads here are simply a means of getting to historical sites and trailheads.

HISTORIC SITES

The Pinery was one of 200 stagecoach stations along the 2,800-mile Butterfield Overland Mail Coach Route. The stations provided fresh mules every 20 miles and a new coach every 300 miles, in order to maintain the grueling speed of 5 mph for 24 hours a day. John Butterfield had seen the need for overland mail delivery between the Eastern states and the West Coast, so he designed a route and the coaches, and acquired a federal contract to deliver the St. Louis mail to San Francisco in 25 days. In March 1857, this was a real feat, and the remaining rock walls at the ruins of the Pinery, which you can see on the Pinery Trail (see "Hiking," below) commemorate Butterfield's achievement.

Located in McKittrick Canyon and accessible by a 4.8-mile round-trip hike, **Pratt Cabin** was built by Wallace E. Pratt in 1931 and 1932, of stone quarried from the base of the Guadalupe Mountains, using heart-of-pine from east Texas for rafters, collar beams, and roof supports. Pratt, a geologist for the Humble Oil Co. (now ExxonMobil), and his family came for summer vacations when the heat in Houston became unbearable. He finally retired here in 1945. In 1957, the Pratts donated 5,632 acres of their 16,000-acre ranch to the federal government to begin the national park. In addition to the grand stone lodge, there are several outbuildings, stone picnic tables, and a stone fence.

Williams Ranch House rests at the base of a 3,000-foot rock cliff on the west face of the Guadalupe Mountains. The 7⅓-mile access road, navigable only by high-clearance 4×4s, follows part of the old Butterfield Overland Mail Route for about 2 miles. The road crosses private land and has two locked metal gates, for which you must sign out keys at the visitor center.

History is unclear about exactly who built the house and when, but it's believed to have been raised around 1908, and it is fairly certain that the first inhabitants were Henry and Rena Belcher. For almost 10 years, they maintained a substantial ranch here, at times with close to 3,000 head of longhorn cattle. Water was piped from Bone Spring down the canyon to holding tanks in the lowlands. James Adolphus Williams acquired the property around 1917, and with the help of an Indian friend, ranched and farmed the land until moving to New Mexico in 1941. After Williams' death in 1942, Judge J. C. Hunter bought the property, adding it to his already large holdings in the Guadalupes.

Another historic site is **Frijole Ranch,** a working ranch from when it was built in the 1870s until 1972. Inside the ranch house is the **Frijole Ranch History Museum** (✆ **915/828-3251**) with exhibits on the cultural history of the Guadalupe Mountains, including prehistoric Indians, the later Mescalero Apaches, Spanish conquistadors, and ranchers of the 19th and 20th centuries. On the grounds are several historic buildings, including a schoolhouse.

OUTDOOR ADVENTURES

Hiking ★★

This is a prime hiker's park, with more than 80 miles of trails that range from easy walks to steep, strenuous, and sometimes treacherous adventures. Among shorter trails, try the **Indian Meadow Nature Trail ★**, with access from Dog Canyon Campground (walk south from the water fountain). This exceptionally easy, .6-mile round-trip stroll follows a series of numbered stops keyed to a free brochure, available at the trailhead. You'll learn about the native vegetation and cultural history of the area as you ramble along this virtually level dirt trail. The name comes from early settlers, who told of seeing Indian tepees in this lovely meadow. The **McKittrick Canyon Nature Trail ★**, rated moderate thanks to its rocky trail and somewhat steep climbs, is .9-mile round-trip, and begins at the McKittrick Canyon contact station. Hiking this trail is a great way to discover the variety of plants and animals that inhabit the canyon, with educational signs along the path telling you why rattlesnakes are underappreciated and how the cactus supplies food and water for wildlife.

The easy .75-mile round-trip **Pinery Trail** (paved and accessible by wheelchair) gives visitors a brief introduction to the low-elevation environment at the park. Interpretive signs discuss the plants along the trail and the history of the area. About .25 miles from the visitor center, the trail makes a loop around the ruins of an old horse-changing station, left over from the Butterfield Stage Route (see "Historic Sites," above). The trailhead is by the Pine Springs

Visitor Center, or accessed from the parking area on U.S. 62/180, located 1 mile north of the visitor center entrance road.

Among the park's longer trails, my favorite is the moderate-to-difficult **McKittrick Canyon Trail ★★★**, which is about 5 miles one way, with access at the McKittrick Canyon Trail trailhead. McKittrick Canyon is perhaps the most beautiful spot in all of Texas, and this trail explores the length of it. The first 2.4 miles to the Pratt Cabin are moderate because of rocky trail conditions; the following mile to the Grotto gains 340 feet in elevation and is also considered moderate; and the strenuous climb to the Notch rises nearly 800 feet in just 1.3 miles. Even so, this is one of the most popular hikes in the park, though not everyone makes it to the Notch.

The canyon is forested with conifers and deciduous trees. In fall, the walnut and ash trees burst into color, painting the world in bright colors set off by the brown of the oaks and the rich variety of the evergreens. The stream in the canyon, which appears and disappears several times in the first 3 miles of the trail, is permanent, with reproducing trout. ***Note:*** Hikers may not drink from, wade in, or disturb the stream in any way.

The first part of the trail is wide and seems quite flat, crossing the stream twice on its way to Pratt Cabin, which is wonderfully situated at the convergence of North and South McKittrick canyons. About a mile from the lodge, a short spur veers off to the left to the Grotto, a recess with odd formations that look like they belong in an underground cave. This is a great spot for lunch at one of the stone picnic tables. Continuing down the spur trail to its end, you reach the Hunter Line Cabin, which served as temporary quarters for ranch hands of the Hunter family. Beyond the cabin, South McKittrick Canyon has been preserved as a Research Natural Area with no entry. Return to the main trail and continue toward the Notch, or head back down the canyon to your car. In another .5 mile, the trail begins switchbacking up the side of South McKittrick Canyon for the steepest ascent in the park, until it slips through the Notch, a distinctive narrow spot in the cliff. Sit down and rest while you absorb the incredible scenery. The view down the canyon is magnificent and quite dazzling in autumn. You can see both Hunter Line Cabin and Pratt Lodge in the distance. Remember to start down in time to reach your car well before the gate closes (see "Fees, Regulations & Permits," p. 408).

To stand at the highest point in Texas, hike the strenuous **Guadalupe Peak Trail ★★**, which goes 4.2 miles from the trailhead at Pine Springs Campground to the top of 8,749-foot-high Guadalupe Peak, where the glorious views make the almost 3,000-foot climb worthwhile. If you have only 1 day to explore this park, and you are an average or better hiker, this is the hike you should choose. Start early, take plenty of water, and be prepared to work. When you've gone about halfway, you'll see what seems to be the top not too far ahead, but beware: This is a false summit. Study the changing life zones as you climb from the desert into the higher-elevation pine forests—this will take your mind off your straining muscles and aching lungs. A mile short of the summit, a campground lies in one of the rare level spots on the mountain.

If you plan to spend the night, strongly anchor your tent—the winds can be ferocious up here, especially in spring.

From the summit, the views are stupendous. To the north are Shumard Peak and Bush Mountain, the next two highest points in Texas, with respective elevations of 8,615 and 8,631 feet. The Chihuahuan Desert stretches to the south, interrupted only by the Delaware and Sierra Diablo mountains. This is one of those "on a clear day you can see forever" spots—sometimes all the way to 12,003-foot-high Sierra Blanca, near Ruidoso, New Mexico, 100 miles north.

> **Leaf Peepin'**
>
> McKittrick Canyon's beautiful display of fall colors usually takes place between late October and early November. It varies, though, so call before going.

Horseback Riding

About 60% of the park's trails are open to horses for day trips, but horses are not permitted in the backcountry overnight. There are **corrals** at Frijole Ranch (near Pine Springs) and Dog Canyon (see "Visitor Information," p. 407). Each set of corrals contains four pens that can accommodate up to 10 horses. There are no horses or other pack animals available for hire in or near the park. Park rangers warn that horses brought into the park should be accustomed to steep, rocky trails.

Wildlife Viewing

Because of the range of habitats here, and also because these canyons provide some of the few water sources in West Texas, Guadalupe Mountains National Park offers excellent opportunities for wildlife viewing and bird-watching. **McKittrick Canyon** and **Frijole Ranch** are considered among the best wildlife viewing spots, but a variety of species can be seen throughout the park. Those spending more than a few hours will likely see mule deer, and the park is also home to a herd of some 50 to 70 elk, which are sometimes seen in the higher elevations or along the highway in winter (I've seen them there myself, and they are enormous!). Other **mammals** include raccoons, striped and hog-nosed skunks, gray foxes, coyotes, gray-footed chipmunks, Texas antelope squirrels, black-tailed jack rabbits, and desert cottontails. Black bears and mountain lions also live in the park, but are seldom seen.

About two dozen varieties of **snakes** make their home in the park, including five species of rattlesnakes. Look for **lizards** in the mornings and early evenings. These include collared, crevice spiny, tree, side-blotched, and Texas horned lizards, and Chihuahuan spotted whiptails. The most commonly seen is the prairie lizard, identified by the light-colored stripes down its back.

More than 200 species of **birds** are known to spend time in the park, including peregrine falcons, golden eagles, turkey vultures, and wild turkeys. You are also likely to encounter rock wrens, canyon wrens, black-throated sparrows, common nighthawks, rufous-crowned sparrows, mountain chickadees, ladder-backed woodpeckers, solitary vireos, and western scrub jays.

Where to Stay & Eat

There are no accommodations or restaurants inside the park. The closest communities with lodging include **Carlsbad,** New Mexico, 55 miles north of the park (see "Carlsbad Caverns National Park," below). **Van Horn,** Texas, is another option, 45 miles south of the park. Beautifully restored in recent years to its original 1929 grandeur, **Hotel El Capitan,** 100 E. Broadway (www.thehotelelcapitan.com; ✆ **877/283-1220** or 432/283-1220; doubles $119–$139), is easily the most distinctive lodging near the park. Check out the photos on the website; the place is pretty nice for this part of Texas.

CAMPING

In the Park

The park has two developed vehicle-accessible campgrounds. Both are open year-round, cost $8 per night per person ($4 for Golden Age and Golden Access Passport holders), and have restrooms and drinking water, but no showers or RV hookups. **Pine Springs Campground** ★ is near the visitor center and park headquarters just off U.S. 62/180. There are 19 spaces for RVs, 20 very attractive tent sites, and two group campsites (call park headquarters for information). About a half-mile inside the north boundary of the park is **Dog Canyon Campground** (✆ **915/828-3251**), accessible from N. Mex. 137, with nine tent sites and four RV sites. Although reservations are not accepted, you can call ahead to check on availability of sites. Campstoves are allowed, but wood and charcoal fires are prohibited.

The park also has 10 designated **backcountry campgrounds,** each with five to eight sites. Be sure to pick up free permits at the Pine Springs Visitor Center or Dog Canyon Ranger Station on the day of or day before your backpacking trip. Water is available at trailheads, but is not available in the backcountry. All trash, including toilet paper, must be packed out. Fires are strictly prohibited; use cookstoves only. You can camp only in designated campgrounds.

A SIDE TRIP TO CARLSBAD CAVERNS NATIONAL PARK ★

One of the largest and most spectacular cave systems in the world, Carlsbad Caverns National Park comprises more than 100 known caves that snake through the porous limestone reef of the Guadalupe Mountains. Fantastic and grotesque formations fascinate visitors, who find every shape imaginable (and unimaginable) naturally sculpted in the underground—from frozen waterfalls to strands of pearls, soda straws to miniature castles, draperies to ice-cream cones. Plan to spend a full day.

Formation of the caverns began some 250 million years ago, when a huge inland sea covered this region. About 20 million years ago, a reef that was once undersea moved upward, ultimately breaking free of thousands of feet of sediment enshrouding it. As tectonic forces pushed the buried rock up, erosion wore away softer minerals, leaving behind the Guadalupe Mountains. Brine from gas and oil deposits mingled with rainwater, creating sulfuric acid that dissolved limestone and created cave passages.

Once the caves were hollowed out, nature took over, decorating the rooms with a variety of fanciful formations. Very slowly, water dripped down through the rock into the caves, dissolving more limestone and absorbing the mineral calcite and other materials on its journey. Each drop of water then deposited its tiny load of calcite, gradually creating the cave formations we see today.

Although American Indians had known of Carlsbad Cavern (the park's main cave) for centuries, it was not discovered by settlers until ranchers in the 1880s were attracted by sunset flights of bats emerging from the cave. A cowboy named Jim White, who worked for mining companies that collected bat guano for use as a fertilizer, began to explore the cave in the late 1800s. Fascinated by the formations, White shared his discovery with others, and soon word of this magical below-ground world spread.

Carlsbad Cave National Monument was created in October 1923. In 1926, the first electric lights were installed, and in 1930, Carlsbad Caverns gained national park status.

Underground development at the park has been confined to the famous Big Room, one of the largest and most easily accessible of the caverns, with a ceiling 25 stories high and a floor large enough to hold six football fields. Visitors can tour parts of it on their own, aided by a state-of-the-art portable audio guide, and explore other sections and several other caves on guided tours. The cave is also a summer home to about 300,000 Mexican free-tailed bats, which hang from the ceiling of Bat Cave during the day but put on a spectacular show each evening as they leave the cave in search of food, and again in the morning when they return for a good day's sleep.

Essentials

GETTING THERE The main section of Carlsbad Caverns National Park, with the visitor center and entrance to Carlsbad Cavern, the park's main cave, is located about 35 miles from Guadalupe Mountains National Park. From Guadalupe Mountains National Park, take U.S. 62/180 northeast to White's City, and turn left onto N. Mex. 7, the park access road. You enter the boundary of Carlsbad Caverns National Park almost immediately and reach the visitor center in about 7 miles. From the city of Carlsbad, head 30 miles southwest on U.S. 62/180 and then 7 miles on N. Mex. 7 to the visitor center.

For airport information, see the "Getting There" section under "Guadalupe Mountains National Park," earlier in this chapter.

VISITOR INFORMATION Contact **Carlsbad Caverns National Park,** 3225 National Parks Hwy., Carlsbad, NM 88220 (www.nps.gov/cave; ✆ **575/785-2232**). Books and maps can be ordered from the **Carlsbad Caverns Guadalupe Mountains Association,** 3225 National Parks Hwy, Carlsbad, NM 88220 (✆ **575/785-2232**).

The visitor center is open daily 8am to 7pm Memorial Day to Labor Day; and self-guided cave tours can be started from 8:30am to 5pm. During the rest of the year, the visitor center is open from 8am to 5pm, with self-guided cave tours from 8:30am to 3:30pm. Tour times and schedules may be modified during slower times in the winter. The park is closed on Christmas Day.

At the visitor center are displays depicting the geology and history of the caverns, bats and other wildlife, and a three-dimensional model of the caverns. Tours and other park activities, both above- and below-ground, are available. There is also a well-stocked bookstore, a restaurant, and a gift shop.

FEES Admission to the visitor center and aboveground sections of the park is free. The basic cavern entry fee, which is good for 3 days and includes self-guided tours of the Natural Entrance and Big Room, is $10 adults 16 and older and free for children 15 and younger. There are additional fees for guided tours. Annual passes and senior passes are good for the entry of four adults.

A general cave admission ticket is required in addition to tour fees for all guided cave tours except those to Slaughter Canyon Cave and Spider Cave. Reservations are required for all guided tours. Holders of annual and senior passports receive 50% discounts on tours. The Kings Palace guided tour costs $8 for adults, $4 for children ages 6 to 15, and is free for children ages 4 and 5 with an adult—younger children are not permitted. Guided tours of Left Hand Tunnel, limited to those age 6 and older, cost $7 for adults and $3.50 for children 6 to 15. Guided tours of Spider Cave, Lower Cave, and Hall of the White Giant are limited to those 12 and older, and cost $20 for adults and $10 for youths 12 to 15. Slaughter Canyon Cave tours, for those 6 and older, cost $15 for adults and $7.50 for children 6 to 15. You can make reservations for cave tours up to 3 months in advance online or by phone (www.recreation.gov; ✆ **877/444-6777**).

REGULATIONS & PERMITS As you would expect, damaging the cave formations in any way is prohibited. What some people do not understand is that they should not even touch the formations, walls, or ceilings. This is not only because many of the features are delicate and easily broken, but also because skin oils will both discolor the rock and disturb the mineral deposits that are necessary for growth.

All tobacco use is prohibited underground. In addition, food, drinks, candy, and chewing gum are not allowed on the underground trails. Those making wishes should not throw coins or other objects into the underground pools.

Cave explorers should wear flat shoes with rubber soles and heels, because of the slippery paths. Children 15 and under must remain with an adult at all times while in the caves. Although strollers are not allowed for younger children, child backpacks are a good idea, but beware of low ceilings and doorways along the pathways.

No photography is permitted at the evening "Bat Flight" programs without a special permit.

Pets are not permitted in the caverns, on park trails, or in the backcountry, and because of the hot summer temperatures, pets should not be left unattended in vehicles. A **kennel** (© **575/785-2281**) at the visitor center has cages in an air-conditioned room, but no runs, and is primarily used by pet owners for periods of 3 hours or so while they are on cave tours. Pets are provided with water, but not food, and there are no overnight facilities. Reservations cannot be made, and pets are accepted on a first-come, first-served basis ($10 per pet).

Free permits, available at the visitor center, are required for all overnight hikes into the backcountry.

WHEN TO GO The climate aboveground is warm in the summer, with highs often in the 90s (mid-30s Celsius) and sometimes exceeding 100°F (38°C), and evening lows in the mid-60s (teens Celsius). Winters are mild, with highs in the 50s and 60s (teens Celsius) in the day and nighttime lows usually in the 20s and 30s (around 0°C). Summers are known for sudden intense afternoon and evening thunderstorms; August and September see the most rain. Underground it's another story entirely, with a year-round temperature that varies little from its average temperature of 56°F (13°C), making a jacket or sweater a welcome companion.

Crowds are thickest in summer and on weekends and holidays year-round, so visiting on weekdays between Labor Day and Memorial Day is the best way to avoid them. January is the quietest month.

Visiting during the park's off season is especially attractive because the climate in the caves varies little regardless of the weather on top, where the winters are generally mild and summers warm to hot. The only downside to an off-season visit is that you won't be able to see the bat flights. The bats head to Mexico when the weather starts to get chilly, usually by late October, and don't return until May. There are also fewer guided cave tours off season, although tours will have fewer people. The best time to see the park might well be in September, when you can still see the bat flights, but there are fewer visitors than during the peak summer season.

RANGER PROGRAMS In addition to the cave tours, which are discussed below, rangers give a talk on bats at sunset each evening from mid-May to October at the cavern's Natural Entrance (times change; check at the visitor center or call © **575/785-3012**). Rangers also offer demonstrations, talks, guided nature walks, and other programs daily. Especially popular are the climbing programs, where rangers demonstrate caving techniques. In recent years, a series of stargazing programs has been presented by graduate students from New Mexico State University. The park also offers a **Junior Ranger Program,** in which kids can earn badges by completing various activities. Details are available at the visitor center.

On the second Thursday in August (usually), a "bat flight breakfast" from 5 to 7am lets visitors watch the bats return to the cavern after a night of insect hunting. Park rangers prepare breakfast for early-morning visitors for a small fee and then join them to watch the return flight. Call park for details.

What to See & Do

EXPLORING THE HIGHLIGHTS BY CAR

No, you can't take your car into the caves, but for a close-up as well as panoramic view of the Chihuahuan Desert, head out on the **Walnut Canyon Desert Drive,** a 9½-mile loop. You'll want to drive slowly on the one-way gravel road, both for safety and to thoroughly appreciate the dramatic scenery. Passenger cars can easily handle the tight turns and narrow passage, but the road is not recommended for motor homes or cars pulling trailers. Pick up an informational brochure at the visitor center bookstore.

CAVING ADVENTURES ★★★

Carlsbad Cavern (the park's main cave), Slaughter Canyon Cave, and Spider Cave are open to the general public. All guided tours must be reserved and have individual fees in addition to the general cave entry fee (see "Fees," above). Guided tours are sometimes fully booked weeks in advance, so reserve early.

Most park visitors head first to Carlsbad Cavern, which has elevators, a paved walkway, and an underground rest area. A 1-mile section of the Big Room self-guided tour is accessible to those in wheelchairs (no wheelchairs are available at the park), though it's best to have another person along to assist. Pick up a free accessibility guide at the visitor center.

The Big Room Tour, Natural Entrance Route, and King's Palace Guided Tour are the most popular trails, and all of them are lighted and paved, and have handrails. However, the Big Room is the only one of the three that's considered easy. The formations along these trails are strategically lit to display them at their most dramatic. This also means that today's visitors can see much more of the cave than early explorers, who were limited by their weak lanterns.

The **Big Room Self-Guided Tour** ★★★ is an easy 1-mile loop that you access by taking the visitor center elevator to the Underground Rest Area or via the Natural Entrance Route (see below). Considered the one thing that all visitors to Carlsbad Caverns National Park must do, this easy trail meanders through a massive chamber—it isn't called the Big Room for nothing—where you'll see some of the park's most spectacular formations and likely be overwhelmed by the enormity of it all. Allow about 1 hour.

The **Natural Entrance Route,** also 1 mile, is considered moderate to difficult, and is accessed outside the visitor center. This fairly strenuous hike takes you into Carlsbad Cavern on the same basic route used by the early explorers. You leave the daylight to enter a big hole, and then descend more than 750 feet into the cavern on a steep and narrow switchback trail, moving from the "twilight zone" of semidarkness to the depths of the cave, which would be totally black without the electric lights conveniently provided by the Park Service. The self-guided tour takes about 1 hour and ends near the elevators, which can take you back to the visitor center. However, I strongly recommend that from here you proceed on the Big Room Self-Guided Tour if you have not already been there.

The **King's Palace Guided Tour ★★** is a moderate 1-mile loop that you access by taking the visitor center elevator to the underground rest area. This 1½-hour ranger-led walk wanders through some of the cave's most scenic chambers, where you'll see fanciful formations in the King's Palace, Queen's Chamber, and Green Lake Room. Watch for the delightful Bashful Elephant formation between the King's Palace and Green Lake Room. Along the way, rangers discuss the geology of the cave and early explorers' experiences. Although the path is paved, there is an 80-foot elevation change.

Ranger-Led Cave Tours

In addition to the popular self-guided and guided tours discussed above, there are a number of ranger-led tours to less-developed sections of Carlsbad Cavern, which provide more of the experience of exploration and genuine caving than the above-mentioned tours over well-trodden trails. These caving tours vary in difficulty, but all include a period of absolute darkness, or "blackout," which can make some people uncomfortable. Because some tours involve walking or crawling through tight spaces, people who suffer from claustrophobia should discuss specifics with rangers before purchasing tickets.

Left Hand Tunnel starts in the visitor center near the elevator. It's the easiest of the caving tours, where you actually get to walk (rather than crawl) the entire time! Hand-carried lanterns (provided by the park service) light the way, and the trail is dirt but relatively level. You'll see a variety of formations, fossils from Permian times, and pools of water. Open to those 6 and older, this tour takes about 2 hours. The moderate **Lower Cave Tour,** a 1-mile round-trip, starts at the visitor center near the elevator. This 3-hour trek involves descending or climbing over 50 feet of ladders, and an optional crawl. It takes you through an area that was explored by a National Geographic Society expedition in the 1920s, and you'll see artifacts from that and other explorations. You'll see a variety of formations, including cave pearls, which look a lot like the pearls created by oysters and can be as big as golf balls. This tour is open to those 12 and older only. Four AA batteries are required for the provided headlamp; sturdy hiking boots and gloves are recommended.

The **Hall of the White Giant Tour,** which starts at the visitor center, is only .5 mile (one-way), but it is strenuous and takes around 3 to 4 hours as you crawl through narrow, dirty passageways and climb up slippery rocks. The highlight is, of course, the huge formation called the White Giant. Only those in excellent physical condition should consider this tour; children must be at least age 12. Four AA batteries for the provided headlamp and sturdy hiking boots are required; and kneepads, gloves, and long pants are strongly recommended.

More Cave Tours

It takes some hiking to reach the other caves in the park, so carry drinking water, especially on hot summer days. All children 15 and under must be accompanied by an adult; other age restrictions apply as well. Each tour includes a period of true and total darkness, or "blackout."

The **Slaughter Canyon Cave Tour ★★** is 1.25 miles round-trip and is considered moderate. The parking area is about a 45-minute drive from Carlsbad and is reached via U.S. 62/180, going south 5 miles from White's City to a marked turnoff that leads 11 miles to the parking lot. Discovered in 1937, this cave was mined for bat guano until the 1950s. It consists of a corridor 1,140 feet long with many side passageways. This highly recommended guided tour lasts about 2 hours, plus at least another half-hour to hike up the steep trail to the cave entrance. No crawling is involved, although the smooth flowstone and old bat guano on the floor can be slippery, so hiking boots are recommended. You'll see a number of pristine cave formations, including the crystal-decorated Christmas Tree, the 89-foot-high Monarch, and the menacing Klansman. The tour is open to children 6 and older; participants must bring their own flashlights.

The 4-hour tour of **Spider Cave** is a very strenuous, 1-mile loop (plus a .5-mile hike to and from the cave). Meet at the visitor center and follow a ranger to the cave. This tour is ideal for those who want the experience of a rugged caving adventure as well as some great underground scenery. Highlights include climbing down a 15-foot ladder, squeezing through very tight passageways, and climbing on slick surfaces—all this after a fairly tough, .5-mile hike to the cave entrance. But it's worth it. The cave has numerous beautiful formations—most much smaller than those in the Big Room—and picturesque pools of water. Children must be at least 12 years old. Participants need four AA batteries for the provided headlamps and good hiking boots. Kneepads, gloves, and long pants are strongly recommended.

BATS, BIRDS & OTHER WILDLIFE VIEWING

At sunset, from mid-May to October, a crowd gathers at the Natural Entrance to watch hundreds of thousands of **bats** take off for a night of insect hunting. An amphitheater in front of the Natural Entrance provides seating, and ranger programs are held nightly (times vary; check at the visitor center or call ✆ **575/785-3012**) during the bats' residence here (the bats winter in Mexico). The most bats will be seen in August and September, when baby bats born earlier in the summer join their parents and migrating bats from the north on the nightly forays. Early risers can also see the return of the bats just before dawn.

Bats aren't the only wildlife at Carlsbad Caverns, however. The park has a surprising number of **birds**—more than 300 species—many of which are seen in the Rattlesnake Springs area. Among species you're likely to see are turkey vultures, red-tailed hawks, scaled quail, killdeer, lesser nighthawks, black-chinned hummingbirds, vermilion flycatchers, northern mockingbirds, and western meadowlarks. In addition, each summer, several thousand cave swallows usually build their mud nests on the ceiling just inside the Carlsbad Cavern Natural Entrance (the bats make their home farther back in the cave).

Among the park's **larger animals** are mule deer and raccoons, which are sometimes spotted near the Natural Entrance at the time of the evening bat flights. The park is also home to porcupines, hog-nosed skunks, desert cottontails, black-tailed jack rabbits, and rock squirrels, as well as the more elusive ringtails, coyotes, and gray fox, sometimes seen in the late evenings along the park entrance road and the Walnut Canyon Desert Drive.

Where to Stay & Eat

There are no accommodations inside the park, but there are two concessionaire-operated restaurants (✆ **575/785-2281**). **Carlsbad Caverns Trading Company,** a family-style full-service restaurant at the **visitor center,** serves three meals daily in the $5 to $10 range. The restaurant is open from 8:30am to 5pm most of the year, with extended hours from Memorial Day to mid-August and on Labor Day weekend. The **Underground Rest Area,** a souvenir shop located inside the main cavern 750 feet below ground, has a snack-bar-style eatery with box lunches. Its hours are coordinated with cave hours.

Seven miles from the visitor center, the small town of White's City has a campground and amenities, but the closest recommended services are in and near the city of Carlsbad, 30 miles northeast of the turnoff to the park on U.S. 62. Here, you'll find several chain and franchise motels and a number of independent and chain restaurants. Motels on the southwest edge of the city, on the road to Carlsbad Caverns, include **Best Western Stevens Inn,** 1829 S. Canal St. (✆ **800/780-7234** or 575/887-2851; $89–$99 double). Also in this area is the **Days Inn,** 3910 National Parks Hwy. (✆ **800/325-2525** or 575/887-7800) with similar rates to the Best Western; and **Super 8 Motel,** 3817 National Parks Hwy. (✆ **800/800-8000** or 575/887-8888; $86–$101 double).

For more information, contact the **Carlsbad Chamber of Commerce,** 302 S. Canal St., Carlsbad, NM 88220 (www.carlsbadchamber.com; ✆ **575/887-6516**).

CAMPING

There are no developed campgrounds or vehicle camping of any kind in this national park. **Backcountry camping,** however, is permitted in some areas; pick up free permits at the visitor center.

There are numerous commercial **RV parks** on National Parks Highway on the way to the park, as well as in Carlsbad.

THE PANHANDLE PLAINS

12

The High Plains of northern Texas might not top the list of the most popular places to visit in the Lone Star State, and most people only stop when passing through en route to other states. Still, in many ways it may well be a cross section of the region: The small-town charm of the Great Plains, the spice of the Southwest, and the polite twang of the South are all present in equal measure. Beyond this cultural intersection, highways have crisscrossed the region since the 1930s, fostering a brood of cheap motels and kitschy roadside Americana. But with big skies and wide-open spaces dotted with newfangled windmills, you can see how even seemingly empty landscapes like this can fill the heart with wonder and wanderlust.

Inhabited by nomadic tribes for much of the past 12,000 years, the Panhandle Plains are distinguished by a high mesa—3,000 feet above sea level—that tapers downhill to the south and east, bordered by spectacular canyons and unique geological formations. In 1541, when Vásquez de Coronado ventured north in his quest for the fabled Seven Cities of Gold, he pounded stakes into the ground to claim the land for Spain—as well as mark his route for a return trip through the mostly featureless flatlands. Thus, the "Llano Estacado," Spanish for "staked plains," was born. Today, **Lubbock** inhabits the center of the mesa that Coronado staked out; **Amarillo** sits on its northern edge.

The late 19th century brought significant change to the area: Ranchers began to graze cattle here, railroads crisscrossed the mesa in all directions, and agriculture took hold as the predominant industry. Million-acre ranches became the norm. During the fall and winter of 1874 and 1875, the indigenous tribes battled the U.S. Army in the Red River War, culminating with the dispersal of Comanches, Kiowas, and Southern Cheyennes to reservations in Oklahoma.

The landscape was irrevocably altered again by the discovery of oil in the 1920s, when ranchers found themselves sitting on "black gold." The Dust Bowl days of the 1930s dampened development, but the area recovered and saw tremendous growth following World War II.

At first glance, the Panhandle Plains might appear monotonous, but the region is actually worth a closer look than you'll get from behind the wheel. The magnificent palette of **Palo Duro Canyon,** the lively nightlife in the university town of Lubbock (Buddy Holly's home), and Amarillo's ranching heritage—from cattle to Cadillacs—are unexpected diversions that make this area a worthwhile stop.

AMARILLO

122 miles N of Lubbock; 267 miles E of Albuquerque, New Mexico

The commercial center of the Texas Panhandle, Amarillo was born when the Fort Worth and Denver City Railway started laying track in the area in 1887, a decade after ranchers began to graze their cattle on the buffalo-grass-speckled plains. When the town was formally incorporated, the name Amarillo—meaning "yellow" literally and "wild horse" figuratively—was adopted from a nearby lake. In a little over a decade, the combination of the railroad and the ranchland led to the establishment of Amarillo's long-standing status as a cattle-shipping capital. To this day, the city "smells like money" most when the Amarillo Livestock Auction is in full swing.

While its agricultural roots remain the cornerstone of the local economy, Amarillo's location on a major east-west highway—Route 66 until 1970 and I-40 thereafter—has long made it a popular stopover for folks crossing the country, with a plethora of motels and restaurants catering to motoring tourists. Amarillo is fairly low-key and nondescript at first glance, but it's a pleasant, inexpensive spot for an overnight stay. Several of its attractions are must-see tourist traps, namely the roadside kitsch of Cadillac Ranch and the Big Texan Steak Ranch. As a destination, Amarillo can be a fun place to spend a weekend, especially for those with a taste for cowboy culture.

Essentials

GETTING THERE

BY PLANE More than 32 commercial flights take off or land on average daily from **Rick Husband Amarillo International Airport (AMA)** (✆ 806/335-1671), off I-40 exit 76 (Airport Blvd.) at 10801 Airport Blvd., 7 miles northeast of the city center. Airlines serving Amarillo include **American, Southwest,** and **United.** Car rentals are available from **Avis** (✆ 806/335-2313), **Hertz** (✆ 806/335-2331), **Enterprise** (✆ 806/335-9443), and **National** (✆ 806/335-2311).

BY CAR Coming from east or west, Amarillo can be accessed via I-40, exits 62 (Hope Rd.) through 75 (Lakeside Dr.). The primary downtown exit is 70 (Taylor/Buchanan sts.), and the airport is located northeast of exit 75.

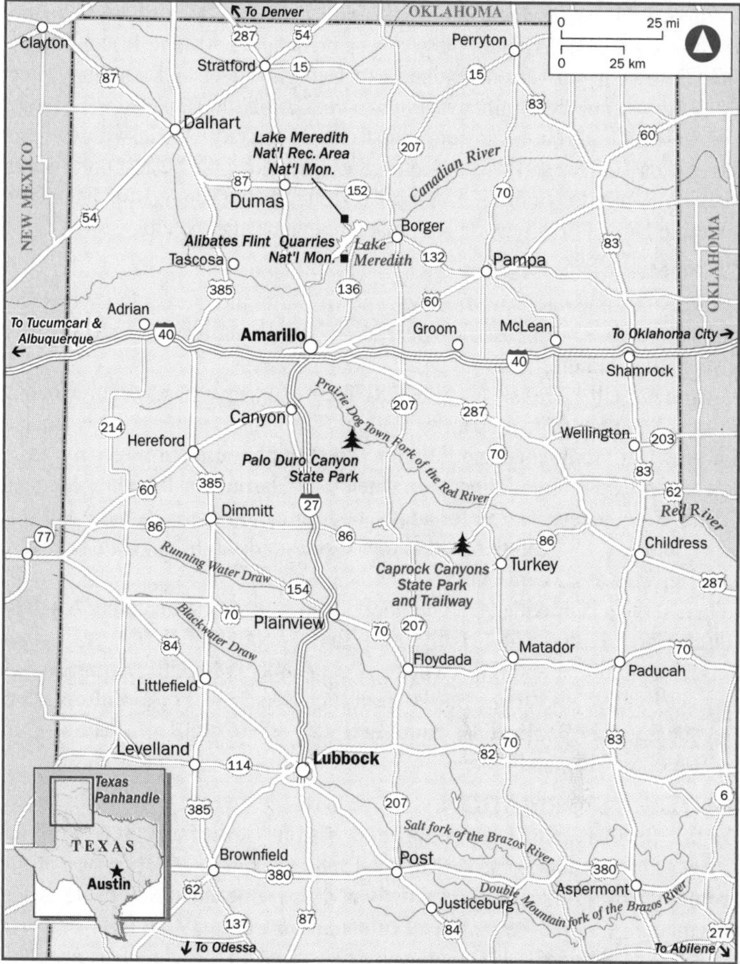

Coming from the north by car, you'll likely enter Amarillo via U.S. 87/287, which takes you through downtown and continues south to Canyon and Lubbock as I-27. If you are coming from the northwest, Texas FM 1061 can be used as a shortcut from U.S. 385; it becomes Tascosa Road as it enters Amarillo. U.S. 60 is the primary route northeast to Pampa and southwest to Hereford, and U.S. 287 veers east beyond the city, to Childress, and, beyond that, Wichita Falls and Fort Worth.

ORIENTATION

I-40 cuts through the heart of Amarillo, skirting the south side of downtown. The city's primary north-south artery is U.S. 87, which splits into four one-way, north-south streets in the downtown area. (From the west, these streets are Taylor, Fillmore, Pierce, and Buchanan.) South of I-40, U.S. 87 becomes I-27, which leads to Canyon and Lubbock. The northern boundary of downtown is 1st Avenue, the southern boundary I-40. The Route 66 Historic District begins at 6th Avenue and Georgia Street and continues west along 6th Avenue for a mile to Western Street. Amarillo Boulevard is a major east-west route through the northern stretch of the city. Along with Georgia Street, Ross-Mirror and Washington streets are among the busiest north-south roads in Amarillo. Loop 335 comprises four roads (Soncy Rd., FM 1719, Lakeside Dr., and Hollywood Rd.) that circumnavigate the city.

GETTING AROUND

Aside from some one-way streets downtown, Amarillo is easy to navigate by car, with relatively little traffic. (Instead of a rush hour, locals like to say they have a "rush minute.")

Amarillo City Transit (✆ **806/378-3095**) operates a bus system Monday through Saturday from 6:30am to 6:30pm. The main transfer point is located downtown at 3rd Avenue and Fillmore Street. Eight different routes run from downtown to the major shopping centers and Harrington Regional Medical Center. Ride tickets are 75¢ for adults, 60¢ for children ages 6 to 12 and students, and 35¢ for seniors 65+ and travelers with disabilities (with Medicare and City Transit ID card only).

Taxi service is provided by a number of cab companies, including **AA Discount Cab** (✆ 806/374-1110), **Ace's Taxi** (✆ 806/676-7263), **AJ's Taxi Service** (✆ 806/206-3621), **Airport Taxi** (✆ 806/358-8350), **Amarillo TX Taxi** (✆ 806/626-5015), **Bob's Taxi** (✆ 806/373-1171), **Bolton Taxi** (✆ 806/236-2240), **Jack & Son Taxi** (✆ 806/626-5015), **Yellow Cab** (✆ 806/626-5015), and more.

VISITOR INFORMATION

Contact the **Amarillo Convention and Visitor Council,** 1000 S. Polk St. (www.visitamarillotx.com; ✆ **800/692-1338** or 806/374-1497) or stop at the **visitor information center,** open daily at 401 S. Buchanan St. For statewide information, visit the **Texas Travel Information Center,** 9700 E. I-40 (www.txdot.gov; ✆ **806/335-1441**) on the city's east side on the south frontage road just west of I-40, exit 75.

FAST FACTS The **Northwest Texas Hospital,** 1501 S. Coulter Dr. (www.nwtexashealthcare.com; ✆ **806/354-1000**), and **Baptist St. Anthony,** 1600 Wallace Blvd. (www.bsahs.org; ✆ **806/212-2000**), are Amarillo's two largest hospitals. Amarillo's main **post office** is located at 2301 S. Ross St. (✆ **806/468-2101**) and is open Monday through Friday 8:30am to 5:30pm and Saturday 9:30am to noon, and closed on Sundays.

What to See & Do

THE TOP ATTRACTIONS

Amarillo Cultural Art District ★ In the fall of 2016, the Texas Commission on the Arts designated an Amarillo Cultural Art District comprising the city's historic downtown and its celebrated part of old Route 66, the Civic Circle, the Galleries at Sunset Center, Amarillo College, the Amarillo Museum of Art, and the Amarillo Little Theatre, where events such as **Jazz-tober** (free Tues-night jazz concerts in Oct), **High Noon on the Square** (Wed noon concerts in June, July, and early Aug on the Potter County Courthouse Lawn), and the **Electric Light Parade** (a night parade in Dec) are held. There are also jazz concerts on Tuesday nights in June on the lawn of the Amarillo Museum of Art and at Sam Houston Park near historic Route 66 at the Star-light Theater. The arts district is also home to **First Friday Art Walks** on the first Friday of each month from 5pm to 8pm at the Galleries at Sunset Center, a converted shopping mall with more than 55 galleries and 100 artists. Art is everywhere in Amarillo, with 102 life-size replicas of the great American quarter horse on display throughout the city to celebrate Amarillo's Western heritage and provide art in public places.

1000 S. Polk St. www.centercity.org/amarillo-cultural-district. ✆ **806/372-6744.**

Cadillac Ranch ★ You've likely seen this quirky roadside attraction in magazines and wondered what it is all about. Texas's iconic Cadillac Ranch isn't a ranch at all: It's an art installation made from 10 vintage Cadillacs (dat-ing 1949–64) half-buried nose-first in a cow pasture along I-40 just west of Amarillo. It was created in 1974 by three members of an avant-garde San Francisco art group known as "the Ant Farm" and funded by the late Stanley Marsh 3, an eccentric Amarillo millionaire. Although it's located on private land, visitors are allowed—even encouraged—to stop by and trespass. The owners don't even mind if folks add creative touches with graffiti and spray paint—the Cadillacs have been painted and repainted countless times, so why not stop and leave your mark?

I-40 W., on the south frontage road btw. exits 60 (Arnot Rd.) and 62 (Hope and Holiday rds.). Free admission. Daily 24 hr.

Route 66 Historic District ★ Just west of downtown Amarillo, this area preserves about a mile of the original Route 66. Once a suburb accessible by trolley car, this Rte. 66 district, now part of the Amarillo Cultural Art Dis-trict (see above) has evolved into a hub for the city's nightlife and shopping. Buildings that once housed drugstores and theaters are now home to eateries, antiques stores, and specialty shops.

6th Ave. btw. Western and Georgia sts. www.amarillo66.com. ✆ **800/692-1338.** Ama-rillo CVC.

MORE ATTRACTIONS

Amarillo has much more to offer than one might expect, including the **Ama-rillo Museum of Art,** on the campus of Amarillo College at 2200 S Van Buren St. (www.amarilloart.org; ✆ **806/371-5050** and 806-371-5392), a repository of regional 20th-century art and Asian exhibits. Families with young children may enjoy a visit to the Panhandle's preeminent children's science museum, the **Don Harrington Discovery Center,** 1200 Streit Dr. (www.discoverycenteramarillo.org; ✆ **806/355-9547**), also home to the innovative **Space Theater**, a domed planetarium and theater showcasing the wonders of space. For an old-fashioned family Midway, hop aboard the vintage rides at **Wonderland Amusement Park** at 2601 Dumas Dr., at Thompson Memorial Park (www.wonderlandpark.com; ✆ **800/383-4712** or 806/383-3344), including old-time roller coasters (such as the popular double-loop "Texas Tornado"), water rides (like "Shoot the Chute"), a carousel, a miniature golf course, and an arcade. Celebrating the story of the region's native peoples through art and culture, the pueblo-inspired **Kwahadi Museum of the American Indian**, located at 9151 I-40 E. (www.kwahadi.com; ✆ **806/335-3175**), is also a dance theater.

OUTDOOR ACTIVITIES

Amarillo offers many opportunities for outdoor recreation, including municipal golf courses, pools, and parks, as well as several lakes, reservoirs, and state parks in the surrounding area. The best recreation spot is **Palo Duro Canyon State Park** (p. 430), about 27 miles southeast of the city.

The **Lake Meredith National Recreation Area** (www.nps.gov/lamr; ✆ **806/857-6680**), located 38 miles northeast of Amarillo via Tex. 136, offers opportunities for boating, fishing, hunting, horseback riding, camping, hiking, swimming, scuba diving, wildlife viewing, and four-wheeling, although varying water levels (depending upon drought conditions) may impact boating options. Aside from boat-launching fees, access to Lake Meredith is free to the public; for more, see "Boating," below. The site is also home to **Alibates Flint Quarries National Monument**, the point of origin for a significant percentage of arrowhead points and flint tools found throughout the Great Plains. Although the monument is closed to most recreational activity, guided tours are offered at 10am and 2pm by reservation (www.nps.gov/alfl; ✆ **806/857-3151**).

Wildcat Bluff Nature Center, 2301 N. Soncy Rd. (www.wildcatbluff.org; ✆ **806/352-6007**), is the best spot for hiking and wildlife viewing in the city itself, with more than 2 miles of moderate trails on its 600 acres of cottonwood-shaded hills. The Nature Center is open Tuesday through Saturday 9am to 5pm; trails are open during daylight hours. Admission is $3 adults, $2 for kids and seniors, and free for kids 2 and younger.

BOATING **Lake Meredith National Recreation Area** (www.nps.gov/lamr; ✆ **806/857-3151**) was once the Panhandle's top watersports destination, but in recent years drought conditions caused lake levels to drop enough to close the marina. At press time the rain was falling again, bringing lake levels up and opening a boat ramp. When full, the main lake occupies 12,000 of the area's 46,000 acres and attracts boaters, windsurfers, water-skiers, and even scuba divers. Lake Meredith also offers a variety of free camping opportunities, including scenic overlooks, shoreline camping, and wooded campgrounds. No reservations are needed; sites are on a first-come, first-served basis. Trailer/RV hookups are not available. However, dump stations with potable water are located near the **Fritch Fortress** and **Sanford-Yake** campgrounds (www.nps.gov/lamr/planyourvisit/camping.htm).

FISHING Catfish and bass are the fish of choice for anglers in the Texas Panhandle, and several spots in and around Amarillo are quite popular. For no fee (you save the cost of a Texas state fishing license), visitors can fish in several "community fishing lakes" in Amarillo's city park system, stocked with channel catfish and/or rainbow trout. These include **Thompson Memorial Park** at Dumas Drive and 24th Avenue, **Martin Road Park** at NE 15th Avenue and Mirror Street, **Southeast Regional Park** at SE 46th Avenue and Osage Street, and **Harrington Regional Medical Center Park** at SW 9th Avenue and Wallace Street. **Lake Meredith National Recreation Area** is another popular fishing spot for the Panhandle. Fishing licenses can be obtained at local Wal-Marts and sporting-goods stores, including **Big 5 Sporting Goods,** 8004 I-40 W. (© **806/356-8115**).

GOLF The City of Amarillo Parks and Recreation Department manages four golf courses: two at the **Comanche Trail Golf Complex,** 4200 S. Grand St. (www.comanchetrail.com; © **806/378-4281**), with greens fees for 18 holes of $15 to $18; and two at **Ross Rogers Golf Complex,** 722 NE 24th Ave. in Thompson Memorial Park (www.amarilloparks.org; © **806/378-3086**), with greens fees of $21 to $24. At both courses, carts are $26 for 18 holes.

HIKING Aside from the hiking opportunities at **Wildcat Bluff Nature Center, Lake Meredith National Recreation Area** has two hiking trails. The **Devil's Canyon Trail** is a moderate one-way trail that leaves from Plum Creek on the north side of the lake and continues into the canyon for 1.5 miles. In the city limits, the **Rock Island Rail Trail** runs from Coulter Street on the west side to 7th and Crockett streets near downtown, 4 miles of jogging/biking/walking terrain in all. The area's best hiking destination is **Palo Duro Canyon State Park** (p. 430), about a half-hour drive southeast of Amarillo.

HORSEBACK RIDING There are several horse-friendly trails in **Lake Meredith National Recreation Area,** in McBride Canyon and alongside Plum Creek on the lake's north side. The National Park Service provides corrals at the Plum Creek and Mullinaw campgrounds, but riders need to bring their own horses. **Palo Duro Canyon State Park** also has horse trails and stables.

MOUNTAIN BIKING The closest mountain-biking trails to Amarillo are 27 miles away in **Palo Duro Canyon State Park** (p. 430). The 3-mile Devil's Canyon Trail at **Lake Meredith National Recreation Area** (see "Hiking," above) is also accessible to mountain bikers. In July 2016, 5 miles of new multi-use trails (part of the Harbor Bay Trail) opened, and plans are underway for 10 additional miles to open in the near future. The new trails are appropriate for intermediate-level hikers, and park officials suggest that before starting out, mountain bikers should become acquainted with the trail, which has several switchbacks.

SPECTATOR SPORTS

FOOTBALL The **Amarillo Venom** (www.govenom.com; © **806/378-4297**) play in the Indoor Football League, with home games at the Amarillo

Civic Center's Cal Farley Coliseum, 401 S. Buchanan St., from February to June. Walk-up ticket prices are $10 to $40.

HOCKEY The **Amarillo Bulls** (www.amarillobulls.com; ✆ **806/242-1122**) play in the North American Hockey League at the Cal Farley Coliseum (aka the Bull Pen), 401 S. Buchanan St. The schedule runs from September to March, with single-game ticket prices ranging from $9 to $23.

RACING Motor-sports enthusiasts can get their fix of racing action at **Route 66 Motor Speedway,** located about 10 miles east of downtown Amarillo at 3601 E. Amarillo Blvd. (www.route66motorspeedway.com; ✆ **806/383-7223**). The oval dirt track is a half-mile long. Races are held on Saturday nights from late April to late September; admission is $12 to $30.

RODEO The **Working Ranch Cowboys Association (WRCA;** www.wrca.org; ✆ **806/378-3096** for tickets) holds its annual **World Championship Ranch Rodeo** in Amarillo during the second week of November. Real working cowboys compete in such events as wild-cow milking, bronco riding, and team penning at the Amarillo Civic Center Auditorium, 401 S. Buchanan St. Tickets are $32 to $42. In October, marksmen on horseback test their skills at the **Cowboy Mounted Shooting Association World Championship** (www.cowboymountedshooting.com; ✆ **888/960-0003**). Several other major equestrian events are held in town during the fall and winter; contact the **Amarillo CVC** (www.visitamarillo.com; ✆ **800/692-1338**) for details.

Where to Stay

Amarillo's location on I-40 makes it an ideal stopping point on cross-country trips: You'll find dozens of chain motels located just off the interstate, including **Baymont Inn & Suites East,** 1700 I-40 E. at exit 71 (✆ **806/372-1425**), with rates of $60 to $85 double; **Hilton Garden Inn,** 900 I-40 W. (✆ **800/321-3232** or 806/355-4400), with rates of $109 to $179 double; and **Motel 6,** 3930 I-40 E. at exit 72B (✆ **800/466-8356** or 806/374-6444), with rates of $40 to $70 double. Room taxes in Amarillo add about 15% to lodging bills.

Courtyard by Marriott ★ If you want to stay in Amarillo's city center, this Courtyard by Marriott is your only lodging choice. Luckily, the striking 10-story redbrick is one of Amarillo's nicer hotels, housed in the handsomely renovated landmark Fisk Building (circa 1927). A lobby mural depicts historic Polk Street. The contemporary rooms come with sweeping city views. The hotel's **Bistro** restaurant serves breakfast and dinner, as well as beer and wine and Starbucks coffee, and several bars and restaurants are an easy stroll away on surrounding blocks.

724 S. Polk St. www.cyamarillo.com. ✆ **806/553-4500.** 107 units. $133–$189 double. **Amenities:** Restaurant; bar; exercise room and access to nearby health club; room service; Wi-Fi (free).

Wyndham Garden Inn ★★ This 10-story, 263-room Wyndham (formerly the Ambassador) is one of Amarillo's better hotels, with an attractive five-story atrium and indoor pool. Rooms have modern, comfortable furnishings and are nicely accented with warm colors and Texas touches of wood and leather. East-facing rooms on upper floors offer good views. The hotel bar and grill has been newly renovated.

3100 I-40 W. (exit 68B on Georgia St.). www.wyndhamhotels.com. ✆ **800/207-4421** or 806/358-6161. 263 units, including 3 suites. $99–$139 double; $300 suites. **Amenities:** Restaurant and bar; exercise room; Jacuzzi; indoor heated pool; Wi-Fi (free).

CAMPING

Several camping options exist in and around Amarillo, with numerous RV campgrounds in the city as well as primitive camping opportunities at Lake Meredith National Recreation Area (see "Outdoor Activities," p. 426). The recreation area does not have RV hookups, but it's free to stay there. See also "Palo Duro Canyon State Park" (p. 430).

Amarillo KOA ★ Located in a secluded spot near the airport on Amarillo's eastern fringe, this campground has pull-through and back-in RV sites, tent sites, and cabins. Facilities include a pet walk, a heated outdoor pool, free Wi-Fi, a playground, a game room, and a gift shop with sundries and RV supplies.

1100 Folsom Rd., Amarillo. www.amarillokoa.com. ✆ **800/562-3431** (reservations only) or 806/335-1792. 124 sites, including 8 regular sleeping cabins (without bathrooms) and studio cabin with bathroom and small refrigerator. $29–$37 campsites; $57–$100 cabins. Located east of Lakeside Dr. (I-40 exit 75) via U.S. 60.

Where to Eat

You'll find numerous restaurants and bars in the 700 block of **South Polk Street** in Amarillo, serving food ranging from Mexican to Asian to pub fare. Burger buffs will want to hit the ramshackle **Coyote Bluff Cafe,** 2417 S. Grand Ave. (✆ **806/373-4640**), a dinky local landmark clad in rusty signs and featuring troughs of iced beer and some of the best half-pound "prairie patties" (hamburgers) in the Panhandle. (They've got hot wings and rib-eyes, too.) Main courses are $5 to $15 at lunch and dinner.

The Big Texan Steak Ranch ★★ STEAK This historic Route 66 landmark is indeed an iconic Texas institution. Even if you've never been to Texas, you've probably heard of this place—or at least its offer of a 72-ounce steak, free to anyone brave (or foolish) enough to wolf it down in under an hour. More than 60,000 people have tried since its introduction in 1959, and only 9,000 have succeeded. A wrestler named Klondike Bill once inhaled two of the dinners within the hour limit, and competitive eater Joey Chestnut finished one in 8 minutes, 52 seconds. Not quite that hungry? Stop here anyway. The restaurant alone is a tourist attraction, with a horse corral, shooting gallery, and motel ($55–$90 double), filled to its cowboy-hat brim with Old West clutter and taxidermy. Costumed cowboy musicians often perform, and there are dances on some summer nights, as well as limos (with longhorn-mounts on the hoods) to ferry guests to and from hotels.

But Big Texan is not just a kingdom of cowboy kitsch. It's also a decent restaurant and home to the **Big Texan Brewery,** featuring craft beers. The big

DON'T PASS UP palo duro canyon

No trip through this part of Texas would be complete without seeing the Palo Duro Canyon, a 60-mile canyon sculpted by the Red River over the past 90 million years and now part of **Palo Duro Canyon State Park** (11450 Park Rd. 5, Canyon, TX 79015; www.palodurocanyon.com; ✆ **806/488-2227** or 512/389-8900 for advance reservations). With 800-foot cliffs striped with layers of orange, red, and white rock and adorned by groves of juniper and cottonwood trees, Palo Duro (Spanish for "hardwood") is a geology buff's dream: The base of the canyon is walled by red shales and sandstones from the Permian period (250 million B.C.); these are topped by colorful Triassic shales and sandstones; and the top of the canyon is made of a pastiche of stones only a few million years old. Of the 200 species of animals that venture into the canyon, you're most likely to see mule deer and wild turkeys. The park also holds the famed **Pioneer Amphitheatre,** the venue for the musical drama *TEXAS* (p. 431); several hiking, biking, and horseback riding **trails;** and a **visitor center/museum** with interpretive exhibits. The park offers 100 campsites, including 7 pull-throughs, 75 back-ins, and 18 tent sites. Primitive sites, equestrian sites, and seven cabins are also available. Fees for day use are $5 adults and free for children 12 and under. Fees are $12 to $24 for campsites, and $60 to $125 for cabins.

thing here are still the thick, juicy steaks. You can also get barbecued ribs, fried chicken, fried seafood, and burgers, and breakfast and lunch are equally hearty.

7701 I-40 E. www.bigtexan.com. ✆ **800/657-7177** or 806/372-6000. Reservations accepted for large parties only. Main courses $6–$14 breakfast, $9–$14 lunch, and $9–$72 dinner. Daily 7am–10:30pm.

BL Bistro ★★★ NEW AMERICAN Amarillo may be a small town, but BL Bistro can hold its own against any big-city eatery. With sleek modern interiors and shaded outdoor dining areas, BL Bistro may well be Amarillo's best fine dining spot. For over a decade, owner/chef Bryan Sanders has served fresh fare to discriminating diners, delighting them with starters like pan-seared calamari, charred edamame, and marinated lamb "Hot Rock" seared tableside. Even more impressive are his main courses, like seared chile-lime scallops and rosemary lamb pasta. Chef Sanders also offers prime steaks, like the hand-cut Black Angus rib-eye. Look for weekly lunch specials, and fresh sushi on Friday and Saturday nights.

2203 S. Austin St. www.blbistro.com. ✆ **806/355-7838.** Reservations recommended. Main courses $12–$34. Mon–Fri 11am–2pm and 5–10pm; Sat 5–10pm; Sun 11am–2pm.

Shopping

Amarillo's biggest enclosed shopping center is the **Westgate Shopping Mall,** 7701 I-40 W., between the Coulter Drive and Soncy Road exits (www.westgatemalltx.com; ✆ **806/358-7221**). The mall's stores include Dillard's, Gap, Forever 21, JCPenney, Eddie Bauer, and more, as well as a movie theater and several restaurants. Westgate is open Monday through Saturday 10am to 9pm and Sunday noon to 6pm.

The **Historic 6th on Route 66** (www.amarillo66.com) offers a wealth of antiques stores and craft shops at 3522 W. 6th Ave. between Georgia and Western streets. Art lovers should head to the **Galleries of Sunset Center,** 3701 Plains Blvd. (www.sunsetartgalleryofamarillo.com; ✆ **806/353-5700**), a smartly converted shopping center that's now home to a collective of some 55 galleries and 100 artists.

Western wear is big in Amarillo. **Cavender's Boot City,** 7920 I-40 W. at Coulter Drive (www.cavenders.com; ✆ **806/358-1400**), has a huge selection of boots, along with hats, belt buckles, jeans, jewelry, and practically every other Western garment under the sun.

Amarillo Nightlife

THE PERFORMING ARTS

The best places to check for performing arts events in Amarillo are **www.artsinamarillo.com** and **www.panhandletickets.com**.

Amarillo Little Theatre, 2019 Civic Circle (www.amarillolittletheatre.org; ✆ **806/355-9991**), produces about 10 plays a year at two theaters southwest of downtown. Established in 1927, ALT is one of the oldest continuously operating community theaters in the country. The ALT Mainstage focuses on musicals and lighter fare, while the Adventure Space produces edgier, adult-oriented productions. Recent shows include *Brighton Beach Memoirs, Young Frankenstein,* and *Hairspray.* Ticket prices range from $12 to $21.

The **Amarillo Opera** (www.amarilloopera.org; ✆ **806/372-7464**) produces two main-stage operas annually, one each in the fall and spring, and an annual spirituals concert on the first weekend of every February. Performances take place at the Globe-News Center for the Performing Arts, 400 S. Buchanan St., and tickets are priced from $15 to $100. The **Amarillo Symphony** (www.amarillosymphony.org; ✆ **806/376-878**) performs classical and pops concerts year-round, also at the Globe-News Center; tickets for most concerts cost between $16 and $52.

Lone Star Ballet (www.lonestarballet.org; ✆ **806/372-2463**) presents a season of local and guest performances from October to April at the

A Texas-Size Musical Drama: *TEXAS*

The nation's biggest outdoor musical drama ***TEXAS,*** a grand summer showcase of song, dance, and amazing fire and water effects, covers the Panhandle's colorful past. It's held Tuesdays through Saturdays from early June to mid-August at the Pioneer Amphitheatre in Palo Duro Canyon State Park. The family-friendly 2-hour show, which has thrilled more than 4 million visitors for more than 50 years, features a cast of singers, dancers, and horses, and finishes with a fantastic fireworks show. Tickets are $14 to $30 adults, $13 to $31 children 12 and under. For an extra $16 ($9 children), enjoy the show's Chuck Wagon Bar-B-Que dinner at 6pm. You can even take kids on a backstage tour. The admission fee to the state park is waived at 5:30pm for those with tickets to the show. Visit **www.texas-show.com** or call ✆ **806/655-2181.**

Globe-News Center. The local company produces *The Nutcracker* annually on the second weekend of December, and occasionally puts on joint performances with the Amarillo Symphony. Tickets are $15 to $50.

NIGHTCLUBS & BARS

The main nightlife district in Amarillo is **South Polk Street** downtown, between 7th and 8th avenues. **Bodega's,** 709 S. Polk St. (© **806/378-5790**), is dance club with DJs. **Crush Wine Bar & Deli,** 701 S. Polk St. (www.crushdeli.com; © **806/418-2011**), is a cozy wine bar and club, and locals seem to like **Butlers Martini Lounge,** 703 S. Polk St. (www.facebook.com/butlers.martinibar; © **806/376-8180**). The **Golden Light Cafe & Cantina,** 2908 W. 6th Ave. (www.goldenlightcafe.com; © **806/374-9237**), is a Route 66 landmark open since 1946, with a grill and oodles of nostalgia and live music for the country-music lover and fans of the Americana music scene.

LUBBOCK

122 miles S of Amarillo; 100 miles SE of Clovis, New Mexico

The first Anglo explorers to happen upon the site of modern-day Lubbock were less than impressed. "It spreads forth into a treeless, desolate waste of uninhabited solitude, which has always been and must continue, uninhabited forever," wrote Capt. Randolph Marcy.

Capt. Marcy would be shocked to see Lubbock today. This city of about 250,000 residents is the economic and cultural center of the surrounding South Plains, the home of Texas Tech University, and the self-described "nursery" for Austin's music scene. Indeed, Lubbock's musical heritage is legendary: Buddy Holly still reigns as the local king, but Tanya Tucker, Mac Davis, Waylon Jennings, Jimmie Dale Gilmore, Joe Ely, and Dixie Chick Natalie Maines are also from this area.

Named after Col. Thomas Lubbock, a Confederate officer, Lubbock was established in 1890 and grew rapidly, its economy built on cotton and cattle and, later, oil and gas. The city has long been a regional hub—hence the nickname "Hub City." One glance at a map and the nickname's appropriateness becomes clear: Lubbock is surrounded by dozens of small agricultural towns.

A town with the second-largest contiguous university campus in the nation, home to a law school and an agricultural school, Lubbock makes a fun stopover for a night, thanks to its lively Depot District and college hot spots. If you're in town during a Texas Tech "Red Raiders" football game, you'll be sure to make friends with diehard fans enjoying tailgate parties in parking lots, fields, backyards, and businesses all over town.

Essentials

GETTING THERE

BY PLANE **Lubbock Preston Smith International Airport,** 5401 N. Martin Luther King Blvd. (www.flylia.com; © **806/775-2044**), sees 70 arrivals and departures daily. Four airlines serve the airport: **American, United, Delta,** and **Southwest.**

Most of major car-rental agencies, including **Avis** and **Hertz,** have desks at the airport. **Royal Coach Towne Car Service** (✆ **806/795-3888**) offers airport transportation in Lincoln Town Cars into the city for $15 to $30.

BY CAR Lubbock sits at the intersection of three major highways on the "Port to Plains" route; I-27 enters the city from the north and becomes U.S. 87 south of Lubbock. Cutting down from Clovis, New Mexico, northwest of the city, U.S. 84 continues southeast to I-20 near Abilene. U.S. 62/82 is the third major highway that runs through Lubbock, entering town from the southwest, where it is the primary route to and from Carlsbad and Roswell, New Mexico, and continuing through the plains to the east.

GETTING AROUND

Getting around Lubbock is fairly stress-free: It is laid out on a standard grid with few anomalies, with I-27 bisecting the city north-south and Loop 289, a major highway, circling it. Downtown is located just west of I-27, accessible via either exit 3 (19th St.) or exit 4 (4th St.). The east-west streets in central Lubbock are numbered, beginning with 1st in the north, and the north-south streets surrounding I-27 are arranged alphabetically, from Avenue A on the east side of the highway and continuing to Avenue X on the west side of I-27. University Avenue and 19th Street outline two sides of the Texas Tech campus, and once you've found those streets, you'll be able to find your way to and from most places you want to go in town.

CitiBus (www.citibus.com; ✆ **806/712-2000**), Lubbock's mass transit system, operates 11 routes Monday through Friday from 5:25am to 7:45pm and Saturday from 6:45am to 7:55pm. No service is offered on Sunday. The main downtown transfer station is located at the intersection of Broadway and Buddy Holly Avenue (the equivalent of Ave. H). Fares are $1.75 for adults, $1.25 for children 6 to 12, 85¢ for Medicare, seniors, and persons with disabilities; and free for children 5 and under. A $3.50 day pass allows for unlimited rides.

Taxi service is provided by **Yellow Cab** (✆ **806/765-7777**). Rideshare lovers and Tech students like using their **Uber** app (www.uber.com) here.

VISITOR INFORMATION

Visit Lubbock, the city's official Convention & Visitors Bureau, at the Wells Fargo Center, 1500 Broadway, 6th floor (www.visitlubbock.org; ✆ **800/692-4035** or 806/747-5232), provides local maps and information on lodging, dining, and attractions.

FAST FACTS The **University Medical Center,** 602 Indiana Ave. (www.umchealthsystem.com; ✆ **806/775-8200**), operates a 24-hour emergency room. The main **post office** is located downtown at 411 Ave. L and is open Monday through Friday from 8:30am to 5pm.

What to See & Do

THE TOP ATTRACTIONS

Buddy Holly Center ★★★ MUSEUM If you're a rock-'n'-roll fan, and even if you're not, don't miss this little museum paying tribute to Lubbock's favorite native son, legendary rock pioneer Buddy Holly, who died at the age of 23 in a plane crash, along with the Big Bopper and Ritchie Valens. Permanent exhibits showcase the life and music of Holly, whose comet-like rise left an unforgettable impact on rock, influencing everyone from the Beatles to the Grateful Dead. As Sir Paul McCartney said, "At least the first 40 songs we wrote were Buddy Holly–influenced." The collection includes interactive exhibits and such memorabilia as Holly's trademark horn-rimmed glasses recovered from the crash site, alongside his guitars and other personal mementos. A 20-minute documentary tells you more about the man and his music. The newest exhibit, introduced in January 2017, features Holly's childhood bedroom furniture, along with other items belonging to the Buddy Holly Educational Foundation of London and the Center. Also not to be missed is the **J. I. Allison House,** adjacent to the Center, where you can walk inside the carefully re-created home of Jerry Allison, drummer for Holly's band, the Crickets, and stand in the very rooms where and Allison and Holly wrote hits like "That'll Be the Day." Across the street from the Center, check out the **Buddy Holly Statue** and the **West Texas Walk of Fame,** honoring Holly and other musical stars from the area. The **Lubbock Fine Arts Gallery,** also located in the Center, has rotating exhibits. Diehard fans can also get directions to Holly's gravesite; his former 1957 home (1305 37th St.); and the historical marker on the lot at 1911 6th Street that marks his birthplace. Don't leave Lubbock without having your photo taken in front by the giant-size replica of Buddy Holly's glasses.

1801 Crickets Ave. in the Depot Entertainment District. www.mylubbock.us/departmental-websites/departments/buddy-holly-center. ✆ **806/775-3560.** $8 adults, $6 seniors, $7 children 7–17 and students, free for children 6 and under. Tues–Sat 10am–5pm; Sun 1–5pm. Closed Monday major holidays.

LHUCA: The Louise Hopkins Underwood Center for the Arts ★★★ ART CENTER Presenting visual, performing, and literary arts, this progressive art center cultivates and celebrates the arts by inspiring creativity and engaging with the community. LHUCA is the force behind Lubbock's First Friday Art Trail events, as well as programs, classes, artists in residence, gallery openings, a clay studio with open space for artists, film festivals, and more in this not-for-profit organization's stunning gallery and classroom space.

511 Ave. K. www.lhuca.org. ✆ **806/762-8606.** Free admission (donations appreciated). Tues–Sat 11am–5pm; Closed Sun–Mon and major holidays.

Museum of Texas Tech University ★★ MUSEUM A cultural treasure house holding some 7 million artifacts and artworks, including dinosaur fossils and vintage Western wear, the Texas Tech Museum covers a lot of bases, from visual arts to science and history to the humanities. Look for both permanent and regularly rotating exhibits—like a recent "In the Blood" exhibit on the natural history and pop culture of vampires. Don't miss the **Moody Planetarium** (public shows: daily $2 adults, $1 students and seniors, free children 4 and under). Next door, the **National Ranching Heritage Center** is dedicated to preserving the country's history of ranching. Here visitors can explore some 40 relocated historic buildings, touring authentic structures like a 1783 *vaquero* corral and an 1850 log cabin. The center hosts several annual events, including a "Summer Stampede" Western Art and Gear Show in June and "Candlelight at the Ranch" in December.

Museum: 3301 4th St. at Indiana Ave. www.depts.ttu.edu/museumttu. ✆ **806/742-2490.** Free admission. Tues–Sat 10am–5pm (until 8:30pm Thurs); Sun 1–5pm. Open until 9pm for First Friday Art Trail on the first Fri of each month. Closed major holidays. **National Ranching Heritage Center:** 3121 4th St. at Indiana Ave. www.depts.ttu.edu/ranchhc. ✆ **806/742-0498.** Free admission. Mon–Sat 10am–5pm; Sun 1–5pm. Open until 9pm for First Friday Art Trail on the first Fri of each month. Closed major holidays.

MORE ATTRACTIONS

American Wind Power Center ★ MUSEUM Dedicated to the American-style water-pumping windmill and related exhibits on wind electricity, this is a unique and worthwhile museum displaying a collection of 200 water-pumping windmills. The center also houses an art gallery and gift shop.

1701 Canyon Lake Dr. www.windmill.com. ✆ **806/747-8734.** Adult admission $7.50; children (5–12 years) $5; seniors (60+) and veterans $6; family of 4 (2 adults and 2 children) $20; active duty military and their household families admitted free with military ID. Tues–Sat 10am–5pm; Sun 2–5pm. Closed Mon and major holidays. Located 1 mile west of I-27 via 19th St.

Science Spectrum Museum & OMNI Theater ★★ MUSEUM Children and tinkerers of all ages will delight in the interactive exhibits at this museum, whose mission is to educate kids about science and technology. It covers a wide-ranging spectrum from fossils to physics. A greeting by an animatronic T-Rex leads you into the dinosaur exhibit, and you can get up close and personal with native lizards, snakes, and turtles in the Demo Dock. New exhibits focusing on physical science include Circuit Benches, Launch Rockets, and Air Cars. The facility is also home to the OMNI Theater, with a 58-foot domed screen.

2579 S. Loop 289 (btw. Indiana and University aves.). www.sciencespectrum.com. ✆ **806/745-2525.** Admission $8 adults, $6.50 seniors and children 3–12, free for children 2 and under. Omni Theater tickets, adults $7, and seniors and children $5.50. Combo Theater/Museum tickets, adults $11.50, and seniors and children $9.50. Mon–Fri 10am–5pm; Sat 10am–6pm; Sun 1–5pm. Closed major holidays.

Texas Tech University ★★★ UNIVERSITY CAMPUS You really haven't seen Lubbock if you haven't visited (or at least driven through) the sprawling Texas Tech University campus. With its Spanish-tile red rooftops, broad boulevards, stately Ivy League–style brick buildings, enormous lazy river pool, and recreation center to rival the best in the U.S., it's an impressive campus. From theaters where big-name acts perform to the giant Texas Tech stadium where a masked rider comes out on a black horse to open the games while fans toss tortillas (yes, it's a thing here), the campus is the pride and joy of the High Plains. Little-known fact: Texas Tech is the second-largest contiguous campus in the United States and is also home to a health sciences center, an agriculture college, and a law school.

Btw. University Ave., 19th St., 4th St., and Indiana Ave.

OUTDOOR ACTIVITIES

Within the city limits of Lubbock, the 248-acre **Mackenzie Park ★**, east of I-27 at 4th Street (✆ **806/775-2687**), is the largest recreation area, with two golf courses (one traditional and one Frisbee); walking, jogging, and equestrian trails; and **Prairie Dog Town,** one of the few active prairie-dog colonies in the urban United States.

Caprock Canyons State Park and Trailway ★ (www.tpwd.state.tx.us; ✆ **806/455-1492**) is a 2½-hour drive from Lubbock, located to the northeast near Quitaque off Tex. 86. Like Palo Duro Canyon to the northwest, this 15,313-acre park provides a startling contrast to the plains in its jagged formations of red rock and diverse vegetation. An abandoned railroad line was converted into a 65-mile trail system that travels along a canyon floor, through a one-time railroad tunnel, and up a steep incline onto the mesa of the High Plains. Hikers, bikers, and horses are permitted on the trail. Several other hiking opportunities exist in the park as well. Primitive backcountry campsites are available for $12 nightly, as well as tent sites for $10 to $14 and sites with partial RV hookups for $17 to $22. Additionally, boaters and fishers can take advantage of Lake Theo, located on the south side of the park. The park charges a $4 adult daily entrance fee, but children 12 years and younger are free.

BOATING Two boat ramps access the spring-fed **Buffalo Springs Lake,** Tex. 835, 5 miles east of Loop 289 (www.buffalospringslake.net; ✆ **806/747-3353**). Gate fees are $10 adults, $9 college students with valid ID, and $5 children 11 and younger and seniors; plus $5–$12 per watercraft and $10 per ATV, UTV, or dirt bike.

GOLF Lubbock has several public 18-hole golf courses, including **Shadow Hills Golf Course,** 6002 3rd St. (www.shadowhillsgolf.com; ✆ **806/793-9700**), with greens fees of $17 to $27 ($25–$35 with golf cart); **Rawls Golf Course,** 4th Street and Texas Tech Parkway on the campus of Texas Tech (www.therawlscourse.com; ✆ **806/742-4653**), with greens fees of $36 to $64, cart included; and **Meadowbrook Golf Course,** 601 Municipal Dr. in Mackenzie Park (www.meadowbrooklubbock.com; ✆ **806/765-6679**), with two 18-hole courses and greens fees of $18 to $36 with cart or $13 to $28 without. Nearby, the **Mackenzie Park Disk Golf Course** is free, although you'll need your own Frisbee.

HIKING Four miles of nature trails snake around **Lubbock Lake Landmark** as well as the 65-mile trailway at **Caprock Canyons State Park** (see above). Several miles of walking and jogging trails, many of which are horse-friendly, are within the city limits at **Mackenzie Park,** 4th Street and I-27 (✆ **806/775-2687**).

MOUNTAIN BIKING There are a few trails at **Buffalo Springs Lake,** Tex. 835, 5 miles east of Loop 289 (see "Boating," above), but Lubbock's hardcore mountain bikers head north to **Palo Duro Canyon State Park** (see "Don't Pass Up Palo Duro Canyon" box, earlier in this chapter) and **Caprock Canyons State Park** (see above).

SWIMMING Lubbock is home to four municipal pools, all outdoor and open from late May to early August: **Clapp Municipal Swimming Pool,** 4600 Ave. U; **Mae Simmons Community Center,** 2004 Oak St.; **Maxey Park,** 4007 30th St.; and **Montelongo,** 3200 Bates St. In season, each is open from 1 to 6pm daily with an admission fee of $2.50 adults and $2 children 11 and under and seniors and active military members with ID. For details, call ✆ **806/775-2670.** The **YWCA,** 3101 35th St. (www.ywcalubbock.org; ✆ **806/792-2723**), has a year-round indoor pool. Swimming costs $5 for a day pass.

SPECTATOR SPORTS

The Lubbock home crowd roots for the **Texas Tech Red Raiders** (www.texastech.cstv.com; ✆ **806/742-4412**), who compete in Big 12 athletics, including football, baseball, and basketball.

Where to Stay

You'll find Lubbock's greatest concentration of hotels and motels in three areas: downtown; off of I-27 between 50th Street and Loop 289; and in the city's southwest corner, off Loop 289 near Quaker and Indiana avenues. Rates are highest on the weekends when Texas Tech hosts home sporting events, graduations, and parents' weekend.

Among the city's many chain properties are **Courtyard by Marriott,** 4001 S. Loop 289 (✆ **800/321-2211** or 806/795-1633), with rates of $116 to $149 double; **Embassy Suites by Hilton,** 5215 S. Loop 289 (✆ **800/362-2779** or 806/771-7000), with suites for $129 to $159; and **Motel 6,** 909 66th St. (✆ **800/466-8356** or 806/745-5541), with rates of $42 to $52 double.

Room taxes in Lubbock add 13% to lodging bills.

MCM Eleganté Hotel & Suites ★ A favorite hotel of many Red Raider parents and alums, and a popular stay for business travelers, this former Holiday Inn is one of Lubbock's largest hotels, located adjacent to the Civic Center. In the hotel's east tower, six stories of rooms surround a sunny atrium, and the property also features a nice indoor pool. Rooms are comfortable, though not fancy, and there is a restaurant downstairs. A free hot breakfast, including fresh eggs cooked to order, is another plus, making it a good choice for families.

801 Ave. Q. www.mcmelegantelubbock.com. ✆ **806/763-1200.** 293 units, including 72 suites. $119–$139 double; $139–$169 suite. **Amenities:** Restaurant; bar; exercise room; small indoor pool; room service; complimentary shuttle to/from airport, campus, and within a 3-mile radius; Wi-Fi (free).

Overton Hotel & Conference Center ★★ This is my first choice for lodging whenever we visit our son at Texas Tech. On the eastern edge of the TTU campus, close to the Red Raiders' Jones AT&T stadium, this AAA Four-Diamond hotel is arguably the nicest hotel in town. Contemporary but with subtle West Texas touches, the 14-story Overton has a large ground-floor conference center and handsome guest rooms, each with a king or two queen beds and great views of campus. Book a room on the Preferred Level for access to the private 14th-floor Club Lounge offering evening wine and snacks and an array of breakfast goodies, too, along with free coupons for a full breakfast buffet downstairs. Rates are reasonable, and the location can't be beat—especially if you're in town for a Red Raider home game; that's when the Overton turns its lobby and one of its enormous ballrooms into a tailgate-style party spot with jumbo screens and a big buffet of good eats.

2322 Mac Davis Lane. www.overtonhotel.com. ✆ **806/776-7000.** 303 units. $149–$204. **Amenities:** Restaurant; bar; preferred-level rooms; exercise room; Jacuzzi; outdoor heated pool; business center; conference center/ballrooms; room service; Wi-Fi (free).

CAMPING

Buffalo Springs Lake, FM 835 (www.buffalospringslake.net; ✆ **806/747-3353**), has one of the most scenic campgrounds in the area, with 33 shady sites and three tent areas. Camping fees are $25 a night for tents, and $35 to $40 per night for full hookups. **Caprock Canyons State Park** (www.tpwd.texas.gov/state-parks/caprock-canyons; ✆ **806/455-1492**) is another popular camping destination, with primitive backcountry sites ($10) and tent sites ($12–$14), as well as sites with partial RV hookups ($17–$22). Campsites are $9 to $12 at **Lake Alan Henry** (www.lakealanhenry.org; ✆ **806/775-2673**), 65 miles southeast of Lubbock. See "Outdoor Activities," above, for complete information on these parks.

Where to Eat

Café J ★ MEDITERRANEAN/NEW AMERICAN This vine-covered restaurant with a Spanish-tile roof is across the street from the Texas Tech campus. Contemporary yet comfortable, with warm colors and soft lighting, it has raised the bar for fine dining in these parts. The menu offers fresh, light options, like pasta primavera, organic salads, seared ahi tuna, and a tasty cream of green chile soup. More filling options include a bubbling crock of French onion soup, a beef tenderloin filet, or scrumptious bacon-wrapped sea scallops served with pumpkin risotto. Desserts also are divine. Art adorns the walls (most of it for sale). The restaurant also has a happening bar, cocktail lounge, and covered patio, and on most Friday and Saturday nights, Cafe J has live music from 10pm on. An a la carte brunch is offered on Saturdays and Sundays.

2605 19th St. www.cafejlubbock.com. © **806/743-5400.** Reservations accepted only for parties of 5 or more. Main courses $7–$15 lunch, $9–$30 dinner. Sun and Tues–Fri 11am–2:30pm; Tues–Thurs 5:30–10pm; Fri–Sat 5:30–11pm. Bars open later.

The Triple J Chophouse & Brew Co. ★ STEAK/BURGERS This Depot District restaurant on the old downtown strip (Buddy Holly Ave.) is one of the reasons I like Lubbock so much—it makes the town seem like so much fun. This Western-themed college joint and microbrew pub is a hit with all ages. Roomy booths and tables line a long seating area below brick walls adorned with horns and Texas photography; the slick bar sits directly in front of the glass-enclosed brew tanks. The menu focuses on beef but also offers seafood, wood-fired pizzas, and comfort food (potpies, rib tips, chicken-fried steak). Steaks are great, so don't fill up on the tempting chips and salsa (not tortilla chips per se; more like crispy fried wontons). Waiters scribble their names in crayon on paper tablecloths, and live music is often playing in back by the bar. It's the kind of place that would make Buddy Holly proud. A longhorn mount hung upside-down shows support for the Red Raiders, not to mention a bit of irreverence toward rivals (particularly the UT Austin Longhorn mascot Bevo).

1807 Buddy Holly Ave., in the Depot District. www.triplejchophouseandbrewco.com. © **806/771-6555.** Reservations not accepted. Main courses $7–$25. Mon–Thurs 11am–10pm; Fri–Sat 11am–midnight. Bar open later.

Shopping

Lubbock is home to the region's largest mall, **South Plains Mall,** 6002 Slide Rd. at South Loop 289 (www.southplainsmall.com; © **806/792-4653**), which houses about 150 stores, including Barnes & Nobles, Dillard's, Eddie Bauer, Sears, Foot Locker, American Eagle Outfitters, and many other stores, specialty shops, and restaurants. Mall hours are 10am to 9pm Monday to Saturday, and noon to 6pm on Sunday.

Lubbock Nightlife

THE PERFORMING ARTS

Built in 1938, the charming, retro **Cactus Theater,** 1812 Buddy Holly Ave. (www.cactustheater.com; © **806/762-3233**), a beautifully restored vintage movie theater in the Depot District, is now the attractive centerpiece of Lubbock's performing arts scene, with stage performances and more. Tickets run $15 to $40.

Lubbock Symphony Orchestra, 1313 Broadway, Ste. 2 (www.lubbocksymphony.org; © **806/762-1688**), performs 10 classical concerts and one pops concert every year at the Lubbock Civic Center Theater (at 6th St. and Ave. O), often featuring guest conductors and musicians from around the world. Ticket prices range from $10 to $60.

Established in 1926, the **Texas Tech University Theatre,** on the Texas Tech campus on 18th Street between Boston and Flint avenues (www.depts.ttu.edu/theatreanddance; ✆ **806/742-3603**), has produced more than 1,000 plays since its founding. Recent productions include *You Can't Take It With You* and *Avenue Q*. The theater also hosts ballets, experimental plays, and one-act play festivals. Tickets are $10 to $12; student tickets $5.

NIGHTCLUBS & BARS

Lubbock has a bustling nightlife, thanks, primarily, to the presence of 35,000 (and growing) Texas Tech students. You'll find the highest concentration of clubs in and around the vibrant **Depot Entertainment District,** located between Texas Avenue and I-27 around 19th Street, including the **Blue Light,** 1806 Buddy Holly Ave. (www.thebluelightlive.com; ✆ **806/762-1185**), known for its live music, singer/songwriter nights, and its hip, young crowd. Also in the neighborhood, you can line-dance and two-step to live country music at **Wild West,** 2216 I-27 (www.wildwestlubbock.com; ✆ **806/741-3031**). **Cricket's Grill and Draft House,** 2412 Broadway (www.cricketsgrill.com; ✆ **806/744-4677**), is a rowdy Texas Tech hangout with nearly 100 beers on draft.

Many restaurants morph into bustling nightspots after sundown, including the **Texas Cafe and Bar,** 3604 50th St. (www.texascafeandbarthespoon.com; ✆ **806/792-8544**). If you imbibe, try the city's signature cocktail, the Chilton. Invented by a local doctor of the same name, the drink consists of vodka, fresh-squeezed lemon juice, and soda, in a salt-rimmed glass—it's tart but refreshing.

PLANNING YOUR TRIP TO TEXAS

13

First thing to know about Texas? It's big. The second-largest state in the U.S., after Alaska, comprises an area of 268,820 square miles/696,200km. If you think you can wrap your head around that, just wait until you try to drive across it. You'd have to drive 894 miles (that's almost 14 hours at 65 mph) to get from the South Texas border town of Brownsville up to the North Texas/Oklahoma border town of Texoma. Texas is even bigger than most European countries; it's 10% larger than France and almost twice as large as Germany, only it doesn't have either country's fabulous passenger rail service or spot-on public transportation. You're going to need a car to get around the Lone Star State.

Given the state's sheer size, it's probably not a surprise that Texas is a true mix of urban and rural. It has 3 of the top 10 cities in the nation in terms of population, as well as some of the largest ranches and open spaces found in the country (the famous King Ranch, for example, comprises 825,000 acres [333,865.65 hectares], with land in six counties). So, given how large the state is, even with the highest speed limit in the USA, travel time by car or train can be lengthy. Don't assume that once you get here it's easy to zip from Dallas to Austin and on to Houston and Galveston in the blink of an eye. Crossing the state takes an enormous amount of time and effort, making regional vacations the way to go for most travelers.

As with any trip, before you start your journey to Texas, a little preparation is essential. This chapter provides a variety of planning tools, including information on how to get here; tips on accommodations; and on-the-ground resources. Also, check out the interactive Texas Trip Planner offered online by **Texas State Travel Guide** (www.traveltexas.com/trip-plan#).

GETTING THERE

By Plane

The state's major airports are **Dallas/Fort Worth International (DFW), George Bush Intercontinental (IAH)** and **William P. Hobby (HOU)** in Houston, **San Antonio International (SAT),** and **El Paso International (ELP).** American Airlines has its hub in Dallas, United Airlines (which merged with Continental) is based in Houston, and formerly regional and now national carrier Southwest Airlines is headquartered in Dallas.

By Car

More than 3,000 miles of interstate highways crisscross this huge state, connecting four major urban areas to each other and to cities in nearby states. Some relevant mileages: Houston to Dallas, 225 miles; Dallas to Galveston, 268 miles; Houston to Austin, 146 miles; and San Antonio to Houston, 189 miles.

If you're planning a road trip, it's a good idea to join the **American Automobile Association** (www.texas.aaa.com; ✆ **800/765-0766**). In Texas, AAA regional headquarters is at 6555 Hwy. 161, Irving (✆ **469/221-6006**); there are also offices in many other cities, including Amarillo, Austin, Dallas, El Paso, Houston, and San Antonio. Members get access to excellent maps, trip planning, and free **emergency road service** (✆ **800/AAA-HELP [222-4357]**).

For information on driving, car rentals, and gas in Texas, see "Getting Around/By Car," below.

By Train

Amtrak (www.amtrak.com; ✆ **800/USA-RAIL [872-7245]**) operates three lines that travel through Texas. The **Sunset Limited** has stops at Beaumont/Port Arthur, Houston, San Antonio, Del Rio, Sanderson, Alpine, and El Paso on its New Orleans–to–Los Angeles run; the **Heartland Flyer** travels from Oklahoma City to Fort Worth (where it connects with the Texas Eagle); and the **Texas Eagle** runs from Los Angeles to San Antonio (where you can connect with the Sunset Limited) and on to Chicago, with stops at El Paso, Austin, Dallas, and Fort Worth. For the names and locations of various railway stations in major cities of Texas, see "Orientation" in the individual city chapters of this guide.

GETTING AROUND

Texas is huge, so it's highly unlikely you'll try to see it all in one visit. Most visitors will explore either one or two cities or a relatively small section of the state. For those visiting major cities, it's easy to fly in, use public transportation, and then fly or take the train to the next city (see the individual city chapters for airline and rail information). However, those who plan to see a variety of Texas locales—within reasonable distance—will find that the most practical way to see Texas is by car. A good option would be to do Austin and San Antonio with a side trip to the Hill Country on your first visit, or San Antonio and Austin on with a side trip to the Texas coast (Port Aransas), Dallas and Fort Worth on another visit, and Houston and Galveston on a third visit. Then perhaps save West Texas for a Big Bend hiking or family trip for another season.

By Plane

A number of airlines offer flights between Texas's major cities; see "Getting There/By Plane," above, and individual city chapters.

Attention visitors to the U.S. from abroad: Some major airlines offer special discount tickets to transatlantic or transpacific passengers through **Visit USA AirPass,** which allows mostly one-way travel from one U.S. destination to another at very low prices. Usually unavailable in the U.S., these discount tickets must be purchased abroad in conjunction with your international fare. This system is the easiest, fastest, cheapest way to see the country. Inquire with your air carrier.

By Car

Driving is an excellent way to see Texas in small chunks—roads are well maintained and well marked, and a car is often the most economical and convenient way to get somewhere; in fact, if you plan to explore beyond the cities—which we highly recommend—it's practically the only way to get to some places. Of course, the main argument against driving is the distance between many destinations covered in this book.

Texas often has some of the lowest gasoline prices in the United States; although prices fluctuate, in 2016 the average price for unleaded gas was $2.06 per gallon, with the lowest prices in the Gulf Coast area (for current prices, check out www.texasgasprices.com). Taxes are already included in the printed price. One U.S. gallon equals 3.8 liters, or .85 imperial gallons.

Major highways that crisscross the state include I-20 from West Texas to Dallas–Fort Worth and all the way to Louisiana; I-35 from the Oklahoma border to Dallas–Fort Worth, Austin, and San Antonio to the Mexican border at Nuevo Laredo; I-10 from El Paso to San Antonio; and I-45 from Houston to Dallas. The "Pickle Parkway" toll road, or Texas State Highway 130, makes

On the Road Again

Texas maintains 77,000 miles of roadways, including interstates, U.S. highways, state highways, and farm-to-market (designated FM on signs) roads. Furthermore, it has some 48,000 bridges on public roads—the most in the nation. It also has the highest speed limit in the nation (85 mph) on sections of certain lonesome highways and toll roads, like parts of Texas State Highway 130 (SH 130), also known as the Pickle Parkway, between Austin and Seguin.

it quicker (at 80–85 mph) to get from Georgetown, Texas (just north of Austin), to San Antonio or South Texas, without going through Austin traffic.

Access points into Texas include I-40 (from Oklahoma and New Mexico); I-10 (from New Mexico); U.S. 69/75 and I-44/U.S. 287 (from Oklahoma); U.S. 77 and I-35 (from Oklahoma); I-10 and I-20 (from Louisiana); I-30 (from Arkansas); and U.S. 77 and U.S. 83 (Harlingen/Valley border crossing). ***Note:*** Expect delays crossing into Texas from Mexico, especially now that the border area is problematic with drug and violence issues.

Once you leave the interstates, a veritable spider web of roads will take you just about anywhere you want to go, at least until you venture into the vast emptiness of the southwest plains. This seemingly uncharted area contains two of the gems of the state, however: Big Bend and Guadalupe Mountains national parks. These two places make it worth the effort to find a way to get there.

Traffic in major cities, such as Houston, Dallas, and Austin, can be congested and frustrating, especially during rush hours, and distances are often great. Away from the cities, however, you'll often find roads to be practically deserted.

Because much of Texas has a relatively mild climate, snow and ice are not usually a problem. However, those traveling to or through Amarillo and other northern sections of the state in winter should check weather reports frequently—being stranded by an ice storm is not entirely uncommon. Be sure to bring plenty of water along and check your radiator in summer; cars can quickly overheat under hot, sultry conditions.

All the major rental-car companies operate in Texas, including **Ace, Advantage Alamo, Avis, Budget, Dollar, Enterprise, E-Z Rent A Car, Hertz, National, Sixt,** and **Thrifty.** International visitors who plan to rent a car in the United States should keep in mind that even though foreign driver's licenses are usually recognized in the U.S., you may want to consider getting an international driver's license. Note that insurance and taxes are almost never included in quoted rental car rates in the U.S. Be sure to ask your rental agency about additional fees for these. They can add a significant cost to your car rental. Many rental-car agencies have non-negotiable age requirements, both minimum-age (generally 25 or older) and upper-age limits (often 70–75 for certain vehicles); find out what the age limits are for rentals in Texas.

Check out **BreezeNet.com** (www.bnm.com), which offers domestic car-rental discounts with some of the most competitive rates around. Also worth visiting are Kayak, Orbitz, Hotwire, Travelocity, and Priceline, all of which offer competitive online car-rental rates.

For anyone considering crossing into Mexico, the border region has received a lot of attention for violence, often drug-related. It's wise to acquaint yourself with the most recent warnings about Mexico and border crossings. Visit the U.S. Department of State at **www.travel.state.gov** for travel alerts and tips for traveling abroad. See also "Texas: Gateway to Mexico," below.

Texas Driving Times & Distances

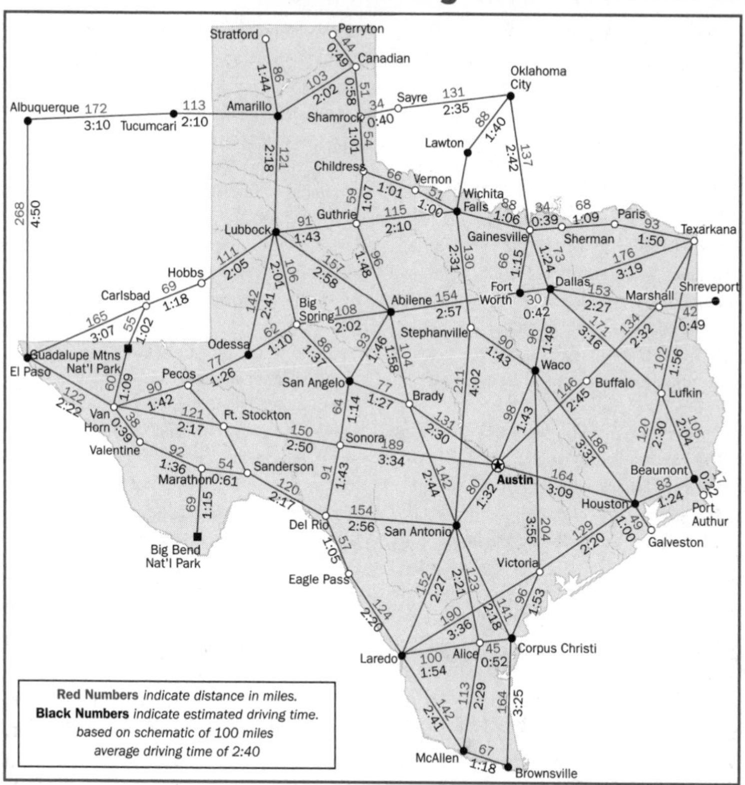

INSURANCE If you hold a private auto insurance policy, you are probably covered for loss or damage to the rental car, and liability in case a passenger is injured. The credit card you used to rent the car also may provide some coverage.

Car-rental insurance probably does not cover liability if you caused the accident. Check your own auto insurance policy, the rental company policy, and your credit card coverage for the extent of coverage: Is your destination covered? Are other drivers covered? How much liability is covered if a passenger is injured? (If you rely on your credit card for coverage, you may want to bring a second credit card, as damages may be charged to your card and you may find yourself stranded with no money.)

DRIVING RULES Texas law requires all drivers to carry proof of insurance, as well as a valid driver's license. Safety belts must be worn by all front-seat occupants of cars and light trucks; children 16 and under must wear safety belts regardless of where they are in the vehicle; and children 3 and

TEXAS: gateway TO MEXICO

Many travelers believe that a vacation in western or southern Texas would not be complete without an excursion across the border into Mexico, to visit the picturesque shops, dicker for colorful pottery and inexpensive jewelry, and sample genuine Mexican food. In our experience, the shopping is especially enjoyable—you really can get some bargains—and the food is often spectacular. Mexican border towns welcome tourists and almost universally accept U.S. currency—in fact, for many of these communities, tourism is the primary source of income.

Remember, however, that a trip across the border, even if you just walk across for the afternoon, constitutes a trip to a foreign country, and the laws of Mexico, not the United States, apply. In addition, these border towns are often hotbeds of drug smuggling, so stick to the main tourist areas and, it should go without saying, never let anyone convince you to carry anything across the border for them.

U.S. and Canadian citizens must carry a passport if they plan on crossing back into the U.S. A Mexican tourist card (available from Mexican officials at the border) is required for those going beyond the border towns into Mexico's interior, or those planning to stay in the border towns for more than 72 hours. Other foreign nationals will need a passport and the appropriate visas.

Travelers driving cars beyond the border towns will need vehicle permits, available from Mexican officials at the border, and those driving cars across the border for any distance at all should first buy insurance from a Mexican insurance company (short-term insurance is available at the border and at travel clubs such as AAA). If you're only planning to cross the border, visit a few shops, sample Mexican

under, or under 36 inches tall, regardless of where they're sitting, must be in approved child seats. Since September 2011, the maximum speed limit on most interstate highways is 75 or 80 mph (with the exception of the 85 mph section of certain highways like Texas State Highway 130, mentioned above); and the maximum on numbered non-interstates is normally 70 mph during daylight and 65 mph at night, unless otherwise posted. For a list of speed limits that have been raised to 75 or higher, go to the **Texas Department of Transportation** website, www.txdot.gov/driver/laws/speed-limits/approved.html. Motorcyclists are required to wear helmets, and radar detectors are legal.

MAPS A good state highway map is available free at any state information center or by mail (see "Visitor Information" on p. 461, later in this chapter). Maps can also be purchased at bookstores, gas stations, and most supermarkets and discount stores.

ROAD CONDITIONS Texas roads are among the best in the western United States, and the state's generally moderate weather keeps snow closures to a minimum. However, icy roads are fairly common in the northern sections of the state during winter, and hurricanes can cause flooding in late summer and early fall along the Gulf Coast. The **TxDOT 24-hour hotline** (✆ **800/452-9292**) food, and then cross back into Texas, consider leaving your car on U.S. soil and walking. This will save you the hassles of having to get Mexican car insurance and any red tape if you are involved in an accident; of course, then you'll end up having to carry any purchases you make across the border.

Warning: It is a felony to take any type of firearm or ammunition into Mexico; you could easily end up in jail and have your car confiscated. In addition, there are a number of regulations regarding taking pets across the border, plus fees, so it is usually best to board pets on the U.S. side.

When reentering the United States from Mexico, you will be stopped and questioned by U.S. Customs officials, and your car may be searched. U.S. citizens may bring back up to $800 in purchases duty-free every 30 days, including 1 liter of liquor, 100 cigars (except Cuban cigars, which are prohibited), and one carton of cigarettes. Duty fees are charged above those amounts, and Texas charges a tax of about $1 per liter on all alcoholic beverages. Items that may not be brought into the United States, or which require special permits, include most fruits and vegetables, plants, animals, and meat.

The above is just a brief summary of the complex laws related to traveling between the U.S. and Mexico. There are more details in the official state vacation guide available from the Texas Department of Transportation (see "Visitor Information" in "Fast Facts," later in this chapter); for complete information, contact **U.S. Customs** (www.cbp.gov; ✆ **202/354-1000**) and the **Mexican Government Tourism Office** (www.visitmexico.com; ✆ **800/446-3942** or 713/722-2581). A good online source of information is **www.mexonline.com**.

provides automated info on road conditions statewide; information is also available online at www.dot.state.tx.us/travel/road_conditions.htm.

For additional information, including charted routes, a mileage calculator, regional maps for download, driving tours, and travel information centers geared to road travel, visit www.traveltex.com/plan-your-trip/laws-highway-info. You can also call **TxDot** ✆ **800/452-9292** for other travel information and trip-planning assistance.

By Train

More than a dozen towns and cities in Texas are linked by rail, with mostly daily service from Amtrak. See "Getting There," above, and "Orientation" in individual destination chapters for more information.

International visitors can buy a **USA Rail Pass,** good for 15, 30, or 45 days of unlimited travel on **Amtrak** (www.amtrak.com; ✆ **800/USA-RAIL [872-7245]** in the U.S. or Canada; ✆ **001/215-856-7953** outside the U.S.). The pass is available online or through many overseas travel agents. See Amtrak's website for the cost of travel within the western, eastern, or northwestern United States. Reservations are generally required and should be made as early as possible. Regional rail passes are also available.

Driving the "Drive Friendly" State

For years, the Texas Department of Transportation (TxDot, as it is called in Texas) has been urging motorists to "drive friendly," and apparently many of them have taken that message to heart, especially in rural areas. When you approach a slow vehicle from behind on a two-lane road, more often than not, that vehicle will pull onto the shoulder, while maintaining speed, to let you pass without having to go into the oncoming lane. Fortunately, most Texas state highways have good, wide shoulders so there's little danger. We're not sure if this is technically legal or not, but everybody in rural Texas does it, including state troopers. However, road rage is not uncommon in Texas, and you should think twice before sending an obscene gesture the way of a driver who has just cut you off—especially if that driver is in a pickup truck with a gun rack on the back (also not uncommon in many parts of the state). Do note that when you approach a stopped emergency vehicle with lights flashing, state law requires that you move a lane away from the emergency vehicle, or slow down 20 miles per hour below the posted speed limit. Failure to comply could result in a fine of up to $200.

By Bus

Bus travel is often the most economical form of public transit for short hops between Texas and U.S. cities, but it's certainly not an option for everyone (most travelers find Amtrak more comfortable and often similar in price). **Greyhound** (www.greyhound.com; ✆ **800/231-2222** in the U.S.; ✆ **001/214/849-8100** outside the U.S. with toll-free access) is the sole nationwide bus line. Texas bus lines with service to and within the state include **Arrow Trailways of Texas, Kerrville Bus Co.** (www.iridekbc.com), and **Valley Transit Co.** (www.valleytransitcompany.com).

International visitors can obtain information about the **Greyhound North American Discovery Pass.** The pass, which offers unlimited travel and stopovers in the U.S. and Canada, can be obtained outside the United States from travel agents or through www.discoverypass.com.

Growing in popularity across the USA is **Megabus** (www.us.megabus.com; ✆ **800/462-6342**) with city-to-city daily express bus tickets as low as $1, linking Dallas, Austin, San Antonio, and Houston in Texas, and offering free Wi-Fi and at-seat power outlets. Make reservations and purchase tickets online; if you do it by phone, there will be an additional $5 charge. A recent search showed a typical Megabus fare from Dallas to Austin was $25 and San Antonio to Dallas was $33, though lower fares may certainly be available.

TIPS ON ACCOMMODATIONS

Across the state, Texas offers a variety of lodging options, from typical American chain motels in convenient or airport locations to luxury hotels, historic hotels, and bed-and-breakfast inns, as well as some pleasant and inexpensive mom-and-pop independent motels, cabins, and ranch-style resorts. A number of hotels really resonate with Texas flavor and charm. To make your lodging an integral part of your Texas experience, we recommend choosing a unique or historic property where available and/or choosing one in the neighborhood where you want to spend most of your time. Quite a few historic bed-and-breakfasts are discussed in this guide, and rates are fairly reasonable—especially considering the wonderful breakfasts prepared at most of them. Why spend $80 or more for a boring motel room and then another $10 to $15 for breakfast when, for just a bit more, you can instead sleep in a handsome inn, decorated with antiques, and be served a delightful, home-cooked breakfast?

The Texas Department of Transportation publishes the *Texas State Travel Guide,* the *Texas Events Calendar,* and a *Texas Campground Guide,* all of which can be ordered by calling ✆ **800/452-9292.**

The nonprofit **Texas Bed & Breakfast Association** (www.texasbb.org; ✆ **979/836-5951**) offers a free directory describing more than 100 member bed-and-breakfasts, country inns, unique hotels, and guesthouses. You can also get lodging information from the **Texas Hotel & Lodging Association** (www.texaslodging.com; ✆ **800/856-4328**). Another good resource is **Bed & Breakfast Inns Online** (www.bbonline.com; ✆ **800/215-7365**), where you can view interior and exterior photos of almost every property profiled, including several listed on the National Register of Historic Places. The site offers last-minute, midweek, and seasonal specials, besides a variety of other packages. The guest house/B&B service I always turn to for the best Hill Country lodging, in Fredericksburg and beyond, is **Gastehaus Schmidt Reservation Service** (www.fbglodging.com; ✆ **866/427-8374**). Of course **Airbnb** (www.airbnb.com) is also a popular option for travelers who want to rent a home, condo, apartment, room (or even a couch) when traveling.

House swaps aren't for everyone—clean freaks and people with control issues should skip this section. But you may find that staying in a private home while its owners stay in yours can be a comfortable and cost-effective alternative to booking a hotel. **HomeLink International** (www.homelink.org; ✆ **800/638-3841** or 813/975-9825) is an established house-swapping service. Home swaps in Dallas, Houston, Austin, and other Texas cities can be found through **Craigslist.org**.

HomeAway (www.homeaway.com), one of the nation's largest vacation rental sites (with homeowners across the country offering both short- and long-term rentals) is based in Austin, and on the website you'll find all kinds of listings for homes in the Texas Hill Country, Big Bend National Park area, along the Texas Gulf Coast, and in major cities.

[Fast FACTS] TEXAS

Area Codes Major area codes in Texas are: Dallas (**214, 972**), Fort Worth (**817**), Arlington (**817**), Houston (**713, 281**), Austin (**512**), San Antonio (**210, 830**), El Paso (**915**), Waco (**254**), Corpus Christi (**361**), Galveston (**409**), east Texas (**211, 936**), and south Texas (**956**).

Business Hours Offices are usually open weekdays from 9am to 5pm. Banks are open weekdays from 9am to 3pm or later, and sometimes

Saturday mornings. Stores typically open between 9 and 10am and close between 5 and 6pm Monday through Saturday. Stores in shopping complexes or malls tend to stay open late, until about 9pm on weekdays and weekends, and many malls and larger department stores are open on Sundays. A growing number of discount stores (such as Wal-Mart) and grocery stores are open 24 hours a day.

Car Rental See "Getting There/By Car," earlier in this chapter.

Cellphones See "Mobile Phones," below.

Crime See "Safety," later in this section.

Customs For details regarding U.S. Customs and Border Protection, consult your nearest U.S. embassy or consulate, or **U.S. Customs** (www.cbp.gov). Also, see the "Texas: Gateway to Mexico" box, p. 446.

Disabled Travelers Most disabilities shouldn't stop anyone from traveling in the U.S. Thanks to provisions in the Americans with Disabilities Act, most public places are required to comply with disability-friendly regulations. Almost all public establishments (including hotels, restaurants, museums, and so on, but not including certain National Historic Landmarks) and at least some modes of public transportation provide accessible entrances and other facilities for those with disabilities.

Trip-Ability.com (www.trip-ability.com) has destination reviews of Houston and Austin, detailing everything from airport, hotel, and restaurant facilities to wheelchair-accessible activities and arts facilities. On a very positive note, San Antonio inaugurated **Morgan's Wonderland** (www.morganswonderland.com; ✆ **877/495-5888**), the world's first theme park for special-needs children and adults and their families, in 2010. This park is fun for kids of all abilities and ages.

The **America the Beautiful—National Park and Federal Recreational Lands Pass—Access Pass** (formerly the **Golden Access Passport**) gives persons who are visually impaired or permanently disabled (regardless of age) free lifetime entrance to federal recreation sites administered by the National Park Service (NPS), including the Fish and Wildlife Service, the Forest Service, the Bureau of Land Management, and the Bureau of Reclamation. This may include national parks, monuments, historic sites, recreation areas, and national wildlife refuges. The pass can be obtained only in person at any NPS facility that charges an entrance fee. You need to show proof of a medically determined disability. Besides free entry, the pass also offers a 50% discount on some federal-use fees charged for such facilities as camping, swimming, parking, boat launching, and tours. For more information, go to www.nps.gov/fees_passes.htm, or call the United States Geological Survey (USGS), which issues the passes, at ✆ **888/275-8747.**

Doctors See "Health," below.

Drinking Laws The legal age for purchase and consumption of alcoholic beverages is 21; proof of age is required and often requested at bars, nightclubs, and restaurants, so it's always a good idea to bring ID when you go out. Do not carry open containers of alcohol in your car or any public area that isn't zoned for alcohol consumption; the police can fine you on the spot. Don't even think about driving while intoxicated.

Minors can legally drink as long as they are within sight of their 21-or-older parents, guardians, or spouses. Where you can or cannot buy a drink, and what kind of drink, is determined in Texas by local option elections, so the state is essentially a patchwork of regulations. In most parts of the state, you can buy liquor, beer, and wine by the drink. However, there are a few areas where you can buy only beer (which Texas defines as having no more than 4% alcohol; anything higher is "ale") and others where you can purchase beer or wine by the glass, but not liquor. There are also some areas that are completely dry—mostly in the Panhandle Plains and near the state's eastern border—and other confusing areas where one county will be "dry" (meaning you have to join private clubs—membership is normally free and immediately granted—to drink in restaurants, and liquor stores will stock beer and wine only) and the county right next to it will be "wet" (meaning you can drink in bars and restaurants).

Driving Rules See "Getting Around," earlier in this chapter.

Electricity Like Canada, the United States uses 110 to 120 volts AC (60 cycles), compared to 220 to 240 volts AC (50 cycles) in most of Europe, Australia, and New Zealand. Downward converters that change 220–240 volts to 110–120 volts are difficult to find in the United States, so bring one with you. Wherever you go, bring a connection kit of the right power and phone adapters, a spare phone cord, and a spare Ethernet network cable—or find out whether your hotel supplies them to guests.

Embassies & Consulates All embassies are in the nation's capital, Washington, DC Some consulates are in major U.S. cities, and most nations have a mission to the United Nations in New York City. If your country isn't listed below, call for directory information in Washington, DC (✆ **202/555-1212**) or check **www.embassy.org/embassies**.

The embassy of **Australia** is at 1601 Massachusetts Ave. NW, Washington, DC 20036 (www.usa.embassy.gov.au; ✆ **202/797-3000**). Consulates are in New York, Honolulu, Houston, Los Angeles, and San Francisco.

The embassy of **Canada** is at 501 Pennsylvania Ave. NW, Washington, DC 20001 (www.cic.gc.ca; ✆ **202/682-1740**). Other Canadian consulates are in Buffalo (New York), Detroit, Los Angeles, New York, and Seattle.

The embassy of **Ireland** is at 2234 Massachusetts Ave. NW, Washington, DC 20008 (www.dfa.ie/irish-embassy/USA; ✆ **202/462-3939**). Other Irish consulates are in Boston, Chicago, New York, and San Francisco.

The embassy of **New Zealand** is at 37 Observatory Circle NW, Washington, DC 20008 (www.mfat.govt.nz/en/embassies; ✆ **202/328-4800**). New Zealand consulates are in Los Angeles, Salt Lake City, San Francisco, and Seattle.

The embassy of the **United Kingdom** is at 3100 Massachusetts Ave. NW, Washington, DC 20008 (www.gov.uk/government/world/usa; ✆ **202/588-6500**). Other British consulates are in Atlanta, Boston, Chicago, Cleveland, Houston, Los Angeles, New York, San Francisco, and Seattle.

Emergencies Call ✆ **911** to report a fire, call the police, or get an ambulance anywhere in the United States. This is a toll-free call. (No coins are required at public telephones.) If you encounter serious problems, contact the **Traveler's Aid Society International** (www.travelersaid.org; ✆ **202/546-1127**). The Texas office is at the Dallas/Fort Worth International Airport (✆ **972/574-4420**). This nationwide, nonprofit, social-service organization geared to helping travelers in difficult straits offers services that might include reuniting families separated while traveling, providing food and/or shelter to people stranded without cash, or even emotional counseling. If you're in trouble, seek them out.

Family Travel Texas is a very family-friendly state, with lots of things for all ages to enjoy. Throughout this guide, you'll find numerous attractions, lodgings, and even restaurants that are especially well suited to kids. See "The Best Family Adventures" in chapter 1, as well as the "Kid Magnets" sightseeing sections in destination chapters.

For a list of more family-friendly travel resources, turn to the experts at Frommers.com.

Gasoline See "Getting Around/By Car," earlier in this chapter.

Health Vacationers in Texas generally don't need to take any extra health precautions beyond those they would take at home. It is worth noting, however, that visitors hiking in the drier parts of the state, such as in the deserts of West Texas or the mountains of Big Bend and Guadalupe Mountains national parks, should carry more water than they think they'll need, and drink it.

When heading into the great outdoors, keep in mind that Texas has a large number of poisonous snakes and insects, and you should be very careful where you put your hands and feet. If you're hiking, stick to designated hiking areas, stay on established trails, and carry raingear. When boating, wear a life jacket.

Unless you're camping out in remote Big Bend and other areas, over-the-counter medicines are widely available, as are generic equivalents of common prescription drugs.

Contact the **International Association for Medical Assistance to Travelers (IAMAT;** www.iamat.org; ✆ **716/754-4883,** or 416/652-0137 in Canada) for tips on travel and health concerns and for lists of doctors. The **Centers for Disease Control and Prevention** (www.cdc.gov; ✆ **800/311-3435**) provides up-to-date information on health hazards by region or country and offers tips on food safety. The website **Travel Health Online** (www.tripprep.com), sponsored by a consortium of travel medicine practitioners, may also offer helpful advice on traveling abroad.

Dietary Red Flags While Tex-Mex cuisine is generally milder than Mexican cooking, travelers who are unfamiliar with hot chiles and jalapeños or who have weak stomachs or ulcers should proceed with caution when eating Mexican. Tap water is potable throughout the state, but not to everyone's liking. Texans are big meat eaters in general, but in larger cities, vegetarian-friendly restaurants are widely available.

Bugs, Bites & Other Wildlife Concerns If you venture into the West Texas desert, snakes, spiders, and scorpions could be an issue, so it's wise to carry appropriate medicines, especially if camping.

Sun/Elements/Extreme Weather Exposure Perhaps the biggest health concern in Texas, with its big sky and blistering heat, is sun exposure. Travelers should make every attempt to protect themselves, including headgear, sunscreen, and sufficient hydration.

Insurance

Travel insurance is a good idea if you think for some reason you may be cancelling your trip. (Texas's occasional extreme weather can affect a trip.) It's cheaper than the cost of a no-penalty ticket and gives you a safety net if something comes up, enabling you to cancel or postpone your trip and still recover the costs. For information on traveler's insurance, trip-cancellation insurance, and medical insurance while traveling, visit www.frommers.com/planning.

Internet & Wi-Fi

The major nationwide Internet connectivity providers are present in Texas, including AT&T, Comcast, Time-Warner/Spectrum, and Verizon, as well as many smaller regional providers. There is free (or in a couple of cases, Boingo membership-required) Wi-Fi Internet access in all the major airports; in Austin's Bergstrom airport, kiosks offering free Internet service are stationed along the concourse and baggage claim. In addition, out on the road, Wi-Fi is available at all Texas Safety Rest Areas and Travel Information Centers.

To find Internet cafes in your destination, check www.cybercafe.com. If you have your own laptop, every Starbucks in Texas has Wi-Fi (www.starbucks.com/store-locator). To find other public Wi-Fi hotspots in your destination, go to www.jiwire.com; its Global Wi-Fi Finder holds the world's largest directory of public wireless hot spots.

Internet access and/or Wi-Fi is available in most hotels in Texas, either in the lobby, business center, or in-room. Most major hotels have Internet kiosks that provide basic Web access for a per-minute fee that's usually higher than cybercafe prices. Also, check out copy shops like FedEx Office (formerly Kinkos), which offers computer stations with fully loaded software (as well as Wi-Fi). Though convenient Internet access may not be present in the smallest towns, you may have good luck at the local library.

Legal Aid While driving, if you are pulled over for a minor infraction (such as speeding), never attempt to pay the fine directly to a police officer; this could be construed as attempted bribery, a much more serious crime. Pay fines by mail, or directly into the hands of the clerk of the court. If accused of a more serious offense, say and do nothing before consulting a lawyer. In the U.S., the burden is on the state to prove a person's guilt beyond a reasonable doubt, and everyone has the right to remain silent, whether he or she is suspected of a crime or actually arrested. Once arrested, a person can make one telephone call to a party of his or her choice. The international visitor should call his or her embassy or consulate.

LGBT Travelers Texas is a largely conservative state, which until 2003 still had laws that criminalized homosexual activity. In 2015 a Supreme Court decision changed all that. Still, small, rural communities tend to be home to religious conservatives who may not hold progressive values. But Texans generally have a "live and let live" attitude, and today gay and lesbian travelers will find that in most parts of Texas they are treated just as any other visitors.

There are vibrant gay and lesbian communities in all of the larger cities, particularly Austin, Dallas, and Houston. Resources for gay and lesbian travelers include **Gay in Austin** (www.gayinaustintexas.com), **My Gay Houston** (www.mygayhouston.com), and organizations such as the **Texas Gay Rodeo Association** (www.tgra.org).

Mail At press time, domestic postage rates are 34¢ for a postcard and 47¢ for a letter. For international mail, a first-class letter of up to 1 ounce costs $1.15 for all countries); a first-class postcard costs the same as a letter. For more information, go to **www.usps.com**.

If you aren't sure what your address will be in the United States, mail can be sent to you, in your name, c/o General Delivery at the main post office of the city or region where you expect to be. (Call ✆ **1/800-ASK-UPS [275-8777]** for information on the nearest post office.) The addressee must pick up mail in person and must produce proof of identity (driver's license, passport). Most post offices are open Monday to Friday 8am to 6pm and Saturday 9am to 3pm, and will hold mail for up to 1 month. Always include zip codes when mailing items in the U.S. If you don't know your zip code, visit **www.usps.com/zip4**.

Medical Requirements Unless you're arriving from an area known to be suffering from an epidemic (particularly cholera or yellow fever), inoculations or vaccinations are not required for entry into the United States. Also see "Health," above.

Mobile Phones Mobile (cell) phone and SMS texting service across Texas is generally good, with AT&T and Verizon generally faring best, and Sprint and T-Mobile lagging a bit behind. If you plan to use your phone a lot while in the U.S., it may be worthwhile to invest in an inexpensive "pay as you go" phone from a local outlet. Depending on the offer of the moment, you may get a generous credit for calls when you buy the phone—enough to last for your trip, perhaps, without having to add more calling time. Various calling plans are available, and although most no longer charge for roaming, additional costs for texting can add up. Definitely discuss the options to determine which one best suits your needs before making a commitment.

Keep in mind that your cellphone signal may be particularly weak in rural areas. If you need to stay in touch at a destination where you know your phone won't work, **rent** a phone that does from **InTouch USA** (www.intouchusa.us; ✆ **800/872-7626**) or a rental-car location, but beware: You'll pay $1 a minute or more for airtime. If you're venturing deep into national parks, you may want to consider renting a **satellite phone** (satphone). It's different from a cellphone in that it connects to satellites rather than ground-based towers. Unfortunately, you'll pay at least $2 per minute to use the phone, and it works only where you can see the horizon (that is, usually not indoors). In North America, you can rent Iridium satellite phones from **RoadPost** (www.roadpost.com; ✆ **888/290-1616** or, outside North America, +1/416/253-4539). InTouch USA offers a wider range of satphones, but at higher rates.

If you have a computer and Internet service, consider using a broadband-based telephone service (**Voice over Internet Protocol,** or **VoIP**) such as **Skype** (www.skype.com), or **Vonage** (www.vonage.com), which allow you to make free international calls from your laptop or smartphone in a cybercafe. Neither Skype nor Vonage requires the people you're calling to also have that service (though there are fees if they do not). Another reliable message and phone service application to set up before you travel is **Whats App** (www.whatsapp.com), though the people you call will need to download the app first.

If you're not from the U.S., you'll be appalled at the poor reach of the **GSM (Global System for Mobile Communications) wireless network,** which is used by much of the rest of the world. Your phone will probably work in most major U.S. cities; it definitely won't work in many rural areas. To see where GSM phones work in the U.S., check out www.t-mobile.com/coverage. And you may or may not be able to send SMS (text messaging) home.

Money & Costs Frommer's lists exact prices in the local currency. The currency conversions provided in the table below are correct at press time. However, rates fluctuate, so before departing from home, consult a currency exchange website such as **www.oanda.com/currency/converter** to check up-to-the-minute rates.

In general, Texas is not overly expensive, especially compared to destinations on the East and West coasts of the United States. You'll find a wide range of prices for lodging and dining, and admission to most attractions is less than $10 (it's sometimes free, especially in the smaller towns). Prices in Dallas, Houston, and Austin are now firmly in line with those in large Southern cities such as Atlanta and Miami. Smaller cities and rural areas are much less expensive, while resort areas such as Corpus Christi can be a bit more expensive, especially during winter holidays. Traveler's checks and credit cards are accepted at almost all hotels, restaurants, shops, and attractions, plus many grocery stores; and ATMs are practically everywhere.

Beware of hidden credit card fees while traveling. Check with your credit or debit card issuer to see what fees, if any, will be charged for overseas transactions. Recent reform legislation in the U.S., for example, has curbed some exploitative lending practices. But many banks have responded by increasing fees in other areas, including fees for customers who use credit and debit cards while out of the country—even if those charges were made in U.S. dollars. Fees can amount to 3% or more of the purchase price. Check with your bank before departing to avoid any surprise charges on your statement.

For help with currency conversions, tip calculations, and more, download Frommer's convenient Travel Tools app for your mobile device. Go to www.frommers.com/go/mobile and click on the "Travel Tools" icon.

Multicultural Travelers Texas has a lamentable history of race-related incidents, and bigoted and racist opinions are still found in some small towns and among some less cosmopolitan Texans.

THE VALUE OF THE U.S. DOLLAR VS. OTHER POPULAR CURRENCIES

US$	A$	C$	€	NZ$	£
1.00	1.32	1.35	.93	1.43	.78

WHAT THINGS COST IN TEXAS	$
Taxi from DFW airport to downtown Dallas	45.00
Double room, moderate	125.00–175.00
Double room, inexpensive	75.00–125.00
Three-course dinner for one without wine, moderate	20.00–35.00
Bottle of beer	3.00–6.00
Cup of coffee	1.00–2.50
1 gallon of unleaded gas	2.14 regular/ 2.62 premium
Admission to most museums	4.00–10.00
Admission to most national parks	10.00

Regrettably, discrimination is still occasionally directed toward African Americans and Hispanics (and, more recently, people of Middle Eastern descent or appearance), as well as openly gay travelers. However, most travelers of color and ethnicity, as well as gays and lesbians, will likely encounter few (if any) problems. African-American travelers may want to be cautious when traveling through the small towns of east Texas, which has a history of thorny race relations. Also, travelers of Hispanic descent or appearance may find that they are stopped by the border patrol more frequently than non-Hispanics around border towns, at San Antonio shopping malls, and at other South Texas–area stores and shopping malls, so be sure to carry a current, government-issued picture ID. See also "LGBT Travelers," above.

Newspapers & Magazines The major daily newspapers in Texas are the *Dallas Morning News*, the *Fort Worth Star Telegram*, the *Austin American Statesman*, the *San Antonio Express News*, and the *Houston Chronicle*. You will also find national editions of the *New York Times*, the *Wall Street Journal*, and *USA Today* in major hotels and kiosks and at most Starbucks coffee shops. Texas-based magazines with local coverage include *Texas Monthly* and *D Magazine*. Alternative (free) newspapers include the *Austin Chronicle*, *Dallas Observer*, and *Houston Press*.

Packing Texas's occasional extreme weather fluctuations may require you to pack for more than one season. Casual dress and Western wear are still seen in much of the state, but the big cities are more cosmopolitan and trendier than ever, and fashionable attire at restaurants, bars, and nightclubs is as much the rule in Dallas–Fort Worth, Houston, Austin, and San Antonio as elsewhere in the country (even if many Texas women have a distinct style of overdressing). Still, the South is becoming more and more casual, especially in the summer when temperatures soar, so you don't necessarily need to dress up as much then, especially in Austin and San Antonio, where locals are a little more laid-back. However, in some nightclubs and nicer restaurants, tennis shoes and (grungy) jeans are not welcome—especially in Dallas and Houston.

Passports Virtually every foreign traveler entering the U.S. is required to present a valid passport. As of June 2009, U.S. citizens entering the U.S. by land or sea must present a passport or other Western Hemisphere Travel Initiative–compliant travel document such as a passport card, enhanced driver's license, or SENTRI card. The passport requirement is waived in some cases for minors.

Entrance and Exit to Mexico: According to Mexican government regulations, "As of March, 2010, all U.S. citizens must show a valid passport, book or card, to enter Mexican territory, by any means of transportation, beyond the border zone (20 kilometers, 13 miles, from the border); no exceptions are made for children. No visa or tourist card is required for stays of less than 72 hours within the border zone. When traveling beyond the border zone, or when entering the country by air, U.S. citizens are required to pay a fee to obtain a tourist card (FM-T), which is available at border crossings, Mexican tourist offices and airports, within the border zone. Major airlines will provide this form during your trip. You must include the following information on the form: numbers of days you will be in the country, passport number, destination, city of origin and other related information . . . Entering the country for other purposes, besides tourism and business, or for stays of more than 180 days, requires a visa and a valid U.S. passport." Further information can also be obtained from a Mexican consulate. For information about visiting Mexico, call **800/44-MEXICO [446-3942]** or visit www.visitmexico.com.

Canadians must carry a Canadian passport, enhanced driver's license/ enhanced identification card, or a "trusted traveler card." Mexican citizens must present a passport with a nonimmigrant visa or a laser visa Border Crossing Card to cross the U.S. border.

Warning: Possession/ importation of any type of firearm, weapon, or ammunition is a felony in Mexico without advance written authorization from the Mexican Embassy in Washington, DC, or from a Mexican consulate in the U.S. It does not matter if you are licensed to carry the weapon in the United States, are a law enforcement or military official, or unintentionally transport it. Mexico has severe penalties for this offense, punishable by fines, confiscation of the weapon, and jail time. Ignorance of the law is not a defense. Even a few shotgun shells in the trunk can cause a big problem. Some cities, such as Nuevo Laredo, also have ordinances prohibiting the possession of knives of any kind or anything that might be considered a knife.

Passport Offices:

Australia **Australian Passport Information Service** (www.passports.gov.au; ✆ **131-232**).

Canada **Passport Office,** Department of Foreign Affairs and International Trade, Ottawa, ON K1A 0G3 (www.ppt.gc.ca; ✆ **800/567-6868**).

Ireland **Passport Office,** Setanta Centre, Molesworth St., Dublin 2 (www.foreignaffairs.gov.ie; ✆ **01/671-1633**).

New Zealand **Passports Office,** Department of Internal Affairs, 47 Boulcott St., Wellington, 6011 (www.passports.govt.nz; ✆ **+0/800/22-50-50** in New Zealand or **+64/4/463-9360**).

United Kingdom Visit your nearest passport office, major post office, or travel agency or contact the **Identity and Passport Service (IPS),** 89 Eccleston Sq., London, SW1V 1PN (www.ips.gov.uk; ✆ **+44/0/300/222-0000**).

United States To find your regional passport office, check the U.S. State Department website (https://travel.state.gov) or call the **National Passport Information Center** (✆ **877/487-2778**) for automated information.

Petrol See "Getting Around/By Car," earlier in this chapter.

Police Dial ✆ **911** for a police or medical emergency. In addition to local police, there are Texas State Troopers, whom you are most likely to encounter on interstate highways, and the legendary **Texas Rangers,** the second-oldest state-level law enforcement agency in the United States. The Texas Rangers have statewide jurisdiction and have been involved in the investigation of major crimes, often across county lines (from murder and kidnapping to public corruption, narcotics violations, and organized crime) and been employed in border security operations and as riot police. (The Texas Rangers were created by Stephen F. Austin in 1823, when he deployed 10 men to protect some 700 newly arrived families after the Mexican War of Independence. A hall of fame and museum dedicated to the Texas Rangers is in Waco; visit www.texasranger.org/today/Coop.htm.)

Safety Most areas of Texas are as safe as any other part of the U.S.; however, large cities such as Houston, Dallas, and San Antonio have their share of big-city crime (a few years back, downtown Houston had a particularly dangerous reputation, as have certain neighborhoods, such as Deep Ellum in Dallas). Border towns, such as El Paso in particular, have seen increased violence focused largely on drug (and in some cases, illegal immigrant) smuggling along the U.S.-Mexico border. To steer clear of stumbling into a drug transaction or police raid, avoid hiking alone in isolated areas along the border and stay in the major tourist areas in border towns. Check travel advisories before crossing into Mexican border towns; some have become increasingly dangerous in recent years. For more information, see "Texas: Gateway to Mexico" on p. 446, and visit **travel.state.gov** for updated travel advisories. Also, see "Multicultural Travelers," above, for discrimination issues and safety.

Avoid carrying valuables with you on the street, and don't display expensive cameras or electronic equipment. Place your wallet in an inside jacket or front pant pocket. Consider using a money belt or other hidden travel wallet, and never leave valuables in the outside pocket of a backpack. Should you stop for a bite to eat, keep everything within easy reach—of you, not a purse snatcher. Women might want to wear cross-body bags, especially if they plan to sightsee on foot in congested areas. And, of course, it's always a good idea to leave expensive-looking jewelry and other conspicuous valuables at home. If you're in doubt about which neighborhoods are safe, inquire with the front desk staff at your hotel or the local tourist office.

Remember that hotels are open to the public and that in a large property, security may not be able to screen everyone entering. Always lock your room door—never assume that once inside your hotel you're automatically safe.

If you must store belongings in a car, place them in the trunk. Burglaries of tourists' rental cars in hotel and shopping parking lots and major tourist sites are always a possibility. Park in well-lighted and well-traveled areas, if possible. Never leave any packages or valuables visible in the car. If someone attempts to rob you or steal your car, do not try to resist the thief or carjacker—and report the incident to the police department immediately. Ask your rental agency about personal safety, and get written directions or a map with the route to your destination clearly marked.

Texas has some of the most lenient gun laws in the U.S., and on January 1, 2016, Texas legislation passed a new "License to Carry" law allowing licensed Texans to carry handguns in plain view in belt or shoulder holsters except in certain places, such as in federal buildings, at sporting events, in some schools, courts or court offices, and other businesses that do not allow it (among other places). So you're likely to see pickup trucks with gun racks and maybe even some folks "packing heat" (carrying a firearm). Remember this while driving in traffic or potentially getting into an altercation in Texas; the other party may just have a gun.

Senior Travel Many Texas hotels and motels offer discounts to seniors (especially if you're carrying an AARP card; see below), and an increasing number of restaurants, attractions, and public transportation systems do so as well.

Members of **AARP** (formerly the American Association of Retired Persons), 601 E St. NW, Washington, DC 20049 (www.aarp.org; ✆ **888/687-2277**), often get discounts on hotels, airfares, and car rentals. AARP offers members a wide range of benefits, including *AARP The Magazine* and a monthly newsletter. Anyone aged 50 and older can join.

The U.S. National Park Service (NPS) offers an **America the Beautiful Senior Pass,** which (as of April 2015) costs a one-time processing fee of $10 and is available either by mail or in person at many federal recreational sites. (The mail-in application requires an extra $10 document-processing fee.) A lifetime pass for people 62 years or older, the Senior Pass allows entry to more than 2,000 sites managed by five federal agencies, such as the National Parks Service and the **Fish and Wildlife Service,** including all national parks, monuments, historic sites, recreation areas, and national wildlife refuges. At vehicle-fee sites, Senior Pass holders and passengers in non-commercial vehicles can enter for free. At sites that charge per person, the Senior Pass allows up to three other people in the pass holder's vehicle to enter the site for free. Besides free entry, the Senior Pass also offers a 50% discount on some federal-use fees charged for such facilities as camping, swimming, parking, boat launching, and tours. While the former Golden Age Pass is no longer sold by NPS, these will still be honored if you already purchased such a pass. For more information, go to www.nps.gov/fees_passes.htm or call the United States Geological Survey (USGS), which issues the passes, at ✆ **888/275-8747.**

Smoking No statewide smoking ban exists in Texas. Many cities in Texas, including Austin, Corpus Christi, Dallas, El Paso, and Houston, have enacted a smoking ban in all enclosed workplaces, including bars and restaurants. Other cities, such as Arlington, Fort Worth, Galveston, and San Antonio, allow some limited exemptions (certain bars and some restaurants).

Student Travel The top spots for college students heading to Texas for spring break are **South Padre Island** and **Port Aransas** for sun and fun and, to a lesser extent, **Big Bend National Park** for serious hiking, but all of the beach areas and parks are popular. The sister cities of **Rockport/Fulton** are often a favorite destination for those who like to fish.

Check out the **International Student Travel Confederation (ISTC)** (www.istc.org) website for comprehensive travel services information and details on how to get an **International Student Identity Card (ISIC),** which qualifies students for substantial savings on rail passes, plane tickets, entrance fees, and more. It also provides students with basic health and life insurance and a 24-hour help line. The card is valid for a maximum of 18 months. You can apply for the card online or in person at **STA Travel** (www.statravel.com; ✆ **800/781-4040** in North America, ✆ 132 782 in Australia, or ✆ 0871 2 300 040 in the U.K.), the biggest student travel agency in the world; check out the website to locate STA Travel offices worldwide. If you're no longer a student but are still 25 or under, you can get an **International Youth Travel Card (IYTC)** from the same organization, which entitles you to some discounts. **Travel CUTS** (www.travelcuts.com; ✆ **800/592-2887**) offers similar services for both Canadians and U.S. residents. Irish students may prefer to turn to **USIT** (www.usit.ie; ✆ **01/602-1906**), an Ireland-based specialist in student, youth, and independent travel.

Taxes The United States has no value-added tax (VAT) or other indirect tax at the national level. Every state, county, and city may levy its own local tax on all purchases, including hotel and restaurant bills and airline tickets. These taxes will not appear on price tags.

Texans like to brag that the state is a great place to live because there is no state income tax. Money for government services has to come from somewhere, however, and one of those sources is you, the traveler. Texas lodging taxes are among the highest in the region, ranging from the basic hotel rate of 6% to 17%, with the highest rate in Houston. Sales taxes in Texas vary by county, but usually consist of the basic state sales tax of 6.25% plus an addition 2%, for a total of 8.25%, slightly higher than most surrounding states.

Telephones Generally, hotel surcharges on long-distance and local calls are astronomical, so you're better off using your **cellphone** or a **public pay telephone.** Many convenience stores and packaging services sell **prepaid calling cards** in

Useful Telephone Numbers

- Texas Parks & Wildlife Park Information ✆ **800/792-111**
- Hunting information ✆ **512/389-4505**
- Fishing information ✆ **512/389-4505**
- Poison Center ✆ **800/POISON-1 (764-7661)**
- Road conditions DriveTexas hotline ✆ **800/452-9292**
- Weather hotline ✆ **512/232-4265**
- U.S. Department of State 24-hour Travel Advisory ✆ **202/647-5225**
- U.S. Passport Agency ✆ **202/647-0518**
- U.S. Centers for Disease Control international traveler's hotline ✆ **404/332-4559**

denominations up to $50. Many public pay phones at airports now accept American Express, MasterCard, and Visa. **Local calls** made from most pay phones cost either 25¢ or 50¢. Most long-distance and international calls can be dialed directly from any phone. **To make calls within the United States and to Canada,** dial 1 followed by the area code and the seven-digit number. **For other international calls,** dial 011 followed by the country code, city code, and the number you are calling.

Calls to area codes **800, 888, 877,** and **866** are toll-free. However, calls to area codes **700** and **900** (chat lines, bulletin boards, "dating" services, and so on) can be expensive—charges of 95¢ to $5 or more per minute. Some numbers have minimum charges that can run $15 or more.

For **reversed-charge or collect calls,** and for person-to-person calls, dial the number 0, then the area code and number; an operator will come on the line, and you should specify whether you are calling collect, person-to-person, or both. If your operator-assisted call is international, ask for the overseas operator.

For **directory assistance** ("Information"), dial 411 for local numbers and national numbers in the U.S. and Canada. For dedicated long-distance information, dial 1, then the appropriate area code plus 555-1212.

Time Almost all of Texas is in the Central Standard Time zone (CST); the only exception is the state's far western tip, which observes Mountain Standard Time (MST). The continental United States is divided into **four time zones:** Eastern Standard Time (EST), Central Standard Time (CST), Mountain Standard Time (MST), and Pacific Standard Time (PST). Alaska and Hawaii have their own zones. For example, when it's 9am in Los Angeles (PST), it's 7am in Honolulu (HST),10am in Denver (MST), 11am in Chicago (CST), noon in New York City (EST), 5pm in London (GMT), and 2am the next day in Sydney.

Daylight saving time (summer time) is in effect from 1am on the second Sunday in March to 1am on the first Sunday in November, except in Arizona, Hawaii, the U.S. Virgin Islands, and Puerto Rico. Daylight saving time moves the clock 1 hour ahead of standard time.

For help with time translations and more, download our convenient Travel Tools app for your mobile device. Go to www.frommers.com/go/mobile and click on the "Travel Tools" icon.

Tipping Tips are a very important part of certain workers' income, and gratuities are the standard way of showing appreciation for services provided. (Tipping is certainly not compulsory if the service is poor!) In hotels, tip **bellhops** at least $1 per bag ($2–$3 if you have a lot of luggage) and tip the **chamber staff** $2 to $3 per day (more if you've left a big mess for him or her to clean up). Tip the **doorman** or **concierge** only if he or she has provided you with some specific service (for example, calling a cab or obtaining difficult-to-get theater tickets). Tip the **valet-parking attendant** $2 every time you get your car.

In restaurants, bars, and nightclubs, tip **service staff** and **bartenders** 15% to 20% of the check (a good way to know how much to tip in Texas is to double the tax, which would make your tip just over 16%). Tip **check-room attendants** $2 per garment.

As for other service personnel, tip **cab drivers** 15% of the fare; tip **skycaps** at airports at least $2 per bag ($3–$5 if you have a lot of luggage); and tip **hairdressers** and **barbers** 15% to 20%.

For help with tip calculations, currency conversions, and more, download our convenient Travel Tools app for your mobile device. Go to www.frommers.com/go/mobile and click on the "Travel Tools" icon.

Toilets You won't find public toilets or "restrooms" on the streets in most U.S. cities, but they can be found in hotel lobbies, bars, restaurants, museums, department stores, railway and bus stations, and service stations. Large hotels, coffee shops, and fast-food restaurants are often the best bet for clean facilities. Restaurants and bars in resorts or heavily visited areas may reserve their restrooms for patrons.

Uber & Other Car-Share Apps Uber and Lyft are no longer operating in Austin and Houston, although they are still available for use in San Antonio and Dallas and many other Texas cities. Austin has several other rideshare app companies, such as FARE, Fasten, RideAustin, and InstaRyde. Check the apps for these and other rideshare companies for more information about the areas where their service is available.

VAT See "Taxes" above.

Visas The U.S. State Department has a **Visa Waiver Program (VWP)** allowing citizens of the following countries to enter the United States without a visa for stays of up to 90 days: Andorra, Australia, Austria, Belgium, Brunei, Chile, Czech Republic, Denmark, Estonia, Finland, France, Germany, Greece, Hungary, Iceland, Ireland, Italy, Japan, Latvia, Liechtenstein, Lithuania, Luxembourg, Malta, Monaco, the Netherlands, New Zealand, Norway, Portugal, San Marino, Singapore, Slovakia, Slovenia, South Korea, Spain, Sweden, Switzerland, and Taiwan and the United Kingdom. However, to be eligible to travel under the VWP, British citizens must have the unrestricted right of permanent abode in England, Scotland, Wales, Northern Ireland, the Channel Islands, and the Isle of Man. (***Note:*** This list was accurate at press time in 2017; however, for the most up-to-date list of countries in the VWP, consult https://travel.state.gov.) Even though a visa isn't necessary, in an effort to help U.S. officials check travelers against terror watch lists before they arrive at U.S. borders, visitors from VWP countries must register online through the Electronic System for Travel Authorization (ESTA) before boarding a plane or a boat to the U.S. Travelers must complete an electronic application providing basic personal and travel eligibility information. The Department of Homeland Security recommends filling out the form at least 3 days before traveling. Authorizations will be valid for up to 2 years or until the traveler's passport expires, whichever comes first. Currently, there is a US$14 fee for the online application. Existing ESTA registrations remain valid through their expiration dates.

Note: Any passport issued on or after October 26, 2006, by a VWP country must be an **e-Passport** for VWP travelers to be eligible to enter the U.S. without a visa. Citizens of these nations also need to present a round-trip air or cruise ticket upon arrival. E-Passports contain computer chips capable of storing biometric information, such as the required digital photograph of the holder. If your passport doesn't have this feature, you can still travel without a visa if the valid passport was issued before October 26, 2005, and includes a machine-readable zone; or if the valid passport was issued between October 26, 2005, and October 25, 2006, and includes a digital photograph. For more information, go to **https://travel.state.gov**. Canadian citizens may enter the United States without visas, but will need to show passports and proof of residence.

According to http://travel.state.gov, under the Visa Waiver Program Improvement and Terrorist Travel Prevention Act of 2015, travelers in the following categories are no longer eligible to travel or be admitted to the United States under the Visa Waiver Program (VWP): Nationals of VWP countries who have traveled to or been present in Iran, Iraq, Libya, Somalia, Sudan, Syria, or Yemen on or after March 1, 2011 (with limited exceptions for travel for diplomatic or military purposes in the service of a VWP country); nationals of VWP countries who are also nationals of Iran, Iraq, Sudan, or Syria. These individuals will still be able to apply for a visa using the regular appointment process at a U.S. Embassy or Consulate. For those who require a U.S. visa for urgent business, medical, or humanitarian travel to the United States, U.S. Embassies and Consulates stand ready to handle applications on an expedited basis.

If an individual who is exempt from the Act because of his or her diplomatic or military presence in one of the four countries has his or her ESTA denied, he or she may go to the CBP website, or contact the CBP information Center. The traveler may also apply for a nonimmigrant visa at a U.S. Embassy or Consulate. Certain other travelers who fall under this restriction may qualify for a waiver of the requirements. U.S. Customs and Border Protection strongly recommends that any traveler to the United States check his or her ESTA status prior to making any travel reservations or travelling to the United States. More information is available on the DHS website.

Citizens of all other countries must have (1) a valid passport that expires at least 6 months later than the scheduled end of their visit to the U.S.; and (2) a tourist visa.

For information about U.S. Visas, go to **http://travel.state.gov** and click on "Visas." Or go to one of the following websites:

Australian citizens can obtain up-to-date visa information from the **U.S. Embassy Canberra,** Moonah Place, Yarralumla, ACT 2600 (✆ **02/6214-5600**) or by checking the U.S. Diplomatic Mission's website at **http://canberra.usembassy.gov/visas.html**.

British subjects can obtain up-to-date visa information by calling the **U.S. Embassy Visa Information Line** (✆ **09042-450-100** from within the U.K. at £1.20 per minute; or ✆ **866/382-3589** from within the U.S. at a flat rate of $160 and is payable by credit card only) or by visiting the "Visas to the U.S." section of the American Embassy London's website at **https://uk.usembassy.gov/visas**.

Irish citizens can obtain up-to-date visa information through the **U.S. Embassy Dublin,** 42 Elgin Rd., Ballsbridge, Dublin 4 (✆ **1580-47-VISA [8472]** from within the Republic of Ireland at €2.40 per minute; **https://ie.usembassy.gov**).

Citizens of **New Zealand** can obtain up-to-date visa information by contacting the **U.S. Embassy New Zealand,** 29 Fitzherbert Terrace, Thorndon, Wellington (✆ **644/462-6000; https://nz.usembassy.gov**).

Visitor Information

Contact the **Texas Department of Transportation,** Travel Division, P.O. Box 141009, Austin, TX 78714-1009 (www.traveltex.com; ✆ **800/888-8TEX [8839]**), for a free copy of the official state vacation guide, which includes a state map and describes attractions, activities, and lodgings throughout Texas.

The Texas Department of Transportation maintains a dozen excellent **Texas Travel Information Centers** around the state, offering free maps, brochures, and one-on-one travel counseling. Locations are as follows: **Amarillo,** I-40 East; **Anthony,** I-10 at the New Mexico state line; **Austin,** 112 E. 11th St., at the capitol complex; **Denison,** U.S. 75 at the Oklahoma state line; **Gainesville,** I-35 at the Oklahoma state line; **Harlingen,** U.S. 77 at U.S. 83; **Langtry,** off U.S. 90 on Tex. Loop 25; **Laredo,** I-35 North at U.S. 83; **Orange,** I-10 at the Louisiana state line; **Texarkana,** I-30 at the Arkansas state line; **Waskom,** I-20 at the Louisiana state line; and **Wichita Falls,** I-44 at U.S. 277/281. The centers are open daily from 8am to 5pm except on January 1, Easter Sunday, Thanksgiving Day, and December 24 and 25. For information, call ✆ **800/452-9292.**

The ever-expanding blogosphere is filled with blogs on things great and public as well as obscure and personal, and weblogs originating in Texas are no exception. Check out the resident blogs in *Texas Monthly* on Texas politics, food, and current events at www.texasmonthly.com/blogs. To sample a whole slew of Texas topics and musings, peruse the many blogs listed at www.networkedblogs.com/topic/Texas and www.ringsurf.com/ring/texasblogs.

Water Tap water is potable throughout Texas, though not to everyone's liking.

Wi-Fi See "Internet & Wi-Fi," earlier in this section.

Women Travelers The old macho cowboy culture still exists in some (usually less-urban) parts of Texas, and it's probably safe to say that Texans historically have a greater tolerance for sexist behavior and comments than in some other parts of the country. In bars and nightclubs, both men and women may act (and dress) in a flirtier manner than you might be used to experiencing. Brazen (although usually harmless) come-ons are not uncommon. Although that doesn't necessarily translate into danger for women going out alone at night, being accompanied by another woman (or man, of course) will make you less of a target for unwanted advances.

Index

See also Accommodations and Restaurant indexes, below.

General Index

A

B

E

F

G

Accommodations

Restaurants

Map List

Photo Credits

p. i: T photography / Shutterstock.com; p. ii: Courtesy of Austin Convention & Visitors Bureau; p. iii: visitsanantonio.com / Bob Howen; p. iv: James Hastie; p. v, top: Alizada Studios / Shutterstock.com; p. v, bottom left: Brian Holsclaw; p. v, bottom right: Valerie Hinojosa; p. vi, top: visitsanantonio.com / Richard Nowitz; p. vi, bottom left: visitsanantonio.com; p. vi, bottom right: visitsanantonio.com / Bernadette Heath; p. vii, top left: Luis Tamayo; p. vii, top right: Marquisphoto / Shutterstock, Inc.; p. vii, bottom: Nathan Vaughn; p. viii, top left: Sten-Erik Armitage; p. viii, top right: Eric Kilby; p. viii, bottom: Lars Plougmann; p. ix, top: Visit Houston (Julie Soefer); p. ix, bottom left: Sean Pavone; p. ix, bottom right: Ted Eytan; p. x, top: Mick49 / Shutterstock, Inc.; p. x, bottom left: David ODell; p. x, bottom right: Arina P Habich; p. xi, top: JB Manning; p. xi, bottom: Scott Wilkes; p. xii, top: visitsanantonio.com; p. xii, bottom left: Elena Fernandez Z; p. xii, bottom right: Kent Ellington; p. xiii, top left: Courtesy of Texas Tourism / Kenny Braun; p. xiii, top right: Nan Palmero; p. xiii, bottom: Dean Fikar; p. xiv, top: Edwin Verin / Shutterstock.com; p. xiv, bottom left: T photography / Shutterstock.com; p. xiv, bottom right: visitsanantonio.com / Donald Nausbaum; p. xv, top: kan_khampanya; p. xv, bottom: Courtesy of Gilley's; p. xvi, top left: visitsanantonio.com / Bob Howen; p. xvi, top right: T photography / Shutterstock, Inc.; p. xvi, bottom: visitsanantonio.com.

Frommer's Texas, 7th Edition

Published by
FROMMER MEDIA LLC

ISBN 978-1-62887-324-5 (paper), 978-1-62887-325-2 (ebk)

Editorial Director: Pauline Frommer
Editor: Alexis Lipsitz Flippin
Production Editor: Erin Geile
Cartographer: Roberta Stockwell
Photo Editor: Meghan Lamb
Cover Design: David Riedy

Cover images: (front) Cowboy chasing cow with rope, ©T Photography/Shutterstock; (back) River walk in San Antonio, Texas, ©F11photo/Shutterstock

For information on our other products or services, see www.frommers.com.

FrommerMedia LLC also publishes its books in a variety of electronic formats. Some content that appears in print may not be available in electronic formats.

Manufactured in the United States of America

5 4 3 2 1

ABOUT THE AUTHOR

"There's no prettier sight than looking back on a town you've left behind," hums award-winning travel writer **Janis Turk** from her favorite Townes Van Zandt song. Wherever the Texas-based travel writer has just been, that's the place she likes best, for as Robert Louis Stevenson writes, "the great affair is to move," and "to travel hopefully is a better thing than to arrive."

Thanks to her nomadic family, Turk was traveling before she could walk, and today she's still more at home on the road than anywhere else. Since her first job as a stringer for a small-town newspaper, she has known the pang of wanderlust, and through years of study, writing, editing, and traveling, she has always sought to travel hopefully and write well.

With degrees in Journalism and Literature, Turk taught at three universities before carving out a full-time career as a travel writer. Author of two Frommer's guidebooks and numerous Web features and reviews, Turk has also written for major newspapers and magazines and appeared as a travel expert on television, including the CNN Airport Network. A few years back, Turk garnered a top award in travel writing at the New York Travel Fest. When she's not running with the bulls in Pamplona, wandering the souks of Morocco, on safari in Kenya, sipping tea in a Bedouin tent in Wadi Rum, or sailing around Cape Horn, Turk loves driving the backroads of the Lone Star State and spending time with her family.

Ever the go-girl, Turk keeps a toe-hold in New Orleans and one eye on the open road, always mapping out her next adventure and humming a traveling song. Janis divides her time between Texas and New Orleans, when she is not traveling.

ABOUT THE FROMMER TRAVEL GUIDES

For most of the past 50 years, Frommer's has been the leading series of travel guides in North America, accounting for as many as 24% of all guidebooks sold. I think I know why.

Though we hope our books are entertaining, we nevertheless deal with travel in a serious fashion. Our guidebooks have never looked on such journeys as a mere recreation, but as a far more important human function, a time of learning and introspection, an essential part of a civilized life. We stress the culture, lifestyle, history, and beliefs of the destinations we cover, and urge our readers to seek out people and new ideas as the chief rewards of travel.

We have never shied from controversy. We have, from the beginning, encouraged our authors to be intensely judgmental, critical—both pro and con—in their comments, and wholly independent. Our only clients are our readers, and we have triggered the ire of countless prominent sorts, from a tourist newspaper we called "practically worthless" (it unsuccessfully sued us) to the many rip-offs we've condemned.

And because we believe that travel should be available to everyone regardless of their incomes, we have always been cost-conscious at every level of expenditure. Though we have broadened our recommendations beyond the budget category, we insist that every lodging we include be sensibly priced. We use every form of media to assist our readers, and are particularly proud of our feisty daily website, the award-winning Frommers.com.

I have high hopes for the future of Frommer's. May these guidebooks, in all the years ahead, continue to reflect the joy of travel and the freedom that travel represents. May they always pursue a cost-conscious path, so that people of all incomes can enjoy the rewards of travel. And may they create, for both the traveler and the persons among whom we travel, a community of friends, where all human beings live in harmony and peace.

Arthur Frommer

NOTES